W9-BRR-816

INTRODUCTION TO MODERN BUSINESS

8th Edition

INTRODUCTION TO MODERN

Prentice-Hall, Inc., Englewood Cliffs, New Jersey 07632

VERNON A. MUSSELMAN
Professor, Business Education, University of Kentucky; and Investment Counsellor

EUGENE H. HUGHES
Professor and Dean, Emeritus, College of Business Administration, University of Houston; and Labor Arbitrator, Santa Barbara, California

In Collaboration with JOHN H. JACKSON
Professor, College of Commerce and Industry, University of Wyoming

BUSINESS

ISSUES AND ENVIRONMENT

Library of Congress Cataloging in Publication Data

MUSSELMAN, VERNON A
Introduction to modern business.

Bibliography: p.
Includes index.
1. Business. I. Hughes, Eugene Harley,
(date) joint author. II. Jackson, John Harold.
III. Title.
HF5351.M86 1981 658.4 80-19587
ISBN 0-13-488072-2

8th Edition
INTRODUCTION TO MODERN BUSINESS
Issues and Environment
Vernon A. Musselman ● Eugene H. Hughes
in collaboration with John H. Jackson

Printed in the United States of America

10 9 8 7 6 5 4 3 2 1

Editorial / Production Supervision by Kim Gueterman
Interior and Cover Design by Janet Schmid
Cover Photograph by © Reginald Wickham
Composition by Typothetae Book Composition
Interior Illustrations by E-H Technical Services, Inc.
Acquisition Editor: Barbara Piercecchi
Manufacturing Buyer: Gordon Osbourne

Prentice-Hall International, Inc., *London*

Prentice-Hall of Australia Pty. Limited, *Sydney*

Prentice-Hall of Canada, Ltd., *Toronto*

Prentice-Hall of India Private Limited, *New Delhi*

Prentice-Hall of Japan, Inc., *Tokyo*

Prentice-Hall of Southeast Asia Pte. Ltd., *Singapore*

Whitehall Books Limited, *Wellington, New Zealand*

CONTENTS

PREFACE

When we speak of the BUSINESS WORLD, we do not speak of a system in isolation. We include activities of national and international scope, personal involvement as consumers and employees, governmental and social involvement, and political involvement. It is the interrelation of all of these systems and organizations which make the study of business so vital and dynamic. Careful consideration of all of these has characterized seven previous editions of Musselman and Hughes.

Today more than ever before the changes taking place in the world around us, in our social, political, and economic environment must be considered in the study of business. This eighth edition retains many features of previous editions. In addition, it reflects the characteristics of this new environment of business.

New Features

Study objectives. Study objectives begin each chapter. They are written to help students know what to expect in the discussion that follows.

In the news. Each chapter opens with a report of some recent happening from the current business scene. These are items of special interest related to the chapter content.

Biographies. A brief biographical sketch of a successful business person is included in each chapter. These are designed to link the concepts in the text to the world in which we live and work.

Chapter questions. Two types of questions follow each chapter: Review Questions and Discussion Questions. The review questions are closely tied to the study objectives at the opening of the chapter. They are specifically answered in the text material. The discussion questions are more analytical and are intended to take the reader beyond the memorization level.

Current issues. Throughout this edition the authors relate the chapter material to our current business environment. In this environment there are many issues on which students and instructors will not agree. "Current Issues" present the pros and cons of some contemporary issues to challenge and stimulate the reader.

Business case situations. One of the most popular features of the previous editions was the business case. In response to requests from users, this edition gives case situations for each chapter.

A new collaborator. John Jackson, University of Wyoming, has joined the author team as collaborator. John is the author of *Organization Theory*, 1978, Jackson and Morgan, Prentice-Hall; *Personnel*, 2/E, 1980, Mathis and Jackson, West; and *Successful Supervision*, 1980, Jackson and Keaveny, Prentice-Hall.

In addition to these new features many important changes and updates have been made in the text material.

Chapter 1. "Business and Our Economic System" is an update and combination of the material formerly included in the first two chapters. The result is a tightened, clearer, and more integrated discussion.

Chapter 10. "Physical Distribution and Energy" combines the discussion previously presented in two different chapters. Their interrelationships and contributions to manufacture and trade are described.

Chapter 16. "Risk Management and Insurance" gives a more comprehensive discussion of risk management, and looks at types of insurance under the umbrella of risk management.

Chapter 18. "Information Management and Computers" was completely reorganized into a new chapter. It retains the basic theme of managing data, the emphasis is placed on the use of computers and micrographics.

Chapter 20. "The Government's Role in Business" has shifted the emphasis to a consideration of the ways that government functions in business. The discussion of taxation has been retained.

Chapter 22. "Career Development in Business" is completely new. It provides practical guidance for the reader and places emphasis on individual student action.

Women and minorities. The discussion of the place of women and minorities in business is no longer in a separate chapter, but integrated throughout the text. The authors feel that as our society progresses, the roles of women and minorities will and should be an integral part of the business world.

The **Glossary** has been greatly enlarged to include both primary and secondary terms discussed.

Reading references have been grouped by major divisions and appear in the back of the book rather than at the end of each chapter.

Improved Study Guide

This student aid has been enlarged over that for previous editions. Its popular features have all been retained.

Principal Ideas in the Chapter
Activities, Problems, and Questions
Applied Readings

The section *Self-Test* has been increased in length and different types of items are used: True-false, completion, multiple choice, and yes-no items.

The answers to the Business Terms exercises which appear in the textbook at the end of each chapter are given in the *Study Guide.* The answers to the Self-Test exercises are included in the back of the Study Guide.

Instructor's Manual

The Instructor's Manual has been greatly enlarged and improved—it is twice as long as the previous edition. Features retained from the previous editions include: chapter outlines, answers to textbook questions and cases, answers to study guide contents, and the three ring binder. New features include annotated lecture outlines, a 60-page film guide, over 100 transparencies (roughly 50% from within the text and 50% additional material), all keyed to the lectures.

Test bank. Adopters of Musselman and Hughes can avail themselves of the Prentice-Hall computer testing service. Our testing service offers two options to the instructor. One option supplies the adopter with either a spirit or a xerox master of the instructor's selected questions. The second option is a computer tape data bank of the selected questions.

To the many users of previous editions who submitted suggestions, the authors are grateful. We also express our appreciation to the numerous business firms and organizations that have permitted us to reproduce illustrations about their companies from their publications. Our special thanks go to the members of our Advisory Board for their significant contributions.

Mary Bacon
Somerset Community College
Somerset, Kentucky

Z. S. Dickerson
James Madison University
Harrisonburg, Virginia

Gregory W. Gray
State University College at Buffalo
Buffalo, New York

Carl M. Guelzo
Catonsville Community College
Catonsville, Maryland

Kathy Hegar
Mountain View College
Dallas, Texas

Garland E. Holt
Tarrant County Junior College
Hurst, Texas

Donald Musselman
James Madison University
Harrisonburg, Virginia

Anthony Porreca
University of Tennessee
Knoxville, Tennessee

Sarah Pyles
Ashland Community College
Ashland, Kentucky

Pierre Rothstein
Oakton Community College
Morton Grove, Illinois

Dennis Shannon
Belleville Area College
Belleville, Illinois

Bruce Walker
Arizona State University
Tempe, Arizona

Jerome M. Kinskey
Sinclair Community College
Dayton, Ohio

Gerry Welch
St. Louis Community College
St. Louis, Missouri

In addition we express appreciation to the following persons for their comments and suggestions: Gene Beckman, Jefferson Community College, Louisville, Kentucky; Wallace Conard, Columbus Technical Institute, Columbus, Ohio; Justin C. Cronin, Boston College, Chestnut Hill, Massachusetts; James Grigsby and Robert Rhile, Lake Sumter Community College, Leesburg, Florida; John J. Marsh, Northern New Mexico Community College, Santa Cruz, New Mexico; Robert Sands, Alfred State College, Alfred, New York; David R. Sargent, United Business Service, Boston, Massachusetts; Clay Sink, University of Rhode Island, Kingston, Rhode Island; and Robert St. Clair, Point Park College, Pittsburgh, Pennsylvania.

John Jackson joined the team for this eighth edition as collaborator. His contributions are many and most valuable. Our deep appreciation goes also to the cooperative staff of Prentice-Hall, Inc., our publisher, including Barbara Piercecchi, for her guidance and direction, and her able secretary, Linda Albelli; to Kim Gueterman, production editor; Marie Lines, copy editor; and Janet Schmid, designer.

INTRODUCTION TO MODERN BUSINESS

BUSINESS AND ITS ENVIRONMENT

PART I

BUSINESS AND OUR ECONOMIC SYSTEM

1

STUDY OBJECTIVES

WHEN YOU HAVE FINISHED READING THIS CHAPTER, YOU SHOULD BE ABLE TO

ONE Define the term economics and explain why we must have an economic system

TWO Discuss the essential components of our private-enterprise economy

THREE State some important national goals and show how they conflict with one another

FOUR Identify the factors of production as they relate to goods and services

FIVE Compare the principal features of capitalism, socialism, and communism

SIX Explain how we can judge the success of an economic system

IN THE NEWS

Barter Is Back, Bigger Than Ever

Barter refers to the swapping of goods with little or no money changing hands. It was carried on extensively during the Colonial period in America.

Barter is making a comeback, and on a national rather than an individual level. Many nations are being squeezed by the high cost of petroleum. These nations are finding it increasingly difficult to come up with the hard currencies they need to pay for it. So they have resorted to what they call trade agreements—a modern form of barter.

The U.S. Department of Commerce reports that between 10 and 20 percent of the $1.2 trillion annual stream of world commerce is in the form of "countertrade."

One example of countertrade is the building of a plant in Hungary, being supervised by Levi Strauss and Company. It is being paid for through a ten-year "buy back" agreement. Levi Strauss receives 60 percent of the plant's production.

Another example is the deal whereby Pepsico is supplying soft-drink syrup to the Soviet Union. In addition, it is aiding in the construction of Pepsi-Cola bottling plants there. In exchange, Pepsico received the exclusive U.S. marketing rights to Stolichnaya Vodka.

Trade experts predict that the kind of barter known as countertrade will boom in the 1980s.

The U.S. is universally recognized as the capital of capitalism, the land of free markets and the home of resourceful entrepreneurs. More than any other country, it has been known for leaving an entrepreneur free to decide prices for his products and set wages for his workers, free to grow and prosper—and free to go bankrupt if he failed. Historically, the U.S. Government has often done much to strengthen those twin pillars of free enterprise, private ownership and unfettered competition.

TIME ESSAY

Business enterprises produce goods and services for our society. These enterprises provide products and services that satisfy customers' needs and create employment. If well managed, they make profits for their owners. Those that fail to meet customers' needs must change or they soon disappear. The Hershey Foods Corporation provides an example of a business changing to meet changed customer needs.

In the past Hershey Foods has been almost totally dependent on the candy business. In recent years, however, the consumption of candy in the United States has declined. So, like many other businesses, the Hershey Corporation has been diversifying to reduce its dependence on one product.

The cost of the components of chocolate candy bars has risen considerably. This caused Hershey to raise the price and reduce the size of its candy bars. These changes occurred at the same time that the population group that buys the most candy (ages five to seventeen years) declined. The net effect was that the Hershey Corporation faced the risk of losing much of its profitability.

Hershey has made several moves to improve its position in providing products people want. The company acquired the Friendly Ice Cream Corporation, a chain of family restaurants, to give it a foothold in the growing fast-food business. Then Hershey acquired the Procino-Rossi Corporation and the Skinner Macaroni Company—regional pasta manufacturers.

We live in a rapidly changing and sometimes bewildering environment. Dealing with these changes—in performing our jobs, in making economic choices, and in using new technologies—requires an understanding of economics.

Some economists believe that the U.S. economy is moving into a new phase. The steady rise in the standard of living of the 1950s and 1960s changed during the decade of the 1970s. People have had to scramble to maintain their living standard against persistent inflation. The American public seems to be changing its expectations about what the future holds. Thus, future consumer buying patterns will be less predictable than in the past.

Economics is usually studied on two levels. One is by observing the behavior of specific units or how a specific company might react to changes in the status quo. This is called **microeconomics.** Or we might study larger segments of the economy, such as total annual production of all companies or total annual consumption of all family units. This is called **macroeconomics.** Both of these vantage points are useful for understanding business.

WHAT IS ECONOMICS?

Economics affects all of us, whether we understand how it does this or not. **ECONOMICS is a science that deals with the satisfaction of human wants through the use of scarce resources of production.** Since all resources are limited, there never are enough to give individuals all that they want. The economic system of a country must deal with the problem of allocating these scarce resources among the competing parties who want them.

An "economic system" results from the way in which people organize natural resources, labor, and management skills to produce and distribute the things they want. In many ways an economic system makes conflicting demands upon us. It may dictate certain behaviors, such as getting a job to provide income, and it may then change the demand for the jobs certain people are trained to perform. Engineers are a good example—ten years ago there was little demand for engineers, now there is a strong demand. At some point in the future we can be sure the demand for engineers will decline again. Individual workers must look out for their own interests—yet may have to join other workers to present a united front to get what they want. The ideal economic system rewards individual achievement—at the same time it encourages everyone to work together for the benefit of all.

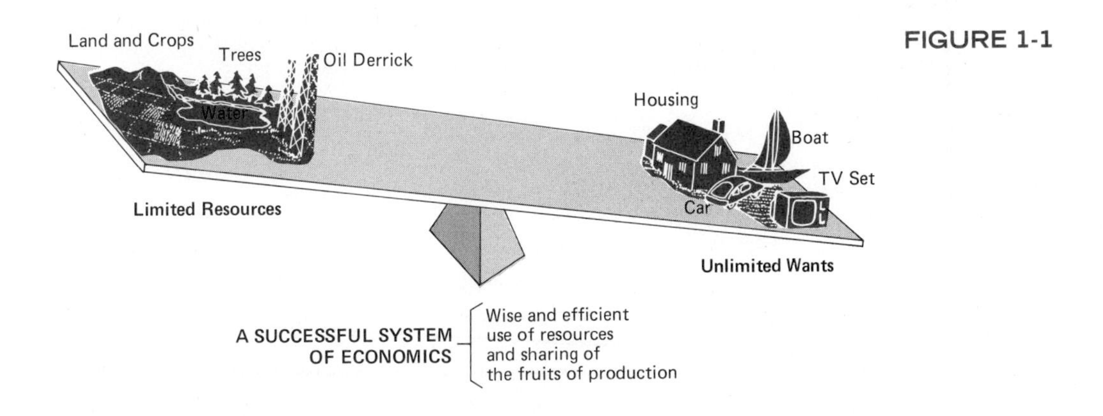

FIGURE 1-1

JOHN D. DeBUTTS

"A boss doesn't get a job done, his people do," believes John D. deButts, former chairman of the board and chief executive officer of AT&T.

"And you have to motivate your people," he says. "Sure, sometimes you have to direct, but even in a directive you should sell your reasons for doing something."

DeButts began developing this managerial style right after he joined the Bell System in 1936 as a traffic department trainee in Richmond, Virginia. "I must have been barking at the operators like a drill sergeant, and one started to cry," he recalls. "I guess that's when I started learning that you have to convince people, not order them."

That early lesson in employee relations stayed with him. For convincing people has been an integral part of his approach to managing ever since, an approach that has taken him through positions at three Bell operating companies—one as company president—and through three separate stints at AT&T.

DeButts also believes that "once a decision is made, a person should let people carry it out in their own way. I don't believe in telling people how to do something. It doesn't develop them and it takes away the enjoyment of the job. Once an objective is set, let 'em go to it."

DeButts places great emphasis on a feeling for people. "I think a good manager must understand human nature, and have compassion for people. The best bosses I worked for had this feeling, this compassion, and I hope I've learned from them."

DeButts spent the first twelve years of his Bell career in Virginia but then started moving rapidly around the Bell System. In 1949 he went to AT&T in New York as an engineer. In 1957 he worked in Washington, D.C., in government relations. In 1959 he became vice-president for operations and engineering and a director of the Chesapeake and Potomac Telephone Companies. And in 1962, at the age of forty-six, he became president of Illinois Bell—and was the youngest of the Bell System presidents.

He returned to AT&T as executive vice-president in April 1966, became vice-chairman of the board in February 1967, and chairman of the board and chief executive officer in April 1972. He retired as chairman in 1979.

DeButts serves on the board of directors of Citicorp (and its subsidiary, Citibank, N.A.), General Motors, Kraft Corporation, and United States Steel and is vice-chairman and a trustee of the Duke Endowment. He also serves as chairman of the Business Council, governor of the United Way of America (and chairman of its corporate development committee), on the executive and policy committees of the Business Roundtable and is vice-chairman of the Conference Board.

DeButts and his wife, Trudie, whom he married in 1939, have two daughters.

THE PRIVATE-ENTERPRISE ECONOMY

There are two basic tenets of a private-enterprise economic system: private ownership of productive resources, and the opportunity (freedom) to make choices. Because productive resources are privately owned, this system is sometimes called **capitalism.** Because citizens can make economic choices on their own as to what they will do, it is also called a **free-enterprise** system. In reality the American system is a mixed economy. Productive resources are largely privately owned. But the role of government is very strong and is becoming more important. Furthermore, individuals and businesses are not completely free to make choices. Therefore the term **private enterprise** seems to be more appropriate than either **capitalism** or **free enterprise.**

As we have seen, resources needed for production are limited, but people's wants are unlimited. Finding and managing scarce resources to fulfill people's needs will always be a problem. Even though people organize for their common good, deciding how to utilize the available resources requires answers to some basic questions in any economic system:

? What goods are to be produced?
Who determines what goods are to be produced?

? How are these goods to be produced?
How do we organize our resources to produce them?

? Who will receive the benefits of producing goods and services?
How will these benefits be distributed?

The manner in which these questions are answered determines the relative roles of private and governmental leadership. As they are answered and implemented, a nation's economic goals become established, and a method of achieving those goals is developed.

In some countries, economic decisions are made by millions of individuals. In other countries, where the major industries are owned collectively (by the government), economic decisions are made by the government. In authoritarian societies, economic decisions are made by a dictator and a few trusted advisers.

In some countries, changes in the arrangements made to answer the above questions take place over time. Hungary and the United States provide two examples.

Making Economic Choices

Making a choice requires selecting among alternatives. To make a choice, a business or an individual must have more than a single opportunity from which to choose. Making the best choice means selecting the best alternative. The best choice might be more earnings (or profits), or it might be more satisfaction through the enjoyment of goods or services. In making such choices, economics suggests that for a given degree of satisfaction, people will choose the cheapest alternative. Or, if costs are the same, people will choose the greatest satisfaction.

To illustrate: A rational business person, when selecting among several pieces of equipment of equal cost, will choose the one that affords the greatest

THE GOVERNMENT SHALL BECOME CAPITALIST AND THE CAPITALIST SHALL BE GOVERNED . . .

In Communist Hungary two examples of a decidedly capitalistic approach to things have been noted recently. The demand for American jeans has led the government to install a Levi's plant. It is Levi Strauss and Company's first plant behind the iron curtain. Hungarian workers for the plant were initially trained in the United States. The Hungarian jeans are basically the same as the American variety and sell at roughly twice the price of those in the United States.

Furthermore, the increasing demand for goods and services in Hungary has led to the establishment of privately owned shops and businesses. A black-market economy based upon private transactions has developed. This second economy takes care of such things as repairing cars, television sets, and homes. It is estimated that two out of three Hungarian workers supplement their income by such private employment. And by caring so well for material needs, Hungary's rulers have quieted political discontent.

In the United States about 41 percent of all families currently receive some government cash payment such as social security, welfare, or veterans' benefits. These payments are financed by taxing the incomes of individuals and the profits of companies. They are a form of income redistribution in which income is taken from one group and given to another. All of this is done with the approval of the elected representatives of the general public.

efficiency of operation or the largest output. A government, when selecting among aircraft of comparable performance and capability, will choose the cheapest.

Setting Individual and Collective Goals

Individual goals. By now it should be obvious that an economy without direction would function very poorly—or maybe not at all—and that a nation's people must work together for the benefit of the greatest number. In the United States most people are relatively free to run their own economic affairs. To begin with,

FIGURE 1-2

Americans can choose the type of work they want to do. This assumes, of course, their willingness and ability to prepare and qualify for such work. In fact, they may often choose either to go into business for themselves or to work for someone else. They are free to spend or to save their earnings, according to their own desires. Yet in all of this, each individual is only a part of the whole.

In the United States and in other parts of the free world, the individual exerts his or her influence upon the system by voting, both at the polls and in the marketplace. We have in this country a private-enterprise economy operating within a democratic political framework. Economic freedom and political freedom go hand in hand, complementing and reinforcing each other. And economic, social, and political freedoms allow people to set and achieve their economic goals.

Collective goals. In addition to individual needs, people have a group of collective wants, such as education, highways, national defense, and a variety of social benefits. In the United States we try to maintain high wages and stable prices, provide a high return on investments, conserve natural resources, increase the production of goods, protect business from unfair practices, and nurture cooperation between management and labor.

Just as an individual's goals give direction to his or her planning and effort, society's choice of goals gives direction to the national economy. But society's goals

ADAM SMITH, THE FOUNDER OF FORMAL ECONOMIC STUDY

Although the subject of economics is almost as old as recorded history, formal recognition of economics as a study began in 1776 when Adam Smith published a book called "The Nature and Causes of the Wealth of Nations". Within six months the supply of these books was exhausted. At that time Smith was known as the father of economics, and his "Wealth of Nations", as it was later called, became the basis of early economic theory.

According to Adam Smith, the best way to run an economy was by relying on the free operation of the "unseen hand" of competition. Competition would ensure that firms offered the best values to consumers or consumers would do business with the competitor. This philosophy of economics—the operation of competitive markets—became the basis upon which the economies of the United States and other Western democracies were established.

Adam Smith argued that government control of production was unnecessary. Businessmen should be permitted to produce the things that would earn them a profit. Smith strongly advocated the principle of "laissez faire" (to let alone), which he also applied to foreign trade by recommending free trade. This meant he was opposed to the mercantilists, a school of economic thought that sought to maintain regulation of excess exports over imports.

To a remarkable degree the policy of free pursuit of self-interest, used as part of other capitalistic theories, has had the results Adam Smith predicted. If Adam Smith were alive today, he would probably observe that many of our current economic problems are the same as when he lived. But today the answers have changed.

are not completely consistent with one another. Indeed, they may often be in direct conflict. For example, an attempt to maintain stable prices may run contrary to the desire for higher wages and dividends. The desire for increased consumption may conflict with the idea of conserving natural resources. New industry in the local community would provide more jobs for local workers, but it might decrease the quality of the environment by polluting the air or water. Increased technological development may cause, at least temporarily, increased unemployment. And free trade among the industrial nations conflicts with the desire for protection through import duties. Although we cannot completely reconcile these conflicting national goals, we can agree that **the overriding economic objective of the American people is the desire for an ever-rising living standard—a higher level of personal income and consumption—subject to conditions that provide for individual and national advancement and freedom of choice.** All this is also conditional upon maintaining an environment that enables us to live a good life.

BASIC RIGHTS OF A PRIVATE-ENTERPRISE SYSTEM

Certain basic rights provide the framework for our economic system. Without these rights the economic system we now have in the United States could not exist. They are intimately related to the social and political freedoms that characterize American democracy. As such, the economic foundations of the private-enterprise system constitute one of the foundations of democracy as we know it:

1. The right to property ownership
2. The right to a profit
3. The right to compete
4. The right of freedom of choice and contract

The relationship of these rights is expressed in Figure 1-3. Our enterprise system is a combination of the rights that belong to each individual.

Right to Property Ownership

Private enterprise is built around the idea of private property. By **PRIVATE ENTERPRISE** we mean **the system under which individuals are free to supply their own capital and operate their own businesses.** Thus, in a private-enterprise

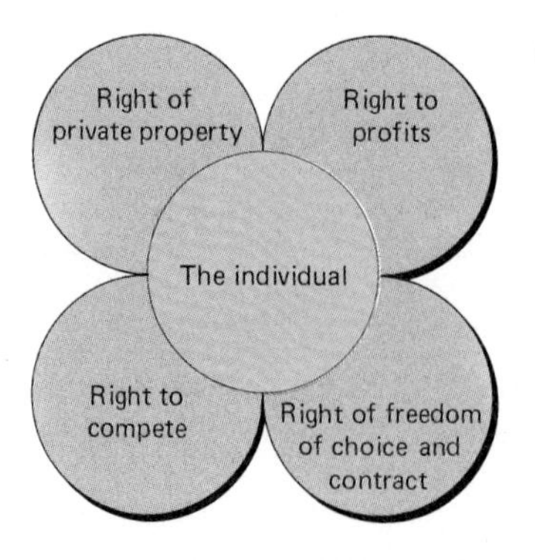

FIGURE 1-3

Basic rights of our capitalistic system.

system, factories, land, and products are owned by individuals and not by the government. Private property includes both tangible and intangible property. Tangible property includes buildings, equipment, and furniture. Intangible property includes shares of stock, patent rights, and insurance policies. The right to own property includes the right to control its use, sell it, or give it to another.

The right to own property is provided for under the Fifth and Fourteenth Amendments of the Constitution of the United States:

> [Fifth] . . . nor be deprived of life, liberty, or property . . . nor shall private property be taken for public use without just compensation.
>
> [Fourteenth] . . . nor shall any State deprive any person of life, liberty, or property, without due process of law. . . .

Many laws have been enacted to protect property owners against theft, confiscation, and embezzlement. In fact, the preservation of this right of private ownership is an essential function of government.

This right of private-property ownership takes place in a free market, which is part of the system used in transferring such ownership. Since capitalism is individualistic, it is not surprising to find that the primary driving force of such an economy is the emphasis on one's self-interest. Yet in pursuing the interests that achieve the most for the individual, the general welfare of society is often served as well.

Some property, however, is owned jointly with the state, and both goods and services are also produced by government enterprise. The U.S. post offices, public schools, and road systems are examples.

The Profit Incentive

The profit incentive is another essential part of capitalism. Adam Smith argued that the right to make a profit is the strongest form of business motivation.

In an economic sense, **profit** is the share of the product or enterprise going back to the owner after all payments are made for capital, materials, and labor, including management. Accountants use the term more broadly. For them,

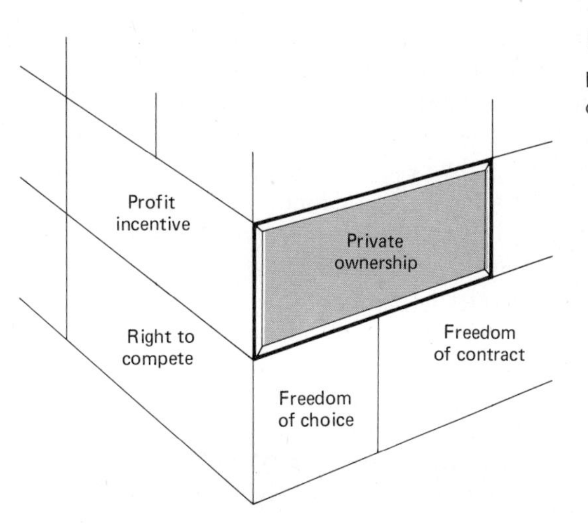

FIGURE 1-4

Private ownership is the cornerstone of capitalism.

PROFIT is **the net increase in company assets resulting from the operation of an enterprise.** Regardless of which definition you prefer, the profit motive is an inherent feature of capitalism. It is the entrepreneur who generally benefits most from profits.

Since the entrepreneur risks time, money, and effort, some argue that he or she should be allowed to make as large a profit as possible. Others feel that profit should be restricted to what is "fair and reasonable." Just what constitutes a fair and reasonable profit, however, is difficult to decide—many factors enter the picture. It is generally agreed that the entrepreneur is entitled to a return on investment. He or she should enjoy a margin of profit to cover possible losses in future years, and a reward for efficiency and ingenuity in management. You should remember that the entrepreneur faces the possibility of losing money instead of making a profit. Indeed another "right" that is often overlooked when talking about private enterprise is the right to fail. Thousands of businesses do just that every year. There are no guarantees of success or profit.

Profit is not an end in itself. It is a beginning. Profit is seed money for more products, more plants, more dividends, more tax payments, and more jobs, more opportunity. Profits can advance the well-being of everyone—rich and poor, consumers and producers, investors and noninvestors.

Profit pictures in the United States have recently been clouded by persistent inflation. For example, despite "record" earnings in 1978, General Motors, then the nation's largest industrial company, earned not one nickel more than it did five years earlier. When the 1978 profit is restated in 1973 dollars, GM earned only 5.5 percent on each dollar of sales—compared with 10.3 percent in 1965. Yet 1978 went on the books as a year of "record" profits because of inflated dollars.

The Opportunity to Compete

Private enterprise under the capitalist system leads to competition. **COMPETITION** is **the practice of trying to get something that is being sought by others under similar circumstances at the same time.** The ground rules and ethics of competitive practices are set up by the members of society through laws. Competition is good for both business and consumers. Self-interest encourages businesses to ask high prices. But when many competitors are bidding for the same business, price reductions ultimately enter the picture. In addition, the aggressive characteristics of one competitor may make him or her more efficient than another. Thus, under competition, managerial practices tend to be kept on a high plane of efficiency.

Competition operates in the market in many ways. Producers compete with one another for the best raw materials at the lowest prices. They also compete for the best factory locations and for the most efficient and productive workers. Wholesale and retail establishments also vie with one another for qualified employees and for the most desirable locations.

Some industrial firms compete principally with rival business enterprises that manufacture identical or similar products. They attempt to match or beat their competitors by making a better-quality or a better-designed product, and by giving better service.

Competition also prevails among firms that produce or sell different but related products. Manufacturers of one line of toys are competing with manufacturers of other toys and games for a share of the recreation market. Similarly,

PROFIT. WHAT ABOUT IT?

Opinion Research Corporation recently conducted a poll among American adults to get a feeling of public attitudes toward—and knowledge about—profit.

The public's estimate of the average manufacturer's after-tax profit on sales was six times the actual amount.

Auto company profits they overestimated at twenty times the actual amount.

Oil company profits they overestimated at eight times the actual amount.

Opinion Research Corporation's conclusions: (1) the public grossly overestimates profits, and (2) when compared with a previous poll, the public's knowledge of profit is worsening.

The poll also revealed that a majority of Americans want the government to put a ceiling on corporate profits.

a radio station competes with both newspapers and television stations for advertising.

One area of competition among entrepreneurs involves price. Entrepreneurs attempt to gain a price advantage over their competitors by lowering costs or increasing the efficiency of management.

Competition among entrepreneurs can benefit consumers in several ways. It leads to better service, for example. In an attempt to gain a service advantage over a competitor, a business owner may air-condition his or her place of business, extend credit to customers, or deliver merchandise to customers' homes. Competition also leads to better products for the consumer and tends to eliminate inefficient entrepreneurs. The business owner who cannot meet the competition—that is, a business owner who fails to provide better service or to produce a better or cheaper product—soon goes out of business.

Competition in certain industries has been reduced because of regulation or noncompetitive practices. Antitrust laws have been passed to help maintain competition in areas where it has faltered. In regulated industries the government is taking steps to increase competition as well. The drug industry is an example. New laws have been proposed that would (among other things) reduce the length of time a drug manufacturer has an "exclusive marketing" right from seventeen to five years. After five years other companies could produce the product, which would increase competition and reduce prescription costs to the consumer.

Freedom of Choice and Contract

Freedom of choice is another right of every person in a private-enterprise society. Many of us are free to either become entrepreneurs or work for someone else. We have the privilege of either manufacturing goods ourselves or distributing goods that others have produced. We can choose the type of goods we will produce or sell, and we can make decisions about our place of residence and employment.

We also enjoy freedom of choice as consumers in a private-enterprise system. We decide whether to buy, where and when and how much to buy, and whether the product or service is worth the price being asked. This right is a distinguishing characteristic of the private-enterprise system.

Another privilege enjoyed by members of a free society is freedom of contract. This is simply the right of every entrepreneur, worker, property owner, and consumer to bargain. This freedom includes the right to exchange goods and services on terms that are acceptable to all parties concerned.

The economic freedoms and the other freedoms of a democratic people are so interrelated that it is impossible to separate them.

William A. Simon, former U.S. Secretary of the Treasury, said it this way:

> By whatever name one wishes to call this category of free human action—free enterprise, the free market, capitalism—it simply means that men are free to produce. They are free to discover, to invent, to experiment, to succeed, to fail, to create means of production, to exchange goods and services, to profit, to consume—all on a voluntary basis without significant interference by the policing powers of the state.

Could a democracy survive without freedom of choice? Would a democracy actually exist in complete absence of freedom of contract? How free would the businessperson be if he or she could not choose the nature of the enterprise? These questions clearly indicate that the foundations of the American economy are also the foundation of American democracy.

"Free enterprise" assumes that individuals are the best judges of their own interests, and that an economic system that makes it possible for them to pursue those interests will achieve the greatest welfare for all.

In the United States we enjoy these economic freedoms:

1. Freedom to make a career choice and a job selection
2. Freedom to change jobs at our own discretion
3. Freedom to invest our savings in the private-enterprise econmy
4. Freedom to choose among a wide variety of available goods and services

Our private-enterprise economy fosters these freedoms and allows them to operate.

ECONOMIC GOALS IN THE UNITED STATES

To understand the American economy, we must consider a number of economic goals that are based on values—values that are widely accepted in this country. These goals can be summarized as follows:

1. *Promote economic growth.* Increase the amount of goods and services available to Americans and at the same time maintain an economy that allows for the distribution of a high level of national income. Promote a high level of stability for prices.
2. *Promote a rising standard of living.* As an increased quantity of goods are produced, a family can live better than before without sacrificing savings.
3. *Maintain full employment.* Useful jobs should be available for all who are willing and able to work.
4. *Encourage price stability.* Stable prices are needed to minimize upswings and downswings in the business cycle and to prevent inflation and deflation in the value of the dollar.

5. *Provide an equitable distribution of income.* This is to be accomplished by maintaining full employment, increasing the productivity of workers, and removing job discrimination.

6. *Ensure economic freedom.* Americans should have the freedom to choose the work they prefer with the right to buy goods freely in the marketplace.

7. *Provide financial security.* Persons who are disabled, aged, dependent, or otherwise handicapped and unable to care for themselves should be eligible for some type of economic assistance and employment training to qualify for work opportunities.

Some of these goals are interrelated. For example, full employment helps to maintain a high standard of living and give workers financial security. Where goals are in conflict, a system of priorities must be developed. Often a goal that helps one group is detrimental to others.

THE FACTORS OF PRODUCTION

The goal of our economic system is to produce the goods and services that will satisfy human wants. Some people believe that production simply means turning out radios, cars, clothes, furniture, and other products. This belief is true as far as it goes. But **production** defined in a broader sense is the process of transferring inputs from human and physical resources into outputs wanted by consumers. These outputs may be either goods or services. Production involves four essential elements, which are called the **factors of production:**

1. Natural resources
2. Labor
3. Capital
4. Entrepreneurship

Figure 1–5 suggests that an interlocking relationship exists among these elements. This becomes more obvious when you think about each of the elements.

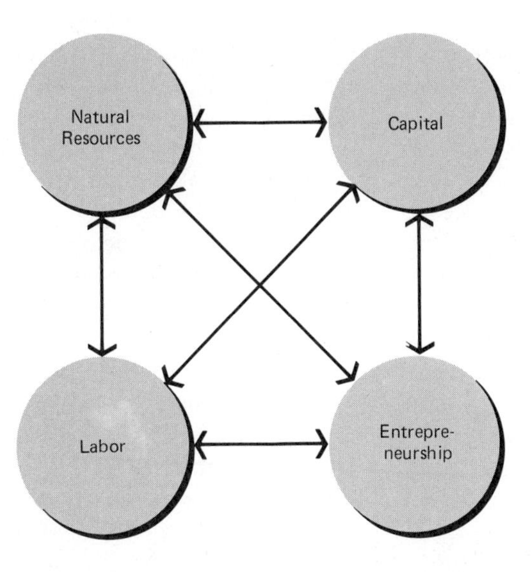

FIGURE 1-5

Relationships among the factors of production.

Natural Resources

Land is one resource that is essential to production. Its most important characteristic is that it is a **fixed resource**. In addition to serving as a location for equipment and buildings, it is capable of producing crops of all kinds and the minerals used in production. From an economic standpoint the reward for the use of land is rent, a monetary return derived from putting it to profitable use. Some economists are alarmed by what is happening to land and its use. Such public issues as land zoning and land-use planning are being raised and challenged in the courts to determine who is responsible for the environment.

On and under land surface lie our known supplies of forests and minerals. Much has been said about our limited supply of petroleum and natural gas. But all other mineral resources are also in limited supply. Although we have an abundance of coal and an adequate supply of iron ore, we are dependent on imports for many essential minerals. We cannot replace the deposits of mineral resources, and we are consuming them at a rapid pace. Annual consumption of industrial raw materials (fuels, metals, minerals, and building materials) is eighteen tons per capita. The mineral deposits lying on the ocean beds have not yet been explored, and they represent our next area of development.

The rich U.S. land area, together with our mild climate, provides one of our most valuable natural resources. It is the principal source of materials that can be replaced—grains, animals, forests, and fibers.

Historically, there has been plenty of clean, pure water and fresh air. But with worldwide industry developing at the present rate, we are polluting the air, lakes, and rivers at an alarming rate. Ecologists and conservationists have called attention to this situation. And both national and state governments have become concerned. Manufacturing industries are spending billions of dollars annually to protect air and water resources.

Labor

Labor is the second factor of production—human effort directed toward the creation of goods and services. Unskilled labor is very available, but highly skilled labor is often scarce in areas where it is most needed. Even during times of high employment there are shortages of certain types of skilled labor.

In the United States we have an adequate supply of labor for both agriculture and manufacturing. There are two discernible trends in the makeup of our labor force: (1) the number of women entering the labor force has been steadily increasing in recent years, and (2) the percentage of people employed in the production of goods is decreasing while the percentage involved in services is increasing.

The reward for labor is wages. If labor forces the selling price of the product up and the price becomes too high, the demand for that product will decline. Changes in the demand for the finished product will inevitably cause changes in employers' demands for labor. Labor is paid two types of income: wages and fringe benefits. In recent negotiations between management and labor, fringe benefits have received increasing emphasis. Fringe benefits now constitute over 35 percent of the total cost of wages in the United States. The amount of wages a worker receives constitutes his or her **money income. The value of that wage in terms of its purchasing power is called REAL INCOME.** During periods of inflation, workers seek to preserve their real income. During periods of unemployment, they are concerned about the loss of jobs.

The largest single category of the labor force is engaged in manufacturing, about one-fourth of the total. The second largest employment segment is trade, with about one-fifth of the total. Government is third, employing one-sixth of the total. The percentage of employed workers in nine selected industries is shown in Table 1-1.

Capital

Capital is another major factor of production. The use of the term **capital** is not restricted to money invested in a business enterprise. Business capital includes all the additions of value that require money to purchase or build—land, buildings, equipment—and that are used in production. **Machinery, equipment, and supplies used in the production of other goods and services are called CAPITAL GOODS.** A farmer's capital goods would consist of his tractors, cultivators, harvesters, trucks, and all other types of machinery and tools. The function of capital goods is to assist labor in production and increase the amount of goods and services produced. Capital provides the tools and other means for labor to produce. Without capital to purchase machinery, farmers would still be producing by primitive means only enough to feed themselves. The result would be a hungry world. The United States feeds much of the rest of the world because of its capital-intensive farming methods.

The Entrepreneur

The history of early industrial development and trade in America is largely the history of U.S. entrepreneurs. It describes people with the pioneer spirit, initiative, and inspiration, and a willingness to work and take risks. An **ENTREPRENEUR is the chief initiator or organizer of a business enterprise.** In proprietorships and partnerships the entrepreneurs take the **risk**. They are the ones who stand to gain

TABLE 1-1
PERCENTAGE OF EMPLOYEES IN NINE SELECTED INDUSTRIES, 1940–1980

Industry	1940	1950	1960	1970	1980 (est).
Manufacturing	25.2	27.5	27.2	25.8	24.1*
Wholesale and retail trade	16.1	17.7	19.4	19.9	20.1
Government	9.8	11.0	14.1	16.7	18.0
Services	8.0	9.2	11.1	15.4	17.0
Agriculture	25.5	18.2	11.8	6.0	4.8
Transportation and public utilities	7.0	7.2	6.5	6.0	5.8
Contract construction	3.0	4.2	4.7	4.5	4.4
Finance	3.3	3.3	4.1	4.9	5.2
Mining	2.1	1.7	1.1	0.8	0.6

*Percent of total

or lose from the business operations. In corporations it is the stockholders who are the risk takers.

Historically, management has been considered to be a right and responsibility of the entrepreneur. However, a distinction should be made between the **owner-manager**, or entrepreneur, and the **professional manager**. The professional manager has a somewhat different set of motives and responsibilities, since he or she is not the sole owner of the enterprise. Management and labor are seldom in agreement as to the value of the contribution each makes to the success of the enterprise. Labor has been gaining more and more input in decision making in large businesses where the work force is unionized. Management brings together, coordinates, and directs the various components of the production process. Managers are responsible for manufacturing operations and marketing. Chapters 4 and 5 discuss in detail the theory, principles, and practices of business organization and management.

OTHER ECONOMIC SYSTEMS

Although capitalism rests squarely on the right of property ownership and the profit incentive, this is not true of other ideologies, such as socialism and communism.

Socialism

The chief difference between socialism and capitalism is found in the area of property ownership. Socialism, like capitalism, is market oriented. But it differs in that the basic industries are owned and controlled by government. The basic industries usually include mineral production, such as coal and oil, transportation and communication, and certain of the major manufacturing industries. The government thus controls the economy and determines the kinds and amounts of goods to be produced. Individuals may own personal property and small business enterprises (particularly distributive businesses), and they are free to choose the occupations in which they work.

The chief weaknesses of socialism are the lack of individual incentive and the inefficiency that results from government bureaucracy. England provides an excellent current example of a socialistic society and the problems that can result. Capitalism rewards accomplishment through the profit incentive; socialism does not. Lacking this incentive, people tend not to dedicate their efforts toward achieving efficient production.

Government-operated businesses are noted for their inefficiency and the lack of executive leadership. Many government operations are overstaffed, and management positions are changed as other persons come into power in political office. Appointments to important positions are made on the basis of personal friendship or as repayment for political favors, rather than one's ability to do the job.

Communism

The Union of Soviet Socialist Republics (Soviet Russia) and the People's Republic of China (Communist China) are the two leading exponents of communism. In contrast to private ownership, communism practices total government ownership. The government owns the means of production, and the people work for the government. (This is sometimes referred to as state capitalism.)

Since the government owns both the land and the factories, there is no way for workers to "invest their savings" in productive enterprises. The government decides what is to be produced, and "consumer needs" rate a low priority in the two countries mentioned when compared with the United States.

The profit incentive does not exist under communism. There is little or no reward for tasks well done, such as our practice of paying dividends or bonuses. And a promotion within a plant hierarchy would mean added responsibilities without the increase in pay that we would usually expect. Most personal incentives available to American workers are absent under the Communist system, including the right to strike or bargain for benefits.

Communism does not recognize rights and freedoms for individuals to the extent that democracy does. The state is supreme, and state officials do the planning. Government leaders determine their successors—leaders are not chosen by a vote of the people.

Capitalism and communism stand at opposite poles. The Communist, seeing the rich person with a fine home, says: "No one should have so much." The capitalist, seeing the same thing, says: "All people have the right to seek as much."

There have been recent reports that the profit incentive is being practiced on a small scale in the USSR. Apparently, production under the commune plan has lagged significantly behind expectations.

No doubt each form of government has its advantages and disadvantages, but the important thing to remember is this: A nation's form of government and the nature of its economic system are interrelated and interdependent. Frank M. Dixon summed it up well when he wrote:

> No matter what the form of a government, there are in fact only two kinds of government possible. Under one system, the state is everything and the individual is an incident. Under that system, the individual is a subject, rather than a citizen. Under that system, the individual has no rights, though they may be termed such; he has only privileges. Under that system, the state is the reservoir of all rights, all privileges, all powers. But this system our forefathers rejected. They declared that all just government derives its powers from the consent of the governed. They affirmed the dignity and the sanctity of the individual. . . . They elected a man-made state, not a state-made man.

Table 1-2 compares capitalism with socialism and communism.

APPRAISING THE ACHIEVEMENTS OF AN ECONOMIC SYSTEM

How would you determine whether an economic system has done well or poorly? It is possible to measure the system in terms of economic growth, productivity, and distribution of personal income.

TABLE 1-2
COMPARISON OF CAPITALISM, SOCIALISM, AND COMMUNISM

Characteristic of the System	Capitalism	Socialism	Communism
Economic markets	Freedom to compete with right to invest.	Limited competition with state-owned industries.	Absence of competition with state-owned markets and industries.
Individual incentives	Profits and wages in relation to one's ability and willingness to work.	Profits recognized. Wages set by state based on workers' needs.	Profits not allowed. Workers urged to work for the glory of the state. Bonuses for exceeding quotas.
Capital sources	Capital invested by owners who may also borrow on credit. Capital may be reinvested from profits. Depreciation is legal.	Obtained from owners and from state-issued bonds for state-owned industries. Depreciation permitted.	State provides all resources to start a business owned by the state. No depreciation.
Labor	Workers generally free to select an employer and an occupation.	Worker allowed to select occupation. State planning encourages employment.	The state determines one's employer and employment.
Management	Managers selected on basis of ability. Managers have freedom to make decisions.	Managers in state-owned industries must answer to the state. Non-monetary rewards emphasized.	Key managers must be party members to qualify. Absence of freedom to make decisions.
Business ownership	Individuals have right to own a business and to contract with others.	State owns basic industries, including steel, mines, and transportation. Other businesses may exist.	State owns all productive capacity, including communes.
Risk assumption	Losses assumed by owners. May transfer business risk to other businesses through insurance.	People assume risks of state-owned industries. Losses taken from taxes.	Economic production owned by the state. Risks assumed by the state. Losses reduce standard of living.

Economic Growth

Of the several measures of economic growth, the one most commonly used is the gross national product. By **GROSS NATIONAL PRODUCT (GNP)** we mean **the total value of all finished goods produced and services rendered in an economy for one year.** In a way, the GNP serves as an index of the degree to which our output is growing (measured in terms of market value). It is the most comprehensive measure of what the people in a given country produce. We often read that the growth rate in such countries as Germany and Japan is much greater than in the United States. When interpreting comparative growth rates, however, we must consider the age span of a country's industrial development. Growth rates are greatest during the early years of industrial expansion. As a nation's industrial development matures, it is harder to attain the same rate of increase as that achieved during its infancy. As a country's population increases, its GNP would naturally grow. So the per capita GNP growth is the more important measure of growth.

THE CASE FOR ECONOMIC GROWTH

Persons concerned with the environment have continually called our attention to the harmful results of economic growth. Growth, they point out, depletes the resources under the earth's surface and denudes our forests. The use of our resources leads to a runoff of chemicals and pesticides into rivers, lakes, and oceans. It pollutes the atmosphere and leads to an excessive concentration of population in cities. In a very real sense, more gross national product means more gross national pollution.

But it evidently is not possible to call a halt to growth and to keep everything else the way it now is. Many of the characteristics of our society are premised on a condition of economic growth. Abolish growth and we halt the workings of society in their present form.

The case for growth rests first upon the fact that a growing population means an increasing labor force. Obviously these people demand jobs and their share of the nation's produce.

Another element in the case for growth is the rising aspirations of people. People demand more and more goods and services per capita, a situation complicated by the fact that there are more "per capitas."

Also, more goods and services will be needed to solve pollution problems. Pollution is inherent in much of production, but, paradoxically, to bring it under control more production is also needed.

The GNP has its limitations as a measure, despite the fact that it is convenient and widely used. (The GNP does not measure the value of *all* the goods and services produced. For example, the food a farmer grows for his own consumption and the services a housewife gives her family are not included.) GNP is limited (with a few exceptions) to goods and services that are exchanged in markets. The GNP for the U.S. is depicted in Figure 1-6.

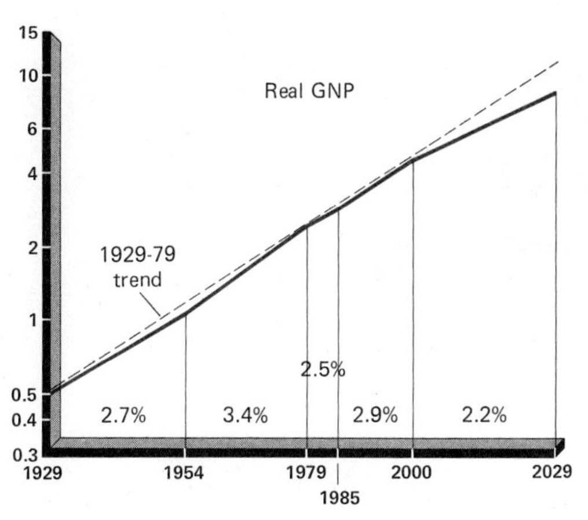

FIGURE 1-6
(Source: Council of Economic Advisers and Bureau of Economic Analysis.)

Productivity

Productivity is another good way to evaluate an economic system. **PRODUCTIVITY** refers to **the output achieved in relation to the input taken to produce it.** (**Input** is the amount of materials and labor consumed to produce goods and services.) The greater the number of goods produced in a given time, the better the system. Increased output leads to higher wages, shorter hours, lower prices, and a greater return to the business owner. There are two ways of measuring productivity: the average hourly output per worker, and the national income per person-hour (one person times one hour equals one person-hour).

The typical worker in the United States today produces approximately six times more than the average worker produced a hundred years ago. This does not mean that today's worker works six times as hard. It means that this ratio is based on dollar value in terms of constant (not fluctuating) purchasing power. The productivity of American workers in the past has been very good. However, the productivity rate in the United States during the past decade has been most disappointing.

Improved Standard of Living

Perhaps the best test of the achievement of an economic system is how well the people fare under it. This is generally called the standard of living. **STANDARD OF LIVING** refers to **people's living level or quality of life—the degree to which their economic needs can be satisfied by the family income.** It is a qualitative rather than a quantitative measure. The best way to measure it would be personal income per person, or family, stated in terms of its purchasing power. The total number of dollars may be increasing, but what will they buy? You will recall that when one's earnings are measured in terms of what they will buy, this is called real income. The growth in buying power of the American worker between 1949 and 1980 is depicted in Figure 1-8. The comparison of living standards of people in the United States and other industrialized nations is shown in Figure 1-9.

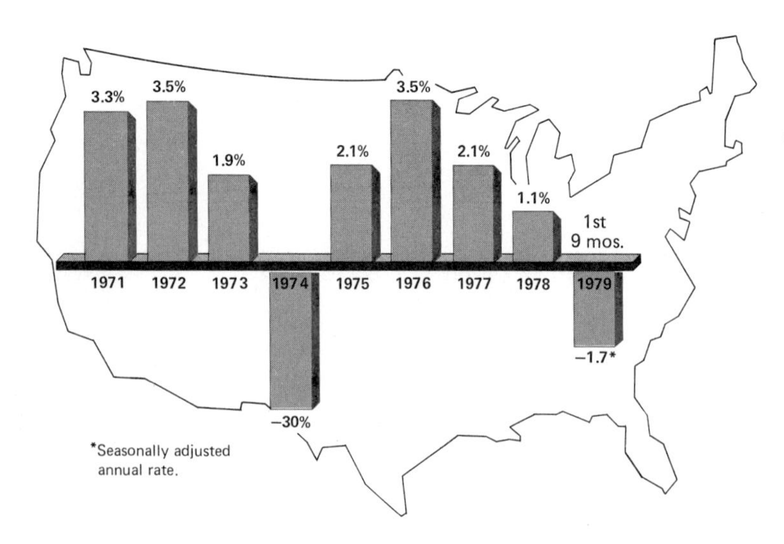

FIGURE 1-7
Productivity—output per person-hour (annual percentage change).
(Source: U.S. Department of Labor.)

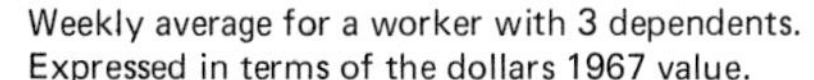

Weekly average for a worker with 3 dependents.
Expressed in terms of the dollars 1967 value.

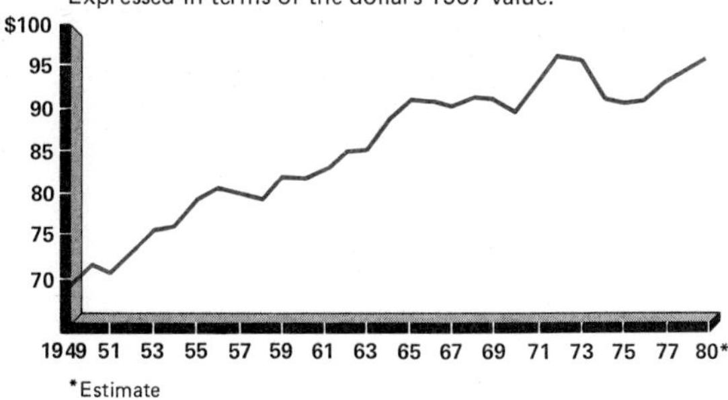

FIGURE 1-8

Paycheck buying power.
(Source: Bureau of the Census and Bureau of Economic Analysis.)

Economic Stability

The history of economic development has always been characterized by cyclical change. The smaller the span between the high and low points of the cycle, the better the economic system. Because nations are economically dependent upon one another, seldom will a country experience prosperity or recession alone. Instead the business conditions characterizing one nation's economy will be present to a similar degree in other countries with which it carries on international trade.

For the past three decades the United States has experienced a period of general prosperity. Periodically there have been minor recessions or adjustments. The most serious of these was the recession of 1974–75, which prevailed throughout the free world. It was a period in which inflation and high unemployment existed together. This was a departure from prior experience when only one or the other was the primary concern of government and business at one time.

The Leading Business Indicators

Information from the U.S. Department of Commerce is important to the business and industrial community. Among the data published regularly is the "Composite Index of Leading Indicators." This index has twelve components, which are appraised monthly. The data for each component are collected monthly and are then combined to form one index. These measures when taken together show how

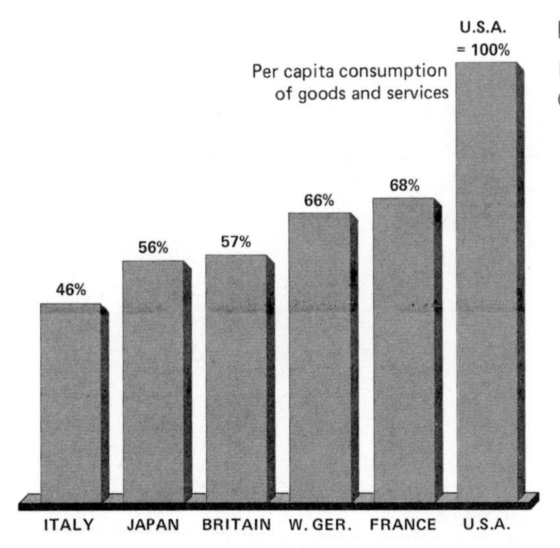

FIGURE 1-9

Living standards.
(Source: United Nations data.)

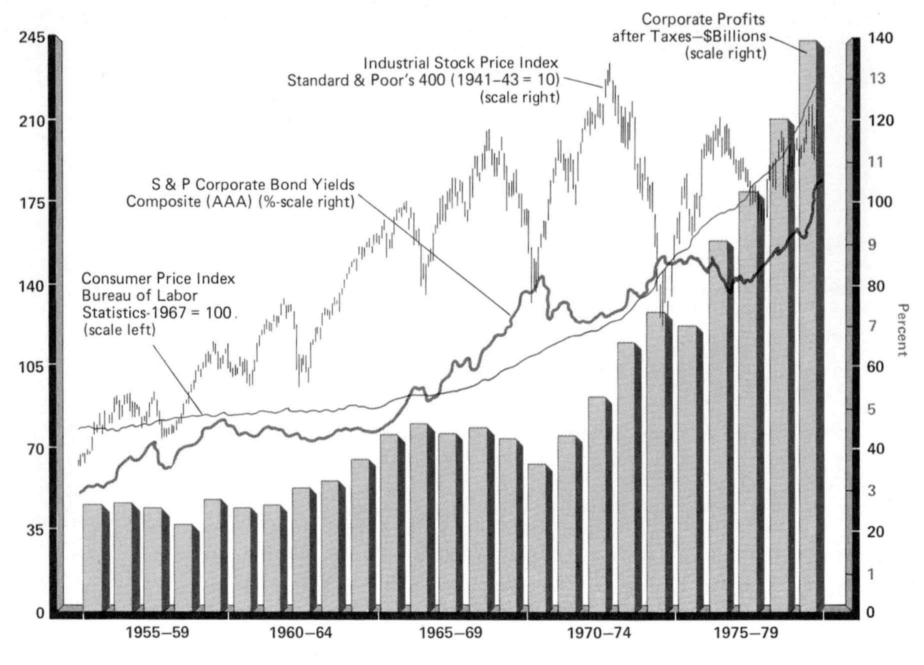

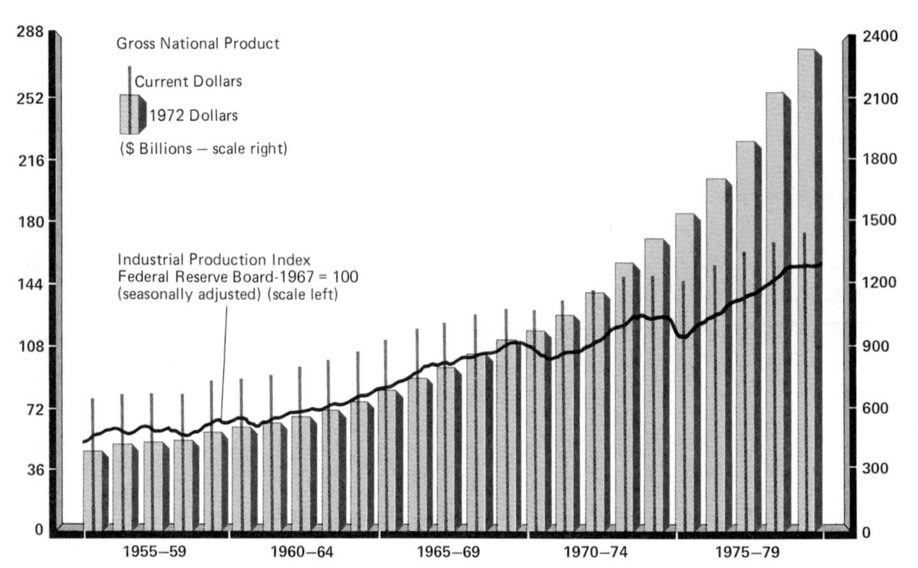

FIGURE 1-10

Trends of stock, bonds, profits, and business since 1955. (Source: United Business Service.)

the general business climate is moving. Changes during a single month may not be significant. But when the composite index shows continued gains month by month, this is an indication that business is improving. The index now in use was revised in 1975. The one used earlier expressed several components in current dollars. It thus failed to make needed adjustments because of inflation. Index movements over short periods may reflect the influence of random events. Examples of such events are unusual or extreme weather patterns; or a prolonged strike by members of a large labor union, such as the teamsters, the dockworkers, or the mine workers.

The components that make up this composite index are shown in Table 1-3.

TABLE 1-3
THE TWELVE LEADERS

1. Average workweek of production workers, manufacturing.
2. Layoff rate, manufacturing.
3. Value of manufacturers' new orders for consumer goods and materials in 1972 dollars.
4. Index of net business formation.
5. Standard & Poor's index of 500 common stock prices.
6. Contracts and orders for plant and equipment in 1972 dollars.
7. Index of new private housing units authorized by local building permits.
8. Vendor performance—percentage of companies reporting slower deliveries.
9. Net change in inventories on hand and on order in 1972 dollars.
10. Change in sensitive prices of key raw materials—excludes foods, feeds, and fibers.
11. Change in total liquid assets—the liquid wealth held by private investors.
12. Money supply in 1972 dollars.

SOURCE: U.S. Department of Commerce, Business Conditions Digest.

SOME ECONOMIC ISSUES

Although our mixed economy has many advantages, it also has its disadvantages. Business, labor, government, and the public must cooperate if our system is to serve the best interests of all the people. The U.S. private-enterprise system has demonstrated its ability to function acceptably, maintain a high living standard, eliminate most poverty, and find ways to reduce unemployment. Many challenging issues still exist, such as the following:

1. How can we best hold down inflation and still expand economic growth?
2. Should the government guarantee everyone who is able and willing the opportunity to work?
3. How large should business enterprises and labor unions become? Are big business and powerful labor unions good or bad for the country?
4. Should more government funds be used to subsidize economic growth?
5. How should the burden of taxes be determined in order to make the payment of taxes more equitable?
6. How can we determine the long-range social and economic costs and benefits of various government programs?
7. How can we balance production growth with the conservation of natural resources?
8. How will the energy needed to fuel the world's industries be distributed and the monetary payments for it be recycled?

These are but a few of the major economic issues facing our nation. Some of them are more complex than others, but all command the attention of persons in public and private positions of importance. In the next several chapters many of these issues are explored in more detail.

Inflation

The years of high and volatile inflation during and following the Vietnam War put an end to over a century of relative price stability in the United States. **Inflation** is a general increase in the prices of goods and services throughout the economy.

Economists have long felt that inflation is a self-limiting process. It is caused by a temporary imbalance between the demand and the supply for goods and services. When either the demand drops or the supply increases, inflation should level off. However, the old idea that inflation carries with it the basis for an economic decline no longer seems to hold true.

Many experts believe that only by rebuilding America's industrial base, and developing new sources of energy, can the persistent rise in inflation be stopped. Productivity in the United States (output per worker) has increased very slowly and has even decreased over certain recent periods of time. This does not necessarily mean that people are not working as hard, but it does indicate that they could use better tools and machines in their work.

CAREERS IN ECONOMICS

Many individuals make their living analyzing economic facts so that business managers, business owners, and government officials will be able to make more intelligent predictions and daily decisions. A career as an economist can therefore be an interesting, challenging, and rewarding area of employment.

The economist works largely in three areas: (1) in business enterprises, (2) in government, or (3) in a college or university as a teacher of economics. To a lesser degree, economists are also employed by independent research firms that provide business with analyses of economic data to aid in solving specific problems.

Business Enterprises

Individual firms are the largest employers of economists. These include banks, insurance companies, manufacturing firms, retail distribution chains, transportation companies, construction companies, and farms. Many business decisions depend upon a better understanding of how the economy is working and what action the firm should take to prevent business losses due to economic fluctuations.

Government

Many economists are employed in the area of government. This includes not only the federal government but also state and local governments. There are also career opportunities in government agencies outside the United States. Much of the government economist's work involves conducting economic studies and collecting and interpreting facts that pertain to the current business scene.

Education

Those who wish to go into economic areas but are not interested in either business or government may have a rewarding career in teaching economics. Most of the individuals who teach at the college level eventually obtain a Ph.D. degree in economics. Some of them work part time as economic consultants to labor unions, trade associations, and small business firms.

SUMMARY OF KEY CONCEPTS

Economics is everyone's concern. It deals with the management of resources in meeting people's wants.

The fundamental economic problem of every society is *wants versus scarcity.* People's wants have no limits, but the resources available are limited.

Individually and collectively we must make *choices.* The law of economics dictates that for a given degree of satisfaction, one will choose the cheapest alternative. When the costs are the same, one will choose the greatest satisfaction.

The basic features of our mixed economy are

a. Private ownership of productive resources
b. The right to earn a profit
c. Competition in the marketplace
d. Freedom of choice and contract

The economic goals of our country are

a. Economic growth
b. Rising standard of living
c. Full employment
d. Price stability
e. Equitable income
f. Economic freedom
g. Financial security

The basic factors of production consist of natural resources, labor, capital, and entrepreneurship.

Socialism and communism as economic systems contrast with capitalism in that they minimize private ownership and competition. Government ownership and planning are emphasized.

When we measure the success of an economic system, some of the criteria used are

a. Economic growth
b. Productivity
c. Rising standard of living
d. Economic stability
e. Index of leading indicators

BUSINESS TERMS

You should be able to match these business terms with the statements that follow:*

a. Capitalism
b. Capital goods
c. Competition
d. Economics
e. Entrepreneur
f. Factors of production
g. Gross national product
h. Private-enterprise economy
i. Productivity
j. Profit
k. Real income
l. Socialism
m. Standard of living

1. The science of using scarce resources to satisfy human wants
2. An economic system based on property ownership and the profit motive
3. Equipment, tools, and machinery used in production

*In this Business Terms Section, the number of business terms sometimes exceeds the number of statements that follow.

4. A person who invests time, money, and effort in a business enterprise and assumes the risks involved
5. The net income left to a business after all expenses have been paid
6. Effort to gain possession of something actively being sought by others
7. The essential components that together make up manufacturing
8. Wages stated in terms of its purchasing power
9. The sum total of all goods and services produced in one year
10. The output of goods produced measured in relation to raw materials and labor used
11. The level of living and quality of life of the people
12. An economic system where the major productive industries are owned and controlled by the government

REVIEW QUESTIONS

1. What is the main economic concern of any country?
2. What questions must the people of a nation answer when deciding how to develop an economic scheme?
3. State and define the essential foundations of our private-enterprise economy.
4. What are the chief economic goals in the United States?
5. What are the essential factors of production in any economy?
6. Which of the economic systems—capitalism, socialism, and communism—encourages each of the following: the making of a profit, rights of labor, competition, right of private ownership, government ownership of the factors of production?

DISCUSSION QUESTIONS

1. Sometimes our national goals are in conflict with one another. What criteria should be followed in resolving such conflicts?
2. In what way is the right to own property a basic right in a capitalistic economy?
3. How are economic, political, and social freedoms interrelated?
4. Which of the economic goals of a private-enterprise economy do you think is most important and why?
5. Which of the factors of production are lacking in most nonindustrialized countries?
6. Select one of the issues mentioned in this chapter, and state your position regarding it.

BUSINESS CASE 1-1

Making Economic Choices

James Peterson owns a large cattle ranch in Colorado, which has been in his family for three generations. He is fortunate because a creek of clear water runs through his ranch and supplies drinking water for his cattle. On the back boundary of his ranch, bordering upon the creek and beyond, are fifty acres of forest. Years ago a sizable deposit of low-sulfur coal was discovered on the opposite side of the ranch.

The Mountain Timber Corporation has approached James about buying his timber. This would yield him a considerable one-payment sum of money. However, he fears that it would denude the land and contaminate the water in the creek. The payment for the timber looms large for the present. But there are important questions about what effect cutting the timber would have on maintaining a watershed for his cattle in future years.

The Western Coal Company has also offered James an attractive contract to strip-mine his land for the coal. This, too, is a tempting offer but would destroy the beauty of that part of his ranch. This coal-deposit area lies under a rolling rugged area, which he views from the front of his home. In fact, it is his favorite view of the countryside.

Although there are no restrictions in the deed to his ranch, James knows that his father constantly resisted opportunities to let the coal be mined. He repeatedly spoke of the beautiful view and vowed to keep it that way for posterity.

Adjacent to the creek is some relatively level and productive ground. But the annual rainfall in this area is insufficient for growing crops. James has wondered about pumping water from the creek to irrigate this portion of his farm. None of his neighbors are irrigating, but if they should all undertake such a practice, there would not be enough water to go around.

The cost of feed has risen recently, and the profit margin on raising cattle has narrowed somewhat. But the economic forecast is for higher beef prices in the future.

So James is faced with making some choices.

1. What choices are available to him?
2. What specific alternatives would enable him to have the "best of both worlds"?

BUSINESS AND SOCIETY

STUDY OBJECTIVES

WHEN YOU HAVE FINISHED READING THIS CHAPTER, YOU SHOULD BE ABLE TO

ONE Describe the different types of environment within which business must function

TWO Define consumerism and describe its role in society

THREE Explain what is being done to give minorities and women fair treatment in business

FOUR Discuss what has caused our physical environment to deteriorate, and offer suggestions for restoring it

FIVE Describe various actions the government is taking to protect and improve the environment

SIX Illustrate how business is attempting to meet its responsibility to society

IN THE NEWS

Equal Opportunity—Equal Rights

The federal government has announced guidelines for ending sex bias in college athletics. The ruling is that sports scholarship money must be distributed proportionately, that is, according to the number of male and female athletes enrolled. For example, if 30 percent of a school's athletes are women, female athletes must receive 30 percent of the scholarship money.

The government will weigh other factors to see if a school is treating women athletes fairly. This includes such things as equipment, locker rooms, and coaching. This does not mean that facilities must be identical, but they must provide equal opportunity.

The corporation is operating in a "pressure-cooker" environment. It is attacked by environmentalists, consumerists, women's liberation advocates, the civil rights movement, and other activist groups.

BUSINESS WEEK, SPECIAL REPORT

We have already seen that business exerts a major influence on our way of life and on economic relationships. In this chapter we consider the responsibility of business to people's lives and well-being. Society is asking the business firm, as a social institution, to accept more responsibility for these things. Years ago the phrase "social responsibility of business" usually referred to social contributions in the local communities, and ethical practices. Today it involves much more, such as giving consumers more information and better service, hiring minority workers and eliminating discrimination, and maintaining a clean physical environment.

BUSINESS ENVIRONMENTS

Business both determines and is the product of environmental influences. The factors that make up the environment are constantly changing. So, in order to survive and prosper, business must also change. By **ENVIRONMENT** we mean **the sum of all the external forces that influence individuals, businesses, and communities.** It includes ethical, legal, economic, political, social, and physical elements—each overlaps and influences the others. All are discussed at length in this chapter.

Modern Business in a Pluralistic Society

Business today is the focal point of many strong and diverse interests. These interests are motivated by self-interest, but they must also be concerned with public interest. Business is dependent upon the public to purchase its goods and services. The public attitude toward business greatly affects the way in which businesses operate and serve.

Figure 2-1 depicts the variety of groups that constitute a pluralistic society. A **PLURALISTIC SOCIETY is the combination of diverse groups that influence**

BUT NOW IT'S NOT BAD FOR YOUR HEALTH . . .

Clairol Inc. accounts for about 75 percent of U.S. hair-dye sales. Recently, however, that achievement was threatened by the actions of federal regulators and an issue of "social responsibility." A substance used in hair colors for sixty years was suspected of causing cancer in humans. Federal regulations would have required Clairol and other manufacturers to post a warning label on their glamorous packages.

L'Oreal, the French cosmetics company, quickly reformulated its hair dyes and succeeded in chipping away at Clairol's share of the market. Nine months later Clairol, too, removed the suspected cancer-causing ingredient. Reformulation saved the hair-color industry, but attention has been called to the more than 125 suspected cancer-causing chemicals currently being used in cosmetics. For some businesses, these opportunities to be responsible societal citizens will pay off handsomely; for others who misread the consumer or fail to grasp the seriousness of the situation, they will spell real problems.

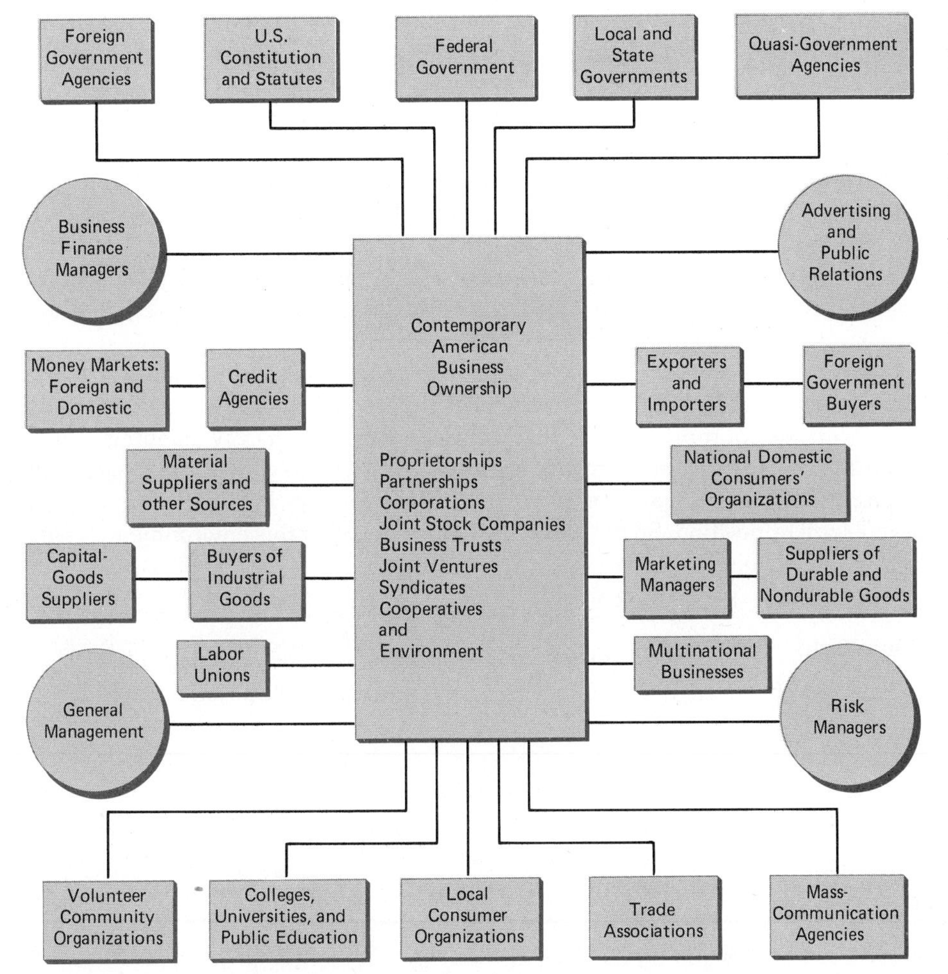

FIGURE 2-1

Business as part of a pluralistic society.

In a pluralistic society, business is a joint venture with other segments of the environment. This venture is not necessarily a conflict for power. Rather, it is an effort to meet the needs of the various groups, including the business firm.

the business environment. In this pluralistic society there are many power centers, each with some but not total independence. There can be a kind of mutual advantage between business and such groups. Business has a responsibility for achieving acceptable community relations. And multiple groups that influence business and government help diffuse power and prevent it from becoming concentrated in a single segment of society. Progress is made through give and take—compromise rather than by arbitrary action. Pluralism represents the efforts of people to reconcile the needs and interests of a variety of organizations.

The Image of Business

For the past decade the institution of business has been battered on many sides. The news has been full of accounts of business scandals, bribery, misrepresentation, price fixing, tax evasion, advertising abuse, and illegal payments. Dozens of individuals and companies have been convicted of such misdemeanors and felonies. Why do such things occur? Is it that certain business leaders became greedy and, in addition to enriching themselves, sought to increase their companies' profits?

Criticism of business has not been restricted to economic, moral, ethical, and political considerations. Business has contributed to the deterioration of our physical environment. Chemical and solid wastes have been dumped into lakes and rivers. Dangerous and poisonous waste materials have been buried in abandoned storage and plant sites.

The storage of nuclear waste generated by the nuclear-power industry raises the specter of another unfavorable situation like that which arose at Three Mile Island. Some commercial reactors that have been used to generate consumer electric power face a shutdown in the 1980s if additional temporary storage is not found.

And temporary storage is clearly not a long-term answer. For twenty years some plants have been "temporarily" storing the toxic waste. Yet no one has the answer to the tough question of what to do with nuclear waste.

Subsurface salt caverns have long been considered optimal disposal sites, but recent studies have raised doubts. Furthermore, different locations that might be considered appropriate sites for storing the waste are hardly standing in line to do so. The government wants to bury the wastes in New Mexico, a state with a long history of nuclear research and uranium mining, but this has met with severe local opposition. So the role of business in solving this environmental issue remains an ongoing concern.

Problems like these have led to the following questions:

1. What can business do to earn a favorable image in the eyes of the public?
2. To what extent is business responsible for improving the physical environment?
3. What is the public's share (through government) of the cost of improving the environment?
4. How can business better meet its obligations to society?
5. How can various groups in society best work to improve business?

In order to improve relations between business, government, and the public, U.S. companies are greatly increasing their public-relations staffs. Personnel are attending congressional hearings and meetings of regulatory agencies. They are attempting to become better informed about the activities of governments. Businesses must also listen to consumers and provide more and better information to the public. Public relations must provide for better two-way communication, not merely "propagandizing."

Mobil's effort to improve its image. The Mobil Corporation recently spent one-fourth of its $21 million public-relations budget in an attempt to improve its corporate image. The company placed ads in leading magazines and newspapers, arguing for mass transit and a national energy policy. Two paragraphs from one of these ads follow:

> In the words of a former chairman of Mobil, "No business is truly safe unless it serves its customers better than they could serve themselves, persuades them that it is doing so, and retains their goodwill in the process. One can't be too sure how long corporations would retain their present opportunities to operate at a profit if making money were their sole contribution to society.
>
> "Mobil tries to be a good employer, a good supplier, a good customer, a good investment, and a socially conscious organization. We try also to be responsive to the aspirations and legitimate needs of minorities and others of the disadvantaged, to environmental problems, and to a host of other concerns. And we would not argue that this is undiluted altruism."

CONSUMERISM

CONSUMERISM is **a movement to inform consumers and protect them from business malpractices**. The consumerism movement focuses on inferior and dangerous merchandise, unfair business practices, and false or misleading advertising. Some consumer groups concentrate on local issues, such as a local business's pricing policies. Other groups concentrate on national issues, such as product safety or truth in lending. Consumerism is a fact of business life today, and the businesspersons who ignore it do so at their peril. The consumer has developed a large constituency and a strong measure of government support.

For many individuals the consumerism movement began during the 1960s because some businesses were not giving the public the kind of products or services it wanted and paid for. But the first major consumer milestone in the United States was reached at the turn of the century. It was then that the Pure Food and Drug Act and the Meat Inspection Act were passed to improve conditions in the food industry. During those years, the idea of self-regulation on the part of business began. This concept led to the movement that eventually resulted in the creation of the Better Business Bureau. Better Business Bureaus are private organizations that exist in most cities. The BBB listens to complaints from consumers and assists them in protecting their rights. The BBB publishes numerous pamphlets which are available to consumers, such as the following:

Tips on Renting a Car
Tips on Home Improvements
Facts about Health Insurance
Facts on Selecting a Franchise
Facts on Home Insulation
Buying on Time
Home Fire Protection
Tips on Energy Saving

Mail Order Profit Mirages	*Truth in Lending*
Multi-Level Selling Plans	*Guarantees & Warranties*
What about Service Calls?	*Read Before You Sign*
Tips on Refunds & Exchanges	*Tips on Sales Contracts*

Rising consumer expectations, along with the increased complexity of products, form part of the base of the consumerism movement. Business managers and the government have developed a keen interest in the rights and values of consumers because of the consumerism movement. The federal and state governments have persons and/or agencies to aid consumers. The U.S. president has a special adviser for consumer affairs.

The Rights of Consumers

Consumers, as individuals and as groups, feel that they are entitled to a fair shake in the business world. Among other things they feel that they have the right to safety, to be informed, and to be heard. These would include

1. The right to fair and honest dealings in business transactions
2. The right to true and complete data about products they may wish to purchase
3. The right to know the true interest rate they are being charged
4. The right to know details about income, expenses, and profits of business whose stock they wish to purchase
5. The right to register complaints about shoddy merchandise and unfair business practices

The expression of these rights has led to fundamental changes in some businesses.

General Motors is quietly testing an idea that would have been unheard of just a few years ago. A program of binding arbitration to settle customer complaints is being run by the Better Business Bureau in a northern state.

Under this program, General Motors agrees to let an arbitrator decide disputes between customers and dealers and to abide by that decision. The program seems to be successful so far. There is evidence that executives in Detroit are concerned that if they do not do a better job of handling consumer complaints, the government will move in. Ford Motor Company is also testing a similar program in another state, and the National Automobile Dealers Association has set up similar plans in forty-four different cities.

Government Consumer Laws

The federal government has enacted much legislation to aid and protect consumers. The major acts and their chief purposes are enumerated in Table 2-1. Some of these laws protect both consumers and businesses. For example, changes in the U.S. law now require that counterfeit merchandise be forfeited. This was becoming a big problem for both consumers and legitimate businesses. Counterfeiters duplicate everything imaginable—from Hennessey brandy and Moët champagne, and Dior and Cardin fashions, to Puma sports shoes, Dunlop tennis racquets, and Coca-Cola.

It has been estimated that over $100 million annually is involved in this counterfeiting scheme. Not only do legitimate businesses lose money but the consumer

TABLE 2-1
FEDERAL CONSUMER LEGISLATION

Legislation	When Enacted	Purpose
Fair Packaging and Labeling Act	1966	Requires packages and labels to carry identity of article, manufacturer's name and location, and quantity of contents, in legible print.
National Traffic and Motor Safety Act	1966	Requires auto manufacturers to notify buyers of defects discovered after delivery and to remedy these defects.
Consumer Credit Protection Act	1968	Requires seller to disclose terms of sale and give facts of actual interest rate and other charges.
Child Protection and Toy Safety Act	1969	Prohibits manufacture and distribution of toys and other child articles sold in interstate trade that have electrical or other hazards.
Truth-in-Lending Act	1969	Requires lenders to inform borrowers of all direct, indirect, and true costs of credit. Both the amount of the finance charge and the annual percentage rate must be made clear.
Fair Credit Reporting Act	1970	Requires consumer-credit reporting agencies to adopt procedures for reporting personal information accurately and fairly.
Consumer Product Safety Act	1972	Regulates product standards and creates a Consumer Safety Commission to maintain product safety standards and give more accurate facts about products on labels.
Privacy Act	1974	Prohibits governments at all levels from requiring persons to give their social security numbers to receive a driver's license, vote, or exercise other rights. Persons have a right to know what information is maintained by federal agencies about them. Sets up a commission to study problems of consumer privacy.
Real Estate Settlement Procedures Act	1974	Requires lenders to disclose to home buyers all closing costs at least twelve days before closing the sale. Penalties for violations can run up to a year in prison and a $10,000 fine.

pays for an item of known quality and receives a cheap imitation. The new law will keep the bogus merchandise that is detected coming into the country out of circulation because the U.S. Customs Department will seize and keep the merchandise.

BUSINESS AND MINORITY GROUPS

Historically, blacks, Hispanics, American Indians, women, and handicapped persons have been discriminated against in hiring and in salary. The government now protects these minority groups against further overt discrimination.

The term **minority group** has long been used by sociologists to identify certain subdivisions of a population occupying a definite level within the social system. For purposes of this discussion, we define **MINORITY GROUP** as a **small division of the population who share a common historical background and cultural patterns different from those of other segments of society.**

Characteristics of Minority Groups

At least three major characteristics are common to various minority groups. First, the group is usually small and therefore plays a lesser role in society than does the majority group. This places the members of such a group at a disadvantage when participating in both political and economic activities.

Second, the group has certain physical characteristics—color, facial structure, hair texture, or something else—that act to physically set members of these groups apart and which may result in automatic exclusion.

Third, minority groups may be accorded fewer social privileges, may be somewhat restricted in their freedom of action, and may be of a low economic or social status.

Federal Civil-Rights Laws

The principal sources of our rights as American citizens are two documents: the Constitution of the United States and the constitution of each state. The first section of the Fourteenth Amendment to the Constitution provides that "no state shall deny to any person within its jurisdiction the equal protection of the laws." Perhaps more than any other language in the Constitution, the equal protection clause has been used to establish and broaden civil rights.

Nearly five generations of minority Americans have lived through amendments to the Constitution and, more recently, through many civil-rights acts to eliminate discrimination against employees. The civil-rights movement has resulted in the passage of several important federal civil-rights laws.

The Civil Rights Act of 1964 launched a major effort to correct discriminating practices. This act made it unlawful for an employer "to refuse to hire, or to discharge any individual, or otherwise discriminate against any individual with respect to his compensation, terms, conditions, or privileges of employment, because of such individual's race, color, religion, sex or national origin. . . ."

The federal government requires businesses and institutions to make provisions for minorities in employment and salary. They must pay women the same salaries as they pay men for identical work categories. Companies doing business with the government must submit reports to show that they are abiding by government laws and regulations. Most businesses, hospitals, and schools fall under some provisions of equal employment opportunity legislation.

A summary of federal civil-rights laws follows.

Summary of Federal Civil-Rights Laws

Civil Rights Act of 1866. "All citizens of the U.S. shall have the same right, in every state and territory, as is enjoyed by white citizens therof to inherit, purchase, sell, hold and convey real and personal property."

Civil Rights Act of 1957. Enacted to prevent persons from interfering with the voting rights of others.

Civil Rights Act of 1960. Strengthens the act of 1957 by requiring stricter enforcement provisions of voting rights. Criminal penalties for bombing and for obstructing federal court orders were imposed.

Equal Pay Act of 1963. Prohibits wage discrimination based on sex. Enforcement is vested in the Wage and Hour Division, Department of Labor. Workers receiving minimum wage under the Fair Labor Standard Act are included.

Civil Rights Act of 1964. Prohibits discrimination based on race, color, sex, and national origin. Prohibits segregation by job classification to deprive employees of equal-employment opportunities. The law also prohibits discrimination in voting, school attendance, hiring, union membership, and the use of public facilities.

Voting Rights Act of 1965. Requires the attorney general to appoint federal examiners to register voters in certain areas.

Age Discrimination Employment Act of 1967. Prohibits age discrimination in employment and encourages hiring older workers based on their ability rather than age. Protects those 40 to 65 years of age from discrimination in employment.

Civil Rights Act of 1968. The act covers 80 percent of all housing for rent or sale. It exempts from its coverage only private individuals owning not more than three houses who sell or rent their houses without the services of a real estate agent and who do not show preference or discrimination in their advertising.

The Voting Rights Act of 1970. Amended the Voting Rights Act of 1965, extending it five more years. Prohibited use of literacy tests for voting and set up uniform residence requirements.

Equal Employment Opportunity Act of 1972. Provides (1) right to employment with companies in interstate commerce having at least fifteen employees, and (2) membership with labor unions that have fifteen or more members. Includes employees hired through a hiring hall or working in an industry engaged in interstate commerce. Opportunities and right to work extended to state and local government employees, including those in public-supported educational institutions.

The Office of Minority Business Enterprise (OMBE) was established in 1969 within the Department of Commerce. Its function is to mobilize public and private leadership and resources to support minority-owned businesses. It coordinates over eighty government programs, which are administered by sixteen different federal agencies. All of these agencies affect minority enterprises in some way.

Government Agencies to Protect Consumers

Several federal government agencies are concerned with serving and protecting consumers. Chief among them are

The Food and Drug Administration
The Federal Trade Commission
The Department of Agriculture

The number of government publications available to help consumers is so great that it is difficult to discover what information is available. In recognition of this problem, the Consumer Product Information Center was established in Washington, D.C., in 1970. The center has the responsibility for making existing publications more available to consumers. Its *Consumer Product Information* catalog includes more than two hundred publications selected because of their special interest to consumers.

WOMEN AND BUSINESS OPPORTUNITIES

The percentage of women in our labor force continues to increase. Women have been ecouraged by changing social values, attitudes, economic considerations, and governmental action. Higher education levels, more women as heads of families, the desire for a higher living standard, and inflation are also contributing factors. In 1980, 41 percent of the labor force were women, and this percentage is expected to increase during the next decade. The growth in the number of women in the civilian labor force since 1950 is shown in Figure 2-2.

Occupations of Women

Occupational opportunities for women continue to improve. About 12 million women worked as clerks in 1976, and the clerical category accounted for one-third of all employed women. But this is changing. Growth rates are fastest in the professional and technical categories. The occupations of the employed labor force by sex for 1975 are shown in Figure 2-3. However, the median earnings of women continue to be below those of men. This is shown in Figure 2-4.

Barriers Keep Falling

The federal government continues to exert pressure to achieve equal treatment for women and men. The Supreme Court has ruled that

1. Employers who have underpaid female workers must equalize their wages with those paid male employees.

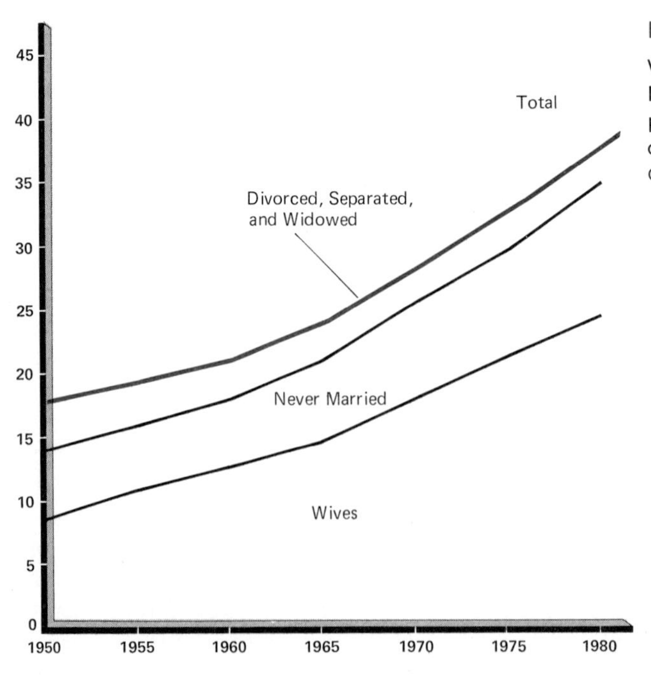

FIGURE 2-2

Women in the civilian labor force—millions of persons 16 years and over. (Source: The Conference Board.)

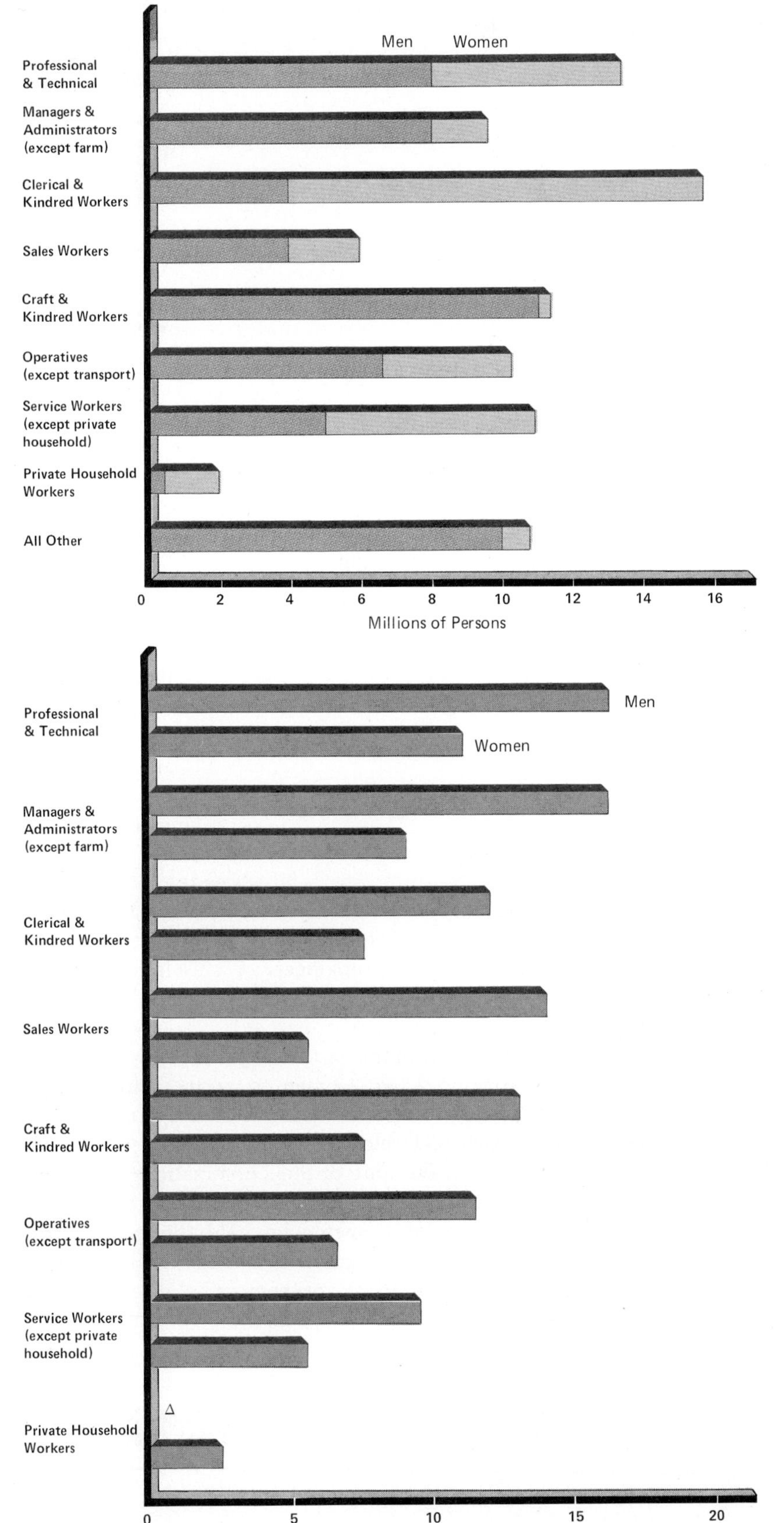

FIGURE 2-3

Occupation of employed persons—by sex. (Source: The Conference Board.)

FIGURE 2-4

Median earnings of selected occupational groups—by sex. (Source: The Conference Board.)

2. Mandatory maternity leave at a set time in pregnancy violates due process.
3. States may not deny women equal opportunity to serve on juries.
4. The "majority age" for men and women must be the same.
5. Employers cannot differentiate in pension plans on the basis of sex just because women live longer than men.

Efforts are being made by business and government to recruit women for supervisory and management positions.

Positions once reserved for men are now open to women. Women currently hold sales jobs in the steel, aluminum, and lumber industries, which were formerly open only to men. Women are being elected to officer positions in labor unions (one out of every five union members is a woman). Women serve on the executive boards of the Amalgamated Meat Cutters and Butchers Association, the International Ladies' Garment Workers' Union, and the American Federation of State, County and Municipal Employees Union.

Some Positive Factors

In 1977 the Small Business Administration initiated a Women's Business Ownership Campaign. This campaign offered businesswomen special assistance in finance and in management, as well as assistance in securing federal contracts. The SBA guaranteed to make available $100 million in loans to women entrepreneurs, each quarter during 1978.[1] The goal of the Small Business Administration for the 1981 year was to award 10 percent of the SBA guaranteed loans to minorities and 10 percent to women.

A decade ago women were clustered in such fields as nursing and teaching. Today the young professional woman has much wider opportunities. The proportion of women now preparing for the professions far exceeds the percentage already so employed. For example, whereas women constitute only 11 percent of the nation's physicians, they constitute 24 percent of its medical students. An estimated ten thousand women are studying engineering. This is ten times as many as in 1970. Women constitute 28 percent of all law students. And women constitute 28 percent of all accountants, compared with only 17 percent in 1960. Figure 2-5 shows how women are gaining in the various professions.

President Jimmy Carter appointed two women to posts in his cabinet. Juanita Kreps was appointed Secretary of Commerce. Patricia Harris was appointed Secretary of Housing and Urban Development, and later became Secretary of Health, Education, and Welfare. At the time of their nominations, these two women between them held nine directorships of U.S. corporations.[2]

There are many other examples of women who hold top management positions. Jane Cahill Pfeiffer, a management consultant, was the first woman vice-president of IBM and later served as chairman of the board of directors of the

[1]Women would not automatically qualify for these loans. Their applications would be processed the same as others.

[2]The New York Stock Exchange, Western Electric, Eastman Kodak, J. C. Penney, R. J. Reynolds, and the Teachers Insurance and Annuity Association for Mrs. Kreps; and IBM, Chase Manhattan Bank, and Scott Paper Company for Mrs. Harris.

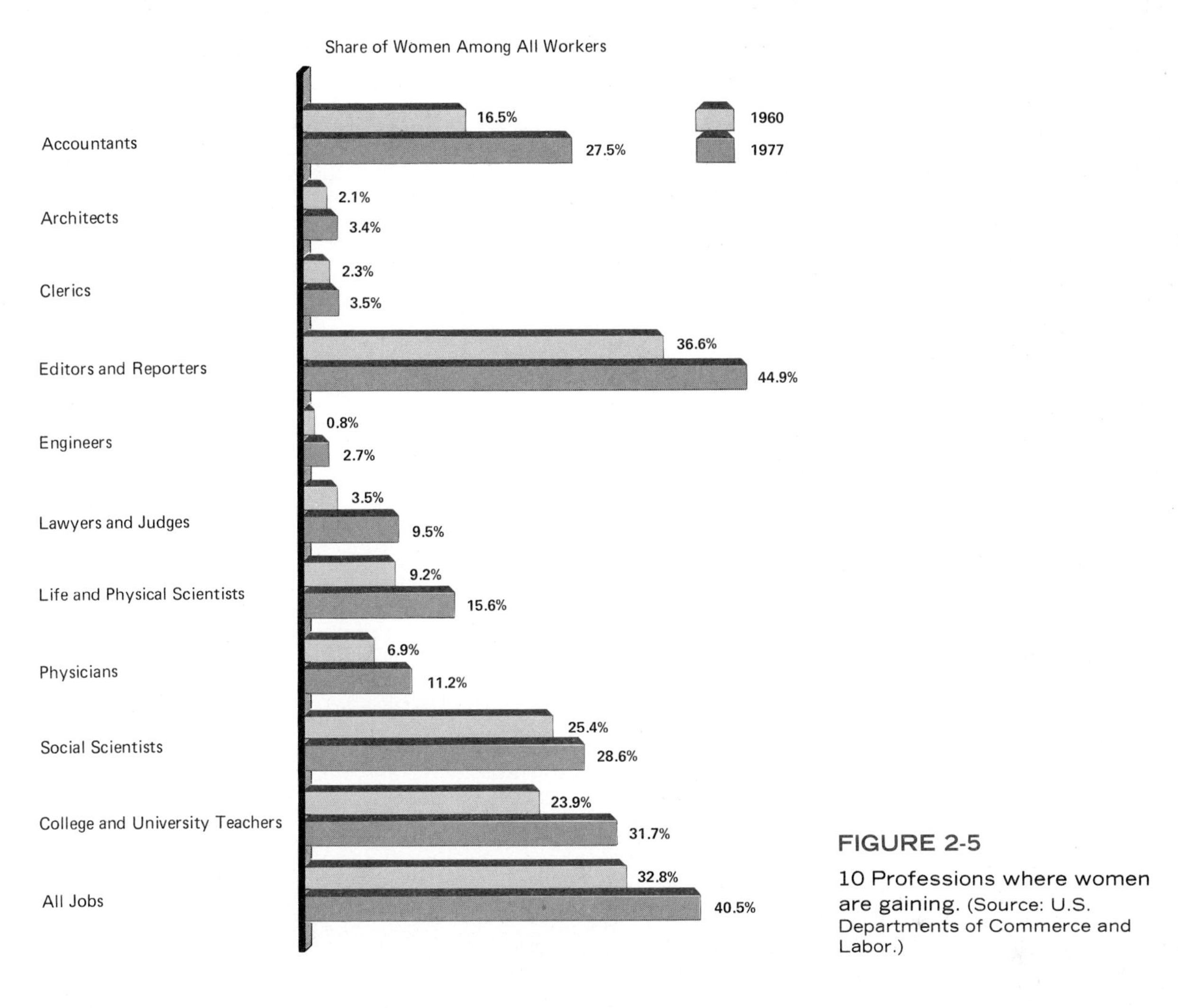

FIGURE 2-5

10 Professions where women are gaining. (Source: U.S. Departments of Commerce and Labor.)

National Broadcasting Company. She also serves on the board of directors of Chesebrough-Pond's and the Bache Group. Marina Whitman, a former member of the president's Council of Economic Advisers, is a board member of Westinghouse, Manufacturers Hanover Trust, and Procter and Gamble. Carol M. Conklin was elected to the position of corporate secretary of General Motors, and Betsy Ancker-Johnson was appointed vice-president of General Motors, in charge of the company's environmental activities.

BUSINESS AND THE PHYSICAL ENVIRONMENT

Of the several economic and social problems facing American corporations, one of the most costly and difficult to solve is that of improving the physical environment. In the late 1960s it was discovered that this nation would run out of clean air and water in urban centers unless something was done to improve the environment. Pollutants of all kinds were destroying the quality of our air and water.

JOHN E. McCONNAUGHY

During the past decade Peabody International Corporation has had a record of continuous and consistent growth, and annual sales have grown from $24 million to $500 million. This achievement was made possible by the company's balance in energy and environment improvement. The five related operational sectors of the company are oil field products and services, testing for safety, clean air, water and fluids, and equipment for handling solid wastes.

In Financial World magazine's 1976 annual survey of security analysts, John E. McConnaughy, Jr., chairman of Peabody International Corporation, was voted the environmental control industry's top chief executive officer for the second straight year.

McConnaughy was appointed chairman and chief executive of Peabody in May 1969.

Before joining Peabody, McConnaughy was with the Singer Company as vice-president—European Consumer Products and was responsible for operations in sixteen countries and sales of some $350 million. He had previously been president of the Singer Company of Canada Ltd. Earlier he held management positions at Westinghouse Electric Corporation in its Consumer Group and Portable Appliance Division.

A graduate of Denison University with a B.A. in economics, McConnaughy received an M.B.A. degree in marketing and finance from the Harvard Graduate School of Business Administration.

McConnaughy is a director of the First New Haven National Bank, and a member of the American Management Association, the American Marketing Association, and the Chamber of Commerce.

McConnaughy is a tennis nut, an avid jogger, and a chess player. He also skis and plays golf, squash, and basketball.

Ecology and Pollution

ECOLOGY deals with **the relationships between people and their environments.** The quality of our environment has rapidly deteriorated in recent years. This has resulted chiefly because of a combination of three factors:

1. The increasing concentration of the population
2. The development of new technologies
3. The rise in economic affluence

Major Forms of Pollution

POLLUTION refers to **the deterioration of the natural environment in which we live and work.** Water and air, which were once clean, are now polluted. The three major areas of pollution are

1. Air pollution
2. Water pollution
3. Solid-waste disposal

Each presents a threat to a healthful environment.

Air pollution. The average person breathes thirty-five pounds of air each day. This is six times as much as the food and drink normally consumed.

By 1970 over 200 million tons of waste products were being released into the air annually. Slightly over 50 percent of the pollution came from the internal-combustion engines of cars and other motor vehicles. Roughly 22 percent came from fuel burned at stationary sources such as power-generating plants, and another 15 percent was emitted from industrial processes.

Air pollution is associated with respiratory disorders and with diseases of the heart. Illness caused or aggravated by air pollution costs the American people an estimated $4.6 billion annually. This is for medical treatment, lost wages, and reduced productivity.

Air pollution corrodes buildings, damages personal property, and harms forests and crops. It causes $12.3 billion in destruction and decay annually.

Water pollution. The sources of water pollution are innumerable. Major sources can be found in almost every variety of industrial, municipal, and agricultural operation throughout the United States. Pollutants present a special threat to ground water supplies. Because of widespread use of high-nitrate fertilizers and concentrated feedlots, nitrates in both ground and surface waters have increased in recent years. Many of our ground waters now exceed the nitrate limits of drinking-water standards. The significance of this fact is that once an underground water supply becomes contaminated, it is virtually impossible to purify it.

The amount of organic waste created by large cities is expected to increase by 300 percent between 1980 and 2020. The development of nuclear energy as a

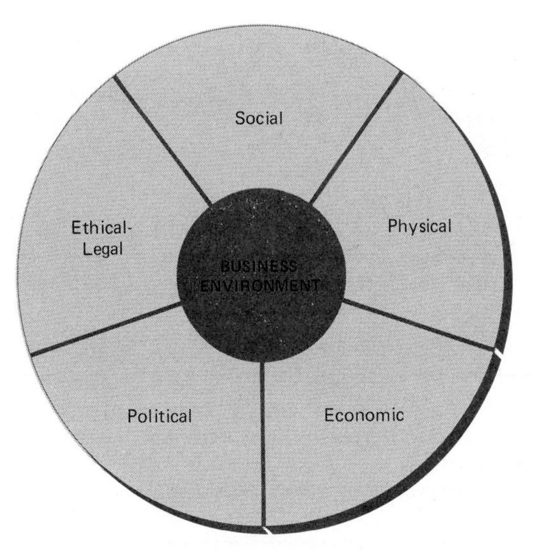

FIGURE 2-6

The business firm interacts with its environments.

source of power has brought a new type of pollution. Radioactive contamination in the form of liquid nuclear waste can cause cancer or a number of other serious conditions harmful to human beings. The nuclear waste-disposal problem becomes more imposing because at the present time there is no safe place to dump this atomic waste material. As Congressman Morris K. Udall, chairman of the House Environment Subcommittee, observes:

> The harsh truth is that eventually, if civilization is to remain on this planet, we need permanent, renewable, clean, and large-scale energy sources that consume nothing and pollute nothing.

Solid-waste pollution. Environmental health cannot be compartmentalized. This is nowhere more evident than in the area of solid-waste management. There are only three repositories for the wastes of society: the earth, its waters, and its atmosphere. The use or misuse of any of these is interrelated with the other two. Restrictions on the use of any one medium as a repository almost invariably lead to increased burdens on, and frequently abuse of, the others.

What to do with solid-waste materials has always been a problem. The simple solution of burning garbage is no longer possible in urban areas because of the air-pollution problem it creates.

Solid wastes include an assortment of products that are no longer usable. In this country we produce about 4.6 billion tons of solid wastes each year. Our annual "throwaway" includes 48 billion cans, 26 billion bottles and jars, 4 million tons of plastic, 7.6 million television sets, 7 million cars and trucks, and 30 million tons of paper. It is estimated that waste collection will soon amount to over 340 million tons per year. The cost of this waste collection and disposal exceeds $10 billion per year.

The Economics of Recycling

Recycling is vital to our industrial economy. It saves energy, creates jobs, provides a supplemental source of raw material for production, and helps turn the problems of litter and waste into economic opportunities.

For example, recycling saves 95 percent of the energy it takes to make aluminum from ore. In addition, it saves precious raw materials and reduces the amount of investment capital needed. A facility to remelt recycled aluminum can be built for one-tenth the cost of new refining and smelting equipment. Alcoa reported that the recycling of aluminum cans rose from 8 million pounds in 1970 to over 330 million pounds in 1978. There are over twenty-five hundred recycling centers in the United States, and they have created fifteen thousand new jobs for workers.

Reynolds Metals Company reported that in the ten years since the program began, it had paid consumers $100 million for used aluminum. During the most recent year, Reynolds recycled more than half the aluminum cans the company made. During that year Reynolds's recycling of aluminum saved a billion kilowatt-hours of electricity.

FIGURE 2-7
Massive recycling of used aluminum beverage cans is credited with saving energy, conserving resources and reducing litter. (Courtesy of the Aluminum Association from De Wys Inc.)

Cost of a Clean Environment

United States businesses were spending more than $13 billion annually in 1980 to prevent pollution, and this increases about 12 percent a year. The Council on Environmental Quality estimates that the cost of cleaning up America will be $271 billion over the next decade:

For cleaner air	$143 billion
For purer water	116 billion
For noise abatement	4 billion
For solid wastes	8 billion

Governments—federal, state, and local—will finance about one-fifth of the cost: private business will pay for the remainder.

LEGISLATION AND THE ENVIRONMENT

The federal government has been very active in enacting laws pertaining to the environment. The first federal law to prohibit pollution of American waters was the Refuse Act of 1899. This act was first enforced in 1970. Since 1965 many laws relating to clean air and water have been enacted. A few of these laws are discussed briefly here.

<u>Water Resources Planning Act of 1965.</u> This act created a Water Resources Council (WRC) and river basin commissions. It authorized national air-quality and emission standards for both stationary air-pollution sources and

automotive vehicles. The act also requires each state to submit plans for achieving national air-quality standards.

The requirements pertaining to pollution and water quality were strengthened by the **Clean Water Restoration Act** of 1966 and the **Water Quality Improvement Act** of 1970.

Solid Waste Disposal Act of 1965. This act authorizes a program to develop methods of solid-waste disposal, including garbage, paper, and scrap metal. It also provides technical assistance to state and local governments in solid-waste disposal programs.

This act was amended by the **Resource Recovery Act** of 1970 and the **Federal Water Pollution Control Act** of 1972.

Air Quality Act of 1967. This act provides for a systematic effort to deal with air pollution on a regional basis. It establishes coordinated action at various levels of government and segments of industry. This act was amended in 1970 to raise the clean air standards. Emission standards for automobiles became effective in 1975. These amendments also created the Environmental Protection Agency, which is discussed below.

Noise Control Act of 1972. This act requires the EPA administrator to set noise standards for products and equipment that are major sources of noise.

Energy Supply and Environmental Coordination Act of 1974. In order to conserve supplies, the Federal Energy Administration was ordered to require electric-generating plants to use coal where it was practicable to do so.

Resource Conservation and Recovery Act of 1976. This act built upon the foundations of the Solid Waste Disposal Act of 1965 and the Resource Recovery Act of 1970. Its stated objective is to promote the protection of health and the environment to conserve material and energy resources. Among other things, it established the Office of Solid Waste within the EPA to direct the way the law was to be implemented.

U.S. Environmental Protection Agency

The U.S. Environmental Protection Agency was established December 2, 1970. Its mission is to integrate and coordinate an attack on environmental problems. Air, water pollution, solid-waste management, pesticides, radiation, and noise are all included. For the first time fifteen federal environmental-control programs have been unified into one independent agency. It is a regulatory agency responsible for setting standards and enforcing compliance.

Standard setting. The EPA must see that the standards it sets will be sufficient to protect the public health and welfare. State and local governments may develop additional controls, but the EPA's direct responsibilities are restricted to protecting health and welfare.

Enforcement programs. The EPA's philosophy has been to encourage voluntary compliance by private industry and communities. If state and local agencies fail to produce effective plans for pollution abatement or if they do not enforce the programs they develop, the EPA must do so.

Research. The EPA's research program is authorized under various major congressional acts. This legislation allots more than one-fifth of the agency's operating budget to scientific study.

Financial and technical assistance. By providing financial and technical assistance to state, regional, and local jurisdictions, the EPA serves as a catalyst for environmental protection efforts. The EPA grants federal funds for the construction and operation of various types of facilities to reduce pollution. It also demonstrates new pollution-control technology.

Since the establishment of the Environmental Protection Agency, the following laws have been enacted by Congress:[3]

Federal Water Pollution Control Act Amendments of 1972
Noise Control Act of 1974
Safe Drinking Water Act of 1974
Energy Supply and Environmental Coordination Act of 1974
Resource Conservation and Recovery Act of 1976
Clean Air Act Amendments of 1977

WHAT BUSINESS IS DOING

Look at a current issue of the annual report of any major corporation and compare it with a similar report issued ten years ago. You will note the increased amount of financial data included. The report will also discuss what the company is doing and spending to meet its social responsibility to the public. It would be impossible to report in detail what all companies are doing. But we do want to provide sketches to illustrate business's effort to meet its social responsibility.

The Other Dimensions of Business is a forty-four-page publication of the Exxon Corporation. The introduction to this publication includes this paragraph:

> It has been a long time since corporate leaders held the view that "the business of business is business." As with so many segments of society, the role of business has changed dynamically over the years. In addition to carrying out its traditional economic and commercial functions, business is acutely aware that it must conduct its activities in a responsible and ethical manner. It has regard for the impact of business operations on the physical environment and a sen-

[3]All the laws mentioned in this section on federal legislation are discussed fully in the publication *EPA Protecting Our Environment,* published by the U.S. Environmental Protection Agency, Washington, D.C. 20460.

> sitivity to the issues affecting the quality of life. Business also helps to support education, health programs, advancement of minorities in employment, community social programs and the arts. Many of the efforts that Exxon and other corporations make in these areas are less known than their familiar products and services. But these efforts form an important, ongoing part of the corporation's daily activities. At Exxon, we feel that it is in the best interest of business to continue to meet public expectations in these areas. We must show through our actions that we believe the prosperity of any business is clearly related to the vitality of the communities in which it functions.

Raymond W. Winkler, environmental conservation coordinator for Exxon says that "the oil industry spends 10 percent of its annual capital investment for conserving or improving the environment."

A recent annual report of the Rockwell International Corporation highlights the activities of its Social Responsibility Committee. As part of its support for higher education, it established a program to aid in the preparation of minority students as scientists. Through its Product Integrity Committee the company embarked on a program to reinforce the high quality of its products.

During an eighteen-month period at Rockwell International, the number of minority employees in professional positions increased from 12.0 to 13.5 percent. During the same period, the number of women in professional categories increased from 5.7 to 7.4 percent. The company budgeted $14 million to ensure compliance with required health standards. During a recent year, it placed $29 million in orders for products from minority-owned firms.

A few years ago a chemical engineer from the 3M Company visited the company plant at Cordoba, Illinois, so that he could help in the development of an industrial herbicide. He discovered that the odor from the herbicide production process was most repulsive. As a result of his report, the 3M Company changed the formula to make the chemical almost odor free. This is one illustration of how the company operates its 3P program (pollution prevention pays). Its purpose is to eliminate pollution at its source rather than clean it up later. Through nineteen different projects, 3M reduced the company's annual pollution burden by 500 million gallons of waste water, 73,000 tons of air pollutants, and 2,800 tons of sludge. The results of this 3P program greatly impressed the Environmental Protection Agency, which featured the 3P program of the 3M Company at a two-day conference in Chicago. More than two hundred companies were represented at that conference.

The Xerox Corporation sponsors a Social Involvement Program. Persons working for the company may be granted a Social Service Leave for one year, with pay. But instead of working for Xerox, they work on social service projects of their own choosing, in their respective communities.

The Xerox program is based on certain fundamental beliefs held by the company. Those listed in the box on the following page seem to be especially pertinent.

Xerox provides leaves of absence, with pay, for highly motivated employees to serve in such projects as rehabilitating the handicapped and giving new hope to those in hospitals and prisons.

A democratic society is strengthened by the close interaction of institutions in the public, private, and non-profit sectors.

We must improve the quality of life where our people live and work.

We must conserve and extend society's higher values by supporting educational, social, and cultural activities.

We must strengthen our pluralistic society by aiding and participating in vital institutions, programs, and public debate.

Corporations can be a positive force in attacking society's problems. These are the problems of business no less than they are problems of individuals and government.

In addition to releasing personnel for one year, the company supports their work through modest contributions to their projects. The program was launched in 1971, and between 1971 and 1979, a total of 240 persons had participated.

The American Telephone and Telegraph Corporation experience. Perhaps one of the most important equal employment cases involves the American Telephone and Telegraph Corporation. The negotiations between AT&T and the government began in 1970. The Equal Employment and Opportunity Commission (EEOC) had initiated action against the company on behalf of its women and minority workers. The EEOC was joined in the decree against AT&T by the Departments of Labor and Justice, and the Federal Communications Commission. In January 1973 an agreement on the issues had been reached, which was submitted to a federal judge in Philadelphia. This resulted in the issuance of a second decree in 1974. This second decree ordered payments to women and minority men who had "*possibly* been discriminated against."[4] The company paid $18 million to approximately twenty thousand workers who were victims of unequal pay practices. It also agreed to wipe out all unequal pay schedules. This cost the company an additional $53 million, resulting from pay increases for a total of seventy-two thousand workers.

The various Bell companies desegregated all jobs in terms of both race and sex. Great progress was made, and in 1974 the company had achieved 90 percent of its targets; by the end of 1976, 99 percent had been met. The decree expired on January 13, 1978. The company had complied sufficiently that the government did not ask that it be extended. Although AT&T was "forced" to improve its pay practices, once it had agreed to do so it was a model of compliance.

In addition to direct payments to employees, the company sustained huge legal, training, and administrative costs. The department responsible for seeing that the terms of the government decree are met requires about 750 full-time employees.[5]

[4]"*Possibly*" because AT&T did not admit discrimination.

[5]A full discussion of this case can be found in the January 15, 1979, issue of *Fortune*, pp. 45–57.

ENERGY, THE ENVIRONMENT, AND CONSERVATION

In the early stages of America's industrial development we depended largely on waterpower and coal. However, petroleum was plentiful and cheap during the 1930s and 1940s. So by 1950 oil supplied 40 percent of our energy needs; natural gas, 18 percent; and coal, only 38 percent. In 1978 oil supplied 46 percent; natural gas, 28 percent; and coal, only 18 percent.

Following the "oil embargo" of 1973 we began looking to nuclear energy to solve our energy dilemma. But various groups protested the development of nuclear plants. Problems remained unsolved regarding the disposal of nuclear waste, and the Three Mile Island incident set back the nuclear-power industry.

CURRENT ISSUE

How Great Is a Factory's Responsibility to its Home Community?

The economic well-being of some small communities is closely tied to that of one or two large industrial enterprises. If such a company closes or moves to a new community, the one that it leaves feels deserted in a number of ways. The statements below all relate to a business that is so deeply embedded in the economic and social life of a community that the community is truly dependent upon the company.

With which of the following statements do you agree and with which do you disagree?

1. The company has at least a moral obligation to remain in the community.
2. The company should explore all possible means by which it might stay and remain a viable business.
3. If the company decides to move to another community, it should offer employment to those workers who wish to move with it.
4. If the company leaves the community, it should pay its discharged workers who have ten years' or more seniority, a year's wages.
5. If the company decides to move, it should be willing to sell the present plant and equipment to the workers at a price considerably below the net asset value.
6. The local community government should offer inducements, such as waiver of taxes, in an attempt to induce the company to remain in the community.

In your opinion, how great or how small is a company's obligation to the life and well-being of the community where it operates?

Delays resulted from such protests, government restrictions, and legal cases. By the mid 1970s it required fifteen years to propose, begin, and build a nuclear-power plant in the United States. This compares with the five to six years required in Europe.

Solar energy offers great promise for the long term, but not much relief in the immediate future. Coal is in plentiful supply, but it pollutes the atmosphere. Periodic labor strikes have slowed the changeover to a greater emphasis on the use of coal.

Conservation

The area that offers the greatest opportunity for conservation in the immediate future is energy conservation. Curtailed allocations of natural gas were in effect during the winter months from 1974 through 1979. Industrial plants and large office complexes responded with strong efforts to conserve energy. As the cost of gas increased, homeowners and businesses alike added more insulation and installed energy-saving equipment.

IBM, in a recent annual report, told of its energy saving for one twelve-month period. The energy saved in its major domestic plants, labs, and headquarters amounted to "31 percent for fuel and 22 percent for electricity from pre-conservation levels of consumption."

The Du Pont Company offers energy conservation consultant services to industry through its Energy Management Services division. One of its studies covering eighteen plants reported an average saving of 22 percent.

The Metropolitan Life Insurance Company of New York, whose offices hold twelve thousand people, estimates that it has cut electrical consumption by 25 percent and steam consumption between 40 and 50 percent. It has done so by turning thermostats down to 68 degrees, by removing every other light bulb in the corridors, and by reducing the number of elevators in service.

Representing Du Pont at a meeting sponsored by the Conference Board, Senior Vice-President Edward G. Jefferson reported that more than 60 percent of Du Pont's energy savings have come from such methods as the following:

1. Tuning controls on steam boilers and furnaces to increase their efficiency
2. Putting steam turbines into plants that need steam for their processes anyway
3. Increasing maintenance to cut down heat waste from steam leaks or poor insulation
4. Recovering heat

PPG Industries includes the following suggestions in its energy-conservation program:

1. Eliminate wasted energy (check for missing or damaged insulation, leaks, spillage, unnecessary steam flow, leaking valves)
2. Improve fuel-combustion efficiency
3. Extract energy from exhaust streams, including recycling of heating water and recovery of steam condensate
4. Use more efficient equipment. Avoid oversized motors, pumps, and compressors

5. Control peak demand by rescheduling operations
6. Reduce heating and air conditioning for unused areas and during nonworking hours
7. Investigate use of high-pressure steam for power generation
8. Reduce lighting in noncritical areas. Make maximum use of natural light

The Exxon Corporation reported that in its home-office building it had, through various conservation measures, reduced the use of electrical energy by 27 percent and gas consumption by 54 percent.

We must, therefore, conclude that an important first step in solving our energy problem is a nationwide effort at energy conservation.

SUMMARY OF KEY CONCEPTS

Business both determines and is the product of environmental influences.

There are many and diverse interests of business: Some are chiefly self-centered; others are in the public interest. As the social, economic, political, and physical forces change, business must adjust to these changes.

One of the major needs of business today is to build public confidence in business as an institution.

Consumerism developed in order to obtain more information and improved product safety and product quality.

The Civil Rights Act launched a movement to give minorities their due in employment, wages, and promotions.

As a result of the Civil Rights Act and further government action, most businesses now have equal employment opportunity for women and minorities.

The Office of Minority Business Enterprise coordinates the various programs administered by federal government agencies concerned with minority businesses.

To improve the physical environment, we are concerned with air and water pollution, solid-waste disposal, and the conservation of natural resources.

Congress has enacted many laws dealing with air, water, and solid-waste pollution.

Business seems to be making an honest effort to deal with its social responsibility to society. This is a long-term and expensive undertaking.

BUSINESS TERMS

You should be able to match these business terms with the statements that follow:

a. Consumerism
b. Ecology
c. Environment
d. Minority group
e. Pluralistic society
f. Pollution

1. The sum of all external forces that influence persons and communities
2. The diverse groups in society that combine to influence the business environment
3. A movement to inform and protect persons who purchase goods and services
4. A small division of the population whose cultural patterns differ from other segments of society
5. A study of the relationships between people and their environments
6. The deterioration of the natural environment

REVIEW QUESTIONS

1. What are the various types of environment in which business functions?
2. What are the "rights" to which consumers feel they are entitled?
3. What is being done to give minorities a fair shake in business and government?
4. What are the major causes of the deterioration of our physical environment?
5. What actions has the federal government taken to restore a clean physical environment?
6. Give some examples of what business is doing to restore a clean environment.

DISCUSSION QUESTIONS

1. What is the meaning of the term *pluralistic society*? What is the basic concern of pluralism?
2. Why has consumerism developed as a force in society?
3. In your opinion, why are there not more women in executive positions in large businesses?
4. How should the cost of cleaning up the environment be divided between business and government?
5. Is the government doing too much, too little, or the right amount in its effort to provide a clean environment? Why do you hold this opinion?
6. Is business as a whole making an honest effort to clean up the environment? Give reasons to support your answer.

BUSINESS CASE 2-1

To Mine or Not to Mine?

The Mills Brothers own two hundred acres of land in eastern Kentucky. They also have title to the mineral rights under their land. For the past five years they have sold their coal at a very low price per ton, and the mining company has paid the cost of mining the coal and restoring the land surface.

The new environmental laws governing this area require greatly increased expenditures. The mining company wants to renegotiate and pay less per ton for the coal. Forecasts for coal indicate that coal will bring a higher price in the future.

The Mills Brothers seem to have three choices:

a. Renegotiate with the mining company, thus receiving a lower price for their coal
b. Offer to let the mining company continue under terms of the old contract
c. Stop mining for the present and hold for a higher future price

1. Which choice would you recommend?
2. What reasons can you give to support your recommendation?

BUSINESS CASE 2-2

A Citizens' Group Protests

The Hart Petro Corporation has applied for a permit to build an oil-processing plant and ocean dock about forty miles from a city of eighty thousand people. This plant is about four miles from a public beach that was heavily damaged by oil spills a few years ago. At that time the company was forced to discontinue drilling for oil off shore. The company also requests permission to construct a seven-mile pipeline from its offshore wells to the proposed plant and ocean dock. According to company officials, about seventy-five persons would be employed in the plant.

To house its employees, the company seeks a permit to build a fifty-unit high-rise apartment in the area. The high-rise would be located about six miles from the plant. The company would construct a separate sewage-disposal plant for the high-rise and would drill water wells. The energy to operate the entire operation is available from the local public-utility company.

At a meeting of the county government, a complaint was filed by an irate citizens' group residing in the nearby city. This group is asking that the project be rejected because it would be a source of air and water pollution and would destroy local wildlife. In response to the complaint, the company offered to post a bond to cover future environmental damages within reason.

1. What issues are involved in this controversy?
2. What more could the company do to earn approval?
3. Would you vote for approval if you lived in the nearby city? Give reasons to support your answer.

OWNERSHIP, MANAGEMENT, AND ORGANIZATION

PART 2

BUSINESS OWNERSHIP FORMS

3

STUDY OBJECTIVES

WHEN YOU HAVE FINISHED READING THIS CHAPTER, YOU SHOULD BE ABLE TO

ONE Identify the principal forms of business ownership

TWO Name other legal forms of business ownership

THREE Describe the advantages and disadvantages of corporate ownership

FOUR List eight provisions found in the articles of partnership agreement

FIVE Distinguish between private and state-owned corporations

SIX Explain how a joint-stock company resembles a partnership

IN THE NEWS

But I Own the Business . . .

Sears, Roebuck and Company is certainly a well-known American business. However, not long ago one of the stockholders, who was also a grandson of the founder, Richard Sears, discovered that not everyone at Sears was willing to listen to such an "owner" of the business.

Carroll Sears, a Chicago resident, ordered a kit to build a two-car garage from the company. The price was $3,800, but he was billed $10,000. He called the store, and although they promised to correct the error, it was not done. They continued to bill him for $10,000. Finally he told those involved that he was Richard Sears's grandson. Even then he had to talk to several people before someone believed him and was willing to solve the problem.

The incident illustrates the different emphases placed on business ownership in proprietorships and corporations. In a "small business" the chances are that most of the employees would have known the founder's grandson.

Choosing the right form of business ownership can be and often is vital to the success of a new venture.

JAMES CASH PENNEY

Every person in the United States can organize a business if he or she chooses to do so. For those who do want to start a business, a common problem is the selection of the appropriate form of business ownership. By **form of ownership** we mean the legal structure of the enterprise. Since there is no "ideal" form of legal ownership, it is difficult to make a choice. Each form has its pros and cons.

In this chapter we will learn about the following forms of business ownership and the ways in which these forms are organized:

1. Sole proprietorship
2. General partnership
3. Limited partnership
4. Joint venture
5. Corporation
6. Joint-stock company
7. Business trust
8. Cooperative
9. Mutual companies

There is no one form of ownership suitable for all kinds of business ventures. Some forms are better for small ventures; others are better for large enterprises. Since the corporation is the most complex form of ownership, we devote more discussion to it than to the others.

THE SOLE PROPRIETORSHIP

The simplest and oldest form of business organization is the sole proprietorship, which has but one owner. It is sometimes called individual proprietorship and is popular today in spite of the concentration of so much wealth in large business

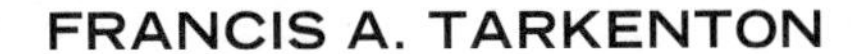

FRANCIS A. TARKENTON

Francis Tarkenton was born in Richmond, Virginia, in February 1940. He attended the University of Georgia at Athens, earning a bachelor of business administration degree. While there he led the Georgia Bulldogs to the Southeastern Conference Championship and Orange Bowl in 1959.

Fran played professional football for eighteen years for the Minnesota Vikings and New York Giants, leading the Vikings to three NFC championships and three Super Bowls in 1973, 1975, and 1976.

Fran's business career began with the Coca-Cola Company. He worked for several years with the advertising agency of Batten, Barton, Durstine and Osborn. In 1969 he founded Behavioral Systems, Inc., and as chairman of the board has expanded the operations from principally servicing the southeastern United States into one of the largest management consultant firms in the country, working with 250 major corporations in all parts of the world.

He has written three books, writes a monthly management article for Delta's Sky magazine, and is a sports announcer with ABC television. Fran owns almost all the passing records in the National Football League and is the No. 1 ranked passer in NFL history. Among his many honors are Most Valuable Player in the NFL 1975, and Outstanding Young Man of the Year in Georgia. He has been active in charity work in both Minneapolis and Atlanta.

Fran has managed to effectively combine his sports, business, and television careers. He is married to the former Elaine Merrell of Atlanta. They have three children.

units. It is common to almost every line of business and is especially appealing to persons who start service-type businesses.

The proprietor of a business is the sole owner of the firm and its assets and is responsible for all the liabilities (debts). An example of a balance sheet for a business owned by George Brown is given in Table 3-1. Brown's total assets are listed as being worth $13,500 while his total debts (liabilities) are $3,900. His

TABLE 3-1
BALANCE SHEET OF A SOLE PROPRIETORSHIP

George W. Brown, TV Repair Shop
December 31, 198__

Assets (owns)		Debts (owes)	
Cash	$2,500	Accounts payable	$3,200
Parts inventory	1,200	Notes payable	400
Merchandise inventory	5,300	Mortgage on truck	300
Tools and equipment	1,500	Total debts	$ 3,900
Truck	3,000	Owner's equity	9,600
	$13,500		$13,500

ownership interest (equity) in the business is the difference between assets and liabilities. In this example it is $9,600. By common definition, a **SOLE PROPRIETORSHIP** is an organization that is owned and operated by one person.

Many of the largest corporations in the United States today began as sole proprietorships. Among these are the Ford Motor Company, F. W. Woolworth, J. C. Penney, Bank of America, S. S. Kresge, and H. J. Heinz. Each started with less owner's equity than George Brown's TV Repair Shop.

A comparison of the total number of sole proprietorships, partnerships, and corporations with their annual cash receipts is given in Figure 3-1. There are nearly 11 million proprietorships, 2 million corporations, and 1.1 million partnerships. You can see that although there are more proprietorships, corporations earn more money. The reason is that the corporate form is usually preferred as businesses become larger.

Advantages of a Sole Proprietorship

A businessperson who selects the sole proprietorship will find that it offers certain advantages, which are explained below.

Ease of starting. The owner himself or herself can determine where the business is to be located, how much owner capital is needed, and how much is to be supplied from personal resources. There are few regulatory requirements to meet.

Ownership freedom and flexibility. The proprietor has complete freedom to make decisions without consulting with others. Any change in decision can be made promptly.

Owner claims all profits. The owner has no one with whom the profits are to be shared. Profits are the reward for taking the risks in the business, and since a sole proprietor takes all the risks, all the profits are his or hers.

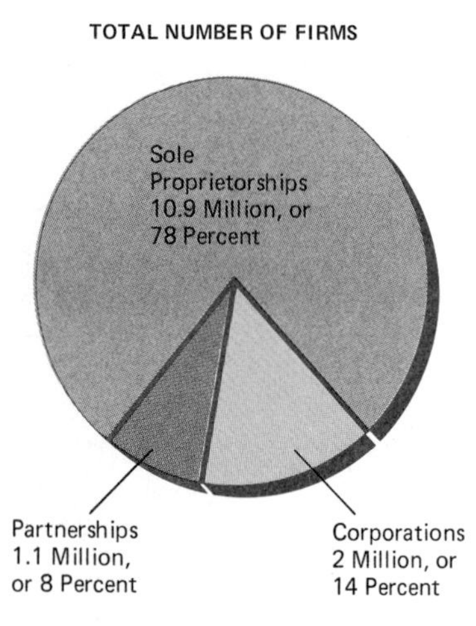

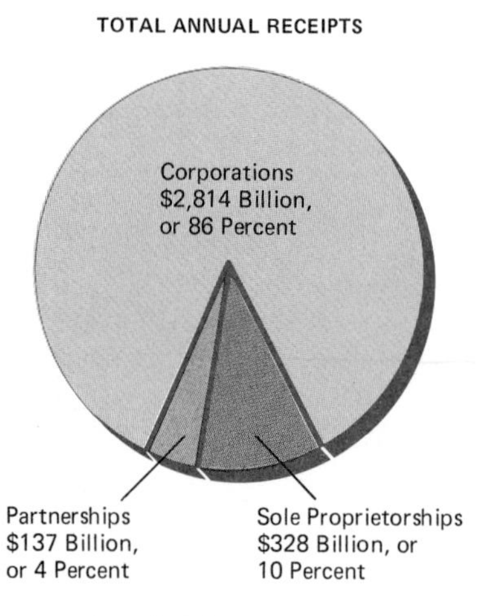

FIGURE 3-1

Number of businesses by forms of ownership and total annual receipts for firms. (Source: Internal Revenue Service.)

Tax advantages. Another advantage of the sole proprietorship relates to income tax. The business itself does not pay an income tax. Instead, sole proprietors pay income tax on the profits they receive as personal income. In this way, income tax is levied only one time on the firm's profits. With corporations, the income to the stockholders is taxed and the income to the corporation is taxed. The sole proprietorship does of course pay property, sales, and payroll taxes.

Disadvantages of a Sole Proprietorship

The disadvantages of a sole proprietorship are explained below.

Owner's unlimited liability. The sole proprietor has complete personal liability for all debts of the firm. This risk often discourages some persons from forming a sole proprietorship. If the firm were to be sued for some reason and lose the suit, the owner would have to pay the settlement. As a business grows, this may become an unacceptably big risk.

Difficulty of raising capital. The amount of capital available to a sole proprietor is limited to the owner's personal funds and any that he or she can borrow. Sole proprietorships usually do not have easy access to large amounts of funds that can be borrowed from commercial sources. Lending agencies are often reluctant to make loans to small firms with limited credit. Consequently, as capital needs increase, the proprietor may find it necessary to change to a partnership or some other form of legal ownership.

Lack of continuity. Although the sole proprietorship is relatively easy to establish, in the event of the owner's death, permanent disability, or bankruptcy, it is legally terminated. This is one of the serious disadvantages of the sole proprietorship. The business has no legal life beyond the life of the founder.

Limitations of size. Most sole proprietorships operate on a small scale. The owner does not have the advantage of consulting with partners or professional managers. And as a firm grows, its managerial resources may be stretched thin

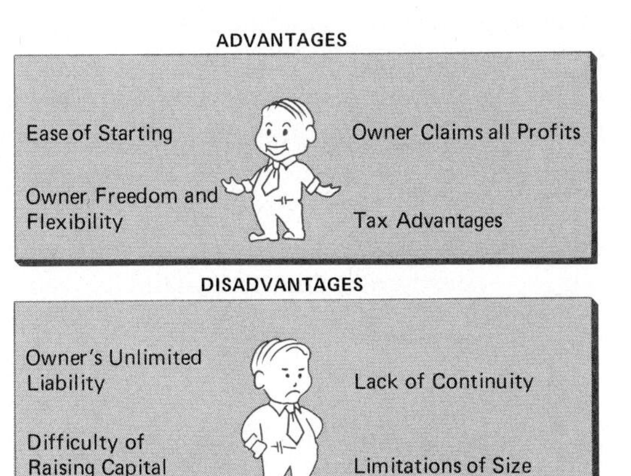

FIGURE 3-2
Advantages and disadvantages of sole proprietorship.

because the firm is small. An owner can successfully manage only a limited number of employees.

THE PARTNERSHIP

Like the sole proprietorship, the partnership has also existed for centuries. Rather than having one owner, in a partnership there are two or more owners. In fact, the law sets no limits on the number of people who may be members in a partnership. At one time the brokerage firm of Merrill Lynch, Pierce, Fenner & Smith had one hundred partners. It is now a corporate subsidiary of Merrill Lynch & Co., Inc.

The Uniform Partnership Act, which has been adopted by most states, defines **PARTNERSHIP** as **an association of two or more persons who are the co-owners of the business.**[1] Authority for the creation of partnerships rests in the common-law rights of voluntary association. Consequently there can be no partnership without the expressed intention of the partners.

General Partnerships and Limited Partnerships

The law recognizes two distinct types of partnership: general and limited. A **GENERAL PARTNERSHIP** is **an association of two or more persons with each general partner as co-owner having unlimited legal liability.** The general partners usually take an active role in the business. Unlike the corporation, the general partnership requires no state charter to operate. Termination of the partnership agreement can occur at any time, depending upon the conditions set forth in the agreement.

A **LIMITED PARTNERSHIP** is **an association in which one or more (but not all) partners have limited legal liability for the debts of the firm.** Each limited partner is not legally liable for such debts beyond the amounts of money he or she invested in the enterprise. It is important to note, however, that limited partners may not participate in managing the business. They are investors rather than participants in the firm's operations. If they do participate in the management, the courts recognize them as general partners, and their liability then becomes unlimited.

Most states have adopted the Uniform Limited Partnership Act, which provides legal sanction and state regulation over limited partnerships. Under this act a detailed statement about the limited partnership must be filed with the county clerk or some other government official. The kinds of information required varies by states. Most states call the document a **limited partnership certificate.**

Kinds of Partners

The law recognizes various kinds of partners in a general partnership. For example, an owner who takes an active role but does not want to reveal his or her identity to the public is a **secret partner.** On the other hand, one who is not active in the firm is a **silent partner.** One who has been a general partner for a long period and owns a large share of the firm is a **senior partner.** The **dormant partner** is both silent and secret. He or she is unknown to the public as a partner and is also not active in the business.

[1]The following states have not adopted the Uniform Partnership Act: Alabama, Florida, Georgia, Hawaii, Iowa, Kansas, Louisiana, Maine, Mississippi, and New Hampshire.

A member of a general or limited partnership who has unlimited personal liability for the firm's debts is a **general partner.** The title **junior partner** is used to identify someone who has been an owner for a short time and is not assuming substantial responsibility.

A **LIMITED PARTNER** is **one whose personal liability is limited to the amount invested in the partnership capital.** Limited partners are not permitted to exercise any managerial functions.

Limited partnerships have been popular in recent years as a form of ownership involving speculative business ventures such as drilling for oil, financing mobile-home parks, and operating cattle-feeding lots. Limited partners have no liability whatever for the debts of the business. They do face the possibility of losing their investment, of course. Moreover their personal assets are in no way liable for debts of the firm.

Forming a Partnership

If you decide that a partnership is the appropriate form of ownership for your venture, a partnership begins with an agreement. It can be written, oral, or implied. However, it makes sense to draw up an agreement in writing.

Partnership agreement.

Written or oral provisions agreed to by the partners are known as a **PARTNERSHIP AGREEMENT** or **ARTICLES OF PARTNERSHIP.** Table 3-2 lists the various elements that constitute common partnership agreements. Some state laws stipulate that a partnership operating under a firm

TABLE 3-2
THE ARTICLES OF PARTNERSHIP

Essential Elements in the Partnership Agreement
1. Name of the partnership
2. Names of partners
3. Location of the business
4. Legal addresses of all partners
5. Nature of the business
6. Intended duration of the partnership
7. Amount of cash or other contributions made by partners
8. Amount of time each partner will devote to business
9. Provisions for salaries or drawing accounts for partners
10. Distribution of profits or losses
11. Duties and responsibilities of each partner
12. Procedure regarding whether books will be closed upon death or withdrawal of a partner
13. Special causes of dissolution in addition to death
14. Methods for resolving disagreements
15. Use of life insurance to purchase protection for surviving partners

name rather than the partners' names must file such name with a county official, together with a list of the partners and their addresses. Each time a partner withdraws or one is added, this procedure must be repeated. If the written agreement does not show how profits and losses are to be shared, then the law presumes they will be shared equally. If you are thinking of becoming a partner, you should choose your partners carefully.

Rights and duties of general partners. Unless waived by the articles of partnership, each partner has certain rights and duties. Some of the more important ones are:

1. The right to participate in the management of the business
2. The right to examine partnership records and financial statements
3. The right to share in the partnership's assets when the agreement is terminated
4. The duty to observe the terms of the agreement
5. The duty to act in good faith when dealing with partners
6. The duty to exercise reasonable care and skill in handling affairs of a partnership involving third parties

General Partnership—Advantages and Disadvantages

The general partnership has several advantages. It can operate in any state with a minimum of legal restrictions. The partnership offers the possibility of raising larger capital resources than the sole proprietorship. It is easy to dissolve, and partners are taxed individually rather than as a business. Duties can be assigned according to the special ability of the partners.

The general partnership has these disadvantages:

1. There is an unlimited liability of general partners.
2. There is the possibility of disagreement because of divided authority.
3. The partnership lacks permanence.
4. It is difficult for a partner to withdraw his or her investment.

Businesses Adaptable to Partnerships

There seems to be no clear-cut method of deciding in advance which kinds of business are best adapted to the general or limited partnership. Any small or medium-sized firm could conceivably operate as a partnership.

In some instances the use of a partnership offers certain advantages. Investment banks and consulting firms are often organized as general partnerships. Such ventures as mobile-home parks and developing shopping centers are adaptable to the general partnership. For many years several of the larger stock brokerage firms were general partnerships. Both Montgomery Ward and Procter and Gamble started as general partnerships. Eventually they grew large and became corporations.

JOINT VENTURES

As another unincorporated form of business ownership, the joint venture has become popular. It was first used in Europe during the seventeenth century to carry out trade ventures with merchants in foreign countries.

The Nature of Joint Ventures

The **JOINT VENTURE** is **an association of two or more persons for a limited purpose, without the usual rights and responsibilities of a partnership.** It is actually a temporary partnership arrangement to carry out a single business operation. After the venture is accomplished, it is dissolved. However, long-running exceptions can be noted, such as Japan's Sumitomo Shoji Kaisha Ltd. Sumitomo is an "integrated trading company" that began on the island of Shikoku 350 years ago. It is composed of more than fifty companies and employs more than 250,000 persons. Such huge trading companies are joint ventures that are involved in domestic trade and in import, export, and third-country trade. They are credited with playing a major role in the economic recovery of Japan following World War II.

Sumitomo displays an incredible breadth of economic interests. It is involved in financing, warehousing, investments in manufacturing, transportation, petroleum, mining, forest products, real estate, and tourism. All activities are directed toward one end—promoting trade. The huge firm feels that exporting to another country is not enough. To help the balance of trade between Japan and the United States, Sumitomo exports American goods to Japan as well as Japanese-made goods to the United States.

A "person" in the eyes of the law can include corporations. So joint ventures can include partnerships between corporations as well as between individuals. It is common for several oil companies to form a joint venture to explore for oil or natural gas. The Alaskan Pipeline Project is an example. The joint venture is also used for large-scale construction jobs to complete specific projects. When used in the sale of securities, it is called an underwriting syndicate. For example, a group of investment banks may join together temporarily to market a new issue of corporate securities. Such a group can easily be organized, since it does not require a charter.

CORPORATIONS

The third major form of business ownership is the corporation. While the sole proprietorship is the most common form of ownership, the business corporation is the dominant economic and social institution in America because of the size of the companies involved. Despite its complexity, it is the most satisfactory form of ownership for large organizations. In writing about the American corporation, Economist John Kenneth Galbraith states:

> The institution that most changes our lives we least understand or, more correctly, seek most elaborately to misunderstand. That is the modern corporation. . . .The modern corporation lives in suspension between fiction and truth.[2]

It is this domination of the corporation that warrants all the attention it receives. The corporation is used for purposes other than business and includes charitable institutions, hospitals, professionals, and municipalities. However, our discussion here is mainly about the modern business corporation whose primary objective is profit.

[2]John Kenneth Galbraith, *The Age of Uncertainty* (Boston: Houghton Mifflin, 1977), p. 257.

What Is a Corporation?

Chief Justice John Marshall of the U.S. Supreme Court defined a **CORPORATION** as "**an artificial being, invisible, intangible, and existing only in contemplation of the law. . . .**"

More recently the U.S. Supreme Court called a **CORPORATION** "**an association of individuals united for some common purpose, and permitted by law to use a common name, and to change its members without dissolution of the association.**" You may be surprised to note the life-like characteristics contained in Chief Justice Marshall's definition of a corporation. This definition suggests that it is a "person," as we noted earlier, separate and distinct from the owners. It can sue and be sued. Corporations are separate legal entities from their owners. Likewise, the owners are separate from the managers in many instances.

A corporation is chartered by a state, and its charter may provide for perpetual existence when so specified in the certificate of incorporation. Some states have more lenient charter restrictions regarding incorporation requirements than others.[3]

Corporations employ numerous people and control vast sums of economic wealth and physical resources. For example, recently the five hundred largest industrial corporations in the United States reported gross revenue of over $1.6 trillion.

Classification of Corporations

Corporations, according to their charter provisions, can be classified as follows:

1. Private or business corporation
2. Public or government corporation
3. Open or close corporation
4. Domestic, foreign, or alien corporations

Private or business corporation.

A business privately operated for profit for the benefit of stockholders is a **PRIVATE CORPORATION.** Examples are the Ford Motor Company, General Electric, and Eastman Kodak. Not all corporations intend to earn a profit. Most states permit the formation of a corporation for charitable, educational, or social purposes.

Public or government corporation.

A corporation chartered by the federal government, a state, or a city for a public purpose is a PUBLIC CORPORATION. The Federal Deposit Insurance Corporation is a well-known public corporation.

Open or close corporation.

A profit-making corporation whose stock is sold on the open market is an **OPEN CORPORATION.** This type of stock is issued by companies that are listed on various stock exchanges and on local (over-the-counter) markets. **A corporation whose stock is closely held by members of the family or by a relatively few stockholders** is called **CLOSE CORPORATION.** In recent years many close corporations, such as the Hughes Tool Company and

[3]Arizona, Delaware, Florida, Iowa, Maine, and Nevada are among the states with fewer incorporation requirements. More corporations are chartered by Delaware than by any other state because the laws of Delaware are the least strict. About one-third of corporations listed on the New York Stock Exchange have a Delaware charter.

the Ford Motor Company, have "gone public" by making their shares available to the public as open corporations. Occasionally a corporation that has traded its shares publicly chooses to "go private" and become a close corporation.

Checker Motors, the maker of taxicabs, passenger cars, and auto parts, also operates taxi and bus services. The company has been exploring a number of schemes that may enable it to go private. The latest plan is to offer holders of the company's 1.1 million common shares $43 a share for their stock. However, the government, through the Securities and Exchange Commission, has expressed concern about making sure that minority stockholders are treated fairly. This concern extends not only to Checker's attempt to go private but to other such transactions.

Domestic, foreign, or alien corporation. A business chartered under the corporate laws of one state is regarded as a **DOMESTIC CORPORATION** of that state. In all other states it is a **foreign corporation.** A company doing business in the United States but chartered by a foreign government is known in the United States as an **alien corporation.**

Advantages and Disadvantages of the Corporation

As a form of business ownership, the corporation when compared with other forms has several important advantages. These advantages are the reason why corporations are the dominant form of business ownership in our economic system. These advantages include the following.

Management Advantages of the Corporation

1. Limited personal liability of each stockholder
2. Life of corporation is almost perpetual
3. Easy to expand its size
4. Easy to transfer ownership
5. Investors not required to manage
6. Allows use of specialists
7. Adaptable to large and small firms
8. Permits concentration of capital

The corporate form of business ownership also has some disadvantages, including the following.

Management Disadvantages of the Corporation

1. Subject to double taxation of income by federal and state governments[4]
2. Greater difficulty and expense in organizing

[4]Corporations are subject to federal and state income taxes. Corporate earnings are taxed, and dividends paid to stockholders are then taxed on an individual basis. This is a form of double taxation. The exception to double taxation is the Subchapter S corporation. It can be taxed as a partnership or proprietorship provided there are not more than fifteen stockholders who have elected to be taxed in the same manner as a proprietorship or partnership. Subchapter S information can be obtained from the Internal Revenue Service's local office.

3. Numerous federal and state government restrictions
4. Lack of secrecy, since corporations file financial reports to owners and the public
5. Impersonal relations between managers and stockholders

Organizing a Corporation

Let us assume that you have selected the kind of business you want to start and that you have decided to incorporate. You made this choice by comparing the advantages and disadvantages offered by the corporation with those offered by a partnership or a sole proprietorship. Your next step is to select the state in which to incorporate. If your principal business will be in Illinois, you should probably incorporate in that state. Before you decide, however, you may want to compare one or two other states' requirements. A local attorney would be one source of information. The attorney could advise you regarding the choice of a state.

After selecting the state in which to apply for a charter, your next step is to contact the state officer to determine what information you must provide for the articles of incorporation. Usually the required information for your application is similar to that listed in Table 3-3. Your charter contains the scope of business, its duration, and the names of incorporators. They are responsible for preparing the articles of incorporation. These articles are, in effect, an application to the state seeking approval to organize the corporation.

The Corporation Charter

At this point your application is ready to be approved. You will receive your corporation charter. Usually a copy is mailed to the clerk of the county in which the company's home office will be located. (This procedure varies slightly in different states.)

TABLE 3-3
INFORMATION FOR CORPORATION CHARTER APPLICATION

1. Name, location, and address of proposed corporation.
2. Names and addresses of incorporators.
3. Intended duration of the corporation—stated number of years or perpetual.
4. Nature of business in which corporation is to engage.
5. Names and addresses of directors and officers.
6. Address of principal business office.
7. Amount of capital to be authorized. This is officially known as the authorized capital stock. It is divided into shares, which may range in value from $1 to $1,000, whether common, preferred, or both.
8. Maximum number of shares of authorized stock to be issued, and whether stock will be par or no-par with or without voting rights.* Shares are in the form of stock certificates, numbered and recorded when issued. Each must bear the signature of officers.
9. Name and address of each charter subscriber to stock certificates, and statement showing total number of shares paid for by each subscriber.

*A detailed explanation of the terms par value and no-par value is given in Chapter 14.

The following items illustrate what a typical charter might contain:

1. Corporation title
2. Name of the state granting the charter
3. Descriptive statement of purposes of corporation
4. Location of corporation's general office
5. Term of years for which corporation is incorporated
6. Number of directors, including minimum and maximum
7. Names of directors and their addresses
8. Amount of capital stock fully subscribed for and purchased
9. Notarization by notary public in the county in which corporation is to maintain its general office

The Corporation Structure

Now the corporation is formed. The first order of business is to elect the officers and vote on the proposed bylaws—the general rules that govern the organization. The bylaws usually specify that the officers are to be chosen by the board of directors. The president may be the highest-ranking officer, but most firms regard the chairman of the board as the top executive.

Corporation officers. In addition to the president, other officers may include the vice-president, secretary, treasurer, and sometimes a controller. In some cases several vice-presidents may be named.

Figure 3-3 represents the structure of a corporation and shows the relationship between the stockholders and the directors and company officers.

Board of directors. The board of directors has the responsibility for the operation of the corporation and developing its policies. Each director, during his or her term of office (usually one year subject to reelection) is expected to

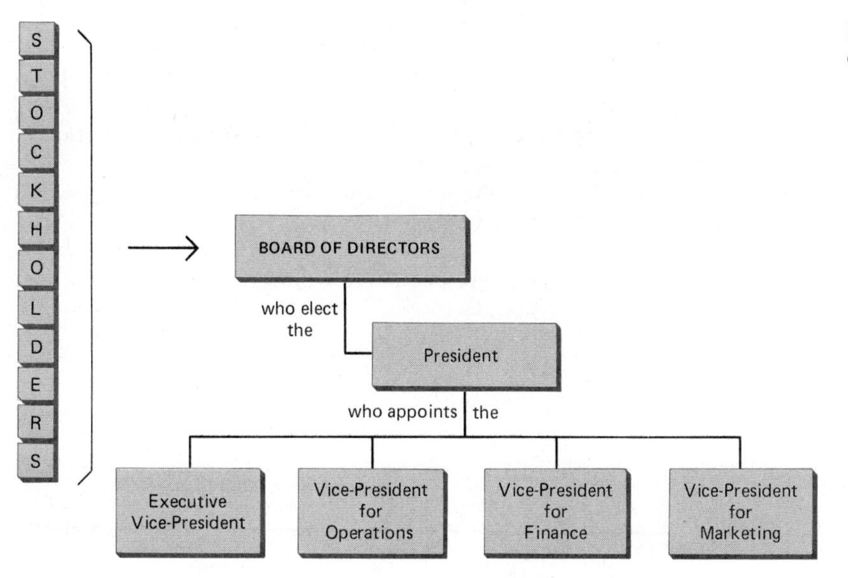

FIGURE 3-3
Corporate organization.

attend the board meetings. A director is neither subject to orders from stockholders nor required to carry out promises made before the election—each director may vote as he or she chooses. However, directors are accountable to the stockholders who elect them. Directors have the following responsibilities:

1. They are expected to exercise reasonable judgment—at least the same degree of prudence that they would exercise over their own affairs.
2. They are responsible for the appointment of corporate officers.
3. They have the sole responsibility for declaring dividends.
4. They cannot be held liable for *honest* errors in judgment.
5. They can delegate decision-making powers to the officers and other employees.

Corporate directors are now being held personally liable for a greater range of actions than at any previous time. For example, if one of the officers of a company

CURRENT ISSUE

Should Corporations Use More Inside and Fewer Outside Directors on the Board of Directors?

Most boards of directors have more outside than inside directors. There is growing public opinion that the way to control the number of corporate bribes, payoffs, and other corporation abuses is by replacing the number of inside directors with outside directors.

With which of the following statements do you agree and with which do you disagree?

1. **Inside directors, who are employees, are more knowledgeable about the company's business.**
2. **Management is frequently reluctant to give outside directors confidential facts about the corporation.**
3. **Outside directors give needed objectivity to executive board deliberations.**
4. **Outside directors can provide expertise that otherwise is not available from inside directors.**
5. **Outside directors may be selected because of their special competence, which gives prestige to the company.**
6. **Since inside directors are employees of the corporation, they are likely to be biased in their opinions on certain issues.**

Do you favor requiring corporations to use outside directors? Why or why not?

fails to get competitive bids for a major purchase, he or she may be held personally liable. Such things as failure to exercise reasonable care in the selection of a bank, investing corporate funds in a proxy fight, or negligent actions can cause a lawsuit. Any acts by a director that result in a loss can be viewed as a potential source of a lawsuit. Thus a high percentage of directors carry liability insurance to protect themselves from such possibilities.

Inside and outside directors. There are two types of corporate directors: inside and outside. **Corporate officers who serve as directors** are known as **INSIDE DIRECTORS.** As a rule, the president and other officers are elected as directors. Some corporations also elect directors from other levels of company employment.

Persons who hold positions outside the corporation and are elected as directors are known as **OUTSIDE DIRECTORS.** Frequently they are prominent individuals and leaders in their own professions or occupations and are chosen for their special qualifications. Recent revelations of corporate payoffs and bribes—especially to foreign governments in order to do business—have resulted in attacks on boards of directors for these unlawful acts.

Sometimes outside directors lack an understanding of business operations because management has failed to provide adequate information. Some critics urge corporations to use more inside directors because they are more familiar with the company's problems. The outside director, however, can act as a brake or as an objective viewer more easily than the insider in some cases.

CORPORATE OWNERSHIP

Although the corporate officers have the responsibility for operating the business efficiently, the stockholders can also play an influential role. Regardless of the size of the corporation, the stockholders are the owners. In small corporations, they do exercise closer control than in giant corporations. They may elect themselves to the board of directors and then appoint themselves to key executive positions.

Corporate Shareholders

Ownership in a business corporation is shown by stock shares. **Common** stock generally carries voting rights. **Preferred** stock, as a rule, does not carry voting rights. Common-stock holders receive dividends only after the preferred-stock holders. This might be important if the company were not making much money. There are several different kinds of shares, which are discussed in some detail in Chapter 14. For the present, our discussion will deal with only one class of stock—common stock.

What do stockholders really own? "Owning a share of stock" is really just what the phrase implies: having a fractional interest in the total entity called the corporation. But this fractional claim is not for a fixed amount payable at any time. It is worth only what someone else will give you for it. From this viewpoint, stockholders own only an unappropriated share of the corporation's net worth on any given day.

Ownership in the corporation can easily be transferred from one person to another by selling and buying shares. A common-stock certificate is illustrated in Figure 3-4. To transfer ownership of this certificate, one must sign it on the reverse side, as shown in Figure 3-5.

Rights of the stockholders. Stockholders have certain legal rights. For discussion purposes, these can be classified as group rights and individual rights. **Group rights** are rights that stockholders may exercise when assembled at regular and special meetings. **Individual rights** are rights that each stockholder has without reference to other stockholders. Stockholder group rights consist of the following:

1. Elect directors
2. Adopt and amend the bylaws
3. Change the charter with the consent of the state
4. Sell or otherwise dispose of corporation assets
5. Dissolve the corporation

In the absence of any state restrictions or the corporate charter, each stockholder has, among others, these individual rights:

1. Buy and sell stock registered in the owner's name
2. Receive dividends in proportion to the number and class of shares owned, provided the dividend has been duly declared by the directors
3. Share in distribution of assets on a proportional basis, as provided in the charter, if the directors decide to dissolve the firm

Stockholders attend the annual meeting of the EXXON Corporation at which time the corporate officers give reports about the corporation's achievements and future plans. Stockholders may ask questions. (Courtesy EXXON Corporation.)

CERTIFICATE FOR LESS THAN 100 SHARES

Number 00000

COMMON STOCK

PAR VALUE $5

TENNECO

INCORPORATED UNDER THE LAWS OF THE STATE OF DELAWARE

TENNECO INC.

THIS CERTIFICATE IS TRANSFERABLE IN HOUSTON, NEW YORK, CHICAGO OR LOS ANGELES

Shares One

COMMON STOCK

PAR VALUE $5

TENNECO

TENS UNITS 1 2 3 4 5 6 7 8 9 0

This Certifies that - - - - - - - - - - - JOHN Q. PUBLIC - - - - - - - - - - - - - is the owner of

SEE REVERSE FOR CERTAIN DEFINITIONS

ONE (1)

FULLY PAID AND NON-ASSESSABLE SHARES OF THE COMMON STOCK

of Tenneco, Inc. transferable on the books of the Corporation in person or by duly authorized attorney upon surrender of this certificate properly endorsed. This certificate and the shares represented hereby are issued and shall be held subject to all of the provisions of the Certificate of Incorporation of the Corporation (copies of which are on file with the Transfer Agent), to all of which the holder by acceptance hereof assents. This certificate is not valid unless countersigned by the Transfer Agent and registered by the Registrar.

Witness the signatures of the duly authorized officers. Dated

CERTIFICATE OF STOCK

SPECIMEN SECRETARY

SPECIMEN CHAIRMAN OF THE BOARD

REGISTERED: FIRST NATIONAL CITY BANK, REGISTRAR

BY AUTHORIZED OFFICER

COUNTERSIGNED: CHEMICAL BANK NEW YORK TRUST COMPANY, TRANSFER AGENT

BY AUTHORIZED SIGNATURE

AMERICAN BANK NOTE COMPANY.

FIGURE 3-4

This stock certificate is typical of the kind issued to stockholders of an open corporation. The reverse side of the certificate is illustrated in Figure 3-5. To sell the shares, it is necessary to indorse the certificate. (Courtesy Tenneco, Inc.)

FIGURE 3-5
(Courtesy Tenneco, Inc.)

TENNECO INC.

The following abbreviations, when used in the inscription on the face of this certificate, shall be construed as though they were written out in full according to applicable laws or regulations:

TEN COM — as tenants in common

TEN ENT — as tenants by the entireties

JT TEN — as joint tenants with right of survivorship and not as tenants in common

UNIF GIFT MIN ACT — .... Custodian ....
(Cust) (Minor)
under Uniform Gifts to Minors
Act........
(State)

Additional abbreviations may also be used though not in the above list.

THE CORPORATION WILL FURNISH WITHOUT CHARGE TO EACH STOCKHOLDER WHO SO REQUESTS THE DESIGNATIONS, PREFERENCES AND RELATIVE, PARTICIPATING, OPTIONAL OR OTHER SPECIAL RIGHTS OF EACH CLASS OF STOCK OR SERIES THEREOF OF THE CORPORATION, AND THE QUALIFICATIONS, LIMITATIONS OR RESTRICTIONS OF SUCH PREFERENCES AND/OR RIGHTS. SUCH REQUEST MAY BE MADE TO THE CORPORATION OR THE TRANSFER AGENT.

For value received, ________ *hereby sell, assign and transfer unto*

PLEASE INSERT SOCIAL SECURITY OR OTHER IDENTIFYING NUMBER OF ASSIGNEE

____

____

PLEASE PRINT OR TYPEWRITE NAME AND ADDRESS OF ASSIGNEE

____

____

________________________________ *Shares*

of the capital stock represented by the within Certificate, and do hereby irrevocably constitute and appoint ________

____

Attorney to transfer the said stock on the books of the within named Corporation with full power of substitution in the premises.

Dated, ________

____

NOTICE: THE SIGNATURE TO THIS ASSIGNMENT MUST CORRESPOND WITH THE NAME AS WRITTEN UPON THE FACE OF THE CERTIFICATE IN EVERY PARTICULAR, WITHOUT ALTERATION OR ENLARGEMENT, OR ANY CHANGE WHATEVER.

THIS SPACE MUST NOT BE COVERED IN ANY WAY

4. Subscribe to additional stock (usually common, not preferred) before it is offered to the public unless this right is waived or revoked by a vote of the stockholders[5]
5. Review and inspect company records
6. Sue directors for misuse of power or fraud
7. Vote at stockholders' meetings, annual or special (generally restricted to common-stock holders)

Many corporations have thousands of stockholders, most of whom are unlikely to attend the annual meeting. A proxy form similar to the one shown in Figure 3-6 is usually enclosed with the notice of the meeting that is sent to each stockholder. The notice in Figure 3-7 was directed to all Southern Pacific Company stockholders, announcing the date and place of the company's annual meeting. This notice includes information about the purposes of the meeting. Those who cannot attend are invited to vote by proxy. The proxy form must be returned

[5]The right of stockholders to subscribe to additional stock before these shares are offered to the public is known as a *preemptive right.* This right can be restricted by charter provisions approved by the stockholders.

PROXY **Southern Pacific Company** PROXY

Annual Meeting of Stockholders, May 17, 1979

The undersigned hereby appoints B. F. BIAGGINI, A. C. FURTH, E. L. HAZARD, G. B. MUNROE, R. S. PERKINS and A. E. HILL, and each of them, proxies, with power of substitution, to vote the shares of the undersigned at the Annual Meeting of Stockholders of the Company, to be held at 4 East 61st Street, New York, New York, on May 17, 1979 at 10:30 A.M., and at any adjournment thereof, for the election of directors, upon the proposals set forth below, more fully described in the Notice of Annual Meeting and Proxy Statement, and in their discretion on all other matters coming before the meeting.

The Board of Directors recommends a vote FOR:
Authority to vote for the election of directors.
FOR ☐ **WITHHOLD** ☐

Proposal 1—Ratification of selection of auditors of the Company and its subsidiaries.
FOR ☐ **AGAINST** ☐

The Board of Directors recommends a vote AGAINST the following Stockholders' proposal:
Proposal 2—Provide limited pre-emptive rights.
FOR ☐ **AGAINST** ☐

The shares represented by this proxy will be voted in accordance with the specifications made; but if no specifications are made, the shares will be voted FOR the election of directors and proposal 1 and AGAINST proposal 2.

(Continued and to be signed on the other side)

(Continued from the other side)

This proxy is solicited on behalf of the Management.

If you plan to attend the meeting, check this box ☐
and an admission ticket will be sent to you.

PLEASE SIGN BELOW AND RETURN IN THE ENCLOSED ENVELOPE.

58205

Dated ________________, 1979

____
Signature(s) of Stockholder(s)

FIGURE 3-6

Corporation proxy form.

Most stockholders vote by proxy using a form similar to the one illustrated here. Usually, a shareholder is entitled to one vote for each share owned. (Courtesy of the Southern Pacific Company.)

SOUTHERN PACIFIC COMPANY
SOUTHERN PACIFIC BUILDING
ONE MARKET PLAZA
SAN FRANCISCO, CALIFORNIA 94105

Notice of Annual Meeting of Stockholders

April 2, 1979

TO THE STOCKHOLDERS OF SOUTHERN PACIFIC COMPANY:

The Annual Meeting of the Stockholders of Southern Pacific Company will be held at 4 East 61st Street, New York, N. Y., on Thursday, May 17, 1979, at 10:30 A.M., for the following purposes:

1. To elect fourteen directors to hold office until the next Annual Meeting of Stockholders and until others are duly chosen in their places and shall have qualified.
2. To act upon a resolution for stockholder ratification of the selection of the auditors of the Company and its subsidiaries.
3. To transact such other business as may properly be brought before the meeting or any adjournment thereof, including taking action upon a resolution proposed by six stockholders, as set forth in the accompanying Proxy Statement, if such resolution is introduced at the meeting. This proposed resolution requests that steps be taken to provide limited pre-emptive rights to the stockholders.

Only stockholders of record on the books of the Company at the close of business on March 22, 1979, will be entitled to vote at the meeting. A list of such stockholders will be available at the meeting and, during the ten days prior to the meeting, at the office of the Transfer Agent, Southern Pacific Company, 130 John Street, New York, N. Y. The stock transfer books will not be closed.

A. E. HILL, *Secretary*

To assure your representation at the meeting, please sign the enclosed proxy and return it promptly in the accompanying envelope. By doing so, you will help the Company avoid the expense of further solicitation.

FIGURE 3-7

Notice of annual meeting of stockholders.

Annually each stockholder receives a written notice of the corporation's annual meeting with management. At that time the stockholders elect directors, ratify the appointment of the auditors, and transact other business properly brought before the meeting. (Courtesy of the Southern Pacific Company.)

by a certain date. A **PROXY** is defined as a power of attorney that transfers to a third party the stockholder's right to vote at the stockholders' annual meeting. A common practice is to send the proxy to a member of the board or to a director named on the form.

Sometimes stockholders become dissatisfied with the existing management. By gathering enough proxies, it is possible to get approval for a proposal that disgruntled stockholders support. Business history contains some interesting cases of bitter "proxy wars" fought to gain control of a corporation.

In 1977 the Securities and Exchange Commission, an agency of the federal government, held extensive hearings on stockholder participation in the operation of corporations. The SEC expressed disappointment that companies had not done more on their own to give stockholders real participation in corporate governance. The SEC has recommended that changes in proxy rules take place to make corporate elections more effective.

Corporation Mergers

A news release announcing a corporation's plans to merge with another corporation is often welcomed by the stockholders but feared by competitors. Many of today's most successful corporations achieved their large size by joining with other companies. For example, General Foods Corporation has merged with a number of companies so that it now owns and markets more than a dozen branded foods that were formerly owned by smaller companies. Examples are Post cereals and Gaines dog food.

Reasons for a merger. The reasons for corporate mergers include the following: (1) to take over a going company to expand a market, (2) to achieve tax advantages, (3) to gain new sources of goods, and (4) to acquire cash reserves.

The managements of the two companies discuss the advantages and disadvantages of the merger. Laws affecting merger and tax effects are reviewed. There is always the possibility that the merger may require approval of the U.S. attorney general to ensure that there is no violation of the antitrust laws.

Or, in the case of regulated industries such as the airline industry, other government agencies may be involved. For example, the Civil Aeronautics Board in 1979 negated a potential merger between Eastern Airlines and National Airlines. If Eastern and National had merged, it would have created the second largest non-Communist airline in the world (United Airlines is the largest). The CAB administrative law judge felt that the merger would lessen competition in the airline industry.

Finally, there is a price-per-share proposal by the offering corporation, known as the **tender-price offer.** Each stockholder has a right to accept or refuse to tender his or her shares at the proposed offering price. This tender-offer method is becoming increasingly popular because it is less costly than a long proxy fight. Tender offers are usually made to the target company's stockholders by mail or through newspaper announcements.

Some companies seeking a merger have taken a different approach. This involves buying the company's stock on the open market paying the market price. That strategy is the gradual buy-in. Among the best-known American corporations to follow this plan are Teledyne, Loew's Corporation (theater owners), and the American Financial Corporation. The idea is to go after a company that would make a good acquisition but to do it at the market price rather than an agreed-upon merger price. This can be accomplished by buying shares on the open market. By taking control of 5 to 20 percent of the shares, a foothold is established if the acquiring corporation chooses to push for merger later. Ultimately the stockholders of the two companies are asked to vote on the issue. Sometimes mergers are very costly due to legal fees, advertising, and the presenting of arguments to government commissions.

Types of Merger Combinations

Merger combinations are of three types: vertical, horizontal, and conglomerate. In most cases it is the larger company that acquires another by buying its assets.

Vertical mergers. A **vertical merger** consolidates several firms **engaged in different steps of producing the same products.** These steps can range from raw materials to end products. For example, a steel company may own coal mines, railroads, blast furnaces, and rolling mills. This allows the steel company to control its source of raw materials as well as the manufacturing process. The company makes steel from the mineral extraction process all the way to the final product.

Horizontal mergers. A **horizontal merger** involves separate companies **engaged in the same business activity** joining together under one ownership. General Motors actually was formed by merging with a number of other automobile companies. This kind of merger tends to reduce competition. General Motors has also expanded vertically by acquiring companies that manufacture automobile bodies, batteries, and accessories. Rather than start new companies, General Motors acquired existing companies.

Conglomerate. A third type of merger is the **conglomerate—a collection of unrelated companies** producing unrelated products. A basic purpose of the conglomerate is to achieve quick growth and thereby increase earnings. Gulf & Western Industries became a conglomerate by acquiring over ninety corporations, and Litton Industries merged with fifty companies.

According to merger specialists W. T. Grimm & Co., in a recent six-month period a total of thirty-seven mergers took place, which involved more than $100 million as part of the transactions. During a six-month period a year earlier, twenty mergers were completed. Says Michael Evans, president of Chase Econometric Associates:

> The high inflation rate means a company has to add at least five percentage points to its rate-of-return calculations. If a company has been getting 15 percent, it must now aim for 20 percent, and there aren't many projects that qualify. As a result corporations are going the acquisition route.[6]

When will the merger spree end? Some economists believe it will continue for several more years. By that time, bidding for companies will push stock prices to the point where the return on investments from mergers may be less than the return from starting new plants. Many economists agree that using corporate cash for acquisitions adds little to capital formation or job creation. Thus mergers should become less popular in future years.

Holding Companies

Any corporation that buys sufficient shares in another corporation is called a holding company, and the acquired firm is a **subsidiary.** The owning company is known as the **parent company.** Some holding companies own all the voting stock of their subsidiaries. But even those that own less than half can take advantage of the right to use management-secured proxies. In this way they maintain effective control over the directors of the subsidiary.

A major holding company in the public utilities field is the American Telephone and Telegraph Company. The AT&T owns a controlling interest in twenty-two companies—mostly regional telephone companies that are also corporations. In the map of the United States illustrated in Figure 3-8, you can see how widely AT&T shares are distributed in the fifty states.

United States antitrust laws prohibit mergers that "may tend to substantially lessen competition or tend to create a monopoly." A proposed merger combination may be stopped by the U.S. Department of Justice if the intent is to monopolize or restrain trade.

[6]The distinction between **merger** and **acquisition** is not sharp. Acquisition means the outright purchase of assets of a company, or a sufficient interest in it, to gain control.

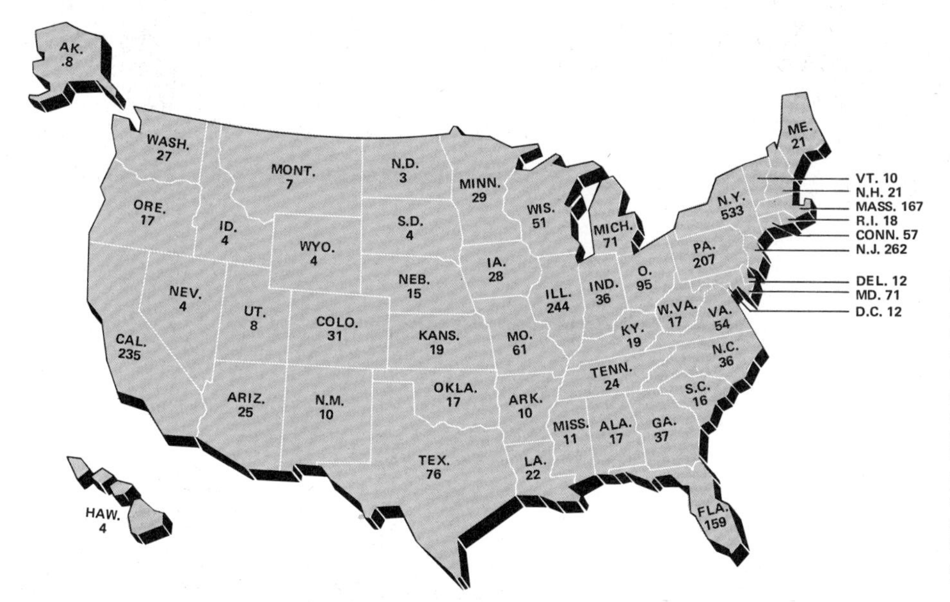

FIGURE 3-8

AT&T common-stock owners live in fifty states and 127 nations. Of the common shares outstanding, women own 31 percent, men 17 percent, financial institutions 34 percent, and joint ownership 18 percent. The number for each state represents thousands. (Courtesy American Telephone and Telegraph Company.)

Public Utility Holding Company Act. In 1935 Congress passed the Public Utility Holding Company Act. Utility company executives spent large sums in trying to defeat this legislation. The act's purpose is to control mergers of corporations and prevent economic concentration of power. Interlocking directorates with banks are prohibited by this legislation, and so is intercompany borrowing.

The issue of whether bigness is badness is not clearly decided yet. Indeed, bigness seems to lead to more concentration of power in the market, which reduces competition. But proponents argue that bigness is a reward for having success-

THE TRUSTBUSTERS GO AFTER CONGLOMERATES

Assaults on conglomerate corporate mergers continue on the Washington scene. Senator Edward M. Kennedy began a movement with a series of fact-finding hearings. In 1979 he introduced a bill in Congress designed to halt virtually all mergers of large corproations. His bill would limit mergers on the basis of size alone: Bigness itself should be added to the list of antitrust offenses because large corporations cause social problems even when they do not impair competition.

It is said that large corporations "overawe" small firms by their sheer economic power and unlimited resources. The argument is also made that when most of an industry is concentrated in the hands of a "few" giants, there can be little competition.

Economist Yale Brozen of the University of Chicago says that Senator Kennedy's attack on large corporations and mergers is no longer intellectually respectable. "What Kennedy really means," says Brozen, "is that no one should have any power except the Washington monopoly." Kennedy has been leading the deregulation movement in Congress for several years. His opponents believe he would do better to concentrate on deregulation and drop the subject of mergers.

fully competed, and that they should not be penalized for doing a good job. According to William S. Knudsen, former chairman of the board of General Motors:

> A big corporation is more or less blamed for being big; it is only big because it gives service. If it doesn't give service, it gets small faster than it grew big.

OTHER FORMS OF BUSINESS OWNERSHIP

Although we have already discussed the major forms of business ownership in the United States, several others warrant mention.

Joint-Stock Company

The joint-stock company was a popular form of business ownership before the rise of corporations. It is a voluntary association of persons operating under articles of agreement. The capital is divided into transferable shares. It is similar to a general partnership, for the owners all have unlimited personal liability. And it is like the corporation, for profits are distributed on the basis of shares held, and income taxes are similarly assessed. It differs from the partnership, for the owners elect directors, who have authority to conduct the business. Also, the firm is not dissolved by the death of one or more shareholders. It is inexpensive to start, because the articles of agreement do not require approval by a government agency. For purposes of income tax, it is taxed in a manner similar to the corporation.

Business Trust

A business trust is unlike any of the other forms of ownership we have studied. It is an arrangement whereby the owner of real property (trustor) may place it in trust with a trustee who agrees to manage it for the beneficiary. The trustor may be the beneficiary. Property may consist of money, real estate, or other assets described in the deed of trust. Certificates of trust are issued to investors, whose liability is limited to the amount invested. Among its advantages are its (1) simplicity of formation, (2) small cost to form, and (3) relative freedom from government regulation. The disadvantages include these:

1. It is taxed as though it were a corporation.
2. Its certificates are not as easy to sell as those of a corporation.
3. Limitations may be placed on the life of the trust. However, death of a certificate holder does not terminate the trust agreement.

The real estate investment trust (REIT) has been popular in the United States since about 1960. Approximately 175 REIT funds have been organized and sold by brokerage firms. Their popularity declined as a reuslt of the economic recession and accompanying inflation of the 1970s, when many people lost a great deal of money in REITs.

Cooperatives

Cooperative associations, or co-ops as they are often called, are another kind of state-chartered business. Co-ops differ from corporations in several ways:

1. They are owned by the user-members. Each owner has only one vote regardless of the number of shares owned.

2. All capital is subscribed to by the members. There is a limit to the number of shares each owner may acquire.
3. Co-ops may pay **patronage dividends**—dividends paid in proportion to the amount of goods each member has bought through the co-op.
4. Directors usually receive no salary. Only managers and regular employees receive a salary.

Kinds of cooperatives. There are basically three kinds of cooperatives. The **producer cooperative** engages in marketing the products grown by members (usually farmers). Some producer co-ops market on a national scale, using such brand names as Sunkist oranges and Sun-Maid raisins. **Buying cooperatives** owned by farmers buy such items as fertilizer, seeds, and supplies. **Consumer cooperatives** are retail outlets where the members may purchase such products as food, gasoline, and tires. The credit union is also a form of consumer co-op which provides saving and borrowing services. Credit unions are discussed in detail in Chapter 15.

Cooperatives enjoy certain advantages not available to corporations. Any savings made by the co-ops are returned to the owners as dividends. These dividends are not taxed as are those paid by corporations; they are regarded as a refund of overpayments rather than as earned income. The federal government provides financial assistance for certain kinds of co-op activities normally not available to profit-making corporations.

One disadvantage of co-ops is that they lack the profit-making incentive found in other forms of ownership. Co-op board members are volunteers who receive no pay for their services. Frequently, the scale of salaries paid employees is lower than for similar work in other forms of business.

Mutual Companies

Mutual companies are similar to cooperatives, since they are owned by those who use their services. A mutual company is chartered in the same way as a corporation, but no stock is issued. There are two primary types of mutual companies: **mutual insurance companies** and **mutual savings banks.** A person who deposits money in a mutual savings bank is automatically a member. Like co-ops, mutuals are generally nonprofit. Earned income may be reinvested or returned to owners as a rebate or dividend. Mutual insurance companies grant their members a reduction in premiums by paying them dividends. Although no capital stock is issued in mutual companies, the mutual still operates as a legal entity similar to a corporation.

SUMMARY OF KEY CONCEPTS

The sole proprietorship is easy to start. The owner receives all the profits and enjoys maximum freedom to manage.

The sole proprietorship has two main disadvantages:

1. It is difficult to raise enough capital.
2. Death of the owner may force an end to the business.

Key advantages of the general partnership are greater financial strength than for a proprietorship and more management know-how. The general partnership is simple and easy to start.

The general partnership has two main disadvantages:

1. Each partner is personally liable for the debts of the business.
2. Death of one partner automatically terminates the agreement.

In a limited partnership, one or more partners have limited liability. Limited partners are not allowed to exercise managerial authority.

The rights, duties, and responsibilities of partners are spelled out in the articles of partnership prepared by the partners.

The corporation offers a means to overcome most of the weaknesses of the proprietorship and partnership in that

1. It offers continuity of existence.
2. Owners are not personally liable for all the debts.
3. It is easy to sell one's stock in the ownership.
4. It permits specialists to be hired to manage the business.

Corporations are allowed to merge provided there is no violation of antitrust laws or other statutes.

A joint venture is formed by two or more persons for a limited purpose without the usual rights and powers of a partnership. A member may not withdraw until the project is ended.

A joint-stock company is a voluntary association of persons with ownership divided into transferable shares similar to a general partnership.

A business trust is taxed like a corporation. Death of a certificate holder does not terminate the trust agreement.

Some other forms of ownership are cooperatives and mutual companies.

BUSINESS TERMS

You should be able to match these business terms with the statements that follow:

a. Corporation
b. Domestic corporation
c. Inside directors
d. Joint venture
e. Limited partner
f. Limited partnership
g. Open corporation
h. Outside directors
i. Partnership
j. Partnership agreement
k. Proxy
l. Sole proprietorship

1. An organization that is owned and operated by one person
2. An association in which one or more (but not all) partners enjoy limited personal liability for debts of the firm
3. A partner whose personal liability is limited to the amount invested in the partnership capital
4. As association of two or more persons who are co-owners of the business
5. A written or oral provision agreed to by the partners
6. An association of two or more persons for a limited purpose without the usual rights and responsibilities of a partnership

7. An artificial, invisible, and intangible entity existing only in contemplation of the law
8. A profit-making corporation whose stock is sold on the open market
9. A business chartered under the corporate laws of some states
10. Corporate officers who serve as directors
11. Power of attorney that transfers to a third party the stockholder's right to vote at the annual stockholders' meeting
12. Persons outside the corporation who are elected as directors of the corporation

REVIEW QUESTIONS

1. Why is the sole proprietorship more popular than other forms of business ownership?
2. Give the reasons why so many small firms prefer the proprietorship and large companies prefer the corporation.
3. Identify some of the provisions usually found in a partnership.
4. What do the stockholders of a corporation really own?
5. What is the difference between a *joint-stock company* and a *joint venture?*
6. What is usually found in the corporation charter?

DISCUSSION QUESTIONS

1. Failure rates are highest for sole proprietorships and partnerships and lowest for corporations. In your opinion, what are the causes for such high proprietorship failures?
2. What accounts for the differences in the amount of capital that can be raised by a sole proprietorship and by a partnership?
3. Why is it considered inadvisable to form a partnership based on an oral rather than a written agreement?
4. Do stockholders in Safeway Stores have a voice in the daily operations of that business? Explain.
5. How do you explain the fact that although corporate profits are taxed and again when paid to stockholders as dividends, yet the corporation is the dominant form of business ownership in large businesses?
6. Give some examples of a public (governmental) corporation, a private corporation with shares on an organized exchange, and a conglomerate.

BUSINESS CASE 3-1

Bellvue Engineering Company

Bellvue Engineering Company, one of the nation's leading engineering-consulting firms, is located in Charleston. The company is owned by Howard Hobart, who started the business in 1965 as a sole proprietorship.

Last year, as a sideline, the firm became an agent for a conveyor-belt manufacturing company and also opened a dealership for Kamron mechanical-lift forks.

Both of these lines are well-known products, and the immediate demand for them is strong. For the third consecutive year the firm's growth in net sales has increased by 25 to 30 percent.

The company is now at the stage where it needs at least five more mechanical engineers. Recently Hobart lost three large contracts for lack of engineers.

A few days ago Hobart was offered a dealership for the entire state. He would represent the largest producer of electronic and mechanical valves and switches used in industrial plants. He estimates that this expansion would require about twenty-five thousand square feet of fireproof warehouse space and five thousand square feet of office space. In addition, three more engineers would be needed immediately.

Hobart estimates that an expenditure of $500,000 will be required to build the new facilities, and about $300,000 in working capital. The company cannot finance these expenditures from current earnings.

Hobart has discussed the possibility of a loan with two local banks, but neither one is interested in a long-term loan. Both banks require more collateral than he is able to furnish. There is also the matter of very high interest rates. Hobart's business expansion into additional product lines depends upon the availability of new capital. Otherwise the alternative is to continue operating the business and change from a sole proprietorship to some other form.

1. What is the main problem in this case?
2. Which form of business ownership should Hobart adopt in order to solve this problem? Why do you recommend that form?

BUSINESS CASE 3-2

Hartford Brothers and Cole

For nearly four decades Hartford Brothers and Cole, a general partnership, has been a leader in industrial construction operating on an international scale. Now the two Hartford brothers are planning to retire, but Cole is not. The brothers would remain general partners, although they realize the risk they will take if they do so. Both brothers would like to find a way to retain a financial interest with a minimum of financial responsibility. Cole is agreeable to working out a feasible plan.

There is evidence that several of the employees would like to become part owners of the business. As many as twenty employees at lower management levels might be interested in becoming part owners.

1. Can the existing partnership be enlarged without revising the partnership agreement?
2. What would you recommend as a feasible solution to the problem?

GENERAL BUSINESS MANAGEMENT 4

STUDY OBJECTIVES

WHEN YOU HAVE FINISHED READING THIS CHAPTER, YOU SHOULD BE ABLE TO

ONE Describe management and nonmanagement activities.

TWO Discuss the contributions made by Frederick W. Taylor and their impact on the rise of a managerial class.

THREE Explain how the managerial class movement began in the 1840s and lasted until World War I.

FOUR Contrast the approaches of the classical school, the behavioral school, and the managerial-science school of management theory.

FIVE Describe what is meant by management functions performed by managers at the different levels of an organization.

SIX Identify and discuss the following management skills: technical skills, human skills, and conceptual skills.

IN THE NEWS

WANTED: Top Professional Manager to Run 1984 Olympics

Needed—Super Executive. Major entrepreneurial track record, top financial skills, ability to deal with foreign governments. Organization-building experience necessary. Pay up to $200,000 per year. Politicians and government officials need not apply.

The preceding want ad could very well have been written for the job opening the Los Angeles Olympics organizers had to fill. An Olympics director has probably never been picked with such care. In Montreal in 1976, politicians managed the games at a cost to the taxpayers of a billion dollars. The Los Angeles leadership felt a top professional manager could turn a profit on the games. The Los Angeles committee proposed to keep 40 percent of the profits and use them for amateur sports in the city.

The person appointed to the position must run what is essentially a private company. The organization has directors, a chairman, and an executive director who operates as president. The position is for seven years, coming to a climax in the summer of 1984. Major sources of revenue will be ticket sales, television rights, and product-licensing fees.

A management that tends to look exclusively at the balance sheet, and not at its people, is going to have trouble with the balance sheet.

GILBERT RICHARDS
Chairman and
Chief Executive Officer,
The Budd Company

Every organization, whether it be a government agency, a social club, an athletic team, a church, or a business corporation, needs competent managers. "A good manager must be able to sort out facts in such a way that he knows which are crucial to an issue." So states Irving S. Shapiro, chief executive officer and chairman of the board of directors of E. I. Du Pont de Nemours.

As the top executive of one of the world's largest manufacturing companies, Thomas A. Murphy, chairman of the General Motors board of directors, makes decisions that affect millions of customers. He is responsible for the well-being of 750,000 employees and the 16,000 dealers who sell and service GM products.

In a sole proprietorship, the owner is also the manager. In a partnership, one partner is often designated as the "managing partner." Business corporations, of course, employ professional managers. These managers may own much or only a few shares.

This chapter concentrates on the theory and practice of general management activities. The most difficult and challenging management tasks are those that require managing people through superior-subordinate relations.

THE FIELD OF MANAGEMENT

Since about 1900 the research and writing of scholars and business practitioners has provided a rich and growing body of management principles and practices. This chapter is an introduction to that field as it relates to business.

What Is Management?

Managers are those individuals who bring together the money, manpower, materials, and machinery necessary to operate a business. They must plan for the future, organize the enterprise, direct the activities of employees, and control the entire business.

In common usage, **managers** are people who make decisions. When several persons get together in an organization, one of them must fill the role of leader to supply orderly and efficient handling of the business affairs. **Management** is the process of getting work done through other persons. Managers do not produce a finished product, nor do they directly sell a product to a customer. Instead they direct others to do these things. Figure 4-1 shows the "*M*'s" of management.

What specifically do managers do? The process of **MANAGEMENT** includes **planning, organizing, directing, and controlling the activities of an enterprise to achieve specific objectives**. Managers perform these functions in varying degrees at different organizational levels. They are the basic managerial tasks.

Management has also been called the art of decision making, since managers spend so much time choosing among alternative solutions to business problems. Table 4-1 lists typical problems that may occur and some alternative ways of dealing with them. These problems occur at all levels. A good example of some major management problems can be found in the college food-catering industry.

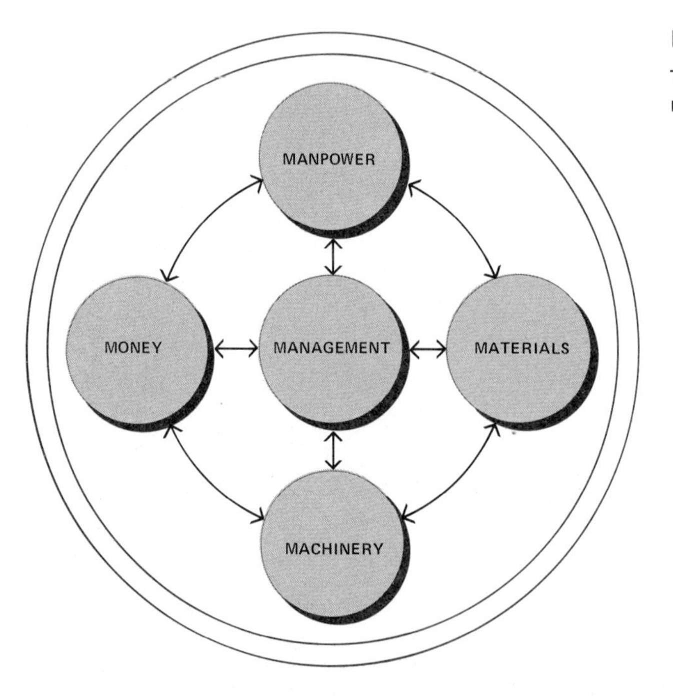

FIGURE 4-1

The M's of management.

TABLE 4-1
TYPICAL PROBLEMS ENCOUNTERED BY MANAGERS

Problem	Alternative Solutions
1. Need to employ more experienced personnel.	a. Revise job requirements to employ more experienced persons. b. Review wage scale to see if it is competitive. c. Develop on-the-job training to upgrade employees.
2. High absenteeism in certain departments.	a. Discuss absenteeism with department manager to find cause. b. Consider changing department managers. c. Talk to employees involved.
3. Trusted employee was caught stealing.	a. Dismiss employee. b. Discipline employee, since this is a first offense.
4. Dissatisfied executive threatens to resign.	a. Review complaint to see what can be done to keep the executive. b. Encourage the executive to stay. c. Let the executive resign.
5. Sharp decline in profits	a. Review operating costs. b. Raise product prices. c. Increase advertising budget.
6. Union trying to organize employees.	a. Improve conditions that employees complained about. b. Agree to bargain with union. c. Hire an attorney and fight the union.
7. Newspaper article charges firm is polluting the air.	a. Employee public-relations firm to explain the company's side. b. Ignore the article. c. File a lawsuit against the newspaper.

QUESTION: For the above problems, what other alternatives can you suggest?

Rising food prices annoy everyone, but especially in the college food-catering business. Providing food for college cafeterias is a big business. Some 11 million students constitute a market worth $2 billion annually.

Greyhound Corporation is a major participant in the market. A study of one Greyhound contract illustrates the problems. Greyhound once won the contract to feed fifteen hundred students at the University of California, Irvine, from Saga Corporation, another major feeder, with a bid of $2.46 per student per day. By March, Greyhound's costs had escalated to more than $3.00 per student, and it was losing $15,000 per month on this operation. It invoked a "pull-out" clause and dropped the contract.

Managing such an operation has many problems besides the rising cost of food. Most contracts contain stipulations that students be provided with specified choices at each meal. There are limitations on how much pasta or poultry can be substituted for meat. College business managers set board rates nearly a year in advance. This causes serious problems in estimating costs. Food companies engage in bidding competition with each other, and colleges often complain of poor hygiene, quality, and service.

Better management seems to be the key to improving results in this industry. Some companies are trying pay-as-you-go systems and credit cards for meals. Computerized food purchasing has cut costs in some instances, and other companies are employing waste-reduction education programs.

Levels of Management

In the organizational hierarchy, large businesses ordinarily have at least three levels of management, which are often referred to as the "management pyramid." These three levels are (1) top or institutional management, (2) middle or administrative management; and (3) operating or supervisory management. These levels are shown in Figure 4-2. As you can see, each level of the pyramid contributes a different amount of major decisions.

Top management. The highest level is top management, often referred to as senior managers or key executives, who have usually had many years of varied experience. This level is composed of the board of directors, the president or chief executive officer (CEO), and other corporate officers. Top management develops broad plans for the company and makes important decisions about such things as mergers, new products, and stock issues.

Middle management. The next level of the management pyramid, known as middle or administrative management, is composed of plant superintendents and/or division managers. These managers have the responsibility for developing the operating plans that implement the broader plans made by top managers.

Operating management. This is the lowest level of the management pyramid. It is primarily concerned with putting into action plans devised by middle managers. Operating managers are often referred to as "first-line supervisors" because they are responsible for supervising the workers who perform the day-to-day operations.

HISTORICAL BACKGROUND OF MANAGEMENT

Before continuing our discussion of the role of managers, let us look briefly at the historical background that helped to produce the "management boom" in the United States, which started immediately following World War I.

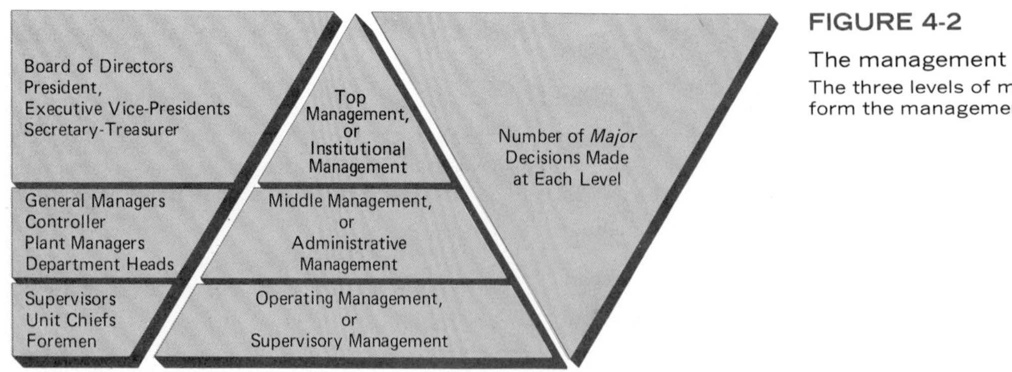

FIGURE 4-2

The management pyramid.
The three levels of management form the management pyramid.

Rise of a Managerial Class

When this nation was founded, most of the work was done on farms by farmers. Only a few craftsmen were available to make such items as pots and pans, hand tools, and furniture. Most consumer goods were sold by traveling merchants. Shops were almost nonexistent in the towns and in the few cities. By 1820, about 71 percent of those employed were farm workers. There were few factories and there was almost no machinery.

The first American industrial revolution began in about 1820 and ended in 1850. During this period Congress enacted high protective tariffs to encourage American business enterprises. The population increased, and many people moved from farms to cities to find employment. New inventions appeared, which caused the growth of new businesses. Eli Whitney introduced the cotton gin, which greatly increased the supply of cotton for the textile industry. Whitney also built a factory to make guns. He believed that his factory could make gun parts using the same specifications, which would promote the concept of mass production.

During this period John Deere and Cyrus McCormick perfected farm equipment. John Studebaker built a factory to make wagon wheels. He later organized a company to make automobiles. The owners of the businesses usually managed them too.

One of the first uses of nonowner managers was by the Delaware and Hudson Canal Company, which constructed a canal extending from Albany to Buffalo, New York. Three railroad companies connecting cities in Massachusetts were chartered in 1830. By 1840 it was possible to ship goods by rail from New York to Washington, D.C. These railroads employed managers using such titles as general agent, passenger agent, freight agent, and claim agent.

The second industrial revolution, which occurred from 1870 to 1900, marked the beginning of large-scale production, business growth, and a decline in farm employment. America symbolized advanced capitalism, great wealth, and large corporations. By 1900 monopolies existed in oil, tobacco, sugar, steel, and whiskey enterprises. A national network of rail transportation had been built, which encouraged new businesses and required managers.

It was during the second industrial revolution that some of the largest American family fortunes were founded. By 1879 oil refined into kerosene for use as a source of light and heat made John D. Rockefeller and his associates powerful and rich. There were the Hill, Gould, Harriman, and Vanderbilt fortunes from new railroads. The McCormick fortune was based on farm machinery, and the Carnegie and Frick fortunes on steel. The business tycoons were conspicuous by their exhibitions of great wealth.

As businesses grew in mining, manufacturing, and transportation, changes also occurred in the service trades and retailing. The men's clothing industry shifted from hand tailoring to machine-made suits.

Workers spent long hours on the job, often under poor working conditions, and received low pay. There were no employee retirement plans, sick leave, or paid holidays. Labor unions were just getting started. Workers were often fired if the employer learned about their union membership.

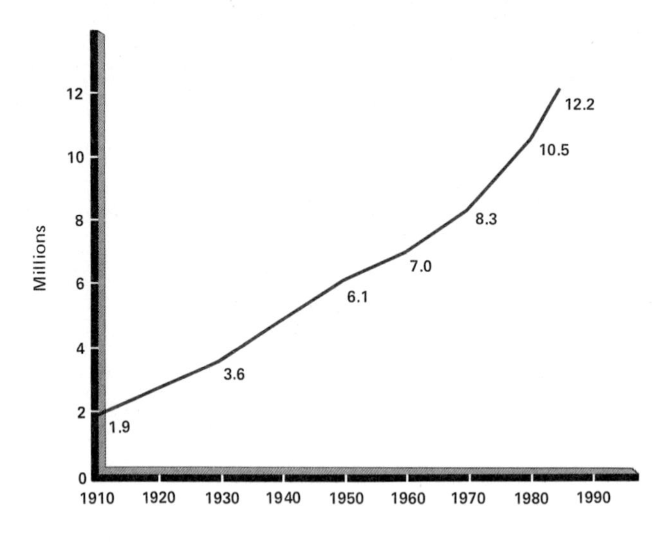

FIGURE 4-3

Managers and administrators (except farmers) employed in the United States 1910–85. (Source: Bureau of Labor Statistics, projected to 1985.)

By 1910 businesses employed 1.9 million managers. Figure 4-3 shows the growth in the number of managers projected to 1985.

The Scientific Management Movement

Business is constantly searching to find more efficient ways to increase productivity and at the same time cut production costs. Prior to 1880, managing a business was mostly regarded as common sense, if not an art. But around 1885 Frederick W. Taylor (1856–1915) joined the American Society of Mechanical Engineers (ASME). Taylor was a self-taught engineer and was one of the first to study work methods using the ASME as a sounding board for his ideas.

A few years before Taylor, Henri Fayol (1841–1945), manager of a French coal mine, also studied management in search of techniques that would improve the production of coal. Fayol decided that management involved planning, organizing, commanding, coordinating, and controlling. He is generally credited with providing Taylor encouragement to search for more scientific methods.

In this country, Taylor is considered the father of the scientific-management movement. Born of a fairly well-to-do family in Philadelphia, he was urged to study law. His poor eyesight, however, forced him to give up this idea. He went to work as a common laborer in the Midvale Steel Company and eventually became chief engineer. He made numerous experiments to set work standards. In one experiment he trained a pig-iron worker who was able to increase his tonnage load from 12.5 to 47.5 tons per day. Taylor also pioneered methods-time-measurement studies. In his opinion, labor-saving machinery or mass production was worthless unless those who managed were able to keep pace with technical improvements.

These are among the several principles of scientific management advocated by Taylor:[1]

1. All managers must be trained to use scientific principles, replacing the old rule-of-thumb methods for solving problems.
2. Managers should select and train their workers rather than let them choose their own work habits and procedures.

[1]Frederick W. Taylor, *The Principles of Scientific Management* (New York: Harper & Row, Pub., 1911), pp. 36–37.

3. Managers should divide work responsibility as evenly as possible between themselves and their workers.

4. Managers should cooperate with workers to ensure that all work is done in accordance with scientific principles.

Other contributions to scientific management. Henry Gantt (1861–1919), an associate of Taylor's at the Midvale Steel Company, is best known for his Gantt chart. This chart is a graphic means of comparing production performance with standards and production goals. As a chart, it is laid out on a horizontal basis for a given number of days or weeks. Each day shows the number of units produced and the number remaining to be produced. Gantt also developed a piece rate by which a worker who exceeded the standard performance would receive a bonus based on a percentage of the base hourly rate. Both the Gantt chart and the Gantt plan are used in the United States.

The husband-and-wife team of Frank and Lillian Gilbreth (1868–1924; 1879–1972) gained fame for their work in motion and time analysis using a motion picture. The Gilbreths studied motions involved in repetitive work tasks to determine which body movements could be eliminated to increase efficiency. They classified bodily movements into seventeen basic elements (search, find, select, etc.). They both worked for numerous companies as efficiency consultants.

Two other Americans, Mary Parker Follett (1868–1933) and Chester Barnard (1886–1961), conducted research on decision-making techniques and on the informal and formal organization. Barnard, an executive himself, tried to determine how to make an executive's job contribute more to the business. In his search to understand the executive's role, he drew constantly on principles of psychology and sociology. He concluded that within an organization there is a definite need for a communication system and that executives who occupy positions in the management hierarchy were important links in the flow of information.

The Hawthorne studies at the Chicago Hawthorne Plant of Western Electric gave further impetus to the development of a behavioral approach to management.[2] A more detailed discussion of the Hawthorne studies is given later in this chapter.

SCHOOLS OF MANAGEMENT THOUGHT

As a result of an expanding interest in management education in colleges and universities, a number of theoretical approaches to the study of management have appeared. Such theories have come mainly from managers and educators seeking to discover more about what to teach prospective managers. Although several theoretical schools of management thought have emerged, we will discuss five. This introduction to the subject includes the following: (1) classical school, (2) behavioral school, (3) management-science school, (4) systems analysis, and (5) management by results.

[2]For a detailed account of these studies, see Fritz J. Roethlisberger and W. J. Dickson, *Management and the Worker* (Homewood, Ill.: Richard D. Irwin, 1965).

The Classical School

The beginnings of the classical school coincided with the formation of large corporations. Much of the early classical literature was written between World Wars I and II. Classical theory defines management in terms of the tasks that managers perform. Advocates of the classical school identified the primary managerial functions of planning, organizing, directing, and controlling—each of which can be divided into subfunctions. The development of managerial skills was directed toward applying these functions.

The organization chart was considered an important tool used by proponents of the classical school. An organization chart shows the authority relationships between superiors and subordinates. The basic approach of this school of management is to first identify what managers do and then to distill from these tasks a set of principles. These principles are then used as a guide in the practice of management.

Early proponents of this school included Frederick W. Taylor, Henry Gantt, Frank and Lillian Gilbreth, Mary Parker Follett, Harrington Emerson, Henri Fayol, and Chester Barnard.

The Behavioral School

Variously called the "leadership," "human relations," or "behavioral sciences" school of management, the behavioral school became popular in the 1950s. This school concentrates on the human aspect of management and emphasizes the need for managers to understand people. Managers should also know how to motivate those subordinates whom they supervise and direct. The behavioral school draws from such disciplines as psychology and sociology as part of the manager's educational background.

The Management-Science School

Unlike the classical school of management thought which identifies management tasks, the management-science school involves mathematics and statistics. Mathematical models are used to solve the operational problems of planning and controlling. A model is a representation of reality. A physical model such as a wind tunnel is one kind of model. Another kind is the mathematical relationships among variables programmed for computers. Management science is a quantitative approach that has provided valuable tools for solving business problems. The computer has made it possible to study problems that previously were too complex to be solved without it.

Systems Analysis

The systems concept was indirectly used by Frederick W. Taylor in his analysis of work performance. The concept of a system means that everything in the system is interrelated and interdependent. It offers a means for viewing internal and external operations of a business. The identifying characteristic of systems analysis is that it deals with problems involving all the component parts, not with separate parts. In marketing, for example, making a decision about price requires considering the impact on all phases of distribution used to market goods (as well as changes that might affect the rest of the organization).

A **SYSTEM** is **an entity made up of two or more independent parts that interact to form a functioning organism**. Systems analysis is the method used to solve business problems by identifying the major parts of the problem and their relationships. Input for such analysis can range from invoices to information

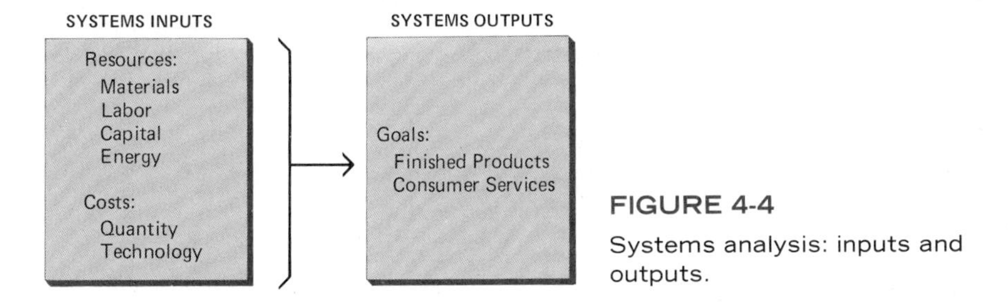

FIGURE 4-4

Systems analysis: inputs and outputs.

contained in reports, such as sales quotas, costs, and prices of various resources. Types of systems inputs and outputs are shown in Figure 4-4. The output is actually the end product of the computer system. The output media may be punched cards, printed pages, or magnetic or paper tapes.

The computer has made systems analysis a more effective tool of management, since it can handle more information than the human mind. However, it does not eliminate the need for managers to perform their tasks of management.

Results Management

Since it was first introduced by Peter Drucker in the early 1950s, results management, or management by objectives (MBO), has grown in popularity. MBO is actually a program to improve employees' motivation and control of their jobs by allowing them to participate in setting their own goals. Employees then know exactly how the job is to be done *and* how they will be evaluated. Figure 4-5 shows the four-step sequence of most MBO programs.

Management by results is a philosophy as well as a program. It focuses on results, *not* the behavior an employee exhibits. It assumes that the results managers or employees produce are the important thing—not how busy they may look.

Those who have used MBO programs believe that they have certain benefits. For example, employees in the program are able to relate their personal performance to the overall organization goals. The program can also improve communications between subordinate and supervisor. MBO has been responsible for promoting positive attitudes on the part of subordinates toward their work.

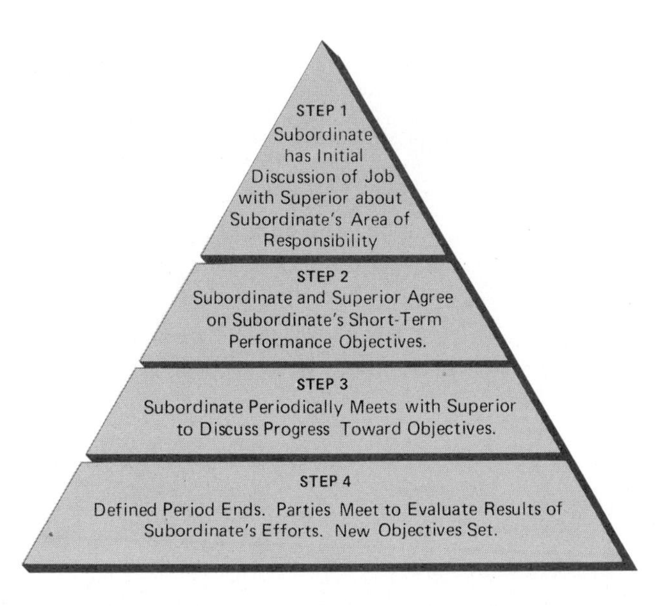

FIGURE 4-5

Steps in management-by-objectives program.

Despite these advantages, there are some disadvantages. Sometimes it is difficult to set precise objectives. In some organizations, employee goals are changing, a fact that management should recognize. MBO will succeed only at management levels where parties are willing to participate. It is essential that the objectives be reasonable and easily measurable. For example, if the objective is to increase sales, the amount of the increase should be stated as a percentage. MBO should not be considered a panacea for all managerial problems. Executives who have established MBO programs say that they worked best when competitive forces were favorable.

MANAGEMENT FUNCTIONS

We previously mentioned that management serves by performing certain functions. These functions are generally known as **planning, organizing, directing,** and **controlling.** Figure 4-6 identifies these functions and indicates their relationships to each other. It is these tasks that managers should be skilled in performing if they are to succeed in their work.[3] The sequence of these functions is not intended to imply an absolute order. Instead these functions might be performed in any sequence dictated by the situation. All four are interdependent, and it is the manager's role to coordinate them. It should be emphasized that these functions are performed at all levels of the management pyramid in varying degrees. We will now discuss each function in detail.

Planning

Planning involves deciding on a course of action. **PLANNING is preparing a plan of action, setting company objectives, determining strategy, and selecting alternative courses of action**. It involves the following activities:

1. Determining the firm's short- and long-term objectives
2. Formulating policies, programs, and procedures

PODC

[3]Management writers differ as to the number of management functions and what they are. Some writers define the functions more narrowly by including such subfunctions as staffing, motivating, innovating, and communicating. The four basic functions listed in Figure 4-6 are considered to include staffing, motivating, innovating, and communicating as subfunctions.

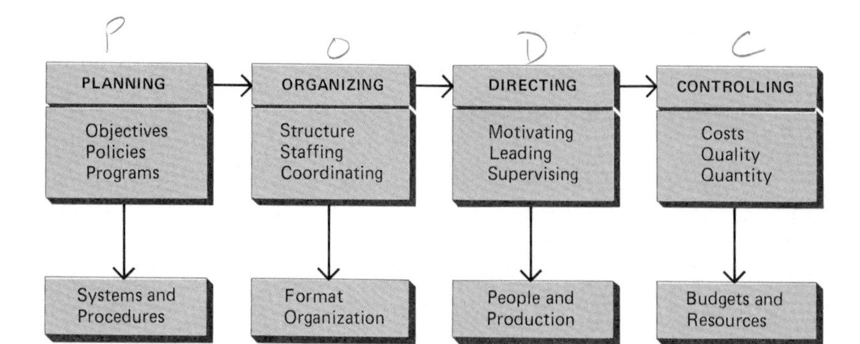

FIGURE 4-6

Functions of management.

Logically, planning seems to be the first function, which is followed by the other three. Some people also regard decision making and policy making as functions. In practice, however, these two activities are more often mingled with one or more management functions.

3. Making periodic follow-up reviews to determine what changes in plans may be needed.

The record industry is a good example of a unique planning problem. CBS, RCA, and the other major record album marketers offer retailers huge discounts on older albums that have not been selling. The retailers can return unsold merchandise for credit on future purchases. So after Christmas they send back records by the millions. When the companies fail to have a good selling album to generate sales, they are stuck with many dollars' worth of returns. But the big recording artists who make the records do not make them at a regular rate. Several bring albums in at the same time, and then the companies go through a long dry period where they have nothing new to offer. The problem requires some major breakthroughs in planning.

Planning is as important for day-to-day activities as it is for years in advance. It is also a continuous process because business conditions are constantly changing. Figure 4-7 illustrates how planning is related to the entire firm and to the stockholders, customers, and general public.

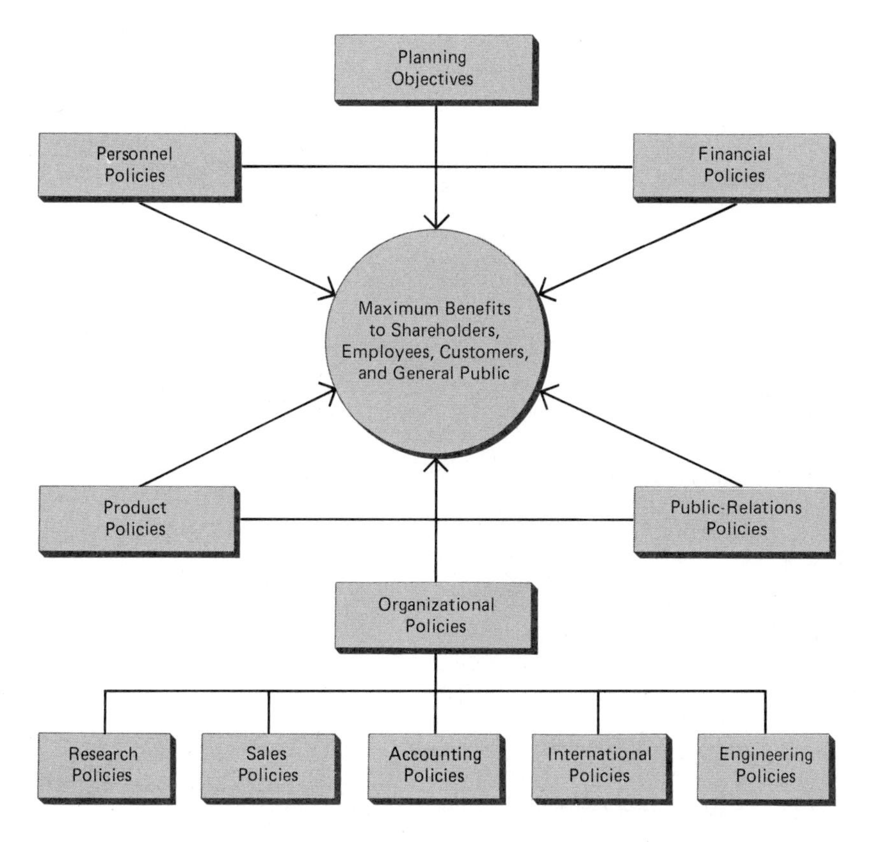

FIGURE 4-7

The management function of planning affects the entire organization.

Planning is closely related to all management functions. It sets the stage for what the organization intends to do.

Steps in planning. Planning is directed toward achieving objectives. Figure 4-8 illustrates how planning progresses through a series of steps. Once plans are completed, the next function is typically that of organizing.

Organizing

ORGANIZING is defined as **the means by which managers coordinate human and material resources within the formal structure of tasks and authority.** This function involves classifying and dividing work activities into manageable units. It includes the following procedures:

1. Grouping work activities according to their interrelationships to ensure more effective teamwork and individual efficiency
2. Defining and delegating individual authority and responsibility for those working in the organization
3. Developing organizational relationships to achieve coordination of effort and communication at different organizational levels

The organizing function includes the total organizational structure—such broad business functions as finance, marketing, production, transportation, and personnel administration.

Directing

As a management function, **DIRECTING** is **achieving organizational objectives by motivating and guiding subordinates.** It is especially important at the supervisory level where the largest number of people are employed. In practice, it is much more than just ordering or commanding things to be done.

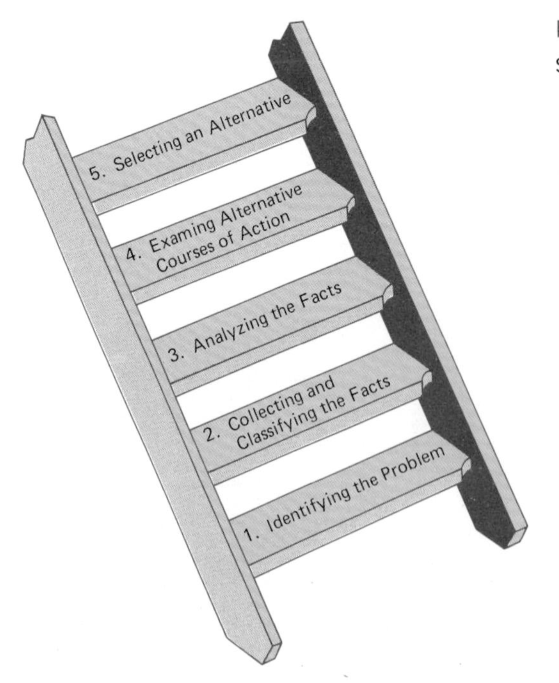

FIGURE 4-8
Steps in the planning function.

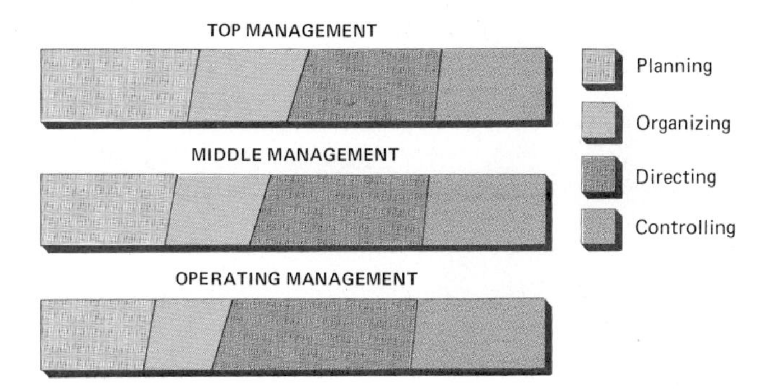

FIGURE 4-9

Proportion of management functions performed at different levels.

A chart showing the approximate distribution of management effort expended in performing their functions in a medium-size manufacturing business.

Controlling

The controlling function is sometimes misunderstood because of the lack of a precise definition. As used here, **CONTROLLING** is **a procedure for measuring performance against objectives.** It deals with the question, Did what was supposed to happen indeed happen—why or why not?

The need for controls springs from the inherent imperfection of things and people. Things that are planned do not happen automatically. Generally, the function of controlling includes

1. Performing routine planning
2. Establishing standards
3. Scheduling work
4. Reviewing costs
5. Exercising supervision
6. Taking corrective action

We have identified and discussed four management functions. These are common to all levels of management, as shown in Figure 4-9.

The sequence that these functions follow is not necessarily rigid—these functions might be performed in another sequence. However, the logic behind the order of these functions is that planning occurs first, followed by organizing, directing, and controlling.

QUALITIES OF EXECUTIVE LEADERSHIP

Now that you are familiar with the functions of business management and the areas of an organization in which these functions are performed, let us turn to the role of the executive. What is the "average" executive like? What qualities make him or her an executive? What skills does he or she use?

What Is an "Executive"?

The terms **executive** and **administrator,** which are often used interchangeably, had their origin in government. Such persons were concerned with the administration and execution of estates, laws, and justice. The terms have since been accepted by business, industry, and other institutions.

An **EXECUTIVE** is **a top-level management person responsible for the work performed by others under his or her supervision.** An executive is the medium from which orders flow to employees. Executives also originate orders, make decisions, and translate company policy. As decision makers, executives use three basic skills, which we will call technical, human, and conceptual. While interrelated, they can be examined separately.

REGINALD H. JONES

As chairman and chief executive officer of the General Electric Company, Reginald H. Jones has brought a fresh vitality and new strategic direction to one of the highly diversified world enterprises. He has at the same time earned the deep admiration and respect of his peers by his tireless efforts on the national scene, challenging the conventional wisdom on capital formation, tax structure, monetary reform, and international economic policy.

Reginald Jones is an example of the new-style chief executive: articulate, world-minded, politically sophisticated, and an activist in the formation of public policy. He is well known for his point of view that most of the problems of business in our politicized economy are external to the firm. This has brought him to the forefront as a vigorous spokesman for the business community.

He has served as chairman of the Business Council, chairman of the President's Export Council, co-chairman of the Business Roundtable, and a member of the Advisory Committee for International Monetary Reform.

Mr. Jones was born in the United Kingdom and came to the United States when a boy. He and his wife, the former Grace B. Cole of New York, have a son, Keith E., and a daughter, Grace S. Vineyard.

Technical skills. These include the ability to use the methods, equipment, and techniques involved in performing specific tasks.

Human skills. These represent the ability to work effectively with others. Such skills require a sense of feeling for others and an appreciation of the rights of others. They are demonstrated by the way the individual recognizes subordinates, equals, and superiors.

Conceptual skills. These include intelligence, verbal ability, and the ability to see the whole enterprise or organization as a unit of operation. Such skills are critical in decision making—one is able to conceive the nature of the problem before attempting to solve it.

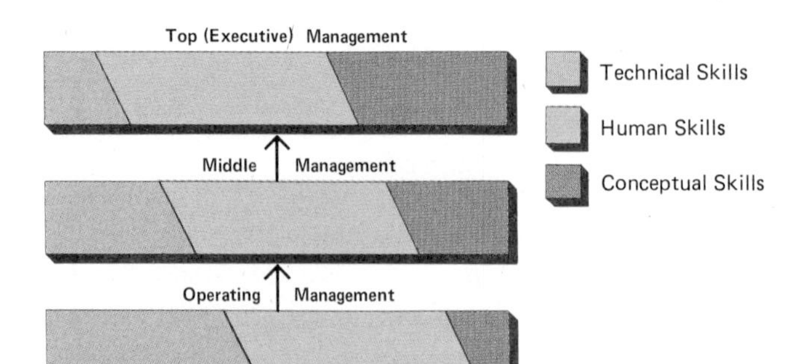

FIGURE 4-10

Managerial skills needed at different levels.

As a manager advances from one level to another, different amounts of management skills are required.

The proportion of these executive skills tends to differ at various levels, as Figure 4-10 illustrates. For example, supervisors at the operating-management level perform more technical skills than middle or top managers. Conceptual skills, by contrast, are more important at the executive level.

Massey-Ferguson's president, Victor Rice, provides a good case study of the kinds of skills necessary at the executive level.

Massey-Ferguson, Ltd., is a Toronto-based farm machinery maker. MFL's troubles started in the late 1960s after a decision not to compete head on with Deere and Company and International Harvester for the North American market. By 1977, 70 percent of MFL's sales were outside North America —in Europe, Latin America, Africa, Asia, and Australia. But that move into the international market was financed with borrowed money.

When farm equipment markets took a dive in 1977, Massey-Ferguson was in trouble. In an effort to cut its losses, MFL sold off some overseas units that had been losing money. President Rice's strategy is to stay with MFL's strong suits—tractors, diesel engines, and combines. Further decisions have been made regarding reorganizing the far-flung organization to gain more control.

Leadership

A business that loses its leader is like a team without its captain; the business, as well as the team, can lose its direction. Some managers rely heavily on the authority that goes with the position they occupy in order to motivate people. Others use both informal influence and formal authority effectively. In business an effective leader is expected to exert a degree of leadership to motivate subordinates. It is through the quality of leadership that the firm's potential is realized.

What is leadership? Some behavioral theories give the impression that leadership is exactly the same as management. But this assumption is not completely accurate. Leaders are found wherever there are groups of people. They may or may not also be managers. **LEADERSHIP is the ability to influence others to behave in a certain way.** In this process the leader influences members of the group and is responsive to their needs. Leadership is useful in any kind of group or organization. And it can mean the difference between success and failure of any kind of organization, in or out of business.

Value of leadership to management. The challenge of leadership to business can be seen by noting some of the major people problems with which management is involved today:

1. What can be done to make workers more interested in their jobs?
2. How can people be motivated to accept change?
3. What is the most effective way to encourage employees to raise their level of output?

4. What causes employee morale problems?
5. What is the most effective way to improve morale?
6. How can management communicate more effectively with subordinates?

Leadership Styles

Certain variations in leadership styles are effective in different situations. One is to make decisions autocratically without consulting the subordinates. Another is to consult with subordinates before making a decision. And still a third is to let the subordinate make the decisions. The three basic styles of leadership are

1. Autocratic leader
2. Democratic leader
3. Free-rein leader

An **AUTOCRATIC LEADER** is **one who makes decisions without consulting subordinates.** A **DEMOCRATIC LEADER encourages the group's participation in making decisions that affect them.** A **FREE-REIN LEADER allows most decisions to be made by subordinates with a minimum of direction from the leader.** Figure 4-11 illustrates the three leadership styles.

Often the question is asked, Which style of leadership is best? The answer depends largely on the specific situation. Some subordinates are too inexperienced to make decisions without consulting their leader. Some problems requiring immediate action must be handled without consultation with subordinates in order to avoid delay. On the other hand, where time is not a factor, the leader may find it desirable to encourage individual or group participation, especially if acceptance of the decision by the group is important.

Are leaders "made" or "born"? Research on this issue is limited. That leadership ability can be taught in all cases is still open to question. All around us we see examples of untaught leaders who seem more successful than those who enroll for training in leadership development. Between these two extremes there are many individuals who are gifted to a moderate degree. For them, self-development provides opportunities to improve leadership ability.

Importance of Employee Motivation

It is essential that managers have an understanding of motivation. After World War II, behavioral scientists began a rather intense study of the subject of motivation. Psychologists generally agree that all behavior is motivated. That is, people generally have reasons for what they do. Behavior is not just random.

Meaning of motivation.

The word **motivation** is derived from the Latin word **movere,** meaning "to move." **MOTIVATION** is **an internal force that makes people move toward satisfying a need.** Such needs as hunger, thirst, power, and achievement can motivate human behavior. Once a motive is active, the individual will act to satisfy that desire or need associated with the motive.

The Hawthorne studies.

The first major study of human behavior at work was conducted at the Hawthorne plant of Western Electric in Chicago during the 1920s. Elton Mayo, a social scientist, and his associates studied working conditions and their impact on the actual productivity of plant and employees.

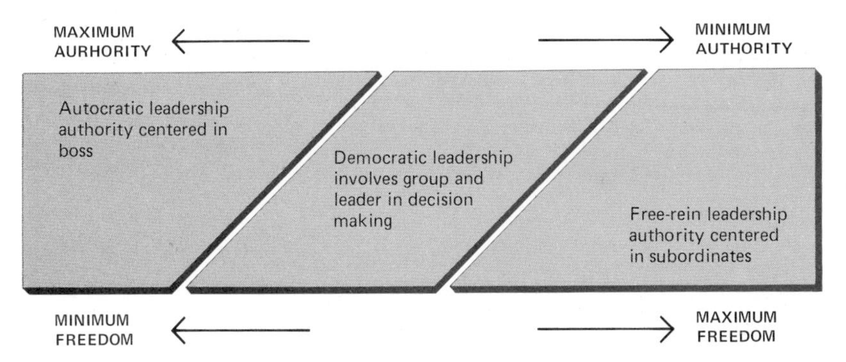

FIGURE 4-11

Patterns of leadership behavior.

Limits of authority and freedom exercised by managers as leaders vary from authority-centered behavior to free-rein behavior in dealing with subordinates.

The Hawthorne studies pointed out the importance of understanding the human factor. These studies were the first to make a systematic analysis of human behavior and management. A major conclusion of the Hawthorne studies was that the kind of supervision given employees has a major impact on the behavior of work groups.[4]

Levels of Employee Needs

One of the best-known explanations of employee needs and their levels was developed by Abraham H. Maslow, a psychologist, who drew up a list of human needs.[5] Maslow noted that only those needs that have *not* been satisfied can motivate human behavior; furthermore, a satisfied need is no longer a motivator, but it can reemerge as a motivator. For example, because you had a big breakfast, it does not follow that you will not want supper. The hunger need has reemerged.

Maslow's theory of motivation emphasizes two basic ideas:

1. People have many needs, but only those needs not yet satisfied influence human behavior.
2. Human needs are grouped in a hierarchy of importance. When one need is satisfied, another higher-level need then emerges and seeks satisfaction.

Figure 4-12 identifies the hierarchy of needs. The basic needs are food, shelter, thirst, and rest. These are followed by safety from external danger needs,

[4]See Roethlisberger and Dickson, *Management and the Worker*, p. 165.

[5]Maslow, *Motivation and Personality* (New York: Harper & Brothers, 1954).

FIGURE 4-12

Hierarchy of individual needs in order of priority.

such as protection from injury, and job security. Higher-level needs include social needs, self-esteem needs, and self-actualization. Those needs at the top of the hierarchy—such as self-actualization or self-esteem needs—are more difficult to satisfy.

It is important to recognize that the Maslow theory does not explain all human motivation at work. Maslow's major contribution lies in his hierarchical concept. He was the first to suggest that once a need is satisfied, a higher-level need emerges. Maslow's need theory has had a strong impact on businesses' approach to the motivation of employees.

CAREERS IN MANAGEMENT

Management trainee is a broad term used for careers in all areas of business. The American business system uses men and women college graduates in many different management areas. These graduates begin in sales, banking, accounting, production, personnel administration, or distribution. And there are all kinds of opportunities related to the production and operation of a business. These positions include supervisors in product manufacturing, factory managers, and so forth.

Management careers may be in line jobs or as staff specialists. Staff managers may include the fact-finding specialists, whose services support the managers who make decisions. Labor relations specialists deal with unions as interpreters of union-management labor contracts. People with management training can work as representatives of such organizations as the AFL-CIO, the country's largest labor organization.

Growing Need for Managers

The work of the manager as a decision maker is not limited to a given industry. On the contrary, managers are needed wherever there are people working together toward a specific goal. This also includes areas of government, as well as hospitals, chambers of commerce, trade associations, and educational foundations.

A recent study conducted by Haskell and Stern Associates, a New York executive search firm, found that "general management" positions will be the hardest to fill in the 1980s. The study surveyed personnel executives and discovered that most companies will need management "generalists" to run their operations in the next decade. But, because many lower-management positions have become so specialized, the supply of "generalists" is scarce. Also tough to find in the 1980s will be computer specialists and engineers. The easiest jobs to fill will be in the legal, sales, and financial areas.

SUMMARY OF KEY CONCEPTS

The strength of any enterprise is its management, who bear a heavy responsibility for operating a successful business.

The functional role of managers is to plan, organize, direct, and control what happens in the business.

The levels of management are top management (the highest), middle management (concerned with the carrying out of policies and plans), and operating management (responsible for supervision).

The scientific-management movement is marked by the beginning of the use of scientific principles in managing a business. Frederick W. Taylor was the first American to apply these principles to business.

Advocates of the classical school of management subscribe to the theory that managers are responsible for performing certain functions: planning, organizing, directing, and controlling.

The behavioral school advocates that the training of managers should include instruction on how to motivate subordinates.

The management-science school makes use of mathematical models and computer science as a tool for decision making.

Managers are known to use three skills in dealing with others: technical, human, and conceptual. **Technical skills** involve the use of equipment, techniques, and methods in performing management tasks. **Human skills** are used in exercising leadership styles. **Conceptual skills** enable managers to view the entire business as one part relates to another.

Good leaders can motivate others to higher levels of achievement. The three basic leadership styles are the autocratic style, the democratic style, and the free-rein style. Autocratic leadership is centered in a leader who makes decisions without consulting others. The democratic leader invites the participation of subordinates. Free-rein leadership behavior allows groups to make decisions.

Maslow noted the presence of a hierarchy of needs, which exist on several levels. Once a given level of need is satisfied, it ceases to operate as a primary motivator. It is replaced by needs of a higher level. Maslow's theory explains the seeming contradiction as to why money is not always the prime motivator.

BUSINESS TERMS

You should be able to match these business terms with the statements that follow:

a. Autocratic leader
b. Controlling
c. Democratic leader
d. Directing
e. Free-rein leader
f. Leadership
g. Management
h. Motivation
i. Organizing
j. Planning
k. System

1. The process of planning, organizing, directing, and controlling activities of an enterprise to achieve specific objectives
2. Means by which managers coordinate human and material resources within the formal structure of tasks and authority
3. Preparing a plan of action, setting company objectives, determining strategy, and selecting alternative courses of action
4. An entity made up of two or more independent parts that interact to form a functioning organism
5. The ability to influence others to behave in a certain way
6. Achieving organizational objectives by motivating and guiding subordinates

7. A procedure for measuring performance against objectives
8. A leader who allows most decisions to be made by subordinates with a minimum of direction from the leader
9. An internal force that moves people toward satisfying a need
10. A leader who encourages the group's participation in making decisions that affect them
11. One who makes decisions without consulting subordinates

REVIEW QUESTIONS

1. What is **management?**
2. What factors caused the development of a managerial class in this country?
3. Identify the contributions made by Frederick W. Taylor's experimentations to progress in the steel industry.
4. At which level of management does most planning occur? At which level does the least planning occur?
5. What is meant by **management functions?**

DISCUSSION QUESTIONS

1. Why would you be interested in becoming a manager?
2. In your opinion, what major qualifications should a successful manager have?
3. Give some of the reasons why the management-by-objectives approach has been widely accepted.
4. Are there really "schools" of management, or are these just ways to approach a problem in trying to solve it?
5. Do you agree that managers must believe in management theories, since they have nowhere else to turn?
6. In what ways can a business improve the qualifications of its managers?

BUSINESS CASE 4-1

Columbia Mills, Inc.

Alvin Rand was the grandson of the founder of Columbia Mills, a large southern textile firm. The company operates two mills in North Carolina and one in Charleston, South Carolina. As president and chairman of the board, Rand made most of the decisions, since he strongly believed in centralized management. His leadership style was often referred to as autocratic. Most of the sixteen middle managers at headquarters and in the various plants resented his style of management.

Jimmy Rand, Alvin's son, is an executive in the company. He feels that he was ignored by his father because he was seldom allowed to make decisions or take part in important matters. Other executives make the same complaint. Morale is low among the management group.

Two years ago profits began to drop. The sales manager proposed that three branch offices be established to give better service to the customers and meet the increasing competition more effectively. This proposal was rejected by President Rand without giving any explanation. The sales manager resigned in protest. Alvin Rand then assumed all responsibility for sales for eight months while searching for a new national sales manager.

The advertising manager resigned when he was not named sales manager. He stated that he did not wish to work for the woman who had been appointed to the job.

When profits again dropped and dividends were reduced, President Rand called a conference of all headquarters executives and plant managers to review the situation. There was talk of a labor strike in two plants. The outlook was grim, and the president asked for help.

The board of directors decided to employ a consulting firm to study ways of cutting costs. The consulting firm proposed the expenditure of a million dollars to install new automated equipment in order to save labor costs.

The consulting firm also recommended that the company negotiate with the union to obtain a new contract replacing the one that expired six months ago. President Rand rejected both recommendations. He claimed that the machinery in the two plants was only fifteen years old and was not worn out. He offered the union a 5 percent wage increase and an improved medical health plan. The President stated that this was the limit of his offer.

During a recent business trip to Chicago, President Rand died. The directors, who were all members of the family, appointed Jimmy Rand president. The position of chairman of the board was not filled.

1. What management principles were violated by Alvin Rand?
2. What are some of the causes of the company's difficulties?

BUSINESS CASE 4-2

What's Wrong with Western Tires, Inc.?

Western Tires, Inc., with headquarters in Phoenix, Arizona, has been manufacturing automobile tires and fan belts for American-made automobiles. These products are marketed under the brand name of Wearwell through tire dealers and service stations as replacement parts. Carl and Lee Busch, brothers, established the company in 1923 and are still the principal shareholders. Carl owns 60 percent of the outstanding common stock, and Lee owns 20 percent. Six employees, including two of the company executives, own the remaining stock.

The company employs 225 men and women, with 23 working in the headquarters offices. Carl Busch is president, and Lee Busch is treasurer and is in charge of all accounting, including the payroll department. Lee has been trying to persuade Carl to install a computer. The plant superintendent has also submitted a request to use a computer for quality-control purposes in the plant. The president says a computer costs too much.

Union grievances are frequently filed, but few ever go to arbitration. Usually the president makes the final decision to make a settlement which the union is willing to accept. In general, the company's executives feel that the president lacks leadership qualities and does not know how to get along with others. He is also unwilling to delegate responsibility.

On several occasions Lee has urged his brother to seek the directors' approval to appoint an executive vice-president. Lee feels that this executive could take over some of the duties now performed by the president.

Last month the president was ill for twenty-four days because of a stroke. Carl's physician has advised him that he must reduce his workload and delegate more authority to others. During Carl's illness the company lost a large contract for five hundred replacement tires. This contract would have been between the company and a fleet owner. When this was discovered, two directors asked the president for an explanation. They wanted to know why he had not authorized his brother, Lee, to negotiate this pending contract.

1. What is wrong with the company organization?
2. What action would you take to solve the company's problems if you were in charge?

ORGANIZATIONAL STRUCTURE AND BEHAVIOR

5

STUDY OBJECTIVES

WHEN YOU HAVE FINISHED READING THIS CHAPTER, YOU SHOULD BE ABLE TO

ONE Distinguish the meaning of the word organization as applied to business from several other meanings

TWO Explain why some firms start with one form of organizational structure and eventually change to another

THREE Contrast a formal organization with an informal organization and give examples of each

FOUR Name six "principles" of organization to be considered in formalizing an organizational structure

FIVE Define the following terms: authority, responsibility, delegation, accountability, and coordination

SIX Explain the difference between the line plan, line-and-staff plan, and functional plan of organizational structure

IN THE NEWS

Making One Organization Out of Two

Chicago-based Gould, Inc., the giant battery maker, recently acquired Philadelphia's I-T-E Imperial Corporation. During the first few months Gould made only minor changes, such as replacing I-T-E's stationery with Gould's letterhead. But then Gould's Chairman William T. Ylvisaker began changing I-T-E's strong group management organization to a divisional management structure.

All but two of I-T-E's top sixteen executives have left or been demoted. And only about half of the two hundred key middle managers have survived. Before the merger I-T-E had five group presidents, who managed the plants or sales under them. Gould changed these to divisions and cut the groups back to two.

Chairman Ylvisaker claims that the transition has gone smoothly. His philosophy is that "two plus two should equal five." This means that when joining two organizations under one management, the combination should be more than either organization considered separately. Ylvisaker feels that "if you leave a subsidiary completely separate, you don't truly get full benefits."

Take my assets—but leave me my organization and in five years I'll have it all back.

ALFRED M. SLOAN

It is said about Americans in business that when three or more meet, their first act is likely to consist of electing officers and dividing up the work.

This is not a new condition. William Allen White (1868–1944), author and newspaper editor, observed that "if four Americans fell out of a balloon they would have a president, vice president, secretary, and treasurer elected before they landed." The highly competitive nature of modern business makes it necessary to try to increase organizational efficiency.

Business firms, like other organizations, did not just "get that way." Someone must take the lead in designing a planned set of relationships in which people interact.

In this chapter we examine the types of organizational structures used in business. Each "plan" for organizing has its strong and weak points. The nature of the business and the way it is managed determine how well a plan for organizing will work.

THE NATURE AND DEVELOPMENT OF ORGANIZATION

There may be differences of opinion as to how a business should be organized. But there is no disputing that proper organization is the backbone of a successful venture. We live in an organizational society. Businesses, governments, unions, athletic teams, hospitals, and educational institutions are all organizations. Human beings need organization to do anything that requires more than one person can accomplish.

The Meaning of Organization

The term **organization** has two different meanings. The first refers to the organization "creature" itself—like General Motors, the Pittsburgh Steelers, or the AFL–CIO. The second meaning refers to organizing as a process. The process of organization may include putting people into jobs and grouping jobs together into departments.

In the process of organization, someone must decide what each person will do and how much authority each person will have. **ORGANIZATION** can be simply defined as **a structure of relationships to get work done.** In business, the firm's objectives are its goals for the long and short term. The organizational structure that is developed should help the firm reach those goals.

Depending upon its nature and size, a business can be organized in several different ways. General Motors is subdivided by **products:** Chevrolet division, Buick division, and so forth. A chain food store, such as Safeway, is organized by **geographical regions.** An oil company, such as Exxon or Mobil, may be divided by **functions:** production, exploration, refining, marketing, and finance departments.

Organizations need a "**hierarchy of objectives**." Every business has its objectives. These may be for the business as a whole or for divisions or departments, or for individual activities. Ideally, all these objectives when summed up should equal the overall organizational goals. This "hierarchy" or pyramid of goals and objectives is illustrated in Figure 5-1.

How Does an Organization Develop?

Most business enterprises begin on a small scale. The owner makes the decisions and performs most of the activities. As the firm grows, such activities as production, marketing, and finance may be handled by different people. Different activities become separate departments, with managers and employees. Eventually the finance department, for example, may become important enough to be headed by a vice-president. Large companies finally become a collection of many different organized activities.

FIGURE 5-1
Hierarchy of organizational objectives.

HUMAN BEHAVIOR IN AN ORGANIZATION

Because people are the primary resource of the firm, understanding how and why they behave is important in solving many kinds of management problems. Managers can learn much from the behavioral sciences (psychology, sociology, and anthropology) as to what motivates and influences people in their work groups. Primary behavioral concerns in work organizations include work groups, motivation, job attitudes, and leadership.

Work Groups and Motivation

Work groups exist in all forms of organizations involving people. But only since 1920 have behaviorists paid special attention to their importance in studying about the behavior of people in the workplace. The needs that people bring to their work are as different as individual personalities. If people work close to one another and share common interests, they tend to develop a feeling of belonging to the group. As members of a team, workers can provide support to other members by helping each other, training each other, and coordinating their work.

In a business organization, a **WORK GROUP is a collection of employees who share a common job and view themselves as a group.** In some cases groups form because workers expect to receive more economic rewards on the job by forming a group. Motivation is the *why* of human behavior. It is an internal drive that causes people to behave the way they do. Different people may have very different motives for doing the same thing. People usually act to satisfy a felt need. Workers may be motivated to join a work group if they feel that their personal needs can be better satisfied by so doing. These needs include security, information sharing, and belongingness. In a unionized plant, being part of a work group may help to protect members from pressure by a management that is seeking better quality and increased production. Employees also may join a work group because of the personal satisfaction they derive from affiliating with others.

Work itself can be a powerful motivator and a force in shaping one's identity. Work **can be significant** and should contribute to one's self-esteem. The question "Who am I?" often brings a response related to an organization or a job: "I work for IBM." "I am a division manager," or "I am an accountant with Ford Motors."

Job Attitudes

Enormous technological advancement in recent years has resulted in the greater use of machines and automatic equipment. Workers in plants sometimes complain that their jobs are boring. They feel that their talents are not being used. They may feel that they are not being given sufficient opportunity to use their skills. The trend toward more automation in manufacturing and agriculture has been challenged by labor unions

Studies have shown that the so-called work ethic is not as strong as it once was in America. The belief that hard work is good in and of itself is part of the work ethic.[1] Such work attitudes are an important part of the behavior of people at work.

[1]Max Weber (1864–1920), the German sociologist, first used the term "Protestant ethic" in 1904 in his book *Protestant Ethic and the Spirit of Capitalism.* This term has since come to mean competition and the desire to achieve in business.

Some of the most profound criticism of work is expressed by junior managers. They dislike misleading hiring practices. They disapprove of such things as job descriptions that promise stimulating training programs but lead nowhere. They are irritated by the seemingly useless rules about dress codes, hair styles, and beards.[2] Such irritants are controllable by business organizations individually and can affect attitudes toward the organization.

Another factor affecting work attitudes is the social unrest in large cities—our main workplaces. Some corporations try to eliminate these problems by moving to rural areas but find that other sets of problems exist in the new locations.

Another part of work attitudes is communication. In a study conducted by a Special Task Force of Health, Education, and Welfare (HEW), the investigators made the following observation: "The most consistent complaint reported to our task force has been the failure of bosses to listen to workers who wish to propose better ways of doing their jobs."[3]

A summary measure of work attitudes is morale. **Morale** is the general attitude of the work force in a business toward their jobs. **Job satisfaction** is another term that means much the same thing.

Leadership

The leadership that a manager in a business organization uses to get people to work is an important part of understanding work behavior. Studies have shown that there is no "one best way" to lead employees. It depends on the leader, the employees, and the situation. For example, allowing convicted killers on a chain gang to vote on what they want to do is probably the wrong leadership style for that situation. Likewise, ordering professional research scientists to do something and demanding that they do it is also the wrong style for the situation.

Good managers obtain more work from their subordinates in a business organization by being good leaders. In addition to recognizing the style that is most appropriate in a given situation, they do not rely only on their position as managers to get things done. They have learned to work within the structure effectively.

The kind of leadership style that prevails in a business organization helps to create the "working climate" for employees. For example, in Texas Instruments the climate that has been created is somewhat different from that found elsewhere.

The TI climate is vital to the success of the Dallas company. The climate stresses a strong work ethic, competition, company loyalty, and rational decision making. The climate is similar to that found in many Japanese firms—assigning personal responsibility for the quality of the work. As in Japanese companies, there is a strong effort made to align company and personal goals. Other similarities with Japanese management climate exist as well. Eighty-three percent of TI's employees are on "people involvement teams," which search for new ways to improve their own productivity. The company looks at its people as being completely interchangeable.

[2]Judson Gooding, *The Job Revolution* (New York: Walker and Company, 1972), p. 40.

[3]Department of Health, Education, and Welfare, *Work in America* (Cambridge, Mass.: MIT Press, 1973), p. 37.

TI feels that it takes five years to train company managers. Those who make it serve in a demanding, no-nonsense climate. And not everyone wants to make it. Some people fit right in, but others bail out quickly. The climate polarizes people—either you fit in or you are rejected.

FORMAL AND INFORMAL ORGANIZATION

Organizations may be largely formal or informal in the way they structure work relationships. The history of the business, the technology involved and the top managers' personalities help determine what the formal organization pattern will be. Every organization has an "informal component" as well as the formal one.

Formal Organization

The **FORMAL ORGANIZATION** is **the system of jobs, authority relationships, responsibility, and accountability designed by management to get the work done.** The formal structure is created to deal with the work that has to be done. It provides a framework for work behavior to take place. The formal organization offers relatively fixed areas within which people work on their own areas of responsibility. At the same time, of course, the work each person does is part of the larger task the business as a whole is trying to accomplish. The formal organization is the part that shows on the organization charts. The informal organization does not.

Informal Organization

An "informal organization" exists in every organization. It is not planned. It just happens—based on friendships and contacts both on and off the job. The **INFORMAL ORGANIZATION** is **a network of personal and social relationships that may have nothing to do with formal authority relationships.**

Informal organizations exist in all businesses because they arise from people interacting, and people will always interact and form friendships. Managers often wish they could do away with the informal organization. It may offer resistance to their formal orders, find nonacceptable ways of getting things done, or keep changes from being implemented. The grapevine is the communication system of the informal organization. Here communications travel quickly by word of mouth. They may pass on valid information or rumor and untruth. The grapevine can, however, work to assist the formal communication system. A major point about both the informal organization and the grapevine is that they cannot be abolished. They *will occur*, and managers would be well advised to learn to work with them.

An example of an informal organization in one work group is given in Figure 5-2. In the work group are three categories of employees: members of the inner group, those in the fringe group, and those in the out group. Hay, Small, Jones, and Jackson belong to the inner group. They all perform similar work and set the general tone for the total group. Ryan, Ricks, and Lee are part of the fringe group. They have not been completely accepted by the inner group. Lane and White belong to neither group. Even though they work in the same department, they are "loners." Ultimately they may become members of the fringe group.

Informal organizations do not necessarily cause poor job performance. Sometimes the informal organization is the best way to supply information needed for job performance.

Understanding Formal Organizational Structure

Certain fundamentals of organization have evolved over the years as items that must be considered when designing the formal organization. These fundamentals include dealing with the following: (1) policy, (2) authority, (3) responsibility, (4) accountability, (5) delegation, and (6) coordination.

Policy. A **POLICY** is **a written or oral statement that serves as a general guide for decision making.** Although policies are commonly made by top-level managers on items of importance, it is the people at lower management levels who make policies work. For example, it may be the policy of one firm to give two weeks' vacation to an employee only after he or she has worked there for two years or longer. Some policies are referred to as "working policies." These relate to specific types of operations or conditions, such as sick leave, promotion, retirement, and vacation.

Authority. **AUTHORITY** is **the power to act and make decisions in carrying out assignments.** In a corporation the authority comes from stockholders and is delegated to directors. They in turn delegate authority to top executives, who may in turn transmit some authority to lower-level managers. Some people have authority because of their knowledge of a subject; others have authority because they control resources or because they have a charismatic quality.

Responsibility. **RESPONSIBILITY** is **an individual's obligation to carry out assigned duties.** In delegating (or assigning) activities, the manager assigns to subordinates a responsibility to carry out tasks. Responsibility and authority should be equal. A subordinate should have the power to carry out responsibilities. The flow of authority and responsibility is downward.

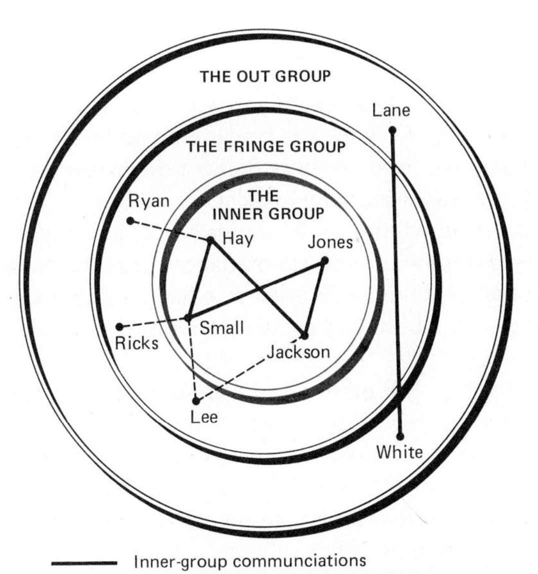

FIGURE 5-2

Example of the informal organization in a work group.

KATHARINE GRAHAM

Katharine Graham is the daughter of Eugene Meyer, a California-born financier, who purchased the Washington Post at auction in 1933. After graduating from the University of Chicago, she worked as a reporter for the *San Francisco News* and later joined the news staff of the *Washington Post*. She also worked in the Sunday and circulation departments. In 1940 she married Philip L. Graham and then devoted her life to being a homemaker and mother of their four children.

When Eugene Meyer retired as publisher of the *Post*, he turned the reins of the newspaper over to his son-in-law, Philip Graham, who led the *Post* to new heights until his untimely death in 1963.

Mrs. Graham became president of the *Washington Post* in 1963, publisher in 1968, and chairman of the board of the Washington Post Company in 1973. As the newspaper's chief executive officer, she has practiced the principle of delegating full authority to capable persons—and then giving them responsibility commensurate with that authority. She has encouraged and supported the paper's editorial writers and reporters. She has urged them to "seek out the facts and stay with the truth." She is highly respected throughout management circles for her business expertise and success in management. Mrs. Graham believes in sound preparation and successful work experience. She urges young people to "prepare and plan for the future as well as for the present."

Accountability. **ACCOUNTABILITY is holding a subordinate answerable for the responsibility and authority delegated to him or her.** Accountability is always upward in the organization, because one is accountable to the superior who delegated the task. A person should be held accountable only to the extent that he or she is given responsibility and authority.

Delegation. **DELEGATION is giving one person the power and obligation to act for another.** Delegation is considered an art of management. It is generally not well practiced. Studies show that a principal reason for managers' failure is their unwillingness or inability to delegate authority. As an organization grows, the manager must be willing to assign authority and responsibility to subordinates in order to have time to perform managerial functions. Figure 5-3 shows how the process of delegation is performed in a formal organization. Authority, responsibility, and accountability are elements involved in making decisions.

Coordination. All parts of a business firm have a common goal, that is, the success of the venture. Therefore all the various efforts must be coordinated. **COORDINATION is synchronizing all individual efforts toward a common objective.** Its purpose is to make sure things happen at the right time and place, and in the correct order. Although personal contact is the most effective means of achieving coordination, other devices are used. These include forms of written communication—bulletins, letters, and procedure manuals. Group meetings can also be effective.

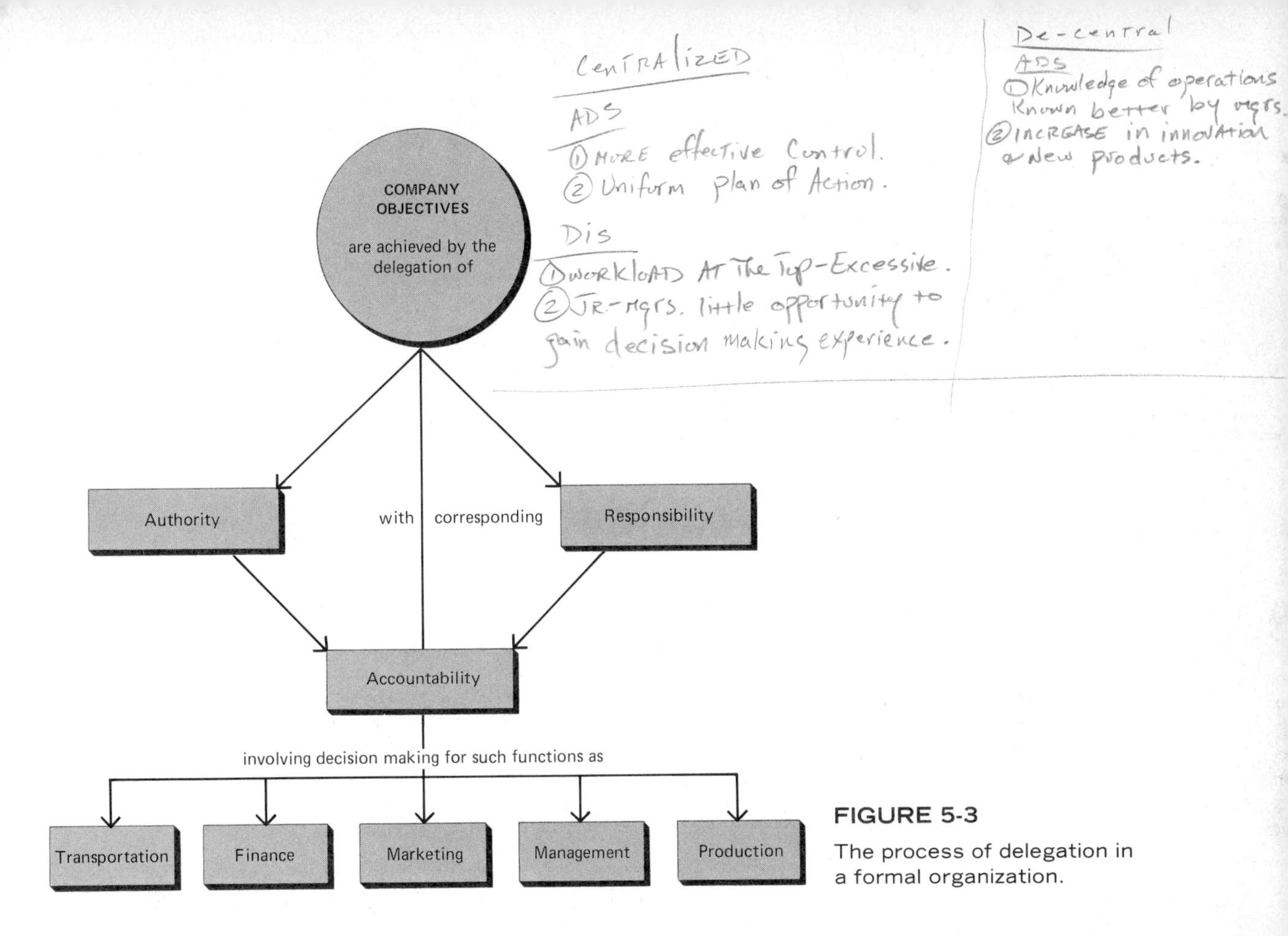

FIGURE 5-3

The process of delegation in a formal organization.

Centralization vs. Decentralization of Management

The terms **centralization** and **decentralization** are often used in management. The issue is, How much authority should management delegate throughout the organization?

Centralized organization. A business that adopts a policy of placing major decision-making authority and control in the hands of a few top-level executives is a centralized management organization. Thus a **CENTRALIZED MANAGEMENT ORGANIZATION is a system that delegates authority and control to a central area, usually the top.** Centralized management is illustrated in Figure 5.4.

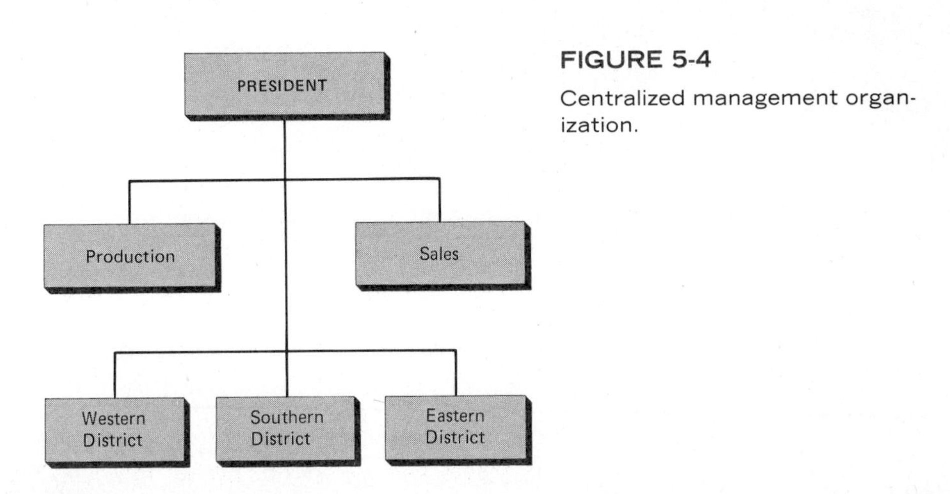

FIGURE 5-4

Centralized management organization.

Advocates of centralization contend that it permits more effective controls and tends to reduce decision-making time. A further advantage is that it allows all units to follow a uniform plan of action. It is popular in department stores and food chains. Central headquarters decides on all policies involving buying, advertising, marketing, accounting, personnel, and credit. Sears, Roebuck and Company is an example of centralized management.

A disadvantage of centralization of management can occur when the business grows rapidly and the workload at the top executive level becomes excessive. Delays can occur in making decisions, and this can result in higher operating costs.

A second disadvantage is that centralized organization offers junior managers little opportunity to obtain decision-making experience. Virtually all important decisions are made at the company headquarters.

Decentralized organization. Many large firms have adopted decentralization of management authority. **DECENTRALIZED MANAGEMENT is a systematic effort to delegate to lower levels all authority except that which must be exercised at the highest level.** Decentralization takes place for different reasons. Some companies decentralize managerial functions because they know that conditions vary from plant to plant. Officials at each plant know their own operations better than centralized personnel. Therefore they can make better decisions. Under decentralization, local managers welcome the opportunity to demonstrate their ability. Figure 5-5 shows how the president delegates authority to the three regional district managers for production and sales.

The organization chart in Figure 5-6 shows how Safeway Stores—America's largest food chain—has decentralized its entire organization. As indicated in the chart, there are twenty-six separate retail divisions. Each has a vice-president who has the authority and responsibility for operating a specific district. Thus authority and responsibility are decentralized. Each region is the equivalent of a fairly large retail operation, and each district is a distribution center for warehousing, buying, advertising, and so on.

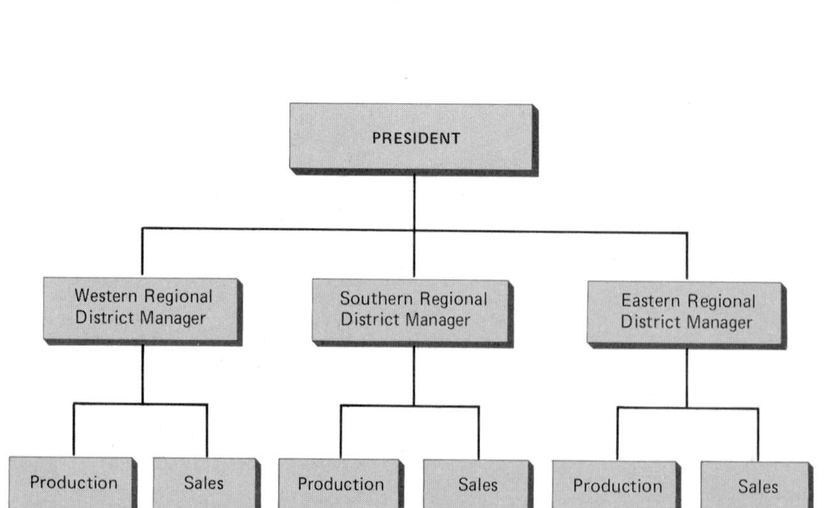

FIGURE 5-5

Decentralized management organization.

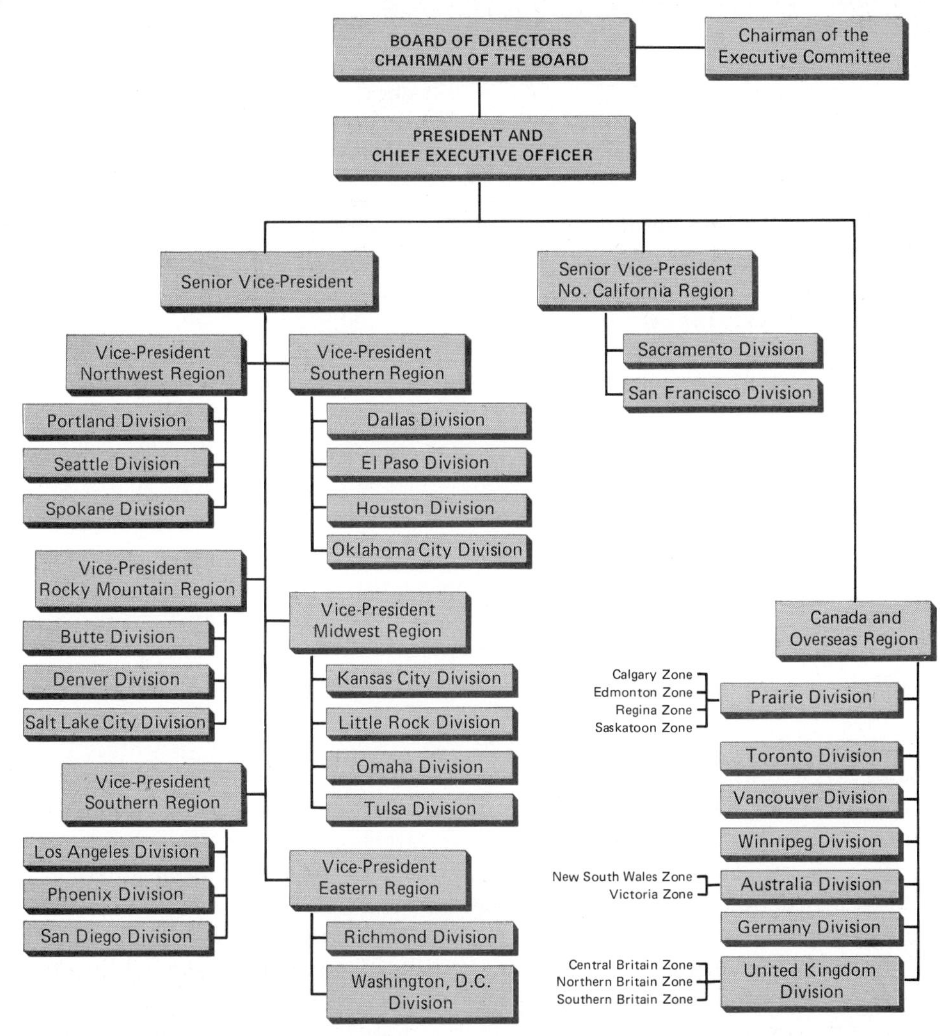

FIGURE 5-6

Organization chart—Safeway Stores, Incorporated.

The Safeway Stores organization is divided into three groups—Supply Divisions, Retail Divisions, and Service Divisions. Only the Retail Division are shown here. These are grouped by geographical regions, each headed by a vice-president. This figure illustrates a decentralized management organization. Each Retail Division vice-president has full power to act within policy guidelines. (Courtesy Safeway Stores, Inc.)

Another advantage of decentralization can be an increase in innovation and new products. For example, ESB Ray-O-Vac recently decided to decentralize for these reasons.

ESB Ray-O-Vac is a large battery maker that has been facing a declining share of the market for its products. The biggest problem has been Ray-O-Vac's inability to bring new products rapidly to market. The long-life alkaline dry cells and maintenance-free car batteries are examples. Both were mastered by Ray-O-Vac's technical people early enough to make the company a leader with these products. But the caution and bureaucracy at central headquarters kept the products from reaching the market in time.

David C. Dawson, ESB Ray-O-Vac's president, moved to decentralize. He removed a layer of corporate management and reorganized along the decentralized model. Four product groupings were organized: Ray-O-Vac for dry cells (for flashlights, radios, etc.), Exide Company for auto batteries, Systems and Electronics Company for several electric products, and Universal Electric Company for appliance motors.

The heads of these divisions now have complete control for their operations and report directly to Dawson. The test of the new organizational form will be how quickly the company can catch up in lost market share.

Principles of Successful Organizational Structure

Before we examine the various types of formal organization plans, we should consider some of the principles that underlie a company's organizational structure. There are accepted principles of organization that are often observed.

Every organization should have an objective. The performance of all parts of the organization should be directed toward the achievement of the same objective. This is known as **unity of objective:** It is necessary to develop effective teamwork within an organization. A distinction should be made, however, between the organization's objectives and individual goals (of executives, supervisors, and workers who make up the organization). The individual worker's goal is not the same as the organization's objective. For example, the objective of raising additional operating funds may be assigned to the chief finance officer. The employees, through their local union, may vote to have as their objective a 10 percent hourly wage increase. The two goals are different and would be achieved differently. Below are the corporate objectives of Safeway Stores, Incorporated. These objectives cover more than the goal of earning a profit and providing a service.

There must be clear lines of authority and accompanying responsibility, beginning at the top and descending to the lowest level. A good organizational structure provides for delegation of authority from, let us say, the president to the vice-president, to the general manager, to the supervisor, and finally to the workers. Thus, authority stems from the highest executive level and is delegated downward. The president of the firm may, for example, assign to the manufacturing vice-president the responsibility for buying raw materials and new equipment. At the same time, the vice-president must have the authority to determine what prices should be paid for these items.

The number of levels of authority should be held to a minimum. Each time a new management level is created, another link is introduced into the chain of command. And the longer the chain, the more time it takes for instructions to pass downward and for information to travel upward. The number of levels depends upon whether the firm is centralized or decentralized. Where there are too many levels, authority is splintered. In such a case, a problem cannot be solved or a decision made without pooling the authority of two or more managers. In many day-to-day operations there are cases of splintered authority; most managerial conferences are probably held because of the need to pool authority before making a decision.

No one in the organization should have more than one supervisor. This is the **unity-of-command principle.** This principle is useful in the clarification of authority-responsibility relationships. Whenever a manager lacks total ability to hold his or her subordinates responsible, the manager's position becomes one of confusion and frustration and it may eventually be undermined.

SPAN OF CONTROL is a limit on the number of positions one person should supervise directly. This principle is an important concept in developing the organizational structure. It places some limit on the number of subordinates who can satisfactorily be managed by a single executive. The span of control depends on many things—the nature of the job, the personalities of the manager and subordinates, and how far apart they are geographically. If the operations have been decentralized, with operating units that are nearly autonomous, it is possible for top-level executives to supervise satisfactorily more people than in situations where more control is necessary.

The organizational structure should be flexible enough to permit changes with a minimum of disruption. Since change is inevitable in any business, the ideal organizational structure is one that permits an executive to make changes without destroying the continuity of the business or the efficiency of the employees. Good organizational structure must not be a straitjacket.

Safeway's Corporate Objectives*

1. To make Safeway stock an increasingly profitable investment for our shareholders.
2. To practice responsible citizenship in the conduct of our business and in community and social relations.
3. To satisfy increasing numbers of customers, at a profit sufficient to assure the continuing healthy growth of the company.
4. To provide attractive, convenient stores staffed with courteous employees, and stocked with the products customers want.
5. To be known for superior perishables—meats, produce, dairy products, and baked goods.
6. To operate efficiently at the lowest costs consistent with quality and growth.
7. To be alert to new ideas, opportunities and change.
8. To strengthen our organization by continuous and systematic training and development of employees and managers.
9. To offer our employees responsibility, challenge, and satisfying rewards for accomplishment.

*Courtesy Safeway Stores, Incorporated.

Types of Authority Relationships

Jobs or positions in business are classified according to the nature of their authority in the organization. These may be **line, staff, functional,** or **project management** authority relationships. Such relationships are not confined to a particular kind of business. Instead, some of each type can be found in every field of business.

Line relationships. A line relationship exists where there is direct authority between each superior and subordinate. This means that each manager exercises undivided authority over his or her subordinate, who reports only to that manager. In Figure 5-7 the application of line authority is shown in the first illustration. The flow of authority is direct and unobstructed.

Staff relationships. Figure 5-7 also illustrates the line-and-staff structure. Notice that the flow of authority is represented by the solid lines and staff relations by the dashed lines. When staff relations are created, persons assigned to these positions are known as staff managers. They furnish special service and advice to line executives.

Since **staff** refers to those in the organization who offer technical and special advice, staff members must be specialists. Their recommendations are made to their superiors, who then decide whether or not their recommendations should be adopted. Examples of staff specialists include legal counsel, research director, engineer, and economist.

Functional relations. Some businesses use a third type of authority relationships, known as functional relations, which is not restricted to managers or departments. This type provides for specialists for each specific major function (hence the name **functional structure**) no matter where in the business the function is performed. For example, a personnel manager exercises functional authority over all people involving personnel relations wherever they are found in the organization. Later in this chapter we will discuss how the functional organization form works.

Project management relations. Project management or "matrix" organizational authority relations violate the unity-of-command principle. A manager may have a regular line role in the organization but may also be in charge of a group of people working on a special project. He or she has an immediate superior

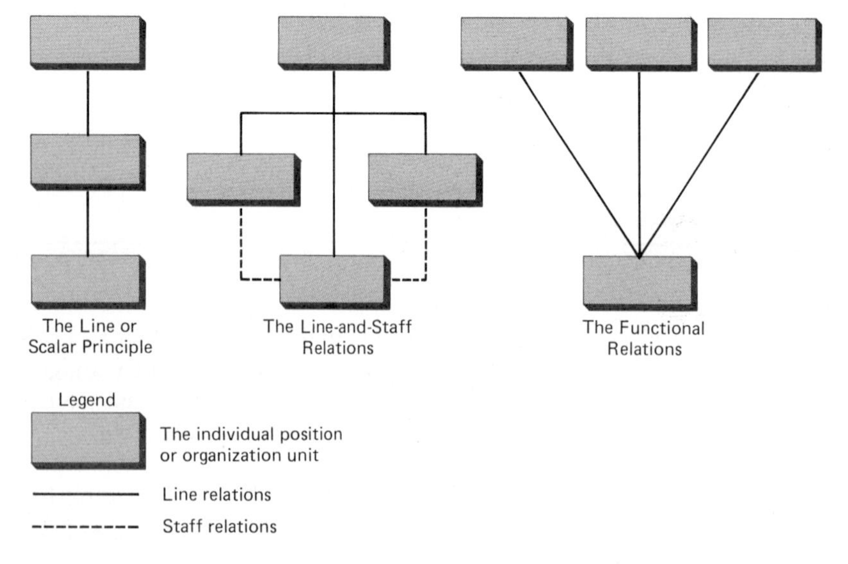

FIGURE 5-7
Three fundamental authority-relationship structures.

in the line organization and reports to a project director as well. The matrix organization is becoming increasingly popular but is limited to certain situations. It is prevalent among companies in the construction and aerospace industries. We will discuss the use of each of these authority relationships as it applies to a specific organizational form.

ORGANIZATIONAL FORMS

Four types of organizational forms are generally found in modern business: line, line-and-staff, functional, and matrix or project form. Each of these has its advantages and disadvantages.

Line Organization Form

The line organization form, shown in Figure 5-8, is the oldest and simplest organization plan used in business. There is a direct flow of authority from top executives to the rank-and-file employees through lower-level executives at one or more managerial levels. Since this direct chain of command is used in military organizations, the line plan is often referred to as the "military" type. It is also related

FIGURE 5-8

Line organization form.

A line organization plan for a medium-size automotive parts manufacturing company in which there is a direct flow of authority from the top executive down to operating employees. Each person has an immediate supervisor. The line of responsibility extends from bottom to top. The line of authority is from top to bottom.

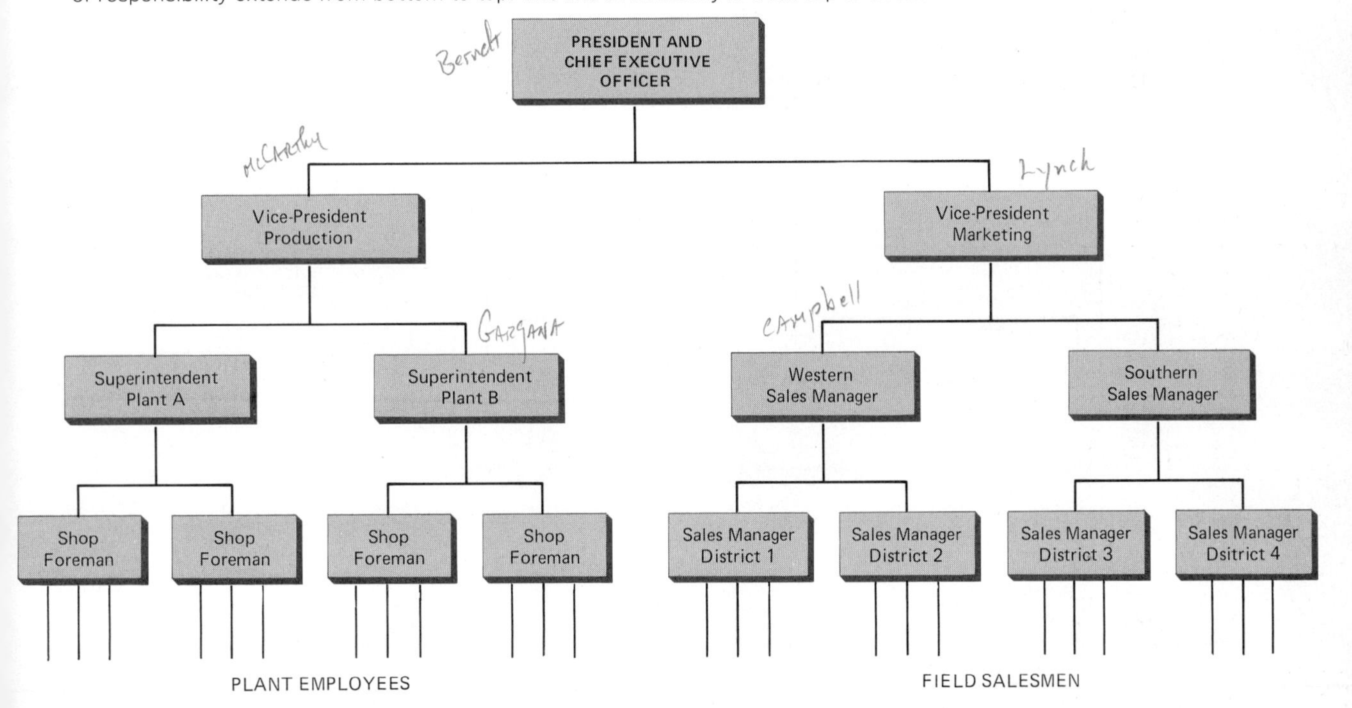

to the "scalar principle," which clearly reflects definite levels of authority within the hierarchy of administration. Each person is responsible to only one boss. Authority flows downward and responsibility upward. This plan is used mainly in small or medium-size manufacturing and service-type enterprises.

Here is a comparison of the advantages and disadvantages of the line organization.

Advantages	Disadvantages
1. It is simple and easy for employees and management to understand.	1. Each supervisor has responsibility for several duties and cannot become an expert in all of them.
2. It permits definite designation of authority and responsibility.	2. The plan overburdens top executives with day-to-day details; little time is left for long-range planning.
3. Each person is responsible to only one boss.	3. The plan fails to provide a specialized staff for more specialized management activities.
4. It permits easy decision making at various levels.	4. It requires supervisors to have a variety of skills in areas of management.

Line-and-Staff Organization Form

Whenever an organization becomes large, the tendency is to modify the line organization by adding staff specialists, as shown in Figure 5-9. As an example, when a line executive is confronted with a legal problem, he or she may call on the legal department for advice. In Figure 5-9 both research-and-development

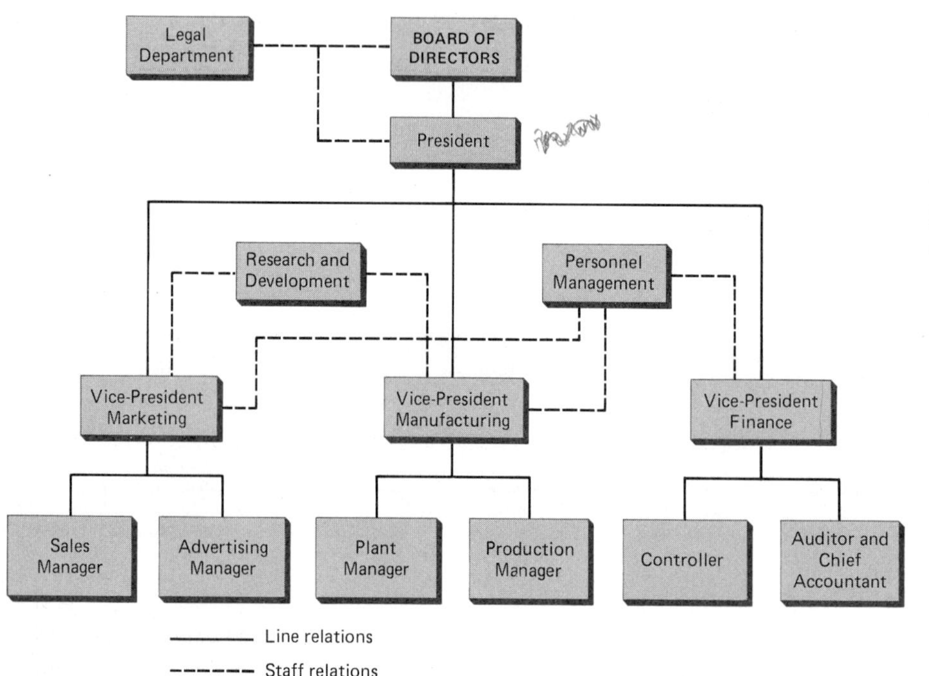

FIGURE 5-9

Line-and-staff organization form.

The line-and-staff organization structure plan provides for a combination of line departments and for staff specialists who are advisers to line executives.

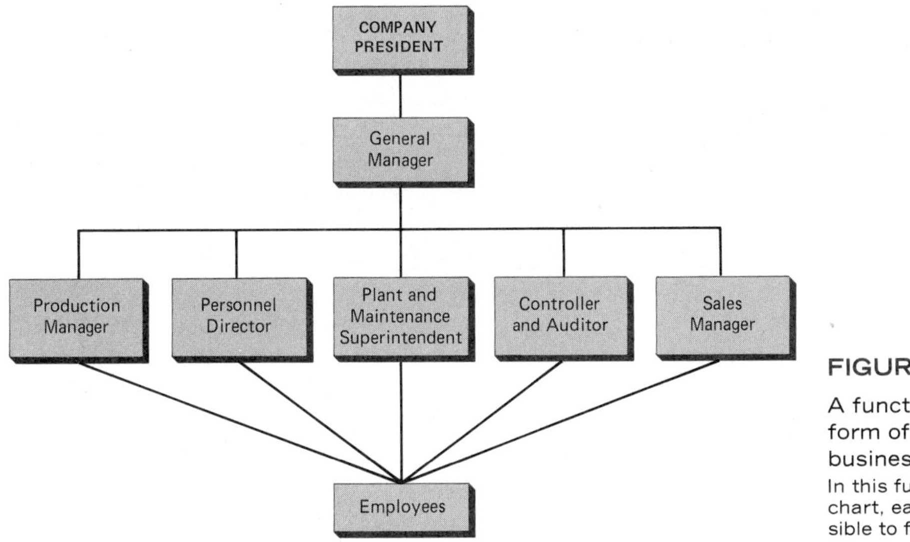

FIGURE 5-10

A functional organization form of a manufacturing business.

In this functional organization chart, each employee is responsible to five supervisors.

specialists and members of the personnel-management department provide staff service to various line executives.

Line executives do the work required to carry on the operations of the firm. Staff people are specialists who serve line executives. Dashed lines are sometimes used in an organization chart to show the flow of advice and communications between staff and line units. The key in determining which members are line and which are staff is the nature of the work performed. Normally, executives in staff departments do not have authority over individuals in line positions. They, of course, exercise authority over employees in their own department or group.

Here is a comparison of the advantages and disadvantages of the line-and-staff form.

Advantages	Disadvantages
1. The plan gives line executives authority to make all major decisions and issue directives to subordinates.	1. Staff specialists tend to overstep by asserting authority of line personnel, causing friction and misunderstanding.
2. It allows qualified technical specialists to advise line executives on the more complex problems of large companies	2. The use of staff specialists tends to increase company overhead.
3. No matter in which department an employee works, he or she rarely reports to more than one supervisor or superior.	3. Decisions may be slowed by line executives who wait for technical and research findings by staff specialists before making a decision.

Functional Organization Form

It is possible to assign authority and responsibility in a pattern different from the line or line-and-staff form. This may be accomplished by giving a manager authority over specified processes or functions. Each functional manager will supervise employees in several different departments, but only on matters concerning his or her specific functional area. In Figure 5-10 you will observe that each employee has five different supervisors. Workers take orders from more than one supervisor,

Mgr. authority over specific functions.-over the employees.

More than 1 Boss on employee - in his specialized Area.

which is at variance with the organizational principle of "unity of command" discussed earlier in this chapter. This plan is not widely used. When a business that has been using this plan expands, the tendency is to change to a line-and-staff plan.

Here are the advantages and disadvantages of the functional form.

Advantages	Disadvantages
1. Each supervisor works exclusively in his or her specialty. The supervisor can grow with the firm.	1. Employees have more than one boss. This can conflict with the unity-of-command principle.
2. Business activities are divided into functions and assigned to specialists. Each specialist performs only one set of duties.	2. Since employees report to more than one supervisor, discipline tends to break down—there are just too many bosses.
3. Each employee can use the advice of various specialists when a problem arises.	3. Overlapping of authority among supervisors may encourage buck-passing and conflict of authority.

Matrix Organization Form

Bring specialists from different parts of Co. to work on specific project.

The matrix organization is used when a project structure is added to another structure. It results in bringing specialists from several different parts of the organization together to work on a particular project. The group is led by a project manager who has responsibility for the entire project. When it is completed, the group is dissolved and its members return to their respective departments.

The matrix organization also disregards the unity-of-command principle. Furthermore, this plan does not agree with the usual line-and-staff concepts. Yet

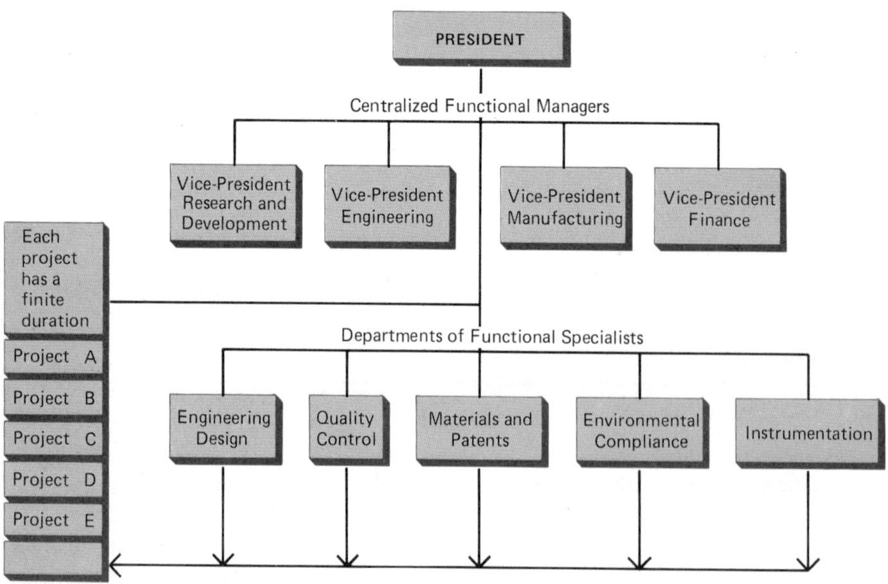

FIGURE 5-11

Matrix or project organization form.

The matrix organization form sets up special projects, and specialists are assigned to the projects as needed. Centralized functional managers exercise authority that flows vertically. Flow of authority exercised by specialists is horizontal, as shown by the arrow. When a project is completed, the matrix personnel return to their home departments.

it works! Some critics of the plan indicate that it discourages informal groups and the traditional supervisor-subordinate relations. On the other hand, the matrix organization allows for maximum use of specialized knowledge, which gives flexibility in the use of knowledgeable persons for difficult assignments. An organization chart for a matrix organization is illustrated in Figure 5-11. The flow of authority is shown by the arrows in the chart.

The project or matrix manager must be extremely competent. This manager functions with two bosses and without the clear authority that is usually thought necessary. Many project managers are engineers. Until recently, however, engineering students have rarely been offered management courses especially tailored to their needs. Now engineering schools, in cooperation with the big companies that hire their graduates, are beginning to offer degrees in engineering management.

More than forty schools now offer degrees in engineering management. The term used is matrix manager. That is where the technical and business aspects of a project blend together.

These programs include required courses in such areas as management decision making in engineering, statistics, behavioral systems engineering, engineering law, and venture management. Most of these programs are offered at night so that engineers who want the training but must work during the day can take advantage of them.

ORGANIZATION CHARTS

A common cause of internal conflict in a business organization is the absence of definite responsibilities and authority. Some employees do not clearly understand their assignments and to whom they report. Solution to this problem can be aided by the proper use of organization charts.

Organization Charts

In discussing the formal organization forms, we presented a chart illustrating each form to indicate how the parts of the organization are related. An **ORGANIZATION CHART** is **the blueprint of the company's internal structure.**

Organizations use charts for various reasons. In addition to showing specific areas of responsibility and authority, charts can improve communication channels. They can identify the difference between line and staff executives. They also help in planning, budgeting, and controlling operations.

Making Organization Charts

One way to prepare a chart is to begin with the highest position. A single rectangular-shaped box at the top of the organization represents the position occupied by the person who holds the responsibility for final decision making. This is often the president or the chairman of the board of directors.

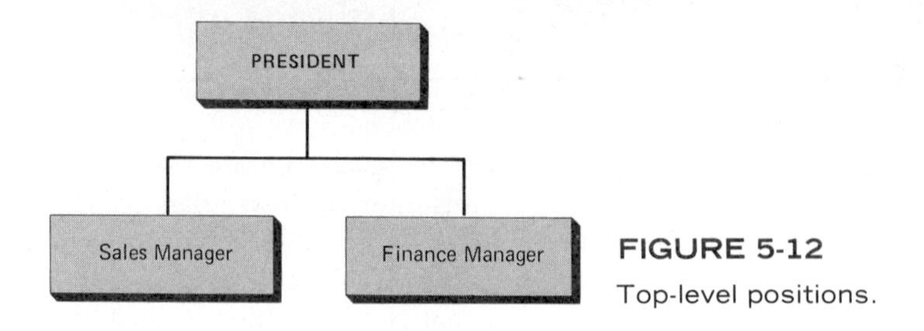

FIGURE 5-12
Top-level positions.

In Figure 5-12 the office of president is the highest position. It is followed by the sales manager and the finance manager.

If two district sales managers, a controller, and a chief auditor are added, the chart will be expanded as shown in Figure 5-13. Now the chart resembles the shape of a pyramid; hence the name "pyramid" chart. The chart will continue to expand as more positions are added. This situation is further illustrated by Figure 5-14, which shows the office of general counsel (a staff position) and four additional staff members. All of these officials report to the president.

Types of organization charts. Companies create organization charts to suit their requirements. There are three main types of organization charts:

1. The vertical chart—Figure 5-8 (the line organization)
2. The pyramid chart—Figure 5-13
3. The horizontal chart—Figure 5-15

Lack of clarity as to who does what is cited as being a major disadvantage of organization charts. But when job descriptions accompany charts, they add a more complete picture. Charts in themselves do not reflect the actual responsibilities of a given position.

For many, the horizontal chart shown in Figure 5-15 is more difficult to understand than the vertical chart. The horizontal chart does not portray a complex and large organization as clearly as does the vertical chart.

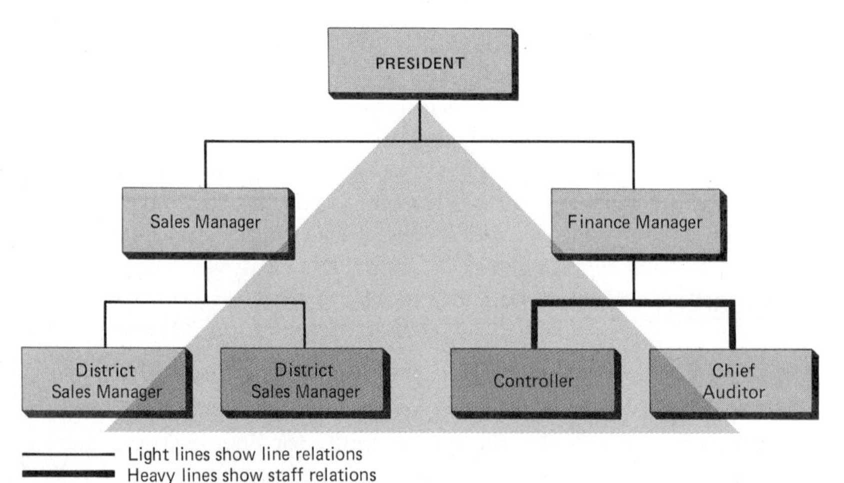

FIGURE 5-13
Partial organization expanded to include another level of management.

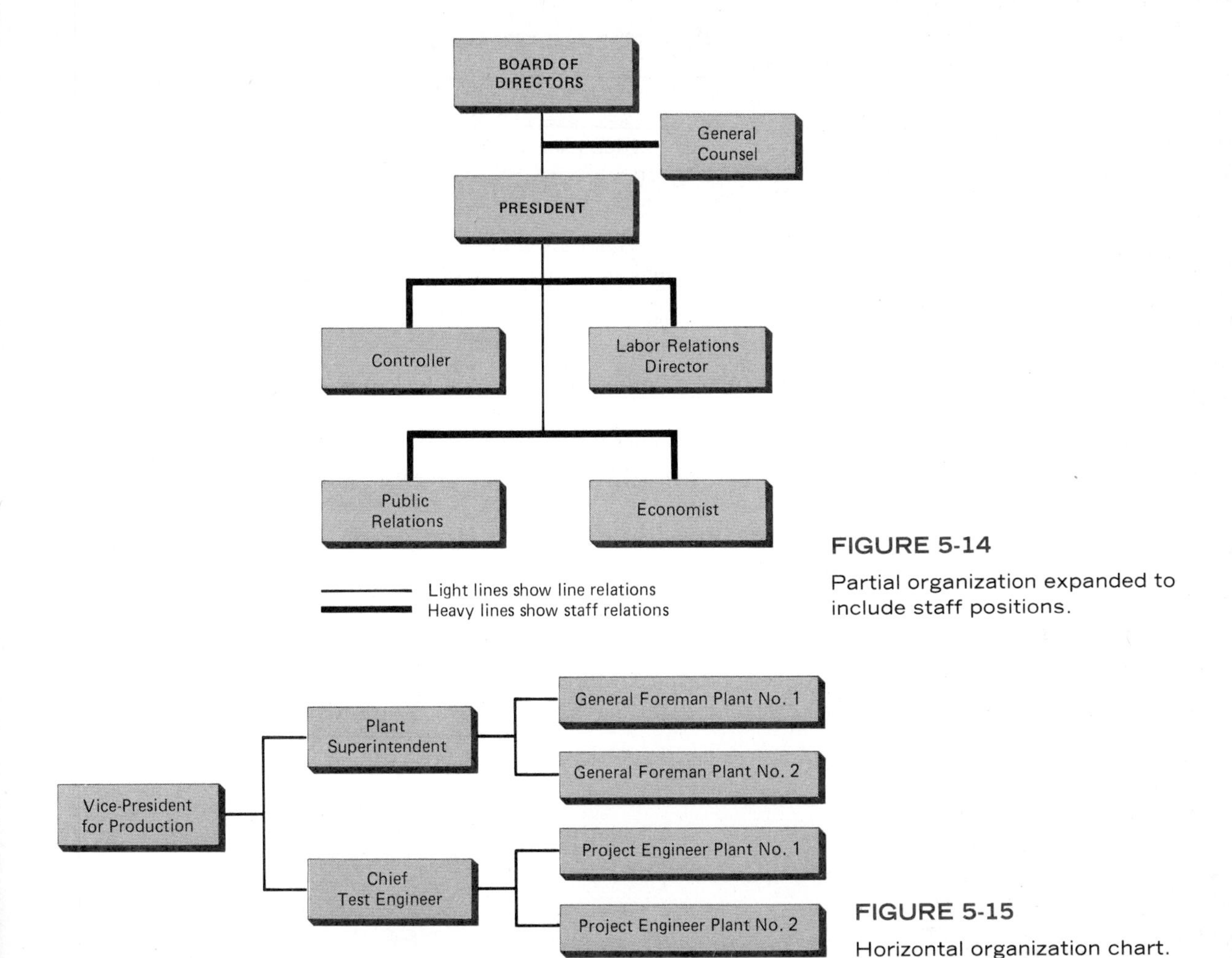

FIGURE 5-14

Partial organization expanded to include staff positions.

FIGURE 5-15

Horizontal organization chart.

SUMMARY OF KEY CONCEPTS

Organization is the internal structure in which people interact in accomplishing the business's objectives. It is an essential tool of management in operating the business.

People are the primary resource of an organization. Managers need to understand how these people behave in dealing with each other.

Every business—small or large—needs some kind of planned organization that will enable the group to work effectively under a central authority.

Operations of the business are performed by personnel who are organized on either a formal or an informal basis. The formal organization is a creation of management. The informal organization is the result of social and communications relationships, which may exist at both managerial and employee levels.

In planning a formal organization, it is essential to provide for the delegation of authority and responsibility. For each employee, responsibility increases with his or her rank and work assignment.

Employees are part of work groups. As individuals, they are motivated by certain wants and needs. Work attitudes constantly change because of a lack of understanding as to what is expected of them.

Four major types of organization plans have been developed. Each can be shown by an organization chart. This chart is a pictorial representation of what employees do and how they relate to each other in performing their work.

The line organization form is a straightforward chain-of-command relationship that shows channels of communication and lines of authority between the superior and the subordinate.

The line-and-staff organization form, as its name implies, combines line and staff functions. Line executives exercise formal authority over others. Staff specialists serve line managers by acting as advisers in special fields.

In the functional organization form, work is organized by departments on functional lines, such as production, finance, and marketing. There is a direct flow of authority for each function.

The project or matrix organization form is based on the project concept. Specialists are temporarily assigned to the project. When the project is completed, the members of the group return to their respective departments.

Organization charts and manuals are useful management tools. The chart is a blueprint of the organization, showing lines of authority. Staff relations are likewise shown.

BUSINESS TERMS

You should be able to match these business terms with the statements that follow.

a. Accountability
b. Coordination
c. Decentralized management
d. Delegation
e. Formal organization
f. Informal organization
g. Organization
h. Organization chart
i. Policy
j. Responsibility
k. Span of control
l. Work group

1. A process for providing a structure of relationships to get work done
2. A collection of employees who share a common job and view
3. A system of jobs, authority relationships, responsibility, and accountability, designed by management
4. A network of personal and social relationships that may have nothing to do with formal authority relationships
5. A written or oral statement that serves as a guide for decision making
6. An individual's obligation to carry out assigned duties
7. Holding a subordinate answerable for the responsibility and authority delegated to him or her
8. The giving to one person the power and obligation to act for another
9. Synchronizing individual efforts toward a common objective
10. A systematic effort to delegate to lower levels all authority except that which can be exercised at the highest organizational level
11. A limit to the number of positions one person should supervise directly
12. A blueprint of a company's internal structure

REVIEW QUESTIONS

1. What are some of the different meanings of the term **organization?**
2. Why does a business change from one form of organizational structure to another?
3. What is the main difference between a **formal** and an **informal** organization?
4. Is there any difference in the authority exercised by a line executive and a staff executive?
5. Why are so many large businesses set up to follow the line-and-staff form of organization plan?
6. Is either the line organization plan or the functional organization plan in conflict with the unity-of-command principle?

DISCUSSION QUESTIONS

1. Make an analogy between a business that earns above-average profit and a football team that wins most of its games each season.
2. What are some of the causes of job dissatisfaction among factory workers and junior managers?
3. If a person is responsible for supervising several employees, why must that individual have authority?
4. What is the difference between **delegation** of authority and **decentralization** of authority?
5. Why do some companies prefer to have a strong centralized managerial structure rather than a decentralized management structure?
6. What are some of the advantages and disadvantages of an organization chart?

BUSINESS CASE 5-1

Baker Bros. Furniture Company

Baker Bros., a Georgia corporation, operates plants in Georgia that manufacture a line of home and office furniture, sold in the southern states. The company headquarters is located in Atlanta.

The managerial policy of the company has been one of decentralization of management in its plants. With the increase in inflation and competition, the company has experienced difficulty in maintaining this policy. After an extended period of discussion, it was decided that this practice would be abandoned.

The directors voted to reorganize the company under a centralization of management. Plant managers would no longer exercise direct supervision at the plants. Instead, each plant would be directly under an operating vice-president at the headquarters. The title of "plant manager" was changed to "plant superintendent." Plant personnel response to this change was one of contempt and protest. The union staged a three-day walkout, making it necessary to close each plant. Two of the managers resigned. The union immediately demanded a greater input in the management decision making at the plant level. The company replied that it was the right of management to reorganize the business. Meanwhile, each plant remained closed.

1. What were the issues in this case?
2. What is your recommendation to the directors?

BUSINESS CASE 5-2

Colonial Corporation

The Colonial Corporation was an established producer of a line of recreational equipment including sleeping bags, tents, and water and snow skis, as well as other items used in camping. Its Hiline brand has had wide acceptance. These products were marketed through brokers who sold to sporting-goods and hardware stores. A recent slump in sales was thought to have been caused by a shortage of gasoline. At the same time it was necessary to increase the prices of all products in the company line. Several members of the family urged the president to sell the business.

Western Industries, a conglomerate, has purchased 55 percent of the common stock with an option to buy the remaining shares within two years. Western has also agreed not to discharge any member of management without giving him or her six months' advance notice.

Two months after taking control, Western sent a management team to review the firm's internal organization. Their study revealed some startling facts, at least from the viewpoint of Western Industries.

The president of Colonial followed the policy that all purchases over $1,000 had to be approved by him. The purchasing agent had only authority to buy goods costing less than $1,000. The president also made virtually all plant decisions involving the hiring and firing of employees, with one exception.

The company's organization chart showed the position of general manager. However, this position has been vacant for several months because the general manager resigned. The president and his son divided the duties of the general manager between them. In a discussion with the son about this business, he summarized his views as follows:

> Our company has always made money, which speaks well for our system. In operating a business, you soon learn who is competent and who is not. I feel that it is essential for me to relieve my father and take over more responsibility for the daily operation of the firm.

1. Comment on the views expressed by the president's son.
2. Have any organization principles been violated by the father and son? Explain.

SMALL-BUSINESS MANAGEMENT AND FRANCHISING

6

STUDY OBJECTIVES

WHEN YOU HAVE FINISHED READING THIS CHAPTER, YOU SHOULD BE ABLE TO

ONE Explain what determines whether a business is considered to be "small" and the importance of small businesses in the total business picture

TWO Identify the advantages and disadvantages of operating a small business

THREE Discuss the factors that contribute to the success of small businesses

FOUR Describe how the Small Business Administration aids small businesses

FIVE Name the principal types of businesses that sell services instead of goods

SIX Explain the importance of franchising in the retail business picture

IN THE NEWS

A Small-Business Franchise Operation That Backfired!

World Team Tennis was an ambitious effort to make tennis popular on a team format. In the fall of 1978 after five years of erratic performance, eight of the ten existing WTT franchises folded. After a search for new franchisees failed, the 1979 season was canceled.

If WTT never manages a comeback, it will at least serve as a good example of problems associated with franchising in a difficult area—professional sports. Although WTT began on a strong note with sixteen teams and such stars as Jimmy Connors, Vitas Gerulaitis, Evonne Goolagong, and Billie Jean King, it did not work for long. The team format, rowdy fans, and players who did not work to make the idea succeed turned off many tennis buffs.

Many top players did not sign with WTT because they did not need the money. World Team Tennis was never able to sign the lucrative television contract that is a key to financial success in professional sports. And the final straw may have been a court ruling that changed allowable tax writeoffs of the franchise purchase price from 90 percent to 20 percent. After all, franchises in WTT were expensive—$200,000 for the franchise and $500,000 capital requirements. This high cost associated with the uncertainty of starting a new league kept investors away. The World Team Tennis franchises appear to have double faulted.

Small business is a symbol of opportunity, enterprise, innovation, and achievement. . . . It stands for something essential to our freedoms.

THEODORE O. YNTEMA
Committee for Economic Development

The history of business in America is the history of the small-business enterprise. Small independent businesses are everywhere and in every line of work. We see them in every community.

Many people want to be their own boss some day. This goal serves as the incentive for thousands to become business entrepreneurs every year. In this country we have a business climate where this is possible. All one needs is an idea, a limited amount of capital, and a will to succeed. Small business is an excellent example of free and open competition in the marketplace.

Many of today's giant enterprises started as one-person operations, including mail-order houses, automobile companies, chain stores, hotel and motel chains, and food-processing plants. Our business history is replete with one-person success stories. The experiences of Penney, Hershey, Firestone, Ford, Eastman, Heinz, Hilton, Hewlett, and Procter are examples of entrepreneurs who started on a small scale.

Thousands of men and women, many holding good positions with established firms, annually resign and start their own businesses. Of course, many of these firms fail, and much time, effort, and money are lost. But the desire for independence causes thousands of Americans to want to become individual proprietors.

This chapter deals with the small-business enterprise. Its purpose is to give you a look at the importance, scope, and problems of the small business. Franchising as a special form of small business is discussed in detail.

SMALL BUSINESS IN THE BUSINESS ENVIRONMENT

There are two ways to enter business on your own. One is to buy a business that is **already established.** The other is to start a **new** business. In either case you need some prior business experience or knowledge before launching your own enterprise.

Buying a Going Concern

There are a number of advantages in buying an established business. These should be carefully considered before starting a new one. One of the major advantages is that the location has been proved. With a new business, research must first measure pedestrian traffic at a given point. Small firms depend largely on drop-in trade rather than telephone orders. Research is often done to determine the size of the automobile traffic and whether adequate parking is available.

Second, a going concern can be evaluated with reasonable accuracy. The actual operating records can be studied. The seller's books may help to determine how well the business has performed during the past several years.

Third, much of the time, effort, and costs related to starting a new firm can be eliminated. The seller has already accumulated an inventory of stock and has assembled the needed personnel. If competent, they can become an immediate help to the new owner. Furthermore, it is possible to begin with a nucleus of customers and to begin operation immediately, without waiting for stock or equipment.

Fourth, the seller may be eager to retire and be willing to make a quick sale by lowering his or her price. Or the price may be reduced in order to settle an estate.

Starting a New Business

For various reasons, some persons prefer to start a completely new enterprise. Some of the advantages of doing this should be noted.

First, starting from scratch allows the owner to choose his or her own location, employees, brand of merchandise, and kind of equipment. Furthermore, a loyal clientele can be cultivated without inheriting any ill will that an existing business may have fostered.

Second, one may find that because of the inefficient management of concerns that are for sale, the market is not adequately served by them. Thus there is a need for a new and efficient firm.

Disadvantages of business ownership. Attractive as being an entrepreneur might seem, there are disadvantages or negative aspects such as the following:

1. Your business income may be less regular than your paycheck as a salaried person. It takes a while before a firm earns a profit.
2. The owner has no one with whom to share the responsibilities. There is a heavy burden of responsibility for meeting payrolls and other expenses. Some owners eventually grow weary of this responsibility.

Advantages of working for someone else. Being a salaried employee offers certain advantages; here are some:

1. You bear little financial responsibility for your employer's losses.

2. Working hours are regular and often shorter than those of the owner. (This advantage may not be so significant if you are a top executive.)

3. Salaried employees have such benefits as overtime pay, paid vacations, medical care, hospitalization, unemployment compensation, and sick leave.

When Is a Business Small?

As a rule, most people apply the term **small business** to the local corner drugstore, service station, or barbershop. This concept may be accurate enough for general use, for most small firms operate on this scale. Public Law 85-536, an amendment to the Small Business Administration Act, states that "**a SMALL BUSINESS concern shall be deemed to be one which is independently owned and operated and which is not dominant in its field of operation.**" In general a small business has few employees, limited capital investment, and low sales. In addition, the Small Business Administration (SBA) defines a small business as one that meets the following standards.

WHAT IS A SMALL BUSINESS?

For business loan purposes, SBA defines a small business as one that is independently owned and operated, is not dominant in its field, and meets employment or sales standards developed by the agency. For most industries, these standards are as follows:

Manufacturing—Number of employees may range up to 1,500, depending on the industry in which the applicant is primarily engaged.

Wholesaling—Small if yearly sales are not over $9.5 to $22 million, depending on the industry.

Services—Annual receipts not exceeding $2 million to $8 million, depending on the industry in which the applicant is primarily engaged.

Retailing—Small if annual sales or receipts are not over $2 to $7.5 million, depending on the industry.

Construction—General construction: average annual receipts not exceeding $9.5 million for three most recently completed fiscal years. Special trade construction: average annual receipts not exceeding $1 or $2 million for three most recently completed fiscal years, depending on the industry.

Agriculture—Annual receipts not exceeding $1 million.

The Committee for Economic Development (CED) offers a slightly different concept for defining small business, by advancing qualitative (rather than quantitative) criteria that distinguish small firms from large ones. The CED considers a company a small business when at least two of the following characteristics prevail:

1. *Management is independent.* Generally, the managers are the owners.
2. *Capital is furnished by an individual owner or a small group.*
3. *The area of operation is local.* Employees and owners reside in one home community. (Markets served need not be local.)

4. *Size within the industry is relatively small.* The business is small when compared with the biggest units in its field. (The size of the top bracket varies widely, so that what might seem large in one field would be small in another.)

As we can see from the CED criteria, a small business is self-initiated, largely self-financed, and closely self-managed and is of relatively small size when considered as part of the industry. In the opinion of the authors, a qualitative definition such as the one used by the CED is the most useful.

An important issue is that most small businesses operate on a small scale and management is independent. It must be remembered that many small businesses service big business. Hundreds of mass-produced consumer goods, although produced by giant corporations, are distributed and serviced largely by thousands of small stores. Only one out of four working Americans is employed by a business that has more than two hundred employees. Nearly 80 percent of American businesses have ten or fewer workers.

Characteristics of the Small Business

Apart from the matter of size, small businesses usually have three distinguishing characteristics: management, capital requirements, and local operation.

Management. The management of a small business is generally independent. Since the managers are the owners, they are in a position to make their own decisions. As a small operator, the owner is both investor and employer. This gives him or her complete freedom of action. Most small businesses are either sole proprietorships or partnerships.

Capital requirements. The amount of capital required is relatively small compared with that required by most corporations. It is supplied by one person or at most by a few persons.

FIGURE 6-1
In 1861 Gilbert Van Camp produced the first factory-canned pork and beans at this site in Indianapolis. Today the Stokely-Van Camp Corporation is international in its operations, with a wide assortment of canned foods—all beginning with a one-man venture. (Courtesy Stokely-Van Camp, Inc., Indianapolis, Indiana.)

Local operation. For most small firms, the area of operation is local. The employer and employees live in the community in which the business is located. This does not mean, however, that all small firms serve only local markets. Small importing and exporting firms and canning and packing plants sometimes operate nationwide.

The main characteristics of the small business and big business are compared here.

Small Business	Big Business
Generally owner-managed	Usually non-owner-managed
Simple organizational structure	Complex organizational structure
Owner knows his or her employees	Owners know few employees
High percentage of business failures	Low percentage of business failures
Lacks specialized managers	Management specialists common
Long-term capital difficult to obtain	Long-term capital usually relatively easy to obtain

Scope of operation. According to the SBA, approximately 75 percent of all nonfarm business establishments in the United States are small businesses. These provide jobs for 58 percent of all private nonfarm workers in the United States. Small businesses account for 43 percent of the gross national product. During the decade of the 1970s about 80 percent of the new jobs created in the private business sector were in companies that employed fifty or fewer persons. Big business overshadows the small firms in manufacturing. Nonetheless there are thousands of small enterprises engaged in manufacturing. These include toy factories, machine shops, soft-drink bottling works, cabinet shops, sawmills, and bookbinding plants.

R. H. Herzig, Board Chairman of the Minnesota Mining and Manufacturing Company said:

> It is the individual entrepreneur, the person with the innovative idea—or the small business—that we should be concerned about. The large growth company isn't and never has been enough for this economy. What the large companies contribute in the way of products, jobs, taxes, and dividends must be augmented by smaller companies.

STRENGTHS OF BEING SMALL

The owner-manager of a small business enjoys freedom of action, flexibility, and being on the firing line.

Freedom of Action

Change is characteristic of business as it is carried on today. There are always new products, more modern machines, and new technology. The small-business owner is in a position to act quickly to meet changing conditions. This is especially important in meeting relatively small market demands. The large company cannot adapt so quickly. And the large company is not geared up to meet a small-market demand. The small retailer can order goods on a short lead time. The large firm orders large amounts of goods and therefore may place orders well in advance.

> Western Auto Supply Company provides a good example of combining some of the strengths of being small with the strengths of being large.
>
> Western Auto is concentrated in small rural markets in the Southeast and Southwest. There are 474 company-owned stores but 3,928 "associate" stores. These associate stores are owned locally—not franchised. Western Auto allows local dealers to use its name in return for purchasing automotive and other products from Western's wholesale operation. The associate stores enjoy the advantages of large centralized purchasing and are able to tailor their selection of goods to local markets.

CURRENT ISSUE

Should I Stay "Small" or Branch Out?

When a small business prospers, the owner naturally thinks about opening additional stores. For retailers this usually requires less capital than for manufacturers. But because a particular business is successful in a given location does not mean that others will be. To begin with, much depends on the quality of management available.

With which of the following statements do you agree and with which do you disagree?

1. A person who has a good thing going should stick with it.
2. Management other than the owner does not have the same interest in the business as the owner.
3. A common cause of small-business failure is overextension, which results in undercapitalization.
4. Launching additional enterprises should be conditional on having managers who are part owners, or at least who share in the profits.
5. A person who is successful in one location can be just as successful in another.
6. We pass this way in life only once, so we should branch out and make all we can.
7. The problems and profits that result from managing several businesses usually do not justify the extra worry and effort.

If you had a successful small business, what factors would determine whether you might enlarge it?

Adapting to Local Needs Most small-business owners are long-time residents of the communities they serve. They are, therefore, in the best position to assess local needs. The local merchant has a close contact with customers and employees and can cater to these local needs and wants. The volume of business is small, so he or she can sell profitably in the small market.

Taking Part Where the Action Is The small business gives the owner (or owners) a chance to participate in management. Often a valued employee's services can be retained by offering him or her an opportunity to become part owner.

DISADVANTAGES OF BEING SMALL

The individual owner faces some handicaps in managing a business and seeing that it succeeds. The owner must be good at everything so that he or she can raise needed capital and compete with larger companies for qualified employees.

Lack of Specialization Business today is very specialized. The individual owner does not have specialized skills in all areas of management. He or she is responsible for personnel, purchasing, finance, advertising, and daily operation. This puts the owner at a management disadvantage. A single owner may be inclined to overdo in his or her strong areas and neglect weak areas.

Raising Needed Capital Since the owner or a few persons furnish the capital, it is quite limited. Unlike the giant corporation, the small independent merchant cannot raise large sums. Cash flow may be sufficient for day-to-day operations. But when a major expansion is at hand, finding needed capital may be difficult.

Attracting Qualified Employees The small business may pay good wages, but it cannot offer the job security provided by large firms. Small businesses usually do not have education and training programs. They offer employees fewer fringe benefits, and promotion opportunities are limited. All of this puts them at a disadvantage in attracting the best-qualified workers. The higher the level of work to be done, the greater the disadvantage. College graduates, for example, prefer to work where there is good opportunity for advancement. The large companies have many more positions, and this makes promotions more likely.

FAILURES AMONG SMALL FIRMS

In every size of business—small, medium, or large—risks are involved. Unfortunately, too many businesspersons are unprepared to acknowledge risk as an important factor. They overestimate their own qualifications and assume they will succeed where others failed. Small firms are vulnerable to economic conditions, competition, and a poor location. As we examine the following reasons, it becomes apparent that there are also other causes of small-business failure.

MUST A BUSINESS BECOME BIG TO BE SUCCESSFUL?

Witco Chemical is a small specialized chemical company. Unlike the large glamour chemical companies such as Dow, Monsanto, and Du Pont, Witco makes its money by buying raw chemical stocks from the giants and manufacturing a line of specialty products which it markets.

"This is not a big company," says William Wishnick, son of Robert Wishnick, who founded the company before automobiles became popular. As a one-armed Russian immigrant, Robert in 1900 was earning his living peddling pots and pans from a wagon in Chicago. One day lightning caused his horse to bolt and run away, destroying his wares. Robert decided to sell chemicals, and Witco was born. Approaching ninety years of age, Robert is still an active member of the board of directors, with headquarters in New York City.

Some market analysts assert that the company's weakness is that it does not dominate its field. However, it is important to note that Witco is number one in the manufacture of white mineral oil used in cosmetics, plastics, and pharmaceuticals. William predicts that the company will soon have $1 billion in sales. "If more rapid growth is what we want," he says, "there are scores of good small specialty companies to buy."

Causes of Failure

Nationwide statistics involving business failures, gathered by the credit-reporting firm of Dun and Bradstreet, reveal that managerial inexperience is a major cause of small-business failure. Poor management is manifested in several ways:

1. Inability to manage and direct others
2. Lack of capital—often an indication of poor financial management
3. Lack of ability in sales promotion
4. Inability to collect bad debts and to curtail unwise credit policies

A detailed list of causes of business failure follows. (Several of these causes overlap, and some are closely identified with the owner's lack of experience and general ability.)

Specific Causes of Small-Business Failure

Insufficient Capital Structure:

Lack of capital to buy adequate stock and equipment
Insufficient capital to take advantage of special merchandise "deals"
Lack of capital to enable one to take merchandise discounts

Use of Obsolete Business Methods and Equipment:

Failure to maintain stock-inventory controls
Lack of credit controls
Inadequate financial and tax records

Absence of Business Planning:

Inability to detect and understand market changes
Failure to understand changing economic conditions
Failure to maintain plans for emergencies
Failure to anticipate and plan financial needs

Personal Qualifications:
Insufficient knowledge of the business
Unwillingness to work long hours when necessary
Failure to delegate responsibility and assign duties
Inability to maintain customer relations
Lack of tact in dealing with employees

Signs of Business Failure

How can a proprietor tell in advance that the business is showing signs of failure? Early signs include the following:

1. Declining sales over several accounting periods
2. Progressively higher debt ratios
3. Increased operating costs
4. Reduction in working capital
5. Reduction in profits (or increasing losses)

As these signs begin to converge, the threat of failure grows, and it becomes more evident that corrective action is necessary. Some positive steps include

1. Reducing operating expenses
2. Striving to improve sales, possibly through increasing advertising
3. Reviewing credit losses to eliminate poor risks
4. Reexamining stock inventories to determine whether they are excessive

Business Failures

In every kind of business, risk is present. But as a group, the probability of failing is significantly greater for small firms. Not all concerns that go out of business actually fail. About half just stop operating, mostly for such reasons as the retirement or death of the owner. Other firms have filed either a voluntary or an involuntary petition for bankruptcy.

Number and rate of failures. Statistics on the number and rate of failures tend to fluctuate from year to year. The failure rate among new businesses is greater than for those that have been established for some time. Figure 6-2 shows that 55.7 percent of business failures occur during the first five years of existence. Only 21.9 percent of business failures occur among firms that have been operating for at least ten years.

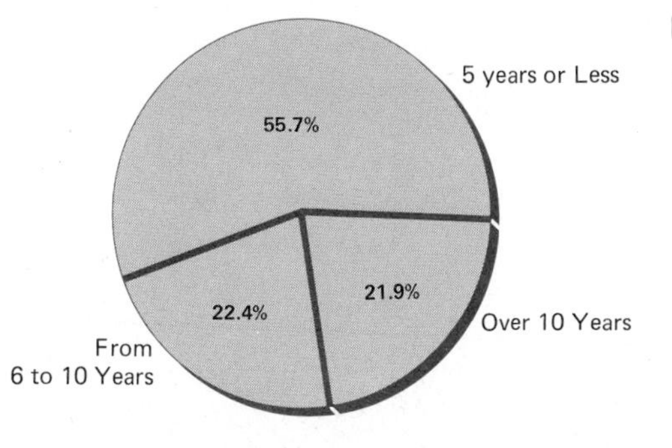

FIGURE 6-2
Business failures by age of firm.

Certain kinds of businesses are more vulnerable to failure than others. For example, small furniture-manufacturing companies have a high failure rate. Small machine shops have a low failure rate. In retailing, where small firms predominate, camera-and-photographic-supply shops and menswear stores have a high failure rate. Retail stores selling appliances, radios, and television sets tend to have a low failure rate.

FACTORS IN SMALL-BUSINESS SUCCESS

Most persons who decide to enter business for themselves have worked for others. They have a pretty good idea of the type of business they want to establish. They must draw upon their business experience in answering certain basic questions. The success of the business depends on answering the following questions correctly:

1. Do I have the breadth of experience needed to manage my own business?
2. Is there room for a new business in the chosen community?
3. Can I raise the capital needed to organize and operate the first year?
4. Is the sole proprietorship suitable for the type of business selected?
5. Do I possess strong emotional factors such as a passion for hard work and long hours?

Management Competence

In the preceding chapter you learned about many aspects of business management. Specifically, we identified what management does and we discussed certain qualities of leadership. Managing a small business requires the same functions as managing a large business. A person must decide if he or she has the competence to manage in all the areas concerned. These areas are the following.

Management Areas

Personnel	Merchandising
Physical facilities	Selling
Accounting	Advertising
Finance	Risk
Purchasing	Day-to-day operations

If a person lacks expertise in certain areas he or she must plan on hiring qualified people to fill those needs.

Determining Capital Needs

Studies show that inadequate capital is a major cause of small-business failures. The smaller the percentage of owner capital in a business, the greater the risk of failure. Capital includes both money used to start the firm and trade credit from manufacturers, wholesalers, and others. A general rule is that the owner furnishes at least two-thirds of the capital. No more than one-third should come from such sources as trade credit or loans.

In estimating capital requirements, a common error is to overlook funds needed for the first year of operation. Most new businesses are not profitable during the early years. One must plan on operating at a loss for a while. During this period the business operates out of capital, not profits. Even after becoming profitable, a given amount of what is called working capital must be available.[1]

Essentially the two capital needs of a business are working capital and fixed capital. Funds spent for goods, supplies, and wages must come from working capital. **WORKING CAPITAL** is defined as **the amount by which current assets exceed current debts.** It consists of cash on hand, demand deposits in banks, inventories of goods, and readily marketable securities that can be converted into cash immediately. It is temporary in nature. **FIXED CAPITAL** is **money invested in buildings, land, equipment, fixtures, and other assets that have a useful life of many years.** These assets are permanent and, in the ordinary course of operations, will not be converted into cash. Fixed capital may be financed by borrowing or from funds supplied by the owner. How much capital is needed depends upon the size of the firm, how the money will turn over, and how profitable the business is.

Capital requirements vary according to the size and kind of venture. Through the use of trade credit, it is possible to reduce the amount of cash supplied by the owner. For service-type firms, such as radio and television repair shops, capital needs may be reduced by cutting back on parts inventories. As a rule, repair parts are relatively easy to obtain on short notice on credit from nearby wholesalers or manufacturers. The general credit requirements to obtain a loan through the Small Business Administration are representative of credit requirements for trade credit as well.

General Credit Requirements

A loan applicant must

Be of good character.

Show ability to operate the business successfully.

Have enough capital in an existing firm so that, with an SBA loan, he or she can operate on a sound financial basis.

Show that the proposed loan is of such sound value or so secured as reasonably to ensure repayment.

Show that the past earnings record and future prospects of the firm indicate ability to repay the loan and other fixed debt, if any, out of profits.

Be able to provide from his or her own resources sufficient funds to have a reasonable amount at stake to withstand possible losses, particularly during the early stages, if the venture is a new business.

[1]Working capital is discussed in more detail in Chapters 14 and 17.

Businesspersons must determine the main sources of available capital in addition to their own. Business-formation capital is of two types: equity and debt.[2] For purposes of this discussion, **EQUITY CAPITAL** is **money invested in the business (by the owner) on which there is no legal obligation to pay interest.** For many small firms, equity capital is the primary source of money. **DEBT CAPITAL** is **money acquired by loan, for which the borrower is expected to return the principal with interest at some specified date.** Borrowing may be for the short term (such as a year) to finance seasonal peaks or long term (five to ten years). The total of equity and borrowed capital constitutes the total amount of fixed and working capital.

Need for a New Business

Established communities usually have most of the various types of businesses for which there is a demand. In fact the older established areas may be losing businesses. But any thriving community is expanding. And as new suburban residential areas grow, shopping centers are soon developed. It is in these new shopping centers that most new businesses are established. Before launching a new business in any area, one must determine if there is a demand for the type of enterprise being proposed. How strong is the competition in the area where one wishes to locate?

FAMOLARE—A SMALL-BUSINESS SUCCESS IN THE SHOE INDUSTRY

Joseph P. Famolare lives in Vermont. In 1974 he began marketing a shoe with a four-wave sole. The shoe with the wavy sole made a hit with young women, and company sales rose to almost $100 million in 1979.

Few of Famolare's acquaintances gave him any encouragement for his new idea in 1974. But it proved successful and profitable. His shoes are now made in twenty locally owned factories in Italy and are shipped to Boston by boat or to Hartford, Connecticut, by plane. They are warehoused in Brattleboro, Vermont.

Choosing the Form of Ownership

In Chapter 3 we discussed several forms of business ownership designed to meet the needs of all kinds of business enterprises, both large and small.

The simplicity of the sole proprietorship makes this form well suited to small firms. But under certain conditions, the partnership and corporate forms are also satisfactory for small-scale ventures. It is important to decide as early as possible which form to use. Here are some questions that you should ask yourself.

[2]Equity and debt capital are discussed in Chapters 14 and 19. The legal meaning is given in Chapter 19.

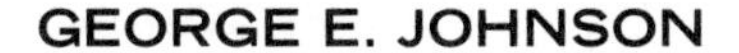

GEORGE E. JOHNSON

George E. Johnson believes that opportunity knocks at least once for every person. He was born in Richton, Mississippi, in 1927 and attended Wendell Phillips High School in Chicago.

Johnson is president and chief executive officer of Johnson Products in Chicago, a company he organized in 1954. The company manufactures over fifty different hair-care and cosmetic products under the Ultra Sheen and Afro Sheen brands. These products are sold throughout the United States and in selected foreign markets. Johnson Products is the largest black-owned manufacturing company in the United States. Since its organization, it has grown into a corporation with annual sales of $41.1 million.

Johnson received a doctor of business administration degree from Xavier University in May 1973. He is on the board of directors of the Commonwealth Edison Company, the Metropolitan Life Insurance Company, the Independence Bank of Chicago, and the Cosmetic, Toiletry and Fragrance Association.

Johnson has served the people of the city of Chicago in numerous ways. Among his main interests are the Chicago Area Council of Boy Scouts, Junior Achievement, the Urban League, Northwestern Memorial Hospital, and the Chicago Community Trust. He has received honorary doctorates from Chicago State University, Clark College, Fisk University, Tuskegee Institute, College of the Holy Cross, Lake Forest College, Babson College, and LeMoyne-Owen College.

Johnson married Joan Henderson in 1950, and they have four children.

How large is my business going to be? Your answer should be useful in determining how much working capital you will need. Should you invite a partner who would furnish some initial capital? If you need more than one partner, would it be better to form a corporation?

How much business risk does the venture involve? You know from your study of proprietorships and partnerships that each may involve unlimited liability. This is one of the reasons that some small firms incorporate.

What about the tax situation? Both the proprietorship and the partnership enjoy certain tax advantages. Each pays only a personal income-tax, at the individual tax rate, on net taxable income including business profits. A corporation, however, pays an income tax on profits, if any; and stockholders receiving cash dividends from the same profits pay a second, personal-income tax. In addition, the corporation may pay an annual franchise tax, and shareholders are subject to stock-transfer taxes.

Many small businesses are organized as a corporation under Subchapter S tax laws. There is a single owner-officer, which gives the limited liability advantage of a corporation, but a Subchapter S organization is taxed as a proprietorship.

A good example of starting a small business to fill a need is that of the Lexicon Corporation of Miami, Florida.

Anastasios N. Kyriakides is the founder and president of Lexicon. Kyriakides came to the United States from Greece when he was fifteen. He learned English while working in a bank and taking courses at Florida International University. Because of his experience in learning English the hard way, he saw the need for computer programs as an assist in learning an additional language.

Kyriakides enlisted the help of Michael Levy, an engineer specializing in microcomputer technology. Together they developed a hand-size computer for learning languages. When one punches out an English word or phrase on the keyboard, the equivalent word in French, Spanish, or some other language appears on a screen. Each language module offers a fifteen-hundred-word vocabulary. In addition to French and Spanish, modules are available for German, Italian, Portuguese, Chinese, Japanese, and Russian.

THE SMALL BUSINESS ADMINISTRATION

The federal government is very active in supervising the affairs of small businesses. In 1953 Congress passed the Small Business Act. This act created the Small Business Administration (SBA) to aid small businesses. The three major areas of assistance to small businesses are

1. Financial assistance
2. Management and technical assistance
3. Assistance in processing government contracts

Small Business Administration Loans

The Small Business Administration is empowered to

> make loans to enable small-business concerns to finance plant construction, conversion, or expansion, including the acquisition of land, . . . equipment, facilities, machinery, supplies, or materials; or to supply such concerns with working capital to be used in the manufacture of articles, equipment, supplies, or materials for war, defense, or civilian production or as may be necessary to insure a well-balanced national economy.

The maximum SBA loan to any one business is $350,000. The amount a business can obtain depends on the case it presents in its loan application. The amount may also be limited by the funds available at the time.

The SBA guarantees that eligible businesses will receive bank loans within certain limits. SBA loans for buildings, machines, and equipment may be for as long as fifteen years. Loans made to provide working capital are limited to six years.

In addition to business loans, the SBA makes disaster loans for up to thirty years. These cover such calamities as floods, earthquakes, and hurricanes. To receive a disaster loan, a business must be located in an area officially declared a "disaster area." The U.S. president or the secretary of agriculture may declare "disaster areas."

Still another type of SBA aid is the "economic opportunity" loan. These loans are made to low-income persons who have the potential ability to succeed in business. The standards for obtaining one of these loans are not as strict as those for regular business loans. The maximum "economic opportunity" loan to any one person is $50,000, and the term is for up to fifteen years. In 1972 this type of loan was extended to honorably discharged veterans of the Vietnam War.

Management and Technical Assistance

Each SBA field office is staffed with specialists in many areas of management. Their services are available to persons in established businesses as well as new business enterprises. The SBA has set up a system of reference libraries. These are available in the Washington office and in each regional office. They contain books, government publications, and other pamphlets, which deal with various aspects of management.

The SBA works with colleges and universities in setting up seminars and short courses. These deal with organizing, planning, staffing, directing, financing, and controlling in small businesses.

The Small Business Administration sponsors a group called SCORE (Service Corps of Retired Executives). This group consists of former business executives who make their skills available to small-business owners. Their services are on a part-time and voluntary basis. There is no charge for their services during the first ninety days. However, the small business that uses their services is expected to pay for their out-of-pocket expenses. SCORE volunteers call the attention of management to company weaknesses and offer suggestions on how to correct them.

In addition to these personal services, the SBA has published booklets dealing with almost every aspect of operating a small business.

Help in Securing Government Contracts

Under a "set aside" program, certain procurement orders may be earmarked for bidding by only small businesses. Under what is called the "production pool" arrangement, small firms may combine their bid where the order is too large for a single business.

SBA works with other government agencies with regard to subcontractors. Such agencies as the Defense Department and the Space Agency have regulations that apply to prime contractors. They must give small firms an opportunity to bid on subcontracts.

The Small Business Administration works closely with the Office of Minority Business Enterprise (OMBE).[3] Lists of such businesses who might bid on subcontracts are supplied to prime contractors.

SERVICE-TYPE BUSINESSES

More than one million business enterprises in the United States are classified as part of the "service trades." Service is an area of business in which small firms are the backbone of the industry. A **SERVICE BUSINESS** is one that is basically

[3]OMBE is discussed in Chapter 2.

labor oriented and provides services rather than goods. The chief areas for small businesses are listed below. In addition, there are many other kinds of "service trades," such as telephone-answering services and services provided by interior decorators, locksmiths, and accountants.

Service-Type Establishments

1. *Communication services*—telephone companies, and TV and radio stations
2. *Entertainment*—casinos, theaters, and sports
3. *Lodging services*—motels and hotels
4. *Personal services*—barber and beauty shops, dry-cleaning shops, photography studios, laundries, and funeral homes
5. *Real estate and insurance*—firms selling property and all forms of insurance
6. *Repair shops*—servicing appliances, radios, TVs, watches, furniture, and automobiles
7. *Restaurants*—cafeterias, coffee shops, and dining rooms
8. *Special business services*—bookkeeping and accounting, collection agencies, credit bureaus, and tax services
9. *Transportation*—automobile agencies, taxicab companies, household movers, and storage
10. *Rentals*—specialized home furnishings, lawn and garden equipment, and medical equipment
11. *Professionals*—attorneys, physicians, and technicians

The service sector is growing faster than other sectors of the economy. More than one-third of all business concerns sell services rather than products. The percentage of the consumer dollar spent for services is increasing (see Figure 6-3).

Nature of Service-Type Businesses

Service-type businesses possess characteristics not common to businesses that produce goods. To begin with, they serve limited markets, and as a result these service establishments have small trade areas. For example, beauticians operate mainly in beauty shops catering primarily to people residing in the local area.

Service establishments exist to perform a service. Few of them maintain much merchandise inventory, and therefore the amount of space needed is reduced. In most cases the sale of goods is incidental to the service function.

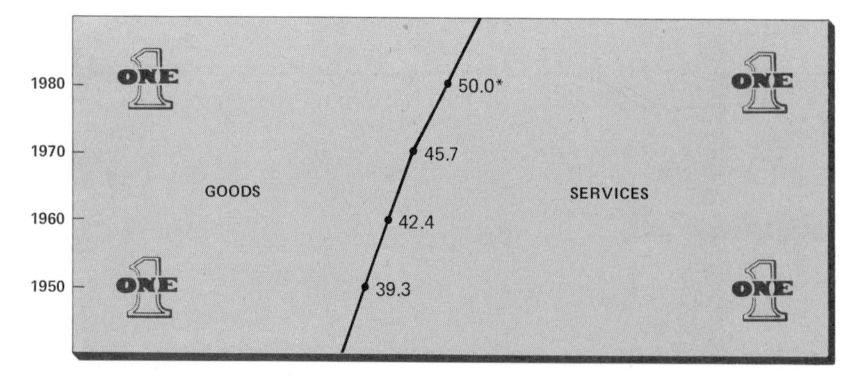

FIGURE 6-3

Percentage of consumer dollar spent for goods and services. (Source: Statistical Abstract of the U.S.)

The level of skill required to render a service is the dominant factor in determining its cost. Some services, such as renting equipment, do not require a high degree of skill. This type of service is relatively cheap. Others, such as making lenses for glasses or making dentures, require considerable skill. This type of service is relatively costly. A service business can start small and add personnel as business volume grows.

The basic charge for the service often includes more than just the direct service rendered. Take, for example, services rendered by electricians, plumbers, collection agencies, and household movers. The hourly labor charge assessed includes the cost of investment in trucks and other equipment used. It also includes an overhead percentage for operating the business office—rent, utilities, secretarial and accounting services, and, of course, a profit for the owner.

FRANCHISING

Franchising is probably the fastest-growing segment of retail business today. Franchising accounts for more than one-third of all retail sales and is growing at the rate of 12 percent per year. Franchising accounts for one-eighth of the gross national product. It is the frontier area in distribution where persons with limited capital may have their own businesses. The best-known example of franchising is the fast-food industry. McDonald's, Kentucky Fried Chicken, and so forth, are franchise operations. However, most car dealers operate under franchise contracts. This is also true of 80 percent of the gasoline service station operators. Franchising is also popular among motels, drugstores, car rentals, and auto-parts suppliers. The data in Table 6-1 show that franchising is indeed a major business form.

TABLE 6-1
FRANCHISING IN THE UNITED STATES

Item	Number
Franchise sales of goods and services	$300 billion
Employment in franchising (includes part-time workers)	5.1 million
Franchise businesses	500,000
Franchise outlets in foreign markets	16,200
Minority franchises	6,800
Percent of total retail stores in the United States accounted for by franchising	31%

SOURCE: U.S. Department of Commerce.

How Franchising Works

The **FRANCHISE** is **a legal licensing agreement between a manufacturer (or operating company) and a dealer for conducting business.** The licensing company is called the **FRANCHISOR**, and the dealer is called the **FRANCHISEE**. The Small Business Administration defines **franchising** as a system of distribution under which an individually owned business is operated as though it were part of a large chain, complete with product name, trademark, and standardized operating procedures.

The parent company (franchisor) permits the dealer to use its name and product, or service. The franchisor gives the local dealer an exclusive territory, counseling, new-employee training, and continuing supervision. National advertising, supplies, and materials are also furnished.

Start-up support may include any or all of the following:

1. Site selection
2. Building plans
3. Equipment purchases
4. Work flow pattern
5. Employee selection
6. Advertising
7. Graphics
8. Grand-opening help

Continuing supervision would include such factors as

1. Records and accounting
2. Consultation
3. Inspection and standards
4. Promotion
5. Quality control
6. Legal advice
7. Research
8. Materials sources

The franchise provides the management at the local level. This includes following established operational and merchandising methods. The franchisee is an independent businessperson. The International Franchise Association regards franchising as "a continuing relationship between the franchisor and franchisee. The sum total of the franchisor's knowledge, image, success, manufacturing, and marketing techniques are supplied to the franchisee for a consideration."

> McDonald's hamburger franchises are a good example of a successful franchise operation. Key to McDonald's success has been very careful control over the quality of the franchisee's operation. Inspectors from the franchisor check periodically to see that all operations are up to standard. McDonald's developed a school for training managers in "the McDonald's way" of doing everything from cleaning the floors to making shakes. This operation is referred to as Hamburger University.

The Contract Agreement

In a franchise, the legal basis of operation is the contract between the two parties. It is an ongoing relationship. However, the parent company may cancel the franchise if the franchise violates the terms of the agreement. The National Association of Franchised Businessmen compiles complaints from franchisees and publishes a list of tips for making franchising contracts. The exact terms of the franchise contracts differ, but in general they include the following provisions:

The Franchisor Agrees to	The Franchisee Agrees to
1. Assign an exclusive sales territory tory to the franchisee	1. Operate the business according to the rules and procedures offered by franchisor
2. Provide a stipulated amount of management training and assistance	2. Invest a stipulated minimum amount in the business
3. Furnish merchandise to the franchisee at a price competitive with the market	3. Pay the franchisor a certain amount (usually as a royalty on a fixed percentage)
4. Advise the franchisee on location of business and design of building	4. Construct or otherwise provide a business facility as approved by the franchisor
5. Offer certain financial assistance or financial advice to franchisee	5. Buy supplies and other standard materials from franchisor or an approved supplier

Some Pros and Cons of Franchising

Like any business, franchising has both advantages and disadvantages. It does not guarantee success. Like most other types of business, its success depends on the effort and skills of the manager. Let us look at some specific points regarding this type of retail operation.

Advantages. One of the major advantages is the training and direction provided by the franchisor. The initial training is followed by continuing supervision. A second advantage is the franchisor's financial help. Start-up costs are high, and the entrepreneur's sources of capital are often limited. If the prospect is considered a good risk, the franchisor often provides the franchisee with financial backing. This is particularly true of such franchisees as automobile dealerships. It is not true of fast-foods and other small investment companies. Furthermore, the franchisee has the benefit of using a recognized trade name, product, or brand title. Such names as Wendy's, Walgreen Agency, Dairy Queen, Holiday Inn, and NAPA are widely recognized. Since most small-business failures are attributed to lack of business know-how, this advantage of a good franchise is obvious.

Disadvantages. The training program some franchisors promise leaves much to be desired. The day-to-day details of operating the business are often omitted. Some franchise agreements allow the franchisees very little freedom to exercise their own ingenuity. Also they may find themselves tied in to a contract forbidding them to buy either equipment or provisions elsewhere. Franchisees seldom have the right to sell their businesses to a third party without first offering it to the franchisor at the same price. Most contracts allow the franchisees to leave it to a member of their family with approval of the franchisor. However, this family member must have the qualifications for a franchisee and must agree to the franchise contract.

WENDY'S STORY

R. David Thomas and his associates established Wendy's in 1969. Thomas describes himself as "a person who always liked good hamburgers." He decided to cater to a distinctive market of people who wanted a better product. He says: "Wendy's limited menu is really the main key to our success. It's so simple that our competitors think that it's complex. There's a limit to how much you can do well in this business. We concentrate on doing only a few things but we do them better than anyone else."

Origin: **The first Wendy's restaurant was opened in Columbus, Ohio, in 1969.**

Objective: **Provide the customer with a "Cadillac hamburger custom made" to the individual consumer's taste.**

Franchise fee: **The franchise fee is $15,000.**

Buildings: **Buildings and real estate are financed by local franchise owners.**

Training: **Two weeks of basic training are provided for new employees —one-week advanced management course for the franchisee and his or her store manager.**

Royalties paid by franchisee: Four percent of gross sales.

SUMMARY OF KEY CONCEPTS

The history of business in America is the history of the small-business enterprise.

Small firms account for 40 percent of all jobs in the field of business.

Although small businesses are most common in retailing, they play a major role in manufacturing and wholesaling.

Small businesses are characterized by independent management, relatively small capital requirements, and service to a small geographical area.

Small businesses enjoy an advantage over large businesses in the freedom of action in management, and flexibility in adapting to local needs and conditions.

Small firms are at a disadvantage in competing with large firms for capital, management specialization, and qualified employees.

Successful businesses must have sufficient working capital and managerial competence, and they must meet a need that exists in the community to be served.

The federal government has taken specific action to help small businesses. The Small Business Administration makes business and disaster loans, provides management and technical assistance, and aids in the procurement of government contracts. It also makes small loans to minority businesses.

Many businesses sell services rather than products. And a service business does not require capital investment for merchandise inventory. So small businesses are found in a wide variety of service, labor-dominated enterprises.

Franchising is a major part of retail merchandising. The franchisor supplies important training, management know-how, and supervision to franchisees.

BUSINESS TERMS

You should be able to match these business terms with the statements that follow:

a. Equity capital
b. Franchise
c. Franchisee
d. Franchisor
e. Lack of capital
f. Service business
g. Small business
h. Small Business Administration
i. Working capital

1. A business that is independently owned and operated and not dominant in its field
2. A common cause of failure among small businesses
3. Funds available to purchase supplies and materials, and pay salaries
4. Money invested in the business on which interest need not be paid
5. An agency created by the federal government to aid small-business firms
6. A business that is basically labor oriented and serves a local community
7. A licensing agreement between an operating company and a dealer
8. The dealer who grants the license in a franchise agreement

REVIEW QUESTIONS

1. What criteria must a business meet if it is to be classified as "small"?
2. How would you describe or characterize a small business?
3. What strengths are characteristic of small businesses?
4. What weaknesses are characteristic of small businesses?
5. In what chief areas does the SBA assist business enterprises?
6. What are the general provisions of the franchise agreement?

DISCUSSION QUESTIONS

1. If you wished to start a small business, how would you go about it?
2. What do you consider to be the chief advantage of a business's being small?
3. If you were starting your own business, what type of business would you organize and why?
4. What factors make for success in managing a small business?
5. Why are small firms so common in service-type businesses?
6. Why is franchising so popular in certain types of retailing?

BUSINESS CASE 6-1

Establishing A New Business

Robert Leach has been working as an automobile mechanic in Winchester, a community of forty thousand people in one of the southern states. He served as a repairman for six years and has been a supervisor for two years. For the past four months he has been thinking of going into business for himself. Robert has saved some money and has a rich uncle who he thinks will lend him some money. He would like to establish a business that sells auto parts and supplies.

To this point, Robert's plans include

1. Description and appraisal of market area
2. Analysis of competition
3. List of potential suppliers
4. Purchasing and pricing procedures
5. Personnel needed and their job descriptions

What important items are missing from Robert's plans?

BUSINESS CASE 6-2

An Expansion Decision

Teng Feng and his wife own and operate the R & K Flower Shop in a community near Chicago. The business specializes in manufacturing artificial flowers, using imported raw materials from Japan. This business has become widely known for its beautiful artificial orchids, roses, carnations, and gardenias.

Until recently, Teng's shop was the only one in his community with artificial flowers for sale. But now a local department store has started selling wax flowers imported from West Germany. Even though Teng's prices are about 10 percent higher than those of his local competitor, his sales volume has held constant. However, Teng knows that one or more of the four young women who make these flowers for him could resign and open their own store. It takes two years to qualify a trainee to produce a lifelike flower at the maximum production rate.

Recently a buyer from a national discount chain offered to buy from Teng annually up to 15,000 artificial orchids, 5,000 roses, and 10,000 gardenias. The price offered was a few cents per flower above Teng's present production cost. Teng believes he could reduce his present unit cost about 10 percent by adding four more employees. These workers would be carried for six months at a trainee wage, and in another six months they would be capable of producing a limited number of flowers, reaching peak production by the end of the second year. Although it might be difficult, Teng thinks he can find four young women to do this kind of work.

Teng questions whether this is the appropriate time to expand. It is an inflationary period, and prices are climbing. On the other hand, this may be a type of offer that will not come again soon. He knows there are some problems facing him. He would need more capital at a high rate of interest. He might not be able to find a sufficient number of trainees. Then there is the possibility of more competition from foreign sources. Is this the time to expand the business?

1. Prepare a recommendation for Teng regarding the issue before him. Support your position.
2. Does Teng have any alternatives open to him?

PEOPLE AND PRODUCTION

HUMAN RESOURCES MANAGEMENT

7

STUDY OBJECTIVES

WHEN YOU HAVE FINISHED READING THIS CHAPTER, YOU SHOULD BE ABLE TO

ONE Explain what personnel managers do

TWO Discuss the relationships between and among job analysis, job description, and job specification

THREE Identify the different aspects of employee staffing

FOUR Distinguish between a promotion and a job transfer

FIVE Describe some leading plans for paying workers

SIX List the different components of a sound staff maintenance plan

IN THE NEWS

Personnel Management Increases in Power and Importance!

Personnel or human resource problems are receiving increasing attention from corporate managers. A survey of over two thousand chief executives showed that 40 percent were spending from five to twenty hours a week on personnel matters. This compares with only 25 percent spending that much time five years ago.

Standard Brands, Inc., provides an example of how the emphasis has changed. In 1977 the personnel department at Standard Brands was composed of a director of labor relations and a director of benefits with a staff of twenty people. It routinely administered employment and dismissal procedures, handled labor negotiations, maintained records, and saw that paychecks were distributed on time. The department rated far below finance, marketing, and planning in power and influence.

Today the old personnel staff continues with its old functions but is now part of a larger Department of Human Resources, with four times as many staff members as formerly. The new department is headed by a corporate vice-president. Management realizes that its most important asset consists of having the right people in the right place at the right time.

This change in the personnel function at Standard Brands is similar to changes taking place in many other companies. These changes have been brought about by two major factors: the flood of new government regulations, and the skyrocketing cost of fringe benefits. Failure to understand and live with the government regulations has resulted in fines in the millions of dollars. With employees' wages much higher than five years ago, and with fringe benefits averaging an additional 35 percent of an employee's paycheck, employers have big investments in employees. They are more concerned than ever with reducing turnover and absenteeism and improving worker morale.

IN THE NEWS

America's most valuable resource is its intellectual capital. We believe a nation succeeds to the extent it encourages the full flowering of its talent.

C. PETER McCOLOUGH
Chairman and
Chief Executive Officer,
Xerox Corporation

Human resources make a business run! Without capital resources and an entrepreneur, there would be no business. But without people to help the owners run the business, nothing would be accomplished.

People do not automatically become productive employees. They must be recruited, hired, matched with the proper jobs, trained, appraised on their performance, and paid acceptable wages. Employees' working conditions must be monitored for safety, their activities coordinated, and records maintained on their performance. If these things are done properly, most people will be satisfied with their jobs.

The management of human resources or "personnel" has seen quite a change from its early days. When the need for a separate unit concerned with "people" problems was first recognized, personnel's role was quite limited. Early human resources management was primarily record keeping, planning the company picnic, and maintaining the retirement records. But the upper levels of management soon began to see the importance of a motivated competent work force. This has changed the role of personnel management in most companies. Furthermore, the federal government has enacted legislation dealing with every phase of human resources management. Hiring, test validation, compensation, child labor laws, health and safety, and pension funding are all subject to federal law. There are severe penalties associated with failure to live within the laws that govern these personnel activities.

Managers have found it necessary to upgrade and professionalize their methods in managing human resources.

Alcoa is an example of the extent to which a company will go to keep people happy when they are transferred. With the high cost of moving, high mortgage rates for new homes, and working spouses, many employees do not want to move.

Alcoa decided that it wanted to move a compensation analyst from Knoxville to Pittsburgh. But he refused to go unless his wife had a job in Pittsburgh too. Alcoa arranged an interview for his wife. It also gave the analyst an interest-free loan to buy a home, as well as an allowance to ease the difference between the old and new mortgage rates. And it paid all moving expenses.

Eastman Kodak and Atlantic Richfield both make an effort to line up jobs for spouses. Moving employees often means helping spouses find new jobs. A recent Merrill Lynch Relocation Management survey showed that 30 percent of the companies surveyed help spouses continue their careers.

Many companies pay cost-of-living adjustments for people being transferred to high-cost areas. State Farm pays managers an extra 37 percent in Anchorage, 27 percent in Honolulu, 26 percent in New York, 24 percent in Boston, 9 percent in San Francisco, 6 percent in Buffalo, and 5 percent in Washington, D.C. United Airlines pays 10 percent extra for employees in Hawaii, and J. C. Penney pays 20 percent extra in New York.

WHAT DO PERSONNEL MANAGERS DO?

Personnel or human resource managers are responsible for a wide variety of items related to people at work. The American Society for Personnel Administration and the Bureau of National Affairs made a study of the costs of various personnel activities. The sample included 227 U.S. businesses. This cost allocation serves as a useful guide in determining whether the personnel department, other managers, or no one is performing the activities. Table 7-1 shows their findings.

TABLE 7-1
WHAT PERSONNEL MANAGERS DO

	Percent of All Companies (N = 227)			
	Costs Allocated to Personnel Department			Costs Not Allocated to Personnel Dept.
Activity	All	Some	None	
Personnel records and reports	89	10	1	0
EEO/Affirmative action	80	15	2	2
Personnel research	79	7	1	12
Insurance benefits administration	75	20	4	0
Wage and salary administration	73	19	5	3
New employee orientation	68	24	6	2
Recruiting/hiring	65	27	7	1
Vacation/leave procedures	64	21	14	2
Pre-employment testing	63	7	5	25
Promotion/transfer/separation procedures	60	31	5	3
Pension plan administration	57	30	10	3
Health and medical services	56	23	14	6
Employee relations/discipline	54	38	5	4
Recreation/social/recognition programs	52	25	13	10
College recruiting	52	11	7	30
Employee communications	46	42	9	3

TABLE 7-1 (Continued)
WHAT PERSONNEL MANAGERS DO

Activity	Percent of All Companies (N = 227)			
	Costs Allocated to Personnel Department			Costs Not Allocated to Personnel Dept.
	All	Some	None	
Performance evaluation	46	32	11	11
Counseling programs	45	26	5	24
Tuition aid/scholarships	44	17	27	11
Union/labor relations	40	16	5	39
Human resource planning	36	30	6	28
Executive compensation	35	22	26	16
Supervisory training	34	44	19	3
Safety programs	34	35	25	6
Management development	33	43	17	7
Community relations/fund drives	33	41	20	5
Food services	33	8	34	25
Management appraisal/MBO	26	28	17	30
Suggestion systems	23	16	11	50
Security/plant protection	21	11	57	11
Skill training	13	38	40	9
Payroll processing	13	27	56	4
Administrative services (mail, messenger, etc.)	12	8	74	6

SOURCE: ASPA–Bureau of National Affairs Bulletin No. 33, December 8, 1977.

Notice in Table 7-1 that "equal employment opportunity/affirmative action" is a major responsibility of personnel departments. That item was of no concern to business fifteen years ago. Changes in federal laws have now made this a top-priority item.

THE ORGANIZATION AND PERSONNEL MANAGEMENT

The personnel function is handled differently in different businesses. In some businesses, all managers are to some extent responsible for the "people-oriented" activities. In others, major personnel activities are centralized in a personnel department. Studies show that as organizations expand, the personnel function becomes a major time requirement for managers. When this happens, the personnel function is usually centralized. Figure 7-1 shows how the personnel department may be given equal status with other departments in the organization.

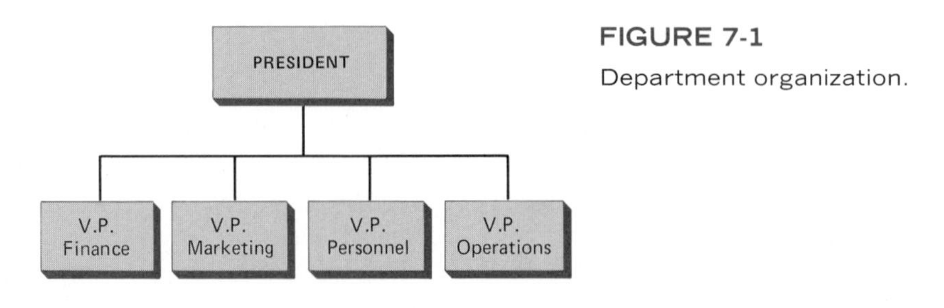

FIGURE 7-1
Department organization.

FIGURE 7-2
Department heads confer about a decision.

Human resources management is usually a staff function rather than a line function. The personnel manager has advisory authority rather than direct authority.

In a staff capacity, the personnel department assists other departments in hiring and training employees and in serving the needs of those employees. But final decisions on personnel matters are made by the department heads.

Sometimes the personnel department is given line authority. In this capacity it does not simply assist or serve other departments. Its staff makes the final decision in hiring, conducts specialized training, and decides who is to be promoted.

Regardless of the organization pattern used, certain personnel activities require considerable attention.

Critical Personnel Activities

In every business organization, certain personnel activities must be implemented to keep the work force productive and morale high. These activities are

Work analysis and design
Staffing
Training and development
Appraisal
Compensation
Maintenance

We will now consider each of these activities in some detail.

WORK ANALYSIS AND DESIGN

Before people can be recruited and selected for jobs, a business must know what work must be done. The way the work is to be divided and assigned to different jobs is the place to start.

A **JOB** is an organizational unit of work. A **job** is made up of a collection of tasks, assignments, duties, and responsibilities. A **position** is a specific work station occupied by the employee. Each employee occupies a particular position, but several positions may involve the same types of duties that make up any one job. The components that make up any job are shown in Figure 7-3.

Work or job analysis is the place to start a personnel examination because it focuses on what people do. The U.S. Employment Service defines **JOB ANALYSIS** as determining, by observation and study, pertinent information about the nature of a specific job. The specific tasks that constitute the job, along with the skills, knowledge, and abilities that are required of the worker, make one job different from all others. **Job analysis includes not only a study of the work itself but also an analysis of the conditions and environment in which the work is performed.**

From the standpoint of the personnel department, job analyses are made in order to

1. Evaluate the work station to see how it relates to other positions
2. Identify activities to be performed
3. Determine the requirements for measuring employee performance
4. Identify potential safety hazards
5. Identify basic information on operational procedures
6. Clarify lines of authority and responsibility
7. Provide the data needed for developing a job classification system
8. Make sure there is compliance with such legal regulations as those of the Fair Labor Standards Act

FIGURE 7-3
Job components.

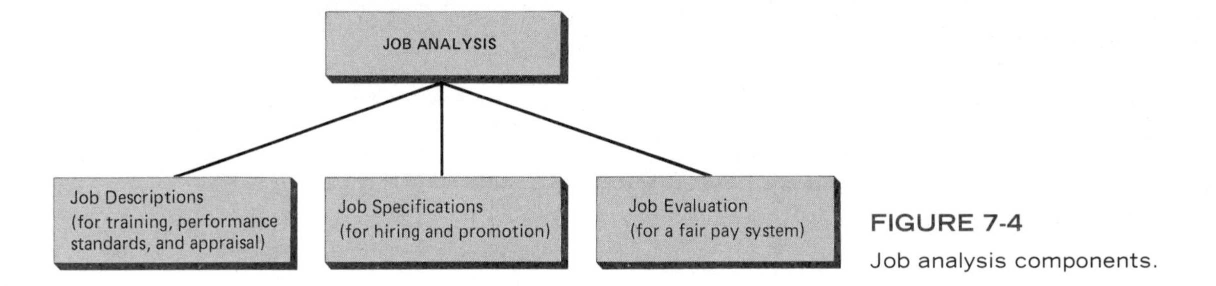

FIGURE 7-4
Job analysis components.

Data for making job analyses are obtained by interview and observation. Certain questions must be answered to give a true picture of the qualifications the worker needs to perform his or her tasks effectively. The information obtained from job analysis is used in one of three ways: for job descriptions, for job specifications, and/or for job evaluation. (See Figure 7-4.)

Job Description

The **JOB DESCRIPTION is a written description of what an employee is to do on a particular job.** Here is an illustration of a job description for a bookkeeper. By examining it you will note that it includes

1. The job title
2. Its distinctive characteristics
3. Specific tasks to be performed
4. The job's relation to other jobs
5. The skills, tools and equipment used, and how they are to be used
6. The materials and supplies used
7. The physical and mental skills required
8. Specific duties and responsibilities assigned to the job

JOB DESCRIPTION FOR BOOKKEEPER

Position ______________________

Incumbent: Patricia Johnson Hours ______________

Salary ______________ Date Job Analyzed: April 28 Date Employed ________

Position Summary

Incumbent is under the supervision of Office Manager: maintains accounting records for income from patient billings, and income payments by Medicare, Medical, and insurance companies; reviews and ages individual delinquent accounts and determines means for collecting payment. Prepares forms submitted to Medicare, Medical, and insurance companies for claims assigned by patients. Reviews accounts receivable preparatory to determining appropriate action for collecting delinquent accounts. Opens all incoming mail and deposits payments in the bank. Maintains daily cash receipts. Explains to patients the nature of the charges made if there is a question. Assists patients' preparation of Medicare, Medical, and insurance forms. Compiles information for submission to an outside agency for computerization of patients' account billings.

Skills: Uses calculating machine, typewriter, copy machine, and transcriber. Also has ability to relate to patient's anxieties and, where appropriate, refer case to the Social Worker. Knowledge of and experience in accounting essential. Understanding of Medicare, Medical rules valuable.

Specific Job Duties

Bookkeeping Duties:

1. Maintain proper records to record income from billings and health-care agencies
2. Perform daily posting to accounts-receivable accounts
3. Maintain a control account to verify patient billings
4. Submit billings for patient accounts. Provide data for use in computerized billing
5. Compile and analyze list of delinquent accounts
6. Submit assigned claims to Medicare, Medical, and insurance companies

Related Duties:

1. Refer delinquent accounts to collection agency
2. Compile daily records for medical doctors showing names of patients admitted and discharged that day
3. Explain the nature of the charges to patients who have complaints
4. Assist patients in completing their claim forms to health agencies
5. Refer special cases who may benefit from help from Social Worker regarding social problems

The description serves management as the basis for job placement and for training, appraising, and transferring employees.

Job Specification

A **job specification** describes the **qualifications** of the person, while the job description describes the job a person is to do. Here is a job specification for an elevator operator's job:

1. *Physical Requirements:*
   Good health.
2. *Education—Knowledge—Proficiencies:*
   Must have minimum of eighth-grade education.
3. *Work Experience:*
   No previous work experience necessary; however, a history of work performed in any capacity would be desirable.
4. *Aptitudes:*
   Should have the ability to learn and retain instructions.
5. *Personal Characteristics:*
   Should be emotionally stable and have the ability to adapt self to varying conditions and work harmoniously with other individuals.

Job Evaluation

A **job evaluation** compares a particular job with others to ensure that it is being fairly priced. Job evaluation can be done in different ways. But the most popular way is to break a job down into identifiable components and then assign points or weights to each component. Finally, each job in the company is evaluated in terms of those components. Factors that are often assigned points are skill, responsibility, effort, and working environment.

EMPLOYEE STAFFING

When it is clear what jobs have to be filled and what those jobs entail, the personnel manager can begin to fill them. Staffing consists of two parts: recruiting and selecting people.

Recruitment

RECRUITING is **the process of forming a pool of qualified applicants.** If the recruiting process provides only as many applicants as there are jobs, there is no **selection.** The company must either take what is available or leave the jobs unfilled.

There are several sources for recruiting new employees:

Present employees
Friends of employees
Former employees
Former applicants
Colleges and universities
Vocational schools
Employment agencies
Labor unions

Recruiting can be done through personal contacts, newspapers, magazines, TV or radio ads, and so forth. When a sufficiently large pool of applicants exists, selection can take place.

Selection and Placement

We have seen that job analysis is the first step in the wise selection of workers. By making use of information obtained during the analysis, the personnel department can carry out the important task of selecting new workers and placing them in the jobs for which they are best qualified. So the next step might be called **applicant analysis.** Employees must be selected without regard to race, sex, religion, or age; that is, business must comply with equal employment opportunity laws.

Application forms.

Almost every business uses some type of application form to obtain information for the applicant's personal file (see Figure 7-5). Such information as name, education, age, address, and telephone number is always included.

The would-be employee's history of work experience is probably the most important information provided by the application form. This record indicates more than the type and extent of the applicant's experience. It also shows whether the applicant sticks with an assignment or changes jobs frequently.

Application forms and interviews could be used to discriminate against protected classes of people. Therefore all questions must be job related. People who have been discriminated against include those in the forty-to-seventy age bracket.

People are living longer in our society, and the average age of the work force is increasing. Table 7-2 lists the life expectancy figures for men and women who are fifty years of age and older.

Job Application Form

File No.__________ Date ________

PERSONAL DATA

PRINT NAME

NAME __________ (MAIDEN NAME) __________
First Middle Last

FULL NAME OF SPOUSE __________ PERSON TO NOTIFY IN CASE OF ACCIDENT? __________ TEL. NO.

APPLYING FOR POSITION AS __________ WHEN AVAILABLE? __________

PHONE NO. __________ SOCIAL SECURITY NO. __________ SALARY OR WAGES EXPECTED __________

PRESENT ADDRESS __________
Street City State Period of Residence

LAST PREVIOUS ADDRESS __________
Period of Residence

BIRTHDATE __________ AGE* ______ SEX* ______ PRESENT EMPLOYMENT STATUS __________

*Note: This information may be asked for but discrimination because of sex prohibited by Federal law. Also, discrimination by age prohibited by law in states with Fair Employment Practices.

☐ SINGLE ☐ ENGAGED ☐ DIVORCED
☐ WIDOW(ER) ☐ MARRIED ______ YEARS

HOW MANY DEPENDENTS? ______ NUMBER, AGES, SEX OF CHILDREN __________

REFERENCES

NAMES OF THREE PERSONS, NOT RELATIVES, FORMER EMPLOYERS, OR PERSONNEL OF THIS COMPANY WHO HAVE KNOWN YOU FOR AT LEAST TWO YEARS, ALSO NAME OF BANK WITH WHICH YOU DO BUSINESS

NAME	ADDRESS	BUSINESS AND POSITION	TELEPHONE (If known)

U. S. MILITARY SERVICE

VETERAN OF U.S. ARMED FORCES? ☐ YES ☐ NO RESERVE STATUS __________ DRAFT STATUS __________

BRANCH __________ SERIAL NO. __________ DATE ENTERED __________ RANK ON ENTERING __________

DATE OF DISCHARGE __________ RANK AT DISCHARGE __________ TYPE OF DISCHARGE __________

IN WHAT THEATERS DID YOU SERVE? __________

MAJOR DUTIES __________

SERVICE SCHOOLS AND OTHER SPECIAL TRAINING __________

EDUCATIONAL DATA

SCHOOLS	NAME AND ADDRESS OF INSTITUTION	DATES FROM — TO Mo.-Yr. Mo.-Yr.	GRADUATED Yes — No	DEGREE RECEIVED	AVERAGE GRADES	AREAS OF SPECIALIZATION
GRADE SCHOOL				—		
HIGH SCHOOL				—		
COLLEGE						
GRADUATE SCHOOL						
TRADE, BUS., NIGHT OR CORRES-PONDENCE						
APPRENTICE SHIPS			—	—		
OTHER						

Form B published by Shepherd Associates, Personnel Consultants, P. O. Box 846, Fort Worth, Texas

FIGURE 7-5
Typical application form.

As people's life expectancy increases, they will choose to work longer. Therefore companies have had to change their former ways of viewing this valuable group of employees. Nearly 25 million Americans are over sixty-five, and that number will increase in the future.

For many years race and sex discrimination cases overshadowed age discrimination. However, the Standard Oil Corporation recently agreed to a $2 million settlement for 160 older workers who were laid off because they were older. The potential for more age discrimination cases in the courts has increased with the passage in 1978 of the Age Discrimination Act.

TABLE 7-2
LIFE EXPECTANCY FOR MEN AND WOMEN

Present Age	Men	Women
50	24.5 years	30.4 years
55	20.6	26.2
60	17.0	22.1
65	13.9	18.3
70	11.1	14.7
75	8.7	11.6
80	6.9	9.0
85	5.5	6.9

Life expectancy is the average number of years of life remaining for persons of a given age. Women at age 50 live almost six years longer than men but at age 85 they are expected to live slightly more than one year longer.

The Employment Interview

Very often the next step in the selection process is to interview the applicant. The chief purpose of the interview is to gather additional information about the applicant to validate answers to any or all questions on the application form. The interviewer attempts to discover how the applicant might fit into the organization and what his or her attitude would be toward the job. The interviewer also explores the applicant's attitude toward work in former jobs, ability to express himself or herself clearly, and personal traits and characteristics. In order to match the right person with the right job, the interviewer attempts to determine the kind of job that would suit the personality and competence of each applicant.

The interview is intended to achieve yet another important function—supplying the applicant with information about the firm, such as its policy on salaries and promotions, working hours and conditions, and skills required.

The usual practice is to conduct a preliminary interview and later a follow-up interview. The purpose of the preliminary interview is to size up the applicants in a general way and to eliminate those who obviously would not fit into the company. This interview may take place even before the application form is completed. The follow-up interview may take place just before the worker is finally accepted or rejected. For this interview, specific items may be covered to ensure that critical questions are not overlooked.

Here are ten questions that help interviewers organize their thinking and reinforce their decisions when hiring new workers:

1. What is the applicant's real reason for changing jobs?
2. Does the previous work record show stability?
3. Is the level of ambition compatible with the job requirements?
4. What has the applicant accomplished on his or her own?
5. Is the applicant's attitude toward former employers positive?
6. Is the applicant's experience favorable?
7. Does the applicant leave a positive or a negative impression?
8. Are there any outward signs of physical limitations—excessive weight, nervousness, chain smoking?
9. How much does the applicant know about his or her own abilities?
10. Are interview impressions consistent with the applicant's work-history record?

Joan Manley

Joan Manley became the publisher of Time-Life Books, not by accident, but by design. She graduated from the University of California in 1954 with a degree in English. Even then she knew that her career goal was focused on book publishing.

Mrs. Manley had the foresight to develop her secretarial skills as an entry into the job market. Although her first job title was that of secretary for Doubleday, she worked in book sales. Her outstanding work in that area soon caught the attention of her superiors. In 1960 one of them, Jerome Hardy, started a new program—Time-Life Books, for Time Inc.—and he offered her a position as his assistant. By 1970 her talents for increasing sales earned her the title of publisher. In 1971 she became the first woman to serve as a vice-president of Time Inc. Mrs. Manley is now group vice-president for books and is also responsible for overseeing the Book-of-the-Month Club, Little, Brown and Company, and the New York Graphic Society, which are owned by Time Inc.

Joan Manley knows that it takes more than just hard work to succeed in management. She says that "a chief executive's problem is always in the future, not in the present." This requires planning for the future, but adjusting and correcting those plans as new developments dictate. This also points up the importance of choosing key personnel correctly. In training her associates, she believes in "maximizing their individual assets—give them maximum freedom but with direction." Mrs. Manley was eager to "serve time" in the various positions she has occupied. She believes in preparing oneself well before accepting new responsibilities.

Tests in Selection

Selection tests can be of two types, aptitude and ability. An **APTITUDE TEST checks on the potential a person has for a certain kind of work.** Aptitude tests and other indirect tests such as IQ or personality tests must be **validated.** That is, the firm must be able to demonstrate that a high score on such a test is related to good performance on the job. Invalid selection tests not only are useless but may discriminate against certain minority groups, and therefore they are illegal. An **ABILITY TEST determines what one can do—not what one's potential might be.** A good example of an ability test is a typing test. These tests must be related to job skills. But establishing validity for ability tests is easier than for aptitude tests.

The physical examination. The company must know whether a potential employee is physically able to perform the work called for in the job assignment. The job might require constant standing, manipulative skills, or keen eyesight.

At one time an applicant was expected to "pass" the physical examination, so that the physician could certify good health. Today the physical examination is used primarily to discover any impairments that might prevent satisfactory performance on the job. This would include not only the job for which a person is applying but also those to which he or she would likely be promoted or transferred. The steps in the employment procedure are illustrated in Figure 7-6.

TRAINING AND DEVELOPMENT

Most managers strongly support employee development. The lower the job level, the greater the available labor supply. Positions that demand the highest skill and specialization often go unfilled for lack of available applicants.

Orientation sessions are one way to familiarize new employees with company policies and procedures. As a part of one's orientation, a person is trained to perform the basic operations essential to the job. The most common types of training are on-the-job training, apprenticeship training, and vestibule schools.

Supervisory training. Because of the greater educational preparation needed for an increasing number of jobs, supervisors must have special preparation for their work. They must possess competencies that exceed those of the personnel whom they supervise.

Supervisory training is basically leadership training in orientation, administration, human behavior, technical knowledge, and instruction. Employees who rank high in desirable personal qualities, who get along well with others, and who exert leadership in group situations are those most often promoted to supervisory positions. Supervisory personnel may be given released time to attend classes, or such classes may be held after the regular workday. In some instances, companies pay tuition and book costs at local colleges or universities.

Executive development. Managers are made, not born. True, they must possess the right personal qualities to become leaders. But as they gain experience, learn the business, and earn promotions, they find themselves a part of company management. Their preparation may include a period of apprenticeship in one or more junior-management positions. But this is usually supplemented by formal courses. Universities offer seminars and workshops for persons who are newly appointed to top-executive positions.

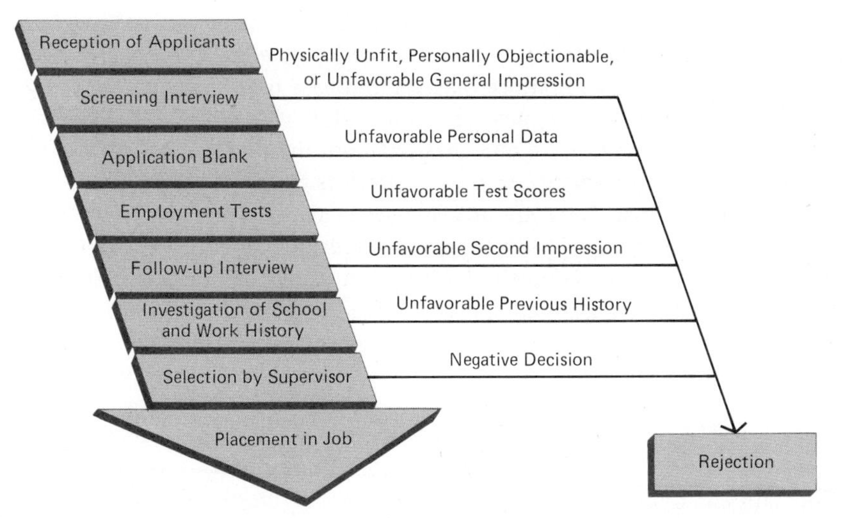

FIGURE 7-6
Selection and employment procedure.

Assessing training needs. It is almost a truism that if some training and education is good, more training and education is better. However, businesses that have sophisticated training efforts tailor them to each person's needs. This is done through a careful assessment of an employee's needs and potential. One good way to assess training needs is to compare performance on the job with the standards outlined in the job description. The manager can then pinpoint areas for improvement and can develop programs to help people improve their performance.

APPRAISAL

One of the most important personnel activities consists of evaluating employees' performance. If employees do not know how their performance compares with what is expected of them, how can they improve? Yet this is also one of the most neglected personnel activities. It is common to hear managers say "They know how they are doing, why should I have to tell them?" Many studies, however, have shown that employees *do not know* how they are doing unless they are told regularly.

Managers resist giving performance appraisals because they can be unpleasant. It is no fun to tell employees they are doing poorly. But it "comes with the territory" and is an important part of managers' work. The personnel department usually helps devise the appraisal system that will be used in the firm. One's immediate supervisor is usually responsible for doing the appraisal.

Multiple ratings. There is considerable evidence that ratings made by one's peers differ greatly from those made by one's superiors. Similarly, there are differences between self-ratings and those made by superiors. Self-ratings seem to overrate ability to get along well with others. Ratings by superiors give more weight to such qualities as initiative, loyalty, and knowledge of one's work.

Self-ratings lead to improved performance in one's assignment, and peer appraisal aids in identifying people with leadership ability. The current trend is toward using a combination of self-ratings, peer judgment, and appraisal by superiors, thereby providing balance in appraisal. The knowledge that superiors are also making appraisals tends to reduce bias and increase objectivity in the ratings made by oneself and one's colleagues. The chief value of the triple-rating procedure is that it provides much more information about the person being evaluated than could be obtained through appraisal by superiors only.

Research shows that there are advantages to using more than one rater. Averaging together the ratings of several persons reduces the effect of a particular rater who may have been prejudiced. A high rating given by an unusually kind and considerate manager might be counterbalanced by one from a manager who emphasizes production success. People who have a wide knowledge of the work and behavior of the person being rated make the best and most reliable evaluations.

Promotion. The term **PROMOTION** refers to **the shifting of an employee to a new position in which both one's status and responsibilities are increased.** Promotions are advantageous to the firm as well as the employee. Management knows that deserving employees have been taken care of, that workers are situated where they can produce the most, and that the cost of orienting and training new people has been reduced. An employee should not be given a promotion when it has not been earned or when others are better qualified or more deserving. When two employees are equally deserving when judged on ability and performance, the promotion usually goes to the person who has been with the company longer. This person is said to have **seniority.**

An advancement in pay that does not involve a move into a new job classification is called a *horizontal promotion.* **An advancement that moves an employee into a job with a higher rank or classification is called a** *vertical promotion.*

If management is to avoid a labor unrest and turnover, it must develop a systematic policy for promotions. Qualified employees become dissatisfied and leave if few opportunities for advancement exist or if promotions are not based on merit.

Transfer

The term **TRANSFER** refers to **the shifting of an employee from one position to another without increasing his or her duties, responsibilities, or pay.** Every business finds it necessary to transfer workers. If workers have been assigned to a job on which their work is unsatisfactory, they may be shifted to another. There are times, too, when the workload is heavier in some departments than in others, or when it is desirable to rotate workers into and out of dangerous positions. Occasionally a transfer is necessary because of personal differences among employees, or because of personality conflicts between workers and supervisors. Workers are often transferred to new communities in order to place employees where they are needed.

When a transfer must be made, management should have justifiable reasons and be certain that the employee will not suffer hardship as a result. Management should tell employees why they are being transferred, and whether their transfers are permanent or temporary.

COMPENSATION

Employee rewards are of two types—financial and nonfinancial. Salary payments are financial rewards and include such forms as insurance coverage, profit sharing, and pensions. Nonfinancial rewards include good working conditions, recognition for exceptional achievement, and other types of job benefits. In this section we will focus on types of monetary payments. If workers are underpaid, they become dissatisfied. If they are overpaid, a company's products may be overpriced in a competitive market.

Equity

An important issue in a pay or compensation system is equity. **EQUITY** refers to **the extent to which employees think a pay system is fair.** If a pay system is viewed as unfair (a lazy or poor worker getting the same raises as better workers, for example), it usually results in a reduction of effort on the job.

Salary and Wages

Most workers in the United States today are paid either a salary, hourly wages, or piece wages. A **salary** is usually expressed in annual terms and is not dependent on the number of hours worked. **Hourly wages** are based on the number of hours spent working. **Piece wages** are based on the number of units produced.

Salary.

Most management and many other white-collar jobs are salaried jobs. There is something of a status symbol associated with salaried work rather than drawing hourly wages. However, salaried individuals may be required to work overtime without additional pay.

Hourly wages.

For some types of work, it is more practical to base wages on the nature of an employee's responsibilities rather than on his or her productivity. In fact, it is often impossible to measure an employee's output objectively. When quality rather than quantity is important, or where the employee is continually interrupted, hourly wages are appropriate. Hourly wages have one disadvantage—they may encourage employees to do less than a "full day's work."

Piece wages.

Under the piece-rate payment plan, a certain sum is paid for each unit a worker produces. The unit payment may be based on the output of an individual worker, or it may apply to the work of a group or even an entire department. Encouraging the workers to "supervise" themselves decreases supervisory costs.

When great emphasis is put on quantity, there is a tendency for workers to sacrifice quality. So management must exercise control over the quality of the units produced.

The wage-price spiral.

Price rises due to inflation have led to increases in what is called the wage-price spiral. It works like this. As prices go up, workers become more determined to maintain their purchasing power. They make wage demands that in turn worsen the rate of inflation which they are trying to outrun. Consider this example.

Eagle-Pitcher Industries of Cincinnati manufactures concrete sewer pipe, auto and truck parts, and other such items. During the 1979—80 recession, sales of these items slumped. Normally one would expect workers to moderate their wage demands under such conditions so they could keep from being laid off. But John W. Painter of Eagle-Pitcher noted that when going into labor negotiations the overriding concern of employees was maintaining their standard of living, not losing their jobs.

Rising labor costs put pressure on businesses to increase their prices in order to maintain their profit margins. The net effect is an upward movement of the wage-price spiral. There is considerable debate as to whether rises in prices or raises in wages give the greatest impetus to the spiral.

Legislation Affecting Compensation

Several major laws can affect the compensation systems a business firm may choose. They are

The Fair Labor Standards Act
The Equal Pay Act
The Walsh-Healey Act
The Davis-Bacon Act
State laws

The Fair Labor Standards Act set a **minimum wage** to be paid to a broad spectrum of employees. Executive, professional, and administrative employees are **exempt** from the act. Government employees are also exempt. The FLSA also contains overtime pay requirements. Generally, pay at one and one-half times the hourly rate is required for time worked over forty hours in any one week.

The Equal Pay Act is an attempt to prohibit wage discrimination based on sex. According to the act, "men and women performing equal work in the same establishment under similar conditions must receive the same pay if their jobs require equal skill, equal effort, and equal responsibility." Corning Glass recently had to pay $1 million in back wages to women under the Equal Pay Act, and AT&T paid over $30 million for violation of this act.

The Walsh-Healey Act requires federal supply contractors to pay a minimum wage. Its formula for calculating overtime differs slightly from that of the FLSA.

The Davis-Bacon Act affects federal construction projects. It requires firms engaged in federal construction to pay the **prevailing wage rate** in the local community. That rate is frequently defined as the average union rate for the local area where the construction is taking place.

State laws tend to cover workers who are not covered by federal laws, especially those in intrastate commerce. A recent survey showed that thirty-nine states and the District of Columbia have their own minimum-wage laws.

Payment Plans

Some firms have set up wage-payment plans designed to reward the worker with added compensation for exceptional performance. Known as wage-incentive plans, they are based on the piece-rate method of making wage payments.

Incentive plans.

Incentive plans are especially appropriate (1) when labor costs are heavy in a cost-competitive market and (2) when production technology is not well advanced.

In 1895 Frederick W. Taylor developed the first wage-incentive plan, now known as the *Taylor Differential Piece-Rate Plan.* Here is how it works. First, a careful scientific study is made of each worker's operations. Then a standard rate of output is established that is within the reach of the average worker. Two rates prevail—one for the worker who fails to reach the standard, and a higher rate for the worker who exceeds it. For example, if the standard output is 100 units per day, a worker who produces fewer than 100 units might receive $0.55 per unit. A worker who exceeds 100 units might receive $0.58 per unit. The worker who produced 98 units would receive $53.90 for a day's work, whereas the worker who produced 105 units would earn $60.90.

A second wage-incentive plan is the *Gantt Task and Bonus System.* Under this plan, if an employee exceeds the set standards by completing the work in less time, he or she receives as a bonus a percentage of the base rate. The bonus is usually figured on a sliding scale, varying from 15 to 35 percent of the base rate. A worker who fails to complete the task in the time allotted receives only the regular hourly rate. There are two special features of this plan:

1. The bonus rate usually begins when the worker does three-fourths as much as the standard. This encourages those who are striving to reach the standard, as well as those who have already passed it.
2. The supervisor is usually given a bonus also, depending upon the amount or number of bonuses paid to the workers he or she supervises.

Two other types of wage-incentive plans are the Halsey and Rowan plans. For both, a standard time is allowed for the completion of a job. If the worker completes the task in less than the allotted time (standard), he or she is given a percentage bonus payment based on the time saved.

A well-conceived wage-incentive plan will include the following objectives:

For management:

1. Lowered costs resulting from increased productivity
2. Improved cost control, leading to production that is more consistent, more uniform, and less variable in actual cost
3. Improved utilization of facilities
4. Improved worker morale, as earnings become proportionate to individual effort

For employees:

1. An opportunity to earn money in excess of base rate and in proportion to individual effort
2. An opportunity for individual recognition
3. An opportunity for a healthful competitive spirit among employees
4. An opportunity for employees to control (at least partially) the level of their standard of living by their own initiative.

Employee profit sharing. **PROFIT SHARING** refers to **wage-payment plans that provide remuneration beyond basic pay schedules.** These extra payments go to all employees, and the amounts are tied directly to the profits earned. The Council of Profit-Sharing Industries has defined **profit sharing** as "any procedure under which an employer pays or makes available to all regular employees, in addition to regular rates of pay, special current or deferred sums based on the profits of the business."

The basic philosophy of profit sharing is to create a "partnership relationship" among employees. It draws labor and management closer together and develops a working relationship and atmosphere favorable to efficient workmanship. Those who advocate profit sharing claim that it creates high employee morale, reduces the number and extent of employees grievances, reduces labor turnover, provides greater security for workers, and improves public relations.

There is, of course, a wide variety of practices in profit-sharing programs. Some plans provide for cash payments. Others provide for deferred payments, which are frequently tied to the issuance of stock. Some of the factors entering into the structure of a profit-sharing plan are

1. Whether the percentage to be paid is a fixed or a sliding rate
2. Whether the percentage is to be applied to profits before or after taxes
3. The amount of the profits to be shared

Eastman Kodak's profit-sharing plan is determined by the amount of the cash dividend paid on the common stock. Employee bonuses are paid on the basis of individual yearly earnings.

One of the best-known plans is that of the Lincoln Electric Company of Cleveland. In this system, each job is evaluated to establish its importance to the company's operations. Then a pay rate is established for each. Workers are rated twice a year and then graded on the quality and quantity of their work, skill, and attitudes. These ratings determine the amount of bonus each worker will receive in relation to his or her base salary.

Labor unions look with disfavor on wage-payment plans that encourage competition among the workers. Union leadership prefers plans that are applied throughout the plant. Union leaders also oppose plans that reward only for increased productivity that results directly from increased personal effort. They feel that wage-incentive plans should also reward workers for increased output based on factors other than a worker's personal skill and effort.

Production-sharing plans. **PRODUCTION SHARING** is similar to profit sharing, for such programs use the cooperative efforts of management and labor. **Rather than shared profits, they represent a sharing of savings that result from reducing production costs.** Savings from production are not the only factors that determine company profits. So it is easier to relate an individual's efforts to the results of a small group.

One of the best-known production-sharing plans is the *Scanlon Plan.* This plan emphasizes the sharing of production savings with *all workers.* It was developed in 1937 by Joseph Scanlon to reduce costs in a steel mill where Scanlon was a union representative. The plan has two basic features:

1. The use of departmental committees to determine the amount of cost savings
2. A direct payment to the workers as a reward for increased efficiency

The basic philosophy of the Scanlon Plan is that more efficient plant operation rests on cooperation from the entire team of company employees.

Under the *Rucker Share-of-Production Plan,* both company and workers share the increased value of goods produced, which results from the joint efforts of management and workers. This plan includes all hourly employees, not just those whose work can be measured. The standards are not based on the number of physical units produced, but on the ratio of sales income to the cost of labor input. It also shows a worker the relationship between the dollars the worker earns and the economic value of the goods he or she helps produce.

The *Kaiser Long-Range Sharing Plan* has received much attention in recent years because it has several unique characteristics. To discourage worker resistance to modern equipment, the plan provides protection against layoffs resulting from increased mechanization. It also encourages vast reduction in materials and supplies as a factor in reducing the cost of production. The profits that thereby result are shared with the workers.

Actually, production sharing is more than a way of giving monetary compensation to workers. It represents labor-management cooperation. In some cases, such as under the Scanlon Plan, the awards for suggestions that improve production efficiency are paid to the group rather than to the individual who submits the suggestions. The emphasis is on teamwork for the benefit of all. With teamwork, production increases of as much as 50 percent have been achieved.

Fringe Benefits

The practice of awarding fringe benefits to employees has grown tremendously during the past two decades. New types of benefits are added each year, and collective-bargaining contracts with unions deal as much with benefits as with direct wage payments.

The earliest benefits to be provided were payments for holidays and vacation periods. Then came hospitalization, legal aid, life insurance, income-tax counseling, subsidized lunches, education payments, sick leave, supplemental unemployment payments, and retirement plans. Currently businesses pay an average of 37 percent of their total payroll in the form of fringe benefits. When the average of weekly earnings was $268.00, the total employee benefits package was $98.81. The significance of this can be seen by considering that a person making $14,000 a year is getting an additional $5,180 in fringe benefits.

Cafeteria-type benefits offer employees the opportunity to choose their individual fringe benefits. The company usually provides a minimum "core" of life and health insurance, vacations, and pensions. The employee buys additional benefits to fit his or her needs with credits earned.

Conoco in Greenwich, Connecticut, has been testing a cafeteria benefits plan among its 731 salaried employees. Ultimately this plan will be offered to all 48,000 employees. The core coverage includes 80 percent of covered medical expenses, $20,000 to $50,000 of life insurance (based on salary), accident insurance, one to five weeks' vacation, and disability benefits.

Employees can then "spend" credits based on their annual salary for more fringes. Most employees choose additional medical coverage; higher life insurance coverage; and hearing, vision, and general health insurance options. Other options could be prepaid legal insurance, group auto insurance, homeowners' insurance, or day care for children. Employees who do not want these options do not have to buy them.

Table 7-3 lists the fringe-benefit costs for a recent year for various industries.

TABLE 7-3
WEEKLY EMPLOYEE BENEFIT COSTS BY INDUSTRY

	Per employee per week
All Industries	$ 98.81
Manufacturing:	
Petroleum industry	148.37
Chemicals and allied industries	124.21
Transportation equipment	121.56
Primary metal industries	112.98
Machinery (excluding electrical)	107.08
Electrical machinery, equipment, and supplies	98.13
Fabricated metal products (excluding machinery and transportation equipment)	98.06
Stone, clay, and glass products	94.29
Instruments and miscellaneous products	93.06
Printing and publishing	91.04
Food, beverages, and tobacco	90.63
Pulp, paper, lumber, and furniture	88.67
Rubber, leather, and plastic products	77.73
Textile products and apparel	53.58
Nonmanufacturing:	
Public utilities	128.48
Miscellaneous (research, engineering, education, government agencies, mining, construction)	113.81
Banks, finance, and trust companies	93.96
Insurance companies	92.12
Wholesale and retail trade	71.52
Hospitals	58.69
Department stores	55.12

SOURCE: U.S. Chamber of Commerce.

Compensation for Management

Today's wage-incentive plans for workers are not as popular as they were two decades ago. However, wage-incentive plans for managers are very popular. Research shows that for managers, pay is a strong incentive for exceptional service when it is directly related to effective performance. A study of five hundred managers at all levels, covering a wide variety of organizations, showed that the majority are concerned with how their salary is divided between cash and fringe benefits. These fringe benefits are usually not taxed. So the more the manager gets in benefits rather than wages, the less tax he or she pays.

The **STOCK-OPTION PLAN** is popular today as a device for rewarding top management. Under this plan, **management personnel are permitted to buy company stock at some future time at the market price of the stock on the date the option was granted.** This plan is viewed as a means by which a company can induce valuable officers to remain with the company.

But a single type of benefit does not always suit all persons in top-management positions within the company. To meet the needs of a group of managers, the so-called cafeteria wage-payment plan is sometimes used. Under this system, several different types of benefits are made available, and each manager is allowed to select the type that would be of the most value to him or her.

EMPLOYEE MAINTENANCE

Employee maintenance refers to several different activities required to maintain personnel at a high level of efficiency. We will discuss health, safety, morale, absenteeism, and turnover.

Employee Health and Safety

Health. An employee who does not feel well is often unproductive. Many companies maintain extensive health services on the premises. It often makes economic sense for management to be interested in employees' physical well-being.

A complete health program provides for first aid, dental services, optical needs, mass X-rays and inoculations, periodic physical examinations, and even psychological and psychiatric counseling. Attention is also given to sanitation and lighting, adequate heat and ventilation, safety, and industrial hygiene. Illness is responsible for the loss of 2 percent of a worker's productive time and 8 percent of all separations from the labor force. Thus the need for an adequate health program can easily be seen.

Currently the biggest health problems facing workers are reported to be alcoholism and drug abuse. It has been estimated that these problems cost American industry over $10 billion a year. Many companies provide counseling services for employees who have such problems.

Safety. A poor safety record in any organization is extremely costly. Accidents may result in physical injury to employees or in damage to machines and supplies, to the physical plant, and to raw materials and finished products. Injuries sometimes cause lost time by other employees, as well as by the injured worker.

It has been said that the true costs of an accident are like an iceberg. Most of them are hidden below the surface and are discovered and measured only through extensive study. Examples of such hidden costs are time spent by management

FIGURE 7-7

A pharmaceutical representative conferring with company physician. (Courtesy of Pfizer Inc.)

FIGURE 7-8
Factory workers wearing safety devices.

in compiling information and reporting the accident, and loss of productive efficiency. Other examples are work that spoils because of lost production time, and costs of training new workers. Approximately 2 million work injuries occur every year, of which one in twenty results in permanent total disability, and one in twenty-three in permanent partial disability. The annual cost of industrial accidents is in excess of $5 billion annually.

Many investigators have done research to determine the causes of industrial accidents. Their purpose has been to work out preventive procedures. They have classified into two distinct types the many factors that contribute to industrial accidents:

1. The personal characteristics and attitudes of workers
2. The impersonal factors—technical deficiencies in the work environment

Personal deficiencies include lack of worker knowledge, improper attitudes, physical defects, reckless indifference to danger, and so forth. Technical deficiencies include inadequate lighting and ventilation, poor design of equipment, improper materials-handling techniques, ineffective safeguards on machinery, and others. However, it is significant to personnel management that four out of every five accidents are caused by personal rather than technical deficiencies.

An effective safety program includes

1. Establishing safety standards and policies
2. Conducting safety inspections
3. Using up-to-date engineering techniques to ensure that equipment and working conditions are satisfactory
4. Educating the workers to become safety conscious
5. Enforcing safety rules and regulations

The techniques used by modern firms in safety education and enforcement include records of injuries, posters, the plant magazine, individual and group conferences, films, training in the use of fire equipment, and manuals that contain safety rules and penalties for infractions.

The federal government's Occupational Safety and Health Administration (OSHA) became effective in 1971. This agency endeavors to serve three major purposes:

1. Develop health and safety standards for persons at work
2. Inspect businesses to see that they comply with the standards
3. Set up record-keeping systems for recording occupational injuries, accidents, and fatalities

How successful OSHA has been in reducing unsafe and unhealthful conditions at work is not yet clear.

Morale

Morale can affect efficiency of operation. Therefore it is of great importance to management, especially to those involved in the personnel function. Research shows that absenteeism and turnover are more sharply influenced by the morale of the work force than by any other environmental factor.

MORALE is **the feeling that individuals or groups have toward their jobs, their associates, and the company.** It is affected by those factors that make up the working environment, including the extent to which one's needs are satisfied in a particular job and as a member of the company's team.

FIGURE 7-9

Good morale through good communication.

Employees relax and read a copy of their company's employee paper, which carries information about employee and company policies. (Photo courtesy of Irene Springer.)

If employees feel that they are being treated fairly, that their salaries are adequate, and that working conditions are good, they are likely to have high morale. **Employee attitude** is similar to morale. Some employee attitudes that indicate high morale are these:

1. Low employee turnover rate
2. few grievances or strike threats
3. High level of compliance with rules and policies
4. Appreciation of working conditions and facilities
5. High production level, with few deliberate work stoppages
6. Evidences of cooperation from employees (union)

Attitudes or performance contrary to these would of course indicate low employee morale.

Morale is the result of a combination of many complex attitudes: workers' personal feelings and biases, their values, economic and cultural environment, degree of security, physical health, emotional stability, realization of job expectations, and the flow of communication between management and the workers.

Absenteeism and Turnover

ABSENTEEISM is **the failure (whether voluntary or involuntary) of a worker to be present at work as scheduled.** According to this widely accepted definition, **tardiness** is also a form of absenteeism. Studies show that there is a close relationship between absenteeism and morale. Excessive absenteeism is an indication of low morale.

Management sometimes uses the rate of absenteeism as an indication of the level of morale. If an employee who is eligible to work twenty-five days during a month fails to work on three of these days, the absentee rate would be 3/25, or 12 percent. By using this same method, the rate of absenteeism for a department or an entire firm could be computed. Rates are sometimes computed for various groups of employees according to age, sex, level of job, and so on. Such analyses make it much easier to determine the causes of absenteeism.

Recent studies of absenteeism seem to show that

1. Absences are most common on Mondays and on days before and after a holiday.
2. Women have fewer absences than men.
3. Older workers have fewer absences than young workers.
4. Supervisors have fewer absences than hourly paid workers.
5. Paid-sick-leave policies do not increase absences when there is a one- or-two-day waiting period before the sick pay begins.

Turnover. High turnover, like absenteeism, is an indicator of low job satisfaction or morale. People leave when the job is not satisfying to them. A certain amount of turnover is acceptable and even good, as it allows for new employees and ideas. But excessive turnover results in untrained persons holding important jobs, and high selection and training costs. It also distracts managers from other important duties.

SUMMARY OF KEY CONCEPTS

Human resources management is usually a staff function. The personnel manager *advises* rather than directs the heads of other departments.

Critical personnel activities include

Work analysis and design	Appraisal
Staffing	Compensation
Training and development	Maintenance

The personnel function of a business attempts to select the right employees, place them in appropriate positions, and keep them as satisfied company members.

Before workers are hired, jobs must be analyzed and job specifications and descriptions must be prepared.

Employee training and development is important, for it provides a company with more valuable workers.

A fair and feasible salary compensation plan rates a high priority in human resource management. This includes an adequate package of fringe benefits.

Wage-incentive plans are less popular today with workers than formerly. But pay incentives are very important to managers.

Employee maintenance helps reduce absenteeism and turnover. Employee morale is a maintenance concern in personnel management.

Considerable attention is given to a desirable working environment. This includes the health and safety of workers.

The federal government has enacted several laws for the protection of workers. The Occupational Safety and Health Administration (OSHA) is quite active in enforcing their provisions.

Employee morale is essential to efficient production. When workers feel that they are being treated fairly and their working conditions are good, morale is high.

Low absenteeism and low turnover are indications that worker morale is good.

BUSINESS TERMS

You should be able to match these business terms with the statements that follow:

a. Ability test	**e.** Job analysis	**i.** Production sharing	**k.** Promotion
b. Absenteeism	**f.** Job description	**j.** Profit sharing	**l.** Recruiting
c. Aptitude test	**g.** Job specification		**m.** Stock option
d. Job	**h.** Morale		**n.** Transfer

1. An organizational unit of work
2. Determining pertinent information about the nature of a specific job
3. A written statement of what an employee is to do on a particular job
4. The process of generating a pool of qualified applicants
5. A test that checks on the potential a person has for a certain kind of work
6. Moving an employee to a new position with increased status and responsibility
7. The shifting of a worker to a new position without increasing his or her duties or responsibility

8. Wage payment plans that provide compensation beyond basic pay schedules
9. Extra compensation based on savings that result from reduced production costs
10. The right of managers to buy company stock in the future at today's market price
11. The feeling that individuals or groups have toward their jobs, their colleagues, and the company
12. The failure of an employee to report for work

REVIEW QUESTIONS

1. What critical personnel activities are of concern to management?
2. How do *job analysis, job description,* and *job specification* differ?
3. What are the various aspects of personnel recruitment?
4. What is meant by *equity* in a compensation system?
5. What specific things are indicative of high morale among workers?

DISCUSSION QUESTIONS

1. How would you summarize the function of the personnel department in one sentence?
2. Which of the steps in the employment procedure do you consider the most important?
3. Compare and contrast job transfer and job promotion.
4. How do *profit sharing* and *production sharing* differ?
5. What are the most important aspects of employee maintenance?
6. How are *morale, absenteeism,* and *job turnover* related?

BUSINESS CASE 7-1

Employee Rights and Attitudes

ADCO Corporation manufactures television sets. When it moved from the Boston area to New Hempshire because of the latter's lower taxes and cheaper labor, it left its workers behind.

ADCO's move caused a great deal of bitterness. The company tried to keep its plans secret until a week before it shut down its Salem factory. All of the Salem workers were refused jobs at the new plant. Since then several of the company's former workers have been driving to Portsmouth, New Hampshire, to tell the company's new employees what they think of ADCO.

The company felt the move was an economic necessity in light of the challenge by Japanese firms. ADCO had lost $1.5 million in the previous year. The cost of production in its former Salem location was simply too high.

Workers did not accept the economic argument. They were angry and wanted answers. The move was made anyway, and ADCO management reports that the company is saving $4 million a year in operating costs. The company president knows that the former employees say that ADCO is a terrible employer. The present employees are considering forming a union. These things do not seem to bother management.

1. In moving from the Boston area to New Hampshire, what could the company have done differently to minimize labor problems?
2. What are the possible long-term effects of this situation for ADCO?

BUSINESS CASE 7-2

Improving Worker Environment

The XYZ Company manufactures parts that it supplies to automobile and truck assembly plants. The employees throughout the plant are quite cooperative and seem proud to be a part of the organization. The labor force is completely unionized. The salary schedule is as good as any in the industry and better than that in most other local factories.

The company management is aware that in recent weeks the various union stewards have held several meetings. The union leadership has not made a list of desired improvements, and there has been no apparent discontent with working conditions. However, the company management knows that the working environment leaves much to be desired. Therefore the personnel department has been asked to recommend specific improvements. Their suggestions include the following (there is unanimity of opinion favoring their adoption):

1. Increasing the number of restrooms
2. Painting walls and ceilings in pastel colors
3. Piping music into the factory

However, management has questioned two additional suggestions. You have been asked to react to both, giving pro and con arguments.

1. That workers no longer be provided the usual fifteen minute "coffee breaks," but that several canteen areas be installed and workers be permitted to take their breaks as they deem desirable.
2. That pay telephones be installed in the factory area so that workers can make outgoing personal calls. Incoming calls, which are received by the receptionist, would be discontinued.

How would you respond to these suggestions?

LABOR-MANAGEMENT RELATIONS

8

STUDY OBJECTIVES

WHEN YOU HAVE FINISHED READING THIS CHAPTER, YOU SHOULD BE ABLE TO

ONE Explain what employees expect to receive from union membership

TWO Report on the historical development of labor unionism in the United States

THREE Identify the largest unions and those industries where unionism is strongest

FOUR Distinguish between the union shop, open shop, and closed shop

FIVE Explain how collective bargaining between management and labor takes place

SIX Describe the different ways that disputes between labor and management are settled

A Longtime Union Foe Loses a Battle

J. P. Stevens and Company, the big textile company, has fought a sixteen-year war against the Amalgamated Clothing and Textile Workers' Union. The company has used a variety of tactics to keep the union out of its southern textile plants.

In a recent ruling, however, the National Labor Relations Board declared the union the bargaining agent for about one thousand workers at the company's plants and warehouses in Wallace, North Carolina. The board went further. It ordered the company to pay the cost of the union's organizing campaign. The board said that its order was based on the company's illegal actions during the campaign, which had "poisoned" the electoral atmosphere. The board also ordered Stevens to reimburse with interest the Labor Relations Board for the costs of investigating, preparing, presenting, and conducting the case.

These extreme measures seem to be a result of frustration with Stevens's apparent philosophy—it is cheaper to pay the fines than to allow the union in. Stevens had lost a representation election once before in court, and it then closed the plant in which the union had won.

One federal appeals court has branded the company "the most notorious recidivist in the field of labor law." The board in the current decision said that "employee rights have been threatened over the years by the efforts of Stevens to destroy the union through persistent violations of the law."

J. P. Stevens will no doubt remain a target for union-organizing attempts in the future.

IN THE NEWS

To the infantrymen, his country's military might is only those buddies he can see, and the equipment they have at hand; likewise, to the wage-earner, "free enterprise" is primarily the way his boss treats him and those around him.

MALCOLM FORBES

Some managers argue that unions are an external force. These managers often resent the idea that a company's employees need an "outside representative." The early history of the reaction of American business to unions has been to fight them. This philosophy is no longer typical, however.

Unions have been content to bargain within the context of America's private-enterprise system. They have not pushed, as unions have in other countries, for government control of the sources of production.

Today many managers view unions as an "internal force" to be reckoned with, since union members are also employees.

The philosophy of unionism in the United States has been somewhat different from that in other countries. Unions are involved in politics through contributions to candidates and political parties. But they have not become politicized to the extent that they have in Europe. The emphasis has remained centered on the job. The result has been a pursuit of bread-and-butter issues—wages, job security, and working conditions—rather than social philosophy.

In this chapter we consider the American work force, the reasons why employees unionize, union history, and labor legislation influencing unions in America. We discuss the common interests between labor and management as well as their disagreements. They agree that they depend on each other and that they must work together. Differences arise, however, in their appraisals of each other's contributions to the success of the business enterprise. We also discuss collective bargaining, dispute resolution, and, finally, the union's role in pension reform.

THE U.S. LABOR FORCE

There were about 102 million persons in the labor force in this country in 1980. This number is expected to reach 106 million by 1985. An ever-increasing number of workers are needed to produce the GNP required to meet the wants of our growing population.

The numbers employed are distributed unevenly among the two sexes and the various age groups that make up the work force. Women make up fewer than half, but this fraction is increasing. The distribution by age groups varies according to the birthrate during different decades. Growth in the labor force is shown in Figure 8-1.

Job Prospects in the 1980s

White-collar workers (including office employees and those engaged in the professions) outnumbered blue-collar workers (those in the factories and on the farms) for the first time in 1956. During the 1980s there will undoubtedly be a continuation of the rapid growth in white-collar occupations and a slower growth in blue-collar occupations. A faster-than-average growth is expected among service workers, and a further decline among farm workers.

The greater growth of white-collar jobs reflects the continued expansion expected for the service-producing industries. There is also an increasing demand for research personnel. The growth of white-collar jobs also reflects an increasing need for educational and health services and a continuing proliferation of paper work. Although the number of blue-collar workers as a group will increase at a much slower rate, the number of skilled artisans will increase at about the same rate as total employment. Employment by major occupational group is shown in Figure 8-2.

The growth in the number of working women over the past decade has been very rapid. More wives have begun to work to fulfill their own career goals and to bring home an extra paycheck. This has led to a growth in the labor force.

Figure 8-3 shows the percentage of women in the labor force.

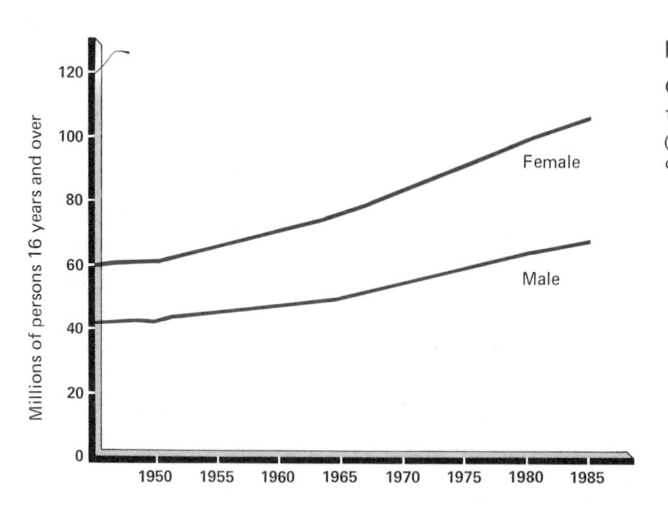

FIGURE 8-1

Growth in the labor force.

(Source: U.S. Department of Commerce.)

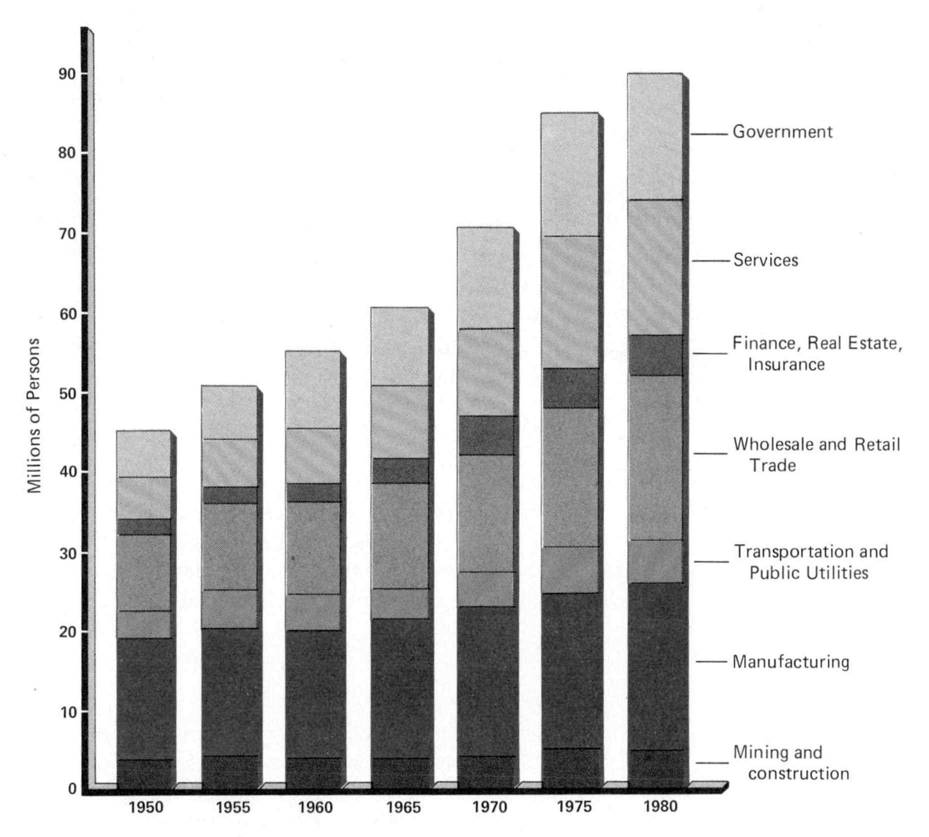

FIGURE 8-2

Employment by occupational group.

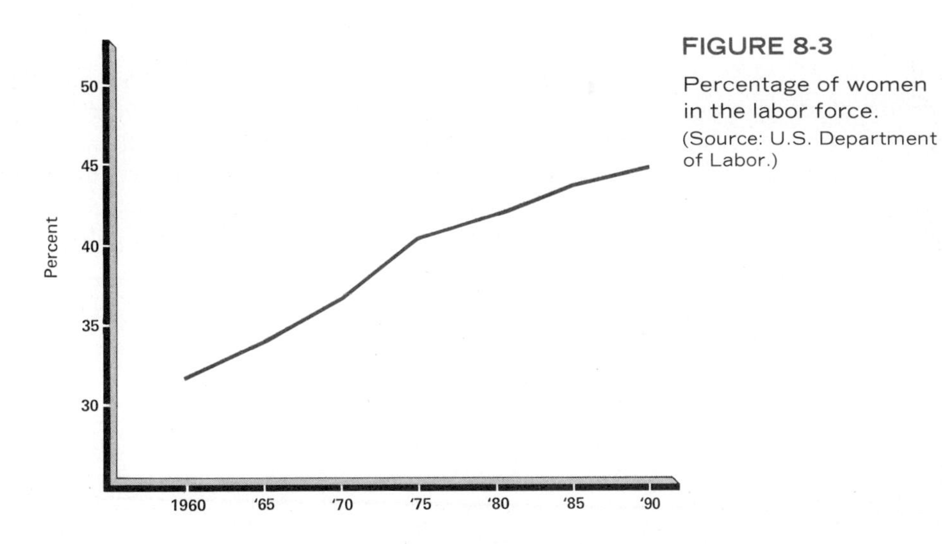

FIGURE 8-3

Percentage of women in the labor force.
(Source: U.S. Department of Labor.)

WHY EMPLOYEES JOIN UNIONS

Several factors can prompt members of the labor force to band together. Perhaps the most important ones in our country are (1) the **added strength** that comes from an effective organization of large numbers working together and (2) the advantages of having **qualified negotiators** when bargaining with employers.

Much insight can be gained from reading the following paragraphs from the preamble to the constitution of the Cigar Makers' International Union of America, organized in 1864.[1]

> Labor has no protection—the weak are devoured by the strong. All wealth and power center in the hands of the few, and the many are their victims and bondsmen. In all countries and at all times capital has been used to monopolize particular branches of business, until the vast and various industrial pursuits of the world are rapidly coming under the immediate control of a comparatively small portion of mankind, tending, if not checked by the toiling millions, to enslave and impoverish them.
>
> Labor is the creator of all wealth, and as such the laborer is at least entitled to a remuneration sufficient to enable himself and family to enjoy more of the leisure that rightfully belongs to him, more social advantages, more of the benefits, privileges and emoluments of the world; in a word, all those rights and privileges necessary to make him capable of enjoying, appreciating, defending and perpetuating the blessings of modern civilization. Past experience teaches us that labor has so far been unable to arrest the encroachments of capital, neither has it been able to obtain justice from lawmaking power. This is due to a lack of practical organization and unity of action. "In union there is strength." Organization and united action are the only means by which the laboring classes can gain any advantage from themselves. Good and strong labor organizations are enabled to defend and preserve the interests of the working people. By organization we are able to assist each other in cases of strikes and lock-outs, sickness and death. And through organization only [are] the workers, as a class, . . . able to gain legislative advantages.

Much progress has been made since 1864, and this preamble would of course be written differently today. It does, however, point out quite clearly one of the advantages of union membership—strength in numbers.

A recent study on why people join unions confirmed the opinion that people organize or join unions primarily to improve the economic aspects of their jobs.[2] **Security, pay, working conditions,** and **company policy** were found to affect union votes more than noneconomic variables do.

[1]*Third Annual Report of the Bureau of Statistics of Labor of the State of New York, for the Year 1885* (Albany, 1886), pp. 544–45.

[2]C. A. Schriesheim, "Job Satisfaction, Attitudes toward Unions, and Voting in a Union Representation Election," *Journal of Applied Psychology*, 63 (1978), 548.

A good example of union job security concerns the job of chicken inspector.

In the old days the chicken inspector would stand beside an overhead conveyor carrying thousands of naked upside-down chickens. And with rapid hand movements, the inspector would go through twenty-six different motions to inspect the chickens for the U.S. Department of Agriculture's chicken inspection service.

However, a recent innovation has changed all that. Now the chicken inspector sits beneath the conveyor and moves only his or her eyes. A two-by-three-foot mirror reflects all sides of the chickens, and inspectors can inspect up to thirty-five thousand birds a day. The mirrors have speeded up the production lines an average of 30 percent. As a result, 25 percent fewer inspectors are needed.

The union representing the chicken inspectors filed suit, contending that the mirrors and speed-up caused "undue inspector fatigue." The union is, of course, also concerned with the 25 percent drop in its membership.

HISTORY OF AMERICAN LABOR UNIONISM

The history of the American labor movement, which dates from the beginning of this country, is colorful and at times marked by violence. Even before the Declaration of Independence, skilled artisans in handicraft industries joined together in benevolent societies. Their primary purpose was to provide members and their families with financial assistance in the event of serious illness, debt, or the death of the wage earner. Although these early associations had little resemblance to present-day labor unions, they did bring workers together to consider problems of mutual concern and their solutions.

During the 1820s, despite several economic slumps, the unions continued to grow. Most unions were small locals, since progress in rapid communication had not been great. But the isolated locals soon learned that by pooling their resources and cooperating with one another, they could more effectively deal with employers and at the same time give help and support to locals in distress.

In 1859 the machinists and the blacksmiths formed locals as part of a permanent national organization. Molders and printers also organized unions. By the end of the Civil War, at least thirty-two national unions had been formed. Some of them still exist today, such as those of the carpenters, bricklayers, and painters. The purpose of these unions has always been the same: to influence wages, obtain better working conditions, and achieve more satisfactory work rules throughout their trade.

The Knights of Labor

The first national union was the Noble Order of the Knights of Labor, which was founded as a local union of garment workers in Philadelphia in 1869. Seventeen years later, this union claimed more than seven hundred thousand members throughout the United States. Internal conflict between those who favored the process of collective bargaining and those committed to political action and social change led to the weakening and dissipation of the Knights of Labor. In time this led to the formation of the American Federation of Labor.

The American Federation of Labor

The Federation of Organized Trades and Labor Unions was established in 1881 through the combination of a number of craft unions. In 1886 another group of unions, which had previously been affiliated with the Knights of Labor, broke away from that group and joined with the unions in the federation. At that time the organization adopted the name American Federation of Labor (A.F. of L.). As an organization, it had little power over its sovereign units, but it did have the power to expel a union or a group of unions from membership.

Historically, the A.F. of L. was predominantly craft unions, although some industrial unions were affiliated with it. Perhaps its most notable and powerful industrial union affiliate was the International Ladies' Garment Workers' Union. The affiliated unions found that by joining together into one organization, they commanded greater strength in securing favorable congressional legislation.

Under the leadership of its first president, Samuel Gompers, the A.F. of L. grew and prospered. Previously, unions had been chiefly concerned with social objectives. Samuel Gompers led the A.F. of L. to emphasize the economic aspects of unions—what is known as **business unionism,** or "bread-and-butter unionism." The A.F. of L. can truly be said to have constituted the cornerstone of the organized-labor movement in America.

For many years the A.F. of L. followed a policy of neutrality in political activity. In addition to business unionism and nonparticipation in politics, Gompers strongly advocated the autonomy of each craft. He felt that this principle was inherent in forming a strong foundation for successful union growth and influence.

The Congress of Industrial Organizations

The A.F. of L.'s policy of a single union for each craft led to the formation of a new labor organization, the Congress of Industrial Organization (C.I.O.). As American industry became more mechanized, there were increasing numbers of workers operating machines rather than following a trade or craft. Understandably, these could not qualify for membership in the "trade" unions. So in 1935, the presidents of eight of the A.F. of L. unions formed what was called the Committee for Industrial Organization.

This new group wanted to organize large industries (such as rubber, steel, and automotive) along the lines of industrial unionism. The feeling became so intense that in 1936, the unions that had associated themselves with the Committee for Industrial Organization were suspended from membership in the A.F. of L. This move resulted in the group's formation as a rival labor organization, which in 1938 adopted the name "Congress of Industrial Organizations." During the next

LANE KIRKLAND

Lane Kirkland became president of the AFL–CIO in November 1979, succeeding the late George Meany. Kirkland was born in Camden, South Carolina, in 1922 and graduated from Georgetown University in 1948.

Kirkland is a licensed master mariner and sailed as deck officer aboard several merchant ships. He held various posts with the AFL–CIO between 1948 and 1958. He was director of research and education, International Union of Operating Engineers, from 1958 to 1960 and rejoined the AFL in 1960. He served as secretary-treasurer of the AFL–CIO from 1969 to November 19, 1979, when he became president.

Kirkland has served on the National Commission on Productivity, the Presidential Commission on Financial Structure and Regulation, the President's Maritime Advisory Committee, and the Committee on Selection of Federal Judicial Officers, among other important services to government. He has also served on the board of directors of the American Arbitration Association, the Rockefeller Foundation, the Council on Foreign Relations, the Brookings Institution, and the National Planning Association.

decade, by advocating the organizing of workers in many fields that had not previously been organized, the C.I.O. grew in power and eventually began to compete seriously with the A.F. of L.

Merger of A.F. of L. and C.I.O.

In the early 1950s the leaders of these two rivals realized that the cause of organized labor would be greatly strengthened if they could join forces. So in December 1955, the A.F. of L. and the C.I.O. unified the two federations into the AFL–CIO. Now four out of five labor unions are affiliated with the AFL–CIO.

The AFL–CIO is a voluntary federation of 121 national and international labor unions, which are in turn made up of 60,000 local unions. **The AFL–CIO itself does no bargaining; it is not a union, but a federation of unions. The bargaining is done by representatives of individual unions or a collaboration of several unions.** The AFL–CIO serves its constituent unions by

1. Speaking for the whole labor movement before Congress and other branches of government
2. Representing American labor in world affairs through its participation in the International Labor Organization—a United Nations specialized agency—and through direct contact with the central labor organizations of free nations throughout the world
3. Helping to organize workers
4. Coordinating such activities as community services, political action, and voter registration

Each member union affiliated with the AFL–CIO remains autonomous, conducting its own affairs, with its own officers and its own headquarters. It is free to withdraw at any time, but as long as it is affiliated, it must observe the items stipulated in the AFL–CIO constitution.

Growth in Union Membership

The economic prosperity that followed World War I and the protective prounion legislation during the 1920s and 1930s brought about rapid growth in union membership. The greatest push for union growth was the passage of the Wagner Act in 1935. From 1935 to 1945 union membership increased fourfold, from fewer than 4 million to almost 15 million. The growth trend in union membership is shown in Figure 8-4. According to the latest figures available when this book was written, there has been a decrease in the absolute number of union and association members.

The degree to which American workers are organized varies greatly throughout different regions and industrial groups. The most highly unionized industries are those that have long been established, such as transportation. Unions in transportation include the Teamsters, the railway unions, and the public-transit unions. Construction, in which the workers are organized on a craft basis, has signed up almost all of those who belong to the construction trades. Table 8-1 lists the most heavily unionized industries. The largest single union in the United States today is the International Brotherhood of Teamsters, which has more than 2.2 million members. It is not affiiliated with the AFL–CIO. The second largest is the United Automobile Workers, with 1.6 million members. The relative size of the ten largest unions in this country is shown in Figure 8-5.

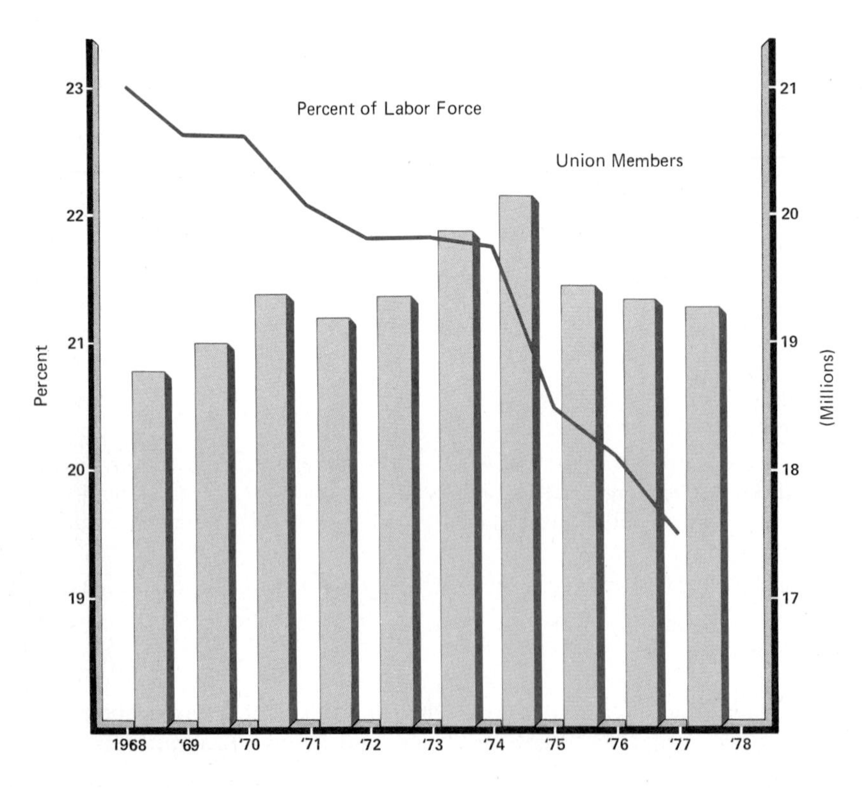

FIGURE 8-4

The big slippage in union power.

As more and more workers have moved out of the industrial sector and into service and white-collar jobs, labor has found it increasingly difficult to gain new recruits. With this trend likely to accelerate, organized labor will probably represent an even smaller percentage of the labor force in the years ahead.

TABLE 8-1
UNION MEMBERSHIP BY INDUSTRY

Industry	Percent of Employees Who Are Union Members
Construction Electrical machinery Ordnance Paper Transportation Transportation equipment	75 percent or more
Apparel Federal government Food Manufacturing Metal fabricating Mining Petroleum Primary metals Telephone Tobacco manufacturers	50 to 75 percent
Chemicals Furniture Leather Lumber Publishing, printing	25 to 50 percent
Agriculture and fishing Government Finance Service Textile mills Trade	Less than 25 percent

SOURCE: Bureau of Labor Statistics, Directory of National Unions and Employee Associations.

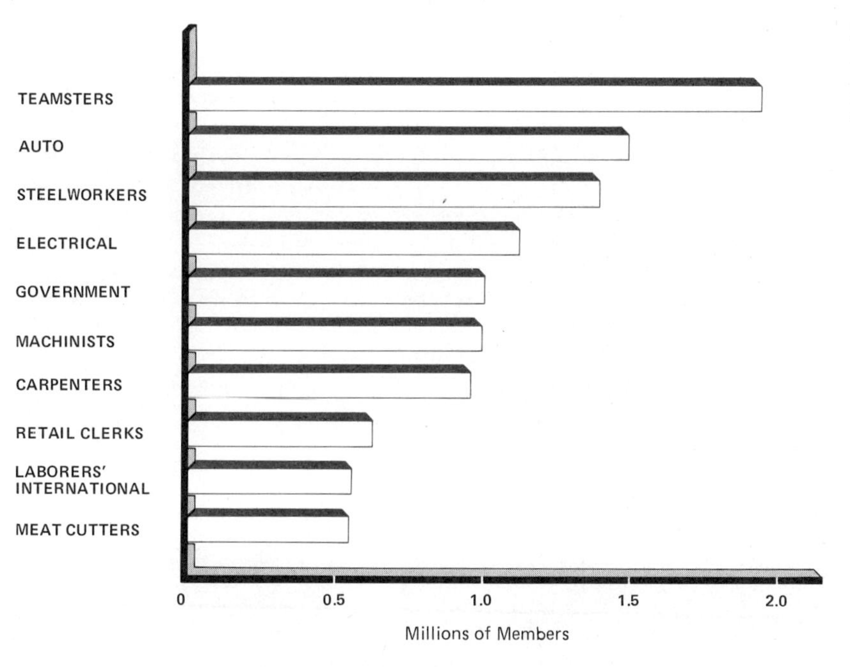

FIGURE 8-5

The ten largest unions, 1980. (Source: Bureau of Labor Statistics.)

One of the areas in which labor unions are making progress in organizing workers is among government employees. This group includes office employees, teachers, firefighters, police officers, hospital workers, and sanitation workers. The number and length of strikes among teachers and sanitation workers in several major cities have frequently made the newspaper headlines. Because of these events, many people believe that government workers should be denied the right to strike. This has reached the stage of becoming an issue; it is difficult to distinguish between their rights and those of other workers.

CURRENT ISSUE CURRENT ISSUE CURRENT ISSUE CURRENT ISSUE CURRENT ISSUF CURRENT ISSUE CURRENT ISSUE CURRENT ISSUE CURRENT ISSUE CURRENT ISSUE CURRENT ISSUE

Should Public Employees Have the Right to Strike?

Traditionally in our society, public employees did not have the right to strike. It was reasoned that the public cannot strike against itself. In recent years strikes of teachers, sanitation workers, and other city employees have made the national news.

With which of the following statements do you agree and with which do you disagree?

1. In order for society to be free, there must be certain abridgements of freedom in certain situations and upon some persons (or groups of persons) within that society.
2. Every worker has the inalienable right to withhold his or her services, and this includes those who work in the public sector.
3. Prohibiting strikes in public employment would be fair, for people would know when they accepted employment that they were giving up that right and privilege.
4. The idea of the right and power of the people to set up governments presupposes every person's duty to obey the established government.
5. Public employees make up 20 percent of the nation's work force. They should not be denied the rights given other workers.
6. Public employees should have the right to strike. However, they should not organize into unions, so that others who wish to work may be hired.

What do you see as the most forceful argument in each case:

a. Supporting strikes by public employees?
b. Prohibiting strikes by public employees?

CURRENT ISSUE

LEGAL BACKGROUND FOR LABOR RELATIONS

The laws that govern labor and labor relations in this country form the basis for the relationship between business and labor unions.

Two distinct types of legislation affecting labor and employers have been enacted. The first pertains to working hours, safety regulations, and health. This group of laws will be referred to as **work legislation**. The second concerns the rights and responsibilities of labor unions and employers. These will be referred to as **labor laws**.

Work Legislation

The earliest control over working hours was applied specifically to women and children. In 1924, Congress unsuccessfully proposed a constitutional amendment granting itself power to regulate the labor of persons under eighteen years of age. All states, however, have laws of one kind or another governing the length of the working day and the use of child labor. Many states have legislation restricting the hours women can work in certain employment. Also, many states regulate the minimum wages that may be paid to workers.

The Fair Labor Standards Act of 1938. The major piece of legislation in this area, the Fair Labor Standards Act, was passed in 1938. It contains provisions related to both wages and hours in industries engaged in interstate commerce. In effect since October 24, 1940, this act originally stated that workers should be compensated at a rate of one and one-half times their standard rate of pay for working over forty hours per week.

This act also sets a floor under minimum wages. The first minimum wage was set at $0.25 an hour and was increased to $0.40 on October 24, 1945. This "floor" or minimum, has repeatedly been raised—to $0.75 an hour in 1949, to $1.00 in 1955, and to $1.25 in 1961.

The act was amended in 1966, raising the minimum wage to $1.60 effective February 1, 1968. It remained at $1.60 until May 1, 1974, when Congress raised it to $2.00. It climbed to $2.10 in 1975, and to $3.35 in 1981. The law specifies that any time an employee is "permitted to work" must be counted as working time. All time spent in physical or mental exertion, whether burdensome or not, that is "controlled or required" by the employer, and pursued necessarily and primarily for the benefit of the employer, is to be counted as working time. Thus the work not requested but nonetheless permitted is working time. If work is permitted away from the premises or even at the employee's home, it is counted as working time.

The law stipulates that an employer may not discriminate on the basis of sex by paying employees of one sex at rates lower than those paid the opposite sex for doing equal work on jobs requiring equal skill, effort, and responsibility and performed under similar working conditions. The federal Fair Labor Standards Act is administered by the Wage and Hour Division of the U.S. Department of Labor.

Other work legislation includes equal employment opportunity laws, Occupational Safety and Health legislation, and child labor laws that are discussed elsewhere.

Labor Laws

The Norris-LaGuardia Act of 1932 contains the first statement of general policy toward unionization of labor ever adopted by the U.S. government. This act gives workers the right to organize into unions. It outlaws the "yellow dog" contract whereby workers, as a condition of employment, would agree not to join a union. And it somewhat restricts employers' use of the labor injunction to halt work stoppages.

The major impact on the legal relations between management and union, however, has come from three pieces of legislation that make up the so-called National Labor Code. Each piece of legislation was enacted to protect one of the three parties involved in the union/management/employee relationship. (See Figure 8-6.)

The Wagner Act, or National Labor Relations Act, was designed to aid unions in their organizing efforts. The Taft-Hartley Act, or Labor Management Relations Act, limited what unions could do. The Landrum-Griffin Act, or Labor Management Reporting and Disclosure Act, was designed to protect union members from their unions. We will consider each in turn.

The Wagner Act. **The Wagner Act of 1935, otherwise known as the National Labor Relations Act, is clearly a workers' law, for its regulations are designed to control the actions of employers.** In fact it is sometimes referred to as "labor's Magna Carta." In general, it guarantees workers the right to organize. This was achieved by making it unlawful for employers to

1. Refuse to bargain collectively with representatives chosen by employees
2. Interfere with the employees' right to bargain collectively
3. Dictate in any way to labor officials about their administrative procedures
4. Discriminate against union members in either hiring or firing
5. Discriminate against employees who take advantage of their rights under the law

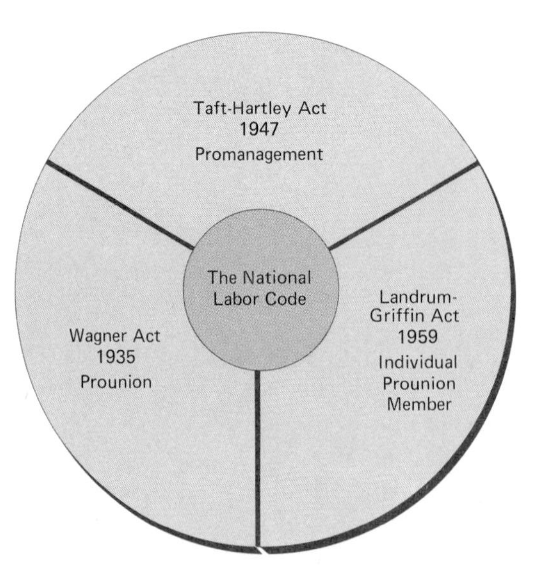

FIGURE 8-6

National labor code.

Legal foundation for union/management relations.

The law established the National Labor Relations Board to administer the provisions of this act in settling disputes. It also serves as a sort of court in protecting workers against unfair practices. Its chief functions are to prevent or correct any violations of the five practices enumerated above and to establish proper bargaining units and organizations to represent the workers. In substance, the Wagner Act has provided an orderly process of democratic elections by the workers. It replaces the former tactic of striking to force the employer to recognize the union as the employees' rightful bargaining agent.

The Taft-Hartley Act. Throughout the history of the labor movement, no single federal law has incurred stronger opposition from unions than the Taft-Hartley Act of 1947, otherwise known as the Labor Management Relations Act. After a bitter battle in Congress, the Taft-Hartley Act was passed over the veto of President Truman. By this time the political climate had shifted in favor of management, largely because of the advantages given to unions under the Wagner Act. The main objective of the Taft-Hartley Act is to equalize the rights and privileges of management and labor. Although the act gives management no new rights, it achieves a balance of power by withholding some of the rights that had previously been extended to unions.

The act holds that it is an unfair labor practice for an employer to

1. Refuse to bargain collectively with employees
2. Encourage or discourage membership in any labor organization
3. Contribute financial or other support to any labor organization
4. Interfere with the organization or administration of any labor organization
5. Discriminate against an employee because of testimony the employee gives under the act

Under the act, unions may not

1. Refuse to bargain collectively with employers
2. Restrain nonstrikers from crossing a picket line or threaten violence to nonstrikers
3. Cause an employer to discriminate against any employee in order to encourage or discourage union membership
4. Force the employer to pay for services not performed (often called "featherbedding")
5. Engage in secondary boycotts
6. Stop work over a jurisdictional or interunion dispute
7. Charge the members excessive or discriminatory initiation fees

Employers as well as workers are permitted to appeal to the National Labor Relations Board against unions in connection with such practices. Certain practices may be subject to court action and lawsuits for damages. Restrictions on the use of injunctions are eased. The Taft-Hartley Act, like the Wagner Act, is administered by the National Labor Relations Board.

Special rules were written into the Taft-Hartley Act for handling controversies or strikes that, in the judgement of the president, create or threaten emergencies by imperiling the national health or safety. In any such dispute or strike, the president is authorized to appoint a board of inquiry to investigate the facts. After that a court injunction can be obtained forbidding the occurrence or continuance of a stoppage for a period of eighty days.

During this **cooling off** or waiting period, efforts are to be made to settle the dispute. If no voluntary agreement can be arranged within sixty days, the employees are polled by secret ballot on whether they will accept the employer's final offer. After all these steps have been taken, however, the injunction must be dissolved whether or not the dispute is settled.

Union opposition to the Taft-Hartley Act has been intense. The act has been denounced as a slave-labor law, and its repeal has been a major goal of the labor movement. Many proposals have been made for changes in the new law by its critics and also by its supporters. For the most part, these changes would ease the restrictions on unions. But revision has proved difficult. This difficulty stems from the problem of reconciling the views of those who were fearful of going too far in modifying the law with the views of those who felt that any obtainable amendments would not be significant. By 1951, practical circumstances had brought about general agreement to repeal the requirement that elections be held to validate union-shop agreements. Experience had shown that in nearly all cases, large majorities of workers voted for the union shop.

The Landrum-Griffin Act. Working under some of the most intense public pressure in years, Congress passed, on September 4, 1959, the first major labor-reform amendments to the Taft-Hartley Act. This act was the Labor Management Reporting and Disclosure Act, commonly called the Landrum-Griffin Act. It is quite correctly titled, for the major portion of the law requires a series of reports to be made to the secretary of labor by both labor unions and business management. Among the reports required are

1. Reports of the constitution and bylaws of union organizations
2. Reports of union administrative policies pertaining to initiation fees, union dues, and other financial assessments; calling of union meetings; qualifications for membership in the union; and the ratification of contracts
3. Annual financial reports by the unions, showing the amounts of assets, liabilities, and cash receipts; salaries of officers; and loans to members, union officials, or businesses
4. Reports of personal financial transactions on the part of union officials that might in any way conflict with the best interests of the union
5. Reports by employers of any expenditures made in order to prevent their employees from organizing; for example, workers hired to sabotage efforts by union representatives at organizing

This law gives employers and union members new protection from union racketeers and unscrupulous labor leaders. Members have more voice in their local union affairs. Local officers must be elected by secret ballot at least once every three years, and national officers every five years. Union members can sue in federal courts if justice is not provided. The law prohibits Communists or anyone convicted of a felony within the previous five years from holding union office. A union official permitting a felon to hold office is subject to a year in jail and a $10,000 fine.

In combination, the effects of the three parts of the National Labor Code seem to be acceptable to union members. U.S. unions appear to be performing largely the way their members want them to. A University of Michigan survey includes the following observation.

A little more than one quarter of union members were dissatisfied with their unions. Unions got good marks in improving wages, benefits, and job security. Their record in handling grievances was not quite as good because rank and filers felt settling grievances took too long.

Some workers (54 percent) felt they had no control over job assigments. And a growing number wanted some control over hours and working days. These two areas may become important bargaining points if unions are able to continue to satisfy their members.

State "Right-to-Work" Laws

You will recall that one of the major objectives of organized labor is the strengthening of the labor unions themselves. But labor has been unsuccessful in getting Congress to repeal Section 14-b of the Taft-Hartley Act. This provision permits the states to enact laws prohibiting the union shop. It has been a strong influence in preventing continued union growth, and its repeal is one of the primary goals of organized labor.

Under Section 14-b of the Taft-Hartley Act, states are permitted to outlaw any form of compulsory unionism, including the union shop. This was a change from the original interpretation of the National Labor Relations Act of 1935 (Wagner Act), which not only allowed the unions the right to negotiate compulsory union-membership agreements but also prevented a state or municipality from nullifying the unions' right in this respect. The right of the states to restrict the types of unions that may be formed (the closed shop, for example) is clearly provided for in Section 14-b of the Taft-Hartley Act. It states:

> Nothing in this Act shall be construed as authorizing the execution or application of agreements requiring membership in a labor organization in any State or Territory in which such execution or application is prohibited by State or Territorial Law.

"Right-to-Work" Today

Florida enacted the first right-to-work law by constitutional amendment in 1944. In 1956 Louisiana repealed a general right-to-work law but substituted a new law banning union-shop agreements in agriculture and in certain agricultural-processing operations. Right-to-work laws dealing largely with agricultural labor have been passed by twenty states, as shown in Figure 8-7. In all, twenty-five states have enacted such legislation, but five have subsequently repealed it.

There are two sides to the argument over right-to-work laws. One, shared by many employers, is that it is morally improper to require workers to join a union in order to obtain or hold a job. This side holds that union-shop agreements are actually intended to perpetuate the bargaining power of nations.

The other side, shared by the unions, holds that right-to-work laws are actually designed to wreck labor organization. Also, any worker who benefits from union activities should be obliged to share in the cost by paying union dues.

Unquestionably, right-to-work laws hinder union growth in those states where such laws exist. Therefore the repeal of Section 14-b is high on organized labor's list of priorities. Several well-organized campaigns have been launched to influence members of Congress to repeal Section 14-b of the Taft-Hartley Act. But such bills have consistently been defeated. Nonetheless, organized labor will undoubtedly be heard from again.

The Union and Closed Shop

Chief among the objectives of organized labor is the maintaining and strengthening of the union, which provides their protection and security. They have achieved the union shop but very much want the closed shop, too.

The union shop. The union shop is the type of union security most commonly found. It recognizes the compulsory union membership of all employees. Management may employ anyone it desires, but he or she will be required to join the union within a stated period of time. The Taft-Hartley Act provides a minimum of thirty days as the grace period before compulsory membership. However, the Landrum-Griffin Act permits a minimum of only seven days for

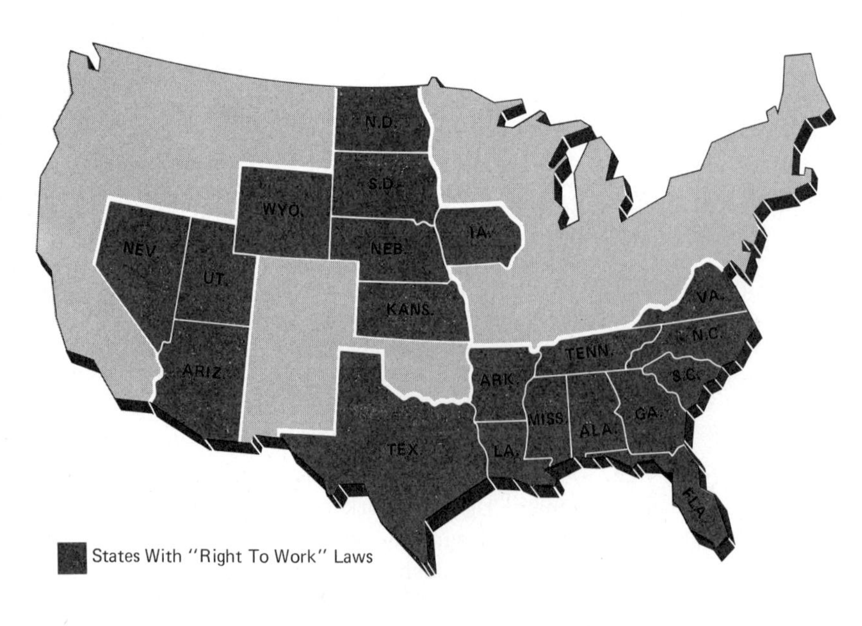

FIGURE 8-7
States with "Right-to-work" laws, 1980.

workers engaged in the construction industry. The Bureau of Labor Statistics reports that among the contracts it has surveyed in recent years, almost three-fourths provide for the union shop.

The closed shop. Under this once-legal agreement, any new employee had to be a member of the union before being hired. In this way, the union was the only source of employment available to the employer. But the closed shop was declared illegal by the Taft-Hartley Act, passed in 1947.

Although the closed shop is now illegal, organized labor has not ceased to work for it. Union leaders are well aware of its value and importance. Therefore this continues to be an issue.

The open shop. In an open-shop situation, there is no union and no effort on the part of management either to promote or to prevent one. Employees are free to choose whether or not to organize. In many such situations, some employees are already members of a union. This makes the open shop an attractive target for union organizers.

COLLECTIVE BARGAINING

The method by which the management of a firm and the union come to agreement on a contract through negotiations is called **COLLECTIVE BARGAINING.** It is called collective bargaining because labor acts collectively—as a group. (Employers also may act collectively.)

Collective bargaining has developed over a period of time as a method of using democratic procedures in employer-employee relationships. The individual exercises his or her voice in the bargaining process through the union representatives. Workers share with other workers and with the employer the responsibility for agreeing on orderly, established bargaining procedures. Procedures such as determining working conditions, practices to be used in promotions and layoffs, and penalties for violation of the work rules are established.

How Collective Bargaining Works

A union becomes the bargaining agent for a group of workers when it is certified as representing the majority of them. Most commonly, this is determined by a secret vote conducted by the National Labor Relations Board. If a clear majority of the workers involved indicate a desire to be represented by the union, then that union is "certified" as the collective-bargaining agent for the employees.

Representatives of the union and of management then meet at the bargaining table and try to reach agreement on a contract. Rarely are the two sides in agreement when they begin their meetings, and rarely is the final product of their deliberations precisely what either side originally wanted.

The first meeting between the negotiation teams usually establishes rules, policies, and schedules for future meetings. Sometimes at this first meeting the representatives of labor formally present their specific proposals for changes in the existing labor agreement. At later meetings, management submits counterproposals. Both groups seek opportunities to suggest compromise solutions in their favor until an agreement is reached.

Collective bargaining is a matter of give and take, with labor and management gradually moving closer together.

Figure 8-8 shows the typical movement on an issue by union and management through collective bargaining. (It could be wages, working conditions, or anything else.) The introduction of other issues can lead to a "trade-off" kind of bargaining. When this happens, one issue may be traded for another. For example, management offers a twenty-cents-an-hour wage increase and no additional fringe benefits, while the union wants twenty-two cents in wages and a new dental-care insurance plan. Ultimate resolution after bargaining might be a seventeen-cent pay raise plus the dental plan.

When union and management representatives have finally agreed on a contract, the union representatives take the contract back to their members. If it does not satisfy the members, they may send their representatives back to continue the bargaining process, or they may decide to reinforce their demands by going on strike.

If labor and management find it impossible to come to an agreement, a third party may be brought in from the outside. This might be a governmental or a private mediator or mediation team.

Once the contract has been ratified by the union and management, it becomes the guiding principle of labor-management relations for the duration of the agreement. All collective agreements run for a specific period of time, usually from one to three years. Months before an agreement is to terminate, representatives of both management and labor sit down together to negotiate terms for a new contract.

Generally, collective agreements cover the workers in a single plant or the workers of a single company that has several plants. The idea of collective bargaining is an accepted procedure in American industry today. In fact, many employers prefer to bargain with labor collectively rather than as individuals.

There are now more than 150,000 collective agreements in force in the United States. On the average, 300 such agreements are concluded every day.

Collective-Bargaining Patterns

The precise form or pattern of collective bargaining varies considerably, depending largely upon the nature of the industry.

Local-market bargaining. As its name implies, this pattern occurs mainly in the local market. The building-construction industry is an example, for building contractors operate essentially in a local market. The work must be done where it is needed, unlike the kinds of manufacturing that can easily be moved from one city to another. Since their product is not transportable, building contractors compete only in the local-market area.

Bargaining takes place between various local unions of construction workers and the local trade association of contractors. These local unions have great autonomy in bargaining, and no attempt is made by their international unions to impose a uniform pattern of wages or working conditions.

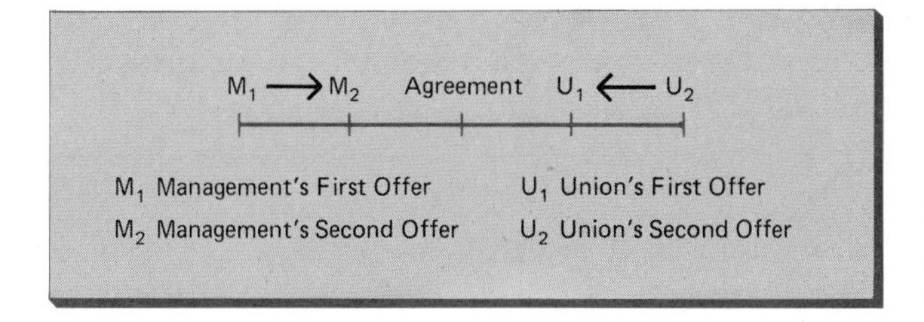

FIGURE 8-8

Collective-bargaining process.

Retail food stores and newspaper publishers are similarly competitive on a local market only, and therefore collective bargaining is customarily done at the local level.

Industry-wide bargaining. The women's apparel industry is a good example of one in which manufacturers compete over a nationwide market. Most of the companies are small-scale producers requiring relatively little capital investment, and labor accounts for a major part of the cost of the finished product.

In this industry the negotiations take place for all employees represented by the union throughout the industry. A standard contract will likely exist for all employees in the industry, with certain local adjustments. The garment manufacturer knows that competitors will be providing wages and benefits to their employees similar to what he or she is providing.

Coalition bargaining. In coalition bargaining, several different unions within a given industry will collaborate in bargaining with an employer. Organized labor favors coalition bargaining because it tends to strengthen bargaining lines where they are weakest—among small and weak unions.

An outstanding example of success in coalition bargaining is the experience of several unions negotiating with General Electric. The General Electric Company had historically insisted on bargaining separately with individual unions. However, eventually eleven electrical unions—all affiliated with the AFL–CIO—formed an alliance, cutting across union jurisdictions, to bargain as a group with GE. The largest and strongest of the eleven unions, the International Union of Electric Workers, took the lead in the negotiations. The AFL–CIO backed the negotiation team by pledging a sum of $8 million to carry out the negotiation effort. It employed a nationwide network of teletype stations in strategic cities to keep union members informed and in line. Although the GE management at first resisted the idea of coalition bargaining, in the end it settled with the coalition group.

THE BARGAINING AGREEMENT

The written labor agreement as we know it today is a peculiarly American phenomenon. It first appeared in the late 1930s, during the time when unions in such industries as rubber, steel, and automobile manufacturing were organized. Before then, labor agreements, which existed principally in the railroad and printing industries, were abbreviated, generalized agreements that left working rules to informal arrangements. Under such generalized agreements, neither party was inclined to curtail its flexibility by agreeing to detailed clauses. Management most wanted the freedom to manage and operate without hindrance from the union, while the union wanted to be free to seize any opportunity to make gains for its members.

Purpose of the Bargaining Agreement

Today the trend is for both parties to spell out every possible detail, so that any dispute that may arise is covered by the contract. Negotiating an agreement now often takes many months of give-and-take negotiation, reflecting union demands and employer resistance. Because agreements are all-inclusive contracts, they generally cover a wide range of topics and conditions, and they range from a few pages in length to a hundred or more. Labor agreements are expected to

1. Indicate clearly the classification of workers to be included and those to be excluded under the terms
2. Spell out detailed rights and duties of the parties concerning working hours, wage rates, overtime, promotions, layoffs, transfers, management prerogatives, and work scheduling
3. Provide procedures for settling grievances and arbitration
4. Define procedures for renewing the agreement

Most contracts stipulate work assignments, to avoid jurisdictional disputes that occur when there is a question about whether certain work should be performed by employees in one bargaining unit or by those in another. Such issues as the subcontracting of work outside the union and the automation of mechanical processes are highly controversial subjects that require lengthy negotiations.

It is generally believed that unions are against technological innovation because it costs their members jobs. The auto industry is an example.

A recent jump in labor-saving devices in auto plants has rekindled workers' fears of automation. Ever since Henry Ford rolled his first Model T off the line in 1913, auto companies have been trying to replace workers with machines.

The auto workers have become concerned about the array of computer applications on the line, and a new breed of robots that have proved they can do the nasty work of welding and painting. The union is fighting back in two ways. The first is to seek early retirement for older workers, thereby reducing the work force faster by retirement. The second is to negotiate more paid time off work. The UAW's spokesman, Vice-President Irving Bluestone, says this tactic has "created" some eleven thousand jobs at GM alone.

Wage increases are a complex issue, often resolved only after a strike. And there are always many questions apart from wages, such as these:

1. Should the employer contribute toward the health plan, or should he or she put the money into improving the retirement plan?
2. Should seniority lists be made up by departments or by job classifications, or should they be plant-wide?

The factors that are generally included in labor agreements are summarized here.

Wages rates and wage-payment policies
Normal workday or workweek
How overtime is to be calculated
Time to be taken for meals, regulations for making up lost time
Working conditions—rest periods, restroom facilities, safety rules and devices, medical care to be furnished
Vacations, leaves of absence, holidays, paid holidays; when vacations are to be taken; how the length of vacations varies with length of service
Selection, promotion, and layoff procedures
Production standards
Seniority—the degree it is to be recognized and how it is to be determined
Transfer of workers to new job assignments
Employment practices for using temporary workers
Welfare workers
Grievance procedures
Strikes and lockouts
Length of the agreement and when it is to terminate

To choose just one of these items for illustration, let us consider the holidays with pay that are given to employees. Table 8-2 shows the holidays and the percentage of union contracts that give that day off with pay.

TABLE 8-2
MOST COMMONLY OBSERVED HOLIDAYS, WITH PERCENTAGE OF UNION CONTRACTS THAT INCLUDE EACH

Holiday	%	Holiday	%
Thanksgiving	98	New Year's Eve	27
Labor Day	98	Employee's Birthday	22
Christmas	98	Veteran's Day	20
July Fourth	97	Floating Day	14
New Year's Day	97	Columbus Day	9
Memorial Day	96	Election Day	8
Good Friday	50	Christmas—New Year's Week	8
Day after Thanksgiving	49	Lincoln's Birthday	5
Christmas Eve	47	Martin Luther King's Birthday	3
Washington's Birthday	36		

Based on an analysis of 400 union contracts selected from the national file of over 5,000 cases.

SOURCE: Basic Patterns in Union Contracts, Bureau of National Affairs

DISPUTE RESOLUTION

The bargaining agreement covers those points that the negotiating parties consider important at the time. However, issues arise occasionally and must be resolved. Most labor agreements describe the procedure to be used when a dispute does arise.

Grievances and Grievance Procedures

Once a collective-bargaining contract is signed, that document governs the union-management relationship. The typical contract specifies what management can and cannot do and what the union's responsibilities might be.

The contract focuses on employee and employer rights. When an employee feels that his or her rights have been violated, he or she can file a grievance. A **GRIEVANCE is a specific, formal dissatisfaction expressed through an identified procedure**. A **complaint**, on the other hand, is a dissatisfaction that is not expressed through the formal grievance procedure. Formal grievance procedures vary depending upon the terms of the contract. But Figure 8-9 illustrates a typical grievance procedure.

As you will note in Figure 8-9, the process can be quite a lengthy one involving many persons. Some grievance procedures include only steps 1, 3, 5, and 7. The supervisor is the key to successful settlement of grievances with a minimum of difficulty. When supervisors are doing a good job, it is at this level that most grievances are settled.

Arbitration. The final step in the grievance procedure, arbitration, is of special interest. An **ARBITRATOR is an impartial labor expert who hears and settles grievances**. Usually the company and union each pay half of the arbitrator's fee, and the decision is binding.

Arbitration is seldom used in conjunction with reaching agreement on the contract itself. It has an important place in settling grievances, and the supply of arbitrators is quite limited. When both parties to the dispute agree to arbitration, the process is known as **voluntary arbitration.** If the union and the company are required by law to submit their dispute to a third party for a decision, the process is known as **compulsory arbitration.** Arbitration is commonly used in labor and industrial disputes when it is provided for in the contract.[3]

Most collective-bargaining agreements provide that specific disputes that cannot be resolved by any of the other established procedures must be submitted to voluntary arbitration for a final decision. The prevailing procedure in collective bargaining is to designate the type of arbitration procedure to be used when grievances cannot be settled without third-party assistance.

A study of 1,254 labor agreements in fourteen industries was completed by the Bureau of Labor Statistics. Three-fourths of these agreements provide for arbitration as the terminal point in the grievance machinery. Of the total number

[3]In all, thirty states have enacted arbitration statutes modeled more or less along the lines of the Uniform Arbitration Act. Naturally the statutes in some states are more comprehensive than in others, but they usually cover at least two of the three primary forms of arbitration practice in the United States—commercial, labor-management, and accident claims.

STEP 1	Employee Dissatisfaction
STEP 2	Discussion between Employee and Supervisor
STEP 3	Grievance Put in Writing Discussion between Union Steward and Supervisor
STEP 4	Meeting between Chief Steward and Supervisor's Manager and/or Personnel Manager
STEP 5	Meeting between Union Committee and Plant Manager
STEP 6	Meeting between National Union Representative and Top Company Executive or Industrial Relations Officer
STEP 7	Arbitration

FIGURE 8-9

A typical grievance procedure.

of workers covered by the arbitration provision, 28 percent were subject to permanently established arbitration machinery. The remaining 72 percent were subject to procedures calling for the selection of arbitrators whenever the need arose.

Of all the arbitration agreements, 93 percent (covering 91 percent of the workers) provided for **automatic** arbitration, or arbitration at the request of either party. Under this procedure, arbitration must be carried out if either party requests it; both parties have agreed in advance to accept the decision as final and binding.

Several private organizations have been established to serve management and labor in settling industrial disputes. The Council on Industrial Relations for the Electrical Contracting Industry, for example, was established in 1920 for the purpose of serving the entire industry. Any segment of the electrical industry in which contractual relations exist between employers and the International Brotherhood of Electrical Workers may make use of the council's arbitration machinery.

The American Arbitration Association (AAA) is a public-service, nonprofit organization. It is dedicated to resolving disputes of all kinds, chiefly through arbitration. The five most common forms of arbitration are: commercial, accident claims, labor, international, and inter-American. The AAA has a list of some twenty-six thousand men and women who are especially skilled in resolving disputes.

In the field of labor arbitration, the AAA makes available to industry and labor a roster of qualified labor arbitrators. Persons may be selected from this list by the parties to a dispute. The person (or persons) chosen hears both sides of the issue and writes the award.

The association publishes a number of pamphlets, bulletins, and research studies dealing with arbitration. It also conducts educational seminars about arbitration and labor relations.

The Government's Role in Settling Disputes

Industrial disputes have long been the concern of the federal government. Whenever a strike jeopardizes the public welfare, the government usually steps in and works for an immediate settlement of the controversy. Two important labor-relations boards are the National Mediation Board, which hears railroad and airline disputes, and the National Labor Relations Board.

Federal Mediation and Conciliation Service.

As an independent federal agency, this service assists businesses and unions by providing a staff without charge to act as mediators and conciliators in labor disputes. The agency also maintains a roster of qualified labor arbitrators. When the parties to a dispute decide to use arbitration, they make a request to the service for a roster of arbitrators, from which they select an arbitrator who hears the dispute and writes the decision.

The arbitrator is paid a fee for the service and is reimbursed for expenses. **The decision (award) is binding upon the parties, for they have agreed to this in the bargaining agreement**. The service, in addition to its central office in Washington, D.C., maintains regional offices in seven metropolitan areas and field offices in over seventy smaller cities. Other services the agency renders include arranging for general educational seminars for labor and management and workshops on labor arbitration.

The National Labor Relations Board.

Probably the leading government organization that aids in the settlement of labor disputes is the National Labor Relations Board, which was created by Congress in 1935 to guarantee labor the right to organize and bargain collectively. The board consists of five members appointed by the president of the United States; each member serves for five years.

There are two types of labor hearings. The first conducts an investigation of employers who are accused of unfair labor practices. The Labor Management Relations Act of 1947 assigned responsibility for this type of case to a general counsel. If the employer is found guilty, the company is ordered to stop interfering with the workers' right to organize; if necessary, the federal courts may be called on to enforce the counsel's rulings.

The second type deals with representation. This type comes under the direct jurisdiction of the labor board, which provides election machinery to determine the workers' preferences on how they want to be represented in collective bargaining.

According to the policy of the board, the workers have the exclusive right, without any interference from the employer, to decide whether they want to be represented by any union, and if so, which union they want. The union that receives a majority of the votes is selected as the workers' official representative. The board also initiates procedures for orderly collective bargaining between the chosen union and the employer.

Several states have conciliation boards to serve in disputes that do not fall under the jurisdiction of the National Labor Relations Board, and several larger cities have mediation boards.

UNION'S ROLE IN PROTECTING PENSION RIGHTS

Organized labor exerted great influence upon members of Congress to provide better protection for their rights earned under private company pension plans. This helped bring about the passage of the Employee Retirement Security Act of 1974. It is considered by many to be one of the most important social laws since the social security legislation. Because of its provisions, the pension entitlements of millions of workers will be safer and more generous than in the past. In general (a) more young workers will be included in company plans; (b) most workers will retain some of their pension rights when they change jobs and; (c) private company plans will be better financed and insured should the companies go bankrupt. The major provisions of the act are:

1. *Self-employed Retirement Benefits.* The amount that self-employed persons are allowed to set aside for retirement on a tax-free basis under the Keogh plan was increased to 15 percent of one's earnings or a maximum of $7,500 per year. This sum may then be taken as a tax deduction.
2. *National Insurance for Pensions.* A system whereby the federal government "insures workers' pensions" was established. The Pension Benefit Guaranty Corporation will insure a workers' vested benefits up to 100 percent of his or her average pay during the five years of highest earnings, with an initial ceiling of a $750 monthly pension.
3. *New Standards on Coverage and Vesting.* There are several provisions that apply here:
   a. All employees twenty-five years of age or older who have at least one year of service with a company must be included in that company's retirement plan.
   b. Employees must be permitted to accumulate pension credits in some orderly and fair manner. (There are three options under which such credits may be calculated.) Vesting refers to the time to which an employee's right eventually to receive a retirement benefit is no longer contingent on his remaining in the service of the employer.
   c. Employees have vested rights in the pension credits they accumulate. There are three options available here: The company may provide ways in which workers who leave the company may receive pension payments when attaining normal retirement age; a worker may transfer pension funds to the retirement program of another company; or he or she may take earned pension funds to invest in an individual retirement account.
4. *Individual Retirement Accounts (IRA).* If workers are not covered by a company pension plan, they can lay aside limited amounts on a tax-free basis in their own personal retirement plan. An individual may annually set aside up to 15 percent of his or her earnings—with an annual maximum of $1,500. This sum may be taken as an income tax deduction.
5. *Report to Employees.* Each worker who leaves a job must be given a summary of his or her pension benefits with the company. This report must also be filed with the Social Security Administration so that it may remind workers upon retirement of any benefits due them from company plans.
6. *Union Pension Plans.* Multicompany pension plans of unions must comply with the rules that apply to other company plans.

SUMMARY OF KEY CONCEPTS

The labor force includes persons employed on farms, in factories, in the professions, and as members of the armed forces. It is currently increasing at the rate of about 1.5 million persons per year. The most rapid growth rates occur in the professions, service occupations, clerical work, and among technicians. Women are a rapidly growing segment of the labor force as well.

Early attempts at organizing the labor force were largely ineffective, with social objectives as their motivation. However, with the formation of the American Federation of Labor in 1886, a definite shift occurred, both in purpose and growth. Under the leadership of A.F. of L. President Samuel Gompers, business unionism was the order of the day, with economic benefits for union members being the chief objective.

The era of most rapid growth occurred during the ten-year period following the passage of the Wagner Act in 1935, when union membership increased fourfold. Then, in the early 1950s, the A.F. of L. and the C.I.O. merged. This strengthened labor considerably, and union membership jumped to 18 million by 1956.

Organized labor has become a way of life in America, and as a political force, labor has greater influence than ever before. The chief objectives or organized labor are increased pay (including additional economic fringe benefits), improved working conditions, and strengthening of the unions themselves.

Labor and management are bound together by common interests and common goals. When they are able to work together to prevent a work stoppage, everyone gains—management, labor, the public, and government.

Bargaining today is done collectively, with labor acting as a unit through its representatives. Some bargaining is done at the local level, but more often it is done on an industry-wide or national level.

The labor agreement covers a wide variety of factors: wage rates, methods of wage payments, working conditions, seniority rights, vacations and holidays, dismissal policies, and the handling of grievances.

Most of the issues between management and labor are basically economic or jurisdictional. Historically, management has looked upon labor as a cost of production, whereas persons who make up the labor force see themselves more as partners in production.

There are private organizations whose sole function is to help management and labor reach agreement. The federal government is also very active in this field, through the Federal Mediation and Conciliation Service and the National Labor Relations Board.

The public, acting through the federal government, has established the policy of the self-determination of workers in deciding who their representatives should be in negotiations with their employers. When it is possible for disputes to be settled without a strike, the general public benefits, as well as management and labor.

Labor was instrumental in influencing pension reform that will make retirement plans safer and better for all employees—union and nonunion.

BUSINESS TERMS

You should be able to match these business terms with the statements that follow:

a. Arbitration
b. Bargaining agreement
c. Coalition bargaining
d. Collective bargaining

e. Grievance
f. Mediation
g. Open shop
h. Right-to-work law
i. Union shop

1. An agreement made between labor and management outlining the terms and conditions of work
2. A situation in which there is no union and no effort on the part of management to promote or prevent one
3. A state law banning the formation of union-shop agreements
4. The process by which management and labor agree on a contract
5. A situation in which several different unions collaborate in bargaining with an employer
6. A worker's written statement of some element of dissatisfaction about his or her work situation
7. The settling of a dispute where labor and management agree beforehand to accept the decision of the "go-between"

REVIEW QUESTIONS

1. What are the chief reasons why employees join labor unions?
2. In which industries are workers most highly organized?
3. Describe the procedure normally followed in collective bargaining.
4. Enumerate the principal items usually covered in a labor contract.
5. What is the difference between an *open shop* and a *union shop*?

DISCUSSION QUESTIONS

1. How does the presence of labor unions in a business help workers who are not union members?
2. How are workers' complaints handled before they reach the arbitration stage?
3. Why are so-called right-to-work laws so strongly opposed by unions?
4. Why is there such conflict between management and labor over the issue of participation in decision making?
5. What, in you opinion, is the number-one issue between organized labor and management?

BUSINESS CASE 8-1

Let's Form a Union!

The Standard Products Corporation stamps out parts that are used in assembling refrigerator cabinets and electric stoves. None of its employees are members of a union. Its wages are equal to those currently being paid by other manufacturers in the community. The fringe-benefits package includes $3,000 of life insurance coverage, with half the premium being paid by the company; free hospitalization benefits; and five paid holidays a year.

Assume that one of your worker colleagues is pushing for the formation of an industrial union with membership open to all employees, including those who work in the office. He has urged you to help him in organizing the union.

1. What factors would influence you in deciding whether to work for organizing a union?
2. What immediate (short-term) advantages to the workers do you see in forming such a union?
3. What long-term advantages would there be in having a union for all workers?
4. What might be some disadvantages to you, as an individual employee, in working for the formation of a union if the effort did not prove successful?

BUSINESS CASE 8-2

Trade-Off

Sam Jackson has a difficult decision to make. He is vice-president of labor relations for a large public utility. Currently a grievance is on his desk and he must decide how to handle it. He is soon to meet with the union vice-president. If they cannot resolve the problem the next step is arbitration, which could be costly.

The case involves an employee who took time off to attend the funeral of a third cousin and wants pay for it. The contract only authorizes payment of wages for employees to attend funerals of immediate family members (usually thought to be spouse, son, daughter, father, mother). However, the employee was very close to this cousin, since they had grown up together. The company's position has been no pay. The company has been concerned that this case could set a precedent that would open the door to paid time off for many funerals.

1. What are the trade-offs in this case?
2. What would you do if you were Mr. Jackson?

PRODUCTION AND OPERATIONS MANAGEMENT

9

STUDY OBJECTIVES

WHEN YOU HAVE FINISHED READING THIS CHAPTER, YOU SHOULD BE ABLE TO

ONE Distinguish between production and manufacturing

TWO State how and when manufacturing was started in the United States

THREE Give reasons to support the assertion that manufacturing is the cornerstone of our business system

FOUR Describe how time and motion studies contribute to scientific management in production

FIVE Identify ways and means by which production operations are controlled

SIX Explain the difference between production and productivity and state why this difference is important

IN THE NEWS

Sears's Misfortunes Affect Many Producers of Goods!

Sears Roebuck is this nation's largest retailer. However, a series of bad decisions and a lack of agreement on its basic strategy recently had a serious effect on the thousands of manufacturing companies that produce products for Sears. As a result of its difficulties Sears decided to reduce inventories, which meant fewer sales for suppliers.

Whirlpool Corporation in the past has sold almost half of its annual output of washers, dryers, air conditioners, and other appliances to Sears. DeSoto Inc., a major manufacturer of paint and furniture for Sears, was hurt as well. Sanyo Manufacturing, a U.S. subsidiary of Japan's Sanyo Electric, had to lay off 20 percent of the thirteen-hundred-person work force at its Arkansas plant.

Sears and its suppliers have had a difficult time trying to boost retail sales. The main reason is that other chains, department stores, and specialists continually nibble away at Sears's customer base. The problems encountered by the manufacturers who supply Sears are only a few of the continuing series of problems that challenge production and operations management professionals.

Mass production is a modernized mode of manufacture that combines uniformity and continuity of motion in all factory procedures and assembly lines, speed achieved by scientific time studies, and precision of every part and operation. It makes uniformity of design, accuracy of part changes, and economy of performance possible.

HENRY FORD

Did you ever stop to think about how to put bristles in a toothbrush? Or how to treat paper pans so that a person can cook in them? Also, why does a disposable lighter that once sold for $1.75 now cost only $0.50?

Almost everything we buy today except fresh fruits and vegetables has been manufactured. The things we buy are the result of some blend of raw materials, labor, and energy. The raw materials come from the earth and oceans. The process of removing raw materials from mines, forests, oceans, and farms is one form of **production**. Production also includes **manufacturing—the process of converting raw materials into finished goods**. Although all aspects of production are important, our discussion in this chapter will emphasize manufacturing.

Business in America operates on a large scale. This is certainly true of manufacturing. It is specialized, mechanized, and automatized. This chapter examines the production processes, operations management, control in manufacturing, and productivity. The following chapter focuses on the management of energy and logistics.

MANUFACTURING: THE CORNERSTONE OF AMERICAN BUSINESS

MANUFACTURING is defined as **the process of using materials, labor, and machinery to create finished products that satisfy human needs or wants.** We have seen earlier that materials, people, machines, and money are frequently called the means of production. Converting them into useful finished goods creates **form utility**.

The lesson of how to produce goods on a mass scale came to us from England where, in the middle of the eighteenth century, the Industrial Revolution was booming. As thousands of laborers and enterprising business-people migrated to America from England and Western Europe, manufacturing developed here.

Early American Manufacturing

In early Colonial days very little was done to encourage manufacturing industries in America. But it soon became apparent to some leaders that if this country was to grow and gain economic independence from Britain, factories must be established.

Alexander Hamilton was one of the first to see the importance of manufacturing. He had visions of this country becoming a strong industrial power. In 1790, as secretary of the treasury, he issued a "Report on Manufactures." He advocated protective tariffs (to give American goods a price advantage), restrictions on imports, and the prohibition of exporting raw materials that were essential for manufacturing. Even before Congress could officially act on his "Report," Hamilton helped to organize the Society for Establishing Useful Manufactures. This was a private organization intended to encourage the production of cotton and linen goods, paper, printing, and public works.

Soon American ingenuity produced sewing machines, flour mills, and shoe factories. Then in 1793 Eli Whitney invented the cotton gin. Thus cotton cloth soon became the cheapest and most popular woven material in America.

The development of the woolen textiles followed that of cotton. John and Arthur Scholfield came to Massachusetts from England and erected a woolen mill at Byfield. Others followed them in the industry, and by 1810 there were two dozen woolen mills in operation. A half-century later, woolen mills had been established not only in New England but also in Texas, California, and Oregon. By 1860 there were over seventeen hundred such mills employing sixty thousand machine operators.

The total number of workers in the manufacturing and construction industries more than doubled between 1820 and 1840. Thus more goods were being made in the factories than in the homes and small shops. By 1850 manufacturing accounted for one-eighth of the total national income. The value of goods manufactured in that year (flour, meal, cotton goods, lumber, shoes, clothing, glass, iron) reached a billion dollars.

Today factories provide employment for millions of workers. In fact, more persons are employed in manufacturing than in any other segment of our business system—approximately 25 percent of the civilian work force.

Manufacturing not only employs millions of workers directly but also supports additional workers in other fields of employment. The Industrial Bureau of the Atlanta Chamber of Commerce reports that the payroll of a factory employing 150 persons supports, on an average, 383 occupied homes, 24 professionals, 6,000 acres of farm products, 18 teachers, and 33 retail stores. All this accounts for $500,000 in annual retail sales, 320 automobiles and the services needed for them, and $2.5 million in tax valuation.

As an example of how a manufacturer supports other businesses and the people who work in them, let us look at the Chrysler Corporation's financial difficulties during the late 1970s. Chrysler was seeking government assistance to bail the company out of serious financial straits.

Senators and congressmen from communities all over the country that would be affected were willing to put pressure on the government to come to Chrysler's aid. Dealers, suppliers, and elected local officials were all mobilized to help Chrysler sell its need for aid. Over 140,000 employees, forty-seven hundred dealers, and hundreds of suppliers would be affected if Chrysler folded. The communities in which each plant and dealership was located would be affected as well.

But potentially the hardest hit would be the city of Detroit. A report compiled by the Department of Transportation concluded that if Chrysler went under, it might take the city of Detroit with it. Loss of the number-three auto maker would destroy the Motor City's economic base for years to come, double its unemployment rate, heighten racial tensions, and force some suppliers into bankruptcy. The federal government came to Chrysler's rescue by guaranteeing one and one half billion dollars in loans in May, 1980.

Manufacturing can truly be called the cornerstone of our American business system. Its economic contribution lies in three areas: (1) it provides employment for millions of workers; (2) it changes the form of raw materials into useful products; and (3) it adds to the value of raw materials.

When you read about manufacturing in the United States in government publications, data are often reported by geographical regions. Figure 9-1 shows what areas are included in the different regional divisions.

The Middle Atlantic and East North Central regions together account for approximately one-half of the country's total manufacturing in terms of number of persons employed and in dollar value added by manufacturing.

FIGURE 9-1

Manufacturing regions of the United States. (Source: Department of Commerce, Bureau of the Census.)

MANUFACTURING ACHIEVEMENTS TODAY

Every day we read about some new technology or some new product that is being developed by American industry.

The International Paper Company has developed a product called Pressware, which is the result of three years of research and experimentation. Pressware containers are made of paper. They have a special polyester coating that keeps them from soaking up grease and cooking juices. These containers can withstand temperatures as high as 425 degrees Fahrenheit.

ANOTHER MANUFACTURING ACHIEVEMENT

Another manufacturing achievement developed by the International Paper Company saves paper. Even the best printers end up printing stacks of wastepaper every day. The reason? High-speed presses do not stop when it is time to change the paper roll. A new roll is just spliced to the tail of the old one and off it goes, traveling as fast as two thousand feet a minute.

But the abrupt change in tension while the new roll is getting up to speed causes the paper to slide, and thousands of misprinted pages can roll off the press. In just one day a printer using standard paper rolls, which measure forty inches in diameter, loses enough paper to print four thousand magazines.

International Paper found a way to cut that waste dramatically with a giant paper roll that measures fifty inches in diameter. This roll has seventeen miles of paper wound around it—five miles more than the standard roll. (Picture 299 football fields placed end to end and you will have some idea of the length.) That extra length means fewer roll changes and a staggering difference in waste.

By eliminating thirteen changeovers per day, one printer saved $190,000 worth of paper per year. This also reduces the chances of costly downtime, for a faulty paper splice can shut down the presses for an hour.

Tires That Don't Go Flat

The Goodyear Tire and Rubber Company has been making flatproof tires for agricultural, industrial, and military use for several years. The company has now extended their use to the mining industry.

In these tires that never go flat, air is replaced with a spongy material called Permafoam. They are immune to spikes, jagged metal, glass, and timber splinters.

The Carpet Fiber Revolution

Technology makes for consumer convenience, and it brings about economy in the use of labor and materials. It also provides new products of higher quality than those they replace. Take the carpet industry as an example.

A mill in Georgia discovered that tufting machines previously used to make bedspreads could also be used to make floor coverings. At nearly the same time, the Du Pont Company developed bulked continuous filament (BCF) nylon. This type of nylon can be put directly on a tufting machine and made into a carpet in a one-step operation.

These twin developments virtually turned the carpet industry upside down. By 1968 synthetic fibers—nylon and polyester in particular—were used in 52 percent of all carpets being made. Today synthetic fibers account for just about all the fibers consumed by U.S. carpet mills.

A carpet made of synthetic fibers will last two to three times longer than a carpet of comparable weight made of wool. The former is also easier to clean, recovers faster when stepped on, can match any aesthetic effect attained by natural fibers, and is less expensive than other flooring materials.

The Contribution of Chemistry

Manufacturing covers many different industries. We cannot consider them all, so let us take chemistry as one example. Chemistry is a $140 billion industry, employing a million people; and it accounts for 6 percent of our gross national product. Chemistry is responsible not only for synthetic fibers but also for pharmaceuticals; plastics; paints, soaps, and cosmetics; and agricultural fertilizers and pesticides.

The chemical industry weighs heavily on the positive side of our country's balance of payments. In 1977 chemical exports totaled $10.8 billion and imports totaled $5.5 billion. This provided a trade surplus of more than $5 billion. The contribution that chemistry makes to production is aptly summarized by Max Ways, formerly a member of the board of editors of *Fortune* magazine.

THE CONTRIBUTION OF CHEMISTRY IN PRODUCTION

Any American who mentally checks the objects in his home or workplace will find few untouched by chemistry. The obvious examples range from medicines to tires, but the less obvious products where chemistry has made significant contributions are probably more important in aggregate. The food supply—of the U.S. and of the world—would be scarcer, dearer and less varied without fertilizers, pesticides and preservatives. TV sets, telephones, computers, all have chemical inputs. One cannot say much about the energy shortage without referring to present and prospective contributions of chemistry to the technology of oil, gas, coal, uranium and electricity. Chemistry plays an essential role in the processing of iron, copper, aluminum and almost every other material we use.

The chemical industry, of course, has caused some problems as well. The environmental and physical effect of some chemicals is very harmful. This can cause serious health problems if the chemicals are not carefully tested prior to their use and carefully controlled if found to be dangerous.

OPERATING PROBLEMS OF A MANUFACTURING PLANT

The production manager is concerned with far more than the effective use of raw materials. This manager must also develop a working organization, as we learned in Chapter 4. One example of an organization chart for production is shown in Figure 9-2. Today, energy for plant maintenance and operation has become a critical factor in production. Limitations placed upon manufacturing by recent environmental standards are also important.

Every manufacturing firm requires the correct physical facilities to carry on its production operation. These include plant location, plant layout, and building design.

Plant Location

The principal factors of plant location are based on the theory that the geographical point selected must balance costs and benefits. Thus attention must be given to several factors that management must evaluate. These factors are as follows:

Selection of Plant Location

Site Factors
Proximity to sales markets
Proximity to related industries
Vulnerability to natural disasters

Cost Factors
Cost of land
Cost of utilities
Construction costs
Cost of taxes
Cost of power, water, and fuel

Service Factors
Educational facilities
Fire and police protection
Health and medical services

Service Factors (continued)
Transportation facilities
Tax regulations and local laws

Resource Factors
Availability of skilled personnel
Availability of unskilled personnel
Availability of raw materials

Miscellaneous Factors
Library facilities
Religious facilities
Public facilities
Employee shopping facilities
Adequate employee housing
Adequate business facilities

Virtually all the factors displayed here can be evaluated from the standpoint of their economic or cost feasibility. For example, what is the cost of shipping finished products to the market by water as compared with truck shipment? Can adequate rail facilities be made available through the construction of spur tracks? Will employees be able to find suitable housing at a price they can afford?

The early history of locating factories in urban centers was one of **CONCENTRATION**. Concentrating facilities in one area provided large numbers of workers in cities like Pittsburgh, Cleveland, and Chicago. The concentration of population also provided a nearby market, as well as a good supply of labor. New England was naturally the nation's first important industrial region. But as the population of the Middle Atlantic States increased, these states first equaled and then surpassed New England as a manufacturing region. In later years the rapid population growth of Los Angeles enabled it to become one of our leading manufacturing centers.

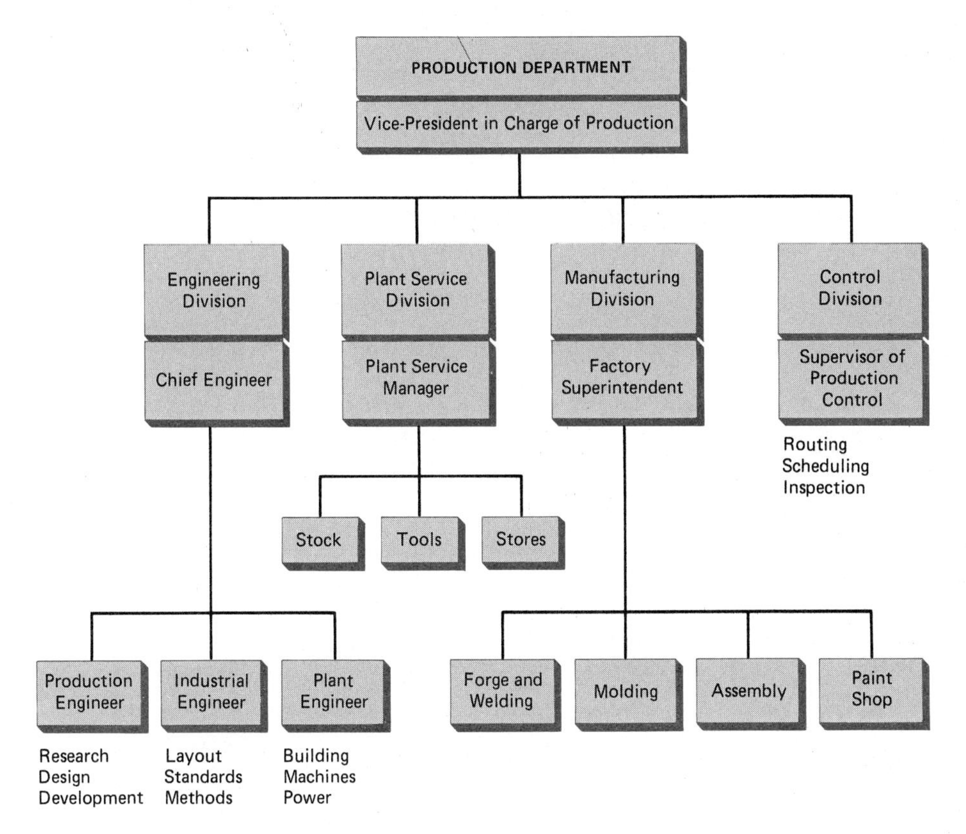

FIGURE 9-2

Production department organization chart.

Currently, **DISPERSION** in manufacturing is the order of the day—building branch factories in different geographical areas. In this way a company can serve several separate market centers. It lessens the extent of loss due to a physical disaster and avoids the high cost of large amounts of land for industrial sites.

WHITE CONSOLIDATED INDUSTRIES AND APPLIANCE MANUFACTURE

White Consolidated Industries did not make appliances until 1967, but in 1978 almost two-thirds of its revenue came from appliance operations.

Between 1967 and 1979 White purchased the appliance operations of seven different companies. These included such large operations as those of Westinghouse Electric, Ford Motor Company, American Motors, and General Motors' Frigidaire Division.

White sells about half of its appliance production as private-label brands through such companies as J. C. Penney, Montgomery Ward, and Western Auto stores.

DIVERSIFICATION is another characteristic of today's manufacturing. Instead of producing a single product, a company makes many different products. Some of the products manufactured by White Consolidated Industries of Cleveland are shown in Figure 9-3.

FIGURE 9-3

The best of two worlds.

Plant Layout

Let us assume that management has carefully weighed all these location factors and has decided on the site for a new plant. The next step is to decide on plant layout. **PLANT LAYOUT** refers to **the arrangement of the work processes to be performed.** Machines and work stations should be arranged so that production operations are carried through to completion with efficiency. A good layout eliminates, as far as possible, wasted motion of both personnel and materials. The amount of space needed for an efficient layout helps determine site selection.

Since management is concerned with producing quality products at a low unit cost, it must make detailed plans for plant layout and the placing of equipment. To keep unit costs low, the layout must permit a free flow of work, a minimum investment of capital, and desirable working conditions for employees. Here are some of the factors that must be considered in planning plant layout:

1. Nature of the manufacturing process
2. Type of product
3. Extent and nature of mechanization
4. Allowances for flexibility and future expansion

The type of building to be erected is closely related to the plant layout needed —in fact, the two are usually planned simultaneously, each influencing the other. If a building is purchased or leased, the layout must be adapted to the building— either as it stands or within the limits of possible changes. The ideal situation is to plan and construct a new building that will give precisely the plant layout desired.

The manufacturing process. If you are going to manufacture only one or two stock products, you can plan a continuous-production process in which the machines are arranged in an orderly sequence. On the other hand, if you are going to manufacture many different products, or if you must make adaptations for special orders, you will usually find it better to group similar machines together.

The steel industry is an excellent example of the *continuous-production* process. The open hearth furnaces burn twenty-four hours a day and are operated by three work shifts. The continuous-production process is also well suited to the glass and rayon industries.

The production of automobiles, appliances, and machines illustrates factory processes that use the **INTERMITTENT PROCESS**. Here, **factory operation may be halted at intervals without damaging the finished product.**

Of course, the differences between continuous and intermittent processes require different types of layouts for plant and equipment.

Type of product. The plant layout best suited to a particular factory is also influenced by the type of product being made. A plant that simply assembles component parts requires one sort of layout. A plant that produces parts and also assembles them requires another. Similarly, whether the article being produced is standard or made to order makes a difference. Made-to-order work does not permit the use of uniform procedures such as those that can be used when

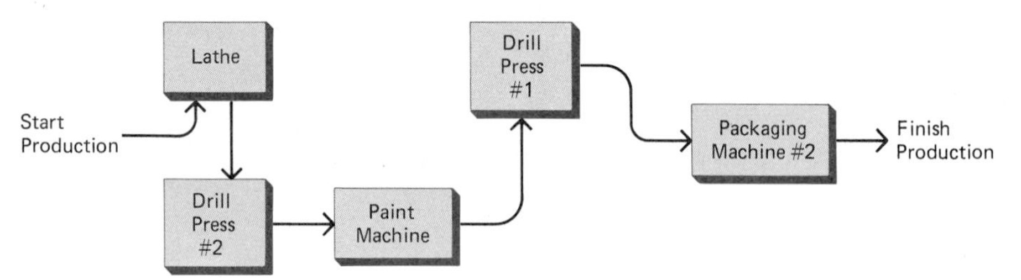

FIGURE 9-4

Product layout in manufacturing. (From *Production and Operations Management* by Everett E. Adam, Jr., and Ronald J. Ebert, 1978. Reprinted by permission of Prentice-Hall, Inc.)

standard products are made. Moreover, specially produced articles are usually shipped shortly after being completed. In contrast, standard articles are often kept on hand for a time and must be stored.

Extent of mechanization. In a plant where most of the work is performed by machines, the layout must promote the free flow of work from one stage of production to another with a minimum of handling. When certain types of workers

FIGURE 9-5

The mass storage cartridge of the computer controls the manufacturing operation. (Source: Photo courtesy of the Control Data Corporation.)

such as machinists or carpenters play a major role in the production process, the layout must provide for freedom of body movement and for the frequent handling of materials.

Automation affects plant layout. Computers can be used for many things, including the running of machines. The item in Figure 9-5 has been at least partially produced on computer-controlled machines.

Building Design

The two most important factors in building design are **flexibility** and **expansion.**

Flexibility. **Flexibility in building design is essential, for it affords versatility and makes buildings less likely to become obsolete**. A building that uses large steel trusses to support the roof provides large working areas free of column obstructions. Placement of the heating and plumbing lines and equipment overhead also frees large floor areas. These free areas enable a company to rearrange layout procedures in the future and keep abreast of technological improvements. They also make it easy and inexpensive to change production processes or to manufacture new products.

The single-story building is the most flexible design because of the ease and economy of knocking out walls and of building additions.

Expansion. The first step in providing for expansion is the acquisition of a large enough land area to allow for larger buildings without reducing parking areas. Multistory buildings that are designed to have new floors added must be structured to bear the added weight. Utility services must be installed that will connect easily with the devices serving the new floors.

In order to place the building properly for best use of loading and docking facilities, railroad sidings, parking areas, and the power plant, the location of the additions must be a part of the original building plan. Long-run factory planning provides for future growth and increasing productive capacity.

SCIENTIFIC MANAGEMENT IN MANUFACTURING

Although people had for many years talked about ways to improve their work procedures, few persons really examined human work movements until the late nineteenth century. We have already mentioned that Henri Fayol, a Frenchman who managed a coal mine, analyzed the basic process of management and is generally credited with giving us the fundamental management principles upon which others have built.

The Influence of Frederick W. Taylor

Some of the contributions of Frederick W. Taylor have been discussed in earlier chapters. Since most of his work was done in factories and shops, scientific management first made its greatest headway in manufacturing. Taylor's observations and research were responsible for instituting new methods and procedures that greatly increased the productivity of workers.[1] He also developed the first wage-

[1]Review our discussion in Chapter 5.

incentive plan, which bears his name. His work formed the basis of contributions from such men as Frank B. Gilbreth, Henry Gantt, Harrington Emerson, and Carl Barth, some of whom were colleagues and collaborators of Taylor.

Time and Motion Study

Among the earliest efforts in scientific management were studies that timed a person's movements and observed that person's work with the intent of eliminating unnecessary or wasted activity.

Motion Study. The purpose of motion study is to develop the most effective method of performing each job by discovering and eliminating wasted motions. The motion-study analyst, who is a trained specialist, breaks down each job into all the elementary motions that the worker uses, such as reaching, selecting, picking up, putting together, and replacing on the conveyor belt. Then the analyst studies both the separate motions and the operations as a whole in order to discover the rhythm of movement, distances covered, coordination, and sequence. After the analyst has completed the study, he or she recommends that certain distances be shortened and that certain movements be eliminated. The analyst tries to advise the worker on the most desirable rhythm and timing, and helps the employee to work out the proper sequence of steps.

Time study. Time study is usually associated with motion study. When the observer breaks down the whole operation into the worker's elementary motions, he or she also determines the time required for each motion by using a stopwatch. He or she selects a location that permits observation of every action of the worker. Each time the worker makes a motion the observer times it and records the time on an observation sheet. The observer also records all work stoppages and delays, and anything else that seems significant. Every elementary motion that the worker makes during the completion of one unit of work (that is, during what is referred to as the "job cycle") must be timed repeatedly. Then the average of all these timings for a single movement becomes the base time for that motion. The total of the averages for all the separate motions involved in one operation becomes the standard time for the complete job cycle.

Sometimes the worker's motions are so rapid that the observer cannot do an accurate job with a stopwatch. Then he or she uses cameras to make what are called "micromotion studies." A large clock having a face divided into hundredths of seconds is placed behind the worker, and a motion-picture camera records both the movement and the position of the clock's sweep hand. By studying the series of pictures the analyst can calculate with great accuracy just how long the movement took.

As we can see, success in time and motion studies requires the full cooperation of the worker being studied. If the worker is not in sympathy with the idea, the results are very likely to be invalid. Then, too, the observer should use a typical worker, not one who is exceptionally fast or slow, efficient or inefficient.

Labor representatives should be invited to participate in time studies. Workers must be given assurance that a study will not be used to force more work from them in less time just to save production costs. If they feel that the result will be higher standards for them to meet for the same pay, they are not likely to be very cooperative.

CONTROLLING THE PLANT OPERATION

The purpose of production control is to maintain a smooth, constant flow of work from raw material to finished product. Thus the product will be completed in the shortest possible time and at the lowest possible unit cost. This requires careful coordination of all the factors that enter into the production process—materials, machines, people, and methods.

Procedural Control

There are four steps in procedural control: (1) **planning,** (2) **routing,** (3) **scheduling,** and (4) **dispatching.**

Planning. **Efficient production is rooted in proper planning. Everything that comes afterward in routing, scheduling, and dispatching reflects the quality of the planning that has taken place in the early stages.** To plan effectively, management must have a realistic knowledge of the plant's limitations and must be constantly informed on the total amount of work in process. (See Figure 9-6.)

Planning is more than setting up overall procedures and objectives. It calls for close attention to specific details. For example, the type and quantity of materials that will be needed must be determined in advance by the production supervisor and other assistants. When a large quantity of material is involved, it is necessary to check the inventory records to see whether a sufficient amount is on hand. Second, if finished parts manufactured by other firms will be used in the assembly process, the number of each kind needed must be determined by the executive in charge of production and ordered in time. Purchase requisitions for these parts, and for any materials that are not on hand, must be issued by the production department to the purchasing department.

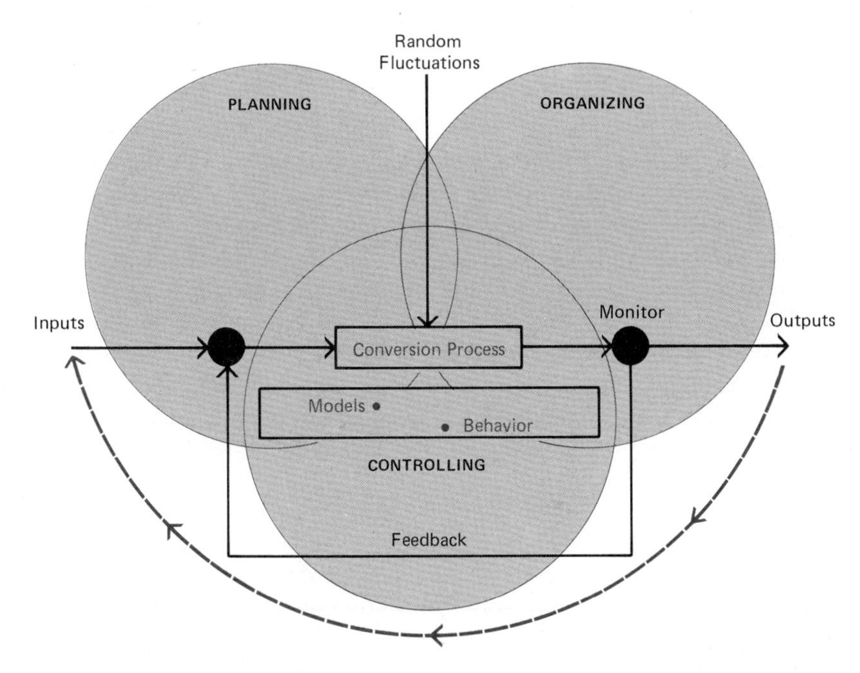

FIGURE 9-6

Production operation and control relationships. (Adapted from *Production and Operations Management* by Everett E. Adam, Jr., and Ronald J. Ebert, 1978. Reprinted by permission of Prentice-Hall, Inc.)

In addition, the work must be distributed to the different departments, the number of workers needed must be determined, the number and types of machines required must be decided upon, and the time for the completion of each stage must be assigned. All this is the responsibility of those in charge of the production department.

In a small industrial plant that employs only a few workers, the supervisor often handles this detailed planning in an informal manner, particularly when the production processes are standardized. On the other hand, in a large industry such as the automobile industry, where dozens of different materials and scores of finished parts from other factories are assembled, management usually sets up a planning department. The complexity of the operation makes such a department a necessity. Each model manufactured is a separate planning problem, and many different operations are performed simultaneously. Although some pass through only one process, others go through several operations before they are completed.

Routing. **Control over the sequence of operations that are performed in the manufacture of a particular article** is called **ROUTING.** When you realize that some articles involve the use of several machines, and that some machines must be used for several different processes, you can see how important routing is in a modern plant. To complicate matters even more, several different jobs are "in process" at the same time.

The person responsible for routing determines the order in which different operations will be performed, which personnel will do the work, and which machines, tools, and supplies will be used. This person must also indicate both the route for each part produced and its relation to the other parts in process. He or she then issues route cards to each department, showing the sequence of operations for each part that passes through that department. Detailed drawings are sometimes prepared to chart all necessary production processes and assemblies.

Scheduling. The scheduling of production work ensures a smooth flow of work through the production process, avoids conflicts and delays in the use of workers and machines, and sets timetables for the arrival of needed materials and the shipping of finished goods in such a way as to keep costs to a minimum. Scheduling is necessary to finish stock items at a rate that will avoid the depletion of items on hand, and to meet time limits on job-order work.

The scheduler must prepare a master schedule that shows the number of items he or she expects to be completed during each week or month. For job-order work, the schedule can be worked backward from the desired delivery date. The scheduler determines a definite time as the date on or before which each operation or part must be completed. Since the scheduler provides the supervisors with schedules for the different jobs, rush orders can be accommodated. And jobs that permit an extra allowance of time can be used to avoid idle periods, thus keeping costs down.

The scheduler must also keep in mind the amount of plant capacity already committed to jobs in process. Also he or she must maintain a balance of work assignments to different departments, thus avoiding overloading. The scheduler is responsible for coordinating the delivery of parts from other plants with the completion of parts within the factory. This avoids overloaded periods for the most frequently used transportation facilities (to avoid delay in delivery of raw materials and finished goods).

Dispatching. The issuing of work orders for each job is necessary for the planning to be carried through, for proper routing to be arranged, and for the schedule to be maintained. The preparation and issuing of these work orders, which entails a good deal of clerical work, is known as **DISPATCHING.** The dispatcher must prepare requisitions for needed materials and supplies and see that the required tools are assembled.

The dispatch clerk must use follow-up routines to keep abreast of the progress of each task. He or she must record the times of starting and completing each task and must deliver work orders and submit reports of completed work. The dispatch clerk uses messengers, pneumatic-tube conveyors, and dispatch boards for delivering and receiving records. He or she must have a systematic filing plan for each type of record. The dispatcher is also responsible for seeing that work progresses in accordance with the routing cards and time schedules. He or she must avoid idle time for machines and people by issuing new work orders as soon as they have completed their tasks. Dispatchers have a responsible job, for they determine how effectively planning is translated into actual output.

Performance Control

Performance control utilizes many techniques. Among the most commonly used are the **planning board, progress charts, standards,** and **inspection.**

FIGURE 9-7

A Boston firm nearly doubles production—through Wassell scheduling. Without adding either equipment or employees, Barnstead, Still & Sterilizer, a large Boston manufacturing firm, has increased production through better scheduling of manpower and order control. Manpower is scheduled on the two VU-9074 Wassell VU-boards, and order control is tracked on three 100—200 85P Produc-Tol Boards, one of which is visible at the far right of the picture. (Courtesy Wassell Organization, Inc.)

The planning board. When several types of work are in progress, involving dozens of different types of machines, management must use some system for exercising overall control. Many modern industrialists set up a visual display called the *planning board.* This shows in detail the plans for three classes of work: jobs in progress, jobs to be started when the work in process is completed, and job orders not yet scheduled. The planning board also provides a separate record for each machine. The shop supervisor can see at the beginning of each day or week exactly what management has planned for the department.

Progress charts. A progress chart serves much the same purpose as a bar graph. Posted on the bulletin board or on a wall, it shows at a glance the dates on which each job must begin, the number of units to be produced, and the date by which each job must be finished. Lines on the chart indicate whether each job is on, ahead of, or behind schedule.

Standards. No production-control system can function effectively without standards. This part of the control system establishes uniform methods of task performance. It also sets standards for quality and for working conditions. Operating standards, which are expressed in terms of time and procedure, indicate the amount of time needed to perform a particular job. This is to provide the data needed for scheduling. The quality-control department establishes an apparatus for use in comparing parts or products with established quality standards. Good standards for working conditions include good ventilation, adequate light, noise control, clean working areas, and freedom from hazards. Periodic lubrication of machines and equipment and a constant supply of materials to all work stations are essential to the proper functioning of this part of the control program.

Inspection. **The most important function of inspection is to enforce standards. Carefully prepared plans and carefully observed schedules are of no value if the finished product proves unacceptable, and establishing standards is useless unless steps are taken to ensure that they are met.**

In addition to maintaining quality standards, inspection serves three other functions:

1. If you can catch defective materials or substandard work early in the production process, you can prevent the waste of additional labor later on.
2. Careful inspection at various stages during the completion of a product helps you to discover points of weakness in the manufacturing process.
3. Thorough inspection of the finished product helps prevent the shipping and delivery of defective or substandard products, and helps you to maintain goodwill and a good reputation among your customers.

Inspection enters the picture even before the production process begins. For example, the receiving department inspects raw materials before accepting them, and the supervisor inspects tools and gauges at regular intervals to make sure they are still up to standard. Since one of the chief purposes of inspection is to see that set standards are being upheld, the worker must be held responsible for poor-quality workmanship. In fairness, however, the worker must first be supplied with sound materials and effective machinery.

How thorough the inspection will be, at what stages it will take place, and who will conduct it are matters of company policy. They depend on the nature of the articles being manufactured and the production processes involved. For example, if you are manufacturing parts for precision machinery that have to be accurate to within 0.005 of an inch, your inspection will be far more elaborate and meticulous than if you were turning out toys, pencils, or paperweights. For most products, a sampling inspection is all that is necessary, but in some cases every item must be inspected (this is called "100 percent inspection").

Through experience, most manufacturers have found that it is better to make the inspection crew responsible to the production manager than to the shop supervisor. Since the supervisor is intent on keeping schedules and pushing production ahead, he or she sometimes shows a tendency to treat quality standards rather loosely. After all, a high rejection rate would slow up production and would reflect adversely on the supervisor and the department.

There are two types of inspection: **centralized inspection,** in which the inspectors are grouped together in one area, and **floor inspection,** in which the inspectors are scattered along the assembly line.

Testing is one phase of inspection; it is especially useful for inspecting completed products. For example, cans are tested under pressure at high temperatures, and automatic washing machines are put through test runs before being boxed for shipment.

PRODUCTIVITY IN INDUSTRY

Production gives us the big picture—the total amount of goods and services being produced balanced against the resources needed to produce it. Total production (output) increases annually because there are more inputs (materials, labor, and capital) each year. **When we interpret output in terms of inputs we are talking about PRODUCTIVITY**—the efficiency of production:

$$\frac{\text{Output}}{\text{Inputs}} = \text{Productivity}$$

Productivity growth is a basic source of improving our standard of living. An increase in the efficiency of production results in more goods and services from the same input of production resources. This translates into a gain in national real income.

Advances in productivity depend in large measure on finding better ways to produce. As David T. Kearns, president and chief operating officer of the Xerox Corporation, said: "Creativity and innovation are hallmarks of America's success. It is in part the responsibility of business to provide the environment and the stimulus to keep this process vital." Without increases in productivity, there can be no increase in the national standard of living.

An example of innovation is the project-center concept used by General Motors in the development of its X-cars.[2] This concept represents a departure from the previous procedures when each division operated separately. It involves the forming of an engineering group that includes experts in customer service and marketing as well as design, manufacture, and assembly. These experts come from the different divisions of the company. The group's purpose was to eliminate unnecessary work and avoid duplication. All the members of the group worked to keep development costs low and to strengthen the respective divisions. The organization design is similar to the matrix organization discussed in Chapter 4.

We are most familiar with labor productivity—measured as the output per worker per hour. But to see the total view of how well the company is moving, we must consider total-factor productivity. This means we must consider the capital input as well as labor.

Total-Factor Productivity

Total-factor productivity in the United States has risen constantly since World War II. However, the rate of increase has recently slowed down. The causes for this are complex, but some probable explanations include

1. The increase in the amount of capital needed for better safety and pollution abatement
2. Less-than-full employment conditions during the past decade
3. A shift in the labor force mix, with a higher percentage of women who, on the average, have less experience than their male counterparts
4. Failure of the capital formation process that allows business to invest in new plants and equipment

From 1948 to 1980, total-factor productivity increased by an average 2.3 percent per year. Labor productivity increased by an average of 3.0 percent, but capital productivity increased by an average of only 1.0 percent per year. (See Figure 9-8.)

[2]General Motors spent four years and about $2.7 billion in the development of the X-cars. The X-cars are the Citation, Skylark, Phoenix, and Omega.

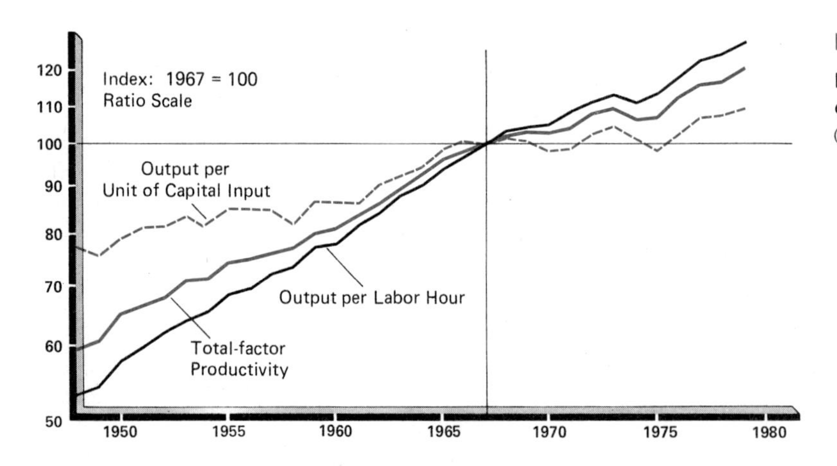

FIGURE 9-8

Productivity in the private domestic business economy. (Source: The Conference Board.)

A good example of the decline in the rate of productivity increase can be found in the U.S. steel industry.

The nation's last big steel mill was built in the 1960s by Bethlehem Steel at Burns Harbor, Indiana. Since then skyrocketing costs and low steel prices have held down earnings and discouraged the building of new mills. Companies contend that they cannot afford new mills on tight profit margins—it is estimated that a new mill would cost $3 to $4 billion.

Industry capacity has increased somewhat (an average of 1 million tons per year), but it has been through the installation of more productive equipment at existing plants. Even then the annual increase is only about 0.01 percent of 1977 steel production.

"There are a lot of old, tea-kettle facilities sitting around out there," says Benjamin Linsky, a University of West Virginia professor who has studied the problem.

The Youngstown works of U.S. Steel is typical. Begun in 1892, it has become less competitive every year. U.S. Steel does not wish to spend large sums of money to fix the obsolete facility, but a recession and a drop in demand for steel may force the closing of this marginal plant. It is estimated that 8 to 26 percent of America's steelmaking capacity is in similar straits.

The farm sector posted the best growth in total-factor productivity—an annual increase of 3.0 percent. The growth rate for manufacturing averaged 2.1 percent annually. The balance of the private economy averaged 1.9 percent annually. The graphs for the three sectors are shown in Figure 9-9.

The average amount of capital per worker in the private economy increased from $28,000 per worker in 1948 to $42,000 per worker in 1976. Both values are stated in 1972 dollars to allow for the result of inflation.

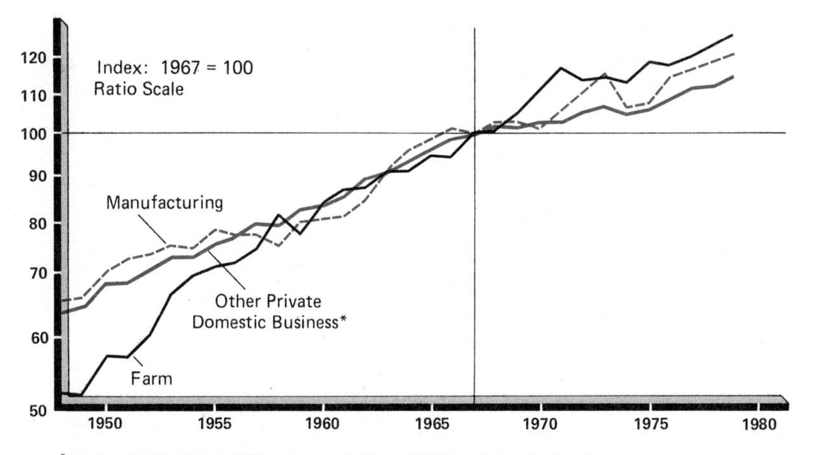

*Services, trade, transportation, communications, utilities, mining, construction.

FIGURE 9-9

Total-factor productivity by major sector. (Source: The Conference Board.)

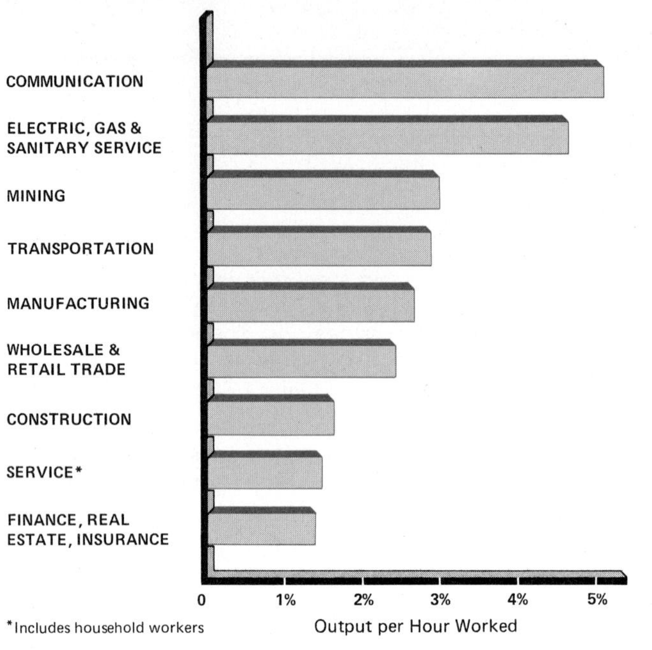

FIGURE 9-10
Productivity by selected sectors—average annual growth rates, 1947–73. (Source: The Conference Board.)

Different industries vary greatly in their total-factor productivity. The leaders are the communications and utilities industries. They are the ones where large increases in the capital stock were caused by major advances in technology. The service industries are at the low end. The annual growth rates for selected sectors of the economy are shown in Figure 9-10.

Rewards of Increased Productivity

As the volume produced increases, the production cost per unit decreases. As productivity rises, the unit cost decreases even faster. As the unit costs are lowered, part of the savings is passed along to consumers. As one example of this, the early cost of a disposable lighter has been reduced from $1.75 to $0.50. Similarly, the first smoke detectors and alarms sold for close to $100 and can now be purchased for $12; electronic digital watches have been reduced from $250 to $10. The price of the Black and Decker quarter-inch electric drill dropped from $24 twenty years ago to $8 now. And every time the price dropped 30 percent, the sales volume doubled.

The Space Frontier

The space shuttle perches atop its mother ship, a Boeing 747 jumbo jet. It is perhaps the most significant industrial development of the past two decades. It may very well be the key to opening the door to a new industrial and manufacturing revolution. Each of these shuttles is capable of making one hundred or more round trips between outer space and the earth.

The space shuttle could give birth to satellites for generating solar energy. It will be able to deploy communication satellites. Materials that are impossible to produce on earth may be manufactured in the zero-gravity shuttle environment.

Some other likely production outgrowths of the space industry are

Ultrapure pharmaceuticals for treating disease
Sophisticated blood and tissue analyses
Single-crystal silicon ribbon for high-performance circuits
New alloys with new and unique qualities
Purer glass for lasers and fiber optics
Monitoring of weather conditions

All of this will stimulate construction projects here on earth to produce and maintain space equipment. NASA estimates that 550 workers would be needed to build a solar satellite. Each satellite would require one hundred thousand tons of materials. It has been estimated that by the year 2000, business in space could reach the sum of $30 billion.

RESEARCH AND DEVELOPMENT

Most of the increase in productivity comes either directly or indirectly from research. **RESEARCH** is defined by the National Science Foundation as **original investigation aimed at discovering new scientific knowledge. Basic research** is research aimed at increasing knowledge. **Applied research** is research aimed at finding a practical use for an idea.

DEVELOPMENT is **the attempt to use new knowledge in the production of useful devices or processes.**

About one-tenth of research and development spending is for **basic research,** and about one-fourth is for **applied research.** Almost two-thirds is spent for development. More than one-half of the money spent for R & D is supplied by the federal government. Most R & D is performed by university staffs and by scientists and engineers in private industry. The way in which government research funds are distributed is shown in Figure 9-11. The National Science Foundation began compiling data on research and development in 1953. The sum

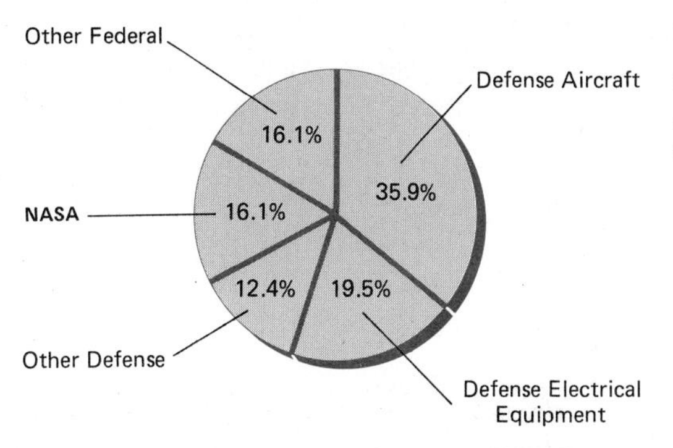

FIGURE 9-11
Federal funding of research and development. (Source: The Conference Board.)

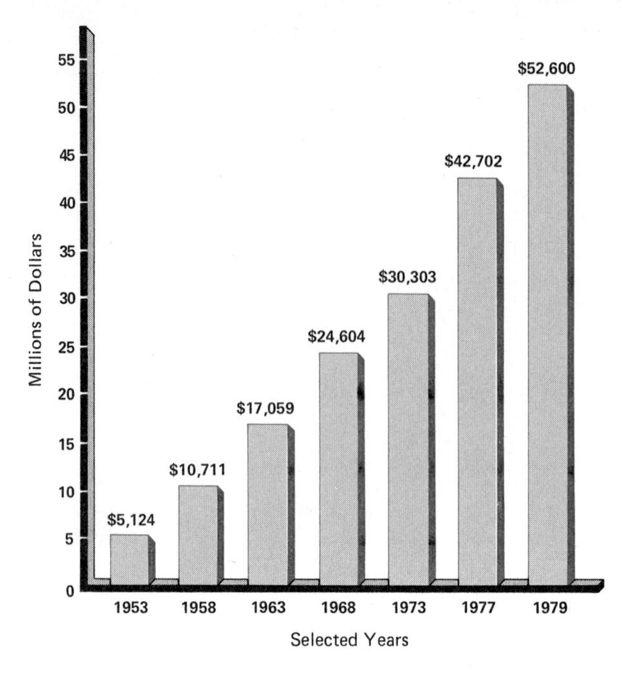

FIGURE 9-12

Total research and development expenditures. (Source: The Conference Board. *Batelle Memorial Institute.)

spent for R & D had increased to $30 billion two decades later and to almost $53 billion by 1979. Expenditures for R & D are shown in Figure 9-12.

R & D is vital in the science- and technology-oriented industries, such as drugs, chemicals, electronics, and aerospace. Intensive competition often forces consumer-goods companies, such as food packagers, soap makers, and toy manufacturers, to create a flow of new products that rely on discoveries in the other industries. At the opposite pole, retailers largely depend on their suppliers to develop new products.

In addition to the development of new products, research and development includes quality control, troubleshooting, testing, and market and economic research.

Product Research

Product research is largely concerned with the improvement of present products and the development of new ones. It is for the most part experimental research carried on in research laboratories. Most large businesses maintain research labs devoted to the discovery, development, and testing of new materials and products.

A considerable proportion of the funds supplied by the federal government has been channeled into research concerned with the military and space programs. The government contributes heavily to experimentation in the biological and physical sciences and in aeronautics, in both state and private universities. It also subsidizes most of the research and development done by private businesses in the aircraft and electronics industries.

Some of the results of research that have increased the productivity of industry are

1. The visual phone system now in use in many large cities. Meetings and conferences are conducted by picturephone—directors' meetings, sales presentations, job interviews.

J. FRED BUCY

Innovation is one of those words executives like to use, generally to impress business associates. It has a quality ring, communicating good intentions, but often the word floats into thin air with hardly a promise of action. J. Fred Bucy is one of that rare breed who, over the years, have actually put innovation to work—and it is worked hard.

That kind of thinking—doing things smarter—was part of the gear Bucy brought with him in 1976 to the office of president of Texas Instruments, Inc., a $2 billion worldwide electronics corporation with seventy-five thousand employees that is intent on reaching a $10 billion annual sales goal by the late 1980s.

Joining TI in 1953, Bucy steadily progressed through engineering and management. Shortly after arriving, he invented seisMAC, TI's first digital data processor for interpreting geophysical data. He then became manager of a major program that helped to revolutionize the geophysical industry.

At the age of thirty-four he was promoted to vice-president and given responsibility for the company's government products. He was elected executive vice-president in 1972, with responsibility for forty-nine plants in nineteen countries.

Along the way, Bucy has made significant contributions, either by personally applying innovative touches or by encouraging his managers to do so.

Among Bucy's most notable and ingenious contributions was the IDEA program (identify, develop, expose, action), which he viewed as a way of creating an environment for nurturing and funding new and fresh ideas without having innovators go through stringent and potentially discouraging procedures.

Bucy received a bachelor's degree in physics from Texas Tech University in 1951, and a master's degree from the University of Texas in 1953. He serves on the boards, councils, and committees of many businesses and government groups. He is married to Odetta Greer Bucy, and they have three children.

2. Fiber optics enable 2,700 computers to talk to each other at the same time. Hairlike glass fibers carry messages on a beam of light. A single optical fiber can carry 150 million bits a second in one direction. Fiber optics will undoubtedly be the dominant cable system for telecommunications by the year 2000.[3]

3. Tiny electronic chips in computers. A small chip that can be held in one's fingertips can hold sixty-four thousand pieces of information. That is thirty-two times more than previous chips. As a result, a set of computer calculations that cost $1.26 in 1952 could be done in 1979 for less than one cent.

[3]Fiber optics may very well be one of the next growth industries. The market for fiber optics systems in the U.S. was only $10 million in 1977. It is estimated by Predicasts, Inc., that this market will soon reach $150 million and will be $1 billion by 1990.

4. General Electric Company announced in June 1979 that it had developed a "revolutionary" new light bulb. It will last five times longer than the typical 1,000-hour incandescent bulb. In addition, it uses only one-third as much electricity to produce the same amount of light. The bulb will cost $10 but is estimated to save $20 of electricity during its lifespan. By the end of the next decade GE hopes to have this new bulb in 10 percent of the screw-in sockets that use bulbs of at least 100 watts. This size market would reduce demand for electricity by 8 billion kilowatt hours per year. This is the equivalent of 14 million barrels of petroleum.

THE METRIC SYSTEM OF MEASUREMENT

Conversion to the metric system is a process that will cost American manufacturing many millions of dollars. But there are benefits too. The metric system (Système Internationale) of measurements was adopted officially by the government of France in 1840, and by the turn of the century thirty-five countries were using it. Today there are more than 130 nations that are either using the metric system or proceeding toward its use. Approximately 90 percent of the world's people use the metric system. Although the United States has not yet officially adopted the metric system, our current system of weights and measures is defined in terms of the system.

Canada inaugurated a voluntary conversion plan to the metric system in 1970 by the establishment of the Metric Commission. Conversion there has been steady but slow because two-thirds of Canada's exports come to the United States, which is still on the old English system.

But the multinational character of large American enterprises is slowly bringing about change. As the large companies convert to the metric system, pressure is brought to bear upon their suppliers to do likewise.

The degree to which a system of measurements affects people in all walks of life was emphatically stated years ago by John Quincy Adams in his "Report to Congress" in 1821:

> Weights and measures may be ranked among the necessaries of life to every individual of human society. They enter into the economical arrangements and daily concerns of every family. They are necessary to every occupation of human industry; to the distribution and security of every species of property; to every transaction of trade and commerce; to the labors of the husbandman; to the ingenuity of the artificer; to the studies of the philosopher; to the researches of the antiquarian, to the navigation of the mariner, and the marches of the soldier; to all the exchanges of peace, and all the operations of war. The knowledge of them, as in established use, is among the first elements of education, and is often learned by those who learn nothing else, not even to read and write. This knowledge is riveted in the memory by the habitual application of it to the employments of men throughout life.

In this country the switch to metrics began officially with the enactment of Public Law 94-168, the Metric Conversion Act of 1975. (It was signed by President

TABLE 9-1			
Measurement Parameter	Unit	SI Symbol	Customary Unit
Length	Meter	m	Inch
Mass	Gram	kg	Pound
Time	Second	s	Second
Temperature	Degree celsius	C	°F
Electric current	Ampere	A	Ampere
Light intensity	Candela	cd	Candle

Gerald Ford on December 23, 1975.) This launched us on a plan of voluntary conversion.

The nine members of the Common Market (European Economic Community) set April 21, 1978, as the cutoff date for metric standards on imports. Since that date imports have not been accepted unless they are labeled in metric dimensions. In order for U.S. manufacturers to ship to Common Market countries, they must give their products' measurements in metrics.

A switch to Systèment Internationale would spur efficiency by reducing the number of product sizes and would eliminate the need to carry duplicate inventories. For example, the Industrial Fasteners Institute developed a set of metric screw-thread standards that lowered the number of required screw-thread sizes from 116 to 25. Adoption of these new standards would lead to a drastic reduction in the inventories suppliers and users would need to maintain.

Conversion would bring major gains to the scientific community, gains that would then filter down to the rest of us. The reason is that information exchange between scientists in different countries of the world would be much easier than at present.

Furthermore, the metric system is easier to understand because it is totally decimalized. And it is coherent in that it features no unwieldy constants. In our system, for example, five hundred foot-pounds per second equals one horsepower. In the metric system, one joule per second equals one watt of power. Similarly, one newton divided by one meter equals one joule of energy. Another aspect of coherence is that there is only one unit for each measure. Metrics makes for a tidier system, simplifying both communication and calculation.

The present international metric system is based on six fundamental units (see Table 9-1).

CAREER OPPORTUNITIES IN MANUFACTURING

One of the chief characteristics of production management is the many different types of positions within this field. Probably no other area of business offers the variety or number of supervisory jobs found in production—in both line and staff positions. Line positions range from department supervisor to plant superintendent. Staff positions include those dealing with all types of supervisory functions, job analysis, time study, and inspection. Large companies require highly specialized personnel to fill certain staff positions.

In addition to the many different positions, there is also a wide variety of industries. Thus those persons interested in production management have a wide choice in selecting a career well suited to their interests and abilities.

Opportunities for advancement in production are quite good. In addition to industrial-engineering functions, production requires the same types of specialized services available in nonmanufacturing enterprises: cost accounting, statistical analysis, personnel management, merchandising, and advertising.

In short, production industries offer most of the career opportunities available in retail merchandising and service businesses. In addition, there are opportunities in production management, planning, development, and plant management.

Most large corporations send their personnel recruiters to college and university campuses to select graduates who have the potential for succeeding in middle- and top-management positions. College courses in industrial management, personnel administration, and marketing management provide the type of background suited to modern industrial management. College preparation speeds the junior manager toward advancement.

SUMMARY OF KEY CONCEPTS

Manufacturing is generally considered the cornerstone of the American business system. It provides employment for 25 percent of all workers, and it indirectly supports millions of others. It increases the value of raw materials by converting them into useful products.

Manufacturers are continually bringing out a stream of new products. As production volume increases, unit costs are reduced.

Every factory needs a location, and for each type of plant some locations are preferable to others. Several factors help to determine the best possible location, such as proximity to raw materials or to markets, adequacy of transportation facilities, and availability of labor, fuel, power, and water.

The first factories were concentrated in large cities, but in recent years dispersion of plant facilities has been the practice.

Production control is obtained through planning, routing, scheduling, and dispatching. Performance control is obtained by time and motion studies and by comparisons of outputs with expected standards.

Inspection is used to maintain standards, catch defective material and substandard work, and discover areas where improvement in the manufacturing processes is needed. Most operations utilize both centralized and floor inspection.

Testing is one phase of inspection. Samples of raw materials are tested to ensure quality products; the completed products are also examined carefully. Mechanically operated products are usually put through test runs as the final production phase before being packaged for shipment.

Productivity lowers the cost of manufacturing and raises the standard of living.

Research and development are essential to increased productivity.

Progress in adopting the metric system of measurements has been slow. Greater participation in foreign business will speed this along.

BUSINESS TERMS

You should be able to match these business terms with the statements that follow:

a. Concentration
b. Continuous production
c. Development
d. Dispatching
e. Dispersion
f. Diversification
g. Intermittent production
h. Layout
i. Manufacturing
j. Motion study
k. Productivity
l. Research
m. Routing
n. Scheduling
o. Time study

1. The process of converting raw materials into finished goods
2. The tendency to locate factories within a single geographical area
3. Arranging work stations within a specific plant
4. Halting manufacturing operations at different intervals
5. Placing factories in a number of different locations
6. Breaking down a specific job operation into its various movement components
7. The sequence of operations performed in making a specific article
8. Ordering the production operations to be carried out
9. Assigning specific times to designated manufacturing operations
10. Amount of goods produced in relation to the amount of labor, money, and material put in production
11. Investigation aimed at discovering new knowledge
12. Using new knowledge in making useful articles

REVIEW QUESTIONS

1. How would you define *manufacturing* so as to distinguish it from other types of production?
2. How does the type of product being made affect plant layout?
3. What do we mean when we say that manufacturing is the cornerstone of American business?
4. What is the difference between *procedural control* and *performance control*?
5. What type of control is attained through dispatching? Routing? Standards? Inspection?
6. What is meant by *total-factor productivity*?

DISCUSSION QUESTIONS

1. Explain how manufacturing provides employment in other segments of business.
2. How are time and motion studies used to increase efficiency in manufacturing?
3. Why do the Middle Atlantic and East-North Central regions lead other regions in manufacturing?
4. Why is productivity important to our economic system and the well-being of our people?
5. Distinguish between *research* and *development*.
6. Why does the federal government allocate so much money for scientific research?

BUSINESS CASE 9-1

To Buy or to Build

The Harper Company is a small plant that assembles small kitchen appliances, which it markets through jobbers. The company receives most of its parts from two other relatively small plants located in the same community. The Harper plant has been earning a good profit and has accumulated a large surplus. The management is considering purchasing the two plants that supply it with parts.

Supplier 1 has been netting about 12 percent profit (after taxes), but Supplier 2 has been netting only 5 percent. Supplier 2 is willing to sell his production operation but will not sell the building in which he operates; however, he has offered a long-time lease on the building. Supplier 1 does not wish to sell but will give a lease on the factory operation and will sell the building in which he now operates.

1. What appear to be the alternatives facing the Harper Company management?
2. Suppose Harper should purchase the one plant available to it and lease the other one. Would you recommend keeping the management at both plants or would you send persons from the Harper organization to head up one or both supplier firms?

BUSINESS CASE 9-2

Control in Receiving Department

The Sisk Company assembles hi-fi record players, radios, and television sets for "private brand" retailers. An audit of the company books revealed that payment had been made for several dozen expensive cabinets that apparently had never been received.

There were three men who worked for Sisk in purchasing and receiving, and their functions overlapped and duplicated one another. Each man initiated purchasing requisitions and checked receiving reports, OK'ing them for payment. It was discovered that one of these men had been working with an outside accomplice, ordering cabinets and OK'ing payment for them when they had never been received by the Sisk Company.

1. How could you determine which of the three men was the guilty party?
2. How could the purchasing and receiving procedures be reorganized to eliminate and make impossible the described practice?

PHYSICAL DISTRIBUTION AND ENERGY

10

STUDY OBJECTIVES

WHEN YOU HAVE FINISHED READING THIS CHAPTER, YOU SHOULD BE ABLE TO

ONE Name the three major components of logistics

TWO Distinguish between the different modes of transportation and when to use each

THREE Describe the role of warehousing in an efficient distribution system

FOUR Describe the basic economic problem underlying the "energy shortage" in the United States

FIVE Indicate which alternate sources of energy seem to offer the most promise for the future

SIX Name the most important aspects of a national energy policy

IN THE NEWS

Out of Your Candy Bar and Into Your Gas Tank

The world has lost its taste for sugar! Oh, certainly not altogether, but since 1974 the supply has far outrun the demand. The all-time-high price of sugar was $1,267.50 per metric ton in 1974. Four years later it had dropped to one-sixth of that price. There have been two main reasons for the change. First, the industrialized nations have experienced a dramatic dietary shift away from sugar. Second, third-world countries that used to import sugar are increasingly growing their own.

What are sugar producers to do? They can hardly warehouse the stuff and hope for better days. The chief of the research arm of the world's largest sugar refiner says, "We are now in the energy business as well as the food business." And indeed sugar is becoming attractive as a building block for many petrochemicals.

Brazil has started an ambitious program to turn sugar into fuel alcohol. The Brazilian government has told local auto manufacturers to develop 100 percent alcohol engines. As this basic food business turns into an industrial business, perhaps we will look back someday and say, "Sugar . . . we used to eat that stuff. What a waste of energy!"

IN THE NEWS

Inflation, unemployment, growth, energy, and the balance of payments are interrelated. Our policies must address all of our diverse economic objectives together.

I would place special emphasis on increasing capital formation and productivity. . . . Increased investment and the higher productivity that flows from it are the sources of rising standards of living and a key to our economic performance in the 1980s.

W. MICHAEL BLUMENTHAL

In the preceding chapter we read about production—the recovery of raw materials and the making of finished goods. But raw materials must be transported to the factories that process them. And manufactured goods must be stored until they are sold. Then they must be shipped to places where they are in demand. The efficient management and handling of materials and finished goods is essential. This is called *logistics* and is discussed in this chapter.

Neither production nor distribution can be carried on without energy. Farming, mining, fishing, and forestry—the sources of raw materials—are all dependent on energy. No manufacturing—the processing of foodstuffs or the manufacture of goods—is possible without energy. Energy is needed to run machines, to heat and cool buildings, and to power trains and trucks. In a very real sense, energy serves as the life blood of production.

Energy is like any other commodity. It must be produced, distributed, and sold. And like most other commodities, it is not naturally available in the right quantities, and in the right places. The energy-producing industry faces many problems in all areas of processing and distribution. In this chapter we will be concerned with various facets of our energy problem and some possible solutions.

LOGISTICS AND PHYSICAL DISTRIBUTION

Much time, labor, money, and energy is used to produce goods to satisfy people's needs and wants. It all starts on our farms and in our forest areas, or in the mines, lakes, and oceans. Raw materials are located just about everywhere. Bringing them together in the right places, at the right times, and in the right quantities

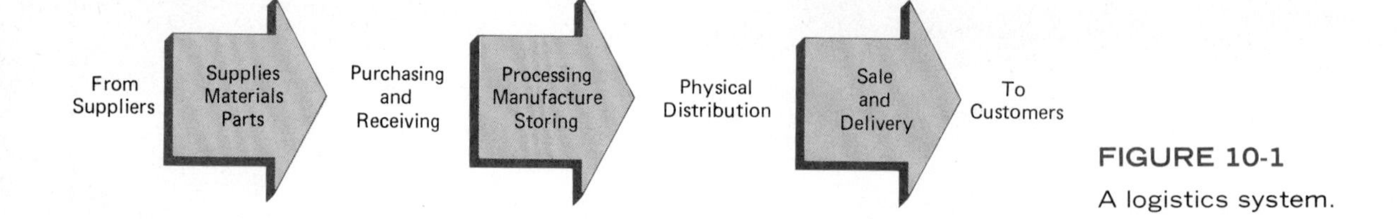

FIGURE 10-1
A logistics system.

requires expert management. Both raw materials and completed goods must be protected while in use and in storage.

The term **LOGISTICS** refers to **the management scheme for providing an orderly flow of materials to the firm and of finished goods to the marketplace.** It embraces the details of supply, product handling, and transportation activities. The logistics operations of a manufacturing enterprise have a dual purpose. First, there must be assembled a wide assortment of raw materials and supplies in the right quantities, at the right time, and at an acceptable price. Second, the logistics plan must deliver the finished products to customers in a manner satisfactory to them. **Logistics operations give time and place utility to goods.**

The first logistics concern of management, then, deals with the details of materials management—purchasing, storing, and handling all types of unfinished goods. The various components of logistical operations account for about one-fifth of the gross national product.

Product Procurement and Management

Raw materials, supplies, and capital goods (machinery and equipment) must be available before production can begin, and all of these must be replaced continually. They must be ordered, received, stored, controlled, and dispersed repeatedly.

Normally a purchasing director is placed in charge of procuring all types of needed materials and equipment. The agent and his or her top assistants develop needed purchasing policies related to quality standards, requisition and buying procedures, and inventory maintenance and control.

In recent years the materials-mangement function in some businesses has been extended to include the purchase of energy. At Du Pont, for example, the Department of Energy and Materials, in addition to buying raw materials, supplies, and equipment, also procures energy, conducts explorations for minerals, and plans alternate energy resources.

At Dow Chemical a similar awareness of the cost of energy has been built into accounting procedures. Periodically a computer at Dow's Midland, Michigan, headquarters is fed reports from the company's seven major divisions. Measurements of energy performance at hundreds of separate operations are combined.

Dow then calculates "net" energy value in BTUs of its products. By comparing the energy used in production with the energy value of the finished product, Dow can tell how much energy it has consumed. Such net-energy analysis can help identify those divisions that are large consumers of energy.

Purchasing Procedures

The steps in routine purchasing are quite common among similar types of businesses. The most elementary steps are these:

1. Laying out product specifications
2. Securing requisitions
3. Surveying market conditions, availability, and prices
4. Placing the order
5. Following up on orders when necessary
6. Receiving the goods
7. Placing goods in inventory

When special orders or materials bidding is done, there may be slight modifications in purchasing procedures. In some instances, samples are submitted during negotiations as a means of establishing standards.

The current emphasis in materials management considers purchasing from the management rather than the marketing point of view. To illustrate, a survey of the one hundred largest U.S. manufacturing companies revealed that the purchasing of materials and services accounts for 52 percent of the sales dollar. At the same time, labor costs consume only 10 to 20 percent. Thus, manufacturing concerns have a greater opportunity for increased profits by reducing the cost of materials than by reducing the cost of labor. The average company can effect a 10 percent increase in profit by reducing supply cost by only 2 percent. Materials management includes to some degree the functions of purchasing, traffic, inventory control, receiving, shipping, and production planning.

Today's purchasing agents are not so much concerned with materials per se as with their function in the production operation. They give more attention to quality and value than to the lowest price, and they may find it advantageous to buy from new suppliers. They are concerned with reducing inventories in items that represent a large dollar investment. (Inventories make up, on the average, 15 to 20 percent of a company's assets.) Modern distribution systems have reduced the need for large stock accumulations, thus increasing stock turnover. The purchasing agent encourages standardization practices. This permits contracting for goods in large quantities at lower prices. It also makes savings possible through competitive bidding according to specifications.

Inventory Maintenance and Control

Remember that storage is an important production cost, for capital is invested in the various kinds of materials for which storage is provided. In addition the cost of labor increases every time materials are handled. Management must maintain a balance among the several factors: having sufficient stores on hand to keep up a normal work flow, buying in quantities large enough to afford attractive prices, and keeping the capital investment in materials and supplies to a minimum.

Should materials be bought as they are needed or in large quantities and stored? If materials on hand will be maintained on short supply, it is imperative to have more than one source from which they may be obtained. And we must be able to depend on these sources to meet our needs on short notice. Also, we must develop methods and techniques for handling materials promptly and moving them to specific demand locations within the plant. On the other hand, if a large inventory will be maintained, purchases are made less frequently and in large quantities. This means we have larger capital sums invested, but quantity discounts might offset such investment costs.

Inventory control. The management of goods and supplies on hand is known as **INVENTORY CONTROL.** There are two aspects of inventory, or product, control: one relates to flow and the other to security. One common practice in inventory control is to issue raw materials and supplies only upon written requisition. Each requisition should be prenumbered, dated, and signed and should show exactly what was issued, to whom, and for what purpose. Standardizing materials when practicable, and establishing limits within which the inventory should be maintained, are also helpful control procedures. Some of the factors that must be considered are

1. Availability:
   a. Number of suppliers
   b. Reliability of suppliers
   c. Efficiency of transport facilities
2. Storage space available
3. Efficiency of handling techniques
4. Rate of consumption
5. Stability of market prices

Decisions on Inventory

You can think of inventories as reservoirs of goods being held available for filling orders. At intervals, products are added to the reservoir as they come off the production lines. Goods are withdrawn from the reservoir as sales are made.

The decision that management faces is to determine at what level goods should be allowed to accumulate, and to what level they should be permitted to fall—setting the upper and lower limits. These control limits are partially determined by the forecast sales volume. The more accurate the sales forecast, the more economical the management of the inventory.

This all demonstrates again the importance of all components of marketing working together. The question of how much inventory to maintain is closely related to the regular flow of finished goods, to promptness in handling goods by transportation agents, to the time required to process orders, and to the sales forecast. Inventory maintenance must be determined by types of products, not by total volume of sales.

Cost considerations. There are three major categories of cost factors: holding costs, costs due to shortages, and replenishment costs.

Holding costs include warehousing expenses, finance costs arising from capital investment in inventories, losses resulting from capital investment in inventories, losses resulting from price changes due to market conditions, insurance on inventory, and losses resulting from spoilage or obsolescence. **Shortage costs** arise from failure to have sufficient goods on hand to fill orders at the time they are received. They include special clerical and handling costs, loss of income because of losing the sale, and; in extreme cases, loss of customers. **Replenishment costs** are usually tied closely to production costs—overtime required to make up shortages, loss of production time caused by equipment breakdowns, and so forth.

ORGANIZATION FOR DISTRIBUTION

The second logistical concern of management is making finished goods available to customers. This includes the management of finished-goods inventories and the movement of goods to customer locations.

There are a number of interrelated parts in the logistics plan: production scheduling, inventory size and control, storage, transportation, size of shipments, and materials handling. The management of the total physical-distribution mix is complex. In some cases even the internal components are in opposition to one another. For example, the production department may want to have a long production run, to keep the unit cost low; marketing may want a large inventory on items that are different—hence short runs to fill deliveries fully and promptly; and finance may want small inventories, to minimize the amount of capital tied up in unsold goods.

According to the National Council of Physical Distribution Management, physical distribution includes

> The broad range of activities concerned with efficient movement of finished products from the end of the production line to the consumer, and in some cases includes the movement of raw materials from the source of supply to the beginning of the production line. These activities include freight transportation, warehousing, material handling, protective packaging, inventory control, plant and warehouse site selection, order processing, market forecasting, and customer service.[1]

For a short definition, we can say that **PHYSICAL DISTRIBUTION** refers to **the movement of goods between producers and users.**

One way in which many firms have established control over physical distribution is to centralize the most basic components of physical distribution yet leave production schedules and inventory control in the production department.

A second arrangement establishes physical distribution as a line-and-staff function on the same level with production, finance, and marketing. Under this arrangement, physical distribution is responsible for materials flow, inventory control, warehousing, customer service, order processing, packing, and shipping.

The centralization of the various aspects of physical distribution can best be accomplished when a firm's operational activities are similar among its different product lines. When the production processes, the materials handling, the marketing channels, and the modes of transportation are similar for the various products manufactured, overall control is much more likely than when these components vary widely.

Sometimes this similarity exists for either the raw materials or the finished goods but not for both. Then the logistics pattern may consist of two different schemes—one for inbound materials and another for outbound finished goods.

[1]Definition by the National Council of Physical Distribution Management, Executive Offices, Chicago.

FRANK BORMAN

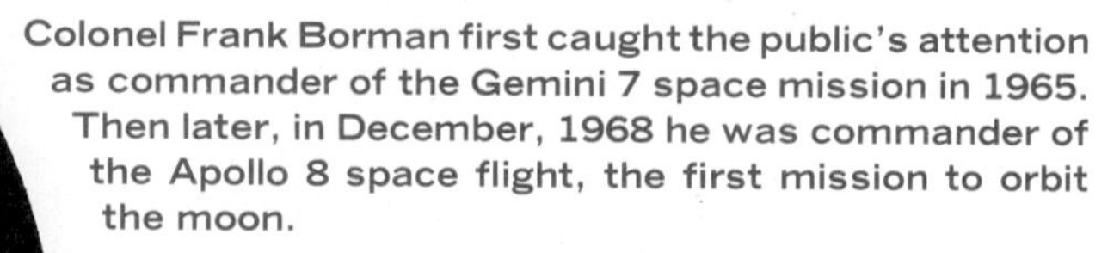

Colonel Frank Borman first caught the public's attention as commander of the Gemini 7 space mission in 1965. Then later, in December, 1968 he was commander of the Apollo 8 space flight, the first mission to orbit the moon.

In 1966 and 1968, Colonel Borman served as special presidential ambassador on trips throughout the Far East and Europe. In 1970, he undertook another special presidential mission—a worldwide tour to seek support for the release of American prisoners of war held by North Vietnam.

Frank Borman's association with Eastern Airlines began in early 1969 when he served as special advisor to the company executives. He became Eastern's vice president in July, 1970, and was elected president and chief executive officer in December, 1975.

President Borman is given credit for changing the policies of Eastern and making it a profitable operation.

Born March 14, 1928, in Gary, Indiana, Colonel Borman received most of his early schooling in Tucson, Arizona. He was awarded a Bachelor of Science degree from the U.S. Military Academy, West Point, in 1950 and a Master of Science degree in Aeronautical Engineering from the California Institute of Technology in 1957. He completed the Harvard Business School's Advanced Management Program in 1970.

In addition to many honorary degrees, special honors and service decorations, he is the recipient of the Harmon International Aviation Trophy, the Robert J. Collier Trophy, and the National Geographic Society's Hubbard Medal.

The breadth and variety of a manufacturer's product line are usually determined before plans are made for solving physical-distribution problems. In other words, the logistics system is usually adapted to the product rather than the product to the logistics plan. Some of the factors that affect the level of customer service are the degree of concentration of customers, the size of a typical order, and the frequency with which orders are received and processed. Other factors are the extent to which the manufacturer must provide storage, compared with the assistance the manufacturer might have received from others in the distribution channel; and the variety and quality of transportation modes from which a choice may be made.

WAREHOUSING AND DISTRIBUTION

Warehousing is an essential part of physical distribution, for most goods are not consumed as soon as they are produced. Orange juice and fresh vegetables are ready for processing only during the harvesting season, yet they are in demand the entire year. Warehousing enables producers to store and move these goods to markets as they are in demand. It also enables manufacturers to gear their production to meet peak seasonal demands without the added cost of overtime or around-the-clock operations. And the proper use of transportation services in conjunction with warehousing helps the manufacturer adjust the operation to fit the time, place, and rate of consumer demand.

The airline industry has been largely deregulated. The airline carriers can decide to add or drop certain routes without government agency approval. Many airlines have dropped flights that were uneconomical. As a result people in many communities feel that they are without adequate air transportation service.

Types of warehouses. There are essentially two types of warehouse operations: private and public. **PRIVATE WAREHOUSES** are owned or leased and are operated by individual enterprises—manufacturers, wholesalers, and retailers —for their own use. They may maintain storage and distribution centers near their plants, or they may maintain branch operations at other locations.

PUBLIC WAREHOUSES make their storage and handling facilities available to any business wishing to use them. Patrons of public warehousing facilities pay for the services they receive on the basis of space and time requirements. Some warehouses store all types of general merchandise; others store only special commodities, such as farm produce or frozen foods. Public warehouses are in operation in all principal market areas in the United States.

FIGURE 10-2
An Electric Clipper stacks palletized bags of flour to a height of 12 feet. This gives the Salerno-Negowen Biscuit Company of Chicago a 33 percent increase in usable storage space. (Courtesy Clark Equipment Company. Industrial Truck Division.)

Shared Services in Warehousing

Distribution costs, like most other costs, are increasing because of a number of factors. These include increasing capital investments in land, buildings, and equipment. Also, expanding inventories caused by a greater variety of products, and an increase in the number of small (less-than-carload) shipments are a factor. These costs in combination have given impetus to sharing warehousing services.

Public warehousing currently operates some twenty-five thousand facilities, and new ones are being constructed at the rate of 12 percent annually. As they move from strictly local operations to national networks, they are able to offer a wider variety of services and increase their efficiency of operation.

One of the services now being shared among warehouses, and by companies utilizing the same facilities, is data processing. This includes invoicing, billing, credit checking, inventory control, accounting, storage, and retrieval. Sharing of services can help the pooling of shipments to constitute full-car or -truck loads. This can effect a considerable savings, for the shipping rate per hundred pounds for a partial load is usually about twice that for a full-car or -truck load. Motor carriers report that small shipments make up 70 percent of their total volume of business. Shared services in warehousing may very well be the idea that will receive the next big push in distribution.

Distribution Centers

In discussing a logistics system in the past, the authors have talked largely in terms of warehousing. But unfortunately, "warehousing" has taken on the idea of depositing goods for an extended period of time. Since this suggests a lack of movement a newer term, **distribution center,** was coined. A **DISTRIBUTION CENTER includes storage, product handling, and preparing goods for shipment.** It puts the emphasis on movement of goods. It expresses better than *warehousing* the concept of prompt and efficient service to customers. The current trend is toward large regional distribution centers rather than small warehouses scattered all over the country.

CHOOSING TRANSPORTATION MODES

Both costs and the acceptable level of customer service are paramount in determining the practicability of establishing a number of distribution centers. But the availability of a variety of types of transportation modes is a very important and limiting factor. Transportation makes its chief contribution to the economy by

1. Widening the market area
2. Giving time and place utility to goods
3. Enhancing specialization in production
4. Reducing the need for maintaining large inventories

Today it is possible to reach a third of the U.S. consumer market within one day, using only five distribution centers. However, to reach four-fifths of the total consumer market in one day would require five times as many distribution points. Thus management can combine the available options in many different ways. Management might choose, for example, to serve one-third of the market through

FIGURE 10-3

Automated distribution center.
This automated distribution center is a part of the IBM plant at Raleigh, N.C. Products and parts are moved by the latest in materials-handling equipment. Up to thirty thousand pallets and three hundred thousand small-parts locations are controlled by an IBM System/370 Model 168 computer. (Photo courtesy of International Business Machines Corporation.)

five distribution centers and reach some fraction of the remaining market by a number of centers above five but fewer than the total of twenty-five. The best choice of number and location of distribution centers would be determined by the relation of costs to revenues and profit margins.

Choosing the kind of transportation cannot be done strictly on the basis of comparative costs. Shipping costs constitute only one of the factors in the physical-distribution mix. The savings in freight costs might very easily be offset by costlier packaging, storage costs, or handling expenses. The appropriate mode of transportation is the one that maximizes efficiency in the total physical-distribution scheme. For example, air freight may be the best choice when time is especially important; for other goods, the greatly reduced rates for water transport may be the best choice.

The percentage of intercity freight movements by different kinds of transportation, as measured in ton-miles, is shown in Figure 10-4. Railroads transport more tons of products more miles, but they haul largely coal, ores, grains, autos, and heavy machinery. Trucks deliver a wider variety of products and reach many more communities.

Types of Carriers

Transportation firms are classified by law as common carriers, contract carriers, and private carriers.

A **common carrier** offers its services to the general public to transport

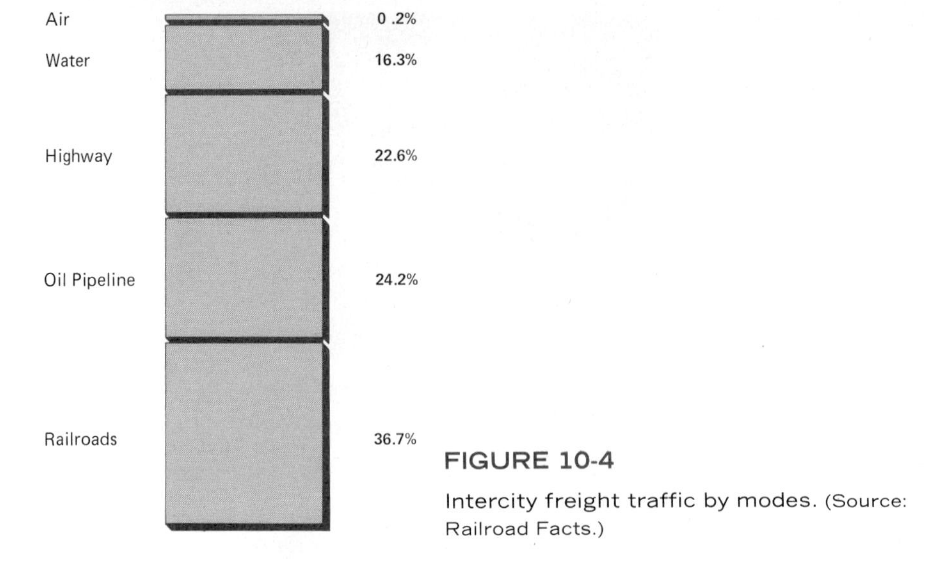

FIGURE 10-4

Intercity freight traffic by modes. (Source: Railroad Facts.)

property for a stated rate and in accordance with standard rules. It is expected to give the same service and charge the same rate to all shippers. Examples of common carriers are railroads, bus lines, intercity freight motor lines, some air-freight lines, most airlines, most domestic water carriers, all freight-forwarding companies, and REA Express. Common carriers are subject to various kinds of state and federal regulations, which are discussed later in this chapter.

A **contract carrier** sells its transport services on the basis of individual agreements or contracts that define the carrier's liability. Some contract carriers specialize, transporting only certain types of goods. Automobile trucking companies, household moving vans, and chartered buses and planes are examples of contract carriers.

A **private carrier** transports its own goods. Manufacturers, wholesalers, and retailers who make their own deliveries in their own trucks are classed as private carriers. Since they are usually small companies operating in small geographical areas, they are subject primarily to local and state regulations.

The Traffic Manager

The traffic manager often heads a "traffic department." Most of the traffic manager's routine work consists of collecting accurate, up-to-date information about tariff rates; selecting common carriers to be used in transporting foods; preparing claims of overcharge, damage, or loss; and auditing freight bills. He or she is also expected to trace lost shipments, supervise the actual handling of freight, and maintain control over back orders.

In addition, the traffic manager

1. Helps consolidate small orders into carload shipments
2. Arranges systematic warehouse-distribution points for less-than-carload lots
3. Studies and perfects ways of reducing losses in shipments caused by improper packaging and handling
4. Selects the most advantageous or strategic destination points for shipments

The traffic manager must know when to use rail, water, truck, or air to transport goods to customers. It is also his or her responsibility to seek adjustments on overcharges caused by discriminatory rates, by preparing such cases and presenting them before commissions and governmental bodies.

REGULATION OF TRANSPORTATION

Because transport companies operate in specific territories by government franchise, they are subject to special government regulations pertaining to routes, consolidation with other companies, rate structures, and curtailment of services. In many instances, regulations are needed to protect the general public and the best interests of transport companies as well.

Most states have commissions that regulate **intrastate transportation** operations—those that occur entirely within the state. These commissions were first concerned with railroads, then later with motor carriers; now it is airport facilities.

Most transport companies cross state lines, and a state regulatory body has jurisdiction only within its own state. Therefore the federal government is responsible for the rules governing **interstate** transportation operations. The passage of the Interstate Commerce Act in 1887 was largely for the purpose of providing railroad regulation. This act created the Interstate Commerce Commission, which dealt with rate discrimination. The act stipulated that the tariffs or rates to be charged were to be reasonable and just. It also stipulated that railroads could not charge a higher rate for a short haul than for a long haul under similar circumstances.

As both transportation traffic and the types of transport companies have continuously increased since 1887, there have been several laws passed broadening the jurisdiction and responsibilities of the Interstate Commerce Commission. The commission was given jurisdiction over interstate pipeline shipments in 1906 and over water transportation in 1940. Now it not only has jurisdiction over the tariff schedules of railroads but is concerned with the appraisal of the value of properties, and with methods of accounting, curtailment of services, financing, and consolidations.

THE ECONOMICS OF ENERGY

The Industrial Revolution of the nineteenth century was the beginning of an energy revolution. It began with the invention of the steam engine as a source of energy that increased the productivity of goods and services. Since then the United States has moved from an era of cheap energy to one in which it is very expensive. This period also witnessed a shift away from coal as our primary energy source to petroleum and natural gas. Coal is available in abundant quantities, but it pollutes the environment. Oil and gas were plentiful, clean, and cheap. Our industrial complex now depends on oil and natural gas as our primary energy sources.

The energy crisis. Here in the United States we face a severe shortage of petroleum products. This has become increasingly evident because of the "oil embargo" of 1973 and the Iranian revolution of 1979.

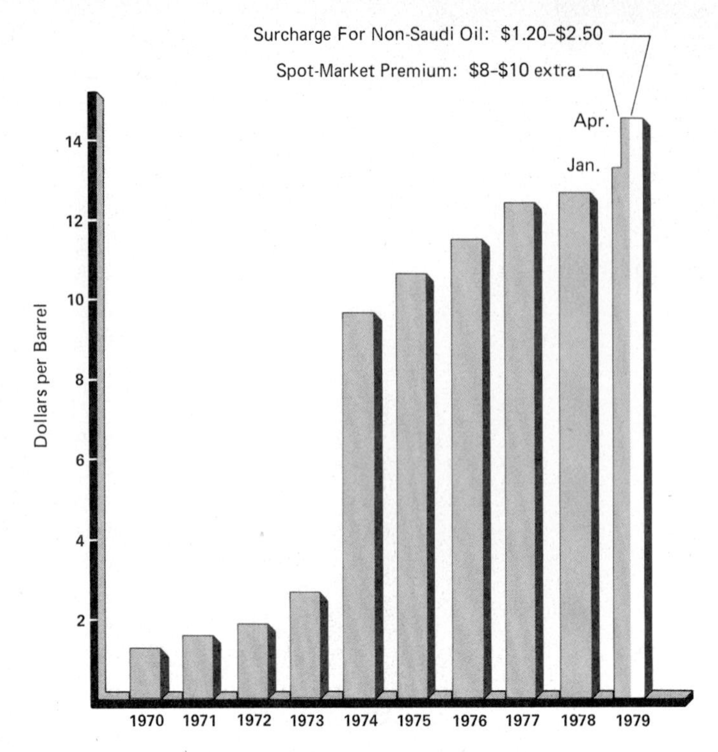

FIGURE 10-5

The oil-price explosion—average realized price for Saudi Arabian "marker" crude. The price of Saudi Arabian light, the benchmark crude, increased elevenfold during the 1970s. This price explosion has continued into the 1980s. Other crudes may be priced higher or lower, depending on their quality and proximity to the market. (Source: World Bank.)

Between 1973 and 1975 the percentage of petroleum that we import decreased somewhat. But by 1976 we were importing a larger percentage than before the 1973 embargo. Also during the late 1970s and the early 1980s, the Organization of Petroleum Exporting Countries (OPEC) continually raised the price of oil. This increase in the cost of crude petroleum is shown in Figure 10-5.

The current cost of energy has increased the cost of manufacturing and distributing everything that business produces. It has been a major cause of the rise in inflation and has been a problem for business, government, and consumers. The price of gasoline rose from thirty-five cents per gallon in 1973 to more than a dollar at the beginning of 1980.

The problem is not that there is a shortage of energy resources. The United States has more energy in the form of coal than the Arab countries have in oil resources. Rather, it is the result of a combination of several factors:

1. Rapidly increasing energy use
2. Maldistribution of energy in relation to production
3. A lack of the needed advanced technology
4. A history of wasting relatively cheap fuel
5. The absence of a functional national energy policy

This may seem strange, since technology and productivity are the twin forces that brought this country to its present position of economic prominence. It may seem strange, too, that so little attention was paid to the first signs of our energy shortage. But when the energy gap showed up at the gasoline pump, the public finally realized that we had a problem. Even then the government took no concerted action to relieve the situation. The energy shortage, then, seems to stem from a combination of the following causes.

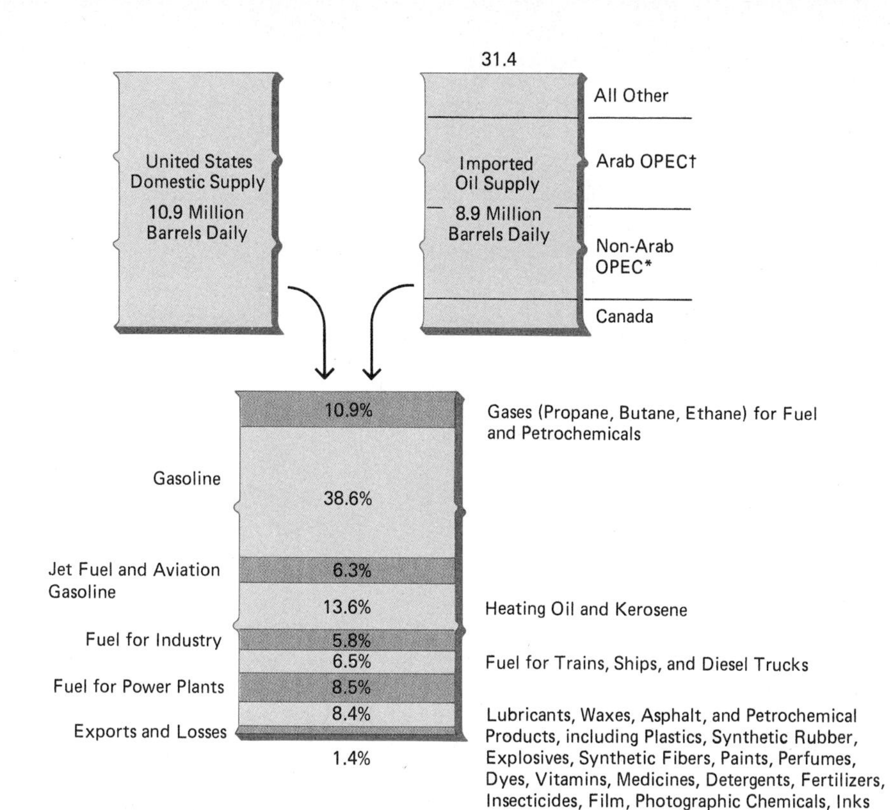

FIGURE 10-6

Rivers of oil flow into the U.S. barrel, 1980.

The United States now uses 19.7 million barrels of oil daily. Of this amount, 1.5 million barrels come from the Alaska Arctic. Some of the crude from the Middle East may go first to Europe, Canada, or the Caribbean for refining before it reaches the United States. (Source: Based on data from *Chevron World* [Standard Oil Company of California].)

Causes of Our Energy Shortages

1. Federal Power Commission price controls on prices at the well of natural gas, dating back to 1954
2. Depressed prices of crude oil and finished petroleum products, discouraging investment in domestic exploration and refinery construction
3. Delays in drilling in certain offshore areas of recognized oil-producing potential
4. Delays in the construction of pipelines to transport Alaskan oil and gas to market
5. Adoption of air-quality regulations, restricting the use of coal and high-sulfur oils
6. Emission-control standards on new-model automobiles, increasing gasoline consumption
7. Record sales of new cars equipped with gasoline-consuming options
8. Delays in the development of alternate fuels as a major power source
9. Rapid growth in production, demanding an ever-increasing supply of energy
10. Too heavy a reliance on oil because of the difficulty of using coal that meets environmental standards

ENERGY DEMAND AND SUPPLY IN THE UNITED STATES

In 1950 the United States produced and consumed more than half the world's output of petroleum. But by 1970 we were importing 33 percent of the petroleum we consumed, and by 1980 we were importing 44 percent. Should the present trend continue, by 1990, we will be importing 50 percent of the petroleum we consume. The sources of our petroleum and how it is used are shown in Figure 10-6.

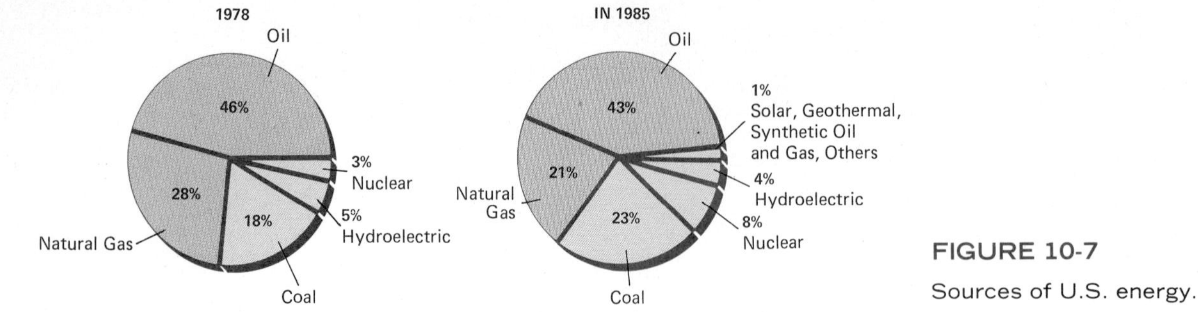

FIGURE 10-7

Sources of U.S. energy.

Primary Sources of Energy

The overall energy market is changing. Coal supplied 38 percent of the energy demand in this country in 1950, but it supplies only 20 percent of it today. The dominance of oil and natural gas as our primary sources of energy is shown in Figure 10-7.

We had high hopes for nuclear energy in the early 1970s. But the objections of various environmental groups throughout the decade have greatly hindered its development. The accident at the Three Mile Island plant in Pennsylvania in the spring of 1979 further delayed its development. Questions of waste disposal and other problems abound. For example, what do you do with an old nuclear-power plant?

About a dozen nuclear reactors in this country are reaching the end of their useful lives. These power plants present a major problem—what to do with them now. "Decommissioning" occurs after a nuclear-power station has reached its thirty- to forty-year planned lifetime.

A controversy is going on as to whether to remove the spent reactor or leave it in place. Dismantling the plants is a major task—with 0.8-foot-thick concrete walls. And this is also expensive—the estimated cost runs as high as $100 million.

Those who argue for leaving the plants in place want either "entombing" (encasing in concrete) or "mothballing" (welding it shut and guarding it). Both of these methods would require long-term monitoring, since elements generated in the process remain radioactive for up to eighty thousand years. Clearly this is another major obstacle for the nuclear-power industry to overcome if it is to provide a reasonable substitute for coal and oil.

The principal source of energy in most regions is oil. The one exception to this is the southwest region where natural gas is the leader. The percentage of our total energy use supplied by different types of sources can be seen in Figure 10-7.

Although we have an abundance of coal, much of it is high in sulfur content. We should eventually be able to use more coal as technology is improved. Converting coal to gas holds out promise for the future, and solar energy is currently receiving considerable attention by both government and private industry. But the perfecting of solar-energy technology will require time.

High-quality, low-sulfur coal in large amounts is available in Montana and Wyoming, but shipping from those areas to population centers has proved troublesome. An interesting idea is the coal slurry pipeline.

FIGURE 10-8

Offshore drilling platform in the North Sea. (Photo courtesy of Bucyrus-Erie Company.)

> **Pipelines carry gas and oil in the world routinely, so why not grind up coal and mix it with water to be pumped in pipelines to its destination? This method is clean, inexpensive, and efficient. However, there are problems. First, the railroads strongly oppose this competition to their coal-hauling revenue and are fighting the pipelines. More serious, however, is the lack of water in the states that have the coal. Montana and Wyoming are both arid-to-semi-arid states and can scarcely spare the water.**
>
> **The Energy Transition Company (ETCO) is working on a plan to turn part of the coal into methanol (wood alcohol) and use that liquid as the carrier in the pipeline instead of water. Both the methanol and the coal would provide fuel at the end of the line. There are many technical and economic problems yet to be worked out, however.**

The Major Energy Markets

The major uses of energy, considered as percentages of the total national consumption, are listed in Table 10-1.

Of course, the consumption in different geographical regions would vary from this national average. These figures show that no one market accounts for more than one-third of the total consumption. Therefore, any effort at reducing consumption should be directed at more than a single group.

TABLE 10-1
NATIONAL ENERGY CONSUMPTION, 1980

Uses		Percentage
Generation and transmission of electricity		17.0
Residential and commercial lighting, heating, cooking, air conditioning, and electrical appliances		23.2
Industrial processes—mining, smelting, manufacturing	27.8	33.4
Petrochemicals; raw materials for plastics, paints, and synthetic fibers	5.6	
Transportation—fuel for cars, planes, trucks, buses, tractors, ships, etc.		24.1
Exports of energy		2.3

ALTERNATE ENERGY SOURCES

A great deal has been written about the development of solar, nuclear, and geothermal energy sources. It has also been proposed that we push forward immediately with the technology needed for liquifying coal and producing synthetic gases from coal and from waste material. All of these hold promise as long-term solutions, but none seems to offer an immediate feasible solution to closing the energy gap. We will look at the potential that each of these has for helping to solve the problem.

Geothermal Development

Geothermal generation is now in operation in Japan, Mexico, New Zealand, the Soviet Union, and the United States. There are now fifty countries interested in geothermal exploration. The most promising zone for such development is the so-called Pacific Ring of Fire. This zone extends from the tip of South America through North America and Alaska, and through Japan, the Philippines, and Indonesia. In the United States the best prospects for geothermal energy are in the West.

Geothermal energy uses the natural heat of the earth. It is captured by drilling wells to bring subterranean hot water and steam to the surface. Steam cannot be transported much more than a mile without its losing both pressure and temperature. Therefore it must be used on site to generate the electricity that can then be transported.

The nation's major geothermal development is the Geysers' field, located about seventy-five miles north of San Francisco. This development was started in 1960 with a 12,500-kilowatt generating plant. By 1980 it had become the largest geothermal development in the world, with a capacity of more than half a million kilowatts. The steam reserves of this field are considered the energy equivalent of a petroleum field of the "giant" class.

The Geysers' field is operated by the Union Oil Company of California. The electricity produced there is distributed by the Pacific Gas and Electric Company. More than one hundred wells have been drilled so far. (On the average, it requires eighteen producing wells to start up a plant that will generate 110,000 kilowatts. A like number of wells must be added over the thirty-year life of the facility.) The Union Oil Company estimates that the Geysers' output can reach 2 million kilowatts by 1990.

There is considerable disagreement as to how large a share geothermal energy will have of the nation's total energy output by the end of the century. This is mainly because so little is known about the resource at this point. Predicting conservatively, this share could amount to 2 or 3 percent. That may be small, but as a fraction of national energy, it represents a significant volume. The projected development of geothermal power is depicted in Figure 10-9.

In the United States the geothermal industry as a whole is still in its infancy. But the potential for this resource is substantial. Experts believe, for example, that there is the geological potential for developing up to 20 million kilowatts of electrical generating capacity in the nation in the next two decades. This would be equivalent to about seven hundred thousand barrels of oil per day.

GENERAL ELECTRIC IS GROWING ENERGY UNDER WATER

Off the coast of southern California General Electric is growing energy. In cooperation with the Department of Energy and the Gas Research Institute G.E. is growing giant kelp, a kind of seaweed. Kelp can be processed into a gas similar to natural gas.

Kelp grows at a rapid rate, sometimes as much as two feet in one day. If it grew that much every day, ten acres of a kelp farm would produce enough kelp to produce 6 million cubic feet of gas in one year.

Solar Energy

In the long run, solar energy offers great possibilities. In the spring of 1975 the General Electric Corporation initiated perhaps the first industrial application of solar energy. The company installed heat-absorbing panels on the roof of one wing of its Valley Forge, Pennsylvania, Space Center. This supplied enough energy to heat the plant cafeteria (20,000 square feet of space) and three-fourths of the hot water used at the Space Center.

During the 1979 fiscal year the Federal Energy Department allocated $500 million for solar-energy research. And according to James Schlesinger, who was then U.S. secretary for energy, "solar energy will soon be the fastest-growing part of our energy supply."

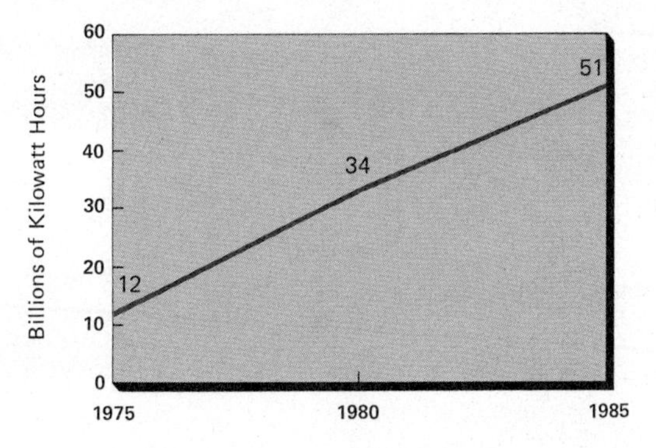

FIGURE 10-9
Projected geothermal-power development.

California has had good luck stimulating the use of solar systems by allowing taxpayers liberal tax credits. As a result, nearly one-third of all solar systems being installed in the United States are in California. These systems are used for heating swimming pools, domestic hot water, and space heating.

The tax credits work like this. When W. A. Spriggs opened a 254-unit apartment complex in Ventura, he included a solar heating system that was essentially paid for by the state. The system cost Spriggs $65,000 more than a conventional heating system. But Spriggs earned a tax credit of $70,000 (25 percent of the total $280,000 cost). For homeowners the tax credit is 55 percent (shared equally between the state and federal governments), up to a maximum of $3,000.

The Council on Environmental Quality predicted that solar energy could account for one-fourth of U.S. energy needs by the year 2000. This report was widely discounted as government policy because of the administration's emphasis on the increased use of coal. However, a solar-energy task force was appointed by President Jimmy Carter with representation from thirty federal agencies. This group predicted that solar energy could contribute as much as one-fifth of U.S. energy needs by the year 2000. The Harvard Business School Energy Project declared that this goal is attainable.

Nuclear Energy

Today's U.S. nuclear-power plants are fueled by uranium. When spent uranium is removed from a reactor, it still contains about 40 percent of its original energy

FIGURE 10-10

The Donald C. Cook Nuclear Plant on Lake Michigan at Bridgman, Michigan. (Courtesy American Electric Power.)

potential. This potential can be recovered through reprocessing, which extends the life of the resource and reduces the radioactive waste.

Nuclear-power plants can be clean. They produce a minimum of waste, emit no smoke or fumes, and consume only a few truckloads of fuel a year. In addition, "thermal effects"—the heat of discharged water—can be and are being controlled when they are of concern, by using such conventional devices as cooling towers. However, many persons fear the danger of possible harmful effects that could result from accidents in nuclear-power plants, and nuclear-waste disposal and decommissioning are major problems.

To illustrate the problems involved in building nuclear-power plants, here is an excerpt from a recent report that the American Electric Power System sent to its stockholders.

Today nuclear reactors provide 13 percent of the electrical energy generated in the United States. The Federal Energy Administration estimates that by the

NUCLEAR: THE END AND THE BEGINNING

Two events took place in July that represent opposite ends of the spectrum that is the lengthy process of planning, designing, building, licensing and operating a nuclear plant.

On July 1 we placed in commercial operation the 1.1-million-kilowatt Unit 2 at the Donald C. Cook Nuclear Plant, Bridgman, Michigan. Thus was completed, for all intents and purposes, the building of the AEP System's first nuclear generating station—over 11½ years after bids had been invited for the first of its two nuclear reactors.

Then, on July 25, we announced the beginning of a four-year study of the possibility of building a nuclear power plant in central Virginia—at the opposite end of the seven-state AEP System from our first nuclear station on Lake Michigan. We plan to study two sites: one in Nelson County at the confluence of the James and Tye Rivers, the other to be selected.

The study is an integral part of our over-all planning for new generating capacity to meet our customers' electric energy needs by the late 1980's and early 1990's. There is no question that, even if there should be substantially greater savings from the conservation of electricity than have been experienced to date, we shall need major additions to our generating capacity beyond what we now have under construction or are committed to build. By beginning to study—now—the technical, environmental and economic aspects of placing a nuclear plant at the eastern end of the AEP System, we will broaden the options available to us in four years, when a decision will have to be made as to what kind of generation to build and where to build it.

Future developments on certain problems now being addressed by government and industry—such as spent-fuel reprocessing, nuclear-waste disposal and licensing delays—may well affect whether nuclear generation proves to be the logical and most economical choice for the area to be studied. We hope that these problems will be resolved by the time that decisions must be made on generating facilities to meet the needs of the 1990's.

year 2000 another 230 nuclear plants will be added to the 72 that were in operation by 1980. For the future, the generation of electrical energy from nuclear-power plants holds good promise. An estimate of nuclear's contribution to electric-power generation for the 1980s is depicted in Figure 10-11.

THE NEED FOR A SOUND GOVERNMENT POLICY

How to deal with the energy problem in this country will continue to preoccupy our government for many years. Periodic energy shortages and high costs retard economic growth, deter industrial expansion, and keep new communities from developing.

President Gerald Ford proposed an energy plan in December 1974, but it was rejected by Congress. However, the Energy Research and Development Administration was established in January 1975 to coordinate government energy programs and to help make the nation self-sufficient in energy. The budget for that year was almost $4 billion. More than one hundred energy bills were introduced in Congress, but the legislators were far from agreement as to what should be done.

One group of bills would establish a federal corporation to explore for new oil and natural gas on public lands. These proposals would also set up a federal purchasing agency to buy and sell oil imports. A second group would tell privately owned oil companies how to do business. A third group would put a "windfall profits" tax on petroleum company profits. Another large group of bills were divided between continuing government price controls and removing them.

In June 1979 the OPEC nations raised the price of crude to a new high—$18 to $23 per barrel. Until then members of Congress and the president could not reach agreement on much of anything in the form of energy legislation. Then on July 15, 1979, President Carter made his fifth address dealing with energy. In this address he proposed the following:

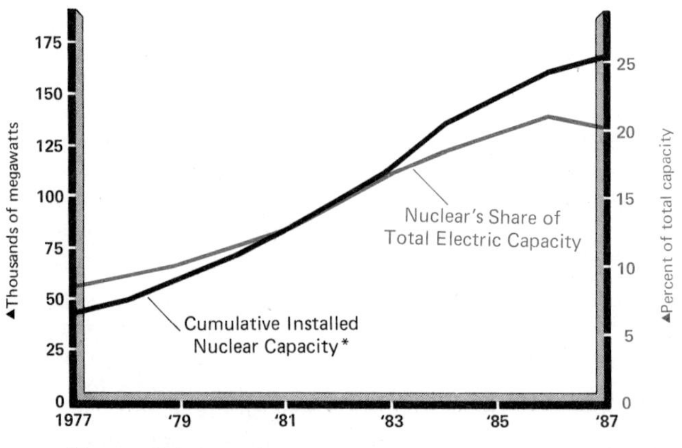

FIGURE 10-11
(Data from *Atomic Industrial Forum*.)

1. The setting of a maximum limit for the nation's use of foreign oil, the amount imported in 1977—8.5 million barrels a day
2. The creation of an Energy Security Corporation to lead efforts to replace 2.5 million barrels of oil imports by 1990—this to be done by developing alternative sources of fuel; and the creation of a national solar bank to achieve a goal of 20 percent of our energy coming from solar power by the year 2000
3. A reduction in utilities' use of oil by 50 percent within the decade
4. The creation of an Energy Mobilization Board, with authority to cut through roadblocks to the completion of our energy projects
5. A mandatory conservation program with quotas for states, counties, and cities; also a standby gasoline rationing plan

CURRENT ISSUE

Should Gasoline Be Rationed to Conserve Energy?

Transportation—fuel for cars, planes, buses, trucks, and ships—consumes about one-fourth of our national energy. Americans have become accustomed to driving anywhere they wish to go in their own automobiles. They seem to be unwilling to conserve gasoline and prefer to pay high prices rather than use less gas.

With which of the following statements do you agree and with which do you disagree?

1. Gasoline rationing would contribute a great deal toward meeting our energy conservation goal.
2. U.S. citizens will curtail their use of gasoline only when forced to do so.
3. Gasoline rationing is an infringement of our right of freedom of choice.
4. There is no way to ration gasoline so as to be fair to everyone.
5. If gasoline were rationed, extra allocations should be given to salespersons and others who must use their cars for business purposes.
6. Gasoline rationing would create an expensive and unjustifiable bureaucracy of federal employees.
7. Gasoline rationing causes automobile owners to shoulder an unfair share of the energy conservation effort.

---

1. Would you favor an equitable system of gasoline rationing? Why or why not?
2. If gasoline were rationed, should it be based on a given number of gallons per car, or per licensed driver in a family? Justify your choice.

CURRENT ISSUE

SUMMARY OF KEY CONCEPTS

Manufactured goods become valuable only when delivered to areas where they are needed.

Logistics is concerned with product handling and the movement of goods. Its dual purpose is to provide an adequate supply of raw materials for production and the delivery of finished goods to the market. It includes physical distribution, warehousing, and transportation.

Manufacturing gives goods *form utility;* logistics performance gives them *time and place* utility.

Effective purchasing procedures and inventory control are essential to the proper handling and efficient use of raw materials.

Warehousing and shipping form the heart and center of distribution. Efficiency in materials handling and control are important aspects of warehousing.

The traffic manager is responsible for the choice of carriers and control over packaging and shipments.

The basic energy problem in the United States is one of depending too heavily on oil and natural gas.

Our increasing industrial development necessitates our greater use of coal and development of alternate sources of energy.

Solar and nuclear energy seem to offer the best opportunities for remedying our overdependence on petroleum and natural gas.

During the 1970s the U.S. presidents and members of Congress could not agree on the components of a sound government policy regarding the use and conservation of energy. The raise in the price of crude to $18 tp $23 per barrel by the OPEC nations in June 1979 spurred Congress to action.

BUSINESS TERMS

You should be able to match these business terms with the statements that follow:

a. Common carrier
b. Contract carrier
c. Distribution center
d. Holding costs
e. Interstate transportation
f. Intrastate transportation
g. Inventory control
h. Logistics
i. Physical distribution
j. Private warehouse
k. Public warehouse
l. Shortage costs

1. The management plan that provides for an orderly flow of raw materials and finished goods
2. The management of materials, supplies, and goods on hand
3. Costs incurred by a business because sufficient goods are not available to fill orders
4. The movement of goods between producers and users
5. A warehouse that makes its facilities available to any and all businesses
6. A facility that provides for storage, product handling, and preparing goods for shipment
7. A shipper that sells its transport services by individual agreements
8. Transporting goods within the geographical boundaries of a single state

9. A transporter who offers services to the general public
10. A materials storage and handling facility whose services are used only by the company that owns it

REVIEW QUESTIONS

1. What are the three major components of logistics?
2. What are the two major aspects of inventory control?
3. What idea does the term *distribution center* convey that *warehousing* does not?
4. What is the chief drawback to using more coal in U.S. industry?
5. What is the chief drawback in nuclear-energy development?

DISCUSSION QUESTIONS

1. What is included in the term *physical distribution* in its broadest concept?
2. What determines whether a company will use public carriers, contract carriers, or private carriers?
3. What are the chief responsibilities of the traffic manager?
4. From an economic viewpoint, what is the basic energy problem in this country?
5. Which of the alternate forms of energy offers the greatest promise for the immediate future?
6. Why has a sound national energy policy been so slow in developing?

BUSINESS CASE 10-1

Solving Logistics Problems

The Hulette Company has experienced a number of logistics problems during the past year. There appears to be jealousy among area heads. Some feel that other "heads" are intruding upon the work for which they are responsible. To say the least, there is a lack of integration of activities and coordination of effort.

Company management is considering the following alternatives:

a. Retain the present organization structure but appoint a "logistics committee"—the several logistics activities would be represented on the committee.
b. Assign dual roles to several individuals by having them function in two or more logistics areas.
c. Reorganize the structure so that most or all logistic activities are under one head.

What do you see as the strengths and weaknesses of each plan?

BUSINESS CASE 10-2

United States Energy Resources

The United States possesses huge quantities of energy source material. There are large pools of petroleum under the continental shelves offshore. There are large reservoirs of oil in the shale and tar sands in the western states. There are large deposits of high-sulfur coal in the eastern states, and large deposits of low-sulfur coal in the western states. We have adequate deposits of the raw material for nuclear fuels.

We have in this country numerous large energy-producing companies with the capital and technology to discover and produce oil, natural gas, and nuclear fuel. We also have the technical capacity to develop feasible solar-energy projects.

The hindrances to harnessing these energy sources seem to be these:

1. Legal action by persons concerned about the environment
2. Government regulation of production and pricing
3. Lack of the necessary incentives for private companies to develop new energy sources
4. Controversies between the executive and legislative branches of the federal government

Assume that you are the energy chief for the United States government with full authority to solve the problem.

1. What would your solution be?
2. How would you achieve a compromise between demands for a clean environment and demands for ever-increasing production?
3. How would you bring about increased conservation practices?
4. How would you divide the cost of exploration and technological development between government and the private sector?

MARKETING

THE MARKETING PROCESS

11

STUDY OBJECTIVES

WHEN YOU HAVE FINISHED READING THIS CHAPTER, YOU SHOULD BE ABLE TO

ONE Discuss the importance of marketing in the U.S. economy

TWO Describe how marketing contributes to the value of raw materials and manufactured goods

THREE Distinguish between marketing functions and marketing activities

FOUR Justify expenditures for the marketing of completed products

FIVE Identify the types of factors that combine to make up the marketing environment

SIX Compare and contrast consumer and industrial markets

IN THE NEWS IN THE NEWS IN THE NEWS IN THE NEWS IN THE NEWS IN THE NEWS IN THE NEWS IN THE NEWS IN THE NEWS

Perrier Proves You Can Sell Water in Bottles!!

For many years about the only customers for bottled water were owners of steam irons and office water coolers. But France's Perrier mineral water has stunned the U.S. beverage industry with a marketing strategy that changed all that.

This new marketing strategy is based on an appeal to health-conscious Americans, a revamped distributor network, and "snob appeal." This meticulously developed marketing campaign segmented the beverage market and tapped the adult segment.

The distributor network was changed from gourmet shops to supermarkets. Formerly 60 percent of sales had been in gourmet shops. Now over 70 percent of sales are in supermarkets and only 5 percent are in gourmet shops. The ad campaign, too, was directed at the affluent and fashionable, with ads in high-fashion women's magazines and TV commercials narrated by Orson Welles.

The naturally carbonated spring water is selling very well as a noncaloric, chic alternative to soft drinks and alcoholic beverages. Sales of Perrier have soared from less than $1 million to over $30 million annually and are rising fast. Perrier could soon have 1 percent of the U.S. soft-drink market—a significant share. The key to the Perrier success is the marketing effort.

IN THE NEWS

Treat customers as guests when they come and go, whether or not they buy. Give them all that can be given fairly, on the principle that to him that giveth shall be given.

GORDON SELFRIDGE

No business or individual is fully self-sufficient—all depend upon others to satisfy needs and wants. We are continually faced with buying decisions in the marketplace as a part of satisfying those needs and wants.

The marketplace is the focal point of all business activity. This is where the business firm presents goods and services competing with other sellers. Here the firm is judged by how well it is able to satisfy consumers. It is also judged by how well it meets customer needs, by how much profit it makes, and by how good its products or services are.

Manufacturing and marketing complement and reinforce each other. What is made must be sold, but we must also know what to make that will sell. If it does not sell it is no longer produced. Not just goods, but services and ideas, are marketed.

This chapter introduces the subject of marketing, with emphasis on marketing functions. Marketing functions involve a variety of activities. These include selection of target customers, product development, promotion, pricing, merchandising, advertising, and shipping. The role of marketing and the marketing concept, as well as marketing functions, are discussed in some detail.

MARKETING IN OUR ECONOMY

The first thing one observes about marketing is activity. The whole marketing process is concerned with the flow of goods from farms, forests, and mines to mills and factories, and from there to different marketing units—warehouses,

JAY VAN ANDEL

Jay Van Andel is a salesman for "free enterprise." He believes that in order to achieve in this country, you must always have a dream. Then your decisions keep you headed in the direction of your dream goal.

Van Andel says that under our system of private enterprise, "you can start your own business whether a fruit stand, a farm, or distributorship, and you can do your own thing in life."

In 1948 Van Andel and his partner, Richard De Vos, sold their business interests in Norwalk, Connecticut. They left immediately for the Caribbean and South America on a year's cruise aboard the schooner *Elizabeth*. The schooner was shipwrecked off the coast of Cuba in March 1949 while en route to Haiti. Van Andel and De Vos were rescued by an American freighter and continued their travels through the Caribbean and South America for another five months.

Van Andel and De Vos returned to Michigan and formed some new business interests. In 1959 they founded the Amway Corporation in Ada, Michigan. The company manufactures over 150 household cleaning and personal-care products and cosmetics. These items are distributed throughout the United States, as well as in Canada, Australia, the United Kingdom, Hong Kong, Malaysia, Germany, and France. Amway Corporation distributes goods through a direct selling organization of some three hundred thousand independent distributors.

Van Andel and De Vos act jointly as chief executive officers of the various Amway companies, generally dividing their responsibilities so that Van Andel handles the business management activities, and De Vos handles the personnel management activities.

Van Andel is active in many civic, government, and trade associations. In 1974 he was the recipient of the Religious Heritage Business and Professional Leader of the Year Award. In 1979, at the age of fifty-four, he was elected to the position of chairman of the Chamber of Commerce of the United States.

When asked by an editor of *Nation's Business* in 1979, "What do you think are the obligations of business?" he replied:

> To the public, business has a responsibility to produce the best goods and services with honesty and integrity. When you do that, you are giving people the best value you can for the price you are charging. Then, you are not only making it possible for people to live well but also producing a surplus of revenue to reinvest, more jobs, and a better standard of living for all.
>
> This surplus produced by the business system also provides for all the other activities in life such as education, the arts, medical care, organized religion, charities, recreation, and even our governmental system, through taxes.

Van Andel is married to the former Betty Hoekstra of Grand Rapids, Michigan, and they have four children.

wholesalers, and retail stores. This continual movement of goods and services in the marketing system is a part of the overall economic system's attempt to meet people's needs and wants.

Marketing Defined

The term **MARKETING** as defined by the American Marketing Association, is **the performance of business activities that direct the flow of goods and services from producer to consumer or user.** This definition shows marketing as encompassing such activities as merchandising, promotion, pricing, selling, and transportation.

To have a **market** there must be a buyer and seller, a product or service, an agreed-upon price, and an exchange. To the economist, the market for a specific good is the sum of all transactions between buyers and sellers of that good at any given time.

Historical Background of Marketing

The early settlers in the United States had few marketing problems. The exchange of goods occurred largely through barter. From a personal point of view, life was usually a matter of producing the necessary food and shelter, mainly by family members. As the colonies' population increased, the need for trading became evident.

Peddlers became the source of family remedies and simple housewares. They obtained their goods from ships that docked in the ports and sold their goods from town to town. And as settlements increased, the storekeeper became the main source of goods. Eventually the general store served as wholesaler, retailer, banker, and the source of many family needs. Each store exhibit included a medley of produce ". . . both a needle and an anchor, a tin pot and a large copper boiler, a child's whistle and a pinafore, a ring dial and a clock, a skein of thread and trimmings of lace . . . a gill of vinegar and a hogshead of Madeira wine."[1]

Early Manufacturers

As manufacturing evolved, industrial goods appeared along with consumer goods, and producers were no longer able to deal directly with customers. The need for a "middleman" developed, and selling was becoming important. The economy, although growing rapidly, consisted mostly of farming, and the supply of manufactured goods had not yet reached the point of meeting the demand. Under these conditions, manufacturers were most interested in concentrating on manufacturing, leaving the marketing to middlemen.

THE MARKETING CONCEPT

The marketing concept, like many other viewpoints, has changed over the years. In the early days of business in America, it was **product oriented.** The idea was to produce as many goods as one could, because the market was limitless.

Following the Civil War, many businesses became very large concerns. The era of mass production developed around the turn of the twentieth century. Situations of excess supply developed in some industries. So some firms turned to increased advertising, more personal selling, and broader distribution. The marketing philosophy shifted from a product orientation to a **sales orientation.**

[1]Fred Mitchell Jones, *Middlemen in the Domestic Trade of the United States 1800–1860* (Urbana: University of Illinois, 1937), p. 44.

After World War II business in the United States prospered. Managers began to see the need to work with their customers. As a result, a new marketing concept developed. This new **MARKETING CONCEPT** has three components:

1. A customer orientation
2. A profit orientation
3. Coordination and integration of marketing activities

Customer Orientation

When buying a car, why are we able to choose from so many models and colors? Because the producer is trying to give customers what they want and will buy. Why did the U.S. car makers shift their production emphasis during the late 1970s to small cars? Because customer demand was for smaller cars that used less gasoline. **Customer orientation** means letting customers' wants guide the firm's production activities. For example, consider "convenience foods."

No one likes what has happened to food prices. These prices keep going up, and the farmers for the most part are not receiving any greater share of the pie. It's the "middlemen," we are told. And so it is. But let us examine the shopping carts of America to see what buyers are doing to cut food costs.

Despite rising food prices, Americans seem to have an insatiable appetite for convenience foods. The typical shopping cart contains ready-to-eat waffles, frozen entrees, prepared vegetables, soda pop, prepared pizza, and so forth. And if the purchaser is questioned as to why not flour, unprepared meat, fresh vegetables, and so forth, the typical response is, "There isn't enough time to cook a big meal."

The nation's big food producers are aware of the irony: People decry high prices but won't buy the lower-priced foods. These producers are rushing to introduce more convenience foods to a waiting market.

Profit Orientation

Perhaps the chief goal of most business concerns is to make a profit. Profits enable a firm to grow and to increase the dividend return to owners. But if a firm is to make a profit, it must also meet the needs of society. It must provide a quality product and a safe product. Profit is at least in part a reward for being socially responsible.

Integration of Marketing Activities

It is necessary to tie together product development, advertising, and sales. Marketing activities must be coordinated with production and financial activities.

The Reliance Electric Company is an example of a firm that not only coordinates marketing activities but applies the new marketing concept.

About twenty years ago Reliance's engineers designed an "ultra-futuristic drive" that used vacuum tubes to convert alternating current to direct current. Although the engineers were pleased and the drive performed well in the lab, it flopped. Why? Essentially, the product did not satisfy the needs of customers. They found that it was too sensitive to withstand dirt and moisture in a plant.

Motivated to overcome years of lackluster performance, Reliance reconstructed its firm in line with the marketing concept. A key change consisted of establishing a group of twelve market managers who worked closely with their customers to obtain information about their needs. Reliance's advertising theme also reflected this new approach: "The man from Reliance has only one engineered drive for you . . . the one you need." In line with another part of the marketing concept, the firm's financial performance improved after the new philosophy was implemented.

The marketing concept brings the marketing person in at the start rather than at the end of the production cycle. It integrates marketing into every phase of business operation.

MARKETING FUNCTIONS

In a market economy there are six "universal marketing functions":

1. Market analysis
2. Marketing communication
3. Market segmentation
4. Product differentiation
5. The valuation function
6. The exchange function

The role and relationships of these marketing functions in the movement of goods are shown in Figure 11-1. Each function is discussed in the paragraphs that follow.

Market Analysis

How does the law of supply and demand function in a marketing situation? Producers must know what consumers want. Consumers want producers to know what they want. This is what market analysis is all about. Both buyers (users) and sellers (producers) are participants. In **MARKET ANALYSIS participants learn about the supply of, and demand for, a given product.**

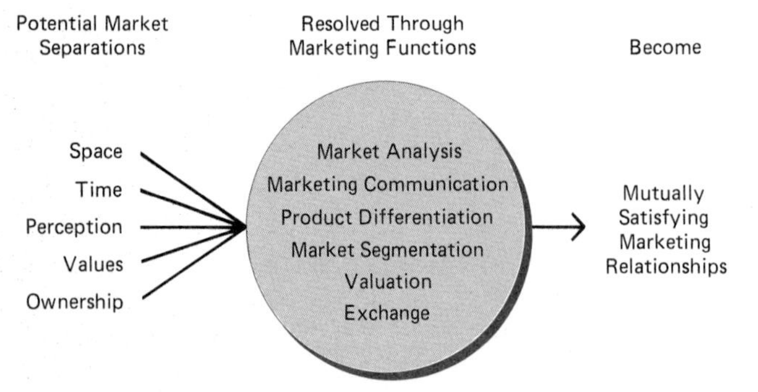

FIGURE 11-1

Role of marketing functions. (From *Marketing Principles* by William G. Nickels, 1978. Reprinted by permission of Prentice-Hall, Inc.)

It is through market analysis that sellers learn who and where their potential customers are. After locating them, sellers gather information about these potential customers that is pertinent to marketing their products. And buyers, through the shopping process, learn about potential sellers. They find out about the cost and quality of their goods. The total of all potential exchanges (between buyers and sellers) of a particular good or service, at any given time, makes up the **market.**

Marketing Communication

Communication is the adhesive that binds market forces together. Through market research, buyers can communicate their wants and desired satisfactions to sellers. Sellers then produce products that meet these expressed needs. Then, through advertising, sellers communicate back to potential buyers. **COMMUNICATION** refers to **the flow of information back and forth between buyers and sellers.** Without communication, the market system does not work very well to control prices. A good example of what can happen with better communication is the removal of the ban on advertising as it applies to lawyers.

Consumers can now "shop" for legal services just as they can for a used car. This does not make the ABA (American Bar Association) happy. The ABA would prefer "self-governance," but that resulted in "minimum fee schedules" and a ban on advertising. After legal advertising began, the price of some services fell as much as 50 percent. Overall the ensuing price competition resulted in no service having a higher price one year after the change than before the change in one study area.

From 1954 to 1976 the number of lawyers being graduated increased by 293 percent. Economic theory predicts that this increase in the number of attorneys should increase competition and keep the prices of their services low. But because of the ABA ban on advertising, this has not been the case.

Now new attorneys can use advertising to build their own practice rather than working for an established firm. This change in the competitive structure of the legal profession should generate downward pressure on prices for legal services.

Since information is the key to correct decision making, this makes communication a very important marketing function. The activities that help sellers carry out the communication function are advertising, sales promotion, personal selling, publicity, and research. The product itself communicates through its design and the attractiveness of its packaging.

Market Segmentation

Can you think of any one product or service that would satisfy all customers? Probably not. Even a basic commodity such as salt requires different package sizes to satisfy various needs. No company has sufficient resources to satisfy all customers, manufacturers, wholesalers, retailers, and so forth. Therefore a firm must select the specific market or markets on which it will concentrate its efforts. The term **market** is used here to refer to a group of people or organizations with unsatisfied needs or wants who have sufficient buying power.

To arrive at markets of a manageable size, a business firm must engage in **MARKET SEGMENTATION. This involves taking a total market and then dividing it into submarkets (or segments) that have similar characteristics.** The individuals or organizations within each segment are similar to one another in terms of their wants, buying power, and shopping patterns.

Common bases for market segmentation include geographical location and such demographic factors as income, age, education, and family size. Rates of usage and personality differences have also been tried as segmentation bases with some success. Some entrepreneurs have even segmented the consumer market into right-handed and left-handed people and have opened shops featuring specially designed left-handed products.

Makers of jogging (or running, if you prefer) shoes have taken a serious lead in market segmentation. The magazine *Runner's World* recently featured no fewer than 103 different kinds of training and racing shoes. For years Adidas was the front-runner in the U.S. market. U.S. manufacturers like Nike and New Balance have seen sales take off. Converse, which has two-thirds of the basketball market, has decided that running is more than a fad and has entered the market.

Nike has introduced a shoe that rides on a cushion of encapsulated air chambers. The shoe took three years and more than a thousand designs to develop. It had to eliminate the problems of going flat and a pogo-stick effect before becoming successful. Further market segmentation is evident as the American manufacturers turn to the European market, casual shoes with "the jogger look," and the whole geriatric market.

After market segmentation and an appraisal of the potential and competition within various segments, a company then selects one or more **target markets.** A marketing mix with one or more custom-tailored components is necessary for each target market. The four major marketing mix components are discussed at length in Chapters 12 and 13.

Buyers also segment their markets. They select the few stores they wish to patronize. And they select the professional persons from whom they wish to purchase professional services.

Product Differentiation

Producers want to make products that best meet the wants of buyers so that they can sell more. They want their goods to be different from those produced by others. Changes may be made in the product itself—design, quality, or appearance. Or they may be made in the packaging, pricing, or labeling. In time the buyers, too, may change what they are willing to pay to receive exactly what they want.

PRODUCT DIFFERENTIATION includes all the ways that buyers and sellers adjust product offers. This is done in order to bring about a product exchange. Product differentiation enables a seller to offer goods that differ from other goods so that they will be preferred over someone else's goods. Take instant coffee as an example. The Nestlé company positioned its TV advertising to establish the distinctive qualities of its freeze-dried Taster's Choice coffee. Procter and Gamble, on the other hand, attempted to differentiate Folger's coffee crystals from those of other competing brands. The idea, in each case, was to emphasize those features that made each product different from competing products.

Procter and Gamble says that it will only market *a new product* if it is superior in some important respect to competitive products already on the market. Unless a product has some point of superiority that appeals to the public, the company feels that it will be difficult for the product to carve out a position in an established market.

The Valuation Function

In valuation, buyers and sellers decide whether the benefits of an exchange are worth its costs. **VALUATION** refers to this **cost-benefit analysis of the marketing exchange.** It is a continual process, occurring both before the exchange and after. Pricing a product is a part of valuation.

A major emphasis in marketing is to see that the benefits exceed the costs. (**Costs** here include such factors as time and effort as well as money.) Values may be changed by either increasing the benefits or lowering the costs.

From society's point of view, the values of the public's satisfaction should exceed both monetary and environmental costs. If the costs of an exchange appear to exceed the benefits, no exchange will probably occur.

The Exchange Function

The goal of all the preceding marketing activity is the **EXCHANGE—a cash-benefits tradeoff.** The exchange function may include financing, storage, delivery, installation, and/or servicing. The exchange does not end the marketing process. Valuation and communication continue, and market analysis may be started again.

Marketing Activities

The functions of marketing are very broad. Within them are many activities that relate to the marketing of goods and services. They include buying and selling, of course, but also such things as brands, display, finance, packaging, and transportation. These many marketing activities are enumerated in Figure 11-2.

MANAGEMENT'S ROLE IN MARKETING

The task of marketing management is to design a "mix" of the marketing functions that is compatible with the buying environment. To do this, marketing people must plan their market strategies carefully.

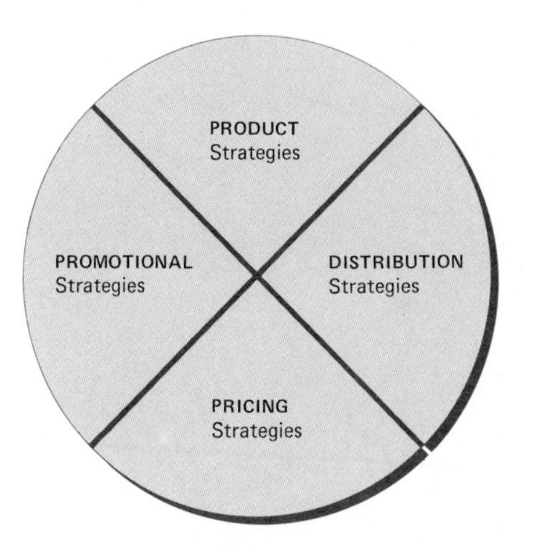

FIGURE 11-2

Decision strategies in the marketing mix.

Marketing Decision Making

Those in management who make basic marketing decisions are influenced by two groups of forces. The first group consists of forces within the business. They can be controlled to some extent. The second group consists of forces outside the business and beyond the influence of management. These two groups can be summarized as follows.

Inside Controllable Forces	Outside Forces
Advertising programs	Competition from other firms
Brands management	Economic changes
Distribution channels	Government controls
Internal organization	Local legal regulations
Pricing	Sociological forces
Product patterns	Technological innovations
Shipping media	Variations in the business cycle

Determining the Marketing Mix

A profitable marketing program depends largely on the marketing mix. Choosing the marketing mix involves a combination of four strategies. The **MARKETING MIX** is defined as **a blending of strategies involving four ingredients: product, distribution channels, promotion, and price.** The offering may consist of a product(s) or service(s), or both. (For example, Western Auto, Goodyear, Firestone, Sears, Wards, and K Mart sell batteries and tires as well as automotive maintenance and repairs.) The four strategies in the marketing mix are illustrated in Figure 11-3.

A business may have more than one marketing mix to satisfy distinct groups of customers. Texas Instruments, for example, has one set of calculators and distribution arrangements for commercial customers and another for consumers. Also, a firm will periodically change its marketing mix because of changes in customers' needs or competition. **Marketing management is directed toward markets and is guided to some extent by environmental factors.**

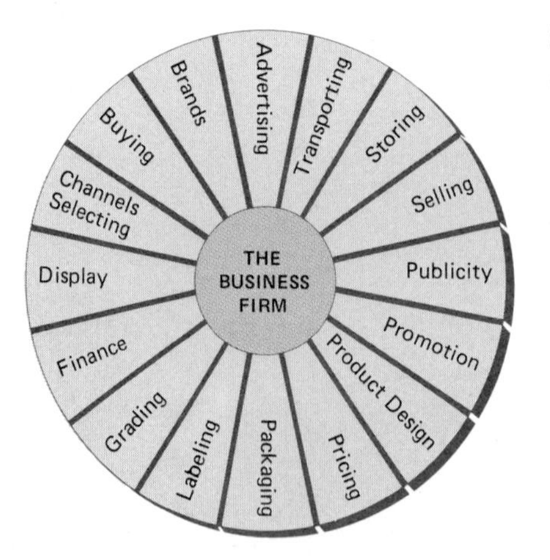

FIGURE 11-3
Marketing activities.

The Marketing Organization

Basically, every company engaged in marketing organizes some of its resources in a specific way to carry out specific strategies. The form of organization used and its complexity depend in part upon the company's size. They also depend on whether the company is a manufacturer, wholesaler, retailer, or service establishment, and the extent to which it has adopted the marketing concept.

Small firms. In a very small firm, the owner-manager is the marketing executive. He or she is truly a "jack of all trades" and quite likely a "master of none." As a firm grows, the owner can delegate some marketing tasks to employees. Eventually the firm may become large enough to support marketing specialists. These are people with special skills in marketing activities, such as advertising, purchasing, or sales. An organization chart for a firm where marketing is centralized is shown in Figure 11-4. This firm is still quite small compared with the giants of industry. However, it has reached a size at which the owner can concentrate more on planning and other top-level administrative activities. For instance, the owner can delegate to the marketing manager the planning for sales strategy.

Large firms. A most interesting form of marketing organization in a large manufacturing firm is Procter and Gamble's brand-manager structure. In 1927 a young executive was assigned total responsibility for an ailing brand, Camay

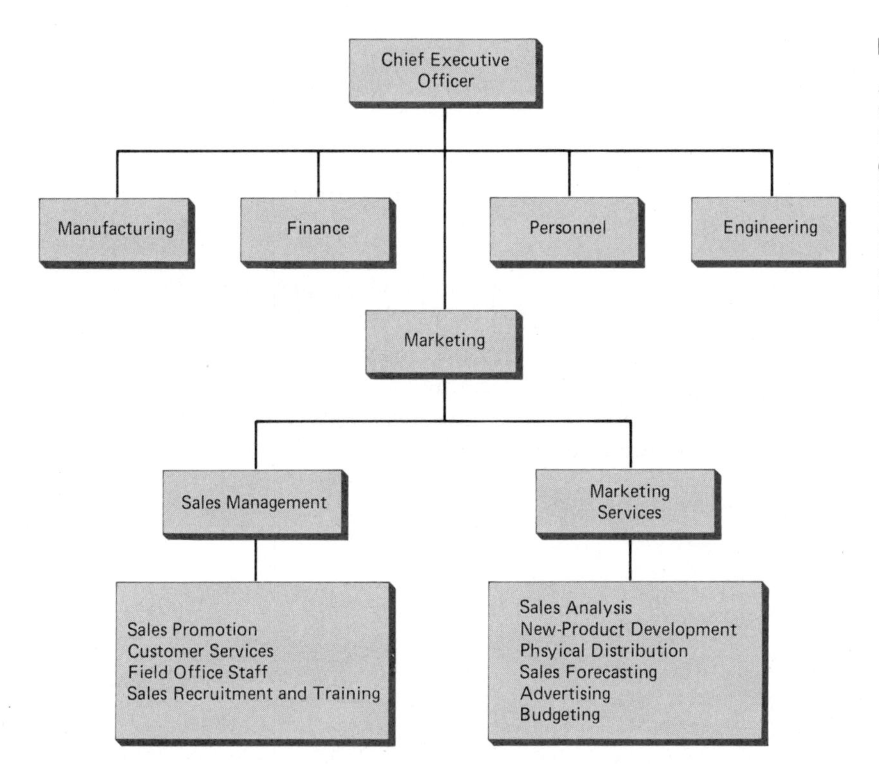

FIGURE 11-4

A company organization where marketing is centralized.

(In this organization all marketing activities are under a marketing manager. The success of the business depends heavily on the firm's ability to market its goods and services through the marketing department.)

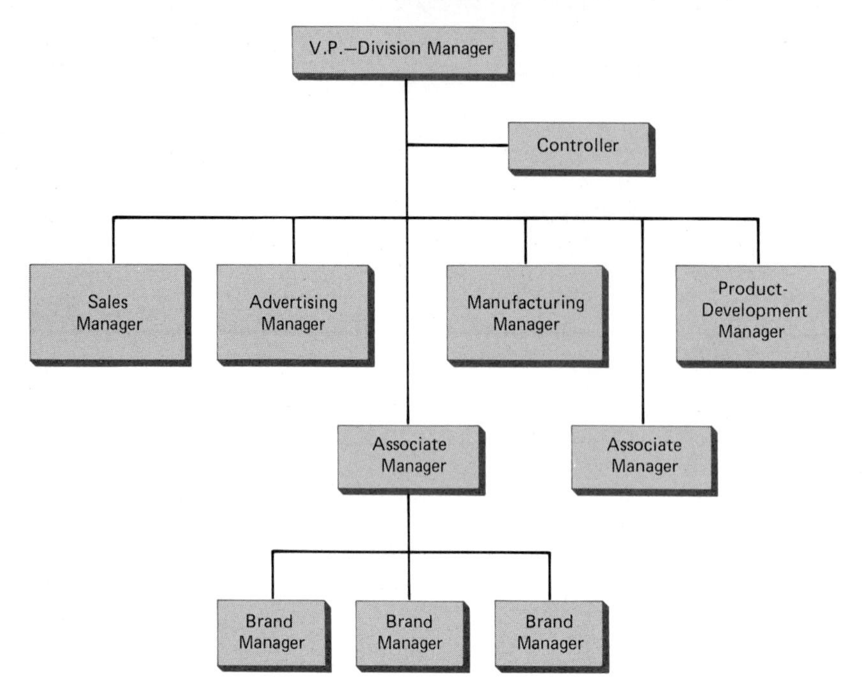

FIGURE 11-5

The brand-manager form of organization in large manufacturing firms.

soap. His concentrated efforts revived the product. This success prompted P&G's brand-manager structure, as shown in Figure 11-5.

Brand managers plan and implement long-range strategies and annual marketing programs for the brand or brands under their responsibility. Doing this entails specific tasks, such as sales forecasting, assisting an advertising agency in creating promotional themes, selecting advertising media, and encouraging the company sales force to put a little extra effort behind the brand.

In the brand-manager structure, the overall marketing program for each brand is coordinated within the advertising department. A basic marketing strategy is planned separately for each brand by a **brand manager** and two or three assistants. This brand group is then responsible for its execution. The brand group is supported by a broad range of staff services (such as market research, promotion development, media buying, and commercial production). It shares joint responsibility for the development of effective advertising with an independent advertising agency assigned specifically to that brand.

One criticism has been that brand managers become too frustrated at having much responsibility but little authority. To overcome such criticism and to achieve a more suitable structure, some firms have emphasized marketing functions or key markets rather than specific products.

THE ECONOMIC CONTRIBUTIONS OF MARKETING

Since our society is dynamic, with constant changes in institutions and activities, it is not surprising that marketing has changed considerably over time. We will discuss several important changes.

The Incentive to Buy

Marketing is really a twentieth-century development. During the nineteenth century, many of the goods manufactured were made to order. Therefore marketing consisted of little more than delivering the goods produced. But as manufacturing capabilities increased, more goods were produced before there were definite orders for them. Eventually the quantity of manufactured goods being produced exceeded the demand for them. Mass-production techniques were forcing the development of mass-marketing procedures. This required large amounts of advertising. Ours is still generally an economy of abundance. This necessitates a marketing system that motivates individuals and organizations to become buyers.

Importance of Services

Marketing is too often thought of in connection with physical products because of two false assumptions. The first is that services do not represent a substantial portion of the American economy. The second is that marketing cannot be applied to intangibles such as services.

Today services account for almost half of the consumer dollar. Certainly, service does make up a significant part of our economy. Figure 11-6 shows how the consumer dollar is divided about equally between goods and services.

The assumption that marketing cannot be applied to intangibles is wrong, for there are numerous successful firms. Holiday Inns, for example, has combined a standardized offering with locations on heavily traveled routes and has become a giant international firm based on services. At the same time, Motel 6 and Days Inns have emphasized economy prices to achieve a profitable share of the motel market. Consider also AAMCO transmission repair shops and Manpower temporary help agencies. They are successful service companies because of distinctive marketing programs. Effective marketing of services involves everything that product marketing does.

The Value-Added Concept

About half the sales price of a product or service pays for the marketing activities required to provide the customer with a finished offering. This was once referred to as the **cost of marketing.** But the word **cost** carries a negative connotation. So the current term is to consider this as the **VALUE ADDED to the offering by performing marketing activities.**

We have already seen that raw materials are enhanced in value by processing them. A finished product or service has little value until it is in the possession of the person who can use it. Thus the money spent in marketing goods adds to their value.

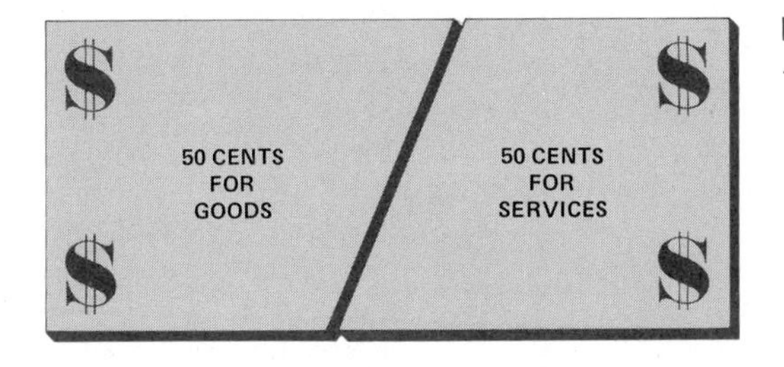

FIGURE 11-6
The consumer dollar.

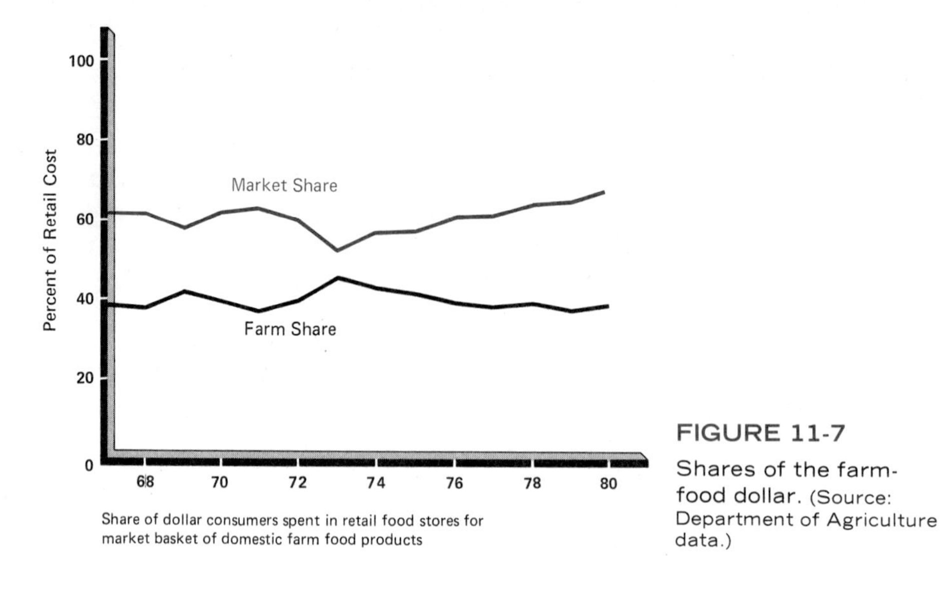

FIGURE 11-7

Shares of the farm-food dollar. (Source: Department of Agriculture data.)

The "cost of marketing" varies with the product involved. For example, for the farm-food dollar, about sixty cents is for marketing. This is shown in Figure 11-7. But cost varies within a given product group. Let us use the farm-food market basket again. It varies greatly—from about sixty cents for the farmer's share for poultry and eggs to about fifteen cents for grains (bakery and cereal products). This is shown in Figure 11-8. This same variation occurs in the different categories of consumer products.

THE MARKET ENVIRONMENT

An unmistakable trend facing marketers is the growing importance of the firm's environment. **MARKET ENVIRONMENT** refers to **all factors surrounding and affecting business operations.** Before looking at different types of environ-

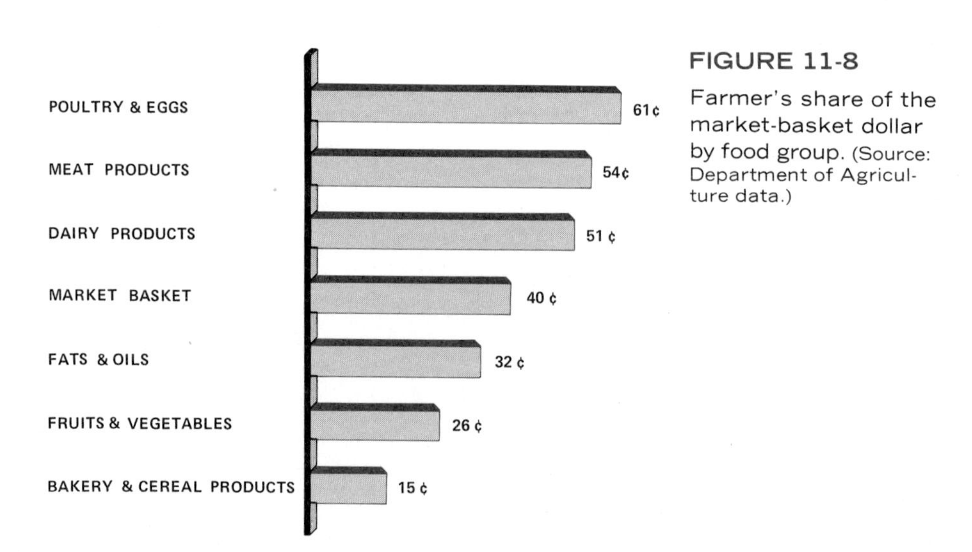

FIGURE 11-8

Farmer's share of the market-basket dollar by food group. (Source: Department of Agriculture data.)

mental factors, we should consider the environment's far-ranging effects on marketing management.

The ban on nonreturnable bottles and cans in Oregon several years ago illustrates how a change in the marketing environment can affect different parties in vastly different ways. Various firms were hurt by the law. Manufacturers of beverage cans experienced a great loss of business. Out-of-state breweries faced higher transportation costs because bottles had to be used. Some parties benefited, however. Bottle manufacturers' volume went up, since returnable bottles became the standard container. And local breweries obtained a cost advantage over distant breweries.

Of course, the primary objective of the ban was a societal benefit—namely, to reduce litter in the form of beverage containers. The point here is that environmental changes pose threats to some firms, *but* they can provide profitable opportunities for others. This basic point applies to all five types of environmental factors discussed below.

Economic Conditions

To appreciate the impact of economic conditions on business, one only has to recall the so-called stagflation of the second half of the 1970s. This combination of recession and severe inflation reduced or eliminated the profits of many companies. Nevertheless, some firms—auto-repair outlets, for example—experienced an increase in business during these "hard" economic times.

The category of economic conditions includes four distinct factors that are beyond a company's control: state of the economy, nature, intensity of competition, and levels of supply. Many economic variables, including gross national product, income levels, rates of unemployment, inflation, savings, and taxes, can influence buying power. With so many complex variables involved, it is difficult for executives to forecast buying power.

A company ordinarily faces one or more direct competitors, such as firms that offer the same kind of product or service. In addition, indirect competition can "steal" customers from a company. That is, firms in different industries might offer a product or service that better satisfies a customer's needs or wants. Thus an airline promoting a vacation package is actually competing with a manufacturer of small travel trailers. Both are offering ways of achieving an enjoyable vacation.

The marketing executive is seeking a **DIFFERENTIAL ADVANTAGE** for the company's offering, **one or more favorable features that are not found to the same degree in competing products or services.** The idea is that this advantage will cause customers to buy the firm's offering. Top quality, widespread distribution, an advertising theme that matches the customer's needs, very low prices, or some combination of these features may be a differential advantage.

General Motors is an excellent example of a firm that has taken advantage of changes in the environment through a series of good decisions.

In the mid 1970s two environmental forces changed Detroit's long-standing automobile-marketing situation. The increasing cost of gasoline, and federal standards requiring manufacturers to increase gasoline MPG on their fleets by as much as 53 percent by 1985, shocked the industry. All U.S. auto manufacturers were dependent on big gas-hungry cars.

General Motors changed its marketing strategy and began to redesign its products. It decided to "down-size" its fleet over a period of years, beginning immediately. GM's "first-strike" strategy paid off big. Ford and Chrysler chose to hold back on down-sizing their big cars, hoping that GM would bear the brunt of familiarizing the public with smaller cars. And GM sales did slip for a while but then caught fire, and its share of the U.S. market jumped from 42 percent to nearly 50 percent.

General Motors also used a very successful marketing gambit in launching its X-car. The car was introduced in the spring of 1979 instead of in the fall, as had been customary with new models. The resulting demand left car dealers without enough X-cars to sell, and customers who wanted these cars had to sign up on waiting lists.

By misreading the shifting market, Ford and Chrysler fell behind. They initially ran ads stressing the larger size of their cars. By saying "Come and get the last of the whoppers" both companies hurt the image of their products in relation to General Motors, since by then the public did not want "whoppers."

Sociocultural Factors

The sociocultural factors of primary concern to marketers are population trends and changes in values. Regarding population, a business firm needs to assess periodically the nature and number of individuals (or organizations) in its present markets. For example, declining birthrates posed a definite threat to the Gerber Company with its slogan "Babies are our business—our *only* business." As a result, Gerber dropped the slogan and expanded its markets and offerings to include geriatric and single-portion food products. On the positive side, some southwestern states and Florida are growing quite rapidly. Retailers in these states face the pleasant prospect of a larger number of potential customers.

Changes in values can be difficult to identify, and nearly impossible to explain or forecast. But because such changes can significantly influence operations, the marketer at least has to decide how to react to such changes when they do occur. Consider two recent, enduring trends in American values and their impact on marketing.

First, there has been a mass acceptance by consumers of purchasing on credit. The opportunity presented by this environmental factor is greater sales than might result on a cash-only basis. But threats are also present. Offering credit can be costly, especially if a high level of bad debts occur.

Second, American society has been oriented toward participation in sports. Many people participate in amateur team sports, and many participate in individual sports such as tennis and golf.

From a marketing standpoint, this orientation means booming demand for the products and services related to tennis, hang-gliding, cross-country skiing, jogging, and other increasingly popular sports. One threat associated with this value change is possible overexpansion, which would cause some sports-related businesses to fail. For instance, how many brands of tennis rackets can the market absorb?

Technological Factors

Technological advances can also affect a firm's possible offerings and the ways in which it can do business. Connected with the sports boom discussed above, various new products have been the fruits of technology: metal tennis rackets, video electronic sports games, and graphite-shaft golf clubs, as examples. In the field of electronics, miniaturized integrated circuits have revolutionized such product categories as calculators and watches.

Advances in computer technology have affected virtually all aspects of business. A notable example is point-of-sale terminals, which are replacing conventional cash registers. These terminals can be hooked up to computers so that sales and inventory levels for all items can be monitored daily.

One marketing opportunity presented by technological factors is increased sales from new products. Another is more efficient marketing operations, often resulting from computer technology. Threats are present, too. For instance, a business could invest a large sum of money that does not result in a saleable new offering or more efficient operations.

Government Legislation

Actions of the federal, state, and local governments all affect marketing operations, often very dramatically. For example, the Congress repealed the "fair trade" laws in 1975. For almost forty years, these laws had permitted manufacturers to set minimum retail prices for their products under certain conditions. Detailed below are facts about one agency and law that in many ways typify the aggressive posture government bodies have assumed in their relations with marketers.

Federal Trade Commission. In 1914 Congress passed the Federal Trade Commission Act. The act states that "unfair methods of competition in commerce are unlawful." It also established a five-member commission with broad investigative and regulatory powers.

Since about 1965, the FTC has stepped up its investigations and regulatory activities. Some FTC activities are intended to maintain competition in industry. Others are intended to protect consumers in their dealings with marketers. Recently the FTC has been particularly concerned about deceptive advertising.

FTC actions have been directed at a wide range of industries and companies, including the cereal, automotive-repair, and funeral industries, as well as grocery retailers and automobile manufacturers. The commission has some "bite" to go with its "bark." It can issue quasi-legal trade regulations related to certain business practices. It issues cease-and-desist orders requiring that an offending activity be halted. It can also enter into consent orders with businesses, under which a firm agrees to halt a disputed practice. The role of the Federal Trade Commission is discussed further in Chapters 13 and 20.

Robinson-Patman Act. This federal legislation was passed in 1936. According to the act, it is illegal for manufacturers and wholesalers to grant different prices to different purchasers of goods of like quantity and quality if such discrimination would lessen competition to the seller's and buyer's benefit.

An interesting provision in the act is that the buyer, as well as the seller, can be found guilty if he or she *knowingly* accepts the discriminatory lower prices. However, the act does permit price differences resulting from attempts to meet competitors' prices and from fluctuating market prices or the threatened obsolescence of a perishable product. As you can see, the Robinson-Patman Act is exceedingly complex. This has made compliance by businesspersons and consistent application by courts very difficult.

Consumerism

In Chapter 2 it was pointed out that business has a responsibility to provide consumers with certain types of information. Business is responsible for providing quality merchandise and refraining from unfair business practices.

Consumerism came on strong in the 1960s and today is a significant environmental factor for most marketers. It seeks to increase the rights of consumers in relation to sellers. Let us restate its primary goals:

1. To obtain complete truth in advertising
2. To ensure that products perform as advertised, are safe, and do not harm the physical environment

Perhaps most importantly, various business firms have initiated special programs coinciding with the goals of consumerism. For example, Gillette has a

CURRENT ISSUE

The Consumer Versus the Producer!

Historically we have said that in our private-enterprise economy, "the consumer is king." Through purchasing, consumers decide what is to be produced. Some consumer advocates seem to be sponsoring a confrontation between producers and consumers. Government mandates and regulations of producers work to favor consumers over producers. Is this good for the country? Are not consumers also producers?

With which of the following statements do you agree and with which do you disagree?

1. Consumers must continually battle producers in order to protect their rights.
2. Consumers are also producers—so what is good for one is good for the other.
3. Government policy seems to favor consumers over producers.
4. The word "consumer" is often used when we should say "person," the "individual," or "people."
5. Taxes on savings work as a disincentive, thus penalizing the "producer."
6. Government regulations favor the consumer over the producer, thus reducing total production.

How can we gain a better balance in relations between consumers and producers?

separate vice-president with responsibility and substantial authority related to product safety. Also, some supermarket chains have added unit pricing, which assists shoppers in comparing prices. Marketing executives need to understand consumerism so they can develop compatible marketing programs.

CONSUMER AND INDUSTRIAL MARKETS

The total American market can be subdivided into "final" consumers and industrial customers. **Final consumers** make purchases for their personal or household consumption. **Industrial customers,** a very broad category, are individuals and organizations that make purchases that they can use for resale or for running a business. Thus a person who buys a calculator for balancing the checkbook belongs to the consumer market. When he or she buys another calculator for figuring markups in a small store, he or she is part of the industrial market.

Industrial customers and final consumers usually want different products or services. They also often have different buying processes. As a result, a firm's marketing efforts ordinarily must be especially designed for each.

Government units at all levels (federal, state, and local) buy sufficient goods to account for one-fourth of the gross national product, a significant submarket to be sure. Two-thirds of all government purchases are made by the federal government. This makes Uncle Sam the single largest customer in the United States.

The Consumer Market

The consumer market is made up of purchases by individuals and households. This market accounts for the largest segment of the gross national product.

Classification of Consumer Goods.

Consumer goods are usually classified as convenience, shopping, and specialty goods. **CONVENIENCE GOODS are low priced and easily available.** They can be readily purchased in nearby retail stores. Groceries, drugs, soft drinks, and cigarettes are classed as convenience goods. **SHOPPING GOODS are bought only after comparing price, quality, and style.** In other words, they are shopped for. Clothing, jewelry, and furniture are examples of shopping goods. **SPECIALTY GOODS are specific items that one wants.** People are willing to spend considerable time and money in order to buy what they want. Cars, boots, designer dresses, stereo systems, and fine cameras are examples of specialty goods.

Stereo systems for cars have blossomed into a lucrative market. Amplifiers, tape decks, speakers, and FM receivers to replace factory-installed units are running at about $1 billion per year. Teenagers and people in the twenty-five to forty-four age group are the heavy buyers. These expensive specialty systems, often $300–$1,500, are expected to increase in sales volume, and the cost may come down as the technology improves. They are classified as specialty items because many of the customers know *exactly* what they want in a stereo system and are willing to pay whatever it takes to get it.

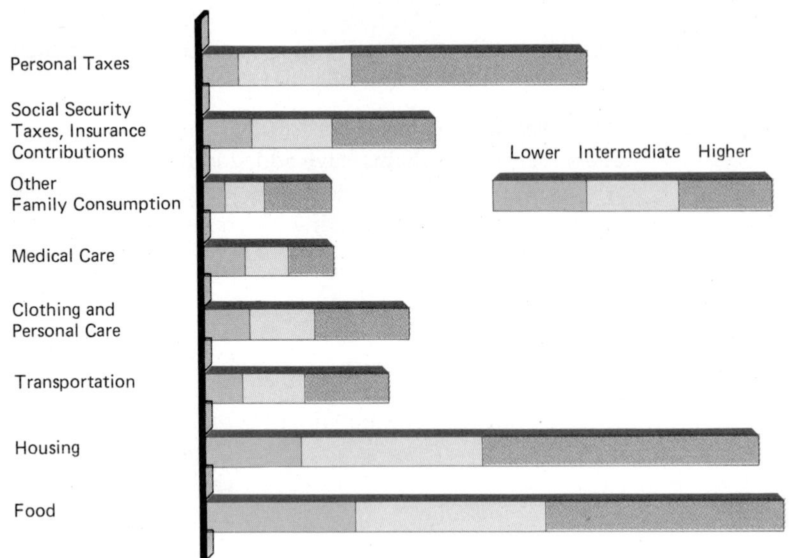

FIGURE 11-9

Budgets for three living standards (family of four), 1978. (Source: Bureau of Labor Statistics and National Consumer Finance Association.)

The lower the family income, the larger the percentage of it that is spent on necessities. The higher the family income, the larger the percentage that can be spent on luxuries, leisure activities, vacations, education, and so forth. The way consumers spend their income is shown in Figure 11-9

The Industrial Goods Market

There is no single market for industrial goods, but several instead. Some dealers sell to a very restricted market, while others handle a wide variety of products. The chief types of industrial goods are

1. Raw materials
2. Industrial equipment and machinery
3. Industrial supplies
4. Tools and other equipment
5. Processed materials
6. Parts and subassemblies

Industrial goods are sold to farmers, miners, lumberers, fisheries, construction contractors, factories, governments, institutions, wholesalers, and retailers. Some marketers will specialize, calling on only one type of market. Others will cover several different types.

The distribution channels through which industrial goods travel are markedly different from those followed by consumer goods. No retailers are needed, and fewer middlemen are used. Consequently, the distribution of industrial goods is usually a simpler process. The most commonly used channels are these:

1. Direct from factory to industrial user, sometimes by way of a factory sales branch
2. From factory to agents (or brokers) to industrial user
3. From factory to industrial distributor (wholesaler) to industrial user[2]

Many types of goods are sold directly to the ultimate users, by the manu-

[2]Marketing channels for both industrial goods and consumer goods are illustrated in the following chapter.

facturers. Approximately 12 to 15 percent of industrial goods are sold through the sales branches of manufacturers. One reason for this short distribution channel is the technical nature of products, such as computers and machine tools. These require expert installation and maintenance service. The best way for the purchaser to ensure getting this service is through face-to-face dealings with the manufacturer. Also, when most of a manufacturer's customers are concentrated in a small geographic area, there is simply no reason to work through a middleman. Finally, many orders for industrial goods are so large that the unit cost of direct negotiations between manufacturer and buyers is negligible.

MARKET RESEARCH

What to produce is always a question facing manufacturing concerns. We have already learned that the consumer votes in the marketplace. If articles are not purchased, they are no longer made. How does a company decide what to produce? This decision is made through market research.

Market research begins with questions the market manager wants to know. It includes all the data desired and determines how these data should be used. Market research follows basically the same steps as other types of research. The sequence of steps is shown in Figure 11-10.

Steps in Market Research

The seven steps illustrated in Figure 11-10 are explained here.

1. *Situation analysis.* This first step consists of surveying all available information related to the company objective. The purpose is to reach an understanding of the problems involved.
2. *Preliminary study.* The preliminary study is the second step of the research process. It includes a wide interview coverage of the field. The market analyst would interview consumers, wholesalers, and retailers.
3. *Selection of research design.* Here the formal plan of attack is described. The methods and procedures to be used are indicated. Often they are tried out and modified.

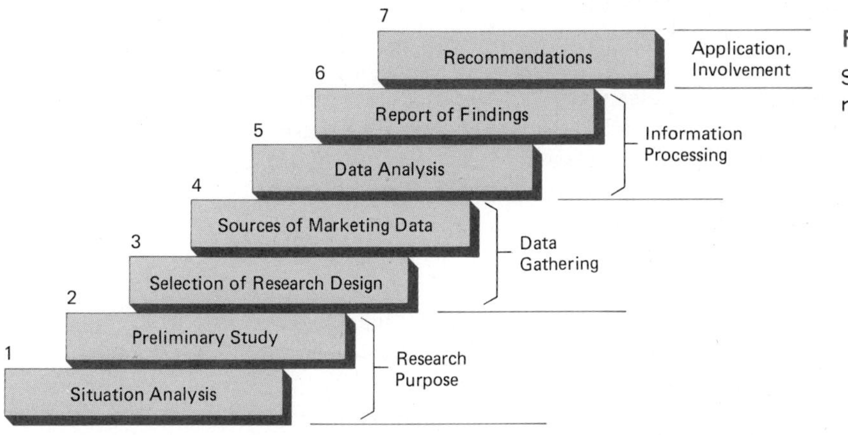

FIGURE 11-10
Steps in the marketing research process.

4. *Sources of marketing data.* Here the analyst details the data sources to be consulted. A set of guidelines is developed. Quite often both primary and secondary sources of data are used.

5. *Data analysis.* The data collected are tabulated, examined, and interpreted.

6. *Report of findings.* This is the written report to be submitted to company management.

7. *Recommendations.* This last step includes the specific recommendations of the researcher. They must be supported by the data collected.

Expenditures for Market Research

Company expenditures for market research vary considerably. One recent study of 250 companies showed that nine-tenths of them spend less than 1 percent of their annual sales on market research. This is quite a contrast with expenditures for product research and development, which often amount to 10 percent and more.

Major factors exert an influence on expenditures for market research: company size, nature of the business, and desire for market leadership. In general, the larger the firm and the more complex its operations, the greater its market research budget. Also, where a company strives for market leadership in its field, the greater its expenses for market research.

MARKETING IN THE FUTURE

Successful marketers have long-range plans for their marketing programs. Several factors will influence marketing in the days ahead. These factors include ecology and energy, world trade, the service sector, and computers.

Ecology and Energy

Until recently marketers catered to the convenience of customers by providing throwaway packaging. However, recycling has now become popular. Recycling means much more than collecting glass bottles and aluminum cans. It includes all types of reusable materials: iron and steel scrap, nonferrous metals, paper, and so forth. The Fort Howard Paper Company makes most of its products from recycled paper. We may be approaching the time when scrap materials will become our major resources—the unmined supply of our backup resource. To conserve our natural resources, goods must be made more durable and easier to repair.

In the United States we have become accustomed to an abundance of materials and energy. Now both must be conserved. The use of energy has in the past increased more rapidly than population, productivity, and gross national product. During the 1970s petroleum became increasingly scarce and expensive. Until solar energy becomes practicable, we will have to trade off between energy development and the environment.

World Trade

No country is self-sufficient. All countries depend upon others for important basic resources. But tariffs and other legal barriers hinder trade among nations. Free trade among nations is given lip service everywhere. But in practice many countries have legal restrictions against "foreign business firms." The European

Economic Community, called the Common Market, has shown how countries can benefit from working together in marketing their products. After five years of painstaking negotiations, the major trading nations signed a world trade pact in April 1979. This agreement reduces tariffs by about one-third over a period of eight to ten years. This will undoubtedly help to increase and improve international trade. International trade is discussed more fully in Chapter 21.

The Service Sector

We saw earlier in this chapter that the consumer dollar is spent about equally for goods and services. The service sector is growing much more rapidly than the manufacture of goods: Health care and communications are two of the leading growth areas. The general purpose of marketing is to bring people and products (or services) together. Personal selling may decline in importance in the communications area as advertising increases in its role in the promotion of communications. Cable TV and two-way cable TV offers great promise, as people can order goods without leaving home. Doctors may make analysis and order prescriptions from their offices while the patients are still at home. It is more economical to move information than people.

Use of Computers

The use of computers in transferring information is discussed in some detail in Chapter 18. Although the emphasis there is not on marketing, computers are becoming increasingly important in marketing. Gathering data, analyzing these data and interpreting and applying them constitute the heart of marketing research. And this is what computers do best. Product design is an important part of an integrated marketing procedure, and computers play a major role in product design. The modern-day marketing concept means that computers will be an integral part of future marketing practices.

SUMMARY OF KEY CONCEPTS

Marketing is a useful and necessary function for virtually all businesses, including manufacturers, wholesalers, retailers, and service firms. It includes those business activities designed to price, promote, and distribute want-satisfying products and services to customers.

Marketing is a twentieth-century development. Effective marketing is necessary to motivate individuals and organizations to become buyers.

Since about 1950 the *marketing concept* has been growing. This new philosophy of doing business revolves around a customer orientation, profit seeking, and integration of all marketing activities.

There are six different marketing functions. These functions are all interrelated and must be coordinated with the production function.

To arrive at markets of manageable scope, a company must divide a total market into homogeneous submarkets. This is called market segmentation. A company selects one or more segments as its target markets and develops a custom-tailored marketing mix for each target market.

Management's role in marketing is to plan and implement one or more offerings, distribution channels, prices, and promotional methods to satisfy selected customers in a profitable manner. Each of these combinations, termed *marketing mixes,* must be compatible with the environment of marketing.

The money spent in marketing goods and services represents the value added to these offerings.

The *marketing environment* includes all factors surrounding and affecting business operations. The five environmental categories are economic conditions, sociocultural factors, technological factors, government legislation, and consumerism.

The largest American markets consist of consumers and industrial customers. Consumer goods constitute almost two-thirds of the GNP.

BUSINESS TERMS

You should be able to match these business terms with the statements that follow:

a. Convenience goods
b. Differential advantage
c. Market
d. Market analysis
e. Market environment
f. Market segmentation
g. Marketing
h. Marketing concept
i. Marketing mix
j. Shopping goods
k. Valuation
l. Value added

1. A buyer and seller, a product or service, an exchange, and an agreed-upon price
2. The process by which participants learn about the supply of, and demand for, a given product
3. Business activities that design, price, promote, and distribute want-satisfying products and services to customers
4. The cost-benefit analysis of the marketing exchange
5. Increasing the value of goods or services because of market activities
6. A philosophy of doing business, emphasizing customer orientation, profit seeking, and integration of all marketing activities
7. A combination of offerings, distribution channels, prices, and promotion used to satisfy selected customers
8. All factors surrounding and potentially affecting business operations
9. Favorable features of an offering that will attract buyers
10. Low-priced goods that are readily available
11. Goods that are bought only after comparing price, quality, and style
12. Dividing a total market into homogeneous submarkets

REVIEW QUESTIONS

1. Why does marketing start before a good is produced?
2. What is the meaning of the term *marketing mix?*
3. What are the six universal marketing functions?
4. What major components make up the marketing mix?
5. How does a marketing organization pattern for large firms differ from that for small firms?
6. What are some important marketing activities?

DISCUSSION QUESTIONS

1. Why is *value added* a better term than *cost of marketing* for the cost of marketing activities?
2. Why is it not true that "the customer is king" according to the marketing concept?
3. As you see it, do changes in market environmental factors constitute threats, opportunities, or challenges to marketers? Explain.
4. Consumers account for much more of the GNP than industrial users. Yet the total sales of industrial goods exceed those for consumer goods. How do you explain this?
5. What is involved in market segmentation? Why would sellers want to segment the market for their products or services?

BUSINESS CASE

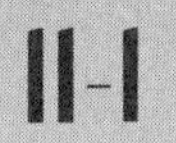

An Opportunity to Enlarge Operations

Harvey Bills operates a used-car business in a city of two hundred thousand people in one of the northeastern states. Although Harvey handles all makes and models, he has more or less specialized in middle-size cars. He has always paid cash for what he bought and has always sold for cash. He has operated as a sole proprietorship. His line of credit is limited but adequate for his operation. He normally has an inventory on hand of about fifty cars at any given time.

Harvey has recently been approached about taking over a new-car agency in the city. This agency represents one of the Big-Three U.S. car companies. It seems to him to be a real opportunity—one that might not come his way again. Of course, he would need more personnel and more capital.

1. What aspects of operating this new-car agency would be similar to what Harvey has been doing?
2. What aspects would be different?

BUSINESS CASE

Will Bookstore Customers Buy Candy?

Georgia Mills operates a bookstore and all-occasion card shop. She has had eight years of profitable experience, and business has grown considerably. She has been visited by a sales representative of a candy manufacturer. He wants her to stock boxes of fine candies. He estimates that to get started, Georgia would need thirty of the one-pound boxes and fifteen of the two-pound boxes. New merchandise can be delivered within two weeks of being ordered. Forty percent of the money taken in would represent the store's profit margin.

The Mills Bookstore is located next door to a successful cafeteria. There are no candy shops nearby, or any drugstores that handle boxed candy.

1. Do you feel that a line of boxed candy is a suitable addition to a bookstore operation?
2. How could Georgia try out the idea but make sure she did not lose money while doing so?

PRODUCT DEVELOPMENT AND MARKETING CHANNELS

12

STUDY OBJECTIVES

WHEN YOU HAVE FINISHED READING THIS CHAPTER, YOU SHOULD BE ABLE TO

ONE Identify those attributes that combine to make a "product," and explain when an item is considered to be a "new product"

TWO Indicate the stages a product goes through from the time it is introduced until it is withdrawn from the market

THREE Describe the most common distribution channels used when marketing consumer goods

FOUR Discuss the main functions performed by wholesalers and other types of middlemen

FIVE Outline the ways retailers help both the wholesalers and the consumers

SIX Name some of the trends in current marketing practices

IN THE NEWS IN THE NEWS IN THE NEWS IN THE NEWS IN THE NEWS IN THE NEWS IN THE NEWS IN THE NEWS IN THE NEWS

Between-Meals Snacks Are Becoming Big Business

The real action in the packaged food industry is currently in salted snacks. Potato chips, corn chips, nuts, pretzels, and other snacks are selling very well. As a result, food companies are flooding the market with new products and are challenging the industry leader, Pepsico Inc.'s Frito-Lay.

Frito-Lay's Fritos and Doritos have long dominated the market, but Planter's and Nabisco have introduced nationwide snack products that have provided stiff competition in test markets. The key to competing with such giants as Frito-Lay is a national distribution system including strategically located production facilities and distribution centers. In addition, either an in-house or a broker-style trucking and merchandising network must be available.

Nabisco is now repackaging an existing line of salted snacks—Mr. Salty pretzels, Flings, and Corkers—in bags. The marketing strategy is to get these items off the cookie and cracker shelves and into the fast-moving salted-foods section. Standard Brands, Planter's Division, is pushing canister packs, which have longer shelf life and more durability than bags. Twice as much product will fit into the same space when using canisters rather than bags. Furthermore, the loss from bags due to breakage and tearing is from 3 to 5 percent. All of this "repositioning" in the marketing strategies of the snack-food companies suggests an increasingly competitive environment and a strong need for product planning and careful evaluation of the marketing channels being used.

IN THE NEWS

The key to successful marketing is superior product performance.

EDWARD G. HARNESS
Chairman,
Procter and Gamble Company

In today's economy goods are produced for sale to others. They are distributed from maker to user by means of marketing channels. But marketing decisions involve much more than just selecting a type of distribution channel. Marketing decisions include such items as the following:

1. The number of middlemen to use
2. How to maintain communication channels between the different levels of middlemen
3. The selection of specific middlemen
4. The geographical deployment of inventory stock
5. The location of distribution centers

This chapter discusses the role that marketing plays in product development. We will learn about products, product lines, the product mix, brands, and product management.

THE PRODUCT

New products are always appearing on the market—consumers' attention is drawn to them daily through advertising. Consumers are constantly being urged to buy new products, and as the family income rises, the variety of goods purchased increases.

But we usually buy more than just a product. In a sense, consumers buy the personal satisfaction that comes from the use of that product. And they often

EDGAR H. GRIFFITHS

Edgar H. Griffiths was elected president and chief executive officer of the RCA Corporation on September 16, 1976. He had been a member of the board of directors since 1972. As president and chief executive officer, he was responsible for all of RCA's divisions and subsidiaries. He became chairman of the company in 1979.

Under Griffiths's leadership, RCA emphasized the goal of steady, consistent earnings growth in an effort to correct the cyclical swings that had marked the company's history. Toward that goal, Griffiths pruned away unprofitable businesses and undertook measures to control costs, increase efficiency, and stimulate sales. At the same time, in keeping with the RCA tradition of technological innovation, Griffiths increased annual outlays for research and engineering. Early in 1979 he announced a decision to proceed with manufacture of the "SelectaVision" VideoDisc System—the first major new consumer product developed by RCA since the introduction of color television.

Griffiths joined RCA at its Camden facility in 1948. A year later he transferred to the RCA Service Company. In 1966 he was named division vice-president, Commercial Services, for the RCA Service Company.

In 1968 Griffiths was appointed president of the RCA Service Company. He held that position until 1971 when he was elected an executive vice-president, Services. Subsequently, he was made responsible for all of RCA's electronics and diversified businesses, which constituted two of the three major business groups of the company.

Griffiths is a member of the Business Roundtable, the Conference Board, and the Emergency Committee for American Trade.

He was born in Philadelphia in 1921 and has a B.S. degree in business administration from St. Joseph's College. He was awarded an honorary LL.D. degree by St. Joseph's in 1977.

buy because of the reputation of that product or the company that makes it. A **PRODUCT** is a combination of attributes that give it customer appeal: style, design, utility, packaging, color, size and prestige.
in qualities, a Lincoln costs considerably more than a Pinto. Mennen's shave cream, Rise, became three products when the company created Rise with lanolin and Rise with menthol, in addition to the regular Rise. Any new combination of attributes can create a new product.

Want satisfaction can be obtained through tangible or intangible qualities. When you want to buy a car, your choice of make and model is determined by a number of tangible physical qualities. These include seating room, number of doors, and the trunk size, as well as the car's color, styling, and design. Your final choice is also influenced by certain social, psychological, or emotional attributes. But there are also the quiet ride, ease of handling, comfort, and how you feel the car will affect your social standing. These intangible factors may be either real or imaginary.

According to Thomas A. Murphy, chairman of the board of General Motors:

> One chief problem facing business today is gaining customer acceptance of products tailored to meet government regulations. Customer satisfaction, as always, remains our primary concern. We will have to satisfy the traditional demands of individual customers in the marketplace, and also meet the broader demands of society, as such demands are expressed by government.

What Is a "New" Product?

A great deal of advertising claims "newness" or improvement for the product being offered. **In a strict sense, a new product is one that serves an entirely new function or represents a major improvement in an existing function.** Felt-tip pens, pocket calculators, videotapes, all-cotton permapress shirts, and instant cameras are examples of "new" products. The real test of newness is what the product does for the ultimate user.

We have become accustomed to seeing new products. Some companies, such as 3M and Du Pont, have a strong reputation for innovation, and research, and new-product development. But whether a product is new depends on its reception in the marketplace. Do buyers perceive an item to be significantly different from its competitive products? This difference might be in design, appearance, or performance.

Services

Providing a service is often the only "product" a business offers. Repair and maintenance people, broadcasters, sports figures, beauticians, consultants, all deal in services. They play a major role in consumer want satisfaction.

We noted in Chapter 11 that about one-half of the consumer dollar is spent for services. This is the fastest-growing segment of business in the United States today.

Generic versus Branded Products

The **BRAND** may be a word, a phrase, or a symbol that gives identity to a particular product or a class of products. Producers do not want you to buy a "soap" or "detergent" to wash dishes. They advertise a brand name, such as Cascade, All, Electrasol, or Calgonite. Companies spend large sums to promote their brand names. Procter & Gamble is well known for the advertising of its various brands. Its brands compete with one another. Brands become symbols of quality, and this attracts buyers and leads to repeated purchases.

Sometimes constant advertising causes a brand name to become a generic term, synonymous with an entire product or service class. For example, the word **Mimeograph** is often used to refer to any type of stencil duplicator. **Scotch tape** is used for any type of transparent tape, and **Xerox** means photocopier. These were all originally brand names. Some manufacturers, such as the Xerox and Coca-Cola companies, spend large sums attempting to protect their brand names. This is done in order to prevent the brand from becoming a generic term. Words that companies once owned but lost as generic terms include **thermos, cellophane, escalator,** and **shredded wheat.**

Coca-Cola has gone quite far to keep "coke" from meaning any cola-flavored soft drink. The company has paid "checkers" to go to restaurants and order a "coke." If the person is served Pepsi or some other soft drink as a coke, action is threatened against the proprietor.

FORMICA'S FIGHT TO KEEP ITS NAME

The Federal Trade Commission wanted to cancel the Formica Corporation's trademark. The FTC argued that, like Aspirin, Formica now describes the product itself—a plastic laminate used on cabinets, counters, and furniture.

This had been considered by many as a major test case that might later affect other names such as Scotch tape, Xerox, and Coke. Had the Commission been successful, the Formica Corporation stood to lose what might be its most valuable marketing tool. However, after two years of hearings before the Trademark Trial and Appeal Board, Congress intervened. In May of 1980 Congress stripped the Commission of various powers, including the authority it used in the Formica case.

National versus private brands. In today's market the brand name is usually the principal method by which the consumer identifies the product. When a housewife shops for a breakfast cereal, she may think of Total or Wheaties. This is the only way the average consumer has of coping with the many brands on the shelves. Most network television commercials feature national brands—the products and services of large companies. For example, any regular viewer of sports events can name the various makes of cars produced by the Ford Motor Company.

But there are also many private brands, such as Ann Page, Scot Lad, Hyde-Park, Riverside, and Kenmore. They are often made by the same companies that make the nationally branded goods. Most private brands are owned by middlemen rather than manufacturers. The market strategy behind private-brand merchandising is to allow a retailer to price its goods slightly lower than nationally advertised goods of equal quality.

Product Line and Product Mix

Specialization is a characteristic of both production and distribution. In marketing, a wholesaler might handle only groceries and other closely related lines. Another wholesaler would deal in pharmaceuticals, while still another would sell hardware or dry goods. Most retailers likewise stay with related product or service lines. In the service area, a business may sell insurance or banking services, operate a small-loan operation, run a dry-cleaning plant, or provide some other specialized type of service.

A firm's product mix consists of one or more product (or service) lines. A basic question is, How many competing brands or lines should be handled?

Another is, What is the best product mix for those lines? Both wholesalers and retailers must decide to what degree they will carry related and unrelated product lines.

PRODUCT LIFE CYCLE

The product management process is not complete when a product or service first hits the market. A product or service moves through five stages during its life:

1. Introduction
2. Market growth
3. Market maturity
4. Saturation
5. Market decline

These stages are illustrated in Figure 12-1 and will now be discussed briefly.

Product-Introduction Stage

The product-introduction stage is the period during which a company first presents a new product or service class to the market. Since start-up costs are large and sales are initially small, a product usually incurs a loss during the introduction stage. Because the product is new and competition is scarce, the product sells for a relatively high price. Customers must be made to want the product. They must be told what the product is, what it will do, and how to use it. Wholesalers must be found to distribute it. Promotion costs are high in order to convince the public to buy it and try it. Often a new product is test-marketed in a restricted area to assess its acceptance by the public.

For example, Fotomat spent several years trying to squeeze a second business into its tiny yellow-roofed huts. It tried pantyhose, repairing shoes, cutting keys, and instant printing. None of these worked well, but Fotomat has a new product—videotape.

Sales of consumer television recorders are starting off slowly as the public begins to accept the new technology. But Fotomat is jumping into the videotape business in the hope of dominating the market. It offers a service for transferring home movies and slides to videotape, and it sells discount-priced blank tape. Furthermore, it is test-marketing prerecorded tapes of movies, as well as golf and tennis lessons.

Market-Growth Stage

During the market-growth stage, sales volume tends to increase rapidly. Rather quickly the product begins to earn a profit for the company. It is usually during this growth period that profits are greatest. As sales volume increases, the unit cost decreases and profit margins reach their peak. But competition develops as the product catches on. This forces down the price and the margin of profit. The sponsoring company may even compete with itself by introducing another brand in this product class.

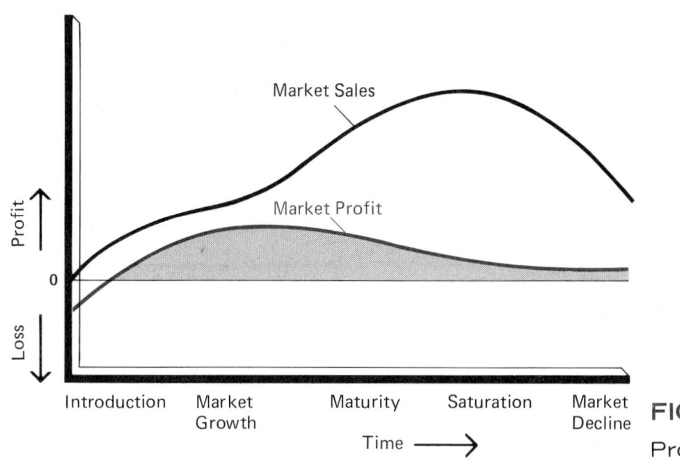

FIGURE 12-1
Product life cycle.

For example, nylon, the first wholly synthetic fiber, was perfected in the 1940s. Within a decade nylon had completely displaced silk in women's hosiery. As nylon reached its peak, new fibers—polyester and acrylics—were introduced. Today a single polyester fiber plant located on three hundred acres of land can produce as much polyester fiber as the amount of cotton grown on six hundred thousand acres.

Market-Maturity Stage

As the product becomes well known, sales continue to increase but at a reduced rate of growth. As competition stiffens, the company must decide whether to reduce prices further or increase promotional efforts. If both steps are taken, the profit margin is reduced to the lowest acceptable level for the producer. Some competitors may leave the market while seeking more viable goods to produce or sell.

Schick, the "other" manufacturer of razor blades, is trying to secure a larger share of that market from Gillette. Schick has about 25 percent of the market, and Gillette has about 58 percent.

Schick has $14 million to spend on advertising to make inroads into Gillette's Atra and Trac II products. It has designed a blade that fits both of the Gillette razors and its own pivot-head razor as well. Since 1972 Gillette has sold over 40 million Trac II razors, and Schick would like the public to refill them with Schick blades.

Saturation Stage

In the saturation stage the market peaks and levels off, and it may start to decline. Few if any new customers buy the good, and repeat orders become smaller. A reduction in total sales is inevitable unless the good is improved or new uses for it are discovered or developed. The profit margin declines still further.

The Market-Decline Stage

During the final stage of the product life cycle, sales decline rather rapidly. New products replace the sales of older articles. For example, color TV sets replaced black-and-white sets. When a company deserts a certain product, competitors absorb that market. Thus for the few producers that remain, there is sufficient market for that product to be produced at a profit. Eventually the product is abandoned because of the small demand for it. For example, rayon was forced off the market by new fibers—nylon, acrylics, and polyesters.

Market Strategy

A **product line** is a "class" of product or service (such as microwave ovens, cars, or clothing). Hence, it consists of various brands. Marketing strategy over the product's life cycle is concerned with

1. The timing of a sales-promotion effort
2. Research aimed at product improvement or new uses
3. The study of new competing products
4. Decisions about possible abandonment

Early in the development stage, advertising is planned for a new product. At first the advertising promotes the whole product class. Later it focuses on a particular brand. Decisions on price must be made from time to time over the product life cycle.

New products are test-marketed in selected areas. Free samples may be distributed. Later coupons may be distributed, good for a discount on the product when purchased. When the product is accepted by the public in the test-market area, the market area is expanded. Many nationally advertised brands were at one time marketed in selected regions only.

PRODUCT MANAGEMENT

Today the need for a product is carefully explored before it is produced on a large scale. Often people are assigned as product managers and given responsibility for coordinating product development and marketing.

Product Planning for Marketing

What happens when management plans to produce an item to meet a market demand? The scope of such planning includes answers to the following decision questions:

1. What attributes should the product have that customers want?
2. In what ways will it differ from competing products?
3. What new uses can this product offer?
4. Can any current company product be modified to meet these requirements?
5. How should it be priced in relation to other similar articles?
6. In what quantity should we make it?
7. What would be effective and efficient distribution arrangements for this offering?
8. When should we launch our advertising campaign?
9. What types of advertising media should we use?

When developing a product to meet a market demand, attention must be given to potential competition and to possible changes in customers' wants.

Stages in Planning

There are seven stages in product planning (see Figure 12-2). Although they normally follow one another, some steps can be performed simultaneously:

1. The first step is *idea generation and screening.* Suggestions for possible new products are explored. Any new suggestion must be compared with company objectives.

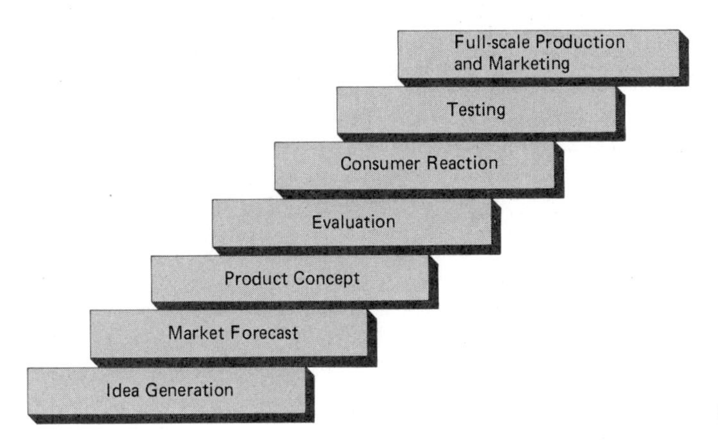

FIGURE 12-2

Stages in product planning.

2. The next step is the *market forecast.* This estimates the size and type of product to introduce. It assesses the overall market potential for the product as such, not for the specific type that might be produced by a particular company.

3. The *product concept* is concerned with the specific qualities of the proposed product. This must be kept in constant review during all remaining stages.

4. This is followed by an *evaluation* or feasibility study, which is done by the engineering staff. It answers the question of whether the product will perform the functions planned for it.

5. *Consumer reaction* is needed at this point, to prevent the waste that would result from proceeding too far in the wrong direction. This is a preliminary sounding of consumer acceptance, often involving in-home consumer use tests.

6. The planned product is then *tested* in the laboratory and in a limited geographic market.

7. The product, if the test results are favorable, then goes into full-scale production and distribution in the *commercial market.* This is the final execution of the total plan.

Withdrawing a Product

Sometimes a company must withdraw a product either because it does not sell or because it is unsafe for users. One outstanding example of the former is Corfam, a synthetic leather product developed by Du Pont. The product was not acceptable to the public and was unprofitable to the company. So it was eventually abandoned after many years and an expenditure of millions of dollars.

Planned product obsolescence.

When management people plan a new product, they may also be planning to drop some of their current products. **Smart management does not wait for one of its products to die. Instead, dropping a product is integrated with the introduction, growth, and maturing of new ones.**

When a product moves into the declining stage of its life cycle, it becomes expensive to maintain. It must remain available to customers, but it is produced in smaller quantities at a higher unit cost. Because of slow sales, it remains in inventory for a longer period of time—and this is costly. Furthermore, it may require more time and attention of the sales force than active products. It may also taint the company image because it does not compare favorably with newer products.

Sometimes the product does not become obsolete, but its design, size, or physical appearance does. In this country consumers are accustomed to changes in styles and fashions. Company management usually leads the way by introducing new styles. The constant automobile body-style changes of the 1950s and 1960s are a good example. Therefore management must strive for constant product innovation to satisfy customers and to make a profit.

THE NATURE OF DISTRIBUTION CHANNELS

For any particular product or service, a CHANNEL OF DISTRIBUTION must be developed. This channel is the *route taken by the title of the product* as it moves from its original producer to its ultimate user. This product flow involves a number of institutions to whom or by whom the title to the good is transferred.

CURRENT ISSUE

Is Planned Obsolescence Detrimental to Consumers?

Planned product obsolescence is a marketing strategy used by companies whose products have reached saturation. By making frequent changes in the design or contents of the model or product, sales are stimulated for producers and middlemen.

With which of the following statements do you agree and with which do you disagree?

1. Planned obsolescence wastes resources and is therefore contrary to the public's best interest.
2. New model changes increase the cost of machine tooling and production shutdown time.
3. Product obsolescence creates problems of liquidating older obsolete models.
4. Planned obsolescence creates employment.
5. Planned obsolescence is necessary to support a high-level economy.
6. Companies whose products have reached the maturity stage would be forced to close if this strategy were not used.
7. Consumers want frequent new models as evidence that they are up-to-date.

Should planned obsolescence be restricted only to those goods requiring resources that are not in short supply?

A marketing channel includes a number of marketing institutions and complementary agencies. Together they transfer title and deliver goods from the point of production through to the final sale. This includes the idea of originating a transaction as well as physical exchange.

Institutions in Marketing Channels

We have already learned about the roles of producers and consumers. All others who play roles in the marketing channel are classified as **middlemen.** These include wholesalers, agents, brokers, commission merchants, jobbers, and retailers.

The Committee on Definitions of the American Marketing Association defines MIDDLEMAN as follows:

> A business concern that specializes in performing operations or rendering services directly involved in the purchase and/or sale of goods in the process of their flow from producer to consumer.

Some middlemen handle the goods physically while others do not. Some of them take title to the goods. The different types of wholesalers and the role of the retailer are discussed more fully later in this chapter.

ESTABLISHING DISTRIBUTION CHANNELS

After the "market" is chosen, the next step in establishing a distribution channel is channel design. Company objectives and consideration of customer needs and desires are basic here. Is it desirable to have company-owned stores? To employ salespersons who represent the company exclusively? To use existing middlemen such as agents, brokers, or wholesalers?

When existing middlemen are used, the movement of goods through them must conform to their practices.

Product attributes also influence channel design. Perishable produce must use channels that entail few middlemen, to avoid unnecessary handling and the chance of delays. If the products are large or heavy, the channel must minimize product handling as the product moves from one transporter to another.

Intensity of Distribution

Is the distribution to be intensive, selective, or exclusive? If intensive, **many wholesale and retail middlemen will be needed in order to saturate a market** with the product. Under **INTENSIVE DISTRIBUTION** the chief responsibility for advertising falls on the producer. Retailers are not interested in spending much money to advertise goods that others also sell. If the distribution is **SELECTIVE, a few wholesalers and a limited number of retailers will be used.** The geographical area to be covered may be restricted. Strategy then is concerned with specialized methods of distribution rather than maximum coverage.

In **EXCLUSIVE DISTRIBUTION only one retailer in any given community would handle the product.** The dealer selected can afford to push the product aggressively because he or she will reap the benefits of these efforts. In exclusive

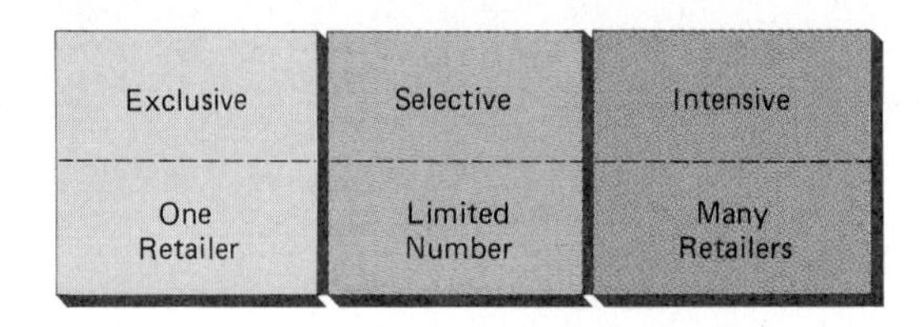

FIGURE 12-3
Intensity of distribution.

distribution the producer might exercise some control over pricing and promotion. In intensive distribution the producer would be able to exercise little or no control.

Selecting Specific Firms

After the channel is designed and the intensity of distribution determined, individual middlemen must be chosen. Middlemen specialize just as producers do. Some concentrate on a few customers and earn good commissions by making large sales. Some give a wide variety of services, while others offer only a few. Some cover wide geographical areas, while others operate reasonably close to home base.

The specific services that the producer wants to have performed, and the intensity of coverage desired, must be matched with those offered by the middlemen available in the territory to be served. Middlemen are interested in representing good companies that make good products, just as manufacturers are anxious to have reputable middlemen representing them.

Six principal factors can affect the choice of middlemen:

1. Reputation of the company's management team
2. Access to the desired market
3. Location of the business
4. Product policies of the middleman
5. Breadth of services to be given
6. Promotion policies of the firm

DISTRIBUTION CHANNELS FOR CONSUMER GOODS

There are intrinsic differences among products and even among various producers of the same product. For this reason there are countless variations in how consumer goods are distributed in this country.[1] (Table 12-1 classifies consumer goods and services.) We will now consider the most direct distribution channel—from producer to consumer. Then we will look at more detailed channels as well.

From Producer Directly to Consumer

The most direct channel for distributing goods is from the producer to the consumer. We have all observed, even patronized, a farmer's roadside stand. The farmer may be selling fresh fruits and/or vegetables. There is no middleman. A few manufactured goods are marketed in this manner. Three basic patterns are used. Makers of vacuum cleaners, cooking utensils, silverware, and cosmetics sell through **house-to-house solicitation.** Examples are Fuller Brush, Tupperware, and Avon. Firms like the New Process Company (clothing), Columbia House

[1]A consumer good is one used by an individual customer rather than a business.

FIGURE 12-4
Here the farmer sells directly to the consumer.

(records), and Ambassador (leather goods) sell by **direct mail.** Sherwin-Williams (paints) and Melville Shoe Company market their goods through **company-owned retail stores.**

From Producer to Processor to Consumer

Most dairies do not own their own herds of dairy cows. Instead they purchase milk from farmers, process it, and distribute it. While the milk is in their possession they process it—pasteurize and homogenize—and bottle it ready for delivery to customers. They may sell only to retail stores, deliver to customers' homes, or both.

For many dairies the milk business is going badly, not because of the channels being used, but because demand for milk is down. To replace lost sales, dairies like Dean Foods, Inc., are developing a variety of other food products, such as low-calorie party dips and chocolate drinks. The existing marketing channels are being used to sell these new products. Because of short shelf life and transportation costs, regional dairies can compete well with such large dairy-food concerns as Borden and Beatrice.

From Manufacturer to Retailer to Consumer

Many kinds of goods, such as automobiles, furniture, appliances, and shoes, are sold directly by the manufacturer to the retailer. This enables the producers to influence the training of salespeople and the way in which the retailer promotes the product.

Since speed is important in the marketing of fashion goods, for instance, buyers for retail stores often place their orders at the sales offices of the manufacturer instead of working through middlemen. And to expedite their dealings

TABLE 12-1
CLASSIFICATION OF CONSUMER GOODS AND SERVICES

Major Category	Subcategories	Examples
Consumer goods	Staple goods	Food, clothing, medical care
	Impulse goods	Gum, popcorn, candy
	Durable goods	Furniture, automobiles

with retail buyers, several manufacturers will join together to display their samples and take orders at a show or fair. An example is the semiannual furniture shows at Chicago, Dallas, and Hickory, North Carolina.

Manufacturers who distribute their goods over a wide area sometimes establish branch warehouses in which they maintain a stock of goods adequate to meet regional demands. By shipping orders directly to retail stores, they render much the same service as the ordinary wholesaler.

A growing variation of this channel is "direct marketing."

Mail solicitation through major mailers such as credit-card companies and oil companies has been used to reduce the cost of billing customers. Everything from $15 wallets to $800 motorcycles is offered in shiny brochures included with customers' bills. Companies called syndicators work with the giant mailers. They pay for selecting merchandise to be offered, preparing brochures, and processing orders. In return the mailers pocket commissions that help offset the cost of computerized credit-card systems. In this format the syndicators never really take possession of the merchandise. They act only as an intermediary between manufacturer (or retailer) and customer.

From Manufacturer to Chain Store to Consumer

The chain organization performs most of the functions that wholesalers render. The chains have buyers who specialize in particular lines of goods. Most chains buy in large quantities, have their own warehouse facilities, and sometimes have their own trucks for delivering goods to retail outlets. Safeway, Kroger, and A&P are well-known grocery chains that maintain their own warehouses.

FIGURE 12-5

Automobiles are sold by the manufacturer to the retailer.
(Source: Photo courtesy of Irene Springer.)

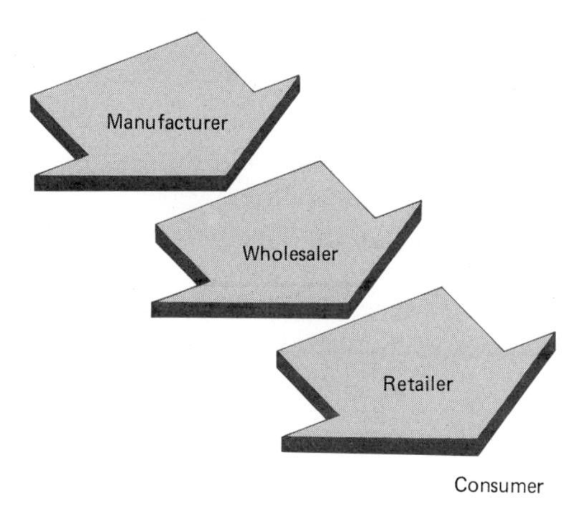

FIGURE 12-6
How do goods get from producer to consumer?

Independent retailers sometimes group together to form a **cooperative chain.** They pool their buying and distribution functions in much the same manner as the large chains. True-Value hardware stores and Associated Grocers are large, successful cooperative chains. In other instances, a **voluntary chain** is organized by a wholesaler who serves a group of retailers by supplying their most important items. The Rexall drugstores and IGA grocers are well-known voluntary chains.

The voluntary chain differs from the retailer cooperative in ownership. In the **VOLUNTARY CHAIN, separate individually owned retail stores make up a group served by a wholesaler.** The retail store owners usually do not own any part of the wholesale firm. In the retailer cooperative, each retail store owns a part of the wholesale organization that serves the group.

From Manufacturer to Wholesaler to Retailer to Consumer

Most convenience goods, such as drugs, hardware, and groceries, move along the route from the manufacturer to wholesaler, to retailer, and then to the consumer.

Wholesalers purchase goods in large quantities from numerous manufacturers. From their collection of a wide variety and types of goods, they supply the needs of retailers. The wholesaler reduces the number of accounts that the manufacturer deals with, and the manufacturer saves the expense of servicing thousands of individual businesses.

The wholesaler likewise saves the retailer money and time. An independent grocery or hardware merchant normally stocks the shelves with thousands of different items. Instead of contacting hundreds of manufacturers, the merchant does business with just a few wholesalers.

MARKETING INDUSTRIAL GOODS

There is no single market for industrial goods—there are several markets. Some dealers sell to a very restricted market, while others handle a wide variety of products. The chief types of industrial goods are

1. Raw materials
2. Industrial equipment and machinery
3. Industrial supplies
4. Tools and other equipment
5. Processed materials
6. Parts and subassemblies

Industrial goods are sold to farmers, miners, lumberers, fisheries, construction contractors, factories, governments, institutions, wholesalers, and retailers. Some marketers will specialize, calling on only one type of market. Others will cover several different types.

The distribution channels through which industrial goods travel are markedly different from those followed by consumer goods. No retailers are needed, and fewer middlemen are used. Consequently, the distribution of industrial goods is usually a simpler process. The most commonly used channels are these:

1. Direct from factory to industrial user, sometimes by way of a factory sales branch
2. From factory to agents (or brokers) to industrial user
3. From factory to industrial distributor (wholesaler) to industrial user

Many types of goods are sold directly to the ultimate users, by the manufacturers. Approximately 12 to 15 percent of industrial goods are sold through the sales branches of manufacturers. One reason for this short distribution channel is the technical nature of products, such as computers and machine tools. These require expert installation and maintenance service. The best way for the purchaser to be sure of getting this service is through face-to-face dealings with the manufacturer. Also, when most of a manufacturer's customers are concentrated in a small geographic area, there is simply no reason to work through a middleman. Finally, many orders for industrial goods are so large that the unit cost of direct negotiations between manufacturer and buyer is negligible.

CONTRASTS IN MARKETING OF INDUSTRIAL AND CONSUMER GOODS

A look at the markets and marketing techniques commonly associated with industrial and consumer goods reveals a number of obvious contrasts.

1. There is a very narrow market for many kinds of industrial goods. This permits sales directly from the producer to the industrial user. For example, the market for certain industrial chemicals is limited mainly to a small group of manufacturers.
2. In the industrial market it is more difficult to discover the party who actually makes buying decisions. It is often difficult for the salesperson of industrial goods to determine which persons in any particular firm really make buying decisions. In the purchase of an item used in manufacturing, for example, the decision may be made by the purchasing agent, the plant superintendent, the supervisor, the product engineer, or the plant manager.
3. Reciprocity of orders between buyer and seller is a common practice in the industrial market, but relatively unimportant in the consumer-goods market. For example, a steel producer may buy its chemicals from the chemical manufacturer that buys its steel. Salespersons of industrial goods may therefore attempt to influence the purchasing department of their firm to patronize their potential customers.

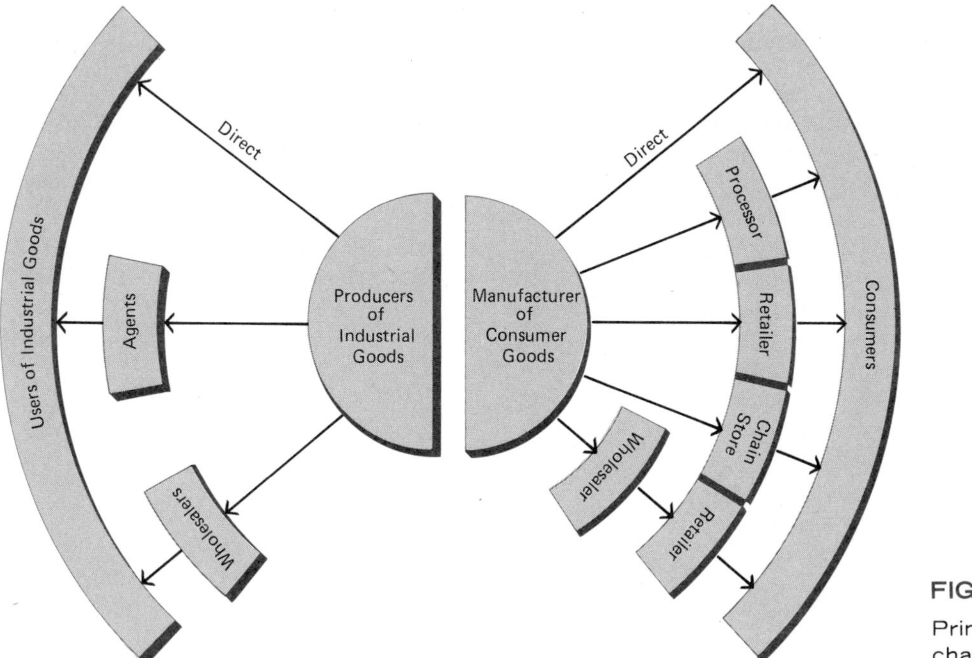

FIGURE 12-7
Primary marketing channels.

4. A single sale of industrial goods often represents a large sum of money. The sale of a single machine, for example, may amount to thousands of dollars, and a contract for materials and parts may run into millions.
5. Buyers of industrial goods are usually well informed and make their purchasing decisions on the basis of the product's proven performance.
6. The demand for certain types of industrial goods is extremely sensitive to changing business conditions. The industrial market suffers more than the consumer market during periods of declining business activity.

The primary channels of distribution used in marketing industrial and consumer goods are illustrated in Figure 12-7.

WHOLESALERS' FUNCTION IN MARKETING

WHOLESALERS are middlemen who buy merchandise for resale, primarily to other business firms rather than to consumers. Their main function is one of assembly and dispersion. They are different from agents, for they buy, take title to, and take possession of the products they handle. Full-service wholesalers provide credit, market information, and pricing suggestions to their customers. In some instances they help with store layout, accounting systems, and other facets of store operation.

The wholesaler is the most important source of supply to many retailers. The small retailer could scarcely operate without a wholesaler's services. The importance of wholesalers in our marketing system can best be understood by investigating how they serve the manufacturer and the retailer.

How the Wholesaler Serves Others

An effective wholesaler serves as a selling agency for manufacturers and a buying agency for retailers. For manufacturers, a wholesaler

1. Informs the manufacturer about such matters as desirable package styling, advertising appeals, and product features. The wholesaler gains this knowledge through close contact with retailers.
2. Provides the manufacturer with thorough coverage of nearly every retailer who might be interested in stocking its product. This is an especially valuable service for manufacturers whose products need wide distribution.
3. Enables the manufacturer to minimize selling cost per unit. The manufacturer of food products, for example, would otherwise have to maintain enough salespeople to call on thousands of retail stores and restaurants.

For retailers, a wholesaler

1. Saves much time in the buying process. Imagine that every clothing store had to buy directly from the thousands of manufacturers whose goods it stocks. If only half these persons called on the retailer once every three months, the retailer would be visited by more than four hundred salespeople daily!
2. Carries a complete line of goods from which the retailer can replenish stock easily and swiftly. So the retailer need not keep a huge supply of goods on hand or tie up large amounts of capital in inventory.
3. Serves as a valuable source of information and advice. For example, wholesalers may give suggestions on display and sales promotion of the goods they sell, as well as ideas on new items available.

TYPES OF WHOLESALERS

The main distinctions among wholesalers, aside from the kinds of products they distribute, involve

1. Whether they take title or possession of the goods
2. The number of functions they perform
3. The type of commission, fee, or regular income they receive

Merchant Wholesalers

Merchant wholesalers—sometimes simply called wholesalers or jobbers—perform more functions than do the other types of wholesalers. They take title to goods; store, deliver, and assemble them; and maintain a regular place of business. Their income comes from selling goods for an amount greater than their cost, rather than from commissions or fees. Merchant wholesalers who provide a wide variety of services such as granting credit, making deliveries, and giving out current trade information are appropriately called SERVICE WHOLESALERS.

Limited-Function Wholesalers

As their name implies, LIMITED-FUNCTION WHOLESALERS render fewer marketing activities than merchant wholesalers, although they do not take title to the goods they handle. For example, the **truck wholesaler** combines the marketing functions of selling and delivery. The truck wholesaler does not grant

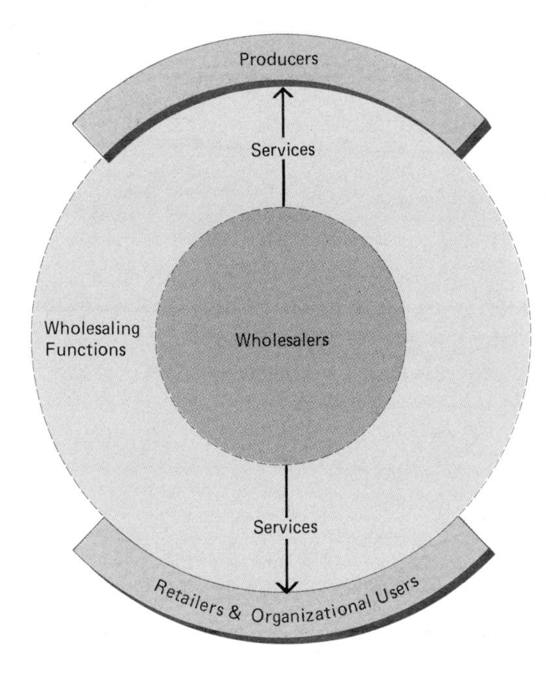

FIGURE 12-8

The position of wholesalers in the distribution channel.
(Adapted from Larry J. Rosenberg, *Marketing*, 1977. Reprinted by permission of Prentice-Hall, Inc.)

credit but collects for each sale. The **drop shipper** sells merchandise that is delivered directly from the manufacturer to the customer. The delivery is called a "drop shipment." Examples are coal, lumber, and building materials that are sold in carload lots.

Agent Middlemen

AGENT MIDDLEMEN are a third category of wholesalers. They do not take title to the goods they sell, and they provide relatively few services. Their main function is to make a sale for the manufacturer or distributor. They are usually paid a commission based on volume of sales. Brokers, selling agents, and manufacturers' agents are classed as agent middlemen.

Commission merchants, unlike these other agents, actually take possession of the goods they market. They usually arrange for the shipment of goods, store them temporarily, sell them, and deliver them to the buyer. At times they grant credit to the buyer. For all these services they charge their clients a commission—a percentage of the sales price. Sometimes they also add their expenses in handling and storing the goods. The majority of commission merchants deal in agricultural products.

Figure 12-8 shows the position of wholesalers in the distribution channel.

RETAILERS' FUNCTION IN MARKETING

Most people are quite familiar with retailing. Woolworth, K Mart, the local druggist, and the convenient grocery store are all retailers. The retailer is a middleman, serving both the consumer and the producer. *Retailers* are business firms that buy goods from wholesalers (and manufacturers) and sell them to consumers. **RETAILING** includes **all the activities related to the sale of goods and services for final consumption.** Retail stores vary greatly in size, kinds of goods and services offered, prices, and organization patterns. Some retail firms have individual owners; others are partnerships, corporations, or cooperatives. Retailing provides employment for about 12 million people.

Retailing and and the Manufacturer

The nearly 2 million retail stores in the Unites States cover the entire nation. They provide producers with a means of reaching the entire population. The manufacturer usually chooses to build the plant in a location near the source of raw materials or where labor is plentiful. Modern means of material handling and distribution enables the manufacturer to sell goods everywhere through retailers. While a single plant will sell goods through many retailers, one retailer will sell goods made in many plants.

CLASSIFICATION OF RETAIL BUSINESSES

Retailing can be carried on either in a store or outside a store. Let us look briefly at each.

In-Store Retailing

In-store retailing usually means that customers visit the place of business to make purchases. Most retail sales are made in stores. These stores can be classified according to their merchandise mix, organizational structure, pricing strategy, and services offered.

Merchandise mix. Some stores specialize, while others offer a broad range of goods. A boat retailer or a florist limits sales offerings to those goods. A department store has a greater breadth of offerings. Some stores carry only one or two national brands, while others offer five of six different brands. Some stores broaden their offerings after they are started. At first Arby's offered only a roast beef sandwich, French fries, and beverages. Later a ham sandwich, a turkey sandwich, and a roast beef platter were added. McDonald's started with hamburgers and eventually added a fish sandwich, a chicken sandwich, and a breakfast menu to its offerings.

Sometimes the merchandise mix changes as customers' tastes change. For example, ski retailers have changed their mix of goods.

Technological advances in ski and boot manufacture have made skiing much easier. Polyethelene foam and fiberglass have replaced the solid wood and metal-lined skis of yesteryear. The result is lighter and easier-to-use equipment. These changes have encouraged skiers to upgrade their gear with more expensive skis, boots, bindings, and ski clothes.

At one time the standard ski wear was jeans and parkas. Now color-coordinated pants, jackets, vests, and so forth, are hot items. As a result, ski apparel sales in retail stores have increased by 40 to 50 percent. The mix of merchandise that ski retailers carry must adapt to customers' wishes.

Organizational structure. Most small retailers start as single proprietorships. As they grow, they may become partnerships or corporations. Your neighborhood druggist or grocer may be an independent merchant or a part of a chain of stores. Some chains, such as Kroger's and Eckerd Drugs, are regional. Others,

TABLE 12-2
THE LARGEST RETAILERS IN THE UNITED STATES, 1978

Name of Company (Headquarters Location)	Sales Volume (In Thousands)	Total Assets (In Thousands)
Sears, Roebuck (Chicago)	$23,486,165	$24,427,084
Safeway Stores (Oakland)	12,550,569	2,835,767
K Mart (Troy, Michigan)	11,812,810	4,836,260
J. C. Penney (New York)	10,845,000	4,837,000
Kroger (Cincinnati)	7,828,071	1,653,029
Great Atlantic & Pacific Tea Company (Montvale, N.J.)	7,469,659	1,334,397
F. W. Woolworth (New York)	6,102,800	2,707,500
Federated Department Stores (Cincinnati)	5,404,621	2,956,431
Lucky Stores (Dublin, Calif.)	4,650,400	1,042,846

SOURCE: Forbes magazine, May 14, 1979.

such as Safeway, Sears, and Goodyear, are national. The largest retailers are chains, as shown in Table 12-2.

In some countries, cooperatives are very popular. In Scandinavia, for example, they are much more popular than they are in the United States.

Franchise operations are extensively used in such areas as automobiles, fast foods, hotels, tire sales, and paint stores.

Pricing strategy. There are essentially two types of pricing stategies: normal-margin pricing and discounting. A store that operates under normal-margin pricing does not use price as its main selling point. It offers goods at prices similar to those charged by the majority of businesses in its line of trade.

A **discount store** normally uses self-service on the part of customers. It has a broad range of merchandise but offers a limited variety of each type of good. Low price is the chief selling strategy.

A number of retailers operate both normal-margin and discount stores. Kresge's is pushing its K Mart operations. Federated Department Stores operates the Gold Circle stores. The Dayton-Hudson Corporation has the Target discount stores.

Services offered. The type of service offered is closely related to pricing strategy. Those who pay higher prices want more service. The completely self-service gasoline station is considered to be a no-service retailer. A supermarket with self-service baskets is a limited-service retailer. Most department stores, such as the May Company, Hudson's, and J. C. Penney, are full-service retailers. They have clerks to wait on customers, offer credit, and provide delivery of goods to the customer's home.

Nonstore Retailing

In addition to retail stores, a large volume of goods is sold through mail-order catalogs, vending machines, and on a door-to-door basis. Most people are familiar with the Montgomery Ward, Sears, and Spiegal catalogs. But Sunset House, United States Purchasing Exchange, Discovery House, and Miles Kimball also

TABLE 12-3
GROSS MARGIN OF RETAILERS

Type of Store	Percent of Gross Margin
Apparel	37
Automobile dealers	14
Drugstores	30
Food	21
Furniture	35
Gasoline stations	24
Hardware	24

distribute their specialty-goods catalogs throughout the country. Mail-order selling makes shopping convenient, and often at reduced prices.

Vending machines are now found in most public buildings and in many factories, warehouses, and stores. This kind of retail merchandising has grown considerably in recent years. Vending sales have more than doubled during the last decade. Vending sales involve multiple activities: buying the equipment, finding the locations, purchasing the goods, stocking the machines, and maintaining the equipment.

Route sales of newspapers and dairy products are examples of another form of nonstore retailing. The Avon lady and the Tupperware representative sell their products to individuals or to groups gathered in homes.

Cost of Retailing

Since retailers perform various marketing functions and are in business to make a profit, they must be compensated in some way. This is accomplished when a retailer buys merchandise at the wholesale price and resells it at a higher retail price. The difference is the margin to cover expenses and (presumably) a profit. Margins vary considerably across types of retail trade. Some examples are given in Table 12-3.

TRENDS IN DISTRIBUTION

During the coming decade there will no doubt be changes in marketing channels and distribution methods. Some of these trends are discussed briefly here.

Growth of Vertical-Marketing Systems

In the past, firms participating in a distribution channel have been independent of other channel members. Producers, wholesalers, and retailers often competed with one another, with overlapping and duplicating services. As all types of middlemen seek ways to maintain or increase profits, they have sought ways to eliminate duplication of effort and services. This will require planned efforts at cooperation with others. This is called a *vertical-marketing system.* It consists of a group of firms joining together in a tightly coordinated manner to provide an efficient distribution system. This system offers important opportunities for cost savings and increased efficiency in distribution. Vertical-marketing systems may be corporate, contractual, or administered.

Corporate systems. In the *corporate* system, the manufacturing and marketing facilities are owned by the same company. The Sherwin-Williams paint company has already been referred to as an example of a manufacturer-owned chain. Firestone, Goodyear, and B. F. Goodrich own and operate many of their retail stores. These are truly integrated marketing plans.

Contractual systems. In the *contractual* system, a number of retailers group together to form a voluntary chain working with a wholesale company. Or the group will organize and operate a wholesale cooperative. Malone and Hyde (a wholesale grocery company), Federated Department Stores, and IGA food stores are examples of contractual vertical-marketing systems.

Vertical-marketing systems will undoubtedly become more prevalent in the near future.

Another contractual arrangement is franchising. Here, one business firm grants a smaller firm the right to operate a specific kind of business. It also provides various kinds of operating assistance, in return for some type of financial compensation. Prominent franchise systems are Wendy's and other fast-food firms, the auto companies, and AAMCO and other automotive-repair firms.

Administered systems. In the *administered* system, one firm in the channel plays a dominant role. That firm coordinates the production and marketing effort. The producer's name, market position, or brand is strong enough to obtain the voluntary cooperation of retailers. Some of the marketing components that are coordinated are advertising, pricing, and point-of-purchase displays. General Electric, General Foods, Magnavox, and O. M. Scott and Sons Company (lawn products) are successful administered programs.

Scrambled Merchandising

SCRAMBLED MERCHANDISING is the broadening of product mixes by retail firms. Supermarkets now carry many nonfood items, and various fast-food restaurants now serve breakfast. The supermarket drugstore carries dairy products and selected grocery items.

This practice seems to be spreading and holds promise of being a dominant part of retailing in the future.

Discount Houses

Discount houses have been in existence for a long time. However, the nature of the discount operation has changed significantly. The first discount house was small:

1. It stocked only a limited number of items.
2. It specialized in some type of goods where the markup margin was high, such as furniture, jewelry, luggage, or small appliances.
3. It did a significant amount of its selling through catalog ordering.

Today the discount retail store occupies thousands of square feet, handles a wide variety of items, displays its merchandise, and operates on a small profit margin. K Mart, Woolco, and Treasure Island stores are widely known.

As prices continue to rise and "shopping time" and gasoline become more valuable, the discount store that brings "everything together in one convenient location" seems destined to prosper in the immediate future. However, the trend is for discount stores to add the more expensive products to their product lines. At the same time the traditional department stores are giving more emphasis to cheaper lines of goods.

As the discount stores and the department stores continue to adopt each other's points of strength, discounting may lose some of its visibility. Price competition may give way to forms of nonprice promotional activities: quality, service, convenience of location, and standard forms of advertising.

More and more retailers are becoming one of two types: large mass merchandisers or small specialized stores.

CAREERS IN MARKETING

Probably no field of business enterprise offers more job opportunities than does marketing. Persons who have the interest and aptitude should have little trouble in establishing a career in marketing. Some areas require special training, such as research, product engineering, art, or copywriting. The chief job areas in marketing are

Personal selling	Buyer
Advertising	Transportation
Marketing research	Product management
Wholesaling	Product testing
Retailing	

Personal selling and advertising are examined in the following chapter. The other job areas are discussed briefly here.

Marketing Research

Marketing research is an important area that has developed rather recently. Most of the business firms that are members of the American Marketing Association have formal marketing research divisions or departments. Like researchers in any other area, marketing researchers should have a knowledge of mathematics, statistics, computer applications, and consumer behavior.

Wholesaling and Retailing

There are almost 2 million retail stores in the United States, and three hundred thousand wholesale firms. Every store must have a manager. A retail manager can run his or her own firm or work for someone else. Twelve million people work in retailing, and the retailing of services is growing most rapidly. Large department stores need department managers, personnel directors, credit personnel, and general merchandise managers. Wholesale businesses need buyers, sales representatives, promotion people, and traffic managers.

Buyers

Every type of business must have buyers or purchasing agents. Many of these persons visit the firms that supply their goods. Others travel to central markets where goods are displayed. Industrial firms and government agencies usually use purchasing agents. Such persons should have a knowledge of shipping, credit, and finance.

Transportation

Shipping costs vary with different modes of transportation. These costs are always paid by the buyer or the seller. All kinds of firms need people with a knowledge of transportation. In addition to industrial firms, wholesalers, and retailers, the airlines and trucking firms offer marketing job opportunities. The industrial companies and wholesalers need people who are knowledgeable in traffic management, materials handling, and physical distribution.

Product Management

We saw earlier in this chapter that product development is an integral part of marketing. Product managers are found in companies that sell both industrial and consumer goods. Product management positions are among the most challenging, most competitive, and most interesting of all the jobs in marketing.

Product Testing

We also noted earlier in this chapter the current emphasis being given product safety and consumer protection. Both businesses and governments employ persons for product testing. Some business organizations have advisers who speak on behalf of consumers regarding marketing needs and procedures. Persons in product testing must know something about consumer market behavior and consumer protection laws.

SUMMARY OF KEY CONCEPTS

Two important components of the marketing mix are *product* and *place.*

A *product* is a good or service produced to satisfy the wants of the ultimate user. To give a product maximum value, it must be distributed to the place where it is in demand.

There are five phases in the life cycle of any marketable product: introduction, growth, maturity, saturation, and decline.

New products are planned to be put on the market. But the deletion of older products from the market is also planned.

A product is considered to be "new" if it serves a new function or makes a significant improvement in an existing function.

Distributing goods from places of abundance to places of demand requires several types of middlemen. The wholesaler and retailer are well known, but agents, brokers, and commission merchants also play major roles.

Distribution channels may be simple and short—direct from the producer to the consumer. Or they may be complex and long—involving one or several middlemen.

Consumer goods usually involve a larger number of middlemen than do industrial goods.

The wholesaler and the retailer work together as a team. The wholesaler performs many services for the retailer. In return the retailer simplifies the distribution process for the wholesaler. The retailer greatly reduces the number of customers the wholesaler must contact to sell goods.

Retailers are classified according to the mix of merchandise handled and their organizational structure, pricing strategy, and services offered.

Current trends in marketing practices include an increase in vertical marketing systems, scrambled merchandising, and a growth in discounting.

BUSINESS TERMS

You should be able to match these business terms with the statements that follow:

a. Agent middlemen
b. Brand
c. Commission merchant
d. Consumer good
e. Distribution channel
f. Exclusive distribution
g. Industrial good
h. Limited-function wholesaler
i. Middleman
j. Product
k. Retailer
l. Scrambled merchandising
m. Service wholesaler
n. Voluntary chain
o. Wholesaler

1. A combination of attributes that give an item customer appeal
2. A word, phrase, or symbol attached to a product
3. Route taken by goods as they move from producer to consumer
4. A business or individual who performs marketing functions between the producer and the consumer
5. Marketing goods through a single retailer in any given community
6. Where independent retailers pool their purchasing and distribution functions
7. A product that is sold to a business that processes it into another good or consumes it in the production process
8. A wholesaler who provides a full set of marketing services to other businesses
9. Middlemen who do not take title to the goods they sell and who give few services
10. A middleman who takes title to goods, stores them for a limited period, but does not offer a wide variety of services
11. A middleman who purchases goods from producers or wholesalers and sells to "consumers"
12. Broadening one's product lines to include types of goods other than the main category handled

REVIEW QUESTIONS

1. What are some attributes that in combination make a product?
2. When is a product considered to be a "new" product?
3. What is a *distribution channel* and why is it important?
4. How do wholesalers serve producers and retailers?
5. What is meant by *scrambled merchandising?*

DISCUSSION QUESTIONS

1. Which stage in a product's life cycle is the most important?
2. Why is product obsolescence sometimes planned for?
3. What types of products are best suited to exclusive distribution?
4. Why are distribution channels for industrial goods less complex than those for consumer goods?

5. How does the commission merchant's method of operation differ from that of other types of agents?
6. How does the role of the retailer differ from that of the wholesaler?

BUSINESS CASE 12-1

How to Market the Goods

The Neal Processing Company has specialized in processing, packaging, and distributing cereal products, cat food, and dog food. The cereals are all sold in cardboard boxes; the cat food and dog food are sold in tins with paper labels around the cans. The company's special identifying insignia has been the use of black and red stripes around the boxes and cans. The company has been marketing its products using its own salespeople who call upon wholesalers and who are paid on a commission basis.

A chain-store buyer has offered to sell for the company its entire cereal line, but he is not interested in the cat food or dog food. The cereal line accounts for the larger sales volume, but the canned products have a greater profit margin.

If the company should accept the chain store as its marketing middleman on cereals and retain its salespeople, the latter would need larger territories in order to receive the same amount of commissions as they have previously earned, since they would no longer handle cereals.

The company wants to keep the black and red stripes for its pet-food products but eliminate them on the cereal boxes should they be sold through the chain store.

1. What advantage would there be to the chain's continuing the identifying black and red stripes?
2. Why should the Neal Company not want to continue the stripes on the cereal packages?
3. What are the chief advantages and disadvantages to the Neal Company in letting the chain store market its own cereal line?
4. Since the same wholesalers have been buying both the cereal and the cat and dog food, how can the Neal Company best market its noncereal products if it makes a deal with the chain-store company?

BUSINESS CASE 12-2

A Broker's Decision to Expand

Henry Knight is an established food broker who lives in a city located in one of the northeastern states. He represents Corporation B, one of the leading processors of canned fruits and vegetables. He also represents a dog-food company, a honey processor, a charcoal producer, and a sugar refiner. He considers his company to be a specialist in canned foods.

Henry employs four salespersons who call on "the trade." This is made up of sixteen wholesale grocery houses located in the central and eastern half of the state. He and his representatives are extremely busy and do well if they can manage to contact each wholesale customer once every two weeks. His two secretaries have all they can do typing orders, handling correspondence, and filing reports.

Corporation B launched a frozen-fruit and vegetable line, which is growing rapidly. The marketing manager of Corporation B has approached Henry about taking on the frozen-food line in his territory. A nearby processor of jams and jellies recently asked Henry to represent that company in the territory he serves.

Three of the wholesalers served by the Knight Company have warehouses in the city where Henry lives. One of these wholesalers has been growing very rapidly and is expanding his operation. In fact, he now serves ten retail stores in two adjoining states and plans to add eight more stores.

A food broker not only sells merchandise for the principals he represents but also helps his wholesalers sell their products in retail stores. When a new store opens, Henry's people spend considerable time making sure that this new store stocks a complete line of products that the Knight Company represents. They also see that the merchandise is displayed properly on the shelves of the retail store.

Henry's problem consists of meeting these new demands with an already overloaded staff. If he takes on additional lines, he will need another salesperson. He feels that to do this might damage his reputation for efficient and personal service. In addition he might be forced to stop traveling the territory himself.

Henry built his business through personal contacts with his customers. So he is not sure what effect this step would have on future business. He is not sure he wants to accept a full-time administrative role.

He knows his commissions would increase significantly if he could add either or both of the new lines. Also, he knows that any increase in sales would mean hiring additional secretarial help. Adding another salesperson and a third secretary would require larger office space, and this would increase his overhead.

1. What alternatives are open to Henry Knight?
2. What factors would influence your course of action if you had his problem?

PRICING AND PROMOTION STRATEGY

13

STUDY OBJECTIVES

WHEN YOU HAVE FINISHED READING THIS CHAPTER, YOU SHOULD BE ABLE TO

ONE Describe the various kinds of plans used in pricing goods and services

TWO Define the term promotion and give examples of the different types of promotion used by businesses

THREE Show how price and promotion fit into the marketing mix

FOUR Discuss motivation and buying motives as they relate to personal selling

FIVE Explain the economic contribution that advertising makes to marketing

SIX Compare the various advertising media and indicate their relative importance

IN THE NEWS

The Strategy Worked for Miller Beer—Will It Work for Seven-Up??

When Philip Morris, Inc., picked John A. Murphy to head its newly acquired Miller Brewing Company, he faced a formidable job. Miller was in seventh place with 4 percent of the beer market. But by introducing new products such as Lite Beer, upgrading the distribution network, and undertaking heavy advertising expenditures, Murphy dramatically increased Miller's sales. Miller jumped to second place, with 19 percent of the market.

Philip Morris recently took over the Seven-Up Company and apparently plans to use the same formula to solve its problems. Seven-Up faces an uphill battle. It ranks third in soft drinks but has only 7 percent of the U.S. market compared with 34 percent for Coca-Cola and 22 percent for Pepsi. Furthermore, its market share has been eroding because the marketing program has lost its momentum.

Murphy has already redirected Seven-Up's advertising campaign and has given it a big transfusion of dollar expenditures. The "Uncola" ad campaign was dropped, along with the ad company that created it, and "America's Turning 7 Up" has been adopted as the theme for the new campaign.

However, turning Seven-Up around might be tougher than it was for Miller. Coca-Cola and Pepsi are sophisticated marketing giants that are not likely to be caught off guard by new packaging, products, or catchy commercials. With beer, the old-line manufacturing-oriented brewery managements were slow to respond to Miller's changes and got burned. It will be quite a challenge for Murphy to work his magic again.

How are customers going to know about our products' virtues unless we tell them?

HARLEY T. PROCTER

We are all aware of prices—the price of a new car, the price of food at the grocery, the price of a pair of shoes. When a business produces a good, it must decide on a price to ask for it. How is this price determined?

Customers do not actually "beat a path to the market to buy a better mousetrap." The producer must attract attention to the product. In other words, it must be promoted. Sellers use several different means to promote their products. We will examine these means, the most familiar one being advertising.

Advertising occurs in different forms, but all have a common objective. Advertising is aimed at increasing sales. It may focus on a company's products or on the company itself.

This chapter examines the role of pricing, personal selling, advertising, and other methods used in promotion.

PRICE AND PRICING OBJECTIVES

PRICE is **the exchange value of a product or service.** It is the amount a **buyer** is willing to pay for a good or service. It can also be the value a **seller** is asking for items he or she is offering for sale. Price is a major factor in competing for sales of both industrial and consumer goods. As a general rule, **the point at which supply and demand curves intersect determines the price for a specific good.** For example, consider the price of a plastic toy. At ninety cents there might be a large demand for it. But at two dollars the demand would decline sharply. Perhaps no manufacturer could afford to make the article and sell it for ninety cents. But at two dollars, several producers would be willing to enter the market.

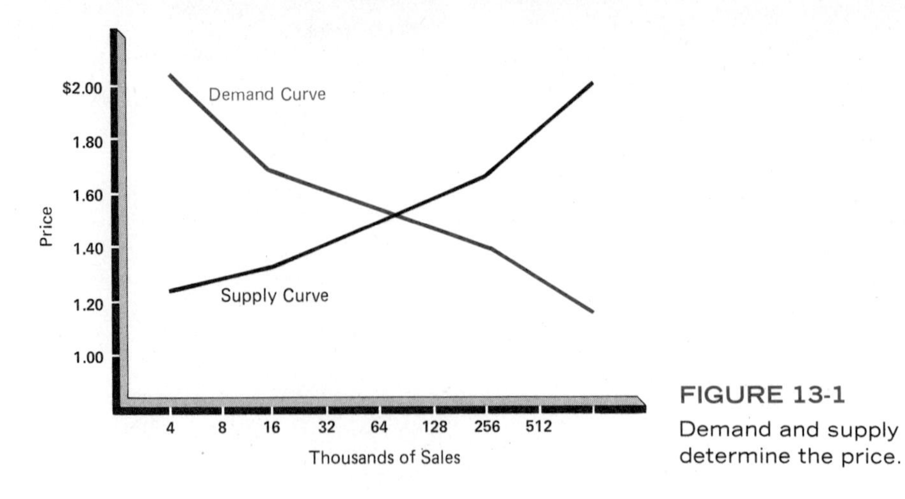

FIGURE 13-1
Demand and supply determine the price.

According to economic theory, the price that would finally be established for the toy would be where a curve representing demand and a curve representing supply intersect. This is illustrated in Figure 13-1.

It is difficult for a producer to establish the "correct" price. When people buy goods in a department store, do they pay cash or do they want credit? Do they take the goods with them or do they want them delivered? Do they want the things they buy gift wrapped? All of these extra services cost money and must be reflected in the price. What is the one correct price that a firm can offer to all potential buyers?

Pricing Objectives

Businesses price goods in order to accomplish certain objectives. A company with a broad line of products may price various goods to achieve different objectives. One article may be priced to maximize profit on that item. Another may be priced relatively low in order to increase its share of the market. Three chief objectives govern pricing practices:

1. Increasing market share
2. Maintaining market share
3. Profitability

Volume Objectives. Both increasing and maintaining market share are volume objectives. The profit margin is set at a low level in order to attract business. Both company image and product line are promoted. Discount coupons are but one device that can be used to increase sales of individual products.

Profitability. Profitability is the "bottom line" in pricing. Management knows that both the quantity sold and the profit margin determine profit. To increase the current price will limit sales. An increase in the price that exceeds the decline in sales would be profitable. If the sales decline exceeds the price increase, it would be unprofitable. For example, let us assume a price increase of 10 percent. If that percentage should cause sales volume to decline by only 7 percent, it would be profitable. But if it resulted in a decline of 12 percent, it would be unprofitable. Management must set its goals before adopting a pricing policy.

PRICING POLICIES

A pricing system must consider several different factors: material and labor costs, overhead expenses, profit margins, and prices charged by competitors. Different approaches to pricing meet different needs.

The Cost Approach

There will be no profit until a firm has recovered its costs. Therefore most companies use some type of cost approach in pricing. The three chief cost-pricing schemes are the cost-plus approach, target rate-of-return, and break-even analysis.

Cost-plus pricing. Some types of business must base their pricing on costs plus a profit. This is especially true where goods are produced to customer specifications. Construction contractors and utilities use this approach. Many wholesalers and retailers also use it.

The usual procedure here is to add a stated percentage of the cost as company profit. The formulas used are

Direct costs + Overhead costs = Total cost

Total cost + Profit margin = Price

This is illustrated in Figure 13-2. The profit margin in this case is $16\frac{2}{3}$ percent of cost.

By using a fair profit standard, cost-plus pricing provides security in an uncertain market, for the seller is relatively safe from price-cutting competition. (This assumes that competitors are satisfied with their present market share.) Competitors are not likely to reduce their profit margins in order to gain a larger market share.

Many services are priced on a cost-plus approach. Here pricing is related to labor costs. Cost-plus is also used in producing goods where one cannot determine ahead of time what the costs may be. The development of a new product for the government illustrates this type of goods.

When a business firm is both a buyer and a seller of finished goods, retail prices may be set by adding a certain sum to their cost. This is called **markup pricing. MARKUP is the difference between a middleman's cost and selling price.** Hence, if a product cost the middleman $40 and is marked to sell for $60, the markup is $20. This represents a markup of $33\frac{1}{3}$ percent. **Markup is generally expressed in terms of percentage of selling price.**

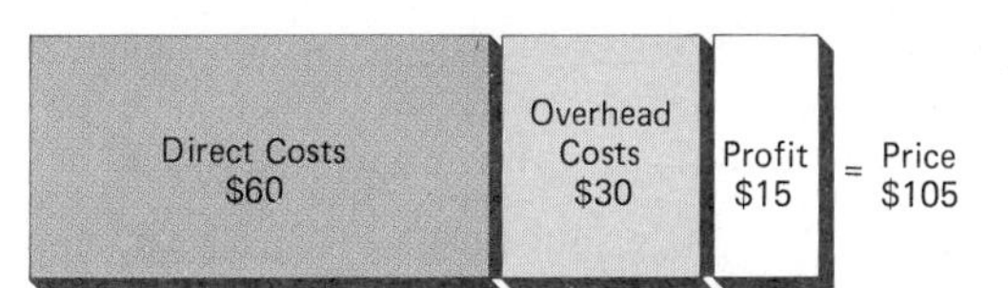

FIGURE 13-2
Cost-plus pricing.

The following steps give the percentage of markup when both cost and selling price are known:

$$\text{Selling price} - \text{Cost} = \text{Dollar markup}$$

$$\$60 - \$40 = \$20$$

$$\frac{\text{Dollar markup}}{\text{Selling price}} = \text{Percentage of markup}$$

$$\frac{\$20}{\$60} = 33\tfrac{1}{3}\%$$

Target rate-of-return. This approach is used when the pricing policy is to earn a specified rate of profit on the amount invested. This varies from the cost-plus approach in that the markup is determined by the rate of return desired. This target rate-of-return may be what is normal in the market. Or it may be what management considers to be a fair return on investment. The desired rate of return may not be maintained constantly. During some periods it may be more or less than the set rate. But over a period of years it should average the set rate.

Target rate-of-return pricing may be difficult where a company has a wide range of product lines or competes in a variety of markets. The problem results from the difficulty involved in estimating direct costs and overhead.

Break-even analysis. Break-even analysis puts more emphasis on sales volume than the cost-plus approach does. For a new product, one would expect to sustain a loss up to a certain point in sales. Management wants to know at what point cost and income would be equal. The break-even analysis hinges on variable costs. Administrative costs and overhead are usually *fixed*. But the price of labor and material varies with the volume produced. It also varies according to supply and demand in the marketplace.

The break-even point is calculated by this formula:

$$\frac{\text{Fixed costs}}{\text{Price} - \text{Variable cost per unit}} = \text{Break-even point}$$

Suppose, for example, that the fixed costs for a small manufacturer are $60,000 for the year. These include basically the cost of keeping the plant open whether anything is produced or not. The costs for raw materials, energy, and labor (variable costs) are $9 per unit produced, and the sales price is $15 per unit:

$$\frac{\$60{,}000}{\$15 - \$9} = 10{,}000 \text{ units, the break-even point}$$

This is illustrated in Figure 13-3. The company must sell ten thousand units to break even and does not begin to make a profit until after that point.

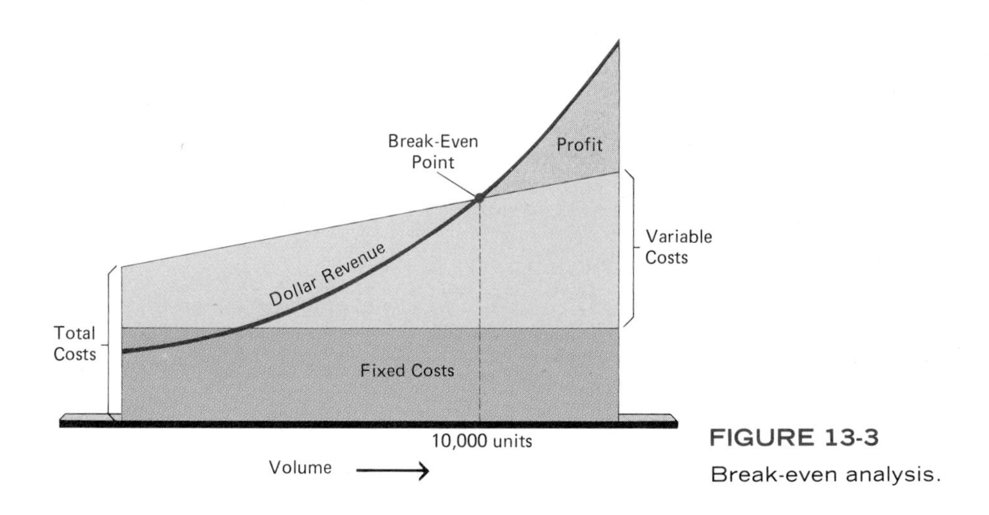

FIGURE 13-3

Break-even analysis.

Pricing Relative to Competition

In some markets, competition is chiefly on a price basis. In this case a company prices its products in relation to those of its competitors. A price might be established to meet competitive prices, or it might be set above or below that of the competition.

At the prevailing price. When pricing at the prevailing price, one does not attempt to meet every competitor's price. Rather, one meets the price of firms whose competition is most severe. This would include those in the same area who might be luring one's customers away.

Pricing above the competition. Many people think that price is an indication of quality. They feel that the more an item costs, the better the quality. So some producers price above the prevailing market price to suggest a higher quality. This can best be done where it is difficult to judge the quality of the goods being purchased.

Carnation Instant Breakfast is a good example. The company brought the product out and it sold very poorly in test markets. But when the company almost doubled the price, sales took off. People equated the higher price with a high-quality product and bought it.

Pricing below the competition. You might question how a producer could price below the competition and still make a profit. One way would be to produce goods of lower quality than those on the market. If a plant is in a labor-surplus region, costs of production might be lower. Another way would be to use low prices as the chief promotional effort. Advertising costs would be kept to a minimum.

PRICE COMPETITION means that **the strategy is to sell goods below the going market price.** Below-the-market pricing is possible only when there is evidence that customers will be attracted to a cost savings. In general, prices below the market mean that choice or selection is limited and that extra services are held to a minimum.

EDWARD G. HARNESS

Edward G. Harness became chairman of the board and chief executive officer of Procter & Gamble in May 1974. He had been president of the company from 1971 to 1974 and an employee of the company since 1940, serving as a member of top management since 1962.

A native of Marietta, Ohio, Harness joined Procter & Gamble following his graduation from Marietta College in 1940. From 1942 to 1946 he served in the air force, emerging as a major.

Upon his return to Procter & Gamble, he held positions of increasing responsibility in the company's advertising department and was named manager of advertising for soap and detergent products in 1960. In 1962 he was assigned general management responsibility for the company's Toilet Goods Division. In 1963 he was elected vice-president of the Paper Products Division. He was named vice-president—group executive and a member of the board of directors in 1966, and four years later became an executive vice-president. In 1971 he became president.

Harness is a member of the board of directors of the Caterpillar Tractor Company and the Exxon Corporation. He is chairman of the board of trustees of Marietta College, vice-chairman of the Conference Board, and a member of the Business Council and the Business Roundtable. He served as a member of the Policy Committee of the Business Roundtable from 1976 to 1979. He is a trustee of the Ohio Foundation of Independent Colleges.

Harness served for two years as co-chairman of the Cincinnati Business Committee, starting with its foundation in 1977. He remains a member of the Executive Committee of that organization. He is a trustee of the Cincinnati Institute of Fine Arts and is a member of the Cincinnati Council on World Affairs and the Cincinnati Historical Society.

Born December 17, 1918, Harness married Mary McCrady Chaney in 1943. They have three children.

PRICING PRACTICES

Management decisions on pricing are much more involved than merely placing a price tag on items offered for sale. Among the aspects that must be considered in pricing are the following:

1. How to establish different prices for different geographical areas or different customers
2. Whether to set a price and maintain it or start high and gradually come down
3. Whether to supply suggested retail prices
4. How to differentiate prices offered to distributors from those given to retailers

The pricing strategy used by 7-Eleven illustrates the complexity of selecting an effective pricing practice.

Nearly everything you buy at a 7-Eleven store can be bought cheaper at a nearby supermarket. The selection is usually very limited; most items include only one brand. The customers are small spenders, averaging only $1.54 on each visit. But 7-Eleven stores are a huge retailing success because they sell **convenience.**

Customers fill their pantries at the supermarket but go to a 7-Eleven for their latest desire—cigarettes, beer, chips, milk, and so forth. The stores are usually open twenty-four hours a day. They are carefully located near apartment buildings or other concentrations of people. Customers return on an average of four times a week.

Pricing of New Products

Pricing policies by producers are modified as a product moves through its life cycle. As an article approaches the end of the market stage and enters the maturing stage, its price is usually lowered. If management decides to increase penetration of the market (that is, obtain as many customers as soon as possible), a low price will be set when a new product is introduced. On the other hand, if management wishes to "skim" the market (that is, obtain large profits per unit), a relatively high initial price will be established.

Pricing strategies are not always apparent from the prices asked. For example, Magnavox is currently selling a home video player that is priced in a way that surprised competitors.

The home video player is a device that plays through any TV set. It will not record TV programs like the home video cassette recorder but plays re-recorded movies, instructional courses, and so forth. These must be purchased separately at a cost ranging from $5.95 to $15.95. The player is the video equivalent of the phonograph.

Price is the primary advantage of the video player over the video cassette recorder. Yet Magnavox's player was initially priced at $695—almost $200 more than its earlier projections and $200 less than its true manufacturing price. Video cassette recorders are currently discounted to as low as $650, and in addition to recording they can play the same prerecorded material as video players.

Price Differentials

A marketing manager can set different price levels for a product in a number of ways. Among them are uniform delivered prices and discounts.

Uniform delivered prices.

Most marketers will vary their prices depending on conditions. One variation is the use of uniform delivered prices. Under this pricing policy, the same prices are charged to buyers irrespective of location. There are three types of uniform delivered prices: (1) freight absorption, (2) basing-point pricing, and (3) zone pricing. Under the freight absorption, the seller is able to offer all buyers a uniform price, regardless of location. The seller absorbs larger freight charges for buyers located far away. Under basing-point pricing, the seller establishes various prices for different geographical locations. If a seller sells outside the local district, he or she would quote a price based on the basing point in the buyer's district. The zone-pricing plan allows the seller to quote prices F.O.B. the buyer's location. The seller charges a uniform price in a single zone. This plan charges some buyers located close to the source of supply and subsidizes those located in a distant area within each zone. The legal aspect of F.O.B. sales is discussed in Chapter 19.

Discounts and Allowances

Discounts are reductions from the published prices of the manufacturer. Several types of discounts are used in pricing. Discounts are available to both wholesalers and retailers. Some of the most commonly used discounts are trade, cash, quantity, and seasonal.

Trade discounts.

Trade discounts are a means of adjusting catalog prices to reflect the cost of a service that the wholesaler or jobber must perform. For example, a full-service wholesaler would be given a trade discount from the price that a limited wholesaler would pay. This would compensate the wholesaler for credit, handling, and transporting costs. Suppose an invoice is priced at $500, with discounts of 20 percent, 10 percent, and 5 percent (sometimes referred to as "chain discount"). The discount would be computed as follows:

$500 –	$100	(20% of $500)	=	$400
400 –	40	(10% of $400)	=	360
360 –	18	(5% of $360)	=	342
	$158			$342

The amount of the discount is $158, and the net price to be paid by the buyer is $342.

Cash discounts.

Probably the most common type of discount offered to buyers to induce them to pay promptly is the cash discount. A **cash discount** is a reduction in the invoice price because one is paying for purchases before the final payment is due. A typical cash discount is $\frac{2}{10}$ net 30. An invoice for $100 dated April 1, with terms $\frac{2}{10}$ net 30, allows the buyer to take a discount of 2 percent ($2) from the invoice price of $100 if it is paid before April 10. If not, the full amount of $100 is due at the end of thirty days.

Quantity discounts.

Another pricing policy is the **quantity discount.** This is offered to the buyer for purchases of large quantities, such as a discount of 10 percent for the purchase of one hundred or more units.

The Robinson-Patman Act of 1936, an amendment to Section Two of the Clayton Act, prohibits varying pricing policies that will place small firms at too great a disadvantage. It prevents sellers from granting special pricing allowances unless these concessions are open to all purchasers on "proportionately equal terms."

OFFERINGS Products Services	DISTRIBUTION CHANNELS	PRICING	PROMOTION Personal Selling Advertising Sales Promotion

FIGURE 13-4
The marketing mix.

Seasonal discounts. Many products have peak seasons when demand is much greater than at other times during the year. Merchants who are willing to purchase and store goods during the off season might be given a discount from the regular price charged. Off-season discounts are justified, for they enable a manufacturer to even out production schedules and make better use of plant facilities.

From a buyer's point of view, the discount must more than compensate for tying up the buyer's additional funds. When delivery of the goods is also accepted, an even greater discount must be received to pay for storage costs.

Promotional allowances. Manufacturers sometimes give middlemen (both wholesalers and retailers) discounts to compensate them for advertising or other promotional expenses. These discounts are usually given for local advertising of national-brand merchandise. Local advertising rates are usually lower than national rates and also have the advantage of capitalizing on the reputation of the local business.

NATURE AND TYPES OF PROMOTION

As a marketing term, **PROMOTION is a firm's efforts to influence customers to buy.** Promotion includes the elements of giving information and influencing customer behavior. Its purposes is to enhance the firm's image or increase the sale of the firm's products.

Promotional efforts are of two main types—personal and nonpersonal. Nonpersonal efforts include advertising, publicity, package design, point-of-purchase displays, and exhibits.

The chief tasks in developing a promotional effort consist of choosing communication media and blending them into an effective program. Seldom does a company rely on a single type of promotional activity. The combination of methods used in communicating with customers is called a **promotion blend.** Promotion is the fourth factor in the marketing mix (see Figure 13-4).

PERSONAL SELLING

A simplified definition of **selling** would be "the art of personal persuasion employed to induce others to buy." Personal selling is the oldest method of selling. This method is unique, for it involves a two-way exchange of ideas between buyer and seller. In our treatment of personal selling we will discuss

1. The behavioral approach in selling
2. The selling process
3. Sales management

Behavioral Approach in Selling

In recent years, marketing executives have received valuable information from behavioral scientists regarding human behavior in the marketplace. The study of behavior starts with an understanding of motivation. **MOTIVATION is an inner force that moves people toward satisfying a need.** Motivation involves a three-stage cycle consisting of a need or want, a drive, and a goal. The drive may be physical, such as the need for water, food, or sleep. Or it may be psychological, such as the need for recognition or security. The drive is the stimulation to act, which is created by the need or want. The third stage, reaching the goal that satisfies the need, is the result of the drive.

For some years now, psychologists have recognized that human behavior is motivated by both environmental conditions and individual characteristics.

Abraham H. Maslow formulated a theory of motivation, which received considerable attention in marketing. He brought together the viewpoints of several schools of psychological thought. Maslow identified a hierarchy of five levels of needs, which he arranged in the order he felt people seek to satisfy them. These needs were covered in Chapter 4 and are reviewed in Figure 13-5.

These needs are significant to marketers. The physiological needs relate to what a product does—automobiles transport persons. Safety needs relate to people's security—homes provide safe and comfortable living quarters. The belongingness needs relate to products that make one more interpersonally attractive or acceptable, and so on.

Consumer Buying Motives

In personal selling as well as in advertising, specific motives are used to appeal to consumers. The shrewd salesperson knows that "if you want to sell a prospect something, you must know something about what makes that person tick." So to understand the consumer, we must recognize the motives that cause him or her to act.

Buying motives are classified as either emotional or rational. **EMOTIONAL MOTIVES are subjective and impulsive in nature.** For example, a man buys a new coat not because he needs it but because he wants recognition. **Emotional motives include hunger, pride, status, safety, and comfort.** Sellers of tangible articles like musical instruments, sporting goods, or furniture rely heavily on emotional buying motives, such as pleasure, comfort, or distinction. Emotional buying motives are often very strong appeals.

RATIONAL MOTIVES are those produced by a logical reasoning process. A product that is bought only after weighing all the advantages and disadvantages

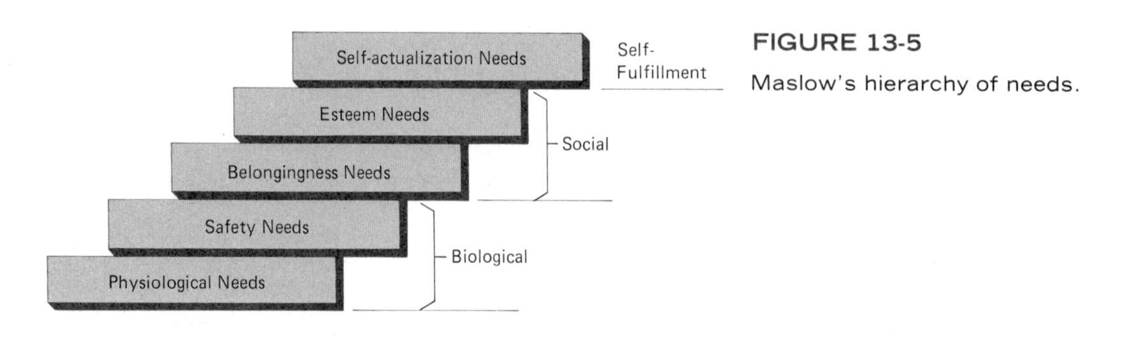

FIGURE 13-5
Maslow's hierarchy of needs.

is not purchased on impulse. Some of the commonly used rational motives are **economy, dependability, fair price,** and **quality.** When selling watches, for example, fair price and dependability are far more convincing buying motives than such emotional motives as security, recognition, or superiority.

A typical buyer may respond to both emotional and rational motives. A decision to buy a certain style of automobile may be entirely emotional, but the choice of brand may well be rational. Also, it is not unusual for a buyer to say the motive was rational, even though it was really emotional. Sellers sometimes recognize this type of behavior and often use advertisements that carry both appeals. The study of consumer buying is complicated. A purely rational motive to one person may be emotional to another. The distinction is generally determined by the amount of time and consideration given to making the purchase.

The Selling Process

Despite the many different types of selling jobs, and the numerous motives used in making a sale, selling can be broken down into specific steps on which the sales presentation is based. Although these steps cannot always be precisely timed or sharply distinguished from one another, they usually occur in the following order:

1. Locating the prospective customer
2. Gaining the prospect's attention
3. Stimulating the prospect's interest
4. Developing the prospect's desire for the product
5. Closing the sale

Locating the prospective customer. **Prospects** are **potential customers.** In some businesses, salespersons are supplied with a list of prospects. In others, potential customers must be discovered by the salesperson. Such customers can be found among one's acquaintances, through inquiries of friends and business associates, through social contacts, and through advertising.

Gaining attention. Obviously the first step in the selling demonstration consists of gaining the prospect's attention. The idea is to prepare him or her for listening to the presentation. Successful salespeople often develop questions or startling statements to do this. One must be careful, however, not to overstate a case. The presentation that follows must deliver what was promised.

Stimulating interest. After gaining the prospective buyer's attention, a salesperson must stimulate interest. The natural procedure here is to follow through with the idea presented to gain attention. Product samples or models are effective in developing buyer interest. A special price discount is another interest stimulator. Developing interest in a service or product is essential to success in selling.

Developing the desire to buy. The sales presentation gradually unfolds as information about a product is given. The buyer must decide that an article or service is worthy and important. It must make a contribution to the buyer. A salesperson must know when to stop the presentation and avoid "overselling" the prospective buyer. The next step is to close the sale.

Closing the sale. The successful salesperson recognizes the precise moment at which the customer reaches a decision, and closes the sale promptly. This may be done by offering the customer a pencil or pen to sign the sales ticket or contract or by actually wrapping the goods. If the sale is to be charged to the customer's account, the salesperson prepares a sales slip and asks, "When shall we deliver your purchase?"

A successful salesperson studies the prospect carefully and discovers which technique will be most effective in closing the sale. For example, the salesperson determines how the customer wishes to pay for the article, and he or she then moves along smoothly to the right closing technique without offending the customer.

One sales manual of instructions says this about closing a sale:

1. When your prospect begins to pause in making the final decision, this is the time to step in and close.
2. Watch your prospect's facial expression. If the prospect indicates by a smile or a twinkle of the eye that he or she is pleased with the article, then get out your order book.
3. Listen to the prospect's voice; if there is a slight inflection or a raising or lowering tone, this is your tip to make your closing remarks.

Some Selling Techniques

Success in selling employs a variety of techniques. Here are a few that are often mentioned by successful salespersons:

1. Find out what your customers' real wants and needs are. Listen as they tell you what they are interested in.
2. Know all about your product and what it can do for your customer. Product knowledge is a "must" in personal selling because it creates customer confidence, builds enthusiasm, and gives a professional touch to the situation. Stress the unique advantage of your product over others.
3. Present a positive rather than a negative approach. The sales presentation is more effective when the salesperson says, "May I help you?" than when he or she says, "You wouldn't like to see our new model, would you?" A negative approach calls for a negative answer.
4. Prepare yourself to handle objections. If the prospect says the price is too high, you might reply, "Yes, the price may be a little higher than you planned. However, in the long run you'll save money because of the superior quality of this product." In any event, don't argue with your prospect about whether a price is too high.
5. Use praise judiciously.

Sales Management

The main task in sales management consists of coordinating the selling efforts of individuals. This is a very personal thing and requires administrative ability, tact, and diplomacy. Various aspects of sales management include the following:

1. Establishing sales-force objectives
2. Planning an organizational structure
3. Recruiting, selecting, and training

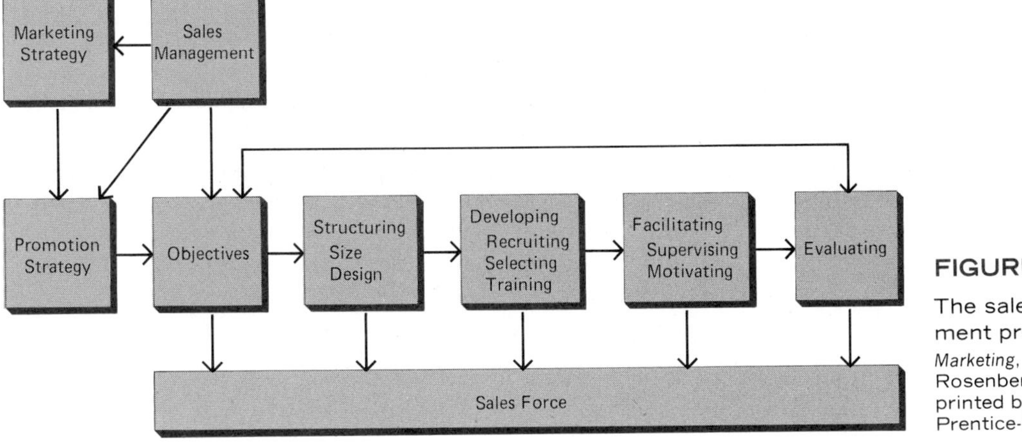

FIGURE 13-6

The sales management process. (From *Marketing*, by Larry J. Rosenberg, 1977. Reprinted by permission of Prentice-Hall, Inc.)

4. Directing the sales force—motivation, supervision, compensation
5. Evaluating and then determining promotions and rewards

This range of sales management activities is illustrated in Figure 13-6.

ADVERTISING

Most companies use a blend of personal and nonpersonal means of selling. More money is spent for advertising than for other types of nonpersonal promotion. The parallel relationship of personal selling to advertising in promoting the flow of goods is shown in Figure 13-7.

To the homemaker, advertising may mean the grocery ad in Wednesday's local newspaper. To the sales manager, advertising is a method of communicating with the public to make the selling job easier. To the accountant, advertising is one of the costs of doing business; and to the economist, it is an integral part of today's business system.

All of us have been influenced to buy certain things because of some form of advertising. It is universally recognized that advertising conveys selling messages and appeals better than other techniques in certain situations.

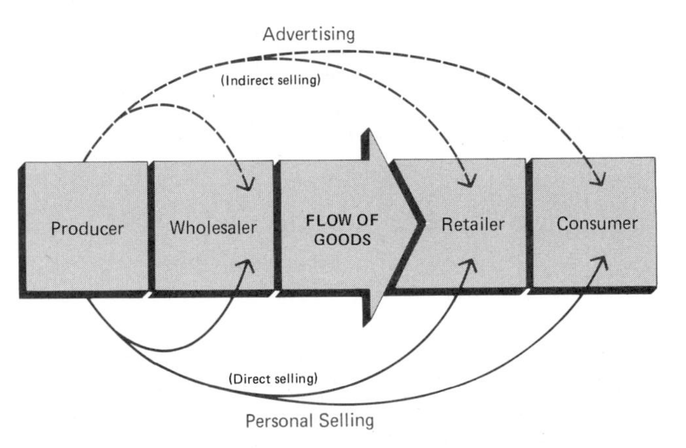

FIGURE 13-7

Personal selling and advertising in marketing.

What Is Advertising?

The Definitions Committee of the American Marketing Association defines **ADVERTISING** as "**any paid form of nonpersonal presentation and promotion of ideas, goods, or services by an identified sponsor.**" Two characteristics are significant in this definition: payment for the advertisement and a sponsor who pays for it. At times it is possible to communicate without cost to the sponsor—for example, through editorial comments by newspapers or magazines about a firm or a product. This type of information is considered publicity rather than advertising. The public-relations department is responsible for the company's publicity. In most businesses, public relations is more concerned with developing an image or a favorable relationship with the public than with directly promoting the sale of products.

Public relations also concerns itself with providing communication to the public when necessary. Such disasters as nuclear-plant failure, airplane crashes, automobiles with serious safety flaws, and oilwell blowouts often require the talents of PR people to communicate with the public. How the company reacts in such emergencies can spell the difference between a temporary loss of goodwill and a permanent loss of business.

Purposes of Advertising

The overall purpose of advertising is to influence the level of product sales and thereby increase the advertiser's profits. Sometimes a firm is forced to advertise because of the actions of competitors or government. Under such circumstances, the opportunity to increase profits may be slim. Yet failure to advertise could result in either reduced sales and less profit or legal action.

As a tool of marketing, advertising generally serves the following purposes (sometimes called "the three R's of advertising"):

1. Retain "loyal" customers: Persuade present customers to keep buying.
2. Retrieve "lost" customers: Slow down the flow of present customers away from the preferred brand.
3. Recruit "new" customers: Increase the flow of customers toward the advertised product. Replace those lost to competitors. Widen the total market.

Types of Advertising

Advertising can be classified into certain types, depending upon the use and purpose.

Product advertising. This type of advertising is designed to sell one or more definite and identified products or services. It usually describes and praises their features and good qualities and may even emphasize their prices. Product advertising is used to sell both consumer and industrial goods. Because consumer and industrial goods have different marketing characteristics, they are sold in different trade channels, to different markets, under different pricing policies, and by different selling methods. Edward G. Harness, board chairman of Procter & Gamble, had this to say about advertising as it relates to products:

> Advertising has no life of its own. It has no unique power to persuade. It is not a separate and distinct force in our society. It should not be praised or criticized for its own sake. It is simply a part of a total marketing process which, to be successful, must be based on a worthwhile product.

Institutional advertising. This type tries to create a favorable attitude toward the seller. It also tries to build goodwill that will generate long-run rather than immediate sales. For example, a manufacturer may run an institutional advertisement to tell the public about the firm's efforts to reduce air pollution. Large corporations can afford to spend money on institutional advertising. Small companies can seldom afford it.

National advertising. This type is used to sell nationally distributed brands by using a medium with nationwide circulation. It is generally associated with advertising by the manufacturer rather than by a retailer or local advertiser. Moreover, national advertising refers only to the *level* of the advertiser. It has no relation at all to geographic coverage. If such a manufacturer places an advertisement in only one city, it is still called national advertising.

Local advertising. **Local (or retail) advertising** is placed by a local merchant. It usually differs from national advertising by being more specific in terms of price, quality, and quantity. In national advertising the purpose is to build a general demand for a product that may be sold in many stores. In local advertising the stress is on the store where the product is sold.

Corrective advertising. Corrective advertising takes place to correct specific false or misleading claims that might have been made in previous advertising. Classic examples of corrective advertising include the following: STP's corrective ads to clarify the claim that STP oil treatment will stop cars from burning oil. Anacin's $24 million worth of corrective advertising disclosing that Anacin is not a tension reliever. Listerine's correcting an earlier claim that it "fights colds." These and other corrective ads have been ordered by courts to rectify misleading information presented in previous advertisements.

Corrective advertising is especially important when the Federal Trade Commission determines that health, safety, or nutrition claims are misleading.

Effects of Advertising on the Price and Public

Advertising alone will not persuade consumers to pay what they feel is an unreasonable price. Yet consumers often believe that a nationally advertised brand is worth a higher price than an unadvertised brand. For example, customers are willing to pay a little more for Armour's canned ham than for an unknown brand. Their experience leads them to think that it will taste better. The consumer may determine this added value by prior use, or he or she may accept the claims of the advertiser. However, if the advertised brand has no important differences, its price may be no higher than that of unadvertised competitors.

Is advertising an economic waste? Critics question the social value of advertising. For one thing, they claim that advertising fails to create new demands and merely results in switching brands. For such consumer goods as toothpaste, cosmetics, detergents, and gasoline—where advertising is highly competitive—the total per capita consumption has risen steadily over the years. To say that all advertising is purely competitive and therefore wasteful suggests that competition itself is wasteful. From the advertiser's standpoint, the potential dollar sales should produce enough gross margin dollars—the excess of sales over cost of goods sold—to pay the advertising costs. Advertising is expected to pay for itself in added sales.

It may be difficult to prove scientifically the economic value of advertising. Yet evidence shows that mass advertising is essential to maintain both mass consumption and mass production.

Truth in advertising. There are, of course, dishonest advertisers. As the watchdog for the American public, the Federal Trade Commission (FTC) is constantly battling with companies about their alleged exaggerations or untruths. What do we mean by "tell the truth"? Is the advertisement expected to tell the literal truth, or merely to give a reasonably accurate impression? On this subject, the Supreme Court has made these statements:

> **Advertising as a whole must not create a misleading impression even though every statement separately considered is literally truthful.**
>
> **Advertising must not obscure or conceal material facts.**
>
> **Advertising must not be artfully contrived to distract and divert readers' attention from the true nature of the terms and conditions of an offer.**

The FTC embarked on a strong truth-in-advertising campaign in the early 1970s. It demanded that advertisers be prepared to substantiate their claims. An FTC resolution states that advertisers are not voluntarily meeting the public's needs for more objective information about their claims. The resolution adds:

> Public disclosure can enhance competition by encouraging competitors to challenge advertised claims which have no basis in fact. . . .

In another area of concern, the FTC is seeking to prevent deceptive price advertising. Typical practices that the commission warns advertisers to avoid are contained in its publication "Guides against Deceptive Pricing." This publication is available to businesses in cooperation with Better Business Bureaus.

A recent study published by the *Harvard Business Review* gives some business executives' views regarding advertising:

1. Only one out of three believes that advertisements really give a true picture of the product.
2. Two out of five believe that the general public's faith in advertising is at an all-time low.
3. Nine out of ten feel that advertisers should be required to prove their claims.

Much advertising can be considered truthful. Still, there are too many unscrupulous advertisers who make misleading or half-true statements about their products. Exaggerated claims for killing germs, curing colds, and producing sleep have been challenged by government agencies.

In 1938 Congress passed the Wheeler-Lea Act, amending the Federal Trade Commission (FTC) Act of 1914. The act gives the FTC power over "unfair or deceptive acts or practices." Several statutes aimed at specific industries grant the

FTC authority to act on matters related to labeling and advertising. Among these statutes are the following:

1. Wool Product Labeling Act of 1939
2. Fur Products Labeling Act of 1951
3. Flammable Fabrics Act of 1953
4. Textile Fiber Production Identification Act of 1968

The Federal Communications Commission also has regulatory power over radio and television stations and network operations. It studies the merits of advertisements broadcast by these two media.

In 1965 Congress passed the Highway Beautification Act, prohibiting advertising billboards and other signs within six hundred feet of the interstate and primary-road systems. However, this law has not had total enforcement in all states.

CURRENT ISSUE CURRENT ISSUE CURRENT ISSUE CURRENT ISSUE CURRENT ISSUE CURRENT ISSUE CURRENT ISSUE CURRENT ISSUE CURRENT ISSUE CURRENT ISSUE

Is Advertising Necessary? Is It Good or Bad?

Advertising is a way of life among American businesses. Many large businesses spend millions of dollars advertising their products. But some people feel that advertising is an unnecessary expense.

With which of the following statements do you agree and with which do you disagree?

1. Advertising is essential under a mass-production economy.
2. Advertising increases company profits at the expense of consumers.
3. Advertising performs a worthwhile service by informing prospective buyers about the merits of new products.
4. Advertising, by increasing the sales of a product, often lowers the product's cost to the consumer.
5. Advertising causes people to buy items they do not need.
6. Advertising fails to create new demands and only results in consumers' switching brands.
7. Advertising often does not tell the whole truth.
8. The cost of advertising raises the price to the consumer.

What is your opinion regarding the role and justification of advertising in the American economy?

CURRENT ISSUE

On January 1, 1966, cigarette manufacturers were first required to place on each cigarette package a health warning reading: "Caution: Cigarette smoking may be hazardous to your health." In 1970 Congress made this warning stronger. Each package must now contain this statement: "Warning: The Surgeon General has determined that cigarette smoking is dangerous to your health."

The most far-reaching federal law affecting advertising is the Public Health Cigarette Smoking Act, effective January 2, 1971. This law prohibits cigarette advertising of any kind on radio and television.

ADVERTISING MEDIA

If an advertising message is to reach its audience, some type of carrier must be chosen. In the field of advertising, these carriers are called **MEDIA.** (A specific advertising medium is sometimes called a **vehicle**.) The success of advertising depends upon both the message and the medium selected. The various media commonly used for advertising purposes are

Newspapers	Outdoor advertising
Magazines	Transportation advertising
Direct mail	Point-of-purchase displays
Radio	
Television	Specialty

The sums of money spent for various types of media are shown in Figure 13-8.

Kinds of Media

Some large companies use almost all of the media listed above. But small companies, for financial reasons, may use only one or two. Many factors must be evaluated in selecting the proper media. These include the cost, extent of coverage (circulation), size of the selection from which to choose, degree of flexibility, timeliness, and nature of coverage (geography).

Newspapers. There are approximately eighteen hundred daily newspapers in the United States, with a combined circulation of 65 million; and there are about seven hundred daily newspapers with Sunday editions, with a combined circulation of over 52 million.[1] In terms of spending, the newspaper is the leading medium. It accounts for 30 percent of the total advertising dollar.[2] This vehicle is very effective when a business is seeking to cover a single metropolitan area. Copy can be prepared and submitted only a few hours before press time, although most newspapers specify that copy be turned in several days in advance. However, the short life of each newspaper edition and the poor reproductive quality of illustrations are two limiting factors. Studies show that the average length of time

[1] *Editor and Publisher Yearbook,* 1979.

[2] Newspaper Advertising Bureau.

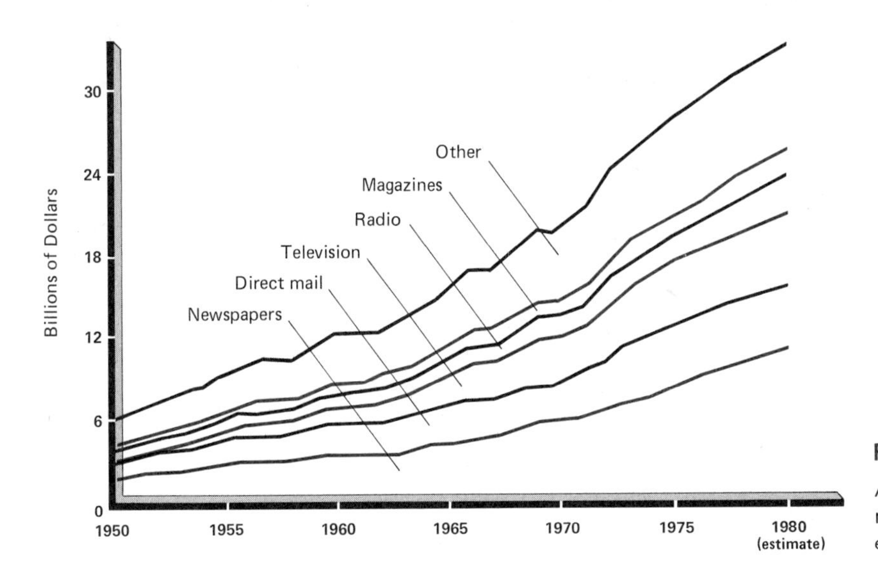

FIGURE 13-8

Advertising expenditures by medium. (Courtesy: The Conference Board.)

a person reads a newspaper is only twenty minutes. The newspaper advertisement is used when the appeal attempts to reach the general public, not a select group.

The twelve companies that spent the most for newspaper advertising during a recent year, in order of the amount spent, are listed in Table 13-1.

Television. Television is a mass medium. It can be used either on a nationwide or on a regional basis, or it can be concentrated on the local market. As with radio, television has the advantage of immediate reception, providing timeliness to an even greater extent than newspapers. A magazine or newspaper may be in print several hours or days before it is read by the subscriber, but the TV message

TABLE 13-1
TOP 12 NEWSPAPER ADVERTISERS, 1978

Rank	Advertiser	Expenditures
1	R. J. Reynolds Industries	$61,093,436
2	Philip Morris	52,013,737
3	General Motors Corporation	46,702,868
4	Ford Motor Company	27,209,744
5	Loew's Corporation	26,666,500
6	RCA Corporation	19,143,498
7	Liggett Group	18,994,769
8	American Brands	18,355,332
9	British American Tobacco Co. Ltd.	16,532,063
10	Delta Air Lines	16,156,072
11	Chrysler Corporation	15,819,958
12	Columbia Broadcasting System	14,842,633

SOURCE: Media records.

TABLE 13-2
TOP 12 NETWORK TV ADVERTISERS, 1978

Rank	Advertiser	Expenditures
1	Procter & Gamble Company	$261,715,300
2	General Foods Corporation	169,427,900
3	American Home Products Corporation	111,136,200
4	Bristol-Myers Company	110,341,400
5	General Motors Corporation	107,826,500
6	General Mills	84,283,200
7	Ford Motor Company	79,510,600
8	Sears, Roebuck and Company	71,367,500
9	Philip Morris	67,054,600
10	Johnson & Johnson	64,979,100
11	Chrysler Corporation	60,988,000
12	Unilever	60,507,900

SOURCE: Net time and program costs from Broadcast Advertisers' Reports, and supplied to leading national advertisers.

is received by the listener at once. Television's greatest advantage is that it combines sight, sound, motion, and demonstration. And for many viewers it does all this in color—a unique combination for advertising. On the other hand, its message is short lived and production costs are high. Expenditures for TV advertising are the second largest.

Ninety-five percent of all American households have television sets, and 80 percent of all adults (eighteen years of age and older) view television daily. It is a mass medium that appeals to all age groups.

Most prime time is given to the national networks. Because of its broad coverage at prime time, advertising on the national network is expensive. The twelve companies that spent the most for network TV advertising during a recent year, in order of the amount spent, are shown in Table 13-2.

Complaints about the frequency of TV advertisements are causing the networks to consider carefully how many ads are "enough." Affiliated stations have been unhappy because the increase in the number of national network commercials reduces the number of advertising minutes they can sell.

Direct-mail advertising. Direct-mail advertising ranks third behind newspapers and television in the amount of money spent. It is estimated that 85 percent of third-class mail and between 10 and 15 percent of first class mail are direct-mail advertising.[3] The chief advantage of direct-mail advertising is that the advertiser can select precisely the audience to be reached, which is not possible with other media. Direct-mail advertising is the most flexible, for it may serve a local, regional, or national market. Also, it offers an opportunity to make one's message personal and provides great flexibility in production design and accurate timing in its scheduling. Direct-mail advertising does not require the purchase of time or space,

[3]Direct Mail Advertising Association.

as do the other media. The cost of direct-mail advertising is for printing, securing mailing lists, and postage.

Magazines. In contrast to newspaper ads, magazine advertising reaches a more selective group. People buy magazines intended for them as members of special groups, such as teachers, doctors, engineers, farmers—and yes, even advertising personnel. Magazines generally are printed on high-quality paper that enhances creative designs and the use of color. Copy must be submitted weeks in advance of the publication date. People keep magazines much longer than newspapers and thumb through them again and again. Magazines provide a wide range of prospects, reaching people with many and special interests.

The W. R. Simmons Company reported that 90 percent of the nation's adult population (eighteen years of age and older) are magazine readers during an average month. The Daniel Starch research organization reported a study covering 12 million inquiries. This organization found that 54 percent of all inquiries to any single magazine ad are received within one week after its publication. Another 25 percent are received during the second week. By the end of the sixth week, 95 percent of the return is in.

Advertising rates are based on circulation. The cost of reaching customers can be determined in this way:

$$\frac{\text{Page rate} \times 1{,}000}{\text{Circulation}} = \text{Cost per thousand readers}$$

The twelve companies that spent the largest sums for magazine advertising in a recent year, in order of the amount spent, are listed in Table 13-3.

TABLE 13-3
TOP 12 MAGAZINE ADVERTISERS, 1978

Rank	Advertiser	Expenditures
1	R. J. Reynolds Industries	$71,517,200
2	Joseph E. Seagram and Sons	69,160,400
3	General Motors Corporation	56,305,300
4	Sears, Roebuck and Company	55,930,800
5	Philip Morris	53,306,800
6	General Foods Corporation	36,234,900
7	Chrysler Corporation	35,357,500
8	Procter & Gamble Company	33,754,300
9	Columbia Broadcasting System	27,117,400
10	American Brands	26,399,200
11	Loew's Corporation	24,147,600
12	Bristol-Myers Company	23,761,500

SOURCE: Leading national advertisers. (Farm papers not included.)

Radio. Radio as an advertising medium is considerably different from what it was before television. Some persons thought that television would destroy radio advertising. To the contrary, it has increased greatly. In total, the more than four thousand AM stations and more than two thousand FM stations reach 80 percent of the population on any given day. Whereas there may be only one or two daily newspapers in a specific market, there are several radio stations. Radio messages are designed for special audiences, such as homemakers, farmers, and youth groups.

Spot advertising on the radio gives individual market selection. The advertiser can therefore tailor the message to the market coverage selected. Spot advertising enables a business firm to present its message at the most favorable time in an individual market. It provides the greatest flexibility in time, wording, station, and market.

The twelve companies that spent the largest sums for network radio advertising in a recent year, in order of the amount spent, are listed in Table 13-4.

TABLE 13-4
TOP 12 NETWORK RADIO ADVERTISERS, 1978

Rank	Advertiser	Expenditures
1	Smith Kline Corporation	$5,153,900
2	Sears, Roebuck and Company	4,388,300
3	General Motors Corporation	3,171,700
4	American Home Products Corporation	3,155,000
5	Schering-Plough Corporation	2,953,200
6	Wm. Wrigley Jr. Company	2,902,400
7	Sterling Drug	2,754,700
8	Warner-Lambert Company	2,678,900
9	Anheuser-Busch	2,483,800
10	Cotter & Company	2,467,700
11	Hartz Mountain Industries	1,947,300
12	Kraft Inc.	1,901,500

SOURCE: Radio Advertising Bureau and Radio Expenditure Reports.

EXPENDITURES FOR ADVERTISING

The total spent for advertising in 1978 was $43.7 billion. When taken as a whole, the amount of money that American corporations spend for advertising equals the amount they pay to their stockholders in dividends. A study recently completed by the Association of National Advertisers shows that for most companies dealing in consumer goods, advertising is among the three largest expenditures. For retailers, advertising ranks as the number-two expenditure, exceeded only by payments for salaries.

TABLE 13-5
ADVERTISING EXPENDITURES BY MEDIUM, 1978

Medium	Expenditures in Millions	Percent of Total
Newspapers	$12,690	29.0
Television	8,850	20.2
Direct mail	6,030	13.8
Radio	2,955	6.8
Magazines	2,595	5.9
Business papers	1,420	3.3
Outdoor	465	1.1
Farm publications	105	0.2
Miscellaneous	8,630	19.7
Total	43,740	100.0
Total national	24,045	55.0
Total local	19,695	45.0

Newspaper Advertising Bureau.

As you compare the listing of the different companies relative to advertising expenditures by various media, you will note the following:

1. The companies that spend the largest sums for advertising spend more for TV ads than for all other types combined.
2. The companies that spend the most for newspaper and radio advertising differ considerably from the leading TV advertisers.
3. Only General Motors ranks in the top twelve in all four categories—Chrysler, Philip Morris, and Sears, Roebuck in three.
4. Only one retailer—Sears, Roebuck—is large enough to rank in the top ten in any category of advertising expenditures.

As you study Table 13-5 you will observe that newspaper advertising ranks ahead of TV, and that direct-mail advertising ranks third, ahead of radio and magazines. This is contrary to what many people think.

The data shown in Table 13-5 are depicted in graphic form in Figure 13-9.

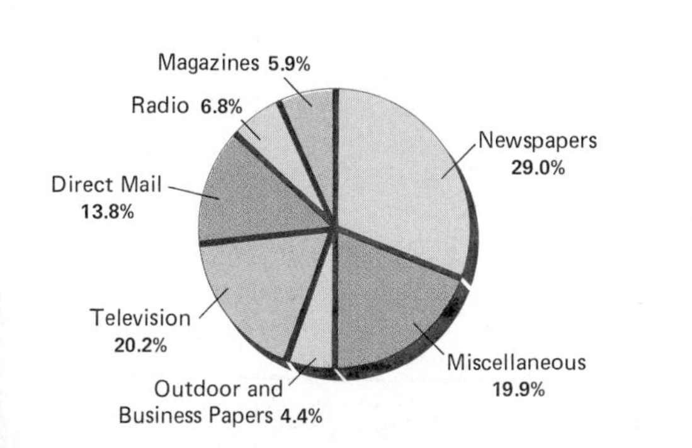

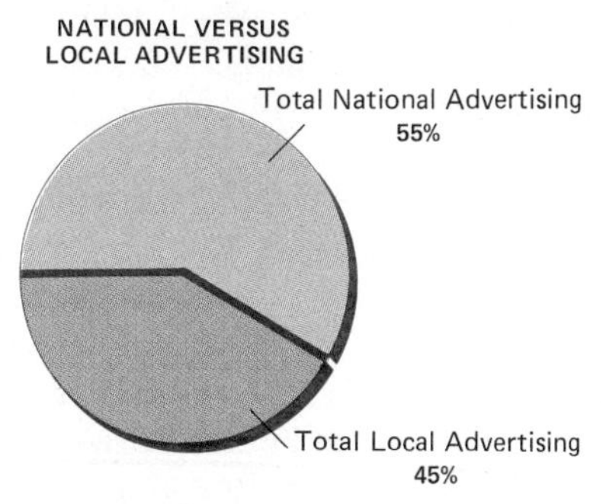

FIGURE 13-9
Advertising budgets by medium, 1978.

OTHER TYPES OF SALES PROMOTION

Other types of sales promotion used by businesses are publicity; point-of-purchase advertising; trade shows and exhibits; samples, coupons, and trading stamps; and outdoor advertising.

Publicity

PUBLICITY is in reality free promotion. **It consists primarily of news stories and personal appearances.** When a new firm is opening for business, publicity appears in the local newspaper. When a business is remodeling, building an addition, or moving to a new location, these also form the basis of stories in the local news media.

Authors, athletes, and other public figures are usually willing and available to make public appearances at department stores and other businesses to promote their activities.

Word-of-mouth publicity from satisfied customers is invaluable. Extra effort to give them top-quality merchandise, fair treatment, and personal service will cause this publicity to be positive and will result in additional sales.

Point-of-Purchase Advertising

Point-of-purchase advertising is used largely in retail stores. It consists of displays inside stores close to the place where the goods are stacked. These displays are intended to stimulate impulse buying—decisions made on the spot without prior planning to buy.

Trade Shows and Exhibits

Both wholesalers and retailers attend regional and national trade conventions where producers exhibit their merchandise. Examples are state and national conventions of food brokers, hardware dealers, and buyers of clothing. Furniture store managers and buyers usually visit several of the leading furniture marts. Trade shows and exhibits are scheduled at different times during the year.

Samples, Coupons, and Trading Stamps

Samples are used to promote new products. They are usually distributed by mail and through magazine and newspaper ads. Sometimes a coupon is used to distribute a free sample—it is good for the entire price of the article. As a rule, however, coupons represent a discount off the regular selling price.

Trading stamps may be given with retail purchases. They are accumulated and exchanged for gifts. S & H and Top Value stamps are perhaps the most widely distributed nationally.

Outdoor Advertising

Billboard advertising is used throughout the nation, in cities and along the highways. Its use is limited because of the space needed for such an exhibit. City buses also display advertisements. To be effective, outdoor ads must be colorful and restricted to short, simple messages. They usually feature pictures and use only a few words. Outdoor advertising accounts for only 1.1 percent of advertising expenditures in the United States.

CAREERS IN SELLING AND ADVERTISING

More than 7 million persons are employed in sales. Some of these persons (slightly more than one-half) are in wholesaling, retailing, and manufacturing. Others sell insurance, securities, or real estate; still others work for banks, utilities, transportation companies, newspapers, TV and radio stations, and service organizations. With the exception of administrative personnel, the financial rewards for salespersons are as good as those offered in any field of business endeavor.

Careers in promotion include preparing floor and window displays in retail stores, as well as preparing all types of advertising copy for in-house displays and local newspapers. Important attributes for advertising personnel include the ability to write, visualize, create and innovate. Advertising personnel must be flexible in viewpoint and must be able to adapt to new situations.

Most work in advertising beyond the local level is done by advertising agencies. These advertising agencies tend to use the following specialists:

1. *Media director*—This person selects the media that best achieve a client's objectives. He or she coordinates the use of several types of media into a feasible plan.
2. *Production specialist*—This person must have a knowledge of printing processes and broadcasting technicalities. The production person's primary job is to keep the project—pamphlet, booklet, or ad—moving through the various processes. (These positions are also needed in publishing firms, printing firms, and company advertising departments.)
3. *Art-and-layout director*—This person, who must possess talent and skill as an artist, is responsible for the quality of the artwork. The director confers with the client, the account executive, and others in the agency to determine the best possible layout and art for the ad.
4. *Account executive*—This person occupies one of the most important and "sensitive" positions in an agency. He or she is responsible for keeping the client satisfied with the agency's work. Besides being a creative individual and a good salesperson, the account executive must be familiar with business practices and have an understanding of marketing, merchandising, and advertising.
5. *Copywriter*—Often called the "idea person," the copywriter prepares the copy—the message the advertiser wishes to present. In the final stages of the copy, the copywriter works with various specialists, including the art-and-layout director and the account executive.

SUMMARY OF KEY CONCEPTS

Two important aspects of the marketing mix are *price* and *promotion.*

Pricing is a basic means of competing with other businesses. The *price* of an item is its exchange value—the amount acceptable to buyer and seller.

The two chief pricing objectives are volume sales and profitability.

The chief pricing policies are the cost approach, and pricing relative to competition.

Practices that make price differentials possible are F.O.B. pricing and various types of discounts: trade, cash, quantity, seasonal, and promotional allowances.

Promotional efforts are either personal or nonpersonal. Personal selling and advertising are the chief types of promotion.

Personal selling involves an oral presentation by the seller to a prospective buyer.

Advertising attempts to reach large numbers through nonpersonal means.

As a tool of marketing, advertising serves to retain loyal customers, reduce lost customers, and recruit new ones. As a social force, it has altered our living habits and has helped to raise living standards.

Economically, advertising has promoted the growth of industry, lowered unit costs, and served to identify families of products under one name or brand.

The more popular advertising media are newspapers, radio and television, magazines, and direct mail. Transportation advertising and point-of-purchase displays are effective, but they are used less frequently. Direct-mail advertising is the most selective, and radio and television advertising is the most flexible.

More money is spent for newspaper advertising than for any other medium. Television ranks second, direct-mail third, radio fourth, and magazines fifth.

BUSINESS TERMS

You should be able to match these business terms with the statements that follow:

a. Advertising
b. Cash discount
c. Cost-plus pricing
d. Emotional motives
e. F.O.B. pricing
f. Markup
g. Media
h. Motivation
i. Personal selling
j. Price
k. Promotion
l. Promotional discount
m. Publicity
n. Rational motives
o. Trade discount

1. The exchange value a buyer will pay for a good or service
2. The difference between a merchant's cost price and sales price for a specific good
3. Basing the selling price of a product on its cost plus a profit
4. A pricing quotation that shows whether the buyer or the seller is to pay the freight
5. A discount offered to middlemen for marketing services rendered
6. A company's sales-communication contacts with customers
7. Sales activities that involve personal contacts between a seller and a buyer
8. Promotional communication that does not cost the company anything
9. Paid forms of promotional communication
10. Stimuli that move a person to action
11. The means selected by an advertiser to communicate the advertiser's sales effort to the buying public
12. A desire to buy goods or services supported by logical reasoning

REVIEW QUESTIONS

1. What factors must be considered when setting up a pricing system?
2. At what three levels are prices set in relation to competition?
3. Under the zone-pricing plan, who pays the freight?
4. What steps are involved in the selling process?
5. What purposes are served by advertising?
6. What is the rank order of advertising media in terms of money spent?

DISCUSSION QUESTIONS

1. How do demand and supply affect product pricing?
2. What is the bottom line in pricing? What factors determine its limits?
3. How is the break-even point calculated?
4. What is the justification for giving discounts for the early payment of goods?
5. What promotional activities would you include for a women's retail clothing store?

BUSINESS CASE 13-1

Pricing a New Product

We learned in the preceding chapter that an item is considered to be a "new product" if a major improvement is made in it. The Haley Manufacturing Company makes a "car-wagon" for children, which is propelled by foot pedals. It has been selling for $32. The company's research department has developed a new technique that greatly improves the car-wagon's working efficiency. The company's production people think this will also save $3 on the cost of producing each one.

Company management is considering repricing the car-wagon. The following courses of action are possibilities:

1. Continue to sell the car-wagon at its present price, but advertise its higher quality.
2. Pass the $3 saving along to customers by reducing the price $3.
3. Split the $3, giving the customer $1.50 and increasing the profit margin $1.50.
4. Since the product is improved, set a new price above $32, and advertise its improved quality.

Choose one of these courses of action, then select from the following list an argument that supports your recommended action:

a. A business is entitled to as much profit as competition will allow.
b. Company management has a moral obligation to its customers to lower prices whenever possible.
c. The company is entitled to a larger profit to recover its research costs.
d. Raising the price shows that the quality is higher.
e. To decrease the price would lower the prestige of the product.
f. The company would increase total profit through increased sales.

BUSINESS CASE 13-2

Advertising a "New Product"

The Kemper Company produces a complete line of assorted jams, jellies, and canned fruits. It has been successful and has experienced an acceptable growth in company sales and profits for the past twenty years. Eighteen months ago it introduced a Star brand of peanut butter, which is packaged in 12-, 16-, and 20-ounce jars.

The Kemper plant is located in Louisiana, and its products are sold in twelve southern and southwestern states. Its complete line of products is sold through six wholesale grocery companies and three large food brokers. The food brokers serve the Memphis, Dallas, and Oklahoma City areas.

In eight of the twelve states, Kemper products are stocked in 80 percent of all independent food stores and voluntary chains. In the remaining four states, distribution ranges from 60 to 75 percent of the food stores. Star brand peanut butter, however, is handled by only half the retail outlets that sell Kemper's other products.

The Kemper management team has decided that it should do something to push its peanut butter item. The six regional sales supervisors have recommended that the advertising budget be increased by $300,000. This budget increase has been approved. However, there was a division of opinion among the company executives. Should they spend this money advertising Star brand peanut butter or all Kemper products, with some emphasis on the Star brand? The choice of advertising media was left to the promotion committee.

1. What types of promotion do you think are feasible in this situation?
2. Which type of promotion would you single out as the one on which the largest amount of money should be spent?

FINANCING AND INSURING THE ENTERPRISE

PART 5

BUSINESS FINANCE AND INVESTMENTS 14

STUDY OBJECTIVES

WHEN YOU HAVE FINISHED READING THIS CHAPTER, YOU SHOULD BE ABLE TO

ONE Identify the three major objectives of financial management

TWO Distinguish between equity financing and debt financing; working capital and fixed capital

THREE Compare the advantages and disadvantages of financing by stocks and bonds as a source of long-term financing

FOUR Explain the difference between income stocks and growth stocks and investment with speculation

FIVE Describe the four important dates related to the declaration of dividends

SIX Discuss the purpose of security markets and the stockbroker's role in serving a client

IN THE NEWS

Discount Dividend Reinvestment—A Good Way to Make Money for Both Corporations and Investors!

The American Telephone and Telegraph Company devised a plan that seems to have caught on with its investors and with other companies as well. Stockholders can now purchase new shares of stock with the dividends they receive on their existing stock at 95 percent of the current market price.

The plan has met with considerable success because investors get a bargain. Not only do they get stock below market rates but they do not have to pay a broker's commission. Since the program was adopted six years ago, about fifty additional companies have adopted similar programs. Overall growth of the discount plan has been phenomenal. It is estimated that last year over $1 billion, or 10 percent of all the money raised by stock offerings, came from stockholders participating in discount reinvestment plans.

The companies that use stock discount programs include such industrial giants as Allied Chemical, International Paper, Standard Brands, and Union Carbide. Smaller companies include American Security, Carter Hawley Hale, and Kemper Insurance.

Dividend reinvestment combined with discount share purchases certainly serves stockholders well. It also serves the companies as a source of cash and capital that can be raised in an orderly, ongoing fashion.

It is frightening how difficult it is to compete in the financial markets.

JOHN D. MORROW
CONOCO, Inc.

The primary purpose of all businesses is to earn a profit by producing and distributing goods or services. To achieve this goal requires a continuous supply of capital to operate the business. (*Capital*, as used here, includes both money and credit.) It is the flow of these capital funds within the firm about which financial management is concerned. If the amount of funds is slowed down, the amount of profit or even the firm's survival will be affected.

Management of capital is a task usually assigned to a financial officer—the treasurer or controller. The financial manager has the responsibility for achieving the following objectives:

1. Evaluate sources of funds and their costs
2. Decide upon fund sources to be used
3. Determine how the funds are to be effectively used

The average enterprise uses two categories of debt financing: short-term and long-term obligations. Short-term financing, which is discussed in Chapter 15, represents debts having a maturity of less than one year. In this chapter we focus on long-term debt obligations of one year or longer. We also examine the security markets.

NATURE OF CAPITAL NEEDS

A firm's profitability is largely determined by the way its capital funds are managed. Therefore the logical course of action is to (1) determine the amount and kind of capital required and (2) plan its use to fit the needs.

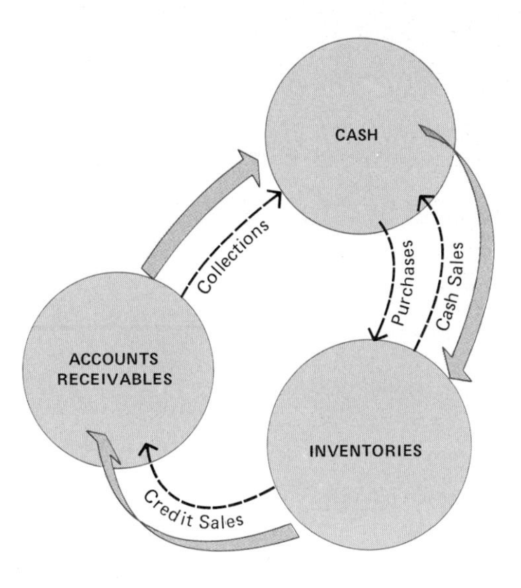

FIGURE 14-1

The circular flow of working capital and the firm's operating cycle.

Types of Capital

The capital requirements of an enterprise can be divided into two main categories: working capital and fixed capital. The use of this capital is reflected by the assets listed on the firm's balance sheet. **ASSETS** are **items of monetary value owned by a business.**

The businessperson often refers to the sum total of current assets as the "working capital" of the firm. These typically consist of cash, inventories, and accounts and notes receivable. Accountants define **working capital** as the excess of current assets over current liabilities. This is sometimes called **net working capital.** For purposes of this discussion, **WORKING CAPITAL** is **the value of the assets that can readily be turned into cash for current use in operating the firm**—the excess of current assets over current liabilities.

Working capital circulates within the firm by revolving from one form to another, as shown in Figure 14-1. This emphasizes its constant change from cash to inventories to accounts receivable and finally to cash. The main purpose of working capital is to provide funds to pay current bills. The task of financial management is to make certain there is neither too much nor too little working capital on hand. Figure 14-2 shows the kinds of current assets used as working capital.

Acquiring **fixed capital** involves a different kind of financial planning than for working capital. Fixed capital is used to purchase assets needed for long periods. Examples are buildings and land. **FIXED CAPITAL** is **money invested in fixed assets to be used over a long period of time.** Since fixed assets are of a permanent nature, they become part of the permanent capital structure. Figure 14-3 illustrates the various kinds of fixed assets used in a business.

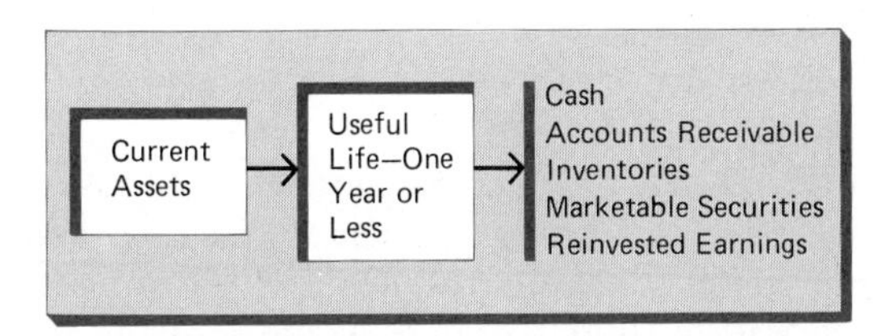

FIGURE 14-2

Working capital assets.

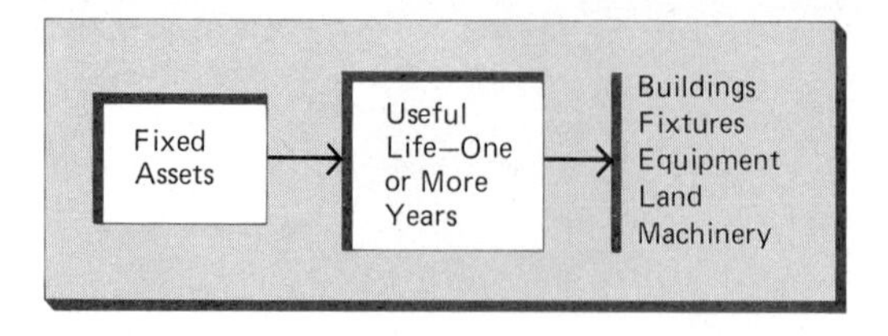

FIGURE 14-3
Fixed capital assets.

The amount of fixed capital required depends on several factors. For one thing, large firms require more fixed capital than small ones. Service-type firms can be started with less fixed capital than manufacturing establishments. Changes in consumer preferences, new competition, and population trends are other factors. All of these factors require planning in advance in order to avoid making errors in fixed asset acquisitions. For most firms, fixed capital assets are the largest investment in the business.

Managing cash for big corporations has taken on a high degree of sophistication. "Cash managers" move millions of dollars with the finesse of a short-order cook. A million dollars can earn as much as $100,000 a year if it is not left idle but is invested in short-term money-market instruments.

Computers help these modern money managers to know daily the amount of cash available. Five years ago about half the cash managers (or asset managers) were about to retire, recalls T. W. Thompson, vice-president of New York's Chemical Bank. Now 80 percent are sharp young MBAs.

At the Monsanto Company Robert Westoby watches tens of millions of dollars flow daily through the company's many bank accounts. He runs a portfolio of investments ranging from $150 million to $350 million, depending on the time of year. He squeezes every dollar he can out of idle funds by investing them quickly in treasury bills, certificates of deposit, banker's acceptances, and so forth. Some cash may only be invested for a very few days, but the net result is additional cash for Monsanto.

LONG-TERM CAPITAL SOURCES

Fixed capital is best obtained from funds provided by owners or creditors who will not be repaid for several years. Regardless of the legal form of business ownership, the following are among the sources of business capital.

1. Owner's equity capital (proprietorships and partnerships)
2. Sales of securities (stocks and bonds)
3. Retained earnings (reinvestment of profits)
4. Lease financing (lease contracts)

Funds originally contributed by the owners as partners or stockholders are classified as a firm's net worth and make up the equity capital.

Small firms are limited in the amount of funds they can raise. Therefore long-term financing for these firms is usually from fixed asset mortgages and other forms of debt capital. Beginning a business on a limited budget is risky because of one's limited availability to raise more funds to operate.

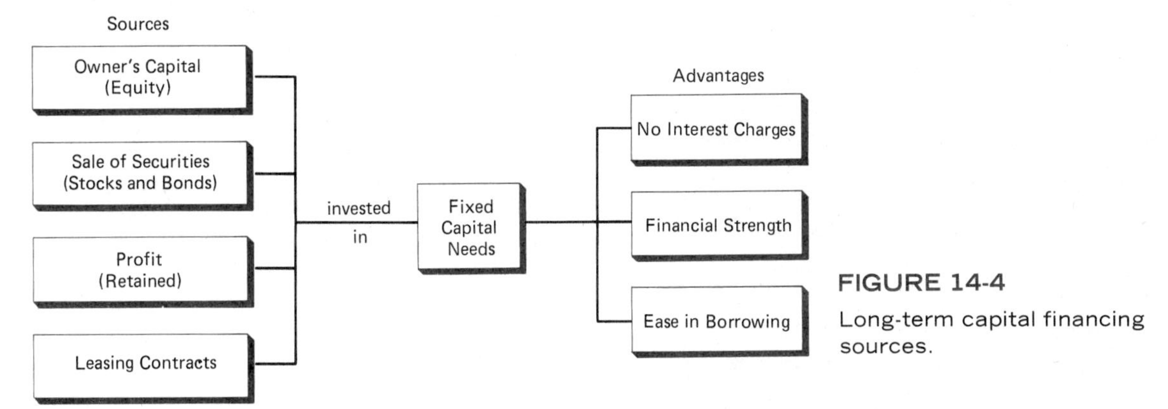

FIGURE 14-4
Long-term capital financing sources.

Big corporations have a distinct advantage, since they are able to sell securities through organized security exchanges. Another alternative for larger businesses is to issue bonds. Figure 14-4 shows various sources of long-term funds and their advantages, for which these funds are used.

Pros and Cons of Equity Financing

The equity section of a balance sheet shows the owner's equity in the business. **EQUITY** is **the ownership claim to the resources of the firm.** Ownership can be either (1) the initial funds or services contributed by the owner, (2) the additional money contributed later, or (3) the reinvested profits earned by the business. The use of equity financing offers the following advantages:

1. There are no interest charges to be paid the owner.
2. A firm financed by equity capital is financially stronger and better able to withstand a business recession than one that uses debt.
3. Assuming the firm is well financed in the beginning, the owner's ability to obtain borrowed capital is improved.

The disadvantages, however, cannot be ignored. One disadvantage is that equity financing is not always a dependable and available source of money. Then, too, the owner may find it difficult to obtain more funds in sufficient quantities to meet various needs. Adding a partner does not always prove satisfactory.

Financing by Sale of Stocks and Bonds

Stock financing generally attracts more capital than can be obtained by other forms of ownership. Corporations can issue more than one kind of stock to satisfy investors. Some investors choose to invest in preferred stocks or bonds rather than in common stock. The major differences between stocks and bonds as a source of funds are as follows.

Stocks	Bonds
1. Owning stock is a direct ownership.	1. Bonds are a direct debt of the corporation, along with interest.
2. Dividends are distributed from profits but are not paid unless declared by the directors.	2. Bond interest is an expense deductible from corporate income.
3. Stocks carry no maturity date, and there is no obligation to repay the owner his or her investment.	3. Bond principal must be repaid at a specific time as stipulated, and bondholders may foreclose if interest is in default.

MARION O. SANDLER

Marion O. Sandler, who grew up in Biddeford, Maine, has come a long way since receiving her B.A. degree in economics from Wellesley College in 1952. At this writing, she is Vice Chairman and a member of the Board of Directors and Co-Managing Officer of Golden West Financial Corporation. In addition, she is Vice Chairman, Co-Managing Officer and Director of World Savings and Loan Association, a subsidiary, also of Oakland, California. As a holding company, Golden West has the second largest savings and loan branch system in the nation and the Company's common stock is listed on the New York and Pacific Stock Exchange.

In 1953, Mrs. Sandler completed the Harvard-Radcliffe Graduate Program in Business Administration. She also holds an M.B.A. degree conferred by New York University Graduate School of Business Administration. As a student, she earned several academic honors. As an undergraduate, Mrs. Sandler was elected to Phi Beta Kappa, a national honorary fraternity. She is also a member of Beta Gamma Sigma, a national honorary society for business school graduates. As a graduate student, she was the first woman to win the Money Marketeers Thesis Prize for the best graduate thesis in the field of investments.

Mrs. Sandler began her career in business as assistant buyer, Bloomingdale's, New York City. Two years later, she joined Dominick & Dominick, a New York securities firm, where she was the first woman admitted to the firm's training program. By 1956, Mrs. Sandler was a security analyst.

Her next assignment was Senior Financial Analyst with the brokerage firm of Oppenheimer and Company, New York City. In this position, she specialized in the analysis of savings and loan associations. Mrs. Sandler was recognized as one of the nation's leading analysts and served as a consultant to various institutional investors such as insurance companies, mutual and pension funds.

In 1963, she and her attorney husband, Herbert Sandler, moved to California. They formed Golden West Financial Corporation and purchased Golden West Savings and Loan Association for $4 million. By the end of 1977, after ten acquisitions, the assets of Golden West increased from $3.9 million to $2.6 billion. It is reported that Mrs. Sandler is very easy to work with provided you meet her high standards.

Retained Earnings

Profit retained in the business is another source of business financing. **Retained earnings** are profits of the firm that have not been paid as dividends to stockholders. As such, retained earnings are the major source of money for future growth. The typical American corporation retains between 35 and 60 percent of its earnings and pays the rest as dividends on common stocks each year. Usually a corporation's financial management will try to maintain a balance between retaining earnings and declaring sufficient dividends to satisfy the stockholders. Some corporations have been known to retain all earnings and declare stock dividends. These dividends are not taxable to the stockholders until the shares are sold.

Lease Financing

Leasing as a method of obtaining assets has become very popular. Originally the emphasis was on real estate leasing, but during the past decade firms have been able to lease all kinds of fixed assets. These items include automobiles, buses, highway and railroad equipment, copy machines, and data-processing equipment. Under a lease arrangement, the lessee (the firm granted the lease) requires less capital than if making an outright purchase. Advantages and disadvantages of leasing from the viewpoint of the lessee are as follows.

Advantages	Disadvantages
1. It helps to free working capital.	1. The cost of leasing is high.
2. It provides equipment needed temporarily.	2. There is lack of accumulation of any equity.
3. It avoids the risk of obsolescence.	3. The lessee acquires no value at end of lease.
4. There are tax incentives.	

LONG-TERM DEBT FINANCING: BONDS

The sale of bonds is widely used by corporations to obtain long-term financing. A **BOND** is **a certificate of indebtedness indicating debt that is owed the bondholder by the corporation.** It is a corporation debt that matures at a stated future date on which interest is paid annually or semi-annually.

Trading on the Equity

The use of debt capital rather than equity capital is one way that financial management can increase the return on equity capital. A corporation may choose to borrow when debt financing appears to be the most economical method of obtaining needed funds. At other times a corporation may find that the retention of earnings is a better way to obtain funds. In general it is considered wise to borrow if more can be earned on borrowed funds than the funds cost. For example, to borrow at 10 percent and earn 15 percent is profitable financing for anyone, incorporated or not. This principle is known as **trading on the equity,** or leverage.

Trading on the equity may work in reverse. If business conditions worsen and earnings on total capital fall below 10 percent, the leverage factor is no longer favorable. The bankruptcy of the W. T. Grant Company was due in part to the company's inability to earn enough to pay the interest charges on its debt financing.

Advantages and Disadvantages of Bond Financing

Financing by bonds offers several advantages:

1. The sale of bonds does not affect management control. Unlike stockholders, bondholders have no voting rights.
2. Bond interest is a deductible expense.
3. Borrowing does not dilute the shareholders' equity because no additional shares are issued.

There are some disadvantages. The debt must be repaid with interest. And the fixed interest charges may become a financial burden during periods of little or no earnings.

Classes of Bonds

There are several classes of bonds. Most corporation bonds are sold in $1,000 denominations. The type of bond used is usually tailored to meet the needs of the individual corporation issuing it. Table 14-1 lists the various kinds of corporate bonds commonly used as a source of long-term debt financing.

Procedures for Issuing Bonds

Trust indenture. Corporation bonds are generally issued with a trust indenture—a contract between the issuing corporation and the trustee. The indenture sets forth the provisions of the bond. These provisions cover the rights and responsibilities of bondholders and a third-party trustee (often a bank). The obligations of a bond trustee are specified in the Trust Indenture Act of 1939, administered by the Securities and Exchange Commission.

Plans for Retiring Bonds

As part of the bond indenture, the issuing corporation is required to include one or more plans for retiring the bonds. This information informs the prospective investor when the bond is scheduled to be retired or paid off. Three plans are used: the serial bond plan, the sinking fund plan, and the call option plan.

TABLE 14-1
KINDS OF CORPORATION BONDS

Name of Bond	Description
Convertible bonds	Bonds convertible into other securities, such as common stock, are known as convertible bonds. The conversion privilege often appeals to the speculative impulses of some investors.
Coupon bonds	A coupon bond is not registered in the name of the owner. At maturity, it is payable to the bearer, with title passing by delivery without endorsement.
Debenture bonds	A debenture bond is not secured by a specific lien on the property but is issued against the reputation of the corporation to support the bond. Such bonds often carry a slightly higher interest rate because they include a higher degree of risk.
Equipment trust bonds (certificates)	This type of secured bond is classified as a chattel mortgage because the security consists of movable goods instead of immovable real estate. These bonds are issued by railroads to buy locomotives or other kinds of rolling stock. The bonds may be sold to a bank or insurance company with a trustee named, who carries out the provisions of the trust.
Mortgage bonds	Bonds that are secured by a conditional lien on part or all of a corporation's property are mortgage bonds. The issuing corporation uses the property, but title rests with the bond trustee.
Registered bonds	A registered bond has the owner's name written on the face of the instrument and on the records of the issuing corporation. A registered bond must be indorsed in order to be sold.
Serial bonds	Bonds of a single issue, but with various dates of maturity, are known as serial bonds.

Serial bond plan. This plan stipulates that a certain number of bonds will be retired annually, based on the sequence of the number shown on the bond certificate. A twenty-year serial bond of $20 million, for example, is really forty different bond issues of $500,000 each that have different yields to maturity. The maturity dates range from six months to twenty years. The shorter maturities of serial bonds usually have lower yields than the longer maturities.

Sinking fund plan. Bonds that provide for a sinking fund call for periodic deposits with the trustee of an amount that will provide enough money to retire the bonds when they are due. This is similar to installment financing.

Call option plan. This plan allows the corporation the right to call or buy back the bond at a stated price prior to the time the bond matures. Calling a bond before it matures might be done by the issuing corporation to take advantage of lower interest rates in the money market or to make way to issue new bonds. The maturity value is changed because the bonds are usually called at a higher price than the par (stated) value. This is a way to compensate the investor for the risk of reinvesting in new securities.

Bond Ratings

Most investors and certain government agencies prefer to rely on "ratings" given bonds and preferred stocks by qualified independent organizations. Two organizations, Standard & Poor's and Moody's, are widely quoted. A rating by either organization is considered reliable. Table 14-2 lists the bond ratings made by these two organizations. Generally speaking, most investors buying for income should consider nothing lower than BBB-rated or Baa-rated bonds.

TABLE 14-2
RISK RATING SCALES FOR BONDS

Standard & Poor's	Rating	Moody's Investors Service
AAA	Highest quality	Aaa
AA	High quality	Aa
A	Good quality	A
BBB	Medium grade, some speculative risk	Baa
BB B	Speculative with defensive qualities	Ba
CCC CC	Very speculative	B
C	Bonds with no interest being paid; may be in default	Caa
D	Lowest rating	C

LONG-TERM CAPITAL FINANCING: STOCKS

The second method by which corporations raise equity funding for long-term use involves the sale of ownership called **stock**. Stock ownership can be either **common** or **preferred.**

Common Stock

When a corporation decides to expand significantly, it may sell stock. Management may use, at its discretion, all the money obtained from this source. There is no legal requirement for the company to pay back to the investors the price of the shares. There is no guarantee of a dividend.

Common stock is issued either as par value or no-par-value. The value printed on the stock certificate is the **PAR VALUE.** Some states use the par value as a basis for taxing the corporation. A company should not issue common stock at less than par value, otherwise stockholders are liable to creditors for the difference between the price paid and the par value. When common stock is sold originally for more than par, the difference is called **paid-in-surplus.** When no stated value is on the stock certificate, it is known as **no-par-value** stock.

Common stock has other values in addition to par and no-par value. Two values commonly used are **book value** and **market value.** Book value is found by dividing the number of common shares outstanding into the total assets minus all debt and minus the preferred-stock value. Book value provides stockholders with some idea of the total dollars per share that have been invested in the corporation common stock and how much would be available should the company liquidate. The market value is easily determined by referring to daily stock-market prices on the financial page of the daily newpaper.

Corporations sometimes "buy back" their own stock. During a period when corporations feel that their stock is undervalued, it may be financially sound to buy up shares of their own stock on the open market. This phenomenon was widely observed during the late 1970s.

During 1977, 1978, and 1979, businesses were pushing corporate takeovers, mergers, and stock repurchases. The single most important reason for the binge of acquisitions and stock repurchases was the replacement value of corporate assets, according to Leon Cooperman, partner in Goldman, Sachs & Co. "It's cheaper to buy than to build," he said.

Cooperman concludes that during that period, companies reduced the amount of stock on the market by about $7.4 billion, through the purchasing of their own stock and the stock of others.

Stockholders' preemptive right. In addition to the right to receive dividends and vote on corporate matters, the stockholder has what is known as a **preemptive right.** This right gives present stockholders the opportunity, based on the number of shares owned, to subscribe to any new issue of common stock. Selling stock on this basis to current stockholders is known as a **privileged**

subscription, or a **preemptive rights offering**. This right is a matter of common law rather than statute law. In about half the states, this right is limited or denied by statute.

To make a rights offering effective, new shares are sold to existing shareholders at a price below prevailing market prices. This offering price, called the **subscription price**, encourages stockholders to buy shares to which they are entitled. For example, if common stock is to be increased by 20 percent through the sale of new shares, each shareholder might receive the right to subscribe to one new share for every five old shares owned. If the shareholder declines to subscribe, he or she may sell the subscription rights. Fractional shares, however, are not traded.

Stock warrants. **STOCK WARRANTS** are **options to buy a specific number of shares, generally common, at a predetermined price.** They are similar to stock rights, for they entitle the holder to buy shares of stock at a fixed price. They differ in that they are offered for a longer time, and they may not expire on a given date. The theoretical value of a warrant depends upon the value of the stock its holder is entitled to buy. For example, a warrant that entitles the holder to buy stock at $25 (exercise price) has a basic or theoretical value of $5 when the stock reaches $30 (market price) on the trading date. The formula is

Market price − Exercise price = Basic price

($30 − $25 = $5)

Warrants are often used to sweeten the sale of a bond issue or preferred stock that might otherwise be difficult to sell.

Stock options. A **STOCK OPTION** is **a privilege given to key executives to purchase company stock under certain conditions of price and time.** For example, a company allows its executives to buy 5,000 shares each of common stock within a time period at $25 a share, which is the current price, without paying a commission. The plan must be approved by the Internal Revenue Service. Later if the market price advanced to $60 a share, those executives would have a realized profit of $175,000 by selling their stock. This plan is often used to provide a long-term incentive.

Stock splits. A **STOCK SPLIT** is **a division of common stock outstanding into additional units.** If you owned 30 shares and received a two-for-one stock split, your 30 shares would increase to 60. Each new share would now be worth half of the original share. The usual reason for a stock split is to bring the market price down into trading range of more investors. If a stock selling for $200 a share has a four-to-one split, the new price "when issued" (w.i.) would be set at $50 a share.

A stockholder owning 100 shares of General Electric common during the mid-1920s would by now have a total of 4,800 shares, mostly because of stock splits. If there had been no splits but the stock continued to rise in price, as it did, GE shares would now be quoted at about $5,000 per share.

Stock dividends. A **STOCK DIVIDEND is a distribution of profits or capital paid in stock.** Sometimes they are paid on a percentage basis. A 10 percent stock dividend means that one new share will be issued for each 10 shares you may hold. Thus if you owned 12 shares at the time the 10 percent stock dividend was declared, you would be entitled to receive 1⅕ (1.2) new shares for each 10 you owned. Since fractional shares are not issued, you would be able to buy on the market enough fractional shares to equal one full share. Stock shares are quoted daily on organized exchanges.

Preferred Stock

In addition to issuing common stock, many corporations raise additional capital by selling preferred stock. This is stock that carries certain preferences over common stock. These are stated on the preferred-stock certificate and in the corporation charter. Here are some of the special features of preferred stock (although these are not necessarily found in all preferred stock):

1. Preference as to assets
2. Preference as to dividends
3. Guaranteed dividends ahead
4. Convertibility
5. Cumulative and noncumulative
6. Preference in liquidation

The board of directors cannot omit dividends on preferred stock and declare a dividend only to common-stock holders. Preferred-stock holders know at the time they buy the stock what the dividend rate will be. Thus if an investor owns 100 shares of 7 percent preferred stock with a $100 par value, the maximum return is $700 in any one year. If the corporation assets are liquidated, holders of preferred stock have a preference over common-share holders when funds from the sale of assets are distributed. As a rule, however, preferred stock does not give the holder voting privileges, whereas common stock does.

Preferred stock may be cumulative or noncumulative. Should the directors decide not to pay a dividend one year, the dividend on cumulative stock carries over to the next year or until it is finally paid in full. Noncumulative stock, however, provides that if the dividends are not paid during the year in which they are earned, the company is not obligated to carry dividends forward.

The use of convertible preferred stock in planning corporate mergers has become popular. Such preferred stock is convertible into some other form of securities, usually common stock. Usually, conversion is at the option of the stockholder. It is usually permitted when the common stock reaches a certain price. If the common stock should reach a high price, holders of convertible preferred would be allowed to exchange their preferred for common in hopes that the common would go higher. Convertibility permits the preferred holder to participate more fully in the company's success if it is achieved but to retain his or her preferred position otherwise.

STOCK EXCHANGES AND SECURITIES MARKETS

Thus far we have dealt with the problems of determining long-term capital needs, the sources of funds, and the types of securities—preferred and common stocks, and bonds—that are used. There is a widespread use of and interest in stocks

FIGURE 14-5

An exterior view of the New York Stock Exchange. (Photo courtesy of Irene Springer.)

and bonds by individual investors, as well as by business firms seeking capital. Thus more than a dozen large and small securities markets, referred to as stock exchanges, have been organized in the United States to provide centers for trading (buying and selling securities at auction).

These markets are meeting places where those seeking capital can negotiate with the representatives of those who have capital to invest.

The organized exchanges are actually auction markets where traders and investors, through brokers, negotiate by setting "asking" prices and making "bids" on securities.

The New York Stock Exchange

Often called the "Big Board," the New York Stock Exchange is a corporation with more than twelve hundred members. Each member has purchased a "seat" on the exchange. This membership gives its holder the privilege of trading on the exchange floor. Members include member-firm corporations, registered traders, floor brokers, and specialists. Member firms are the brokerage houses that deal with the public. Their seats are owned by firm owners. Registered traders buy and sell stocks for their own personal accounts. Floor brokers help commission brokers to expedite orders. Specialists are exchange members assigned to certain stocks for which they will make a market. They may also buy and sell for their own accounts.

More than 2,100 stocks of almost 1,600 companies were listed and traded on the New York Exchange on July 31, 1980. The price of exchange seats has ranged from a low of $17,000 to a high of $625,000. The New York Exchange was 188 years old in 1980.

The American Stock Exchange

Also located in New York City, the American Stock Exchange was started in the 1850s and is the second largest stock exchange. It was known as the New York Curb Exchange until 1953. It has a full membership of approximately five hundred seats and 400 associate members. A total of 1,200 stock issues representing more than 1,150 companies were listed and traded on the American Exchange on July 31, 1980. Its listing requirements are less stringent than those on the New York Exchange.

Regional and Local Stock Exchanges

The principal regional exchanges are the Midwest Stock Exchange in Chicago, the Pacific Stock Exchange, and the Philadelphia Stock Exchange. Other regional exchanges are located in Boston, Cincinnati, Honolulu, Chicago (the Board of Trade), Salt Lake City (Intermountain), and Spokane.

In addition to these regional exchanges, there is a huge local over-the-counter (OTC) market where unlisted stocks are sold. This market is not a particular location. Rather it is a method of doing business where some fifty-five thousand unlisted securities are bought and sold by a large group of brokers and dealers. As agents, they make a market for those who want to invest or sell. This market is known as the "third market." It is patronized by large institutional investors, including mutual funds and insurance companies. The commissions are negotiated rather than determined by auction. Prices of OTC securities are supplied by the National Association of Securities Dealers to newspapers through NASDAQ, its automated system for reporting quotations.

Foreign Stock Exchanges

One of the oldest stock exchanges in the world is the London Stock Exchange. It lists and trades about seven times the number of issues listed on the New York Stock Exchange. The Paris Stock Exchange (Bourse) is an active market. Exchanges in Switzerland include Zurich, Geneva, Basel, and Lausanne. The Toronto Stock Exchange has over one thousand listed securities. There are nine exchanges in Japan, with the largest being in Tokyo.

Coming: A Centralized Securities Market

The long-awaited formation of a central market for securities and a campaign toward reform finally became possible in 1975. Congress, by enactment of the Securities Acts Amendments, provided the Securities and Exchange Commission (SEC) with authority to implement such a market. The general objective is to establish a nationwide system so that all investors will have their orders executed in the specific market that offers the best price for a specific stock.

A nationwide system linking all existing markets electronically would be required. Stock brokers and dealers could route orders to all markets trading the stock in order to obtain the most favorable execution. A central file would establish storage of all limit orders. The Intermarket Trading System linking all the regional exchanges, and the New York and the American exchanges, with the National Association of Security Dealers would create a central market. So far, however, total market reform as mandated by Congress has been a slow process and has not yet been accomplished.

Function of the Securities Markets

Within our economic system, securities exchanges operate as marketplaces where buyers meet sellers through authorized agents. It is possible for two persons in widely separated areas of the United States, through their brokers, to trade with each other without personal contact. You may wonder why you cannot buy a stock directly from a corporation listed on the exchange, just as you buy an automobile from your dealer. The reason is that a corporation has only so many shares outstanding. If you want to buy 10, 25, 100, or 1,000 shares, you usually must buy from someone who already owns (or a combination of several who own) that number of shares. You must buy from a broker who is the agent for each party.

There are certain facts worth keeping in mind about buying or selling stock on an exchange:

1. When you buy stock, you buy from another person through a broker.
2. When you sell stock, you sell to another person through a broker.
3. The exchange provides the marketplace for the sale.
4. The exchange neither buys, sells, nor sets the price of your stock.
5. Through their daily operations, the exchanges provide a continuous market with a constant release of market information.

Stock quotations. Many newspapers publish daily stock quotations of listed securities on a national, regional, or local market. Figure 14-6 shows a partial list of stocks, with explanations given in the margins. For example, sales recorded in lots of 100 shares are "round" lots. Orders for less than 100 shares are "odd-lot" sales. Price quotations are in dollars and fractions ranging from 1/8 to 7/8. A quotation of 25⅝ indicates that the price of the stock is $25.625 per share.

The symbol *P/E* means "price-earnings ratio." This is an analytical ratio that refers to earnings divided into the price of the stock. A stock selling at $30 with annual earnings per share of $2 has a P/E ratio of 15. The P/E ratio is a highly regarded measure of stock value because it gives an indication of corporate success measured against the current stock price. For instance, if a stock has a very high ratio ranging from 25 to 40, this does not necessarily indicate high

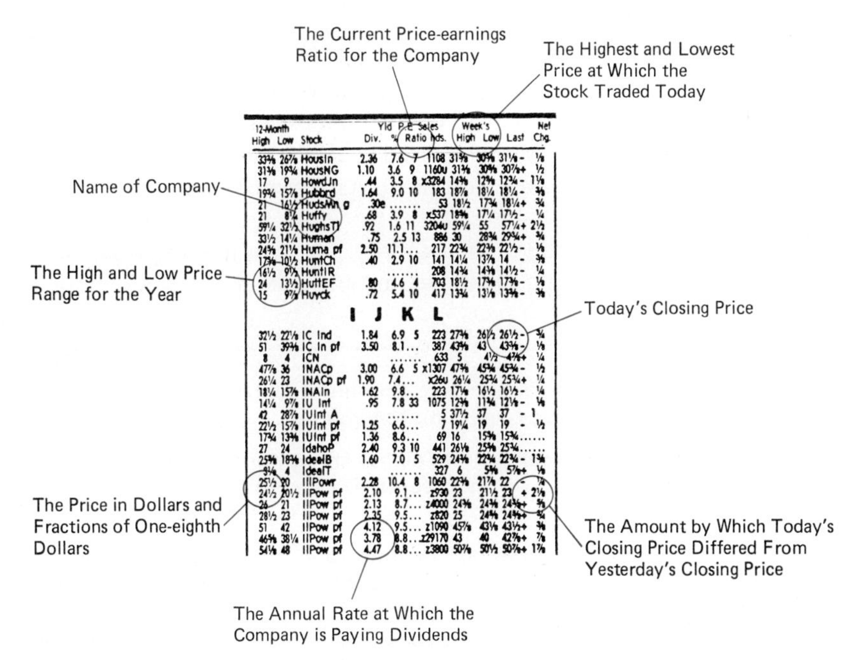

12-Month High	Low	Stock	Div.	Yld %	P-E Ratio	Sales 100s	Week's High	Low	Last	Net Chg.
33¾	26⅞	HousIn	2.36	7.6	7	1108	31⅝	30⅝	31⅛	−⅛
31⅜	19¾	HousNG	1.10	3.6	9	1160u	31⅜	30⅝	30⅞	+½
17	9	HowdJn	.44	3.5	8	x3284	14⅜	12⅝	12¾	−1⅛
19¾	15⅞	Hubbrd	1.64	9.0	10	183	18⅞	18¼	18¼	−⅜
21	16½	HudsMn g	.30e	...	...	53	18½	17¾	18¼	+¾
21	8¼	Huffy	.68	3.9	8	x537	18⅝	17¼	17½	−¼
59¼	32½	HughsTl	.92	1.6	11	3204u	59¼	55	57¼	+2½
33½	14¼	Human	.75	2.5	13	886	30	28¾	29¾	+¾
24⅜	21⅛	Huma pf	2.50	11.1	...	217	22¾	22⅜	22½	−⅛
17⅜	10½	HuntCh	.40	2.9	10	141	14¼	13⅞	14	−⅜
16½	9½	HuntIR		...	...	208	14¾	14⅜	14½	−¼
24	13½	HuttEF	.80	4.6	4	703	18½	17⅜	17⅜	−⅛
15	9⅞	Huyck	.72	5.4	10	417	13¾	13⅛	13⅜	−⅜
		I J K L								
32½	22⅛	IC Ind	1.84	6.9	5	223	27⅜	26½	26½	−¾
51	39⅜	IC In pf	3.50	8.1	...	387	43⅝	43	43⅜	−⅛
8	4	ICN		...	...	633	5	4½	4⅞	+¼
47⅞	36	INACp	3.00	6.6	5	x1307	47⅜	45¾	45¾	−½
26¼	23	INACp pf	1.90	7.4	...	x26u	26¼	25¾	25¾	+¼
18¼	15⅞	INAIn	1.62	9.8	...	223	17⅛	16½	16½	−¼
14¼	9⅞	IU Int	.95	7.8	33	1075	12⅜	11¾	12⅛	−⅛
42	28⅞	IUInt A		...	...	5	37½	37	37	−1
22½	15⅞	IUInt pf	1.25	6.6	...	7	19¼	19	19	−½
17¾	13⅜	IUInt pf	1.36	8.6	...	69	16	15⅜	15¾	......
27	24	IdahoP	2.40	9.3	10	441	26⅛	25⅝	25¾	......
25⅜	18⅜	IdealB	1.60	7.0	5	529	24⅜	22¾	22¾	−1⅜
8¾	4	IdealT		...	...	327	6	5⅜	5⅞	+⅛
25½	20	IllPowr	2.28	10.4	8	1060	22⅜	21⅞	22	−⅛
24½	20½	IllPow pf	2.10	9.1	...	z930	23	21½	23	+2⅛
26	21	IllPow pf	2.13	8.7	...	z4000	24⅜	24⅜	24⅜	+⅝
28½	23	IllPow pf	2.35	9.5	...	z820	25	24⅜	24⅜	+⅜
51	42	IllPow pf	4.12	9.5	...	z1090	45⅞	43⅛	43½	+⅜
46⅝	38¼	IllPow pf	3.78	8.8	...	z29170	43	40	42⅞	+⅞
54⅛	48	IllPow pf	4.47	8.8	...	z3800	50⅞	50½	50⅞	+1⅞

FIGURE 14-6

The meaning of daily newspaper stock-market quotations.

quality. Rather, it means earnings currently are low, with future earnings expected to be higher. Generally, speculative investment stocks sell at either extremely low or extremely high P/E ratios. Companies with outstanding growth potential tend to have higher P/E ratios than income stocks.

Bond quotations. Corporate bonds are quoted daily in many newspapers but in a different manner than stocks. Most bonds are quoted in denominations of $100, although the face value is $1,000. For example, a bond quoted at 97 in your newspaper means that the trading price is $970 on that date. It is selling for 97 percent of par—the price of its denomination. Stocks are quoted at the exact price for which they are being bought or sold. Bonds are grouped into several categories, such as domestic corporate bonds, U.S. government bonds, and foreign bonds.

The fulcrum around which the bond yield varies is the interest rate. It is fixed for the life of the bond. As a rule the bond yield is stated as a percentage of the face value of the bond. Thus a bond paying 7 percent interest on $1,000 yields the investor $70 per annum ($70 ÷ $1,000). If the market price drops to $900, the yield goes up. But if the market price increases, the yield declines.

SECURITY INVESTMENTS AND THE STOCKBROKER

Investing in common stocks as a source of wealth is a convenient and affordable way to participate directly in the private-enterprise system. A corporation offers its shares of common stocks in order to obtain capital for the business. Once these stocks are sold to the public, they become investment securities for the owners.

Role of the Stockbroker

Whether you live in Chico (California) or Chicago, if you decide to invest in a stock, you begin by consulting with your local stockbroker. Most likely he or she has the title of "registered representative," or "account executive."

The main function of a stockbroker, who is usually a member of a brokerage firm, is to buy and sell securities for customers. As a compensation, the broker is paid a commission fee.

Women stockbrokers are still in the minority, but their number is growing. Furthermore, women are showing an increasing interest in the stock market.

A few years ago most of the clients that women stockbrokers dealt with were men. But today things are beginning to even out.

At Merrill Lynch about 10 percent of the eighty-three hundred brokers are women. The women brokers say that about 80 percent of their clients are men.

Most women brokers say that they are seldom rejected because they are female. The male clients seem to think a successful woman broker has to be twice as good as a man to get where she is.

XON	MOB	T	F	AC
55½	3s42	10-s 58-1/8	4s42	2s39¼

FIGURE 14-7
Reading a stock-market ticker tape.

Once you have selected a broker and have arranged to open an account, your next step is to discuss your investment objective with the broker. Then you and your broker would discuss several stocks and bonds that seemed to satisfy your investment objectives.

Many brokerage offices are equipped with a large ticker-tape screen that electronically displays security transactions seconds after they happen on national exchanges. In Figure 14-7 a segment of this ticker tape shows the names of the stocks, the number of shares traded, and the most recent price. Only the price is shown when the sale is for 100 shares. For multiples of 100, the number of hundreds of shares is given. For sales above 1,000 shares, the exact number is given. Each stock has its own symbol. Following is an explanation of the stock symbols and numbers shown in Figure 14-7.

XON – 100 shares of Exxon Corporation at $55.50 per share

MOB – 300 shares of Mobil Corporation at $42 per share

T – 1,000 shares of American Telephone and Telegraph Company at $58.125 per share

F – 400 shares of Ford Motor Company at $42 per share

AC – 200 shares of American Can Company at $39.25 per share

Investment versus Speculation

Among Americans, common stocks are the most popular security investment. They are easy to buy, can be bought in small or large lots, and can easily be converted into dollars.

Definitions. The term **INVESTMENT** refers to **the purchase of securities that offer safety of principal and satisfactory yield equal to the risks. SPECULATION** is **the assumption of above-average risks for which there is anticipation of a higher financial return.** The stock trader who speculates tends to deemphasize dividends and is willing to accept more risk, hoping that large profits can be made in a short time. A **PORTFOLIO** is **a collection of investment securities owned by the investor.**

It is often suggested that before investing in any stock, one should have enough money in a savings account to meet an emergency and a reasonable amount of life insurance for protection. Assuming your reserve funds are adequate, what is your first step in beginning an investment program?

Choosing your investment objective. In contrast to the speculator, the investor determines his or her investment objective by considering one or more of the following:

1. Safety of principal
2. Growth in the value of the asset
3. Income from dividends

Safety of principal. If investors are unwilling to risk the possible losses inherent in common stocks, then good-quality bonds and preferred stocks may

TABLE 14-3
SELECTED COMMON STOCKS WITH GROWTH POTENTIAL

Name of Corporation	Recent Price	Annual Dividend	Per Share Earnings	Percent Yield	P/E Ratio
Abbott Laboratories	$39	$1.00	$2.95	2.6	13
Hewlett-Packard*	58	.40	4.00	0.7	15
International Business Machines	63	3.44	5.10	5.5	13
Lilly (Eli)	58	2.10	4.55	3.8	13
Xerox	61	2.40	6.80	3.9	9
Schlumberger	92	1.10	4.90	1.2	19

*2-for-1 split July 30, 1979.

SOURCE: Financial reports and stock prices, January 7, 1980.

be purchased. These securities offer the greatest protection for the investor. At the same time they may continue to pay a good yield on the investment.

Selecting growth stocks. The investor who chooses growth stocks to satisfy the growth objective selects companies whose earnings are expected to ourperform those of other companies. Common stocks of growth companies generally exhibit the ability to achieve consistent and above-average sales and earnings.

Growth investors, in contrast to income investors, are not interested in buying stocks for current income. Instead they hope the growth shares will increase in value, which will allow them to sell the stock for a long-term gain. Table 14-3 shows a portfolio of common stocks noted at one time for their growth prospects. Observe that these stocks all offer low percentage yields and have high P/E ratios. The annual paid dividends represent but a small part of the total earnings per share. The managements of these companies have adopted a policy of reinvesting earnings rather than declare larger dividends. The foresighted buyer who invested $10,000 in IBM common stock in 1950 for its growth prospects now has stock valued well above $500,000.

Choosing common stocks for income. Choosing common stocks for income is relatively easy as compared with choosing growth stocks. First you look

TABLE 14-4
SELECTED COMMON STOCKS WITH HIGH-INCOME POTENTIAL

Name of Corporation	Recent Price	Annual Dividend	Per Share Earnings	Percent Yield	P/E Ratio
Carolina Power & Light	$19	$2.08	$3.20	10.9	6
Commonwealth Edison	20	2.60	2.75	13.0	7
Middle South Utilities	13	1.58	2.46	12.2	5
New England Electric	22	2.36	3.30	10.7	7
Oklahoma Gas & Electric	13	1.60	1.50	12.3	9

SOURCE: Financial reports and stock prices, January 7, 1980.

TABLE 14-5
PORTFOLIO INVESTMENT OBJECTIVES

Securities	Safety	Growth	Income
Common stocks	Least	Best	Varies
Preferred stocks	High	Varies	Steady
Bonds	Highest	Very little	Very steady

for a company that has a consistent record of paying high dividends. Then you determine whether the company has maintained a record of periodic increases in the amount of the dividend. A stock that costs $50 per share and pays $4 in annual dividends will yield an 8 percent return ($4 ÷ $50).

Table 14-4 lists several companies noted for their high dividends. These companies have a low P/E ratio but a high percentage yield, the opposite of growth companies. As you can see in Table 14-4, these are public-utility stocks, which seem to offer high dividends. Table 14-5 compares investment objectives with kinds of securities.

Securities-Analysis Sources

In arriving at investment decisions, it is critical that investors be informed about changes occurring in the financial markets. Two of the most complete security services are Moody's *Investors' Service* and Standard & Poor's *Industry Surveys.* Standard & Poor's also offers *Dividend Records, Called Bond Record,* and the *Outlook,* available by subscription. The securities services sold on a subscription basis include among others the following:

1. *United Business Service,* 210 Newbury St., Boston, Mass.
2. *Value Line Investment Service,* 5 East 44th St., New York, N.Y.
3. *Stock Picture,* a composite of 1,700 charts, published by M. C. Horsey & Company, Salisbury Md.

Stock averages. Two widely used statistical averages concerning daily stock-market quotations are the Dow Jones (DJ) and the *New York Times* market index. The DJ averages, published by the *Wall Street Journal,* consist of four groups of stocks and five bond-price indexes. The DJ industrial average, which is the granddaddy of stock-market averages, consists of the thirty industrial companies shown in Table 14-6. The dates in parentheses indicate when each company first appeared in the average. On June 29, 1979, Chrysler Corporation and Esmark Inc. were deleted from the list. These companies were replaced by IBM and Merck & Company. Other DJ stock averages include twenty transportation companies, previously known as the "railroad" average, fifteen utility stocks, and a DJ composite average of sixty-five stocks.

The *New York Times* stock average consists of twenty-five industrial companies, twenty-five rail stocks, and a fifty-stock composite average.

Standard & Poor's 500 Stock Price Index is widely used. It is composed of four hundred industrials, forty utilities, twenty transportation, and forty finance companies (banks, investment, and life insurance). In 1966 the New York Stock Exchange began publication of its common-stock index reflecting the price changes of all common stocks on the Big Board. The American Stock Exchange index covers stocks on that exchange.

TABLE 14-6
DOW JONES INDUSTRIAL AVERAGE OF LISTED COMMON STOCKS, NEW YORK STOCK EXCHANGE

Allied Chemical Corporation	(1925)	International Harvester Company	(1925)
Aluminum Co. of America	(1959)	International Paper Company	(1901)
American Brands Inc.	(1896)	Johns-Manville Corporation	(1930)
American Can Company	(1916)	Merck & Company, Inc.	(1979)
American Telephone and Telegraph Company	(1916)	Minnesota Mining and Manufacturing Company	(1976)
Bethelehem Steel Corporation	(1928)	Owens-Illinois Inc.	(1959)
Du Pont	(1924)	Procter & Gamble Company	(1932)
Eastman Kodak Company	(1928)	Sears, Roebuck & Company	(1924)
Exxon Corporation	(1928)	Standard Oil of California	(1924)
General Electric Company	(1897)	Texaco, Incorporated	(1916)
General Foods Corporation	(1915)	Union Carbide Corporation	(1928)
General Motors Corporation	(1915)	United States Steel Corporation	(1914)
Goodyear Tire & Rubber	(1930)	United Technologies	(1933)
Inco Ltd.	(1928)	Westinghouse Electric Corporation	(1916)
International Business Machines Corporation	(1979)	Woolworth (F. W.) Company	(1924)

The Mechanics of Placing an Order

Let us assume that you have opened an account with a local broker. In consultation with the broker, you have decided to buy 100 shares (a round lot) of U.S. Steel Corporation. Your broker quotes U.S. Steel at $22 a share, with a P/E ratio of 5. The broker will ask you, "Do you want to buy at the market?" (meaning the current market price). You say "Yes," so your order becomes a market order. The broker executes your order, which takes place with remarkable speed.

Within five days the broker sends you a bill showing the amount of the transaction, commission, and taxes (if any are levied). Subsequently, your stock certificate is delivered to you by mail, or you may decide that you want your broker to keep the shares for you and act as your agent. All certificates must clear through a duly appointed transfer agent, who is responsible for all stock transfers. Stocks held by brokers in a custodian account for clients are insured under the Securities Investor Protection Corporation (SIPC) for $100,000 per each account. Replacing lost bond or stock certificates is a costly and time-consuming process. Figure 14-8 lists some vocabulary terms used in security investments and financial news.

Brokerage commission. For many years all brokerage firms charged a uniform commission. In 1975 these firms adopted a system of negotiated commissions. In other words, different brokers could charge different prices for their services. In the example above, the commission on a purchase of 100 shares of U.S. Steel at $22 per share would be about $51. "Discount" brokers, or those who merely buy and sell stocks for you and do not provide research services, have gained credibility. Today some fifty firms make up this new segment of the securities industry.

FIGURE 14-8
TERMS USED IN INVESTMENT AND FINANCIAL NEWS

BLUE-CHIP STOCKS: High-quality stocks of companies with consistent earnings and dividends with well-regarded management.

CHURNING: Excessing trade in a customer's account without acceptable justification. The purpose of churning is usually to generate more commission.

CYCLICAL STOCKS: Corporate stocks whose securities fluctuate with the business cycle. Examples of cyclical industries are autos, cement, machinery, and steel.

DECLARATION DATE: This is the date, set by directors, that the dividend is declared, either as a "regular" or as an "extra" dividend.

EX-DIVIDEND DATE: The date on which a stock sells ex-dividend (without the dividend). On and after this date, the buyer does not receive a previously declared dividend. On this date the market price is usually lowered by the amount of the dividend.

FLOWER BOND: Certain U.S. Treasury bonds that are purchased at a discount and may be turned in at par later for payment of federal estate taxes. The bonds must have been owned by the decedent at time of death.

FULLY DILUTED EARNINGS: Earnings computed on the basis of all securities that could be converted into common stock, thereby reducing earnings per share.

LIMIT ORDER: An order to buy or sell stock to be executed by the broker as indicated by the buyer or seller. A limit order to buy specifies a price below the market; a limit order to sell indicates a price above the market.

MARGIN BUYING: Most security brokers will arrange to help their customers buy securities on margin. This means that the customer pays for part of the purchase and borrows from the broker for the balance. These securities are held as security by the broker until full payment is made on the loan. If the market price of the stock drops below a certain point, the broker will ask the buyer to put up more margin to protect the loan. If the buyer is unable to do this, the broker sells the stock using the funds to cover the loan. Any funds left over may be returned to the borrower. Buying on margin enables investors to buy more shares with less of their own funds. Margin requirements are set by the Federal Reserve Board. Margins in the past have ranged from 40 percent to 100 percent of the purchase price.

WHEN ISSUED: The term "when issued" (w.i.) refers to conditional transactions in securities that are authorized but not yet issued. One may see price quotations for new stock issue, often after a stock split, marked w.i. "Discount" brokers, or those who merely buy and sell stocks for you and do not provide research services, have gained credibility. Today some fifty firms make up this new segment of the securities industry.

In 1978 discount brokers received about $90 million in revenue, or about 7 percent of all retail stock commissions. This was an increase from 3 percent the year before. Discount firms are making long-established full-service brokerage firms take notice.

The president of Paine-Webber, Inc., one of the nation's largest brokerage houses, recently warned a group of brokerage officials that they should diversify. Getting into other areas could be a safeguard against potential loss of business to discounters. The management at Merrill Lynch—the nation's largest broker—states that it, too, is aware of potential competition from the growth of business going to discounters.

Security-Market Options

Another method of investing in stocks involves calls and puts. These are option contracts to buy or sell shares at a specific price. A **call** option is a contract to buy, and a **put** option is a contract to sell. In 1973 the Chicago Board of Trade opened the Chicago Board Options Exchange (CBOE). Now option trading has expanded to the New York Stock Exchange, American Exchange, Midwest Exchange, the Pacific Coast, and Philadelphia-Baltimore-Washington exchanges.

Call option. A call is an option to buy 100 shares at a set price known as the "exercise price," or "striking price," within a specified time period. The striking price is set near the current market price in multiples of $5 or $10. If the stock is selling for $48 per share, the striking price might be set at $50 per share. The last day an option may be exercised is the **expiration date**.

The writer (seller) of the option is paid a premium for giving the buyer the right to buy the option. The writer is expected to deliver the stock when the option is exercised. The Options Clearing Corporation, which serves all the option exchanges, guarantees that the stock will be delivered if the option is exercised and that the seller will be paid.

Put options. A put gives the option owner the right to sell a specified number of shares of a designated stock at a fixed price within an agreed time period. Suppose you bought 100 shares of Coca-Cola at $20 per share. The price jumped to $40. Your paper profit is $2,000. Now you decide not to sell your stock. You think it will go higher. But to protect yourself, you buy a six-month's put. Later your stock declines to $32. You could exercise your right to "put" the stock to the option seller and force him or her to take delivery of 100 shares at $40. You would still be out the price of the put, but that is less than taking a loss of $800 ($8 × 100). On the other hand, if Coca-Cola advanced to $49, you would be out the cost of your option, but you now have stock that has increased $900 in value ($9 × 100).

OTHER LONG-TERM FINANCING SOURCES

We have already noted that large sums of capital for long-term use are obtained from the sale of stocks and bonds and retained earnings. Other financial institutions such as life insurance companies, mutual funds, pension funds, and savings and loan associations also supply long-term business financing.

Life Insurance Companies

The assets of life insurance companies have now reached more than $350 billion. Much of this is invested in corporate stocks and bonds, real estate, and mortgages on real estate. Life insurance companies finance the construction of commercial buildings, shopping centers, and apartments.

Mutual Funds

Mutual fund is a name coined to identify investment trusts and companies created for the mutual investment of funds contributed by several persons. Technically a mutual fund is a corporation whose assets are shares of stock owned by the fund shareholders. The corporation is managed by professional investment managers, who select the fund's investment portfolio.

Mutual funds are especially attractive to persons with money to invest who lack the skill or the time to make investment decisions. These funds are chartered by the state to sell their own stock to investors seeking the advantages of diversification and professional management. Investors may make monthly or one-time purchases or even quarterly investments in varying amounts. Profits are distributed in cash or are reinvested in the fund.

Pension Funds Many companies and labor unions provide funds for employee pensions. These funds invest large sums in common and preferred stocks and in real estate. Today the pension funds are valued at approximately $160 billion. These funds are regulated by the U.S. Department of Labor, the Pension Benefit Guaranty Corporation, and the Internal Revenue Service, as provided for in the Employee Retirement Income Security Act of 1974.

Savings and Loan Associations Savings and Loan Associations (S&Ls), sometimes known as building and loan associations, accept time deposits from savers. These funds are the major source of home mortgages, supplying more than half of all capital used to build housing. These mortgages are usually amortized on a monthly installment plan. About 30 percent of the approximately six thousand associations are chartered under federal laws and require the term "federal" in their title. The remaining 70 percent are state chartered. Most of the associations are members of the Federal Home Loan Bank System, similar to the Federal Reserve. Deposits are insured up to $100,000 per account by the Federal Savings and Loan Insurance Corporation, similar to the FDIC serving commercial banks.

With passage of Public Law 96-221, S&Ls after December 31, 1980 were authorized to compete with commercial banks.[1] This legislation permitted S&Ls to offer interest bearing checking accounts or NOW accounts (negotiated order of withdrawals). In addition, S&Ls may make consumer loans, issue credit cards, engage in trust and estate services, and raise capital by issuing mutual certificates.

REGULATION OF SECURITIES MARKETS

Control over the securities market is now a responsibility of both the states and the federal government. But it was not until the stock-market crash of 1929 that federal laws were passed to prosecute market manipulators and swindlers. Subsequently statutes were enacted by states and the federal government.

State Laws All states have various kinds of laws controlling security sales. These are dubbed "blue-sky laws" because they represent an attempt to stop the sale of the "blue sky" to unwary investors. Such laws seek to protect the public against fraudulent stock offers. In most states the securities commissioners enforce these laws.

Federal Laws The first federal statute dealing with the sale of stocks and bonds was enacted in 1933. The principal securities laws enacted since 1933 are summarized in Table 14-7.

[1]For further details about Public Law 96-221 (Depository Institutions Deregulation and Monetary Control Act of 1980) see Chapter 15.

TABLE 14-7
FEDERAL REGULATIONS OF SECURITY MARKETS AND SALES

Legislation	Purpose
Securities Act of 1933	Known as the "truth-in-securities law," this act requires that full disclosure of new securities be given in a registration statement and prospectus.
Securities Act of 1934	This law authorizes the SEC to administer market securities. All brokers and dealers engaged in interstate trade must register with the SEC and comply with SEC rules. The SEC and Federal Reserve Board jointly set margin requirements. The act prohibits transactions regarded as trading abuses involving over-the-counter markets.
Maloney Act of 1938	Serving as an amendment to the Securities Act of 1934, this act allows investment bankers to form associations for self-regulation. The National Association of Securities Dealers was created to regulate OTC securities.
Investment Advisors Act of 1940	All persons serving as security advisers must register with the SEC. Although registration is intended to guard against fraud, it does not indicate any degree of expertise or favorable results.
Investment Company Act of 1940	This law created the framework for the mutual-fund industry by requiring investment trust companies to register with the SEC. The term mutual funds is another name for what are technically known as investment companies.
Securities Act Amendments of 1964	The Securities Acts of 1933 and 1934 were amended in 1964 to cover securities sold over-the-counter which were assigned to the SEC. Dealers and brokers selling OTC stocks must register with the SEC.
Securities Investor Protection Act of 1970	This act created a nonprofit corporation—the Securities Investor Protection Corporation—(SIPC, pronounced sip-ic)—to protect individual accounts with brokers. If a member broker or dealer is insolvent, SIPC protects brokerage accounts up to $100,000, of which $40,000 covers cash in accounts. SIPC does not protect customers against market losses from price declines. Some brokers carry added $500,000 extra protection per client. Funding for SIPC comes from assessments made on member firms.

SUMMARY OF KEY CONCEPTS

All businesses require capital. The largest single investment by an owner or owners is in fixed assets, which include land, equipment, and buildings.

The primary objectives of financial management are to

1. Obtain an adequate supply of capital and credit
2. Evaluate alternative sources of funds and their costs
3. Manage the financial resources of the business wisely

Business uses long-term financing for continuing operation and acquiring fixed-capital assets. The two main sources of long-term financing are equity (owner) capital and debt capital.

Equity capital is supplied by owners and partners of small firms and by stockholders of corporations. Other sources of capital are profits retained and reinvested and lease financing.

If a business is able to earn more than the cost of interest on borrowed money, it is advantageous to obtain debt capital. This concept is called "trading on the equity," or financial leverage.

Bonds do not affect management control, since bondholders have no voting rights in the affairs of a business. Bonds do not dilute the stockholders' equity. They are a deductible expense.

There are certain financial disadvantages to bonds as a source of funds. They are a debt that eventually must be paid. Fixed interest charges on bonds can become a financial burden during the time when earnings are declining.

Common stock is a popular source of long-term capital. There is no fixed dividend rate stated or guaranteed. While common-stock holders assume the greatest amount of risk, they stand to make maximum gains when profits are high.

Corporations issue preferred stocks. Dividends on preferred stocks take priority over common stocks. Preferred-stock dividends often exceed bond interest.

Stock exchanges are marketplaces where securities are bought and sold. The sale of securities is used for starting new firms and for expanding old firms.

Securities bought by investors should be acquired in accordance with an investment objective. The three major investment objectives are (1) safety of principal, (2) dividend income, and (3) growth of capital (growth stocks).

Bonds and preferred stocks are forms of investment with a high safety-of-principal factor. Stocks of corporations whose sales and earnings are expanding more rapidly than the general economy and more rapidly than the average growth in that industry are growth stocks. Stability and regularity of income are two characteristics of income stocks.

BUSINESS TERMS

You should be able to match these business terms with the statements that follow:

a. Assets
b. Bond
c. Equity
d. Fixed capital
e. Investments
f. Portfolio
g. Speculation
h. Stock dividend
i. Stock option
j. Stock split
k. Stock warrants
l. Working capital

1. Assets that can readily be turned into cash for current use in operating the firm
2. Items of monetary value owned by a business
3. Money invested in fixed assets to be used for a long period of time
4. The ownership claim to the resources of the firm
5. The purchase of securities that offer safety of principal and satisfactory yield equal to the risk
6. Options to buy a specific number of shares, generally common, at a predetermined time
7. A privilege of key executives to purchase company stock under certain conditions of price and time
8. A division of outstanding common stock into additional units
9. A distribution of profits or capital paid to stockholders
10. A certificate of indebtedness indicating debt that is owed the bondholder by the corporation
11. The assumption of above-average risk for which there is anticipation of commensuratively higher financial return
12. A collection of securities owned by an investor

REVIEW QUESTIONS

1. What is *working capital* and how is it used in a business?
2. What major factors determine the amount of required fixed capital?
3. What are four sources of long-term capital financing?
4. Describe the difference between *book value, market value, par value,* and *no-par value* common stock.
5. From the investor's viewpoint, what are the main features of preferred stock?
6. How do growth stocks differ from income stocks as an investment?

DISCUSSION QUESTIONS

1. From the owner's viewpoint, what advantages does equity financing offer?
2. A corporation may prefer to sell bonds rather than issue more common stock. Why?
3. From the corporation's viewpoint, why pay dividends in stock rather than cash?
4. Explain *margin buying of stock* and how brokers protect their interest in a declining security market.
5. What is the main purpose of the Securities Investor Protection Corporation, and who benefits?
6. Discuss the meaning of the term *trading on the equity.*

BUSINESS CASE 14-1

Should the Decker Company Expand?

The Decker Appliance Company, which produces a line of home appliances, has an excellent reputation for high-quality merchandise. The company sells its appliances to two chain stores under separate private-label brands. The two chains buy virtually the entire output of Decker products each year. Both companies have contracts that will expire in another ten months. Each chain has informed the Decker management that it would like to sign a new three-year contract that would result in a substantial increase in the company's annual production. To do this, the company would have to expand its plant by adding new and more modern equipment.

Tentative estimates indicate that a proposed production expansion would involve the need for new financing amounting to $1 million.

The Decker Company, a close corporation owned by four members of the Decker family, is capitalized at $5 million with 100,000 shares of common stock outstanding, with a par value of $50. The company recently retired its preferred stock. There are no bonds. Its credit is the highest rating available, according to Dun and Bradstreet.

The stock is sold over-the-counter, but transactions seldom occur, since there are only about 500 shares held outside the Decker family. The last quoted price was $40 per share. The dividend last year was $2.80 per share, with annual earnings of $500,000. As an investment, the stock yields 7 percent.

At a meeting of the stockholders and the board of directors, various proposals were discussed. One plan consisted of financing the expansion from earnings and leasing.

A second plan consisted of amending the charter and increasing the number of shares of authorized common stock from 100,000 to 200,000. The company would then sell 25,000 shares of common at $40 per share. This would produce $1 million.

1. If you were a stockholder of the Decker Company, how would you feel about expanding the plant's production?
2. Which plan for financing the expansion do you prefer?
3. What risks do you see in increasing production?

BUSINESS CASE 14-2

Helen Mead—A Neophyte Investor

Helen Mead graduated from college five years ago. She is single and has a good position as a computer programmer with a large oil company.

Ms. Mead has a wide circle of friends and has an active social life. At the same time she is setting aside money in a savings account. She has purchased a reasonable amount of life insurance. Several of her friends are interested in the stock market. Although she expects to be able to invest as much as $4,000 soon, she feels that she needs some financial advice.

1. Is Ms. Mead ready to pursue an investment program?
2. Is she ready to set her investment objective?
3. What can she do to become better prepared as an investor?

CREDIT AND THE BANKING SYSTEM

15

STUDY OBJECTIVES

WHEN YOU HAVE FINISHED READING THIS CHAPTER, YOU SHOULD BE ABLE TO

ONE Explain the purpose of credit and how it is used in business

TWO Identify the various kinds of credit instruments and their uses

THREE Distinguish between money and credit

FOUR Understand the operations and purposes of the Federal Reserve System

FIVE Discuss how the Federal Reserve controls the supply of money and credit

SIX Contrast the kinds of services provided by commercial banks with other sources of short-term and intermediate-term financing

IN THE NEWS IN THE NEWS IN THE NEWS IN THE NEWS IN THE NEWS IN THE NEWS IN THE NEWS IN THE NEWS IN THE NEWS

Make $ on Your Checking Account!

Commercial banks now offer automatic transfers from consumer savings to checking accounts. With transfers made automatically (through prior arrangements with their banks) consumers can keep more money in interest-bearing savings accounts. Automatic transfers reduce the volume of checks returned for insufficient funds. (This is a cost for everybody concerned.) They are also expected to make it easier for consumers to meet the minimum balance requirements on their checking accounts.

Automatic transfers extend only to consumer accounts. Corporations, partnerships, and other organizations are excluded. A majority of mutual savings banks can also offer automatic transfers.

Voluntary for both banks and consumers, automatic transfers can be made only on the written authority of the customer. It must be given when the customer signs up for the transfer program. Arrangements may be made for banks to transfer funds automatically from interest-bearing accounts at thrift institutions, such as savings and loan associations. In that case, all three parties, of course, must agree to the transfers in advance.

Although ordinarily waived, banks have the right to require 30 days' notice for withdrawals from savings accounts. Regulations governing automatic transfers require that banks prominently disclose the information that they reserve this right.

The advent of automatic transfers has created uncertainties for both banks and the monetary authorities. There are concerns about the pricing and packaging patterns that will emerge. There are also uncertainties about the effects of this new service on the money supply and the conduct of monetary policy.

IN THE NEWS

The biggest problem facing commercial banking today is not the new competition but the old regulations.

WALTER B. WRISTON
Chairman, Citicorp

In the preceding chapter we examined long-term financing and described how it is done when relatively permanent investments in new equipment, plants, and warehouses must be made. Little has been said, however, about the way an established business obtains credit for short durations. Funds of this nature are needed to finance debts having a maturity date of less than one year. This is commonly referred to as short-term financing. Funds are also needed for intermediate-term financing, which involves loans having a maturity of from one to ten years.

In this chapter we discuss money, credit, and our banking system, which supplies money and credit. We will also explore the Federal Reserve System and other financial institutions, including those that provide consumer credit.

MONEY AND ITS FUNCTIONS

For more than two thousand years, money has been a desirable commodity. Such items as seashells, salt, tobacco, and pieces of metal have sometimes served as money. Today we know how to control the value of money without changing the quantity. Money is used in a market economy where most output is bought and sold.

MONEY is **anything generally accepted in exchange for goods and services.** In this sense, money serves as a medium of exchange.

Our Money Supply

Our money supply in the United States is composed of three kinds of money:

1. Coins

2. Currency (paper money)
3. Bank deposits (demand deposits)

As a means of explaining what constitutes the nation's supply of money, economists use the cryptic symbol M_1 to represent the money supply. M_1 consists of currency and coins plus demand deposits (checking accounts) on deposit in commercial banks. This is money readily available for spending.

A second symbol, M_2, includes M_1 plus time deposits (savings accounts held by commercial banks), but it does not include large certificates of deposit. The symbol M_3 includes M_2 plus deposits in mutual savings banks, savings and loan associations, and credit unions.

Money performs three major functions: (1) as a medium of exchange, (2) as a standard of value, and (3) as a store of value.

Medium of exchange. As a medium of exchange, money is the means by which goods are bought and sold. An employee works in order to be paid in money, which is used to buy the things he or she wants. Likewise, the seller offers goods on the market for money.

Standard of value. Money is a standard of value in that it is the unit by which all values are measured. In a society where specialization and exchange prevail, there is a need for a simple standard of value in the form of money.

Store of value. Individuals owning money may use it in many ways. They may spend it, hold it in a checking or savings account, or hold it in some other form. When it is used as a store of value, money is saved and not spent. The fact that money can be accumulated makes it acceptable to sellers who want to use it as a store of value.

Qualities of Money

For anything to work as money, it must be acceptable in trade as a convenient medium of exchange. It must possess certain qualities. Even though governments may declare money to be "legal tender" (acceptable in payment of a debt), it must be acceptable to those using it. A store owner would rather close the shop than surrender goods for money that he or she regards as worthless. For money to be acceptable, it must possess divisibility, durability, portability, and stability, and it must be difficult to counterfeit. Table 15-1 lists and explains these attributes.

CREDIT AND CREDIT INSTRUMENTS

Credit touches the lives of almost everyone, and in different ways. It is such an important part of business that our economic system is often characterized as a "credit economy." An understanding of credit, therefore, is essential for personal use as well as for business activities.

Meaning of Credit

The word **credit** comes from the Latin word **credere** meaning "to trust." (*Creditum* is "a loan.") When related to business, **CREDIT** is **the ability to secure goods or services in exchange for a promise to pay later.** Credit is also regarded as a

TABLE 15-1
ATTRIBUTES OF MONEY

Types of Quality	Explanation
Divisibility	For money to be acceptable, it must be readily divisible into units of value to facilitate making change. Paper money and coins satisfy this quality. Bank deposits are even better because they can be withdrawn in the amounts desired.
Difficulty in counterfeiting	People have long been tempted to make their own money. Governments take elaborate precautions to reduce counterfeiting as much as possible. Special paper and ink help to make it more difficult to counterfeit.
Durability	The quality of durability is essential. Money should not deteriorate rapidly with frequent handling. Currency and checks may not always pass the durability test to perfection, but they are preferred to apples or bushels of wheat.
Portability	Money must be easy and convenient to transfer. This implies relatively high value per unit of size and weight. People prefer paper money to silver dollars because paper money is light in weight.
Stability	Money is considered to have stability when its purchasing power (the value of goods a dollar will buy) is fairly constant. When prices in general are increasing, the value of money is decreasing. When prices are decreasing, the value of money is increasing. Thus far, gold has approached the quality of stability more than any other commodity.

function of management, dealing with such matters as the approving of credit transactions, investigation of credit risks, and collecting of accounts.

From certain points of view, credit can be better understood if it is explained rather than defined. Credit involves two characteristics. First, there is the element of *faith* on the part of the creditor in the willingness and ability of the debtor to fulfill the promise to pay. When such faith is present, the creditor is willing to give goods, services, or money. The second element of credit is *futurity:* In every credit transaction, the lender accepts some risk over a period of time. Credit instruments always involve a *time* during which the creditor's confidence is placed in the debtor's promise to pay. And until payment is made, there is always a *risk* that it will not be made. By these characteristics, credit instruments are distinguished from other commercial documents that resemble them.

Functions of Credit

Credit serves business in several ways. First, it makes capital available that would otherwise be idle. In exchange for payment of interest for the use of their funds, people entrust their personal savings to banks and other financial institutions. They, in turn, lend these savings to businesses. A direct result of the use of credit has been the development of new businesses.

Second, like money, credit also serves as a medium of exchange. Through its use, transactions can be accomplished quickly, with a minimum of work, and without the exchange of money. Without credit, the high level of economic activity would disappear.

Third, credit is a tool of business promotion that enables the entrepreneur to adjust the volume of capital to the varying needs of the business. By borrowing additional capital, a business can increase production during peak business activity. By extending credit, a business can induce customers to buy, thus gaining a competitive advantage over the entrepreneur who does not give credit.

Trade Credit

Trade credit differs radically from other forms of short-term credit, primarily because it is not obtained from a financial institution. An example of this type of credit is the common "open-book account" extended by credit managers. This has become the most common source of working capital. In accounting language, it is accounts receivable for the seller, and accounts payable for the buyer. It starts when goods are sold to the buyer on a thirty-, sixty-, or ninety-day credit. Other than the invoice, no formal instrument is involved.

Reasons for trade credit. A firm may be willing to grant credit to increase sales. If a firm's sales volume can be raised without spending large amounts on new production equipment, it is possible to spread the fixed costs over a large number of units and reduce the unit cost of production.

From the debtor's viewpoint, use of trade credit occurs largely because debtors are unable to obtain adequate financing from other credit sources, such as banks and finance companies. Commercial banks are either unable or unwilling to assume the costs or the risk inherent in many trade-credit sales. On the other hand, the seller can assume both, because trade credit is about the only avenue open to stimulate sales without resorting to long-term credit of some kind. Many firms would find it difficult to maintain suitable inventories in the absence of trade credit.

Credit managers estimate that open-book accounts constitute about 85 percent of the total volume of retail and wholesale sales in the United States. The seller enters into no formal written agreement acknowledging the debt. Instead the seller relies on the buyer to pay for the goods at the appropriate time. However, since the seller's record alone is not the best legal evidence of debt in the event of a dispute, it is common practice to support these credit transactions with sales slips or delivery receipts.

Trade-credit debt accounts are traditionally payable in thirty days. Wholesalers, jobbers, and manufacturers may sell goods on such terms as "2/10, net 30." This means that a discount of 2 percent on the amount of the invoice will be allowed if the buyer pays the bill within ten days, and that the entire amount is due in thirty days. The buyer's ability to take the discount promptly is evidence of satisfactory financial condition. Business firms often use trade credit to acquire inventory and operating supplies.

When interest rates begin soaring, companies resort to an old trick—slow payments of bills. When the rate gets above 8 or 9 percent, they delay payment as long as possible. The first hint that this is likely to occur appears when companies forgo their cash discounts that many suppliers offer for paying bills early.

As money gets tight, a number of elaborate tricks are employed. The computer is blamed for delaying payment, and checks are drawn against faraway banks. In some instances checks take a week or more to clear. Some customers postdate checks, pay only part of the amount due, or "forget" to sign the checks.

"It is becoming more attractive to use suppliers' money," admitted the treasurer of a large industrial customer that is holding off paying bills.

How the value of corporate securities is affected by the money market is illustrated by a $1 billion offering of IBM notes and debentures.

The IBM Offering

On October 4, 1979, the International Business Machines Corporation began offering $1 billion in debenture bonds and notes. This was then the largest private offering at one time on record.

Within a week the Federal Reserve raised its discount rate to 12 percent, and many leading U.S. banks raised their prime rate to 14 percent. By this time only 60 percent, or $600 million, of the IBM notes and debentures had been sold.

The IBM bonds paid 9⅜ percent and the notes 9½ percent. Because these fixed rates were by that time so far below the interest rate in the money market, the value of both the notes and the debentures dropped almost five points. Those large markdowns caused what was probably the greatest loss to Wall Street underwriters for any single money-marketing venture.

One stock market analyst estimated that the underwriters, as a group, lost almost $20 million on the $400 million of notes and debentures, which had to be marketed on the resale market.

Credit Instruments

In addition to the use of open-account or trade credit which business uses, working capital may also be obtained through the use of credit instruments for short periods. These instruments can be divided into two broad groups: **promises to pay** and **orders to pay.** The first group comprises promissory notes. The second includes drafts of all kinds and trade acceptances.

Negotiable promissory note. This is the legal instrument in the promise-to-pay category used by commercial banks or business firms. The borrower signs a note stating the terms of the loan, its length, and the interest rate to be charged. Most notes are for thirty to ninety days.

In Figure 15-1, which depicts a negotiable promissory note, Joseph Doe, Jr. (the maker), agrees to pay the East End State Bank (the payee) $100, with interest at 9 percent, sixty days from the date of the note. A promissory note has an advantage over open-book accounts because it represents prima facie evidence of the debt. (*Prima facie evidence* means that the evidence is sufficient to establish the fact in question unless rebutted.) Another advantage of the promissory note over the open-book account is that when the instrument is signed by the debtor, it acknowledges the accuracy of the debt at the time he or she agreed to it.

The note may be written so that it bears interest either at maturity or at specified intervals during the period of debt. Or it may be discounted, in which case the interest is deducted from the principal at the time the note is made. For example, Tom Jensen elects to borrow $1,500 from his bank at 10 percent interest for sixty days. When he signs the note, the bank accepts it and pays him the

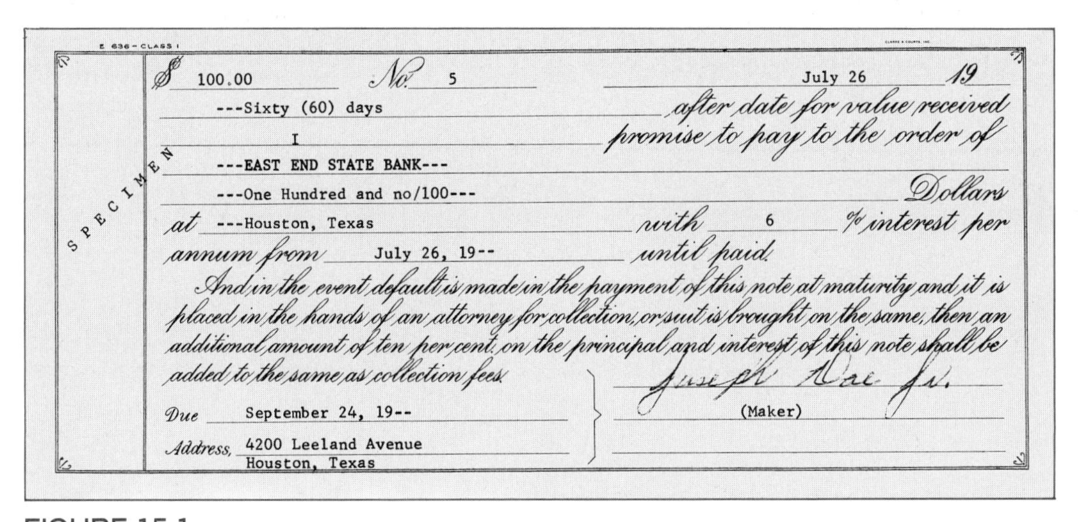
E 636—CLASS I

SPECIMEN

$ 100.00 No. 5 July 26 19

---Sixty (60) days after date for value received

I promise to pay to the order of

---EAST END STATE BANK---

---One Hundred and no/100--- Dollars

at ---Houston, Texas with 6 % interest per annum from July 26, 19-- until paid

And in the event default is made in the payment of this note at maturity and it is placed in the hands of an attorney for collection, or suit is brought on the same, then an additional amount of ten per cent on the principal and interest of this note shall be added to the same as collection fees

Joseph Doe Jr.
(Maker)

Due September 24, 19--

Address, 4200 Leeland Avenue
Houston, Texas

FIGURE 15-1

A negotiable promissory note. (Courtesy East End State Bank, Houston, Texas.)

money. If he used a discounted note, the bank would subtract $25 (interest for two months) from the amount of the note and pay him $1,475. Tom would repay the full amount of $1,500 at the end of sixty days. **Interest deducted in advance** is **BANK DISCOUNT.**

Banks or other lenders often ask the borrower to obtain the signature of a third party as a cosigner of a promissory note. Thus the cosigner becomes an accommodation indorser because that person is liable too for the debt.

Drafts or bills of exchange. Thus far we have discussed the use of promise-to-pay instruments of credit. Let us turn now to the order-to-pay instrument. The one commonly used for short-term credit is the draft or bill of exchange. (These terms are used interchangeably.)

A **DRAFT is an unconditional written order made by the drawer, addressed to the drawee (second party), ordering the drawee to pay a specific sum to a third party (payee).** A draft differs from a promissory note in that it is drawn by a creditor and not a borrower. It is also an order to pay, not a promise to pay. **A draft payable on demand** is a **SIGHT DRAFT. A draft payable at a fixed future date** is a **TIME DRAFT.** Another form of draft used by a bank is a bank draft. It may be drawn upon an out-of-town bank in which the bank maintains deposits.

Figure 15-2 illustrates a sight draft in which Richard B. Brown is the drawer of the draft. It is payable on demand to Joseph Doe, Jr. (payee), from Brown's account in the First City National Bank (drawee). This draft is issued to Brown through the courtesy of the East End State Bank as an accommodation.

Trade acceptance. **A trade acceptance** is another form of trade credit in addition to the open account and promissory note. **It is a draft drawn by a seller of merchandise ordering the buyer to pay the amount of the purchase at a fixed date.** The buyer expecting to honor the draft accepts it by writing "Accepted" on the face of the draft and adding his or her signature and the date.

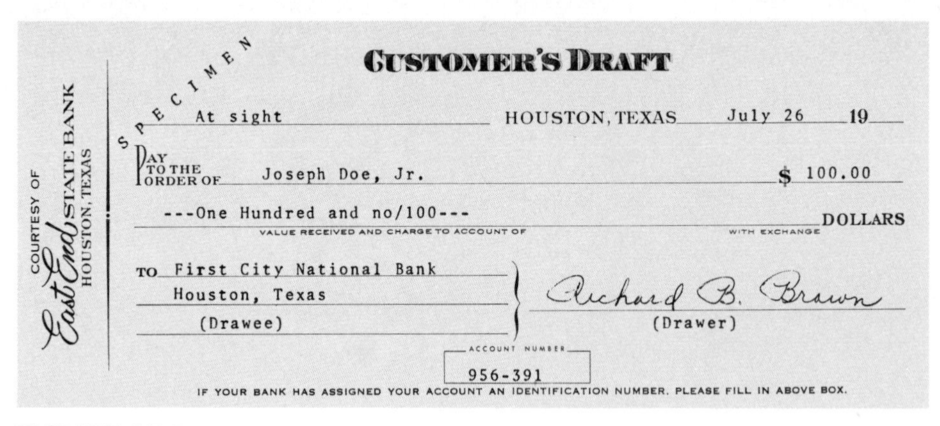

CUSTOMER'S DRAFT

SPECIMEN

COURTESY OF East End STATE BANK HOUSTON, TEXAS

At sight HOUSTON, TEXAS July 26 19

PAY TO THE ORDER OF Joseph Doe, Jr. $ 100.00

---One Hundred and no/100--- DOLLARS

VALUE RECEIVED AND CHARGE TO ACCOUNT OF WITH EXCHANGE

TO First City National Bank
Houston, Texas
(Drawee)

Richard B. Brown
(Drawer)

ACCOUNT NUMBER
956-391

IF YOUR BANK HAS ASSIGNED YOUR ACCOUNT AN IDENTIFICATION NUMBER. PLEASE FILL IN ABOVE BOX.

FIGURE 15-2

A sight draft, payable upon presentation. (Courtesy East End State Bank, Houston, Texas.)

The buyer also designates the bank at which the draft will be paid when due. It should be noted that the seller is both the drawer and the payee. The buyer is the drawee and the acceptor.

When a trade acceptance draft drawn by the seller on a named bank is accepted, it is a bank acceptance. The bank's responsibility is then substituted for the buyer's. Bank acceptances are used in foreign trade transactions where the parties may not know each other.

If the buyer's credit is good enough for a trade acceptance to be marketable, the seller may elect to sell the draft before it is due. The seller is able to receive immediate payment by doing so.

Cashier's check. A check drawn by a bank against its own funds is a **CASHIER'S CHECK.** Banks issue cashier's checks to pay their obligations or to transfer funds. Bank customers can obtain a cashier's check to make a payment for goods. Payment is guaranteed by the issuing bank.

FIGURE 15-3

A bank check that is over one hundred years old. The check is payable to a named payee or bearer rather than to his order. The named payee may deposit it without a required indorsement. The ordinary bank check is the simplest and most commonly used form of draft. In this example the drawer is the depositor. (Courtesy J. E. Weaver from the collection of J. E. Weaver, Woodland, California.)

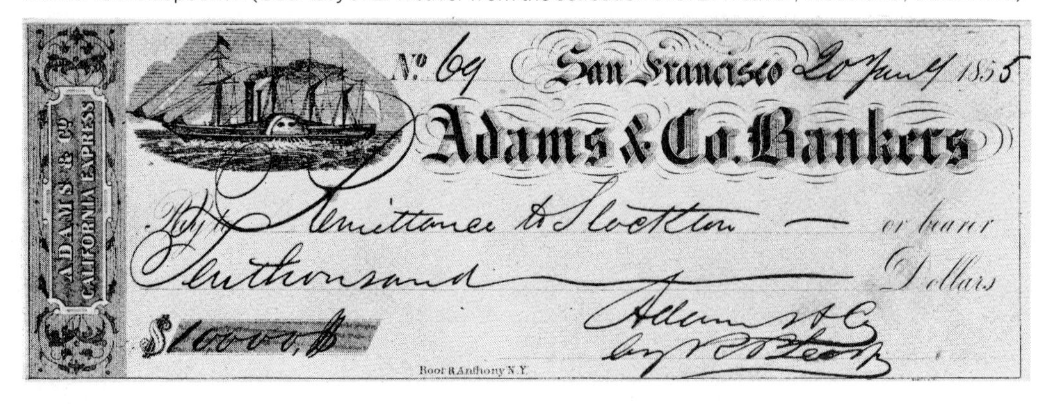

ADAMS & Co. CALIFORNIA EXPRESS

No 69 San Francisco 1855

Adams & Co. Bankers

or bearer

Dollars

Root & Anthony N.Y.

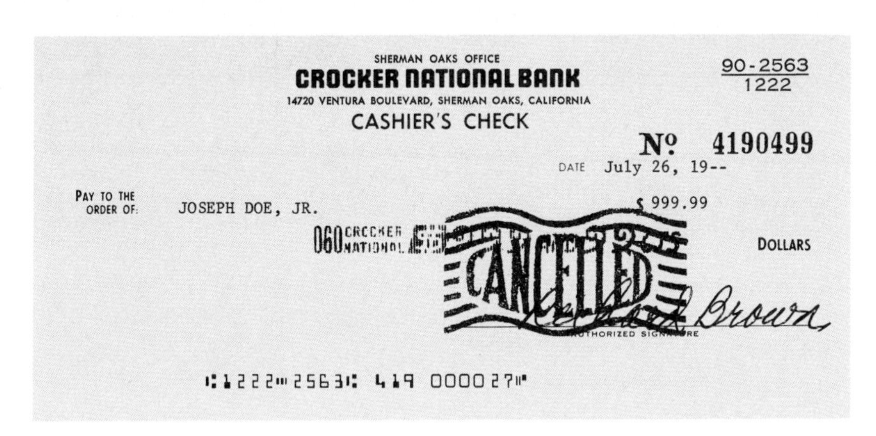
SHERMAN OAKS OFFICE
CROCKER NATIONAL BANK
14720 VENTURA BOULEVARD, SHERMAN OAKS, CALIFORNIA
CASHIER'S CHECK

90-2563
1222

No 4190499

DATE July 26, 19--

PAY TO THE ORDER OF: JOSEPH DOE, JR. $999.99

DOLLARS

CANCELLED

AUTHORIZED SIGNATURE

FIGURE 15-4

A cashier's check.

A cashier's check—a check drawn by a bank against itself. This type of check may be purchased from a bank for remittance purposes. (Courtesy Crocker National Bank, San Francisco, California.)

Figure 15-4 illustrates a cashier's check. Notice that it differs from a regular check in that it is signed by the bank's cashier and drawn on the bank's funds, not on a correspondent bank. **A bank that maintains an account relationship with another bank or engages in an exchange of services is a CORRESPONDENT BANK.** Banks in large cities act as correspondents for banks in smaller cities.

Among the services that a correspondent bank performs for other banks are the following:

1. Collecting checks, drafts, and other credit instruments
2. Accepting letters of credit and traveler's checks
3. Making credit investigations of firms in cities

Certified check. If a bank's customer wishes to make payment to a person who would otherwise refuse to accept a personal check, he or she could obtain a certified check. **A check that is guaranteed by the bank both as to signature and as to payment is a CERTIFIED CHECK.** An officer of the bank certifies the check by writing "accepted" or "certified" on the face of the check and then signing it. The amount of the check is immediately withdrawn from the depositor's account and is held by the bank pending the cashing of the check. Certified checks are mainly used in real estate and securities transactions in which payment

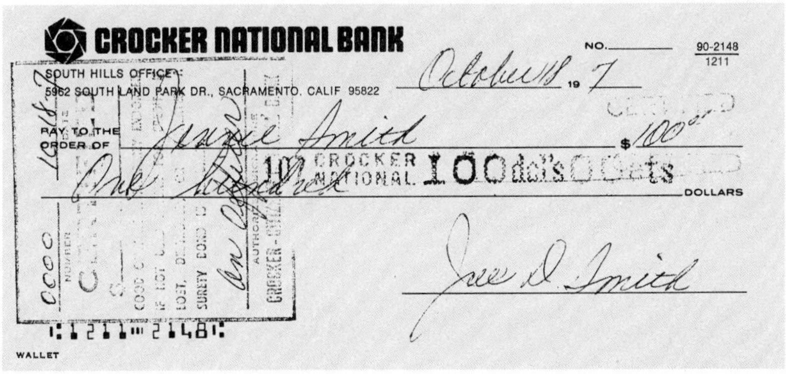

FIGURE 15-5

A certified check.

A certified check is safer because the bank guarantees payment. (Courtesy Crocker National Bank, San Francisco, California.)

in cash or by check is required. The drawer of a certified check cannot stop payment on it. The drawer should redeposit the check if it is still in his or her possession, rather than destroy it.

Figure 15-5 illustrates a certified check. Joe D. Smith is the drawer of the check, Jennie Smith is the payee, and Crocker National Bank is the drawee bank. Jennie Smith will be paid $100 from the account of Joe D. Smith.

OUR BANKING SYSTEM

An efficient and safe banking system is a primary requirement for providing the financial needs of business. Business owners and managers rely heavily on banks for capital funds, some of which come from personal savings held by banks for depositors. These funds are made available for short-term and intermediate-term loans.

Dual Banking System

A unique characteristic of our banking system is its dual nature involving both state and federal regulations and examinations. Banks are the financial institutions through which the monetary policy of the federal government is carried out. The economy must have a responsible system of banks capable of maintaining the confidence of the public.

In each state, a banking department or division supervises banks and enforces the state banking regulations covering various aspects of banking in that state.

Much of the stability of our banking system is due to the Federal Reserve Bank. Federal Reserve Banks are called "bankers' banks" because they provide financial services to financial institutions.

Commercial Banks

We have in the United States about 14,700 commercial banks. About one-third of these are national banks, and the other two-thirds are state banks.

Commercial banks chartered by the state are **STATE BANKS**. Each state has an agency that reviews bank charter applications issued by the state in which the bank is to operate. State banks that qualify may become members of the Federal Reserve System. These banks may also have depositors' accounts insured by the Federal Deposit Insurance Corporation (FDIC). Most of the large state banks are members of the Federal Reserve, but many small ones are not.

Commercial banks chartered by the federal government are **NATIONAL BANKS**. These banks tend to be larger in size. All national banks are approved by the Comptroller of the Currency, an arm of the U.S. Treasury Department. All national banks must be members of the Federal Reserve and are subject to regulations by the Fed. While regulations affecting state and national banks may vary in practice, from the individual depositor's or borrower's viewpoint, there is very little difference.

Commercial banks are the backbone of our banking system. In addition to supplying the largest part of the total money supply, commercial banks perform two important financial functions.

1. They accept deposits from business firms and individuals in the form of checking (demand deposit) or savings (time deposit) accounts.
2. They use these deposits to make loans to businesses and individuals. The making of such loans, on which, of course, the bank charges interest, is the bank's main source of income.

Commercial banks also provide numerous services, such as the following:

1. Collect notes, drafts, and bond coupons
2. Prepare and mail dividend checks for corporations
3. Administer trust funds and estates
4. Prepare foreign-trade documents
5. Furnish commercial letters of credit
6. Provide payroll service to businesses
7. Rent safe-deposit boxes
8. Supply financial advice to firms and individuals

Under a new federal law, Public Law 96-221, commercial banks are authorized to pay interest on checking accounts. Formerly, interest was paid only on savings accounts.

Table 15-2 lists the ten largest commercial banks in the United States. BankAmerica in California is the nation's largest bank, with deposits in excess of $84 billion.

TABLE 15-2
AMERICA'S TEN LARGEST BANKING COMPANIES RANKED BY DEPOSITS

Rank	Bank Name and Location	Deposits in Billions of Dollars
1	BankAmerica (San Francisco)	$84.9
2	Citicorp (New York)	70.2
3	Chase Manhattan (New York)	48.4
4	Manufacturers Hanover Corporation (New York)	38.1
5	J. P. Morgan & Co. (New York)	30.2
6	Chemical New York Corporation (New York)	28.9
7	Continental Illinois Corporation (New York)	24.0
8	Western Bankcorp (Los Angeles)	23.6
9	Bankers Trust New York Corporation (New York)	22.4
10	First Chicago Corporation (Chicago)	21.1

SOURCE: Annual Corporate reports for 1979.

Women's Banks

An interesting adaptation of banking has been the "women's banks" in San Diego, San Francisco, Los Angeles, Richmond, Greenwich, Washington, and Denver. These banks were started during the height of the feminist movement in the 1970s. They were formed by women to meet the financial needs of women. Their early appeal was to women who had been denied credit because they were female—unmarried or divorced. These banks' early histories have been full of problems typical of young "minority" banks. For example, the First Woman's Bank of New York faced some major difficulties immediately after its founding.

In its first two years of operation, New York's First Woman's Bank lost almost $2 million of its $3 million initial capital. The result was a 63 percent staff reduction, the departure of three of its top four officers, and a new president—Lynn Salvage. Ms. Salvage found that the bank had overdone the support of women at the expense of the rest of the market. She explained: "We felt an obligation to give credit to every woman who came through the door. We were a soft touch."

Ms. Salvage set to work to reverse the bank's misfortunes. She substituted quarterly statements for monthly statements for small savers. She borrowed ten managers (only one woman) from other New York banks, tightened credit guidelines, and enlisted the Ford Foundation as a major investor.

Commercial-bank loans. Loans made by commercial banks may be secured or unsecured. Secured loans are those that require some form of collateral furnished by the borrower. **COLLATERAL** is property or security deposited with a creditor to warrant payment of a debt. Usually the collateral can be marketable assets with a value that can be identified and easily measured. Unsecured loans do not require collateral.

In addition to stocks or bonds, the common collateral instruments used for short-term loans are (1) warehouse receipts, (2) chattel mortgages, and (3) accounts receivable.

Warehouse receipts. A document used as evidence of the deposit of goods in a warehouse and for a contract for storage is a **WAREHOUSE RECEIPT**. The receipt may be either negotiable or nonnegotiable. In case of default of the loan payment, the goods may be seized and sold at auction to benefit the lender. This type of financing is encouraged by provisions of the Uniform Commercial Code.

Bills of lading. When goods are shipped by rail or truck, the shipper receives either a **straight** or an **order bill of lading**. The straight bill of lading is nonnegotiable. It conveys title to the goods and must be surrendered to the transportation company before the goods can be delivered to the buyer. Still, it cannot be indorsed to another party. The order bill of lading is a negotiable instrument.

As such it is a contract between the shipper and the carrier covering terms of transportation. A contract is sent to the buyer and when he presents it he is entitled to receive the shipment.

In intrastate shipment, bills of lading in most states are governed by the UCC. In those states that have not adopted that part of the UCC, they are governed by Article 7 of the Uniform Bills of Lading Act. Bills of lading used in interstate transportation are regulated by the Federal Bills of Lading Act.

Chattel mortgages. Chattel mortgages may be used as security for a loan on personal (movable) property. Typical chattels include automobiles, household appliances, and agricultural equipment. When a chattel mortgage is used, title passes to the buyer immediately, but the seller retains a lien on the movable property until the loan is repaid. Several states require that chattel mortgages be recorded.

Accounts receivable. A business may pledge its accounts receivable (money customers owe the firm) as collateral for a loan. Commercial banks and commercial finance companies are the main sources of accounts receivable loans. In some lines of business, factoring companies convert accounts receivable into cash. Under this plan the accounts are sold outright to the factor. The customer is not aware that the account has been sold to a bank or finance company, since the company continues to make all collections and the retailer or wholesaler may continue to serve its customers. Beginning in 1965 banks could own factoring companies after it was determined by the Comptroller of the Currency that it was a proper area of business for a national bank.

Mutual Savings Banks

Mutual savings banks are the oldest type of savings institution in this country. The first ones were organized in 1816 in Boston and Philadelphia. There are at present about 467 savings banks located in eighteen states and in the Commonwealth of Puerto Rico.[1]

These banks were organized to promote savings. Since early commercial banks did not provide savings accounts, mutual savings banks were formed for this purpose. These savings deposits are invested by the bank in real estate mortgages, bonds, and other investments. The difference between the income from loans and investments and the interest paid to depositors is the gross profits of the banks. Mutual savings banks are chartered by the state and are entitled to membership in the Federal Deposit Insurance Corporation. Accounts are insured up to $100,000 in any one bank. Commercial banks accept savings deposits in those states unwilling to charter mutual savings banks.

Under Public Law 96-221, mutual savings banks can now be federally chartered. This law allows them to lend up to 5 percent of their assets in commercial and business loans.

[1]The following eighteen states charter savings banks: Alaska, Connecticut, Delaware, Indiana, Maine, Maryland, Massachusetts, Minnesota, New Hampshire, New Jersey, New York, Ohio, Oregon, Pennsylvania, Rhode Island, Vermont, Washington, and Wisconsin.

HISTORICAL BACKGROUND OF AMERICAN BANKING

Banking is a very old business. Long before the Constitution vested power in Congress to create money and control its value, groups of private citizens had established banks. The first bank was the so-called Massachusetts Bank founded in 1681. Borrowers pledged their land as collateral in the form of notes, which banks held as security. The First Bank of the United States was chartered for twenty years—from 1791 to 1811. A Second Bank of the United States was also chartered for twenty years—from 1816 to 1836. From 1836 to 1863 there were no national banks, and wildcat banking was at its peak. Almost anyone could start a bank. Since banks were considered the "patent medicine" for the ills of business, they were used to try to cure everything that was wrong. Many investors in banks lost their money because of bank failures.

In 1862 the National Currency Act was passed to charter national banks. It required the founders of a bank to pledge $50,000 in capital. By 1890 most banks (80 percent) were under a national charter—few banks were authorized by state governments.

Following the money panic of 1907, Congress decided it was time for more federal intervention. In 1908 Congress appointed a National Monetary Commission to study banking reforms. The Glass-Owen Act of 1913 created the Federal Reserve System, which is still America's central bank.

The stock-market crash in October 1929 helped to produce a complete collapse of the economy. The Banking Act of 1933 was passed to stabilize our banks. The Federal Reserve Board was authorized to regulate interest on savings accounts and to control bank reserves in order to stimulate the economy.

THE FEDERAL RESERVE SYSTEM

At present the Federal Reserve System is composed of 5,668 member banks, 12 Federal Reserve Banks, and 24 branch banks. In addition, there are three important related groups: a Board of Governors, the Federal Open-Market Committee, and the Federal Advisory Council, all of which are shown in Figure 15-6.

The Board of Governors is appointed by the president of the United States with approval of the Senate. Each of the seven members is appointed for a fourteen-year term unless the appointee is replacing a member whose term has not expired. Every second year, the term of one member expires and that member is replaced. Anyone serving a fourteen-year term is not eligible for reappointment. This board is regarded as autonomous and nonpolitical, in the sense that it is free from control by any executive branch of the federal government.

Major Functions

The Federal Reserve System performs two major functions. One is to supply certain basic banking services, such as acting as a clearinghouse for checks, serving as a fiscal agent for the government by distributing currency and coins, and supervising the operations of the member banks. The second function is a dual one: to maintain a sound credit policy for all member banks (by controlling the volume of credit in circulation so as to avoid sharp fluctuations in the business cycle), and at the same time to promote a high level of consumer buying. This

PAUL A. VOLCKER

Paul A. Volcker became a member of the Federal Reserve Board on August 6, 1979. He was designated as chairman of the board for a four-year term.

Volcker was born on September 5, 1927, at Cape May, New Jersey. He received a B.A. degree from Princeton University in 1949 and an M.A. degree in political economy and government from the Harvard University Graduate School of Public Administration in 1951. He attended the London School of Economics in 1951–52. Volcker's first association with the Federal Reserve System was as a summer employee at the Federal Reserve Bank of New York in 1949 and 1950. He returned to the New York Bank in 1952 as a full-time economist and remained with the Federal Reserve until 1957 when he became a financial economist at Chase Manhattan Bank. In 1962 Volcker joined the United States Treasury as director of financial analysis, and in 1963 he became deputy under secretary of the treasury for monetary affairs. From 1965 to 1969 he was a vice-president of Chase Manhattan Bank. In 1969 he was appointed under secretary of the treasury for monetary affairs, where he remained until 1974. During this time Volcker was the principal United States negotiator in the development and installation of a new international monetary system departing from the fixed exchange rate system installed following World War II. He spent the 1974–75 academic year at Princeton University as a senior fellow in the Woodrow Wilson School of Public and International Affairs.

Volcker became president and chief executive officer of the Federal Reserve Bank of New York on August 1, 1975. He continued in that office until he became chairman of the Federal Reserve Board. As president of the Federal Reserve Bank of New York, Volcker was a continuing member of the Federal Reserve System's principal monetary policy-making body, the Federal Open Market Committee. He was elected vice-chairman of the FOMC on August 19, 1975. As chairman of the Federal Reserve Board, Volcker is chairman of the FOMC.

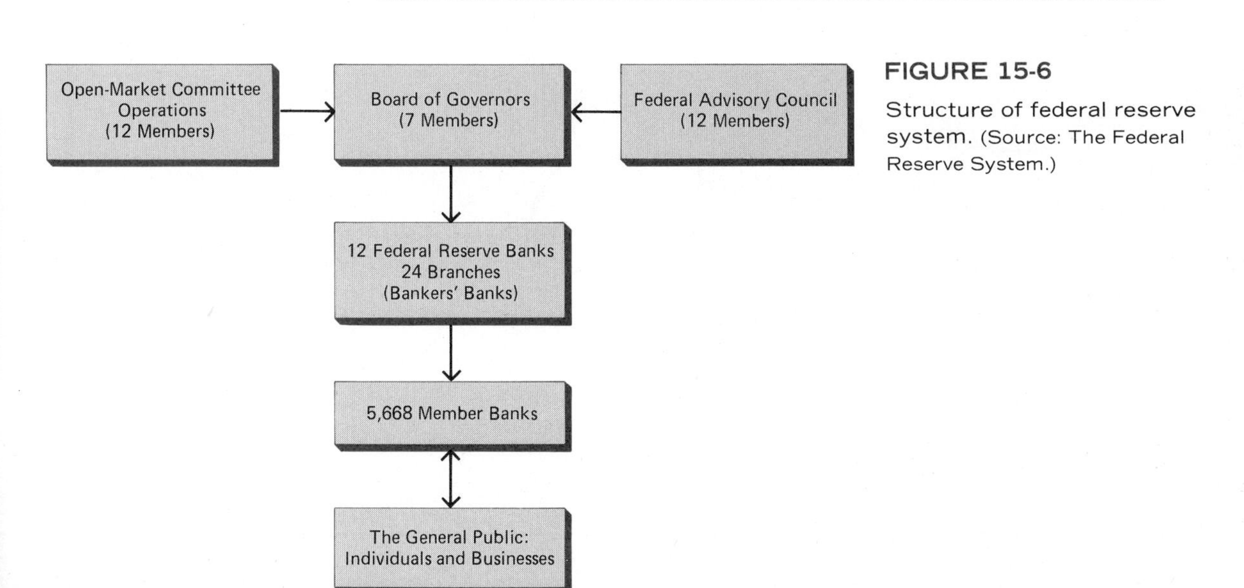

FIGURE 15-6

Structure of federal reserve system. (Source: The Federal Reserve System.)

is a significant function because it serves the entire economy. (The methods by which credit and the circulation of money are regulated are described later in this chapter.)

Federal Reserve Banks

The United States is divided into twelve Federal Reserve districts (see Figure 15-7), each with its own Federal Reserve district bank, located in the twelve cities listed in Table 15-3.

Federal Reserve district banks. Each of the twelve Federal Reserve district banks is a separate corporation with its own nine-member board of directors. Class A and Class B directors are elected by member banks from each district. The Board of Governors appoints three Class C directors. They cannot hold stock of a member bank but may be an employee or officer of the bank.

Branch banks. Within the twelve districts, there are also twenty-four branch banks in addition to the twelve district banks. For example, in district 12 the Reserve district bank is in San Francisco. Branch banks are in Los Angeles, Portland, Salt Lake City, and Seattle. These four branch banks, together with the Federal Reserve district bank in San Francisco, serve all the member banks in the 12th district.

FIGURE 15-7

The federal reserve districts. Boundaries of federal reserve districts and their branch territories. (Courtesy Board of Governors, Federal Reserve System.)

TABLE 15-3
THE FEDERAL RESERVE BANKS OF THE UNITED STATES

District	Bank Location	District	Bank Location
1	Boston	7	Chicago
2	New York	8	St. Louis
3	Philadelphia	9	Minneapolis
4	Cleveland	10	Kansas City
5	Richmond	11	Dallas
6	Atlanta	12*	San Francisco

*Includes Alaska and Hawaii.

Contributions of the Federal Reserve System to the economy. Federal Reserve Banks are called "bankers' banks" because they provide financial services to the total monetary operations of this country. They play a vital role in helping to maintain a sound banking system and a stable economy. The Federal Reserve System is only one of several forces affecting business conditions. However, it has managed to eliminate many of the banking evils that existed before enactment of the Federal Reserve Act. Over the years the system has provided a second line of defense against bank runs by enabling the member banks to discount commercial paper in order to meet demands for cash. The Federal Reserve System and the Federal Deposit Insurance Corporation have made banks much safer than they used to be.

Member banks. All national banks must become member banks in the system. State banks may become members provided they can meet the requirements. Table 15-4 lists the number of national and state banks that are members of the Federal Reserve.

TABLE 15-4
TOTAL NUMBER OF BANKS AND THEIR DEPOSITS, 1978
(DEPOSITS IN MILLIONS OF DOLLARS)

Kind of Bank	Numbers	Deposits
Federal Reserve member banks	5,668	$683,611
Nonmember commercial banks	9,039	255,898
Total commercial banks and deposits	14,707	$939,509
Classes of member banks:		
National banks	4,654	$520,168
State banks	1,014	163,444
Total	5,668	$683,612
Classes of nonmember banks:		
Commercial banks	9,039	$255,898
	14,707	
Mutual savings banks	467	134,916
Total all banks	15,174	$390,814
Total all deposits for all banks		$1,074,426

SOURCE: Federal Reserve System.

Among the advantages of membership are the following:

1. Member banks can borrow from the Federal Reserve.
2. Membership adds financial stability to the member bank.
3. Currency can be obtained immediately from a Federal Reserve district bank.
4. Eligible commercial paper can be discounted and advances obtained from the Federal Reserve.
5. Member banks are audited by Federal Reserve auditors.
6. Deposits up to $100,000 for each depositor are insured in each member bank by the Federal Deposit Insurance Corporation (FDIC).
7. Member banks participate in the clearing of checks.

Operational and Credit Functions

The Federal Reserve's primary function is to control the economy's credit and supply of money. This is the function of a central bank. It performs this function by using three important tools:

1. Reserve requirements
2. The discount rate
3. Open-market operations

Reserve requirements. The Federal Reserve has for years required member banks to keep on deposit in Federal Reserve banks a reserve account. The amount of each reserve has varied with the size of each member bank's deposits. Control of these reserves has enabled the Fed to increase or decrease the money in circulation. A growing number of banks have complained that it was too expensive to have these funds on deposit and not earn interest. Annually more banks have withdrawn from the System. Effective September 1, 1980 under Public Law 96-221, reserve requirements were expanded. All depository institutions that accept deposits from the public are required to keep a reserve account in the nearest district bank. This now gives the Fed more direct control in regulating supply of money. These reserve funds are noninterest-bearing. While the reserve requirement is mandatory for all banks and savings institutions, not all must become a member of the Federal Reserve System. In the past about 60 percent of the nation's banks were exempt from these reserve requirements.

Table 15-5 shows how the multiplying effect works to accumulate reserve deposits in order to increase the supply of money. Let us assume that the prevailing member-bank reserve requirement set by the Federal Reserve is 20 percent.

Bank No. 1 accepts a $100 deposit, withholds $20 for its reserve, and is allowed to lend or invest $80. This meets the 20 percent reserve requirement.

The $80 is lent to another depositor and becomes a credit to his or her account. That depositor writes a check for $80, giving it to a new recipient who deposits it in bank No. 2, which now has $80 in demand deposits. Bank No. 2 withholds $16, or 20 percent, as required reserve and immediately lends $64, the remainder, to one of its customers.

This same process continues until $500 becomes the grand total. The total amount of money lent is $400. The total reserve is $100. The $100 deposit has now increased to $500, which is added to the total money supply.

TABLE 15-5
MULTIPLYING CAPACITY OF RESERVE MONEY THROUGH NEW DEPOSITS*

Transactions	Deposited in Checking Accounts	Money Lent	Set Aside as Reserves
Bank 1	$100.00	$ 80.00	$ 20.00
2	80.00	64.00	16.00
3	64.00	51.20	12.80
4	51.20	40.96	10.24
5	40.96	32.77	8.19
6	32.77	26.22	6.55
7	26.22	20.98	5.24
8	20.98	16.78	4.20
9	16.78	13.42	3.36
10	13.42	10.74	2.68
Total for 10 banks	446.33	357.07	89.26
Additional banks	53.67	42.93†	10.74†
Grand total, all banks	500.00	400.00	100.00

*Based on an average member-bank reserve requirement of 20 percent of demand deposits.

†Adjusted to offset rounding in preceding figures.

The discount rate. The interest rate charged by Federal Reserve district banks on loans to member banks is called the **DISCOUNT RATE**. There are times when a member bank needs money for a short period. A member bank can borrow from a Federal Reserve Bank in two ways: it can sell or rediscount promissory notes or other commercial paper, which is called **rediscounting**, or it can borrow on its own secured notes in much the same way as a business borrows from a commercial bank. This latter transaction is known as obtaining an **advance**. Under the law each Federal Reserve Bank sets the rediscount rate and the rate on advances that apply to member banks of that district. The rates are subject to review by the Board of Governors.

The Federal Reserve Board may raise or lower the discount rate. By raising the rate, borrowing is reduced because borrowers must pay higher interest rates. Or the board may lower the discount rate to stimulate the economy by encouraging borrowing.

Open-market operations. A more common way to control the money supply is through the Open-Market Committee. Open-market operations consist of the purchase and sale of government securities on the "open market" rather than by direct dealings with the Treasury.

When the Board of Governors decides it is time to increase the nation's money supply, the Open-Market Committee buys Treasury bills (short-term bonds) or longer-term bonds. These purchases are mainly made in the New York City area from dealers in securities. The purpose is to increase bank reserves, which in effect makes new money available to member banks to make more loans.

Conversely, a decision to sell government bonds would serve to reduce the overall money supply. Any effort by the Federal Reserve to control our money supply and credit involves the responsibility for making "monetary policy." In contrast, government fiscal policy relates to all practices involving government tax and spending policies. The primary responsibility for monetary policy is with the Federal Reserve System through the system's board of Governors and the Open-Market Committee.

Regulation of margin requirements. In Chapter 14 we discussed the use of margin when buying securities, and we noted that the Federal Reserve has the power to set margin requirements. Regulating margins is a means of encouraging or discouraging lending. The smaller the margin required of the buyer, the more one can borrow against the purchase price of the stock. The higher the margin required, the less one can borrow against the purchase price. However, as a tool to control the money supply, it has proved to be of little value.

Clearing bank checks. Americans write about 27.5 billion checks annually to pay for goods and services. The process of returning these checks to the banks on which they are drawn is performed with amazing speed and accuracy. This procedure is called the clearing process.

Commercial banks in large cities operate collectively a "clearinghouse association," which is not directly part of the Federal Reserve System. Commercial banks in a given city send their representatives to exchange checks drawn on other banks in that city. The cost of operating the clearinghouse is paid by the local commercial banks that participate. Out-of-town checks are sent to the Federal Reserve Bank. These checks are separated by Reserve districts and exchanged. This process is known as the **transit process**. Figure 15-8 illustrates the transit process step by step, involving check clearance concerning banks located in two Federal Reserve districts. In this case firm A draws a check to pay firm B in a different Federal Reserve district. If both parties involved have checking accounts

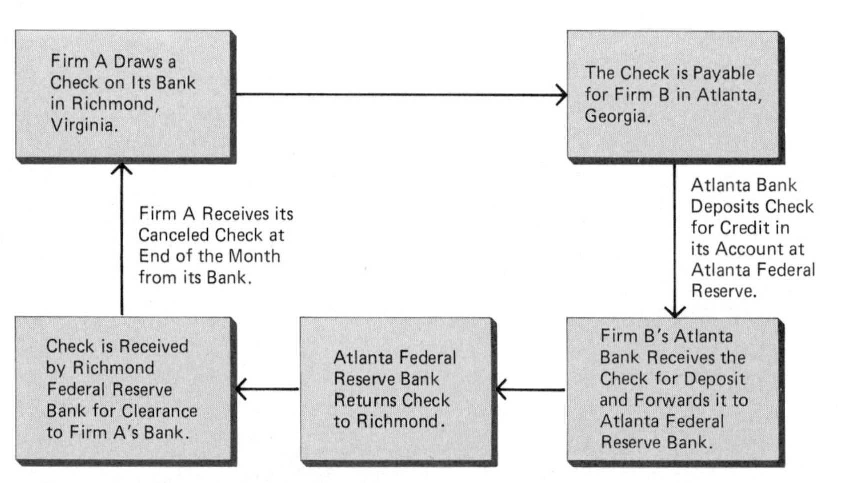

FIGURE 15-8

Step-by-step journey of a bank check through the federal reserve system.

in the same bank, check clearing becomes a simple matter of increasing the checking account of firm B and decreasing the checking account of firm A. Actually the parties involved live in different cities. The Federal Reserve System becomes involved in the check clearance as illustrated in Figure 15-8.

ELECTRONIC BANKING SERVICES

A broad range of banking services are performed electronically without the use of paper. This process is known as EFT, an acronym for Electronic Fund Transfer.

The most obvious of these electronic instruments is the automated teller machine (ATM). It makes deposits, withdrawals, and account transfers. It is easily activated by a "debit card" and a secret security code. ATMs furnish customers ready access to their bank accounts twenty-four hours a day, seven days a week.

Department stores use electronic terminals instead of cash registers at their sales counters. Some are hooked directly to a master computer system and are used to help maintain inventory records.

MAJOR SOURCES OF CONSUMER CREDIT

Large-scale consumer credit is essentially an innovation of the twentieth century. **CONSUMER CREDIT** is **credit granted to consumers to promote personal consumption.** The loans are repaid on the installment basis. The availability of consumer credit and its rapid growth have profoundly altered consumer buying habits and decisions. At first, consumer credit was used largely to buy durable goods such as home appliances, automobiles, and furniture. Now nearly all kinds of goods are bought on consumer credit plans providing for installment payments. Who supplies consumer installment credit? As shown in Figure 15-9, most installment credit is furnished by commercial banks, finance companies, and credit unions.

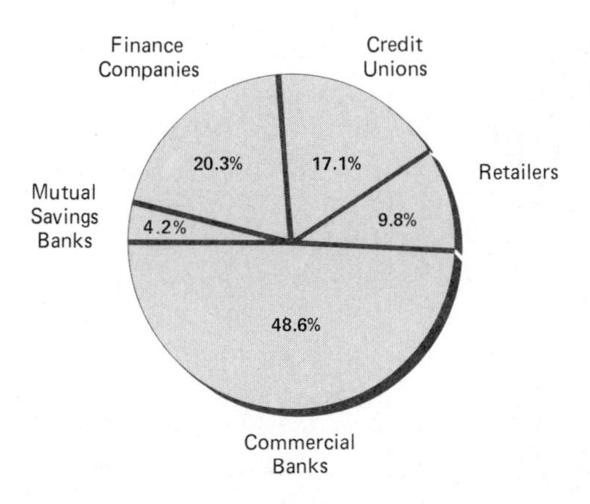

FIGURE 15-9

Chief sources of consumer installment credit, 1978. (Source: Federal Reserve Board.)

Finance Companies

Although finance companies perform a diversity of services for consumers, their main purpose is to supply short-term credit financing. Two types of commercial finance companies have developed: (1) consumer finance companies and (2) sales finance companies.

Consumer finance companies. Sometimes known as "small loan companies," consumer finance companies specialize in short-term loans, mostly under $1,000. These loans are used for financing business inventories, for making small personal loans, and sometimes for providing short-term working capital for small firms. The loans are repaid in installments and usually carry a high rate of interest.

Finance companies have recently moved into lending to businesses as well.

A recent study by the Federal Reserve of New York found that finance companies have become an important source of financing to smaller businesses. The finance companies borrow in the "commercial paper market" where their notes (usually in denominations of $100,000 or more) are sold. The money received then becomes a source of funds to firms who cannot borrow in that market. More than half of the finance company business consists of financing inventories of finished goods and equipment.

Sales finance companies. Not all installment sales credit is financed directly by the seller. Sales finance companies buy installment sales contracts from dealers or merchants who receive notes or contracts from their customers. More than 50 percent of the new-car sales and about 70 percent of the used-car sales are financed by these companies. General Motors Acceptance Corporation (GMAC), which finances General Motors' car sales, buys these contracts from GM dealers. These companies have several advantages over commercial banks in financing installment sales. They can assume greater risks, since they are not subject to banking rules, and they can operate in all states while some banks cannot. They are able to work closely with companies that produce the articles sold by the dealer. By selling customers' accounts, retail dealers are able to obtain the full amount of their sales in cash. This enables the dealer to maintain working capital for the operation of the business.

Credit Unions

Credit unions have been in existence since 1908 when parishioners of the Roman Catholic Church of St. Mary started one in Manchester, New Hampshire. These credit unions grew slowly until after World War II.

A **CREDIT UNION is an organization formed by individuals on a cooperative basis to make loans to its members and encourage them to save.** Systematic savings are promoted through the purchase of credit union shares as an investment. Loans are made to members for any "productive" purpose. These organizations are established by occupational groups, religious groups, fraternal organizations, labor unions, and the military. They are chartered by either the federal or a state government. Students on college campuses have formed credit unions.

Under Public Law 96-221, credit unions now compete more directly with banks. They have permanent authority to issue share drafts. These are check-like drafts members write to withdraw funds on deposit to pay bills. They can raise their interest on loans from 12 to 15 percent. They may make loans to individuals for cooperative housing units. Insurance coverage has been raised from $40,000 to $100,000 per account under the National Credit Union Share Insurance Fund (NCUSIF).

HOW TRUNCTION IS USED IN FINANCIAL INSTITUTIONS

A new technique called trunction is being used to reduce paper flow and cut operating costs in banks and other financial institutions.

Trunction as the term is used in the banking industry, refers to the nonreturn of canceled checks to customers after payment has been made. Instead of returning your canceled checks, your bank would microfilm each canceled check. Meanwhile your checks are held a few months and then destroyed, which saves filing space. Approximately forty thousand checks can be stored chronologically on a microfilm tape four inches in diameter. A copy of any check can be retrieved in a matter of seconds if you have a need to see it.

For many years the public has been sold on the value of having checks returned with the monthly statements. Proponents of trunction are suggesting that the bank is doing you a favor by not returning your canceled checks.

One of the first banks to use trunction was the Valley National Bank in Phoenix, which adopted the plan early in 1979 at five of its branches. About half of its customers joined the plan. One of the first savings institutions to use trunction was the Wilmington (Delaware) Savings Fund Society in 1977. The first year this society saved $70,000, in personnel costs, and $100,000 the second year. A few credit unions are using trunction to handle their share drafts. A share draft is a check form used by a credit union member to withdraw money from a credit union account.

Credit Cards—Plastic Money

The growing credit-card craze has made this the age of plastic money for those credit-card users who say "Charge it." With a credit card you can buy almost anything on credit. American Express, Diners Club, and Carte Blanche are the main travel-entertainment cards used by executives because of their convenience and because of the tax records they offer. Other charge cards are issued by oil companies, car-rentals, airlines, and department stores.

The big struggle for supremacy is between two giants—VISA and Master Charge. VISA is owned by Visa U.S.A., a profit corporation owned by the issuing banks. The sponsor of Master Charge is the Interbank Card Association, a nonprofit organization whose member banks share operating revenues and costs. Both organizations charge cardholders interest on the unpaid balance beyond a certain number of days. Goods and services at many stores that honor credit cards are priced higher to cover the service-charge fee collected by credit-card companies. These fees range from 2 to 9 percent per sale. VISA and Master Charge do a combined business of about $40 billion annually. Approximately 18 million families own three or more cards, for a total of $50 billion each year.

REGULATIONS OF FINANCIAL INSTITUTIONS

In concluding our discussion of banks and other financial institutions, we will summarize the regulatory role of government.

Regulatory Measures Congressional authority to regulate money and credit is chiefly based on Section 8 of the U.S. Constitution. Under this provision, Congress has certain rights, which include the following: borrowing money, coining money, paying debts, and regulating commerce.

CURRENT ISSUE

Should Credit Purchasers Pay Higher Prices?

An ever-increasing amount of consumer goods are being sold on credit. Department stores issue their own company credit cards. National credit cards such as VISA and Master Charge continue to increase in popularity. Stores that recognize these national credit cards must pay from 3 to 9 percent for that service. Is it right to charge cash customers the same as those who buy on credit?

With which of the following statements do you agree and with which do you disagree?

1. **The cash customer subsidizes those who buy on credit.**
2. **Whether one pays cash or buys on credit is a matter of personal customer choice.**
3. **The easy availability of credit cards to most families encourages the use of credit. This in turn makes goods cost more.**
4. **The use of customer credit increases sales volume, and this in turn tends to lower prices.**
5. **Since retailers save the cost of credit when customers pay cash, the cash customer should be given a discount off the price equal to the cost of credit.**

---

1. **Is the cash customer being discriminated against?**
2. **Should buying on credit be prohibited? Why or why not?**

The Federal Reserve Act. Under this legislation enacted in 1913, the Federal Reserve Board has the power to examine and control commercial bank reserves and the supply of bank credit. Reserve Board Regulation Q sets maximum interest rates on time deposits. Regulation Z also was adopted, effective 1969, by the Board of Governors to implement Title I and Title V (General Provisions) of the Consumer Credit Protection Act (Truth-in-Lending Act).

Federal Deposit Insurance Corporation. The FDIC is another government agency charged with bank regulation. Few people now worry about safety of their bank deposits because the FDIC offers deposit protection to participant banks.

Under the provisions of Public Law 96-221, deposits in banks are insured by FDIC. In 1980 the maximum coverage for each account was raised from $40,000 to $100,000. The FDIC also makes periodic inspection of insured banks. Figure 15-10 illustrates the scope of insurance protection for a family of three with individual and joint accounts.

Truth-in-Lending Act. Otherwise known as the Consumer Credit Protection Act, this legislation became effective July 1, 1969. It ensures accurate and complete disclosure of credit terms to consumers. Loan companies, banks, retailers, and other businesses engaged in installment consumer selling must supply complete facts about the cost of consumer loans.

Fair Credit Reporting Act. This act, which became effective in April 1971, gives individuals access to their credit-information file. Any incorrect facts on file about a person's credit must be changed. Those who can prove that credit-bureau reports deliberately wronged them can sue for court costs and actual damages.

Depository Institutions Deregulation and Monetary Act of 1980. Acclaimed as the Magna Carta for thrift and savings institutions, Public Law 96-221 became law March 28, 1980.

This law calls for a gradual deregulation of regulation Q during the next six years. This regulation was issued by the Federal Reserve to set maximum interest

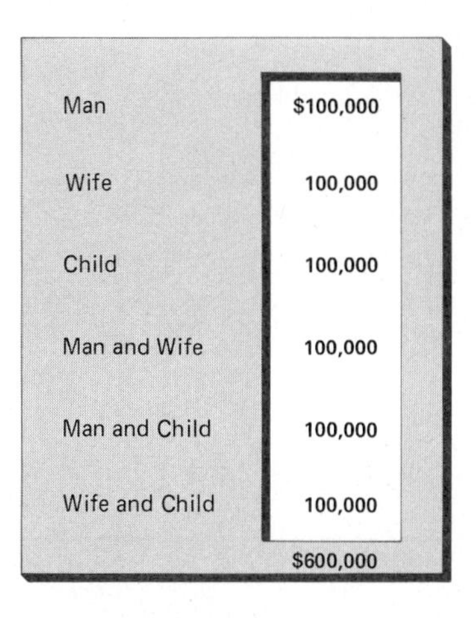

Man	$100,000
Wife	100,000
Child	100,000
Man and Wife	100,000
Man and Child	100,000
Wife and Child	100,000
	$600,000

FIGURE 15-10

Maximum insured coverage for a family of three with individual and joint accounts.

rates on time and savings deposits. The idea behind Public Law 96-221 is to place thrift institutions on a more equal basis with banks in order to promote competition. Individuals may have checking accounts that pay interest. All financial institutions are required to keep funds on deposit with the Federal Reserve in order to strengthen the Federal Reserve's control of the nation's money supply, a key element used by the Fed to fight inflation. Earlier in this chapter other provisions of this law were explained in the discussions dealing with banks, S&Ls, credit unions, and mutual savings banks.

SUMMARY OF KEY CONCEPTS

Every business uses a variety of credit for short-term and intermediate financing. Credit is the basis of all loans.

Credit instruments are based on either promise-to-pay or order-to-pay negotiable instruments. The open-book account and the promissory note are promise-to-pay documents. Drafts and trade acceptances are order-to-pay documents.

Short-term credit is available through such credit arrangements as bank loans, installment credit, and loans granted by finance companies. Security for short-term business loans may be corporate stock, order bills of lading, warehouse or trust receipts.

Commercial banks are the principal sources of short-term business loans. These banks also supply a variety of financing services. They accept demand and time deposits, discount negotiable instruments, serve as trustees of funds, supply financial advice, and issue bank drafts.

Commercial banks are either state or national banks. State banks are chartered by the state government. National banks receive their charters from the federal government.

All national banks must be members of the Federal Reserve System and subscribe to the Federal Deposit Insurance Corporation. State banks may be members of FDIC if they meet its requirements.

The broad objective of the Federal Reserve System is to control the supply of money and credit to promote price stability, encourage economic growth, and help maintain high employment.

During periods of inflation or deflation, the Federal Reserve is responsible for determining monetary policy. Three devices—regulation of bank reserves, regulation of the discount rate, and open-market operation—are used.

In addition to regulation of commercial banks by the Federal Reserve, loan companies, finance companies, and credit unions are also subject to federal controls.

The Consumer Credit Protection Act requires finance companies and others engaged in installment consumer selling to publish, at the time of the credit sale, the cost of finance charges and terms of annual interest.

The Fair Credit Reporting Act, a federal law, permits people to see information about them on file in retail credit bureaus. If the credit bureau is unable to verify the facts, it must delete them from the records.

BUSINESS TERMS

You should be able to match these business terms with the statements that follow:

a. Bank discount
b. Cashier's check
c. Certified check
d. Consumer credit
e. Correspondent bank
f. Credit
g. Discount rate
h. Draft
i. Money
j. National banks
k. Sight draft
l. State banks
m. Time draft
n. Trade acceptance

1. Anything generally accepted in exchange for goods or services
2. A draft payable on demand
3. A check drawn by a bank against its own funds
4. A draft drawn by the seller of merchandise ordering the buyer to pay the amount of the purchase on a fixed date
5. Interest deducted in advance
6. Commercial banks chartered by the federal government
7. A draft payable on a fixed date
8. Credit granted to consumers to promote personal consumption
9. Interest rate charged by the Federal Reserve district bank on loans to member banks
10. Commercial banks chartered by the state
11. A bank that maintains an account relationship with another bank or engages in an exchange of services
12. An unconditional written order made by the drawer addressed to the second party (drawee) that orders the drawer to pay a specific sum to a third party (payee)
13. A check guaranteed by the bank both as to signature and as to payment
14. The ability to secure goods and services in exchange for a promise to pay later.

REVIEW QUESTIONS

1. What are some of the reasons for the use of trade credit?
2. What is the difference between a *promise-to-pay* instrument and an *order-to-pay* instrument?
3. What is the difference between a *cashier's* check and a *certified* check?
4. Give several examples of the kinds of service that commercial banks perform for business.
5. Who owns the Federal Reserve System? Is the Federal Reserve subject to control by Congress?

DISCUSSION QUESTIONS

1. Should bank membership in the Federal Reserve be optional?
2. Is the federal government exercising too much, too little, or the right amount of power in supervising consumer credit?
3. Should all banks be required to participate in the Federal Deposit Insurance program?
4. Do you believe credit unions should be allowed to offer demand deposit checking accounts to compete with banks? Explain.
5. Why do consumer finance companies generally charge higher interest rates than commercial banks on short-term loans?
6. What is the main reason for the growth of credit unions?

BUSINESS CASE 15-1

Alamo Pump Corporation Has Growing Pains

The Alamo Pump Corporation was organized in 1969 to manufacture water pumps for irrigation systems and industrial plants. The corporation owns three important patents related to water and steam valves. Its products are sold mainly through farm implement dealers. Alamo's general office is in San Antonio, Texas. Its stock is locally owned.

Last year the corporation earned 5 percent on sales of $1 million and paid a dividend of fifty cents per quarter on twelve thousand shares of common stock. During peak production periods, usually during the summer months, Alamo often experiences a shortage of working capital, which requires one or more short-term bank loans. However, the new treasurer, a stockholder, is critical of this practice of borrowing. He contends that the corporation should plan to avoid peak production periods. Following is a recent simplified balance sheet.

ALAMO PUMP CORPORATION

Assets		Liabilities	
Cash	$ 50,000	Notes payable	$ 10,000
Accounts receivable	800,000	Accounts payable	300,000
Merchandise inventory	70,000	Common stock (20,000	
Machinery	100,000	shares, $3 per share par	
Land and buildings	100,000	value)	60,000
		Surplus	750,000
Total assets	$1,120,000	Total liabilities and capital	$1,120,000

1. Do you agree with Alamo's treasurer?
2. What is Alamo's main problem, and how can it be solved?
3. What other sources of short-term credit can you suggest?

BUSINESS CASE

The Future for Beta Electronics

Beta Electronics is a partnership owned by Charles Greenwood, a well-known physicist, and his son, Jarvis Greenwood. The father owns 90 percent of the partnership, and the son 10 percent. The firm has been in business four years. It manufactures electronic circuits for highly specialized equipment. Currently the firm has a backlog of orders which can be filled only by a substantial increase in production. Profits for last year were 32 percent higher than for the previous year. Prospects for this year suggest a higher net profit. There is only one other small company engaged in this kind of business and one large company. Last year, after rather generous salaries were paid to company managers and employees, net profits were $145,000.

The partners have engaged a financial consultant. He has recommended that the company incorporate and sell stock only on the local market—a community of 850,000 people. The firm's banker suggests that the partners consider a five-year loan. To expand, it is estimated that the firm will need $400,000 additional capital. This amount will cover the cost of enlarging the present plant and equipment where forty-eight employees now work. Engineers predict that total expansion will require one year. No one has indicated whether more competition will develop in the near future.

1. What specific problems should the partners consider before making a decision?
2. What recommendation would you make to the partners?

RISK MANAGEMENT AND INSURANCE

16

STUDY OBJECTIVES

WHEN YOU HAVE FINISHED READING THIS CHAPTER, YOU SHOULD BE ABLE TO

ONE Identify the types of risk that face businesses and describe how businesses can protect themselves

TWO Explain which types of risk can and cannot be covered by insurance

THREE Define the term insurable interest and state who may or may not have an insurable interest in property or another's life

FOUR Discuss the components of a risk management program

FIVE Explain how potential losses can be avoided, reduced, or transferred by methods other than insurance

SIX Show how hedging can transfer the risk of price changes to others

INFORMATION AND DECISION MAKING

ACCOUNTING AND FINANCIAL STATEMENTS

17

STUDY OBJECTIVES

WHEN YOU HAVE FINISHED READING THIS CHAPTER, YOU SHOULD BE ABLE TO

ONE Describe the purpose of accounting in a business organization

TWO Identify the groups outside the business who are interested in accounting reports

THREE Name the main financial reports prepared by accounting departments and explain how they aid management

FOUR State what a balance sheet shows about the financial condition of a business

FIVE Outline the principal means used when interpreting financial reports

SIX Explain how budgets are prepared and how they help in financial planning

The Annual Report Is Becoming a Marketing Tool!

The annual report issued by management to stockholders on the financial and other operations of the company has long been considered the accountants' stronghold. Recently, however, the annual report has taken on a new shape and purpose. Many companies are trying to turn it into a basic marketing tool. As such, the report is designed to build the image of the company as well as provide product and financial data.

Companies are devoting space in the reports to corporate social responsibility, and political and environmental issues. For example, reports issued by R. J. Reynolds, Time, Abbott Laboratories, and Dow Chemical have all carried essays on government red tape and regulation.

St. Paul Insurance is one company that is trying to use "plain English" in its annual report. The reader need not be familiar with accounting language in order to understand the report.

IN THE NEWS

. . . There is no doubt that measurement standards have an impact on behavior. The way you keep score determines in part the way you play the game. But it would be a great mistake if standard-setting bodies were to start establishing standards because of the economic effect they have . . . .

JOHN C. BURTON
Former Chief Accountant
of the SEC

The keeping of business records is as old as business itself. Babylonians and Assyrians were among the first to record the names of persons who paid taxes. Under the Roman republic, accounting reached a high degree of perfection. The Romans were good administrators, and good administrators know the value of good accounting records.

Accounting has become the chief source of numerical data needed to operate a business. Small, medium-size, and large companies depend upon accounting as a source of information for decision making. The introduction of the computer into accounting has reduced the number of persons needed to record the various kinds of transactions manually. Computers now provide owners and managers with a wider assortment of facts not previously available to them.

After reading this chapter, you will understand why accounting is the language used for communicating facts about changing financial conditions in business. Accounting informs managers how well the business is doing. It gives answers to such questions as How much profit has the business produced? How much tax is owed? and Has the owners' equity increased?

ACCOUNTING DATA SERVE VARIOUS GROUPS

Accounting is the process of recording and reporting financial information about a business. It includes the activities of recording, classifying, interpreting, and reporting financial data.

W. MICHAEL BLUMENTHAL

W. Michael Blumenthal was elected to the board of directors of Burroughs Corporation in 1979. He became vice-chairman of the board in February 1980.

Born in Germany in 1926, Blumenthal received a bachelor of science degree in business administration from the University of California at Berkeley in 1951. He received a master of public affairs degree, and master's and doctorate degrees in economics from Princeton University in 1953 and 1956, respectively. He has subsequently been awarded numerous honorary degrees.

Blumenthal has had a distinguished career in business, government service, and education. After teaching economics at Princeton University from 1954 to 1957, he joined Crown Cork International Corporation where he rose to vice-president and director.

In 1961 Blumenthal joined the U.S. State Department as Deputy Assistant Secretary of State for Economic Affairs. He became an ambassador in 1963 and served for four years as the President's Deputy Special Representative for Trade Negotiations under Presidents Kennedy and Johnson. In this assignment, he was chairman of the U.S. Delegation to the Kennedy Round of Trade Negotiations.

Blumenthal joined the Bendix Corporation as president of Bendix International in 1967. He assumed the top executive position of chairman of the board, chief executive officer, and president in 1972.

Following a ten-year career with Bendix, Blumenthal returned to Washington in January 1977 as the sixty-fourth U.S. secretary of the treasury. He served in that position until his resignation in August 1979.

Blumenthal is a member of the boards of directors of the Chemical New York Corporation and its subsidiary, Chemical Bank; the Pillsbury Company; and the Equitable Life Assurance Society of the United States. He is also a member of the boards of trustees of the Rockefeller Foundation, the Council on Foreign Relations, and the Asia Society.

Managers Accounting provides the basis for measuring the quantitative standards of performance and progress. Manufacturers need to know their production costs as well as their sales results. Retailers need data from which to calculate sales, costs, and income. Inventory records are needed for control purposes. Payroll and other costs must be known before profits can be determined. Financial reports and budgets enable management personnel to decide how much a business will sell and, therefore, how much to buy.

Accounting reports are essential for systematic planning within an organization. If a company is manufacturing a dozen products, cost accounting can supply important data on each product. This would include the relative cost of production and distribution for each product, and the amount each will contribute to earnings. These data are used in deciding which products to push and which to discontinue.

Owners

In a corporation the stockholders need to know about the firm's financial position. Investors who own corporate stock receive periodic financial reports from management. Such a report often includes a letter to the stockholders from the company president. It explains the trends in company sales and profits and the outlook for the future. The letter is usually followed by abbreviated data on earnings, expenses, and profits. A comprehensive annual report is also included. This report contains a detailed balance sheet and an operating statement. Together these show the financial condition of the business, the amount of profit, the dividends being paid, and the amount of earnings being reinvested in the business.

A recent study on the uses of the annual report found that it rates as the most important source of investment information for investors. All respondents rated financial statements as the most important part, and the pictures and president's letter as the least important.

Furthermore, the study found that investors who place the highest importance on the annual report have had some special preparation in accounting, finance, or management.

Creditors

Accounting reports normally prepared at the close of the business year are the most reliable source of information on the financial condition of any business. If a business wants credit with a bank, the loan department of the bank analyzes the firm's financial statements in considering whether or not to grant the loan.

How does a creditor (a person to whom the business owes money) measure a firm's ability to pay? The creditor can use any of the "three *C*'s" of credit—character, capacity, or capital—but chances are he or she will look closely at the firm's capital as revealed in its accounting reports. Financial reports may, of course, reveal a firm's capacity as well as its capital, but creditors have more confidence in an actual statement of capital. Credit losses are usually high in cases where adequate accounting data are not available.

Sometimes the availability or lack of good accounting information can make the difference between survival and bankruptcy. For example, Chrysler Corporation's efforts to obtain federal financial help depended heavily on the company's accounting data:

> During the early part of Chrysler's attempt to get federal financial help, several concerns were expressed by government representatives. The director of the FTC's Bureau of Competition said that it might "be impossible to judge the soundness of Chrysler's forecast for improved sales unless the company [gave] more detailed information."
>
> Other federal officials were skeptical about Chrysler's argument that it needed help immediately.

Financial statements also serve as the basis for a firm's financial "rating" by such agencies as Dun and Bradstreet and banks making loans to the business. People who invest in stocks and bonds almost invariably review a firm's rating and financial reports when they are considering purchasing its securities.

Government Agencies

Various government agencies have an interest in the accounting records of a business enterprise. For tax purposes, both federal and state laws require private businesses to file financial statements.

The government is quite specific as to how tax data must be reported. In one recent case the IRS attempted to dictate to a chicken-raising unit of the Rocco Company how it must report its income:

> The chicken and turkey unit lost money the first year. Using the cash-accounting method, Rocco filed a consolidated tax return with a $2.4 million loss. However, the IRS perceived that if the company had used the accrual method of accounting, it would have had a profit.
>
> The IRS argued that it could force Rocco to use accrual accounting and make Rocco pay $455,000 in income tax. The case went to tax court, and the court decided the use of cash accounting was acceptable and the IRS could not "pluck" this taxpayer.

In this case the government lost, but often taxpayers must conform to IRS approaches to accounting for tax purposes.

Contributions made by business to the Federal Old Age and Survivors Insurance Program and to the state and federal unemployment compensation programs are based on a firm's payroll records. Computation of state sales taxes and federal excise taxes also requires accurate accounting records.

Accounting records such as time cards and payroll analyses enable the government to determine whether a business is complying with minimum-wage laws and rules pertaining to hours and overtime payments. All corporations whose stock is listed on a nationwide stock exchange are required to file reports of their financial operations with the Securities and Exchange Commission quarterly, and also prior to offering new capital stock to the public.[1] When the federal government is purchasing goods on a cost-plus contract, it requires detailed accounting reports from the seller, covering production operations and costs.

Labor Unions

Financial information reflected by a firm's income and expense statements is the basis for demands made by labor during collective-bargaining sessions. Demands for wage increases and added fringe benefits are usually accompanied by arguments and data based on the firm's profits. Labor unions give more attention to a company's financial statements today than ever before. Union officials often know as much about the factors that affect a firm's profits as does the firm's management. Increases in rates of productivity, reductions in unit costs, and trends in profits are among the factors that union leaders study carefully.

> President Jimmy Carter attempted to end a labor strike against the Rock Island Railroad which was severely disrupting Midwest grain traffic during the 1979 harvest season. The president sought to show that the Rock Island was without enough money to continue operations so that other railroads could take over its grain-hauling business until the strike ended. However, a federal judge

[1]The Securities and Exchange Act is discussed in Chapter 14.

reviewed the company's accounting records and rejected the government argument that the railroad was out of cash. He found that the railroad would show a profit for the month even though the strike continued.

Both in making wage and benefit demands and in deciding whether or not to strike, unions must consider company financial statements.

Accounting and Bookkeeping

The terms **accounting** and **bookkeeping** are often used interchangeably, although they are not synonymous. **BOOKKEEPING** is the routine recording of financial transactions for use by accountants. **Accounting** is a much broader term. Accountants devise accounting systems and forms to record transactions and determine how they should be classified, consolidated, and interpreted. Accountants participate in decision making on such things as company policy. Bookkeepers, because of their limited training, are restricted to routine tasks.

ACCOUNTING PROCEDURES AND METHODS

We have noted that one of the functions of accountants is to determine the record system best suited to a particular business. Without such procedures and methods, gathering and classifying business data would lack uniformity and usefulness for its users.

The Accounting Process

The flow chart in Figure 17-1 shows the kind of details involved in the accounting process. Its purpose is to provide persons inside and outside the business with specific financial data. The process starts with the question of what entry is needed and ends with the final preparation of reports to serve several different users.

Recording transactions. The first step in the process of recording data involves making entries in the appropriate journals. Here all entries are entered in chronological order and an explanation is given for each. The journals (books

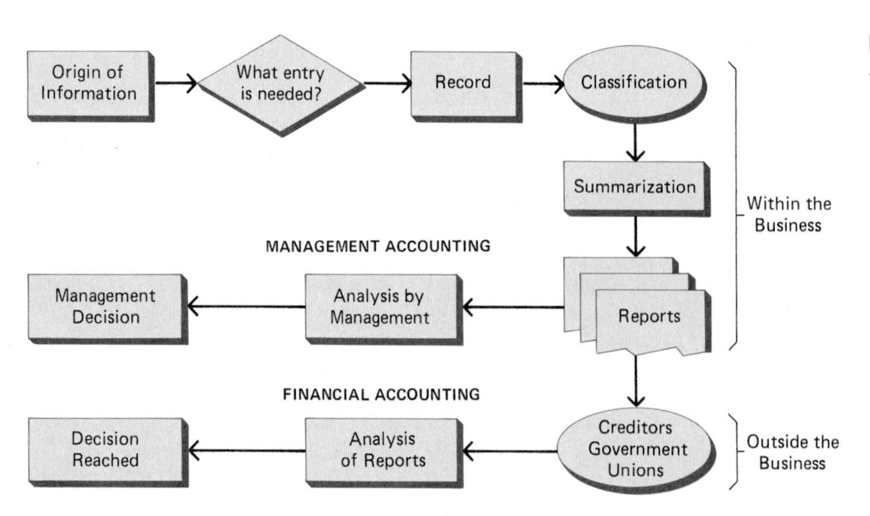

FIGURE 17-1
The accounting process.

of original entry) most commonly used are the cash book, sales journal, purchase journal, and a general journal for miscellaneous entries. The sources of these entries are the various business papers that result from business transactions. There should be some sort of written record as the authority for each tranaction entered in the journals.

Classifying transaction data. After the daily entries have been made in the journals, the second step is to **transfer data to accounts in the ledger. This process is called** *posting.* Whereas transactions are recorded in order in a journal, they are classified by accounts in the ledgers. For example, transactions pertaining to sales might appear in several different journals, but all entries involving sales would be brought together in one place (the sales account) in the ledger. By reviewing the sales account, a merchant can tell how the sales have fluctuated from day to day or from month to month. When it is time to prepare a financial statement, the totals are taken from the ledger.

Interpretation of summary statements. **The final and most important step is drawing conclusions from the financial statements. They reveal many aspects of a firm's financial condition, and their analysis requires precise knowledge of accounting.** An accountant is able to determine whether a business can pay its current obligations and whether a company's debts are excessive. These facts may serve as control factors and are used by management to formulate financial policy to meet changing conditions. Budgets for the next accounting period may be prepared by examining a firm's financial reports.

Reporting financial data. A particular business may require any special type of report at any time. However, the two major reports prepared regularly are the **balance sheet** and the **income statement**. These are generally referred to as financial statements. They are both discussed fully in the next major section of this chapter.

The Accounting Period

Profits and losses are computed for a given period of time, whether for one month, six months, or one year. **This time period** is known as **the ACCOUNTING PERIOD, or fiscal period.** For tax purposes, the accounting period is one year. But a business may elect to use either a calendar year or a fiscal year. Most businesses try to avoid ending the fiscal year on or about April 15, which is the date that annual income-tax returns are due.

The Accounting Equation

There are two types of equities in a business—equity of the creditors, and equity of the owners.

The total value of the assets must equal the total equities. This is shown in the form of what is called the **BASIC ACCOUNTING EQUATION:**

Assets = Liabilities + Owners' Equity

You will see shortly that the balance sheet is an enlargement of the accounting equation.

FINANCIAL STATEMENTS

We have already noted that the two most important financial statements derived from the accounting process are the **balance sheet** and the **income statement**. We will now study the contents of each and observe various methods of interpreting the data in each. Both statements are produced to give management and others a financial picture of the business.

The Balance Sheet

The **BALANCE SHEET** is **a statement of the financial condition of a business or institution on a specific date.** It is like a physician's report of an individual's physical condition. It is true at the moment, but the picture will change when new transactions occur.

The balance sheet is a statement of assets, liabilities, and owners' equity.

Assets. **ASSETS include all items owned by the business that have value.** Examples are cash, merchandise, accounts receivable, land, buildings, and equipment. Current assets include cash and other items, such as merchandise and accounts receivable, that will be converted into cash within a period of one year. Fixed assets are those whose life extends longer than one year. Fixed assets normally include items needed to operate a business, such as buildings and equipment. Fixed assets are to be used rather than bought and sold for a profit.

Liabilities. **LIABILITIES** refers to **a firm's indebtedness.** Examples include accounts payable, notes, taxes, mortgages, and bonds. Like assets, liabilities are classified as current and long-term, depending on whether or not they will fall due within a year. Notice the examples of current and long-term liabilities in the balance sheet of the Halstead Company (see Figure 17-3).

Owners' equity. Owners' equity is also called capital. It is the difference between the total assets and the total indebtedness:

Assets − Liabilities = Owners' equity

In a corporation the sums paid in (invested) by the owners are called capital stock. The profits earned over the years and reinvested by the business are called retained earnings (or earned surplus). The total of capital stock and retained earnings constitutes the equity of the owners.

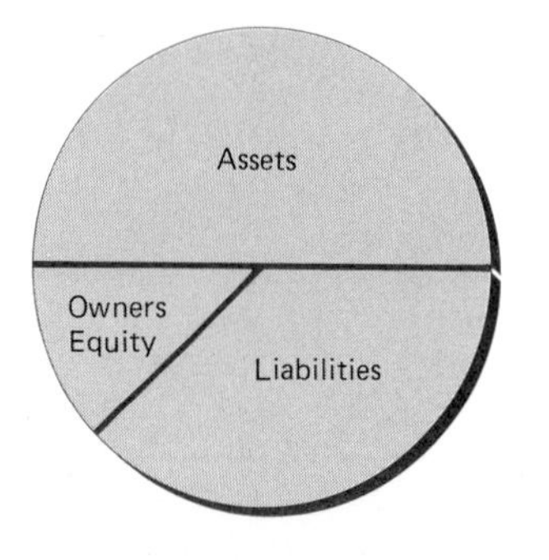

FIGURE 17-2
Owners' equity.

FIGURE 17-3
BALANCE SHEET FOR HALSTEAD CLOTHIERS DECEMBER 31, 19__

Assets		
Current assets:		
Cash	$148,075	
Accounts and notes receivable	310,800	
Merchandise inventory	151,020	
Total current assets		$609,895
Fixed assets:		
Buildings and equipment	250,575	
Less allowance for depreciation	190,430	
Total fixed assets		60,145
Total assets		$670,040
Liabilities and Owners' Equity		
Current liabilities:		
Accounts and notes payable	$143,700	
Taxes payable	7,050	
Total current liabilities		$150,750
Long-term liabilities:		
Mortgage payable		243,830
Total liabilities		394,580
Owner's equity:		
James Halstead, capital		275,460
Total liabilities and capital		$670,040

The Income Statement

Not all the essential facts about a firm's financial condition are provided in the balance sheet. It reveals only facts about the firm's assets, liabilities, and ownership. No mention is made of the income and expenses and of whether the business earned a profit or sustained a loss.

The INCOME STATEMENT shows the firm's operations and reflects its profit or loss status. Whereas the balance sheet shows a firm's financial condition on a given date, the income statement shows the results of operations over a period of time.

FIGURE 17-4
INCOME STATEMENT OF THE HALSTEAD CLOTHIERS
For the Year Ending December 31, 19__

			Percentage
Sales	$828,090		
Less sales returns	42,800	$785,290	(100.0)
Cost of goods sold*		482,695	(61.5)
Gross profit on sales		$302,595	(38.5)
Less expenses			
Administrative expenses	$ 65,700		(8.4)
Selling expenses	210,038		(26.7)
Total expenses		275,738	(35.1)
Net income from sales		$ 26,857	(3.4)

*Supporting Schedule Cost of Goods Sold

Beginning Inventory	$142,280
Purchases	491,435
Merchandise available to sell	$633,715
Ending inventory	151,020
Cost of goods sold	$482,695

Income. As we noted in Chapter 1, the chief purpose of a privately owned business is to earn a profit. This is achieved by selling products at prices higher than their cost. This produces *income*, which increases the owners' equity in the business.

In a retail establishment, the income must exceed the combined cost of goods purchased and the expenses incurred in operating the business. **NET INCOME** is **the amount left after subtracting all costs and expenses.** To have a net income, a manufacturing enterprise must sell its products at a price that exceeds the combined cost of raw materials, labor, overhead, and selling and shipping costs. It is now required that a corporation report both net income before federal income taxes and net income after taxes. Income earned from the normal course of business operations—the manufacture and/or sale of goods—is sometimes shown under the caption *operating income.* Income from interest earned or discounts taken on bills payable is shown as nonoperating or *financial income.*

Cost of goods sold. A wholesale or retail establishment buys its goods to resell. So their cost plus transportation charges constitutes the cost of goods sold. For a manufacturing firm, this cost includes raw material, transportation expense, and labor, in addition to operating expenses generally lumped together as overhead.

Expenses. **When payments are made for services received, they result in a direct decrease in the owners' equity. These decreases are called EXPENSES** and are frequently classified as administrative, operating, or selling expenses. Administrative expenses include management costs and various office expenses. Operating expenses include the depreciation of equipment and machinery, factory labor, and utility expenses. Selling expenses include salaries and travel expenses for salespeople, advertising costs, and shipping expenses.

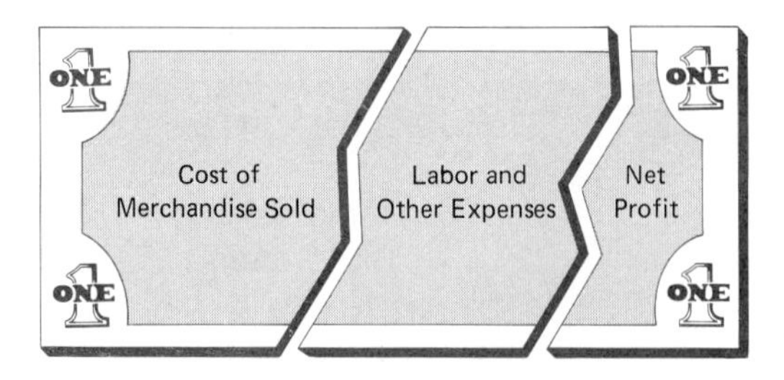

FIGURE 17-5
What becomes of the income.

APPRAISING OPERATIONAL RESULTS

Regardless of how accurately records are kept or how complete summary statements are, the value of most accounting data lies in how these data are analyzed and interpreted. In a small business, the bookkeeper prepares the financial statements and the owner interprets them. In a large business, however, accountants prepare the statements and the chief accountant and the administrative officers interpret them.

Financial Analysis through Comparisons

Financial analysis takes many forms. Here we want to consider various comparisons of different types of data.

Comparison with past performance. Probably the most frequently used comparison shows a relationship between current performance and that of the preceding period (year, quarter, or month). For such a comparison to be valid, the data for both periods must be recorded and analyzed in the same manner. This type of comparison, in which pertinent figures are listed side by side, shows the trend in business operations.

For example, Nordman Corporation of Amherst, Ohio, a manufacturer of equipment for applying paints, adhesives, and coatings, records material prices daily, monthly, quarterly, and annually. These material prices can then be compared with past prices, and the increase in costs can be carefully plotted. This plotting permits accurate forecasts for future material costs.

Comparison with planned goals. Comparing actual results with the performance that was planned for earlier is important. To what degree were the objectives set earlier achieved or exceeded? In addition, one must seek an answer to the question, What was responsible for the difference? That is, did the trend in the entire industry shift? Were there changes in the overall economy? Were the changes peculiar to our situation?

This type of comparison focuses on problems and new opportunities. Management can then decide whether more vigorous efforts are needed to achieve objectives or whether the goals and objectives should be modified.

Comparison with competitors' achievements. Data showing industry averages are provided for most types of businesses. A special accomplishment or significant deviation compared with one's competitors would show up as being above or below the averages.

In addition to broad categories of data published in government documents, valuable data are often supplied by cooperative trade associations. These associations make periodic reports to their member companies. Comparative data are usually available on costs and profit ratios, and sometimes on prices or pricing policies. Company salespeople also gather information and report on competitors' activities in their geographical regions. Where one's competing companies are publicly owned corporations, published annual reports are available for comparison purposes.

Use of percentages. Another statistical tool that management uses is percentages. For example, various items in the income statement, such as cost of goods sold, administrative expenses, and selling expenses, are shown both in dollar figures and in percentages of income from sales. The income statement for Halstead Clothiers (Figure 17-4) shows these percentages in the column on the right. An examination of that statement shows that the cost price of the goods sold was 61.5 percent of the selling price, making the gross profit 38.5 percent of the selling price. Both the dollar amounts and the percentages of the administrative and selling expenses are shown. The net income of $26,857 represents a rate of 3.4 percent of sales.

Sometimes the income statement is broken down according to departments. In this way, management can see at a glance how the various departments compare with one another in total sales, costs, and profits.

Ratios That Measure Financial Strength

As noted earlier in this chapter, the balance sheet shows the total picture of assets, short- and long-term debts, and ownership equity. Management is often interested in a breakdown of selected items listed on the balance sheet. Many of these relationships are in the form of ratios: current ratio, liquidity ratio, working-capital ratio, and debt-to-equity ratio. A ratio shows the relationship between two numbers. It is found by dividing one number by the other one. Ratios are not sufficient when used alone but are significant when combined with other data.

The current ratio. One of the most commonly used ratios is the **CURRENT RATIO. It is found by dividing the current assets by the total of current liabilities.** This ratio gives management an indication of the solvency of the business and the firm's ability to pay its debts. What constitutes a desirable ratio depends on the nature and type of business. In a business where the turnover of merchandise is slow, as in a jewelry store, there will be a greater need for cash and a larger current ratio than where the turnover is rapid, as in a supermarket. A department store would have one current ratio, and a motor vehicle dealer would have quite a different one.

Using the values shown on the balance sheet in Figure 17-3, the current ratio for Halstead Clothiers is 4.05:

$$\frac{\text{Current assets}}{\text{Current liabilities}} = \frac{\$609{,}895}{\$150{,}750} = 4.05$$

This compares favorably with the ratio of 3.86 shown for family clothing stores in Table 17-1.

The liquidity ratio. This is a ratio of cash and its equivalent (marketable securities and accounts receivable) divided by current liabilities. It is a supplement to the current ratio. It shows whether a company can meet its current obligations or pay larger dividends. It is sometimes called a quick ratio, or the **acid-test ratio.** The absolute minimum acceptable liquidity ratio would be 1.

Working capital. **WORKING CAPITAL is the excess (in dollars) of current assets over current liabilities.** It is closely related to the current ratio. It is the same information stated in terms of dollars rather than as a ratio. Working capital indicates a firm's ability to meet its operating expenses and to buy additional goods for resale. If a firm has enough capital on hand, it can take advantage of attractive buying propositions that it would otherwise have to pass up.

Using the figures appearing in Figure 17-3, we see that the working capital for Halstead Clothiers is $459,145:

$$\begin{array}{ccc} \text{Current assets} & - & \text{Current liabilities} \\ \$609{,}895 & - & \$150{,}750 \quad = \$459{,}145 \end{array}$$

TABLE 17-1
CURRENT RATIOS FOR SELECTED TYPES OF RETAIL BUSINESSES

Type of Business	Number of Stores	Current Ratio
Automobile dealers	92	1.53
Clothing—family	97	3.86
Clothing—men's and boys'	220	2.87
Department stores	333	3.06
Discount stores	98	2.21
Furniture	158	3.70
Hardware	92	3.79
Jewelers	138	1.70
Radio and TV	63	2.20
Shoe stores	102	4.05

Debt-to-equity ratio. This ratio gives an index of the relationship between the capital furnished by the owners and the borrowed capital. Today the management of most companies uses the financial leverage of borrowed capital. That is, the management attempts to earn more with borrowed capital than the interest cost it must pay. In a sense, the spread between owners' equity and debt represents the safety margin that ensures that the indebtedness will be repaid.

Using the figures for Halstead Clothiers as reported in Figure 17-3, we have a current debt-to-equity ratio of 54.7 percent:

$$\frac{\text{Current debt}}{\text{Owners' equity}} = \frac{\$150{,}750}{\$275{,}460} = 0.547, \text{ or } 54.7 \text{ percent}$$

Ratios That Measure Operating Results

Thus far we have discussed ratios used to measure the financial strength of a business. At this point, let us focus on ratios relating directly to measuring the operating results. Two such ratios discussed here are the inventory turnover and the return on investment.

Inventory turnover. The **INVENTORY TURNOVER** ratio is **the number of times the value of stock on hand (inventory) is sold during the year.** This ratio is found by dividing the cost of goods sold by the average inventory. It reflects how many times a business sells the goods kept on hand. A high inventory turnover is desirable, for it means the investment in goods is being kept to a minimum. The figure normally used is found by averaging the beginning and the ending inventory. Using the figures from the income statement for Halstead Clothiers (Figure 17-4), we have these calculations:

$$\frac{\text{Beginning inventory} + \text{Ending inventory}}{2} = \text{Average inventory}$$

$$\frac{\$142{,}280 + \$151{,}020}{2} = \$146{,}650 \text{ (average inventory)}$$

$$\frac{\text{Cost of goods sold}}{\text{Average inventory}} = \frac{\$482{,}695}{\$146{,}650} = 3.3 \text{ (inventory turnover)}$$

This figure of 3.3 compares favorably with the figure of 3.7 shown for inventory turnover for family clothing stores in Table 17-2.

Inventory valuation. In determining inventory valuation, the time during which the inventory costs are incurred is important. Among the generally accepted methods used to determine the **time** sequence of costs for inventory accounting are **last-in, first-out** (LIFO) and **first-in, first-out** (FIFO).

During the inflationary period of the 1970s, many firms switched to the LIFO method of inventory accounting. LIFO is an inventory valuation by which cost of goods sold is based on the most recent purchase of goods. By using recent prices, the cost of goods sold reflects a higher price that must be paid to buy new goods or raw materials. Using LIFO reduces the profit shown on the income statement because it raises the cost of goods sold. However, those favoring LIFO argue that it provides a more accurate statement of actual profits than does FIFO. During inflationary periods, taxes are lowered because profits are reduced.

FIFO inventory valuation assumes that the first items bought were the first ones used in production or first sold. Thus the value of the inventory on hand would be close to current market prices. During times of inflation, the higher inventory value increases profits shown on the income statement. Thus the amount of income taxes to be paid would also be higher.

Figure 17-6 compares the two methods of inventory valuation. Each method can have an effect on profits before taxes. In Figure 17-6 FIFO profits are $7,200 and LIFO profits are $5,400. The inventory valuation method used also makes a difference in the movement of cash in and out of the firm (cash flow). For example, in Figure 17-7 there is a deficit for FIFO and a cash flow total of $516 under LIFO.

In Figures 17-6 and 17-7 the accounting figures are the same in each case except for the pricing of inventories. The beginning inventory is 1,000 items

TABLE 17-2
INVENTORY TURNOVER RATIOS FOR SELECTED TYPES OF RETAIL BUSINESSES

Type of Business	Number of Stores	Inventory Turnover
Automobile dealers	92	6.7
Clothing—family	97	3.7
Clothing—men's and boys'	220	3.8
Department stores	333	5.5
Discount stores	98	5.2
Furniture	158	4.6
Hardware	92	3.9
Jewelers	138	16.7
Radio and TV	63	5.0
Shoe stores	102	3.7

FIGURE 17-6
COMPARISON OF INVENTORY PRICING

	FIFO	LIFO
Beginning inventory		
1,000 units @ $10	$10,000	$10,000
Purchases		
1,100 units @ $12	13,200	13,200
Total available for sale	$23,200	$23,200
Sales		
900 units at $18	16,200	16,200
Cost of goods sold		
900 units at $10 each	9,000	
900 units at $12 each		10,800
Profit (before taxes)	$ 7,200	$ 5,400
Federal income tax @ 46 percent	3,312	2,484
Profit (after taxes)	$ 3,888	$ 2,916

carried on the books at $10 each, and the inventory at the end of the accounting period is 1,200 items with a current cost of $12 each. Sales during the period were 900 items at an average price of $18.

Return on investment. Many company managers consider this ratio the single most important index of overall operating performance. It is obtained by dividing earnings by total capital. For a corporation, total capital would include common and preferred stock, retained earnings, and borrowed capital. This ratio is considered an indication of how well management has used the total resources available within the business.

In the case of Halstead Clothiers, this would be

$$\frac{\text{Net income}}{\text{Capital}} = \frac{\$26{,}857}{\$275{,}460} = 9.75 \text{ percent}$$

The national average figure for family clothing stores is 8.3 percent.

Return on sales. One of the most interesting ratios is earnings as a percent of sales. This varies greatly by type of business. It is relatively small for grocery stores, motor vehicle dealers, and discount houses (less than 2 percent) and much higher for jewelry stores, household appliances, and hardware stores. Where this percentage is small, the stock turnover is usually large.

FIGURE 17-7
CASH POSITION AT END OF ACCOUNTING PERIOD

	FIFO	LIFO
Income from sales	$16,200	$16,200
Cost of goods purchased	−13,200	−13,200
	$ 3,000	$ 3,000
Taxes paid	− 3,312	− 2,484
	$ 312*	$ 516

*Deficit amount

For Halstead Clothiers, the return on sales is

$$\frac{\text{Net income}}{\text{Sales}} = \frac{\$26{,}857}{\$785{,}290} = 3.42 \text{ percent}$$

The national average return for family clothing stores is 3.27 percent.

THE FINANCIAL ACCOUNTING STANDARDS BOARD

The national professional organization of practicing CPAs is the American Institute of Certified Public Accountants (AICPA). In 1959 the AICPA created the Accounting Principles Board. The purpose of this board was to set forth accounting principles and policies to be followed by the accounting profession. This board was besieged from all sides during its thirteen-year existence. It came under fire early, being charged with failure to correct alleged abuses. The final result was that on July 1, 1973, it was replaced by the Financial Accounting Standards Board (FASB). The FASB was established as a private independent board. Whereas its predecessor set forth "principles," the FASB uses the term **financial accounting standards.**

Two of the basic premises of the FASB are that when a standard is established

1. It should be responsive to the needs and viewpoints of the entire economic community, not just the public accounting profession, and
2. It should operate in full view of the public through a "due process" system that gives interested persons ample opportunity to make their views known.

One of the most controversial FASB rulings is Standard No. 8, which relates to inflation accounting. It deals with the valuing of fixed assets and says that fixed assets are to be shown in annual reports at current values rather than historical cost figures.

The board will permit a company to experiment with one of two alternatives. A corporation may present key operating, asset, and market data using current costs to determine whether corporate performance has kept pace with the ravages of inflation. Or a company may disclose essentially the same information in constant dollars by adjusting its numbers with the official consumer price index to show whether its purchasing power has been maintained.

In theory, the standards should help investors analyze, for example, whether a rather handsome earnings increase is due to good company performance or simply the result of inflation.

THE USES OF BUDGETING

We have observed from time to time that planning is one of the most significant aspects of business management. Much of the financial planning of business is based on budgets. A **BUDGET is a financial plan showing anticipated income**

and outlays for a given period. Budgets are usually prepared for both individual departments and the business as a whole. If the expenditures for a department equal the amount appropriated, we say that its budget is **balanced.** When the expenditures exceed the amount budgeted, we say that the department has operated at a **deficit.**

Purposes of Budgets

A well-prepared budget helps management in several ways. Perhaps its primary function is to serve as a guide in planning financial operations. It also establishes limits for departmental expenditures. Although budgets are at best only estimates, they are usually accepted as the limits within which a department is to operate. If there must be an overexpenditure in one area, an attempt is made to curtail expenses in other areas.

Another important purpose is to encourage administrative officials to make a careful analysis of all existing operations. On the basis of their analysis, present practices may be justified, expanded, eliminated, or restricted.

Types of Budgets

Perhaps the most important budget to be prepared—certainly the first one—is the **sales budget.** This is an estimate of the total anticipated sales during the budgetary period. One method of preparation commonly used is to have each salesperson estimate the sales increase he or she can achieve in the territory served. As a rule, these estimates are broken down by principal lines or, in some cases, by individual items.

Another approach is to begin with a line graph of sales for recent years and to project it for the budgetary period. Any factor or new development that is expected to increase or decrease future sales must be taken into account. This could include such things as changes in equipment or office procedures. In this way, management can make a fairly accurate forecast of total sales and sales by products. It can then determine the expected gross income.

In this same manner, budgets are prepared for production operations, raw materials and supplies, sales expenses, advertising, labor, plant expansion, and any other activity that requires an important expenditure.

Steps in Budgeting

The first step is to make preliminary plans for the period ahead. All the important phases of the business operation must be studied. The records of past peformance are the starting point. Then estimates for the budgeting period are prepared.

The second step is to plan and keep records of expenditures during the budgetary period. These records should be broken down into several budget categories. They must be accurate, up to date, and relatively easy to interpret. Records of this sort enable management to make periodic comparisons to see whether actual expenses are falling into line with the estimates.

The third step is to study any departure from the original estimates. In some cases, management may decide to alter the budget. Such a situation might be created by unusual capital costs, such as building enlargement or modification that had not been anticipated, or by the unavoidable replacement of heavy equipment that suddenly becomes obsolete. However, in most cases management will take steps to bring expenditures into line with the original estimates.

Budgets are generally prepared in the accounting department from data furnished by other department heads. Sometimes this procedure is reversed, and the department heads prepare their budgets from data supplied by the accounting department.

Budgets Used for Control

If management is to have a fully effective cost-reduction program, constant pressure must be applied to costs. And budgets are the tools that management uses for control purposes. When they are well prepared and based realistically on past performances, they

1. Reveal weaknesses in the organization
2. Make it easier to fix responsibility
3. Make possible comparisons that show trends in performance
4. Help maintain balance among the divisions of the organization

Budgetary control helps shape overall plans, set performance standards, and coordinate activities into a unified whole. It is achieved through the use of forms that show at a glance both the budget estimates and up-to-date records based on actual performance. If there should be any deviations from the budgetary plan, they are called to the attention of management. For example, if materials or supplies are being consumed at an abnormal rate, immediate attention is given to improving the materials-control procedures. And if sales of a particular product are declining rapidly, or if sales are falling off in a given territory, immediate investigations are held to correct this situation.

Budgetary control includes the development and use of three basic budgets: income, cash, and capital.

The **income budget** includes estimates of both gross and net income. The **gross-income** estimate is based on sales forecasts. The **net-income** estimate results from subtracting anticipated expenses from the estimated gross income. Preparing this budget requires perception and analysis of factors outside the business itself. The trends for the industy as a whole and for the regional economy play an important role. Even the best and most accurate forecasts may prove invalid because of unforeseen price competition or research developments. Or a sudden shortage of essential raw materials may curtail operations severely.

The CASH BUDGET (or forecast) **estimates the amount of cash to be received during a future accounting period and the amount needed to pay for all anticipated disbursements.** (It also shows the amount of cash on hand at the beginning of the period and the amount expected to be on hand at the end of the period.) It represents a combination of the financial position of the business at the beginning of the fiscal period and the expected results during the period. Basically, it shows two things: the cash available for the period and an itemized list of expected demands for funds. An example of a cash budget is given in Figure 17-8.

The **capital budget** indicates how the sums for capital expenditures are to be allocated to the major departments. Like all budgets, these estimates must be kept flexible. Changes in market operations may change plans for expansion. Labor difficulties, even those of suppliers, may force a delay into a future fiscal period. Also, unexpected surplus funds may earn more through various investments.

The income and capital budgets are primarily the responsibility of the operating departments. But the cash budget is solely a financial function. The income and capital budgets are a coordinated plan of action to achieve company objectives. The cash budget reflects the anticipated results of those plans.

Budgetary estimates and performance records give attention to areas where action is needed. Yet the actual control over funds, materials, expenses, and so on, must be exerted by individuals. The budget as a control tool is no better than the knowledge and understanding of the people who prepare it or of those who live with it. Management should create a climate that stimulates interest in budgets and a desire to use them as guides against which to measure actual performance.

Zero-Base Budgeting

Until recently budget planners started with the current year's expenditures. Then they decided how much more—or less—to propose for the period ahead. Under this method of budgeting, the person preparing the budget was required to justify only the increase in the amount requested.

ZERO-BASE BUDGETING is a system by which the organization's entire proposed budget must be justified in order to be approved. Under zero-base budgeting, one starts from scratch and decides first on program requirements. Zero-base budgeting received national recognition when President Carter advocated its use by the government. Since then much controversy has arisen as to its use by business firms.

FIGURE 17-8
CASH BUDGET

Item	Monthly Average for Year	Month		
		January	February	March
Receipts:				
Accounts receivable collections	$12,000	$11,700	$12,200	$12,000
Disbursements:				
Accounts payable paid	$ 2,300	$ 2,500	$ 2,800	$ 3,000
Direct labor	2,200	2,400	2,700	2,700
Indirect labor	850	850	850	850
Variable manufacturing expenses	1,000	1,100	1,200	1,300
Insurance and taxes	150	150	150	150
General and administrative expenses	2,800	2,800	2,800	2,800
Selling expense	500	500	600	600
Total disbursements	$ 9,800	$10,300	$11,100	$11,400
Initial cash		$ 6,500	$ 7,900	$ 9,000
Cash change resulting from operations		1,400	1,100	600
Cumulative cash	6,500*	7,900	9,000	9,600
Desired level of cash		6,400	7,600	8,400
Cash excess		$ 1,500	$ 1,400	$ 1,200

*December 31.

Under zero-base budgeting, the budget planners must

1. Set specific program objectives
2. Define products or services to be required
3. Establish standards to be met
4. In some cases, suggest more than one spending level—the minimum level might very well be below the current spending

Zero-base budgeting has certain advantages. It reveals budget items that cannot be justified and therefore should be dropped. It treats all departments alike because they are bound by the same standards. It provides increases where they can be justified and involves more people in the decision-making process. It combines planning and budgeting into a single process.

Among its disadvantages are the following. The process may take more time, and therefore it may cost more to prepare the budget. Sometimes reliable cost data are difficult to obtain, and the manager is unable to justify the budget expenditure. More coordination among the departments is necessary. Without complete coordination, managers may be reluctant to use this kind of budget system. Where jobs must be justified, it may lead to managerial frustration in case the budget is not approved.

CAREERS IN ACCOUNTING

No matter which specialization in business you choose to follow, you will find that the study of accounting will be valuable to you in several ways. Accounting is closely related to every facet of business. In fact, accounting has been called the "language of business." It offers a wide variety of career opportunities.

Fields of Accounting

Accounting practice can be divided into three areas: private or industrial, governmental, and public.

Private accountants. In private businesses, accountants usually start as junior accountants or clerks. Accountants are needed proprietorships, partnerships, corporations, hospitals, schools, and nonprofit organizations. Private accountants may serve as managers, auditors, cost analysts, tax specialists, and financial managers.

Government accountants. Government accountants are those employed by local, state, and federal agencies. The accountant in government may take an examination given by the Civil Service Commission or a state merit system. The applicant is then assigned to a separate government agency or bureau. Both the Federal Bureau of Investigation and the Bureau of Internal Revenue employ numerous persons with accounting backgrounds. The applicant may be employed as an accountant, cost analyst, auditor, or tax specialist.

Public accountants. Individuals and independent organizations that specialize in selling their accounting services to businesses and individuals are called **PUBLIC ACCOUNTANTS.** The public accountant installs accounting systems, audits accounting records, prepares financial statements, and advises clients on taxes and other matters. Public accounting firms are increasing their services to clients to include consulting on problems relating to taxes, management, and corporate strategy.

Accounting as a professional field. The certified public accountant is the top member of his or her profession. The term **certified public accountant** (CPA) is the professional certification for public accountants. The CPA designation is issued by the State Board of Accountancy of each state. About three-fourths of all states require prospective CPAs to be college graduates. Some states require U.S. citizenship; others do not. Most states require at least two years of accounting experience as a prerequisite for taking the examinations. All states require CPA candidates to pass an examination administered by the American Institute of Certified Public Accountants. The examination covers accounting theory, accounting practice, auditing, and business law.

It is not necessary to have a CPA certificate to practice private accounting. But without it, one cannot practice public accounting and certify accounting statements.

The CPA does not recommend his or her client's firm as an attractive investment or a good credit risk for a loan. Moreover, the CPA does not guarantee the accuracy of the client's financial statements. The CPA does, however, certify that the information presented in the financial statements conforms to the generally accepted accounting principles sanctioned by the profession.

Most colleges of business administration offer advanced courses in accounting to prepare the student for the CPA examination. These include accounting systems, accounting theory, auditing, cost accounting, income taxation, and CPA problems.[2]

Other career opportunities. In addition to the three main fields of accountancy, there are other specialized areas providing career opportunities, such as

1. Bank auditing
2. Budget officer
3. Cashier
4. Computer programmer
5. College accounting teacher
6. Systems installer
7. Systems analyst
8. Income-tax specialist

SUMMARY OF KEY CONCEPTS

The accounting department of a business enterprise provides owners and managers with data about finances, sales, operations, and profits.

Reports to stockholders usually go beyond the balance sheet and income statements. They include sales and earnings by product lines, dividends and stock prices, and gains or losses due to currency translations on international sales.

In appraising the results of operations, the financial reports usually show comparisons with previous accounting periods, percentage distribution of the sales dollar among the

[2]Further information about a career as a CPA can be obtained from the American Institute of Certified Public Accountants, 1211 Avenue of the Americas, New York, N.Y. 10036.

major expense categories, and ratios that indicate the degree of liquidity enjoyed by the business.

Some of the more commonly used comparisons are current achievements (a) with past performance, (b) with planned goals, and (c) with the achievement of competing companies.

Commonly used ratios include the current ratio, working capital, inventory turnover, return on investment, and debt-to-equity ratio.

Budgeting is an important management function that is dependent upon data prepared by the accounting department.

There are several types of budgets normally prepared by a business enterprise, but budgetary control is centered on the income, cash, and capital budgets.

Accountancy is an excellent career choice for those who like to work with figures. It offers employment opportunities at beginning positions and is also rich in opportunities for promotion. Accountants are needed by every medium-size and large business enterprise, by service institutions, and by the government.

BUSINESS TERMS

You should be able to match these business terms with the statements that follow:

a. Accounting equation
b. Accounting period
c. Assets
d. Balance sheet
e. Budget
f. Cash budget
g. Current ratio
h. Expenses
i. Inventory turnover
j. Liabilities
k. Net income
l. Public accountant
m. Working capital

1. The period of time for which profits (or losses) are calculated
2. The formula Assets = Liabilities + Owners' equity
3. The statement of the financial condition of the business
4. Items of value that are owned by the business
5. The debts owed by the business
6. The sum left after subtracting all costs and expenses from gross income
7. Payments for services that reduce owners' equity
8. An amount calculated by dividing current assets by current liabilities
9. The amount by which the current assets exceed the current debts
10. The turnover of the investment in merchandise
11. A financial plan that shows anticipated income and outgo for a period of time
12. An estimate of the amount of cash to be received and spent
13. An accountant who offers his or her services to the general public

REVIEW QUESTIONS

1. Explain how accounting data can aid business managers in making business decisions.
2. a. Who has an equity in the assets of a business?
   b. What are the three elements of the basic accounting equation?
3. What does the balance sheet show about a business?
4. What does the income statement show about a business?

5. How is budgeting related to planning?
6. What is the difference between a certified public accountant and a public accountant?

DISCUSSION QUESTIONS

1. How would a prospective stock purchaser and a union-member employee differ in evaluating a company's financial statements?
2. Which financial statement gives a prospective purchaser of the business the more helpful information?
3. Name three important ratios used in interpreting financial statements and tell how each is obtained.
4. Select one important ratio and explain how it would be a help to management.
5. a. What is zero-base budgeting?
   b. What are its values?

BUSINESS CASE 17-1

Halstead Clothiers—To Buy or Not to Buy?

As we progressed through this chapter, we considered much financial data for Halstead Clothiers. This business is for sale at a price of $276,000. The current net capital investment is $275,460 (see Figure 17-3). The net income for last year was $26,857 (see Figure 17-4). This represents a return on investment of 9.75 percent. Other data given include a current ratio of 4.05, working capital of $459,145, a debt-to-equity ratio of 54.7 percent, an inventory turnover of 3.3, and a return on sales of 3.42 percent. Tables 17-1 and 17-2 show median figures for a selected group of family clothing stores for the current ratio, and for inventory turnover. Your research found that the median figures for selected data for family clothing stores as a group include:

Net profits to sales	3.27 percent
Current debt to net worth	43.2 percent

1. On which factors does Halstead Clothiers fail to match up as well as the median for family clothing stores?
2. Considering all the information available to you, would you recommend purchase?
3. What other information would you like to know about this business if you considering buying it?

BUSINESS CASE 17-2

Planning and Budgeting

The Bachus Company, an independently owned department store, has four departments: ladies' clothing; men's clothing; household furnishings; and radios, TVs, and home appliances. Although the company has never kept detailed records by departments, the inventories have always been prepared by departments. And sales, purchases, and salaries records for the past year are all available.

They can be analyzed to see what amounts should be allocated to the different departments.

The company president has asked each department head to submit a plan and budget for the coming year.

Assume that you are to set up guidelines for the department heads to follow and supply them with the data they need.

1. Explain how you would proceed to get the information needed and in what form it should be presented to the president.
2. What types of budgets would you ask for?
3. What kind of information should be included in each type of budget requested?

INFORMATION MANAGEMENT AND COMPUTERS

18

STUDY OBJECTIVES

WHEN YOU HAVE FINISHED READING THIS CHAPTER, YOU SHOULD BE ABLE TO

ONE Explain how the handling of masses of information can be woven into a system

TWO Name the steps involved in processing information

THREE Describe how computers serve businesses in processing data and in decision making

FOUR Name the steps involved in decision making

FIVE State what the term micrographics covers and explain how the use of film can aid in storing, retrieving, and utilizing data

SIX Explain how an open-office layout saves space and increases efficiency

IN THE NEWS IN THE NEWS IN THE NEWS IN THE NEWS IN THE NEWS IN THE NEWS IN THE NEWS IN THE NEWS IN THE NEWS IN THE NEWS

Executives Have Found That Computers Can Help with Daily Routine

Some top executives and government administrators have found that they can push buttons instead of shuffling papers and can thereby accomplish more work. A computer keyboard can be keyed to provide a daily calendar for the executive and key subordinate as well. The executive who wants to schedule a meeting can see at a glance when everyone is free.

The computer can also be used instead of the mails. It can send messages to other computers equipped with similar keyboards and screens. This "automated office" is portable as well. An executive can carry a light-weight computer terminal, plug it into a telephone, and dial the computer in the home office. He or she can work at home, in the hotel room when on business, or wherever.

A minicomputer drives the system. It can provide a combination card file, telephone log, and filing cabinet. Users can retrieve everything from old letters to voucher forms and can have them printed on paper.

Such automated offices are still somewhat experimental but can provide productivity gains among managers and professionals. During the past fifteen years the jobs of typists, insurance clerks, and newspaper reporters, among others, have been changed considerably by improved information-management techniques using the computer. As Roy Ash, chairman of A-M International Corporation, says, "If you really look at what management is, it is analyzing, synthesizing, and conveying information."

IN THE NEWS

As we bring together word processing, data processing, telecommunications, phototypesetting, and other functions, we must ensure we don't create an electronic booby trap. Our technical ability to interconnect systems and devices cannot be allowed to override our common sense. In the early days of data processing, labor costs went up rather than down; teams of expensive programming talent were needed just to make computers work. In our industry, we must make systems operate in the language of people, not the language of machines.

ROY L. ASH
Chairman of the Board
AM International, Inc.

Management decisions are based on up-to-date data. So a business's information-management system must be an effective one. The availability of complex business information requires some modern scheme for processing it.

Business data must be organized and stored systematically so that they can be retrieved quickly. For this reason the effective handling of records is a "business must." Many companies have installed their own high-speed electronic equipment. Others contract for computer services or share time with other users through computer service centers. As more minicomputers come on the market, additional companies will be able to install their own data-processing equipment because their cost will be more affordable.

Systematic decision making is an ongoing procedure, not an occasional process. New decisions are being made continually, and earlier ones are being reviewed. One thing that separates managers in high-level positions from those in lower-level positions is their ability to accept and fulfill decision-making responsibilities. This includes being able to live with the results of their decisions.

In this chapter we will look at the "systems concept" as it is applied to information handling. Then we will discuss computers and their role in processing data and examine the decision-making process as used in management.

THE SYSTEMS CONCEPT APPLIED TO INFORMATION HANDLING

Most people ordinarily view an activity such as decision making as consisting of only what they can see. But closer examination often shows that the activity includes several minor actions, operating together in an orderly fashion. These minor actions are a part of the activity as a whole, and they operate together. Operating together in unity, they give "system" to the activity. For the purpose of our discussion here, we will use the word **SYSTEM** to refer to **any series of related items or events whose interrelation is woven into an organizational pattern.**

The use of the "systems-and-procedures" approach has modernized the way office records are managed, bringing with it time and dollar savings. A records-management system includes a whole group of procedures that are coordinated for efficient handling of business information.

Computers now process all kinds of business information. At first computers were used for handling the routine tasks performed by records clerks and calculating-machine operators. Later they were used for ordering goods and parts, making travel reservations, scheduling production operations, and assisting in the design and control of manufacturing operations. Today businesses have systems for using computers in processing data that cut across departmental functions and boundaries.

The major uses of the records-management system in a business include the planning of work methods and procedures, forms design and control, quantity and quality of work (routing, scheduling, dispatching), cost control and budgeting, and space utilization and procedures.

The Diebold Group, Inc., concluded from one of its recent research surveys that approximately 10 percent of new plant and equipment expenditures are for computer systems.

Stages in System Development and Utilization

Developing a business's information-management system consists of the following five stages:

1. Assessment of problems and needs. The department manager determines the types and quantities of information that need to be handled. (In all probability, systems analysts would assist in this assessment.)
2. Preparation of system proposals by the staff, allocation of resources, and recommendation of an operating budget.
3. Design, implementation, testing, and conversion of the systems-development project.
4. Development and procurement of hardware, installation system testing, and completion of plans for operation and maintenance.
5. A "try-out" operation, evaluative comparison of expected and actual outcomes in terms of costs, benefits, and so forth, and a determination of improvements and/or future systems development.

WHAT IS DATA PROCESSING?

Most persons probably think of data processing as the handling of large amounts of numerical information by machine at a very rapid rate. However, data processing in its simplest form includes *any* kind of information handling: When a shipping clerk prepares invoices for payment, when a records clerk sorts checks, or when a typist prepares statements of account to send to a customer, this is data processing.

We can process information by hand or by machine. In every office a great deal of information is processed by hand. Some data must always be processed by hand to a certain degree in order to get these data into the proper form to be processed later by a machine. Today, however, we handle most accounting and statistical data by machine, and save time. A typical information-management system can now provide much useful information that was not available to managers a few years ago.

An Example of Data Processing

One of the best ways to explain how business data are handled is to examine a typical business transaction involving merchandise. As an example of data processing, let us consider some supplies that must be ordered, received, and paid for.

Computation. Every purchase order describes and states the amount of the items wanted and lists the item cost and the total cost of the goods ordered. This latter figure is arrived at by multiplying the price per unit by the number of units. (This figure may, however, differ from the total cost of purchase; other charges may be added.) So **computation** is a necessary operation.

Communication. After the order form is prepared, it is sent to the company from which the goods are to be purchased. This operation can be called **communication.** At a later date there will be other instances of communicating information—such as when the goods are shipped by the seller, and when a check is issued in payment for the shipment.

Recording and filing. There are several records to be made in connection with the transaction we are using as our illustration: a record of the order, of the receipt of merchandise, of the obligation to pay for the goods, and of the payment that is made later. So the process of **recording** is another essential operation in the proper handling of a business transaction. And records do not just float around; they must be kept together somewhere, so they are usually filed according to some prearranged plan. When records are systematically arranged in specially prepared storage cabinets, we usually call this **filing.** But when data are recorded by a computer, the term **storage** is commonly used. So the filing or storing of information is another operational function in handling data.

Coding. Before records are stored, they are usually classified according to the nature of the transaction involved. It is easier and faster to record information by machine if it is stated numerically than if words are used. So the goods to be ordered in our illustration need to be classified—assigned an identification number. This is usually called **coding**, and it speeds up the operation when large quantities of data are involved.

Sorting. If you were responsible for paying for merchandise purchased, how would you remind yourself to do this on or before the particular day that the invoice falls due? One way would be to write yourself a note on your desk calendar pad. You might actually make the note on the sixth of the month, but you would put it on the page of the calendar pad that is dated the sixteenth, the date the bill is to be paid. A better way might be to file the invoice under the date of the sixteenth, and then on the sixteenth issue your check. However, you would at the same time have to prepare checks to pay all the invoices previously filed as being due on that day. So it is clear that when preparing several invoices for filing, you would arrange them in order according to their due dates. This is called **sorting**, and it is another important function in data processing. (Note that whereas in our illustration we sorted invoices and prepared them for filing by hand, in electronic data processing, the basic data instruments would be sorted rapidly by machine.)

Summarizing. The final phase of data processing is vital because it is important to know how many invoices are paid each day and the total amount spent in order to pay them. A list of all invoices paid on a particular date, the amount of each invoice, and the total paid would constitute a summary of this group of business transactions. **Summarizing** is therefore another essential function in handling large quantities of data.

The seven operations we have discussed are

1. Coding
2. Computing
3. Communicating
4. Recording
5. Sorting
6. Storing
7. Summarizing

These operations together make up the basic elements involved in data processing. We can define **DATA PROCESSING**, then, as **that group of operations performed in handling units of data from the original entry to the final entry.** A **data-processing system** would be the total method used to carry out the seven basic elements of data processing to accomplish the accounting, statistical, and reporting functions of business management.

THE COMPUTER

For centuries, mathematicians have sought a machine that would be capable of performing arithmetical calculations rapidly. In about 1880 W. H. Adhner invented the pinset calculator, which could perform arithmetical operations mechanically. And in 1885 William Burroughs developed the first mechanical adding machine for use in business. During the same year Herman Hollerith introduced the electronic punch-card calculating system. In 1944 Howard Aiken of Harvard University designed the Mark I, which was a mechanical computer. It was operated by a system of telephone relays, mechanized wheels, and tabulating equipment. In 1946 J. P. Eckert, Jr., and J. W. Mauchly of the University of Pennsylvania developed the first electronic computer. It was called the Electronic Numerical Integrator and Calculator. Five years later UNIVAC I, the first commercial computer, was built for the U.S. Department of Commerce by Remington Rand (now Sperry Rand). It was used in the office of the Bureau of the Census.

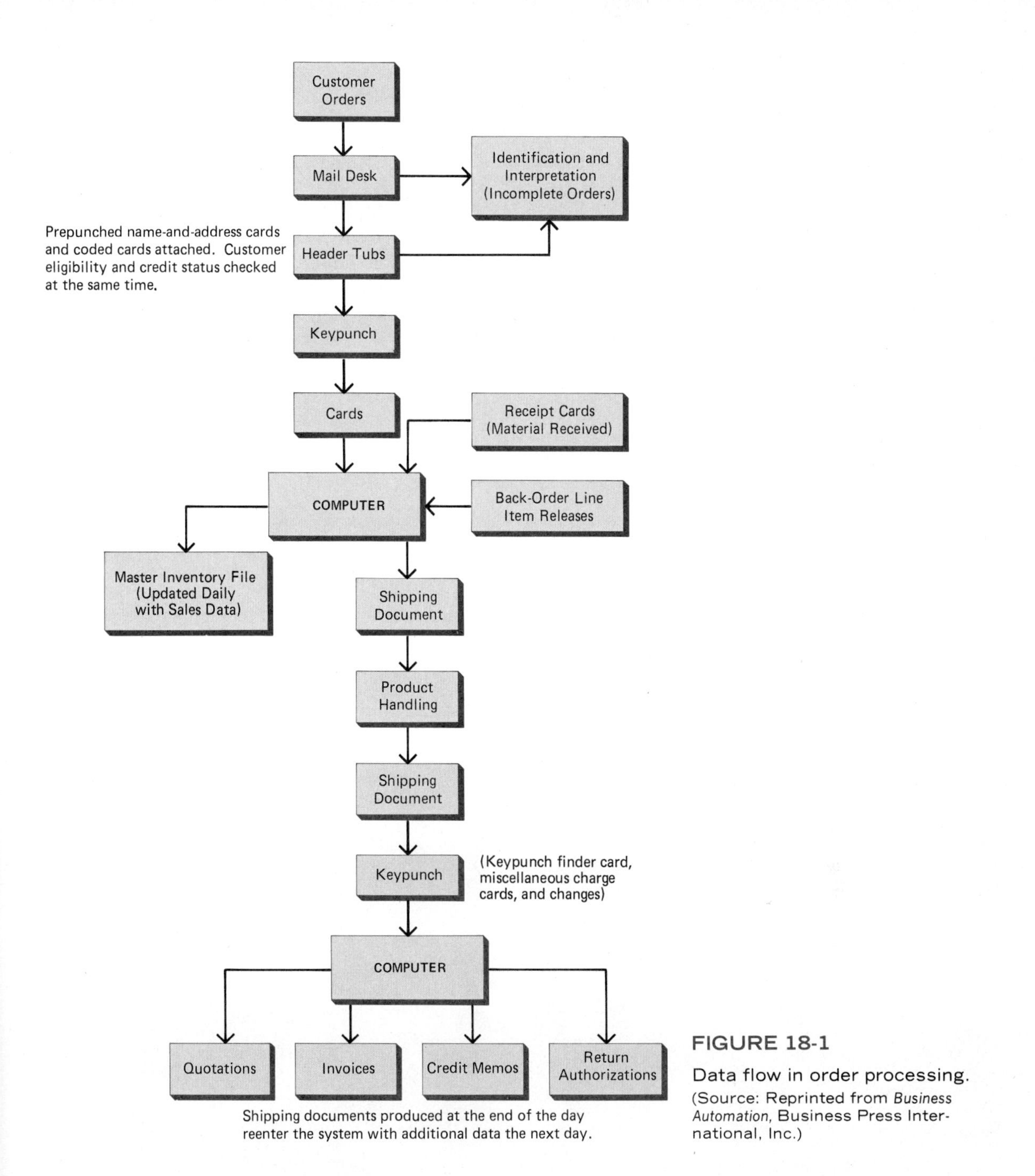

FIGURE 18-1

Data flow in order processing.
(Source: Reprinted from *Business Automation*, Business Press International, Inc.)

Unlike its predecessors, it used binary arithmetic and permitted the storing of instructions in its memory system.

Perhaps the work of the computer can best be illustrated by comparing it with an adding or a calculating machine. As with these simpler machines, the three basic elements involved are the input, processor, and output units. But the similarity stops there, because in the calculating machine, the keyboard is inevitably the means of putting information or data into the machine. And the output is achieved through some type of simple printing mechanism.

The Binary Number System

Digital computers operate by opening and closing electrical circuits. The circuit is either open, permitting the electrical impulse to go through, or it is closed. Therefore the binary number system is used instead of the more familiar decimal system. A comparison might be made to an electric light bulb—it is either on or off. Similarly, within the computer, transistors are held in either a conducting or a nonconducting state, and specific voltage potentials are either present or absent. These binary modes of operation are signals to the computer in much the same way that light or the absence of light is a signal to a person. Since an electric current can indicate only an "on" or an "off" situation, only two symbols are registered by the computer—either a 0 (for the "off" position) or a 1 (for the "on" position). In any single position of binary notation, the 0 represents the absence of any assigned value and the 1 represents the presence of an assigned value.

The memory component might consist of electronic rods, screens, thin film, or magnetic cores. These memory components serve as a sort of electronic filing cabinet. They have the capacity for storing huge amounts of information in a small space, and for reading this information out of storage automatically and at electronic speeds.

FIGURE 18-2
High-speed UNIVAC 490 Real-Time computing system manufactured by the Sperry Rand Corporation's UNIVAC Division. This is the installation at the Keydata Corporation, Cambridge, Mass., one of the nation's first on-line, real-time, and time-sharing computer centers. (Courtesy International Business Machines Corporation.)

Unlike the decimal system, which employs the digits 0 through 9, the binary system employs only two digits–0 and 1.

64	32	16	8	4	2	1 . . . value of each position
0	0	1	0	1	0	1 equals 21

The lowest-order position in the binary system is called the 1-bit and it can only have two conditions, 0 or 1. The next position is called the 2-bit; the next, the 4-bit; the next, the 8-bit, etc. . . each of which can have one of two conditions, 0 or 1.

Another example:

64	32	16	8	4	2	1 . . . value of each bit
1	0	1	0	0	1	1 equals 83

This is just another way of writing the quantity 83. Sixty-four ones, plus sixteen ones, plus two ones, plus one one, equals eighty-three units.

FIGURE 18-3

The binary number system.

COMPUTER HARDWARE

HARDWARE is computer terminology for the machines and equipment that make up a computing center. There are three components that constitute the computer hardware: the input unit, the processing unit (the processor), and the output unit.

The Input Unit

The input unit feeds data into the computer system. Its purpose is to enable the operator to "communicate" with the computer. It performs its function by translating codes from the external form (cards, magnetic tape, or punched paper tape) to the internal form in which data are stored in the memory unit. The data translated might be numbers to be used later in arithmetical calculations, instructions that tell the computer what to do, or numbers and letters to be used in names and addresses.

The **card reader** converts holes in cards into electrical impulses and transmits the information to the memory unit of the computer, ready for processing. Similarly, the **tape reader** performs this function when the input medium is tape instead of cards. The important factor here is that this "reading" of data by the card or tape reader is done independently of human attention.

Instead of a card reader or tape reader, the **optical scanner** may be used with the input medium. The optical scanner reads each character from some input medium and translates it into electrical impulses that are then transmitted to the computer for processing. Scanning devices are programmed to read and evaluate certain numerals, characters, and symbols. Rays of light scan a field on a document, form an internal image, and compare it with an image that has been programmed into the scanner's memory component. If the scanner finds the corresponding image, it accepts it and moves on to the next figure. The optical scanner makes possible the use of invoices, journal records, adding-machine tapes, and accounting-machine tapes as input media, instead of the usual punched

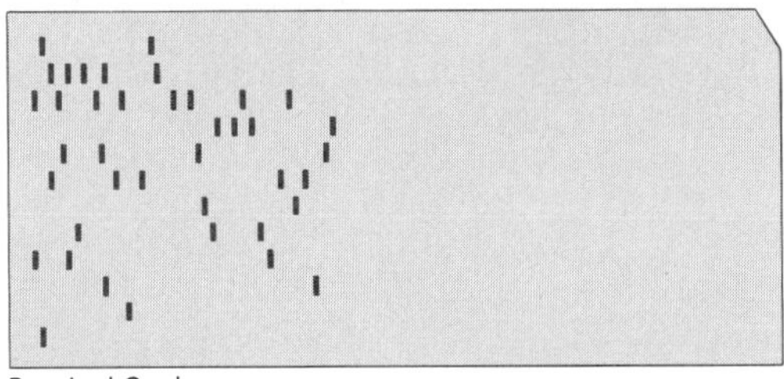

Punched Cards

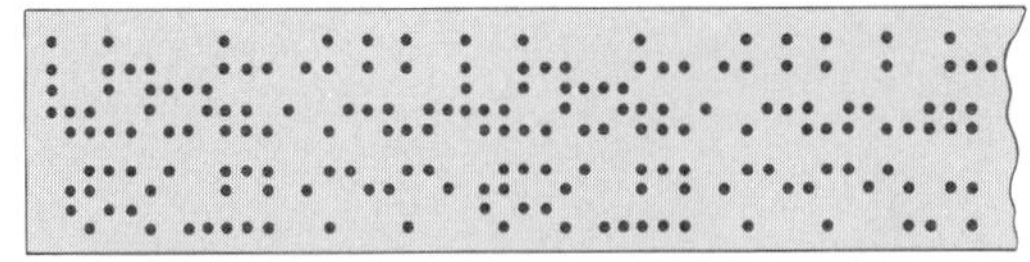

Punched Paper Tape

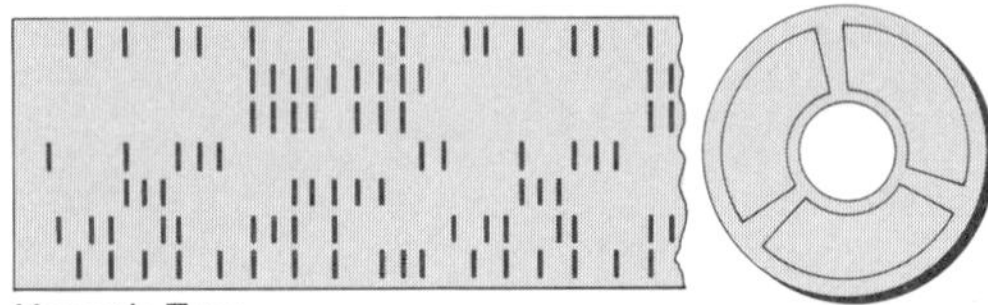

Magnetic Tape

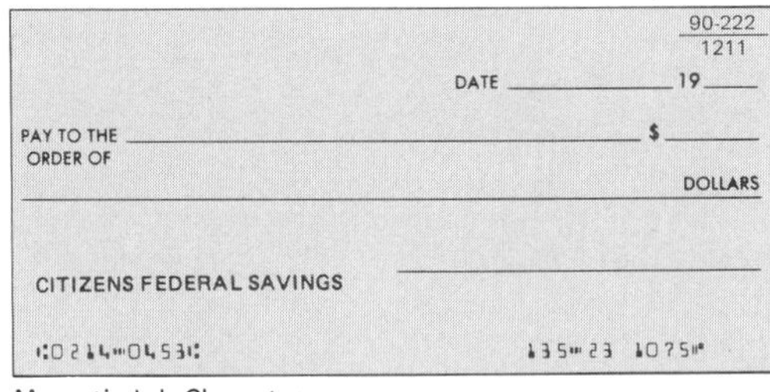

Magnetic Ink Characters

FIGURE 18-4

Input media.

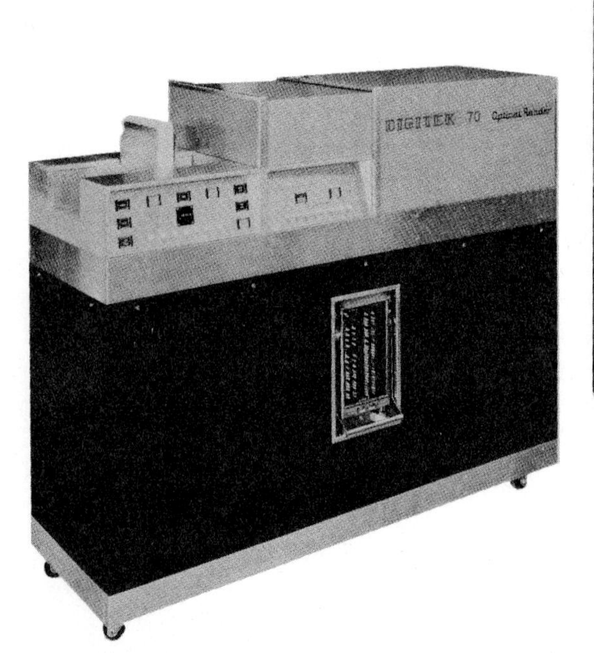

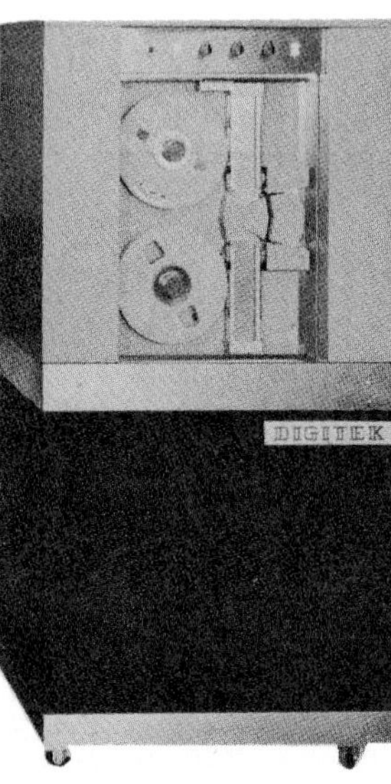

FIGURE 18-5

Digitek Optical Reader can read pencil-marked data from source documents at a basic speed of 2,500 sheets an hour, and transfers this information directly to magnetic tape. (Courtesy Optical Scanner Corp.)

card or punched tape. Ordinary pencils may be used on specially prepared forms for reading by optical scanners. The optical scanner represents the coming thing in data processing.

The Processing Unit

The processor (C.P.U.) forms the heart of the computer. It contains the memory or storage and the circuitry that performs the mathematical operations. In the first generation of computers, the circuitry was based on vacuum tubes, such as those that were used in radio sets. The speed of operations was approximately five hundred additions a minute. These units used a great amount of space, heat, and electricity and were plagued by the problem of tubes burning out.

Later models greatly reduced the size and cost of the computer. They also increased the speed, storage capacity, and reliability. The second-generation computers (1959–65) replaced the vacuum tubes with transistors. The third-generation computers (1965–70) made use of microelectronics (miniature circuits). This increased the packing densities of circuits by a factor of 100. They had the capacity to handle several programs at the same time.

During the 1970s the third-generation computers were greatly improved. While increasing the circuitry, they greatly reduced the size of the processor. Minicomputers were born, and by the end of the decade microcomputers were in use. Microcomputers are used in homes and can be purchased in consumer retail outlets, such as Radio Shack. Their circuits are based on silicon chips much smaller than the eraser of a pencil. Their tiny size shortens the distance the electric pulses must travel and lessens the steps needed to tie elements into one circuit.

The computer memory. The processor's center of operations is the memory or storage component. All data being processed by the computer pass through it. Immense quantities of data are therefore immediately available to the commands of the computer. The memory holds the input data, the intermediate result of calculations, the program of instructions telling the computer what to do, and the final results to be "read out."

Several types of memory units are used in computers. One is the **magnetic core**, which is used in most of the high-speed computers. Magnetic cores are made of special magnetic material shaped into circles, or "doughnuts," the size of pinheads. Each core can be magnetized at any time in one of two directions, one standing for the binary 0, and the other for the binary 1. Thousands of these cores are strung on criss-crossed wires, arranged like the strings of a tennis racket, inside a square frame. The frames are stacked one on top of another to make a basic memory unit.

The stacking arrangement places the cores in columns. Each of these columns is assigned an **address**, which is a specific location within the memory unit. Each column of cores can store either one fact or one instruction expressed in binary code. The stored data can instantly be "read out" from any address and used in working a problem. If desired, the data can be erased from any address and replaced with a new fact or instruction.

A recent advance in computer memory that has not yet been widely marketed is the "bubble memory." Data are stored in magnetic spots that look like bubbles floating on the tiny semiconductor chip. Development of the bubble memory, which can store five hundred thousand characters on a single fingernail-size chip, will change the computer technology radically.

Giants in the data-processing industry, such as IBM and Texas Instruments, are basing much of their future strategy on low-cost storage devices. But it has taken longer to get into production than anyone expected. Recently Bell Laboratories, which invented the device, has come up with a new design that should speed production.

The bubble memory has several advantages over other methods. Probably the greatest is its low cost and high reliability. There are no moving parts and it is quite small. It is now a U.S.-dominated industry, but the Japanese are pouring money into the bubble memory and will probably provide stiff competition.

There are several types of auxiliary storage: electronic rods, disks, drums, and magnetic tapes. In each case the data stored must be read into the C.P.U. for the arithmetical operation.

The capacity of a memory unit is measured in words. A **word**, which is a technical term, is defined as a group of binary digits that is treated as a unit and is stored in one location. A **location** is a unit storage position in the main internal storage, in which one computer word may be stored or from which it may be retrieved.

The magnetic disk for storage in computers was introduced in the mid-1950s. Since that time the disk has been greatly improved. Today, a single 8-inch disk can store as much information as 120 of the original 24-inch disks used in

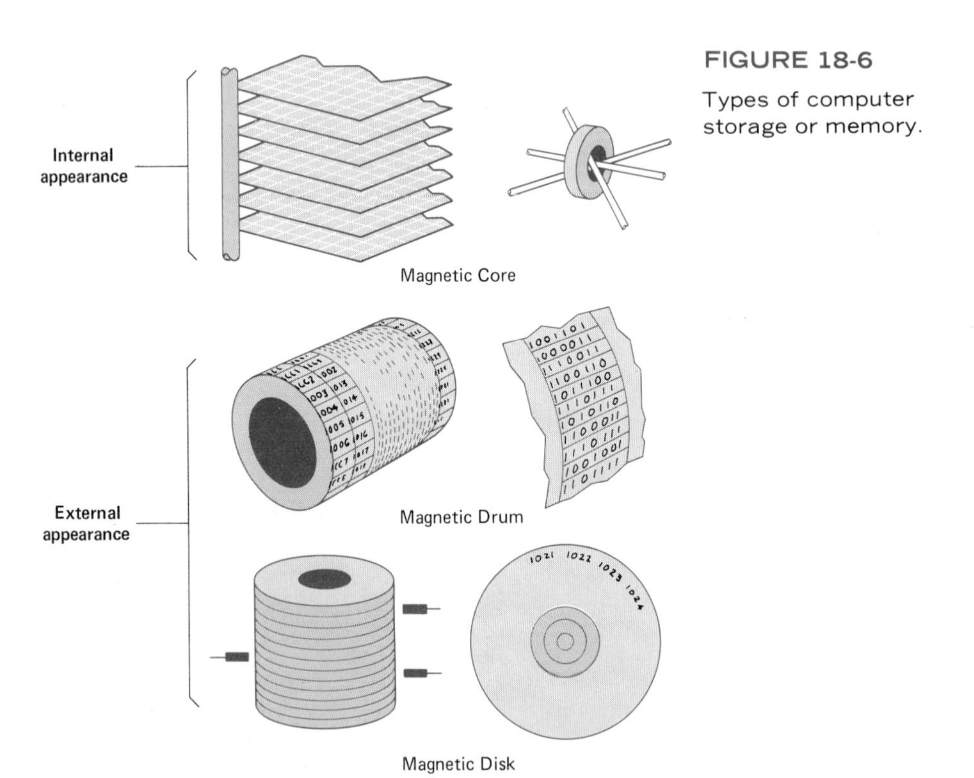

FIGURE 18-6

Types of computer storage or memory.

the 1950s. The cost has come down along with the size. Information storage that used to cost $150 can now be stored at a cost of one dollar.

The Output Unit

After information has been processed, it is printed out in the form of a report; this is called the **printout.** The equipment used is in the form of a high-speed printer, and several printers can be placed on the line with the central processor simultaneously.

In connection with a printed report, the output may take the form of a punched tape or a punched card, magnetic tape, magnetic disk, or cathode-ray tube, depending on the type of output. It is desirable to have a record of the report on magnetic tape when there is a need to process the data further by the use of computers, or to prepare a new copy of the report at a later date.

The output report is the end product of the computer. Some of the types of information that can be produced by a printer are statements of accounts, journals, trial balances, financial statements, bills, invoices, checks, payroll reports, or just lists of names and addresses.

COMPUTER SOFTWARE

SOFTWARE is the term used to refer to **the instructions to the computer. The instructions to a computer telling it what to do are in the form of a PROGRAM.** The person who writes these directions is called a **programmer.** A program consists of a set of coded instructions that inform the computer which data are to be picked up to be used, where the data are stored, what mathematical computations are to be performed, the order in which each operation is to be done, and what is to be done with the output. This program is first written out by hand or on a typewriter and is then transferred to cards or tape so that it can be fed into the computer.

There are four basic considerations in the preparation of a program:

1. Defining the problem to be solved
2. Outlining each logical step required to reach the solution
3. Writing the program in machine or symbolic language
4. Translating the program into machine language if the program has been written in symbolic language

Programs must be written in a language that the machine "understands." Each step is written out in a carefully prepared sequence. There are several languages used when preparing programs. One common language is called Common Business Oriented Language (COBOL), and another is called Formula Translation (FORTRAN). Still another is the Beginner's All Purpose Symbolic Instruction Code (BASIC). COBOL resembles English and can be used by different types of computers. It utilizes the numerals 0 through 9, the twenty-six letters of the alphabet, and a dozen or so special characters, such as the dollar sign, the asterisk, and parentheses.

Computers can be programmed to do many things. An interesting current use is interactive computer modeling in planning or making management decisions.

Sophisticated business models can be constructed and programmed. Planners can then ask "what if" questions of the computer to see what would happen if the company raised prices, cut inventories, acquired another firm, and so forth.

The computer allows managers to "play games" with their businesses without taking risks. R. J. Reynolds has developed a model to predict cash flow at any given point and predict shortfalls that might occur in any division. The impact of such shortfalls on company goals can be predicted from the model.

The Public Service Gas Company of New Jersey tests its corporate plan once a day against a model incorporating costs and equipment use. A financial decision such as a cutback in purchases of fuel during an unexpectedly warm winter week can be tested. As William E. Scott, executive vice-president, said: "Within twenty-four hours we would know the impact of [an oil embargo] and could begin reacting."

ADVANTAGES OF COMPUTERS IN PROCESSING BUSINESS DATA

The two primary advantages of electronic computers in handling information are their incredible speed and their high degree of accuracy. Information is more complete and more immediately available than when processed by hand or mechanically. By operating the computer center during the night, management can have reports that are as up to date as the close of business operations the preceding day. And without the aid of computers, management probably would not have access to these reports in such a timely fashion.

Computers can do a complete accounting job, and they can handle as many as five separate accounts simultaneously—and the limits of their versatility have not yet been reached. New electronic typing calculators combine the electric typewriter with a high-speed electronic computer. They are used to process material in which mathematical calculations are part of the typing operation. Any typist can type in the correct information and numbers, and these machines automatically calculate and then type out the answer.

Electronic data-processing machines are used in the following activities: payroll, inventory, expense accounting, sales statistics, accounts receivable, computation of commissions and dividends, property accounting, and invoicing. The use of electronic machines in processing information saves time and money through the elimination of duplicated effort.

An example. The typical sales-order entry can serve to illustrate this point. As a rule, an order for goods is originated by a salesperson who writes out a sales order and mails or telegraphs it to the home office. When this order is received, a production order is typed. It repeats the name and address of the purchaser and most of the other information written on the sales order by the salesperson in the field. A copy of much of this information is included in the report that goes to the accounting office, and it is typed out again in the billing and shipping departments.

Actually, less than 10 percent of the information typed on the sales invoice and on the bill of lading is new information—that is, different from that first typed when the production order was prepared. With electronic data-processing equipment, as much as 80 percent of the information on the sales invoice is written automatically from a magnetic or punched tape. A separate record is prepared on tape for each regular customer, bearing the customer's name and address and all other information needed for any sales invoices issued to him or her. This information is typed only once; thereafter it is reproduced automatically through the use of the tape. New information, such as the purchase-order number, date of order, quantity ordered, unit price, and total amount, is added to the tape by the machine operator.

BUSINESS APPLICATIONS OF DATA PROCESSING

It is of course impossible to describe fully the thousands of applications of data processing in business and industry. We can only deal briefly with a few examples.

In Industry

Computers serve General Electric very well at its Appliance Park operation in Louisville, Kentucky. Here, in a single location, are grouped several plants that might have been built in several different communities. In one large building the company manufactures washing machines and dryers; in another building, electric refrigerators and freezers; and in still another, stoves. And such small appliances as disposal units, dehumidifiers, and mixers are fabricated in still another building. In fact, seven major operations are carried on, each in a separate building.

In one central office at the Park, there is a computer center. Smaller installations of electronic equipment are located in several other buildings serving the different production operations. By having all these computer operations located close to each other, all production plants can use the center. A small office crew operates the computers during the night. Thus an up-to-date inventory can be ready for management the following morning. Here is dramatic proof of what was said earlier: The speed of the computer makes possible the preparation of reports for management that would otherwise be of little value when finally ready to distribute.

Another example of the business use of computers is in controlling energy costs:

> Honeywell sells energy management systems that regulate air conditioning, heating, and lighting in large buildings. On air conditioning alone, Mercy Hospital in Miami estimates that it saved $160,000 per year after installing a $50,000 computer. A large Chicago real estate firm estimates that electricity use has been cut in half since the installation of computers in several Chicago-area office buildings.

ARMANDO CODINA

Armando Codina believes in the "American Dream"! He came to the United States as a refugee from Cuba at the age of thirteen. His few possessions hardly filled a suitcase, and his English vocabulary consisted mainly of two words—hamburger and coke.

In 1970, with a loan of $18,000 arranged through the Small Business Administration, Codina started the Professional Automated Services of Miami, Florida. It began as a one-man operation, but eight years later the company employed 220 persons and was serving more than one thousand clients. In September 1978, at the age of thirty, Codina sold his business to the Itel Corporation of San Francisco for several million dollars. He has continued as president of the company now operating as a subsidiary of Itel—Itel-Pas, Inc.

Codina has served the Miami community in numerous ways. He is currently chairman of the Catholic Homes for Children, a member of the board of governors of the University of Miami School of Medicine, chairman of the Small Business Council of the Greater Miami Chamber of Commerce, and a trustee of the Dade County Institute of Art.

As a millionaire by the time he was thirty years of age, Codina's experience is truly a classical example of business success, the American way.

Mr. and Mrs. Codina have two children.

In Government

The Internal Revenue Service (IRS) has an Automatic Data Processing System: the National Computer Center, Martinsburg, West Virginia. The center operates twenty-four hours a day, seven days a week. The computers update, maintain, and analyze a centralized master file of more than 100 million accounts. There is one for every business and individual who files a tax return. Taxpayers file their returns with the ten Regional Service Centers. There the information is transcribed from the returns and documents and then validated, key verified, and converted to magnetic tape through a direct data entry system.

These taped output files from the service centers are used as input data at the National Computer Center. Here the information is applied against the master file to update taxpayer accounts. From this operation, tape files are generated that will be converted to microfilm and distributed to the service centers for use as research material. Refund data on tape are sent to Treasury Disbursing Offices, where refund checks are printed and mailed to taxpayers. And tape files of bills, notices, and mailing labels are forwarded to service centers to be printed and sent to taxpayers.

By having data on all taxpayers in the national file at Martinsburg, the IRS can easily check on those who fail to file returns. It can also tell whether a taxpayer owes anything for an earlier year before paying a refund. If tax credit from past years has been forgotten or overlooked by the taxpayer, the IRS will pick this up. It can also match information on wages, dividends, and interest on taxpayers' returns with information received from employers and financial institutions. In fact, businesses can now file their tax returns on magnetic tape, provided their tape is compatible with IRS equipment. The IRS is already receiving millions of taped returns a year. Most of these are No. 1099 (dividend-payment) or W-2 (tax-withholding) report forms.

In addition to the IRS and the Bureau of the Census, nearly all other areas of the federal government use electronic computers for data processing. The Defense Department is one of the largest users.

In Banking

Banking operations depend heavily upon computers for processing data. It is estimated that in the 1980s banks will be processing over 60 billion checks a year. Each check is sorted and cleared many times—first by the bank where it is originally deposited, then by one or more clearinghouses, and finally by the bank where the drawer maintains an account.

To help in sorting, identification numbers are printed in magnetic ink in the lower left-hand corner of each check. Large banks and the Federal Reserve Branch Banks electronically sort all the checks they handle.

Branches of many large banks are wired to a central computer for "on-line processing." Deposits or withdrawals are entered on the keyboard console in the branch bank. The branch is connected by a leased telephone line with the computer in the home bank, where each customer's account information is stored in the memory unit. In seconds, the transaction performed at the branch is recorded in the main bank, and its results are reported back to the branch.

Automated teller machines are becoming popular in the large banks. Computers are being used to dispense cash automatically. This frees human tellers from the task of counting cash. Banks are using computers when "cashing checks" at teller windows. The customer keeps the original while the transaction is handled electronically. Truncation is the next step. Here the paper check is held at the first bank it comes to. All other data is handled electronically.

But the real breakthrough is an approach to an almost completely cashless society. The financial institutions in this country are moving toward a nationwide electronic payment-transfer system. Utility bills and installment payments would be made automatically by the banks for their customers. An automated clearing system would shift funds from one bank to another without checks. In 1980 there were about 60 million VISA cardholders in the United States and 80 million worldwide.

This nationwide payment-transfer system would include all types of financial institutions, not just banks. The stock exchanges are studying a scheme that would give stock purchasers a report of the number and type of stock certificates they own, rather than issue individual stock certificates for each purchase.

BANKING EMPLOYEES WORK AT HOME

The management of the Continental Illinois Bank in Chicago is experimenting with the idea of allowing employees to work at home. Two women from the trust department, using computer terminals in their homes, now perform the same tasks that they formerly performed on the bank's premises.

In Insurance Companies

Most insurance companies find the electronic computer ideal for keeping policy-holder information up to date. Information on premium payments, loans against policies, cash reserves, and dividend payments can be made available at a moment's notice. The data-processing service has made this possible for even the small companies, through shared-time facilities. The minicomputer is also allowing the small company to handle its records electronically.

The loan departments of insurance companies have also found magnetic tape and the automatic typewriter helpful in the study of financial reports. When a business applies to an insurance company for a loan, it is asked to submit a copy of its financial report. If the loan application is for a large amount, the financial report is investigated thoroughly. The report on the application may be updated many times. As new data are reported, the financial report is revised and reprinted. Under the traditional method, the entire report had to be checked each time for accuracy in copying. By using magnetic tape that reproduces verbatim all the old data in the report, only actual changes need to be verified. The work is done at speeds much faster than that of the highest-skilled human typist, and the old data in the report need not be proofread for accuracy.

In Retailing

For several years, retail stores have been using computers to automate the point-of-sale process. Scanning systems are used to record basic information. Thus mistakes at the register are fewer. Formerly separate systems were used for inventory control, purchase orders, etc. These are now being interconnected. Retailers are also placing orders with suppliers by computer.

Data-Processing Service Centers

The recent trend in computers has been toward small units as well as large systems. Yet the development of the small unit has not led to as many installations in small businesses as one might expect. The reason is that in some small businesses, the computer would not be used very much. Thus it might not "pay its own way," as every worthwhile piece of equipment should. Out of the need for the part-time use of computers, "time sharing" has developed. As practiced in computer service centers, time sharing allows many businesses to use the same computer. These service operations (or bureaus) have complete equipment installations and a full staff of specially trained personnel. In addition, they maintain a depository of hundreds of different types of programs—even complete data-processing accounting systems. Part-time users have only terminals installed in their businesses. These terminals are used for sending and receiving information to and from the center. Through these centers, the advantages of electronic data processing are available to businesses, educational institutions, and hospitals that cannot afford even limited computer installations. This aspect of data processing is expanding rapidly.

General Electric Information Services is just such a service center. It has three large computer systems installations, one of which is in the Netherlands. It serves more than five thousand customers in twenty-three different countries.

Xerox Computer Services is another large data-processing service center. It maintains twenty offices in fourteen different states. It serves more than two thousand terminals with clients in thirty-six states. The Xerox and GE service centers are representative of dozens of other data-processing service centers located throughout the country.

Commercial banks have also entered the computer services business.

Computer services can include more than simply time sharing. Girard Bank in Philadelphia now offers complete "back office" management for smaller banks as well as routine services such as check clearing. And Valley National Bank of Arizona now offers a new computer service—analyzing cash register receipts for retailers who are not borrowers.

MICROGRAPHICS

Microfilm has taken its place in the business operation right alongside the typewriter and the computer. It represents a new force in information-management productivity. **MICROGRAPHICS is a method of filing information on film so that a record can be retrieved in seconds.**

Microforms, in a few square feet of space, duplicate documents that formerly required thousands of square feet. Micrographics can be linked with computer, facsimile, and word-processing techniques to form a total information-handling system.

Advantages of Film Systems

The advantages of micrographic systems over paper storage and retrieval systems include the following:

1. Microform records need only 2 percent of the storage space required by the same amount of records stored on paper.
2. Duplicate microform files can be placed in a second location for protection against destruction by fire.
3. Information is recorded in a fixed sequence, giving protection against misplacement or loss.
4. Computer-recorded data can be transferred to film in less time than for a printout on paper.
5. Paper copies of original documents can be produced from microform images.
6. Sending microform records by mail is much cheaper than shipping the more bulky paper records.

Computer Output Microfilm

Computer output microfilm (COM) is a way of retrieving computer-generated data and recording these data on microfilm at very high speeds. With COM, information stored in a computer memory can be captured on film in one-tenth the time needed for a paper printout. With present technology, integration of microfilm into automated data-processing systems is both feasible and economical. Microimage terminals are relatively low cost and provide efficient alternatives

FIGURE 18-7
Kodak microimage terminal.
(Courtesy Eastman Kodak Company.)

to disc storage. A single roll of 16-mm microfilm can retain the images of more than ten thousand letter-size documents at a fraction of the cost of the disc pack.

A Kodak microimage terminal is illustrated in Figure 18-7. When used with the computer in a distributed information network, this Kodak IMT-150 terminal relieves the computer of many control functions required by older computer-assisted retrieval systems. For example, the computer can load a block of data consisting of a number of addresses of microfilm images into the terminal's memory and then go on to other tasks. The terminal's microprocessor can then be used to search out the document images without tying up valuable computer time.

In effect, the intelligent microimage terminal becomes an on-line peripheral to the host computer. In turn, it can direct immediate retrieval and hard-copy output from a library of virtually millions of source documents or computer-generated images.

There are many business applications of computer output microform (COM). In banking, both the front and the back of incoming checks can be filmed. This gives protection until the checks have been cleared and paid. In engineering, drawings can be filmed, providing for quick reference duplication. Insurance companies can film accounting records, policyholder files, and premium and dividend payments. In law enforcement, mug shots, fingerprints, and arrest records can be stored and accessed on microforms. Libraries can film rare published materials, card-catalog data, and circulation records. In medicine, patients' medical records, laboratory reports, supply and drug inventories, and X-rays can be stored on COM. In publishing, catalogs, parts lists, and magazine morgue files can be filmed and stored on COM. In the wholesale trade, catalogs, directories, and manuals—in addition to accounting records, vouchers, and bills of lading—can be recorded on COM.

THE DECISION PROCESS

For the purposes of this discussion, we will restrict our definition of **DECISION MAKING** to **the process of choosing, by scientific means, a specific course of action from among several possible alternatives.** Businesspersons are generally considered to be pragmatists. **Pragmatists** are those who stress the practical consequences of an idea. According to a pragmatist, it is important that a plan be feasible and useful.

Decisions can be grouped under two broad categories: policy decisions and administrative decisions. As applied to business, **policy decisions** are deliberate and specific decisions by managers that usually establish a policy. **Policies** are general guides to action for the organization to follow. The larger the organization, the more important it is to see that policies are applied at all levels of the organization.

Administrative decisions translate company policies into action by determining how policy will be carried out. For example, if top management decides to build a new plant to produce a new product, this is a policy decision. Selecting the employees and managers to run the plant is the administrative decision.

Steps in Making a Decision

The decision-making process is concerned with choosing from among alternative courses of action the one that appears to offer the most promise. This process involves the following steps:

1. Situation analysis and problem definition
2. Gathering, analyzing, and interpreting data
3. Seeking plausible solutions
4. Evaluating alternatives and choosing a course of action

It is important that these steps be performed as listed to maintain a logical, orderly, and careful analysis of all the facts. Moreover, it is important that no step be omitted.

The objectives of a business determine many of the decisions. Assume that the demand for a factory's products dictates an enlargement of production facilities. The objective, then, is to enlarge facilities. The first decision is whether to build an addition to the present plant or to construct a new one. If the latter is chosen, many other decisions must be reached on size, design, location, equipment, and so on. In each of these decisions, many alternatives may be feasible. But specific choices from among them must be made.

Computers Aid in Management Decisions

Up to this point we have emphasized the services that a data-processing system renders a business enterprise in a specific location. Now we will see how and why large corporations use centralized computer systems to coordinate a wide (and widespread) variety of activities.

Before electronic data-processing equipment, most large corporations had to use telephone or telegraph leased-wire services to provide a complete communications network between their far-flung industrial plants and offices. Now, with an electronic data-processing system hooking them up, such traditional intracompany communications networks can become an integral part of a computing center's operations. When production, sales, and financial data are all communicated into a company's home office, management has up-to-the-minute information on which to base its decisions.

In addition to intracompany communications, the telecomputer center often handles conventional inventory and payroll records. Then, too, there are customers' orders. The central computer's storage component always has the latest information on exactly how many units of every product are on hand in every warehouse so that all orders, together with shipping instructions, can be sent immediately to the warehouse that is nearest the customer.

The cash analysis is an item of real interest and significance to management. Extremely large corporations have funds deposited in hundreds of different banks throughout the country. A centralized telecomputer system can, in a matter of minutes, give management a complete status report on the corporation's cash balance.

Sales records and customer billing may also be kept current. Under conventional records systems, there is a five-to-ten-day delay in recording sales and in customer billing. The computing center provides instant information and permits simultaneous recording and customer billing. In addition, company management may have a daily report on total company sales, broken down by products, by regions, or in any other way that management would want such data.

Such data handling improves decision making at all levels. It frees divisional accounting managers from mountains of paper work and enables them to function as true financial planners.

PRODUCTIVITY AND THE BUSINESS ENVIRONMENT

A top priority facing America in the 1980s is increased productivity, and therefore some important and difficult decisions must be made. Perhaps the lowest productivity is in the area of information management in today's office. Ours is an information- and service-based economy. In the United States there are 45 million white-collar workers as opposed to 30 million blue-collar workers. It has been estimated that by the end of the 1980s there will be a 52 percent increase in clerical jobs. During the decade of the seventies, white-collar productivity rose only 4 percent while for industry as a whole it was 90 percent.

Louis Harris, in addressing a conference on office management, said:

> Unless employees come to feel truly involved in the decisions that most affect their office environment, this aspect of democracy in the workplace (open planning) might become another "hot" issue over the next ten years rather than a tool for solving a communications problem, with the stakes being productivity in the workplace.

The open-office system represents an attempt to improve office efficiency. Office managers who have adopted the open-office arrangement report a space

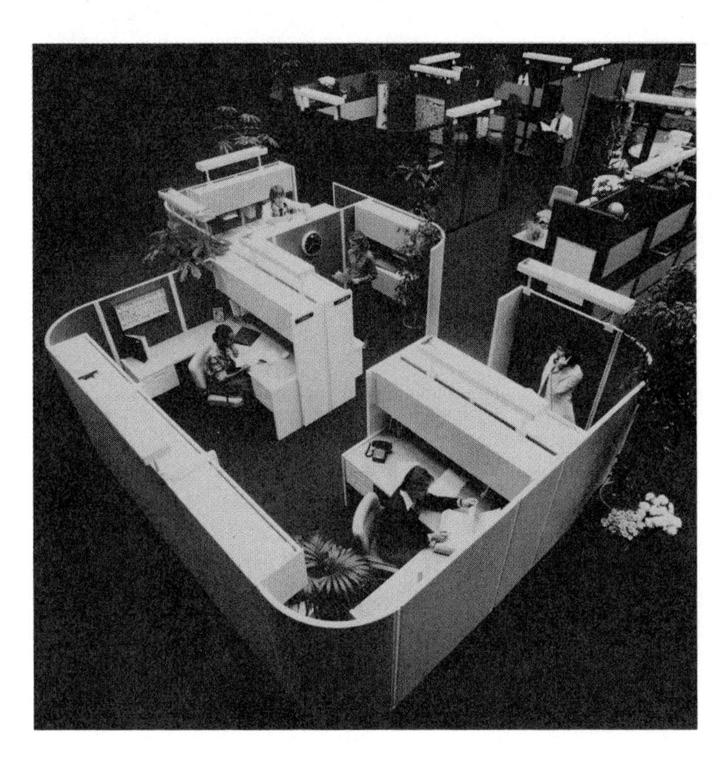

FIGURE 18-8

Open-office arrangement. (Reprinted with the permission of Westinghouse Architectural Systems Division.)

saving of 20 percent and an energy saving of from 30 to 50 percent. It also contributes to better productivity by designing the layout to fit people's needs and individual tastes. People working in a comfortable environment increase office efficiency.

The Tampa (Florida) Wholesale Company adopted the open-plan arrangement in its accounts payable department. The subsequent reduction in personnel resulted in a productivity increase of 15 percent. The open-office arrangement is illustrated in Figure 18-8.

CAREER OPPORTUNITIES IN DATA PROCESSING

Every business executive is a decision maker. Any large business has a number of positions that require the interpreting of data and reaching of conclusions. Decisions are based on information, and these data must be assembled, organized, and interpreted. A person involved in this work might hold any of a number of titles, such as research specialist, economist, statistician, data-processing manager, or systems analyst.

The demand for researchers and statistical workers is generally greater than the supply. One's initial employment might be as a statistical clerk, statistical analyst, researcher, or data processor.

Positions may be found in manufacturing, trade, government, and educational institutions. Promotion leads to department head, director of research, or administrative assistant. Advancement depends on one's ability, breadth of preparation, and experience.

When handling information by computers, the administrative and supervisory position would break down as follows

The *data-processing manager* plans, coordinates, and directs the data-processing activities of the entire organization. He or she must supervise the work of others and should possess high managerial as well as technical skills.

The *manager of computer operations* directs the computer installation, schedules computer time, allocates personnel, maintains the program library, and controls operations within the computer center.

The *systems analyst* creates an ordered system for data collection, processing, and the production of useful information. He or she improves controls and decision making and, at the same time, makes the most efficient use of available data-processing equipment. The largely abstract nature of the work, like that of the computer programmer, requires strong logical and creative abilities.

The *computer programmer* must work closely with the systems analyst to define the problem, analyze data and report requirements, prepare a detailed flow chart of the logical solution, convert this logical diagram to coded instructions for the computer, and test the program to remove errors. Programmers must completely understand the business or scientific problem they are attempting to solve. They must be able to work with a team or alone and be able to communicate with management personnel. They must be sticklers for detail, be logical thinkers, and have no end of patience.

Actually, in data processing, a person's title does not delineate clearly just what the work is. One person with the title of programmer may spend most of the workday writing out specific directions for the computer. Another programmer may spend most of the workday developing problems and even doing systems design.

SUMMARY OF KEY CONCEPTS

The ever-increasing load of paperwork has made rapid processing of information a necessity.

The computer has made available to management up-to-the-minute information that was not previously possible.

The basic components of information handling are coding, computing, communicating, recording, sorting, storing, and summarizing.

Digital computers use the binary number system. In any single position the current is either *on* or *off*, indicating the presence or absence of an assigned value.

A computer installation would include some type of input unit that feeds data into the system, the memory or storage unit, the calculator, the control panel, and the output (printout) unit.

Almost every aspect of modern business operations utilizes the services of computers—manufacturing, wholesaling, retailing, and finance. In addition, governments, hospitals, and schools use computer systems.

Businesses that are too small to have complete computer installations may use the services of data-processing centers.

Decision making is practiced at every level of management—from low-level supervisors to the chief executive.

The steps in making a decision are the same regardless of the level at which it is made. One begins with an identification of the problem, and the final step consists of deciding upon a specific course of action.

Micrographics is a rapidly developing area of records management. It conserves space and is economical and flexible.

BUSINESS TERMS

You should be able to match these business terms with the statements that follow:

a. Data processing	d. Micrographics	g. Program
b. Decision making	e. Optical scanner	h. Storage
c. Hardware	f. Processor	i. System

1. A related series of items with interrelationships, organized into a discernible pattern
2. Operations performed in handling information from original entry to final entry
3. Another name for the memory or filing unit
4. The equipment that performs the work in a computing center
5. The instructions to a computer telling it what to do
6. A method of filing information on film so that a record can be retrieved in seconds
7. The arithmetical or computing part of a computer installation
8. The choosing of a specific course of action from among several alternatives
9. A device that reads characters and symbols and translates them into electrical impulses

REVIEW QUESTIONS

1. What do we mean by the term *system* as applied to the management of records?
2. What are the stages in developing an information system?
3. What are the seven operations in processing information?
4. What types of equipment (hardware) would be found in a typical computer installation?
5. What is a computer program?
6. What steps are involved in making a business decision?

DISCUSSION QUESTIONS

1. Besides being faster, what advantages do computers offer over hand and mechanical methods?
2. What contribution does a data-processing center make to our business system?
3. What specifically is involved in making a business decision?
4. In what specific way does a computer aid in making management decisions?
5. What are the advantages of micrographics over handling printed materials?

BUSINESS CASE 18-1

A College Computer Problem

A small college is contemplating the installation of a small computer. You are a member of the committee appointed to recommend whether or not to make the installation. The main problem is that no single aspect of the college program has sufficient need to utilize the equipment full time. The matter of time apportionment is also somewhat of a problem in that all the departments interested in using the equipment want it some time between 8 A.M. and 5 P.M.

1. Which aspects of the administrative office functions might be interested in using the computer?
2. Which academic departments might need the computer equipment for instructional purposes?
3. How would you schedule all potential users so as to make the maximum use of the equipment and also satisfy everyone's needs?

BUSINESS CASE 18-2

A "Going into Business" Decision

David South is thirty-four years of age, is married, and has two school-age children. He has recently been discharged from the Naval Reserve, in which he learned the baker's trade and practiced it for five years. He has returned to his home community of 160,000 persons. There is a downtown business district, and sizable shopping centers are located at the edge of the residential section, in each quadrant of the city area.

David would like to go into the bakery business in his community.

1. What questions must David answer in deciding whether to open a new business, buy out an established bakery, or work for one of the going concerns?
2. If he should decide to open his own business, what specific problem areas require him to make big decisions?

LEGAL ENVIRONMENT: BUSINESS LAW AND ETHICS

19

STUDY OBJECTIVES

WHEN YOU HAVE FINISHED READING THIS CHAPTER, YOU SHOULD BE ABLE TO

ONE Explain the main purposes that law serves in business

TWO Identify the differences between common law and statutory law

THREE Describe how the judicial system functions in the United States

FOUR Discuss the essential elemenets of a valid contract

FIVE Name the requirements that an instrument must satisfy if it is to be negotiable

SIX Explain when the title to goods passes if they are sold C.O.D., F.O.B., at auction, or under installment contracts

IN THE NEWS

IBM's Antitrust Case Has Been in the Courts "Forever"!

The government filed suit against IBM in 1969 claiming that the computer giant was monopolizing the computer industry. The government is seeking to have IBM dismembered into several independent businesses.

The trial actually began in 1975, and there have been many time-consuming problems. As of this writing the trial has used ninety thousand pages of testimony and has introduced over four hundred documents as evidence.

In 1979 IBM appealed to the U.S. Court of Appeals for the removal of U.S. District Judge Edelstein, who had been hearing the case. IBM's attorney, T. H. Barr, contended that the company was not receiving a fair trial. Barr argued that Edelstein had ruled against most of the company's motions and had showed "hostility" toward its witnesses and lawyers. The judge also required the company to search through many documents to produce information the government should have requested during pretrial proceedings. Barr stated that if IBM were forced to continue with Edelstein as judge, the final outcome would undoubtedly be reversed in a higher court. Then the lengthy case would have to start over. IBM predicted that the case would last another five years.

The Justice Department attorney argued that IBM could not establish its charges of bias against the judge. He also noted that he knew of no instance where the judge had ever been removed in the middle of hearing a case.

Only time will tell the resolution of this case. But it is clear that much more time is going to be needed to resolve this legal business-government battle.

Law is the witness and external deposit of our moral life.
Its history is the history of the moral development of the race.

OLIVER WENDELL HOLMES, JR.

The law is a living, vital, and changing force. Laws are the rules that organized societies rely on to help members enforce and mediate disputes. As the English jurist Edmund Plowden said, "The letter of the law is the body of the law, but the sense and reason of it is the soul." Laws mean little unless they are enforced. William Pitt (1708–78), First Earl of Chatham and an English statesman, said, "Where law ends, tyranny begins." If there is any doubt about this, contemplate a world without law.

Laws that serve as a legal force in the business environment are referred to as **business law.** When business disputes arise—as they often do—they must be settled, not by force or other illegal means, but by the application of law. Thus one purpose of law in business is to settle disputes. Another purpose is to establish order. Still a third is to provide protection.

If you are thinking of a business career, a general understanding of legal terms and principles is important. It can help you determine whether you must seek legal counsel. In a courtroom situation, you would do well to recall the old saying, "A man who serves as his own lawyer has a fool for a client."

THE FOUNDATIONS OF LAW

Before we explore the applications of law to business transactions, let us review the historical background of law.

Legal Sources

There are two main sources of law in the United States: **common law** and **statutory law.**

Common law. Common law is unwritten law, or case law. It is based on court decisions that become legal precedents.[1] Common law is for the most part unwritten and had its origin in England. It was later adopted by other English-speaking countries, including the United States. Common law is an attempt to develop what is called in law equity. **EQUITY** is defined as a branch of unwritten law that grants an adequate or fair remedy. Louisiana is the only state whose laws are not based on common law. It has a legal system founded on the French Civil Code.

Statutory law. The other source of law is statutory law—written law consisting of formal enactments (statutes) by governmental bodies. The U.S. Constitution (the supreme law of the land), federal treaties, and state constitutions are part of statute law. Statutes pertaining to business transactions have been codified. This group includes the Uniform Commercial Code (UCC), a subject discussed later in this chapter.

Classification of Law

Law can be classified as common or statutory law, depending on its origin. Our legal system also can be classified as public or private law, depending on the nature of the issue raised.

Public law. Laws dealing with topics the public is concerned about are classified as **PUBLIC LAW.** Examples of public law are international law, constitutional law, criminal law, and administrative law.

International law covers a body of rules that other nations recognize as binding in their conduct toward one another. **Constitutional law** deals with the legal principles of the Constitution. **Criminal law** defines conduct deemed to be a crime.[2] **Administrative law** covers acts by commissions, such as the Federal Trade Commission, which administer legislative functions.

Private law. Sometimes known as civil law, private law is a collection of codes, rules, regulations, and laws dealing with the rights of individuals (property rights, contract rights, and torts).[3] Business law is a subclass of private law and is examined later in this chapter.

Statutory laws can be established by legislation at three levels of government, as shown in Figure 19-1.

[1]Under common law, when each decision rendered by a court becomes a precedent for subsequent decisions, this is known as the doctrine of *stare decisis*. This is a Latin phrase meaning "to stand by decided matters."

[2]A *crime* is a felony or misdemeanor. A *felony* is a criminal offense such as murder, arson, and grand larceny. These are punishable by imprisonment. Drunkenness, disorderly conduct, and assault are *misdemeanors*. Imprisonment for such is generally not in a state penitentiary but in a city or county jail for less than one year.

[3]A *tort* is a civil (private) wrong. It includes libel, slander, false imprisonment, and fraud. *Slander* consists of defamatory words spoken or gestures. *Libel* is a wrong against an individual in the form of written defamation—in print or picture. *False imprisonment* is unlawful restraint of liberty. *Fraud* is a deliberate act of deceit to deprive one of a right. *Misrepresentation* is misleading another by a misstatement of actual fact.

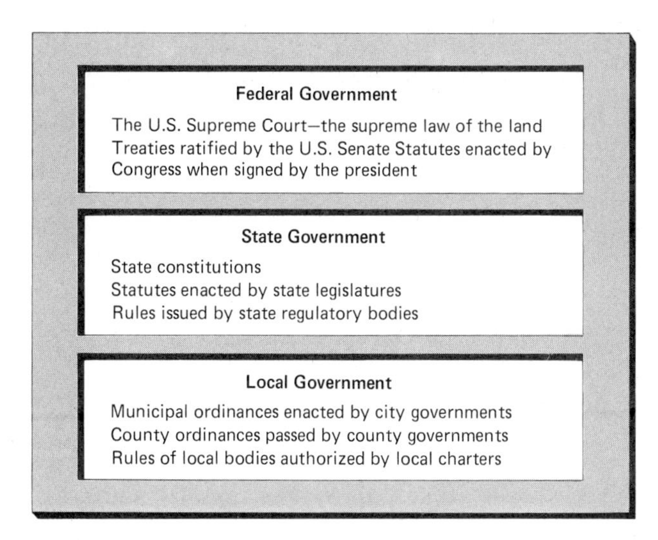

Federal Government
The U.S. Supreme Court—the supreme law of the land
Treaties ratified by the U.S. Senate Statutes enacted by
Congress when signed by the president
State Government
State constitutions
Statutes enacted by state legislatures
Rules issued by state regulatory bodies
Local Government
Municipal ordinances enacted by city governments
County ordinances passed by county governments
Rules of local bodies authorized by local charters

FIGURE 19-1
Levels of statutory law in the United States.

THE JUDICIAL SYSTEM

The branch of government authorized to hear controversies between parties and to apply the law to these disputes is the **JUDICIAL SYSTEM.** The judicial system operates at several levels.

Federal Court System

The federal court system is provided for by Article III, Section 1, of the U.S. Constitution: "The judicial power of the United States shall be vested in one Supreme Court, and in such inferior courts as the Congress may from time to time ordain and establish." Figure 19-2 shows the various levels of the federal court system.

The U.S. Supreme Court, which is also the highest court of appeals, is the court of last resort. It decides constitutional issues, cases to which the states may be a party, and matters involving diplomatic staff.

The two main routes for appealing decisions to the U.S. Supreme Court are shown in Figure 19-3. The Supreme Court is the only federal court established by the U.S. Constitution and not by Congress. However, Congress does determine the number of federal justices and their salaries.

The Supreme Court hears a variety of business-related cases. It may either choose to rule on these cases or choose not to rule and let the decision of a lower court stand. For example, the Court recently heard the following cases.

The Court invited the solicitor general to file the views of the federal government on whether the Court should hear a case involving Sears, Roebuck and the state of California. The case involves exempting from property taxes goods in California warehouses to be shipped to other states.

The Court also let stand a lower-court ruling against the family of the late Texas oilman H. L. Hunt. This case involved allegations that Hunt violated commodity futures contracts' commission limits.

The Court also declined to hear an appeal by Grumman Corporation over calculation of state tax to be figured in bidding on government contracts.

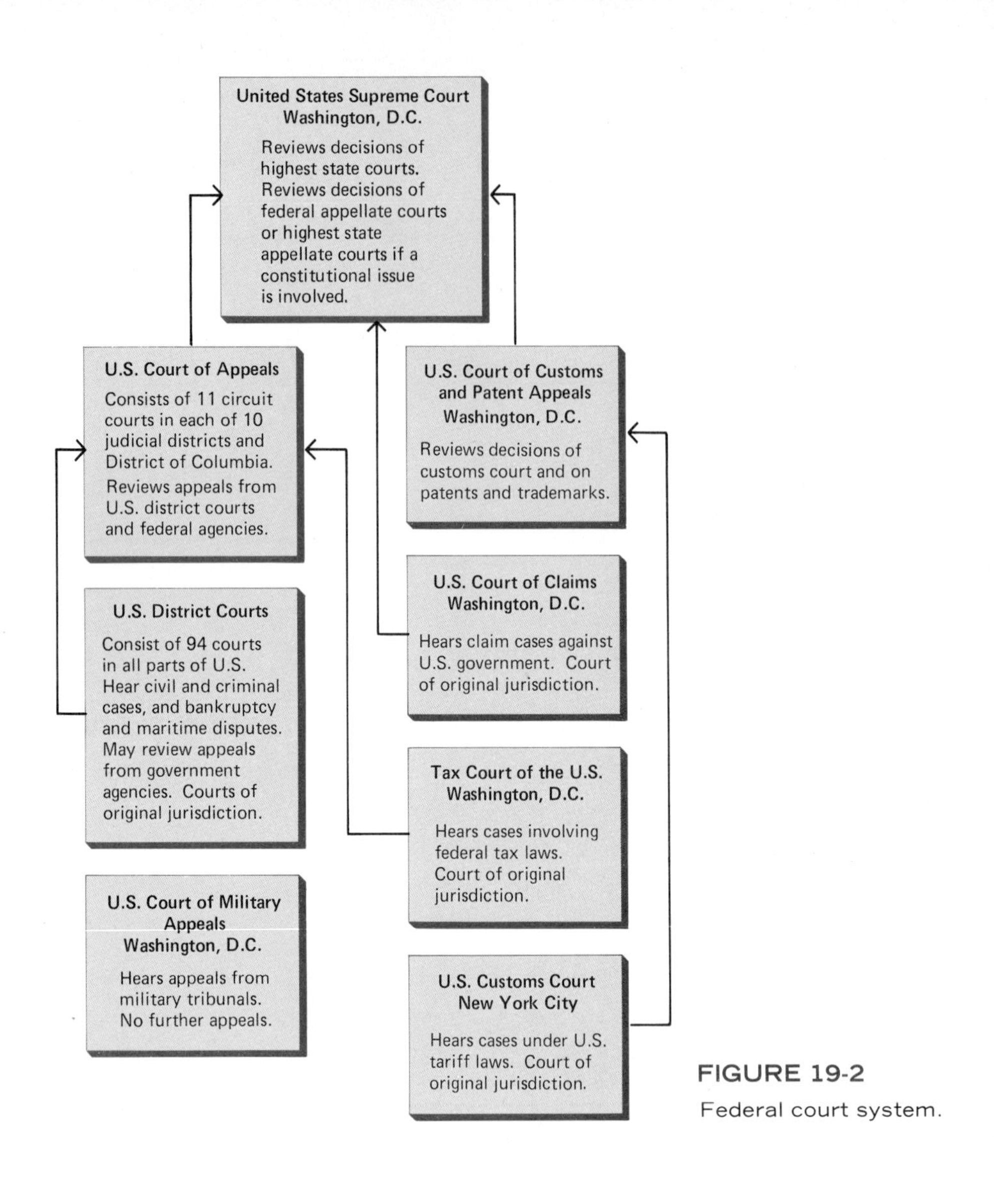
United States Supreme Court
Washington, D.C.
Reviews decisions of highest state courts. Reviews decisions of federal appellate courts or highest state appellate courts if a constitutional issue is involved.
U.S. Court of Appeals
Consists of 11 circuit courts in each of 10 judicial districts and District of Columbia. Reviews appeals from U.S. district courts and federal agencies.
U.S. Court of Customs and Patent Appeals
Washington, D.C.
Reviews decisions of customs court and on patents and trademarks.
U.S. District Courts
Consist of 94 courts in all parts of U.S. Hear civil and criminal cases, and bankruptcy and maritime disputes. May review appeals from government agencies. Courts of original jurisdiction.
U.S. Court of Claims
Washington, D.C.
Hears claim cases against U.S. government. Court of original jurisdiction.
Tax Court of the U.S.
Washington, D.C.
Hears cases involving federal tax laws. Court of original jurisdiction.
U.S. Court of Military Appeals
Washington, D.C.
Hears appeals from military tribunals. No further appeals.
U.S. Customs Court
New York City
Hears cases under U.S. tariff laws. Court of original jurisdiction.

FIGURE 19-2

Federal court system.

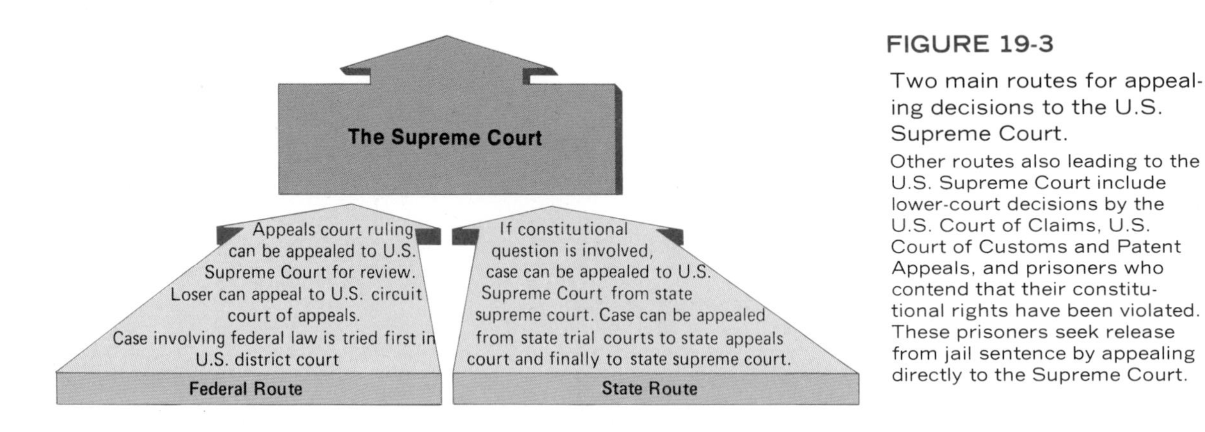
The Supreme Court
Appeals court ruling can be appealed to U.S. Supreme Court for review.
Loser can appeal to U.S. circuit court of appeals.
Case involving federal law is tried first in U.S. district court
Federal Route
If constitutional question is involved, case can be appealed to U.S. Supreme Court from state supreme court. Case can be appealed from state trial courts to state appeals court and finally to state supreme court.
State Route

FIGURE 19-3

Two main routes for appealing decisions to the U.S. Supreme Court.

Other routes also leading to the U.S. Supreme Court include lower-court decisions by the U.S. Court of Claims, U.S. Court of Customs and Patent Appeals, and prisoners who contend that their constitutional rights have been violated. These prisoners seek release from jail sentence by appealing directly to the Supreme Court.

State Court System

Each state has its own court system. Figure 19-4 shows the organizational structure and composition of the state court system. State courts vary as to what they are called. But common to all states are courts of original jurisdiction for civil and criminal matters. Most states have lower courts with specialized or limited jurisdiction. These courts include "small claims" courts, "probate" courts, and "justice of the peace" courts.

The general trial courts hear both criminal and civil matters. Appeals from the general trial courts are made directly to the state supreme court and through the state appellate courts. State and federal courts operate with a minimum of overlapping jurisdictional authority.

Remedies through Court Action

Our American legal system provides for a dual system of remedies obtained from the courts: **remedies at law** and **remedies at equity.**

The term **equity,** derived from the Latin **aequitas,** means "equality" or "justice." A civil action in which the plaintiff seeks correction of an injustice

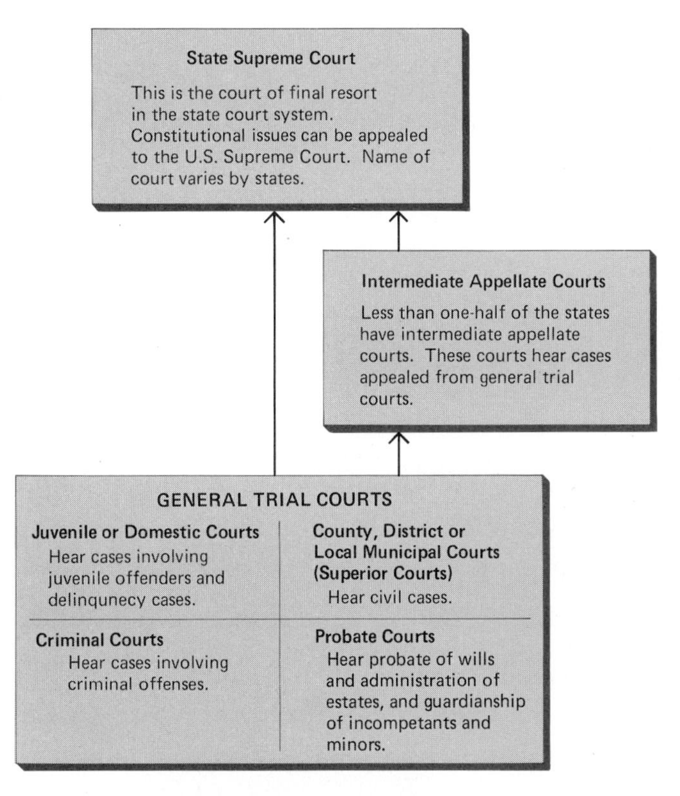

FIGURE 19-4

State court system.

Each state court system varies as to title and number of courts. Each state has only one supreme court, which is limited to questions of law as opposed to issues of fact.

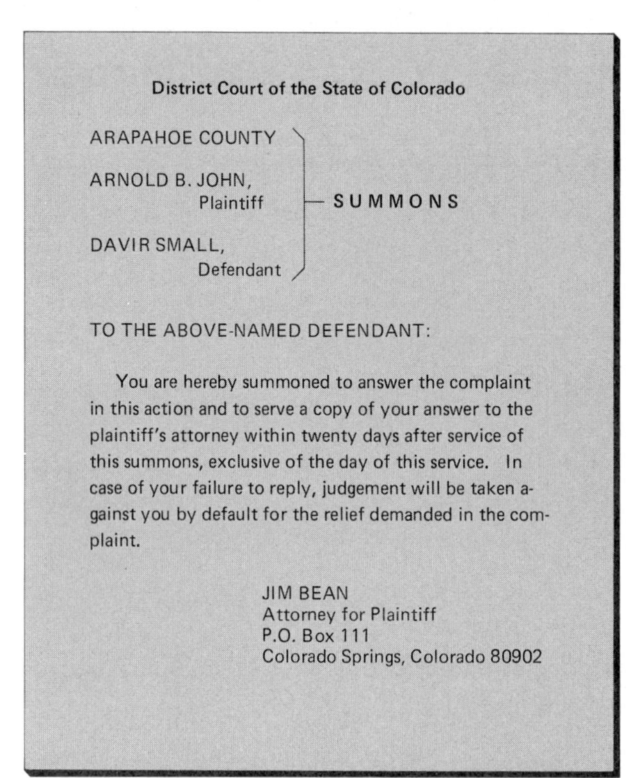
District Court of the State of Colorado

ARAPAHOE COUNTY

ARNOLD B. JOHN,
Plaintiff — SUMMONS

DAVIR SMALL,
Defendant

TO THE ABOVE-NAMED DEFENDANT:

You are hereby summoned to answer the complaint in this action and to serve a copy of your answer to the plaintiff's attorney within twenty days after service of this summons, exclusive of the day of this service. In case of your failure to reply, judgement will be taken against you by default for the relief demanded in the complaint.

JIM BEAN
Attorney for Plaintiff
P.O. Box 111
Colorado Springs, Colorado 80902

FIGURE 19-5
Summons.

is known as a suit in equity. It is different from a suit in law, which is an action by the plaintiff to seek monetary damages. A few states require that suits in equity be tried in special equity courts.

A common remedy at equity is to seek a court injunction restraining one party from continuing an injurious action against another. In general, remedies from courts of law can provide (1) the restoring of real or personal property to one from whom it has been unjustly withheld, and (2) the awarding of monetary damages suffered by the plaintiff.

In a court of law, either party has the right to have the issues of fact determined by a jury—the fact-finding body. Judges decide the issues of law. But in a court of equity, there is no right to trial by jury. The IBM case at the beginning of the chapter is an example. The judge makes the decision based on facts and law.

When the counsel and the client decide to file an action against the defendant, the "attorney for the plaintiff" files a complaint with the court against the defendant. A summons similar to that in Figure 19-5 is issued. **The complaining party in a court action** is the **PLAINTIFF. The party against whom an action at law is taken** is the **DEFENDANT.** The purpose of the summons is to notify the defendant that a suit has been started.

BUSINESS LAW

Several areas of private law directly relate to the business community. Among these are the following.

The Uniform Commercial Code (UCC)

Since the 1950s there has been a trend toward the adoption of a uniform code applicable to a variety of recurring business transactions. Originally, business laws varied from state to state. Firms doing business in several states were often confused by the lack of uniformity of statutes regarding business transactions.

To achieve a nationwide uniformity, the National Conference of Commissioners on Uniform State Laws and the American Law Institute agreed on a uniform code. In 1952 the Uniform Commercial Code, known as "the Code," was published and circulated among the states. In 1958 it was revised, and in 1962 the Code became a model for state laws on most areas of business and consumer law. Most of the provisions of the UCC have been enacted as law by the legislatures of the fifty states. The adoption of a uniform code has been recognized as an important step in reducing confusion in interstate trade.

The UCC regulates transactions involving sales, commercial paper, bank deposits, letters of credit, and warehouse receipts. It also includes bills of lading, bulk transfers, securities, and contract rights. In the discussions that follow in this chapter, many applications of the Code will be observed.

Law of Contracts

In business many transactions involve contracts. A **CONTRACT** is **an agreement between two competent parties in the form required by law that is legally enforceable.** Figure 19-6 shows the five elements that must exist if a contract is to be enforceable:

1. Mutual assent
2. Competent parties
3. Consideration
4. Lawful purpose
5. Required form

Mutual assent. The contract must contain an offer and acceptance without any counteroffers. An advertisement to sell an article at a given price is not a genuine offer; courts have ruled that advertisements only invite offers. There must also be absence of fraud, or undue influence (duress).

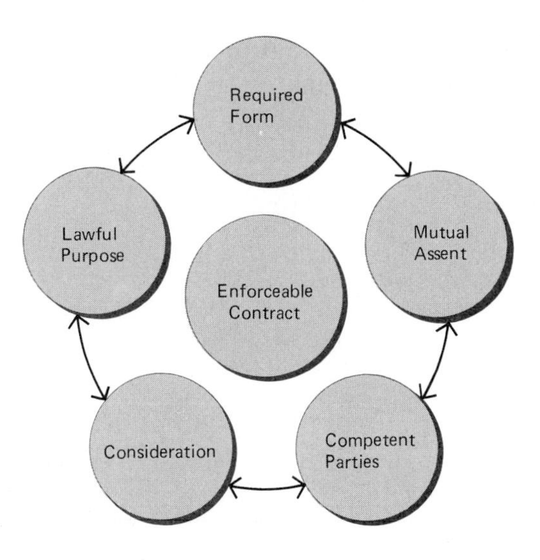

FIGURE 19-6

Required elements for a valid contract.

JOHN B. CONNALLY

John B. Connally is an attorney who has been successful in both government and business. He gained national attention while serving three terms as governor of Texas, from 1963 to 1969. Prior to being elected governor, Connally served as secretary of the navy (1961). Later he also served as secretary of the treasury (1971 and 1972) and as special adviser to President Nixon (1973).

Connally is currently a senior partner in the Vinson and Elkins law firm in Houston, Texas. He is a director of the First City Bancorporation of Texas, Justin Industries, Continental Airlines, Dr. Pepper Company (Dallas), Falconbridge Nickel Mines, and the Houston Chamber of Commerce and is special counsel to the American General Companies in Houston.

Connally married Ida Nell Brill in December 1940. They have two sons and one daughter.

Competent parties. To make an enforceable contract, the parties must be legally competent. Not everyone is competent to make a binding contract. Under common law, insane persons, convicts, and persons under the age of twenty-one do not have the right to contract.[4] In Colorado, Mississippi, and the District of Columbia, the age of twenty-one must be attained before a person can make a binding contract. All other states have set the legal age at either eighteen or nineteen. Formerly many states regarded persons under twenty-one as minors. Such persons could not make enforceable contracts except for necessities (food, clothing, and shelter).

Consideration. Ordinarily a promise as part of a contract is not binding unless it is supported by consideration. **CONSIDERATION** is **something of value pledged in exchange for a promise.** It may consist of money, goods, services, or even another promise to do or not to do something a person has a legal right to do. For example, Jones agrees to buy an automobile from Bailey for $600 and gives Bailey a $10 down payment. Here the consideration is the $10 exchanged for the automobile. Jones has a legal obligation for $590, and Bailey has an obligation to deliver the automobile.

Lawful purpose. To be binding, a contract must involve a lawful purpose. In states where gambling is illegal, promises to pay gambling debts, even when in writing, are not enforceable. A contract for payment of interest in excess of the legal rate (known as usury) is not binding.

[4]The Twenty-sixth Amendment, adopted in 1971, gives suffrage to persons at age eighteen. It does not allow persons between eighteen and twenty-one the right to make a marriage contract without parental consent. Each state has the right to enact laws to determine their legal status. The Uniform Minor Student Capacity to Borrow Act, passed by several states, permits loans to minors for payment of education costs in colleges and universities. These loans are enforceable under conditions of this legislation.

Required form. All contracts do not need to be written to be enforceable. Oral agreements are enforceable, although there may be some difficulty in trying to prove any disputed facts.

The most common contract provisions are contained in the Statute of Frauds, which was adopted in England in 1677. This statute has since been adopted in various forms by different states.

Section 2-201 of the UCC modifies the Statute of Frauds concerning a contract for the sale of goods for $500 or more. This modification provides that unless otherwise agreed to, a contract for the sale of goods for $500 or more is not enforceable unless the contract is written. The written language must be sufficient to prove the parties agreed to the sale. The contract shown in Figure 19-7 contains the essential elements that are binding on both parties.

AGREEMENT

THIS AGREEMENT, made this fifth day of August, 19__, between Fred Herbert, hereinafter called "the employee," and Robert Lee, hereinafter called "the employer."

WITNESSETH:

In consideration of their mutual promises contained herein, the parties hereto agree as follows:

The employee agrees to perform his duties for the period of two (2) years from the date hereof as cashier in the store of the employer and agrees to serve faithfully the said employer in the best interest of said employer.

The employer agrees to pay the said employee the sum of one hundred dollars ($100.00) a week, payable weekly on the last working day of each week during the term of this agreement.

IN WITNESS WHEREOF, the said parties have hereunto set their hands on this, the date first above written in this agreement.

Witness: John Smith (for both parties)

Fred Herbert

Robert Lee

Date August 5, 19__

FIGURE 19-7

An agreement or contract.

An agreement between two parties.

Remedies for breach of contract. For various reasons not all contracts, whether oral or written, are carried out. When a contract is breached (broken), the injured party may decide to pursue legal remedies. ("Injured" and "remedies" may seem like strange terms, but they are part of the legal vocabulary.) For example, the injured party can avoid carrying out part of the agreement, acting in effect as though there had been no contract. The right to cancel a contract is known as the **right of rescission.**

Or the injured party may bring an action for actual damages. Even if this person has not had an actual loss from the breach, he or she is still entitled to a judgment for a nominal damage. The term **NOMINAL DAMAGE** refers to a **trifling sum of money awarded to a person in recognition of a technical infraction by the defendant of the plaintiff's rights.** These awards are often for one dollar.

A third remedy is for the injured party to ask for "performance of the contract" by the defendant. A court does not always compel performance if there is some other adequate remedy at law. As a rule, damages in excess of actual loss (for the purpose of punishing the defendant) cannot be recovered for breach of contract. Such damages are called **punitive damages** (for punishment).

A much publicized case for performance of contract involves the Westinghouse Electric Corporation.

> Westinghouse contracted with several utility companies to deliver 50 million pounds of uranium for their generating plants at $10 per pound. These were long-term contracts. In 1975 Westinghouse renounced the contracts, claiming that it was commercially impractical to deliver the uranium at that price. At the time uranium was selling for $26 per pound.
>
> Westinghouse lawyers argued that meeting the contract obligations could cripple the company. The utilities responded with claims exceeding $2 billion.
>
> Judge Robert Merhige, Jr., ruled in Richmond, Virginia, that Westinghouse should not be excused from its obligations but that the utilities were not entitled to the amount of damages they were claiming. The judge hoped that the businesses would resolve the problem out of court. Said Merhige, "These cases should be settled as business problems by businessmen."

The statute of limitations. Each state has a statute-of-limitations act requiring that an action at law be started within a time limit after the infraction. Beyond that time the remedy is barred. The statute does not have the effect of discharging the contract. It is a defense for breach because no legal action was taken during the prescribed time.

Law of Agency

One of the most common legal business relationships is that between a principal and his or her agent. An **AGENT** is **one who is authorized by another to deal with a third party for the other person. The person for whom the agent acts is the PRINCIPAL.** The usual way of creating an agency is by verbal or written appointment. A formal written appointment is called a **power of attorney**. A proxy form is an example of an agency relationship. When stockholders are notified of a forthcoming corporation meeting, they are given a proxy form. For example, if a stockholder will be unable to attend the annual meeting of stockholders to vote, he or she may appoint another stockholder to be his or her agent to vote the shares.

Duties of principal to agent. The principal is obliged to compensate the agent for services according to the contract; to reimburse the agent for necessary expenses unless otherwise agreed; and to pay for losses sustained by the agent.

Duties of agent to principal. The agent is expected to obey the instructions of the principal; to exercise due skill and loyalty to the principal; and to account for money or property entrusted to the agent.

Obligations of principal to third parties. The principal is liable to the third party for all lawful agreements made by the agent. The principal is also liable for any damages caused by the agent in performing his or her normal duties.

LAW OF PROPERTY

The term **property** refers to a right to own and use anything if you own it. The law of property not only is an important part of the free-enterprise system but involves your right under the Constitution to own property. This right cannot be denied without due process of law. Daniel Webster said that due process denotes "law which hears before it condemns; which proceeds upon inquiry; and which renders judgment only after trial."

Kinds of Property

The law recognizes different classes of property, generally classified as real and personal. Property is also classified as tangible and intangible.

Real property. Broadly classified, **REAL PROPERTY** is the land and anything permanently affixed to it that in a general way is immovable. Trees and shrubbery, when planted, are real property. Buildings and fences are also considered real property when they are attached to the soil.

Personal property. Property that is movable and otherwise not classed as real property is **PERSONAL PROPERTY. Tangible** personal property includes fixtures, goods, furniture, clothing, jewelry, and so forth. **Intangible** property has no physical existence. It is only the right to property and includes stocks, bonds, accounts receivable, insurance policies, and bank accounts. Mortgages, letters of credit, checks, and money orders are also intangible property.

How Property May Be Acquired

Property may be acquired in several ways. The most common is by purchase. Other ways are by gift, by inheritance (descent), by legacy (will), and by deed.

Deed of conveyance. The written instrument that transfers title to real property (real estate) from one party to another is called a deed. It is used whether acquired by gift or purchase. To be lawful, it must be in the form required by the state in which the real property is located.

In most states there are two types of deeds. The quitclaim deed transfers whatever interest and use the grantor may have in the property. It does not warrant

The State of Texas, } **Know All Men by These Presents:**
County of HARRIS

That JAMES GREEN, a widower not since remarried

of the County of HARRIS State of TEXAS for and in consideration

of the sum of Ten Thousand ($10,000)--

--- DOLLARS

to be paid, and secured to be paid, by the grantee

hereinafter named -- as follows:

The sum of one thousand ($1,000) dollars to be paid on the delivery of this instrument, the receipt of which is hereby acknowledged, and the further sum of seventy-five ($75.00) dollars the first day of each and every month thereafter until the purchase price has been paid in full. All of said sums except the first payment of one thousand ($1,000) dollars are to be represented by promissory notes in the amount of seventy-five ($75.00) dollars and to bear interest at the rate of six (6) per cent per annum from date until paid,

have Granted, Sold and Conveyed, and by these presents do/es Grant, Sell and Convey, unto the said WALTER H. JENSEN

of the County of HARRIS State of TEXAS all that certain

TRACE OR PARCEL OF LAND DESCRIBED AS FOLLOWS, TO-WIT:

Lot Three (3) Block Six (6) in the OPAL Addition, City of South Houston, in the County of Harris and State of Texas.

TO HAVE AND TO HOLD the above described premises, together with all and singular the rights and appurtenances thereto in anywise belonging unto the said Grantee, his

heirs and assigns forever and he do/es hereby bind

heirs, executors and administrators, to Warrant and Forever Defend, all and singular the said premises unto the said grantee, his

heirs and assigns, against every person whomsoever lawfully claiming, or to claim the same, or any part thereof.

But it is expressly agreed and stipulated that the Vendor's Lien is retained against the above described property, premises and improvements, until the above described note , and all interest thereon are fully paid according to face and tenor, effect and reading, when this deed shall become absolute.

WITNESS this hand at, South Houston

this 25th day of November 19

Witness at request of Grantor:

Veedee Greenwood
Carol Griffin

James Green
Walter H. Jensen

FIGURE 19-8

Warranty deed.

A warranty deed used to convey title to real property. This type of deed may also contain statements, usually by the grantor, that other things will be done or are true.

the title. The quitclaim deed may be useful in obtaining a release to use the property. It gives the buyer the least protection.

The **WARRANTY DEED is a written instrument that warrants title to real property without defects.** The warranty deed cannot transfer a better title than the grantor (owner) had. However, the grantor covenants that he or she has valid title to the property and that he or she will indemnify the grantee if a loss is sustained due to a defective title. To become effective, a warranty deed must be recorded by the new owner. (A warranty deed is shown in Figure 19-8.)

Abstract of title. Some states use an abstract of title to accompany the warranty deed at the time the title is recorded. An **ABSTRACT OF TITLE is a written summary of all conveyances, mortgages, and liens affecting the title.** A prospective buyer may request that he or she be furnished an abstract of title. The seller's attorney usually performs the title search of real property records on file in the local recording office to determine whether there are any defects. If so, the buyer may then decline to buy the property until such property defects are corrected. States that do not use a title abstract allow title companies to insure the title by issuing a title insurance policy.

Real Property Ownership

The highest form of ownership that one can possess in real property is an **ESTATE IN FEE SIMPLE.** A fee simple estate is one of inheritance. This means that upon the death of the owner, the property descends to his or her heirs unless it has been transferred by a will. Real property can also be rented or leased or used as security for a loan (mortgage).

Community property. In certain states property acquired by husband and wife during their marriage—except that acquired by will, gift, or descent—is owned jointly.[5] Some states provide for right of survivorship as part of the community-property law. Others permit only half the property belonging to the deceased spouse to descend to his or her heirs. However, in these states husband and wife may each file a separate state income-tax return. Each reports only half the common income. (The federal income-tax law allows the filing of separate returns.)

Lease. When you own your own business, you may find that it is more satisfactory to lease real or personal property than to own it. Your agreement with the landlord (owner) to use the property is a **lease.** Your landlord is the **lessor** and you are the **lessee.** Under the Statute of Frauds, a lease for longer than a year must be in writing to be enforceable. The ground on which Radio City is located in New York City is leased for ninety-nine years. The more formal written lease, such as that shown in Figure 19-9, usually contains the following:

1. Date of agreement
2. Names of lessor and lessee
3. Property description
4. Duration of lease
5. Manner of paying rent
6. Responsibility for making repairs
7. Liability for injury to third party
8. Right to sublet or assign

[5]States that have community-property laws are Arizona, California, Idaho, Louisiana, Nevada, New Mexico, Texas, and Washington.

The State of Texas,
County of

Know All Men by These Presents:

Made this 2nd day of MARCH , A. D. 19 , by and between

Smithson R. Conway--, known herein as LESSOR,

and Rollo J. Jenkins---
--, known herein as LESSEE,

(The terms "Lessor" and "Lessee" shall be construed in the singular or plural number according as they respectively represent one or more than one person.)

WITNESSETH, That the said Lessor does by these presents Lease and Demise unto the said Lessee the following described property, to-wit: Lying and being situated in the County of WALLER , State of Texas, and being A single family dwelling located at 1301 First Street in the town of Hempstead, con-six (6) rooms and bath.

for the term of twelve (12) months beginning the 2nd day of MARCH A. D. 19 and ending the 1st day of MARCH, 19 , paying therefor the sum of Twelve hundred ($1200)-------------------------------------- DOLLARS, payable monthly installments the second day of each month in advance.

upon the conditions and covenants following:

First. That Lessee will well and PUNCTUALLY pay said rents in manner and form as hereinbefore specified, and quietly deliver up said premises on the day of the expiration of this lease, in as good condition as the same were in when received, reasonable wear and tear thereof excepted.

Second. That the said premises shall be used for Family residence by the lessee and his immediate family.

and for no other purpose.

Third. That Lessee will not sub-let said premises, or any part thereof, to any person or persons whatsoever, without the consent of said Lessor, IN WRITING, thereto first obtained.

Fourth. That on failure to pay the rent in advance, as aforesaid, or to comply with any of the foregoing obligations, or in violation of any of the foregoing covenants, the Lessor may declare this lease forfeited at Lessor's discretion and Lessor or Lessor's agent or attorney shall have the power to enter and hold, occupy and repossess the entire premises hereinbefore described, as before the execution of these presents.

IN TESTIMONY WHEREOF, The parties to this agreement have hereunto set their hands in duplicate, the day and year above written.

Smithson R. Conway, LESSOR

Rollo J. Jenkins LESSEE

FIGURE 19-9

A lease.

A lease for a period of one year.

Lease agreements have become popular methods for financing both small and large enterprises. Lease-financing is discussed in Chapter 14.

Mortgages. One **MORTGAGES** property when it is pledged as security for a loan. A mortgage against real property is called a real estate mortgage. A mortgage against personal property is called a **CHATTEL MORTGAGE.** When a person who holds a mortgage against property sues to take title to it, this is called a **foreclosure.**

LAW OF NEGOTIABLE INSTRUMENTS

A negotiable instrument expresses a contractual obligation that can be transferred from person to person by delivery, or by indorsement and delivery. No one knows exactly when negotiable instruments ("commercial paper") were first used, but they probably appeared in some form or other during the Middle Ages. The law at that time, known as "the law of merchant," was eventually taken into English common law when the colonies adopted the English system. In later years the several states enacted laws pertaining to "commercial paper," which term was eventually changed to "negotiable instruments." The law of negotiable instruments is now part of the UCC.

Kinds of Negotiable Instruments

Under Article 3 of the UCC, negotiable instruments can be classified as bank drafts, checks, certificates of deposit, bonds, and promissory notes. Although negotiable instruments are contracts, they differ from ordinary contracts in two ways. In all negotiable instruments there is an element of negotiability not found in all other contracts. The second difference is a *presumption of consideration* in all negotiable paper. Since a negotiable instrument can be transferred by negotiation, this makes it possible for the transferee to acquire a better right to it than the transferor had. This characteristic goes to the very heart of the law of negotiable instruments.

Requirements to Be Negotiable

The Uniform Commercial Code provides that to be negotiable, a credit instrument must adhere to certain requirements, which can be summarized as follows:

> UCC Section 3-104: *Form of Instrument.* A negotiable instrument must be in writing, payable in money, and be signed by the person putting it into circulation (the maker or drawer); and promise to pay must be unconditional.
>
> UCC Section 3-105: *When Promise or Order Is Unconditional.* An unconditional promise or order is not made conditional by the fact that the instrument is subject to implied or constructive conditions.
>
> UCC Section 3-106: *Sum Certain.* The sum payable must be certain in amount whether paid with stated interest, by stated installments, or with a stated discount.
>
> UCC Section 3-107: *Money.* An instrument is payable in money if the medium of exchange in which it is payable is money at the time the instrument is made.
>
> UCC Section 3-108: *Payable on Demand.* To be payable on demand, the instrument must be paid at sight or on presentation.
>
> UCC Section 3-110: *Payable to Order.* To be negotiable, the instrument must be drawn payable to order or to any person specified with reasonable certainty. Adding the words "or order" after the name of the payee makes the instrument negotiable.

A distinction should be made between instruments payable "to bearer" and those payable "to order." Negotiable instruments (such as checks and drafts) marked "payable to bearer" on the face are freely transferred without indorsement, the same as money. Title passes by delivery. But an instrument payable "to order" requires the indorsement of the named payee before it may be negotiated. If it is lost or stolen before it is indorsed, title will not pass.

It should be evident from this discussion that such instruments as leases, wills, warranties, and sales tickets do not possess all the requirements of a negotiable instrument and therefore are not negotiable. (Our more commonly used negotiable instruments—checks, drafts, promissory notes, and certificates of deposit—are discussed in Chapter 15 regarding their uses in domestic finance.)

$ 100.00 September 25 19 8X

For value received I *promise to pay to* ALEX BROWN

or order --- One Hundred and no/100 --- *Dollars, in Lawful Money of the United States of America, with interest thereon, in Lawful Money, at the rate of* 9 *per cent. per* ANNUM *from date until paid, payable in* four *installments of not less than* $ 25.00 *in any one payment, together with the full amount of interest due on this note at time of payment of each installment. The first payment to be made on the* first *day of* November *19* 8X, *and a like payment on the* first *day of* each month *thereafter, until the whole sum, principal and interest, has been paid; if any of said installments are not so paid, the whole of said principal sum and interest, to become immediately due and collectible at the option of the holder of this note. And in case suit or action is instituted to collect this note or any portion thereof* -- I -- *promise to pay such additional sum as the Court may adjudge reasonable as attorney's fees in said suit or action.*

Due December 1 *19*8X

At FIRST NATIONAL BANK
Portland, Oregon

No. 65

JOY FOX
4200 Main Street
~~Portland, Oregon~~
(Maker)

AICO-UTILITY Line Form No. 80-042 Installment Note

FIGURE 19-10

A negotiable installment promissory note.

A negotiable promissory installment note is shown in Figure 19-10. The maker of the note, Joy Fox, agrees to pay Alex Brown at the First National Bank in Portland, Oregon, four installments of $25 each, together with interest at 9 percent.

Instruments payable to bearer. As we have seen, the payee of an order paper must be named with reasonable certainty. The same exactness is not required for negotiable instruments payable to bearer. Actually a negotiable instrument may be made payable to bearer without naming him or her. For example, a check payable to the order of "cash" is negotiable, although the payee is not named.

Instruments payable to two or more payees. Sometimes negotiable papers are drawn to the order of two or more payees, together or in the alternative. For instance, instruments payable to "A or B" are in the alternative. The instruments, therefore, may be negotiated by either A or B. But instruments payable to "A and B" together are not in the alternative and must be negotiated by both. Both parties must indorse the instruments in order to negotiate them. The UCC has incorporated most of the provisions of the original Negotiable Instruments Law.

How negotiable instruments are transferred. Transfer of these commercial papers from one person to another is by the simple process of **indorsement,** a signature that should appear on the back of the instrument.[6] The person to whom the instrument is transferred is the **indorsee.** This person is also the **holder in due course,** which means that he or she must either be in possession of the instrument properly indorsed or be the bearer of the instrument, having been named

[6]The spelling *indorsement* appears in the Uniform Commercial Code. The spelling *endorsement* is also acceptable.

as the payee. A holder in due course is one who acquires the instrument under the following conditions:

1. It must be complete and regular on its face.
2. The holder must have given consideration (value) for the paper.
3. It must be accepted in good faith.
4. The instrument must be accepted without notice of defects in the title or defense against payment.

If you accept a bank check by indorsement under these conditions, you are a holder in due course and the legal owner of the check. You may enforce collection of the instrument against prior parties regardless of their claims or defenses.

Forms of Indorsements

The individual named on the face of a negotiable instrument can transfer his or her rights in it by signing his or her name on the back of the instrument and using one of four indorsement forms recognized by the Code: blank, restrictive, special, and qualified (illustrated in Figure 19-11).

Blank indorsement. In a blank indorsement, the payee writes only his or her name on the back of the check, writing it exactly as it appears in the instrument. If the payee's name is misspelled in the instrument, the payee should indorse it with the incorrect spelling and then with the correct spelling. An instrument indorsed in blank is payable to bearer. If it is either lost or stolen and falls into the hands of someone else, the new holder may recover on it.

FIGURE 19-11
Forms of indorsement.

Restrictive indorsement. In a restrictive indorsement, the indorsee is the only person to whom payment is legal. If the check is lost or stolen it cannot be cashed; it can only be deposited to your account. This is known as a restrictive indorsement because the negotiability of the check is limited. The most common form of restrictive indorsement is "For deposit only" (signed). "For collection only" may also be used.

Special indorsement. In a special indorsement, the payee indicates the name of the person or firm to whom he or she wishes to transfer title by writing the words "Pay to the order of . . ." and signing his or her name below this phrase. Another name for special indorsement is "full indorsement."

Qualified indorsement. When you indorse a check you received from someone else to a third party for payment of a debt, you are still responsible for the debt if the check proves to be uncollectable from the first payee. To escape this liability, you may elect to use "Without recourse" as part of the indorsement. The form of indorsement does, however, transfer title of the instrument.

LAW OF SALES OF PERSONAL PROPERTY

Personal property (chattels) consists of all property other than real estate. Personal property includes clothing, furniture, food, jewelry, motor vehicles, animals, books, and securities. The basic principles of the law of contracts apply to the law of personal-property sales. Under Article 2 of the UCC, additional rules have been adopted to cover personal-property sales. We will now discuss these rules, which cover such items as warranties, remedies, and passage of title.

Elements of a Sale

The sale of goods is an agreement by which the seller transfers title to goods to the buyer for a sum of money or some other consideration, such as property. The person selling the goods is the **VENDOR.** The person who buys the goods is the **VENDEE.** A bill of sale is one way to transfer title to tangible personal property, and a deed, as we have noted, is used to transfer title to real property. Some goods are sold on consignment. If they are damaged, lost, or do not work properly, who is responsible for the loss? It is important to know when title to personal property passes from the vendor to the vendee.

When Does Title Pass?

The general rule as to the passing of title is that the buyer ordinarily can obtain no better title to goods than the seller had.

Cash sale. In a cash transaction, the title to goods generally passes immediately. Generally the one who holds title must bear the loss.

Goods sold C.O.D. In C.O.D. (cash on delivery) sales, title passes to the buyer when the goods are delivered by the seller to the common carrier (transportation company). Generally the seller designates the carrier as his or her agent to collect the purchase price as part of the condition of delivery.

Goods sold F.O.B. The term **F.O.B.** means **free on board.** During the early history of this nation, goods were shipped on canal boats or railroad cars. The shipment was said to be "made on board." Charges for shipping on board were set by either the shipping point or the destination point, known as the F.O.B. point.

When goods are sold "F.O.B. factory," title passes to the buyer when the goods are delivered to the carrier at the shipping point. The buyer pays the shipping charges. Any damages en route are a problem for the buyer, not the manufacturer or seller.

If goods are sold "F.O.B. destination," title passes to the buyer when the goods reach their destination. In this case the seller is to pay the transportation charges. The seller must bear the risk to the point of destination unless the goods are insured.

Goods sold at auction. In sales by auction, UCC Section 2-328 provides that title passes to the buyer when the auctioneer announces, by the fall of the gavel or some other manner, that the sale is final.

Sale on installment plan. Under the UCC, possession is transferred to the buyer for an installment sale, but title remains with the seller as security until the price is paid. Risk of loss is assumed by the buyer as soon as the goods are delivered.

Sale on approval. Goods are often sold with the understanding that the buyer has the privilege of returning them. This is known as a sale on approval. Section 2-326 of the UCC provides that in the absence of a contrary agreement, the title and risk of loss remain with the seller until the sale is agreed upon by the buyer.

Sale on consignment. A consignment sale differs from the ordinary sale in that the title remains in the hands of the shipper, known as the consignor, until such time as the goods are sold by the retailer, known as the consignee. A consignment sale allows the consignor to control the price and to reclaim the goods in case of bankruptcy.

Product Liability

The liability for the safety of articles manufactured is known as **product liability.** Who pays when a product is unsafe and someone is injured? Who pays when an otherwise safe product is misused and someone is injured? The courts' approach to product liability has changed recently. The new rule of law is much tougher than the former one. Strict liability is the rule now being followed. It, in effect, puts the product, its packaging, and its promotion on trial. The old rule of law was that manufacturers or sellers were liable only when they were negligent or unreasonably careless.

The costs of this new approach to product liability are enormous, estimated at over $3 billion a year. The change in the rule of law has resulted in cases like the following.

To scent a candle, a teen-ager poured perfume made by Faberge, Inc., over a burning wick. The perfume ignited and burned a friend. The friend sued Faberge for failing to warn buyers that the perfume was flammable and won $27,000.

A construction worker riding in a forklift without a roll bar was injured when the truck rolled over on steep terrain. The court ruled that it was up to the manufacturer to demonstrate that the forklift's benefits outweighed its risks. Otherwise the mere fact that there had been an injury showed that it was defectively designed.

A paralyzed high-school football player won a $5.3 million dollar judgment against Riddel, Inc., a maker of football helmets. The helmet was never introduced at the trial.

Warranties

Warranties are important to buyers who purchase goods on the basis of statements made about the products by the seller. Later the buyers may discover that the goods have defects or are not what they were represented to be.

A **WARRANTY** is **an express or implied promise made by the seller about the goods to induce the buyer to purchase them.** Warranties must be statements of fact and not personal opinions. The UCC recognizes two categories of warranties: express and implied.

Express warranty.

An **express warranty** is any statement of material fact, oral or written, by the seller about the characteristics of the goods. Its purpose is to induce the buyer to purchase from the seller. For example, the seller may state to the buyer, "This article is all wool." If the buyer relies on that statement, the buyer has recourse against the seller if he or she later learns that the product is half wool and half polyester.

Implied warranty.

A warranty that is not specifically stated in certain terms but is implied by law is known as an implied warranty.[7] Fitness for a particular purpose is one kind of implied warranty. Boats are usually "implied" to float, for example. Another kind of implied warranty is that tile to the goods is clear and also that the merchandise delivered agrees with the sample or description shown the buyer.

[7]California was the first state to enact a product-warranty law to protect consumers. This law requires California manufacturers to designate service facilities available to fulfill promises in the warranty. It does not require the manufacturer to provide any warranties. But if a warranty is made for the goods, the manufacturer must see that such services are available to the customer.

Magnuson-Moss warranty Improvement Act of 1975. For the first time, a federal law sets specific standards for sales warranties. This legislation, which became effective July 4, 1975, does not compel manufacturers or retailers to use a warranty. *But if they do,* the warranty must be either a "full" or a "limited" warranty. However, the price tag must be higher than $10.

Specific standards for a full warranty include the following information:

1. The parts of a product that are covered or not covered
2. What recourse buyers have to obtain satisfaction
3. What the warrantor agrees to do if an item is defective or breaks down
4. The period of the warranty

The act also specifies the remedies available to the buyer in case of breach of warranty.

A company may elect to use a limited warranty. This restricts the warrantor's obligation to whatever he or she may elect that is less than the full warranty. The title "limited warranty" must be conspicuously labeled.

Bailments

The essence of a bailment contract is that one person (the bailor) places personal property with another (the bailee) for some purpose. It is understood by the parties that the articles will be returned to the bailor when that purpose has been served. Since there is no passage of title, this means a bailment is not a sale.

The law requires that ordinary and reasonable care be exercised by the bailee while holding the articles. Common carriers, such as airlines and bus companies, have a bailment relationship with those who entrust their baggage to the carrier. Examples of bailment also include borrowing your neighbor's automobile, leaving your watch in a jewelry store for repairs, and storing a trunk in a public warehouse.

INSOLVENCY AND BANKRUPTCY

Most businesses are started with the expectations they will succeed. However, in our competitive system, not all firms survive. When failure does occur, the owner is often unable to pay the debts. When this happens, the owner is considered to be **insolvent.** When insolvency occurs, bankruptcy can be declared voluntarily by the debtor or requested by creditors. The Federal government under the Bankruptcy Act governs the distribution of the firm's assets (or individual) when insolvency happens.

BANKRUPTCY is a state of insolvency in which the property of a debtor is taken over by a receiver or trustee in bankruptcy for the benefit of the creditors. The U.S. Constitution provides for national uniform bankruptcy laws.

Originally, bankruptcy was conceived as a method by which fraudulent debtors were charged with failure to pay their debts. Often they were imprisoned.

Later English common law recognized that bankruptcy could be caused by personal misfortune or misconduct.

Bankruptcy may be either voluntary or involuntary. If the debtor takes the initiative and files a petition in bankruptcy, this is called **voluntary bankruptcy.** Under this action the debtor seeks (1) to have his or her assets distributed among the creditors in payment for debts, and (2) to become free of such debts with the right to start over.

INVOLUNTARY BANKRUPTCY is a petition filed against a person (debtor) by his creditors seeking to have him adjudged by the court as bankrupt. If there are fewer than twelve creditors, one creditor may file the petition. But if there are more than twelve, three must join in the filing. To do this, the creditor or creditors must prove the debtor committed one or more acts of bankruptcy, as defined in the Bankruptcy Act:

1. removing or concealing business assets
2. transferring, while insolvent, part of his or her property to one or more creditors
3. allowing any creditor to obtain a lien upon his or her property and failing to discharge the lien within 30 days
4. admitting in writing his or her inability to pay his or her debts
5. making a general assignment of his or her property for benefit of creditors
6. accepting or permitting while insolvent, the appointment of a receiver or trustee to take charge of the property

Bankruptcy proceedings, of course, are under the control of a federal district judge. The chief officers of the court are the referee, and trustee. The referee in bankruptcy generally is in almost complete charge of proceedings. The creditors are brought together and they elect a trustee who liquidates the assets and distributes them among the creditors. Claims against the bankrupt's assets are paid in the following order:

1. administration and court costs including trustee's expenses
2. wages due employees earned prior to bankruptcy
3. expenses for disposing of assets
4. taxes due federal, state, or local districts
5. debts set by law due persons entitled to priority

ETHICS IN BUSINESS

Now that we have examined certain laws pertaining to business transactions, let us turn to the subject of ethics in business. One theme in this discussion is that if business would conduct itself ethically, perhaps fewer laws would be needed.

Understanding the Meaning of Ethics

Ethics is a segment of philosophy concerned with values of human conduct. The term **ETHICS** refers to a code of conduct that guides an individual in dealing with others. Ethics relates to the social rules that influence people to be honest in dealing with others. Ethical rules differ from legal rules. Ethical rules are not enforced by public authority, whereas legal rules are. Society expects businesspeople to act ethically. Their responsibility also applies to those not in business. In fact, society expects businesspeople and politicians to maintain even higher standards than others because it is the price they are supposed to pay for being in the public eye.

Implicit in ethics is the concept of **equity,** a commonplace legal term meaning "justice." The Emperor Justinian I (483–565) said that equity means "to live honestly, to harm nobody, and to render every man his due."

Ethics and morals seem to be related. The term **morals** refers to a code of

CURRENT ISSUE

Should U.S. Laws Restrict American Companies from Investing in Ventures in Foreign Countries That Violate Human Rights?

Some Americans feel that U.S. corporations should not be allowed to invest in countries that violate human rights. Others take a contrary position, holding that business is business and that foreign politics is separate from business interests.

With which of the following statements do you agree and with which do you disagree?

1. The United States has a responsibility to work to improve the welfare of persons who live in other countries.
2. Trade restrictions are an effective means of strengthening human rights.
3. Attaining a higher worldwide morality is as important as making profits.
4. The United States should not become involved in the internal affairs of other countries.
5. The idea of free trade among nations should not become entangled with human rights considerations.
6. If a U.S. company did not do business in those countries where human rights are violated, its participation in international trade would almost cease.
7. We have no accepted criteria by which to judge others when human rights are being violated.

What is your opinion regarding American companies doing business abroad? That is, should they become involved in the politics of the host countries?

conduct that is often part of our religious beliefs. Most religions have beliefs, perhaps differently stated, that essentially say, "Do unto others as you would have them do unto you."

Making Business More Ethical

Society has a right to expect businesspersons to be ethical. When business fails to meet the expectations set by society, or when business does not comply with the basic social codes of conduct, then society—through the government—often demands that business be required to maintain higher ethical standards.

Many people are cynical about the conduct of business. People in general do not want to be taken in by business or anyone else. This sort of cynicism is often expressed by those who believe that business is based only on greed and that profit is the only goal of business. Neither is necessarily true.

Meanwhile, what has business done to become more ethical? Underlying all managerial behavior is each individual manager's personal set of values. These values are not the same for all managers. Certainly businesses do seek profits. However, as we have seen, profit is only one value underlying business decisions. Every company exists to make money and would not survive if it did not, but there are ethical constraints on the process.

It has been proposed that industries draw up their own codes of ethics, which members of the industry would accept and apply. One of the heartening signs of our times is that businesspersons are becoming increasingly concerned about the ethical implications of their work.

Regional and national trade associations are engaged in promoting codes of ethics for their membership. A **trade association** is a voluntary organization composed of a group of competitors, usually in a single industry, who desire to promote their interests. There are approximately twelve thousand of these associations representing a variety of businesses.

The American Institute of Certified Public Accountants, the American Management Association, and the National Association of Insurance Agents are among the professional associations that have adopted a code of ethics.

Conflict-of-Interest Issue

One of the most discussed ethical problems is the conflict-of-interest issue involving business executives. In this type of situation an executive makes a decision as president of company A and approves, without regard to competitive bidding, the purchase of a large order from company B. The executive owns stock in company B and by virtue of this large order the executive will benefit substantially.

What is wrong with this practice? Is it a violation of any law? In most cases it is not. But it may be if it can be established that company A acted in restraint of trade by circumventing bidding standards. This practice is, however, a violation of ethics. Another conflict of interest is to use privileged information obtained by one's official position to acquire personal gain. Businesspeople who accept high government office are expected to sever their financial interests in those firms that have government contracts. This is to avoid a conflict of interest. This seemingly excellent regulation has some interesting sidelights.

High-level officials at the SEC (Securities and Exchange Commission) are forced to go beyond the disclosures required of top business executives. The law also does not allow them to make any contact with the agency until one year after they leave.

It is difficult to attract competent people to the government agency under these conditions. The SEC is made up almost exclusively of lawyers whose specialty is securities law. Most law firms will not allow a lawyer with such skills to return to the firm after serving on the SEC if he or she cannot work on securities. Therefore many good lawyers hesitate to leave their practice to serve with the SEC. The SEC has traditionally attracted bright young legal talent because a term of service with the agency offers the possibility of lucrative private employment later.

Ethics in the Accounting Profession

The accounting profession has a code of ethics that the certified public accountant (CPA) is expected to observe. Certified public accountants are forbidden to violate confidential relations between themselves and their clients. And CPAs must not allow their name to be associated with business forecasts in a manner that suggests privileged information. Few professional groups have taken their code of ethics more seriously than have the CPAs.

SUMMARY OF KEY CONCEPTS

The two main sources of law in the United States are common law and statutory law. Common law is unwritten law, or case law. Statutory law is written law.

Laws concerned with the rights and liabilities of individuals, partnerships, and other organizations are private laws. Under the U.S. Constitution, each state has the right to enact its own laws. The Uniform Commercial Code embraces the area of business law.

In the judicial system, federal courts are concerned with cases involving federal jurisdiction, and state courts are concerned with cases involving state laws.

A *contract* is a binding agreement between two or more competent parties. To be binding it must contain the following elements: mutual assent, competent parties, consideration, and lawful purpose—and required form in some instances.

The law recognizes two kinds of property: real property and personal property. Real property consists of an interest in land. Personal property includes objects that are movable and not attached to the soil.

A warranty deed is used to convey title of property ownership. A quitclaim deed conveys the use of property without warranty of title.

A negotiable instrument is a contract that can be transferred by indorsement. Examples of negotiable instruments are checks, notes, and drafts. Under the UCC an instrument, to be negotiable, must meet certain requirements.

A negotiable instrument may be payable "to bearer" and "to order of." Title passes by indorsement if the instrument is payable to order of a person. If payable to bearer the instrument is transferred without indorsement, the same as money.

Agency is another legal relationship. The parties to agency are principal and agent.

Each state has a statute of limitations requiring that a legal action be started within a certain time after the infraction. Beyond this date, the remedy sought is barred.

Ethics is broader than law. It involves a violation of a moral standard concerning the difference between right and wrong.

BUSINESS TERMS

You should be able to match these business terms with the statements that follow:

a. Abstract of title
b. Agent
c. Chattel mortgage
d. Consideration
e. Contract
f. Defendant
g. Equity
h. Ethics
i. Judicial system
j. Mortgage
k. Plaintiff
l. Public law
m. Real property
n. Vendee
o. Vendor
p. Warranty
q. Warranty deed

1. A branch of unwritten law that grants a more adequate or equitable remedy than is available under common law
2. Law that deals with topics with which the general public is concerned
3. The branch of government authorized to hear controversies between parties and to apply the law to these disputes
4. The party against whom legal action is taken in the courts
5. Something of value pledged in a contract agreement in exchange for a promise or property
6. An agreement between two competent parties which is legally enforceable
7. One who is authorized to act on behalf of another in dealings with third parties
8. The land and anything permanently affixed to it that in a general way is immovable
9. A written instrument that warrants title to real property without defects
10. A written summary of all conveyances, mortgages, and liens affecting the title
11. A pledge of property as security for a loan
12. A mortgage pledging tangible personal property as security
13. The person who sells merchandise
14. An express or implied promise made by the seller about goods to induce the buyer to purchase them
15. A code of conduct that guides an individual in dealing with others

REVIEW QUESTIONS

1. What purposes does the Uniform Commercial Code serve?
2. What are the two main routes for appealing decisions to the U.S. Supreme Court?
3. What types of remedies are available to the injured party in the case of a breach of contract?
4. What requirements must an instrument meet if it is to be negotiable?
5. When does the title pass to the buyer under an installment contract?

DISCUSSION QUESTIONS

1. Why do managers of a business need a knowledge of business law?
2. Explain what is meant by the elements required to make a contract binding on both parties.
3. Explain the difference between an *express* and an *implied* warranty.

4. When should a person use a blank indorsement on a check? A full indorsement? A restrictive indorsement?
5. Why is conflict of interest considered a problem in ethics?

BUSINESS CASE 19-1

West Lumber Company vs. H & S Construction Company

Sam Long, owner of the West Lumber Company in Boise, Idaho, brought an action to collect a debt from the H & S Construction Company, a partnership owned by Charles Henderson and Jim Sellers.

The facts show that on June 12, 1981, Henderson introduced Jim Sellers to Sam Long as a partner in the H & S Construction Company. At that time, Long recalled that he had done business with Henderson about five years ago when Henderson was in the construction business by himself. Because Henderson had always paid his bills promptly, Long instructed his cashier to obtain an up-to-date credit rating about the H & S partnership.

On June 16 Henderson bought a small amount of building materials, which he paid for by check. And during the next thirty days he placed several more small orders, which he also paid for by check.

On October 15, 1981, Henderson placed another order, which totaled $9,800. He paid the full amount of the bill by check ten days later. The following day the bank informed Long that Henderson's check had been returned due to insufficient funds. Unable to locate Henderson, Long called Sellers, who stated that he was no longer a partner. He disclaimed liability for this debt. Two months later Long filed suit against the partnership to recover the debt.

1. Who is liable for the debt? Why?
2. What precaution might Long have taken to avoid this suit?

BUSINESS CASE 19-2

A Sale on Approval

Helen Ray ordered two fur coats from a local department store. Each of the coats was valued at $1,500 and was to be delivered to her home in the same city on approval for three days. When the coats arrived, the ticket clearly showed that this was a sale on approval. Two days later the coats were destroyed by a fire that started from an unknown origin in Helen's home. The fire occurred on a Saturday night, and since Sunday was the third day of the three-day period, Helen was unable to notify the store because it was not open.

On the following Monday Helen reported the loss to the store and refused to pay for the coats, claiming that she had no insurance protection and that the title had not actually passed to her because the transaction was a sale on approval.

1. Who is liable for the loss?
2. What is the rule in this case?

GOVERNMENT AND WORLD BUSINESS

PART 7

THE GOVERNMENT'S ROLE IN BUSINESS

20

STUDY OBJECTIVES

WHEN YOU HAVE FINISHED READING THIS CHAPTER, YOU SHOULD BE ABLE TO

ONE Describe several ways that the federal government encourages business

TWO Explain why business is dependent upon, and affected by, governmental monetary policies

THREE Identify the types of business that are supervised by governments through the issuance of licenses, franchises, and charters

FOUR Understand the functions of the chief agencies through which the federal government regulates businesses

FIVE Define public policy and explain how it relates to business

SIX Discuss the ways that taxation affects private businesses

IN THE NEWS

The U.S. Textile Industry: The Government Will Help Decide Its Future

The ten largest U.S. textile companies average a meager 3.3 percent return on sales. Thus most of the five thousand companies in the industry have little capital to invest in badly needed equipment for modernizing. Furthermore, tradition-bound management has clung to outdated ways of doing business. Now events are about to occur that will force a change in this industry, and the government will be directly involved.

Textile and clothing imports are continually increasing, and U.S. regulations on employee safety and environmental protection require immediate action. It is estimated that during the next decade the industry must spend $22.5 billion to modernize.

A significant portion of this money will have to go to meet Occupational Safety and Health Administration requirements that cotton dust in mills be reduced. Cotton dust is believed to cause "brown lung disease," a serious ailment found among textile workers. But while the textile industry is blasting the government's intervention in employee health, it is also arguing that the government is doing too little to help it in the import competition area. The industry wants the government to protect it from competition, especially from Japan and China.

In order to adapt to the pressures of the future, the textile industry will have to rely on many mergers of smaller companies into larger companies. The change from a labor-intensive industry to a capital-intensive industry will require the greater capital-generating ability of larger firms. And of course the government will keep a close watch on such mergers to make sure they are in the public interest. The American textile industry's future will greatly depend on U.S. government decisions.

Does anyone believe for one moment that the progress we have made would have been possible under bureaucratic control of any government? This country was founded upon the principle of the regulation of private effort, of making rules for the game and under that system alone can we look for the same success in the future which has been ours in the past.

ROGER BABSON

Business in the United States has changed greatly since Congress passed the first law regulating business. The main purpose of this law, the Interstate Commerce Act of 1887, was to regulate the nation's railroads. Today business is influenced by government more than at any previous time in history. At local levels there are codes and ordinances that establish areas for use by business. Building codes provide minimum specifications for construction details. States, counties, and cities grant licenses to operate various kinds of businesses. Both federal and state laws govern wages, safety standards, and civil rights. There are laws to prohibit monopolies that would restrain trade or prevent competition. More recently federal and state controls regulate energy resources and causes of pollution. Labor laws and consumer legislation affect almost every phase of business.

Taxation is also an area of increased public concern. The mounting costs of government place a heavy burden on businesses and consumers.

Not all government intervention is designed to curtail and restrict business, for government provides a variety of services to business. In this chapter we will examine the role of government as it relates to the following activities:

1. Authority and functions of government
2. Encouragement and protection of business
3. Maintenance of a sound monetary system
4. Patents, copyrights, trademarks, and franchises
5. Regulation of business enterprises
6. Regulation of public monopolies
7. Taxation and business
8. Sources of revenue and types of taxes

AUTHORITY AND FUNCTIONS OF GOVERNMENT

The founders of the American government provided for a federal system, with political power divided between the national and state governments. Our basic laws are described in the U.S. Constitution and the constitutions of the fifty states. In enacting these laws, the federal government derives its authority from the people. The basis of this authority is the Constitution of the United States. Article I, Section 8, of the Constitution gives Congress the power to make all the laws "necessary and proper" to carry out its duties. In addition to the broad powers granted to Congress, the Constitution provides certain specific powers, such as the following.

Collect taxes	Establish post offices
Levy duties	Establish systems of courts
Designate roads	Patrol coastal waters
Coin money	Provide for national defense
Grant patents and copyrights	Fix standards of weights and measurements
Regulate trade between the states	Make laws to enforce private contracts
Pay debts of the U.S.	

Special protection to property is also provided by the Constitution. This includes "due process of law"—any person brought to trial must be accorded the rights to which he or she is entitled. Your right to due process of law is even more important in protecting your personal freedom than in protecting your property rights. The courts have ruled that the Fifth Amendment guarantees that no person shall be "deprived of life, liberty, or property without due process of law."

This, then, is the legal background in which government and business interact. The authors of our Constitution apparently understood the conditions necessary for the growth and encouragement of business enterprise.

What Is Government?

Broadly defined, **government** is **the center of political authority having the power to govern those it serves.** Whether at the local, state, or national level, government has the power to regulate and maintain orderly relations. In this role it is a **protector.** Government maintains an orderly legal and economic system as required by the people. At all levels, government has the right to establish public policy.

Powers of government originate in two ways: (1) through enactment of laws and (2) through judicial interpretation of laws. The role of government in business has increased because of public demand to protect the people and to provide new services.

In relation to business, government acts to (1) encourage the production of goods and services through private enterprise and (2) see that the pricing of goods and services is maintained in accord with the public interest. The government attempts to see that competition is maintained in the buying and selling of goods and services. It also encourages economic growth and price stability. Maintaining these powers over the business economy is not always easy, however.

In recent years the governments of the United States and Canada have experimented with controls on prices and / or wages to maintain price stability. Both efforts met with very mixed results.

In the United States, wage and price controls led to a rash of price increases before and after the controls. They also caused shortages of supplies in some areas.

When the wage controls expired in Canada, the nation experienced an annual rate of about 7 million lost workdays in strikes as unions rushed to catch up in monetary benefits.

In a "free-enterprise economy" the ideal is a completely free price system in the voluntary exchange of goods and services. In a "modified free economy" such as ours, the government plays an active role. It is expected to prevent practices that restrain trade against the public interest.

Michael Blumenthal, former president of the Bendix Corporation and former secretary of the U.S. Treasury, said:

> It is now time for all of us to realize that our present problems have become too big and too complex to be solved by business alone . . . business needs government and government needs business. We must find new ways of organizing into new forms of government-business relationships to solve the problems of the day.

Reasons for Government Control of Business

The reasons for government control of business can be summarized as follows:

1. To protect the welfare of the individual and to promote higher standards of public health, safety, morals, and general well-being
2. To maintain equality of opportunity for all persons regardless of their sex, national origin, or religion
3. To restrain business from engaging in practices that would be harmful to the public, such as making false and misleading statements about a product or service, failing to support warranties of goods, and manipulating prices for the deliberate purpose of gaining an unfair advantage
4. To protect small firms from unfair competitive abuses by big firms
5. To prevent unfair practices resulting from mergers or other forms of combinations, such as price fixing
6. To conserve our national resources, notably forests, fuels, and water, and to prevent dangerous contamination of the atmosphere

GOVERNMENT ENCOURAGES AND PROTECTS BUSINESSES

The federal government makes many positive contributions to the success of the American business system. It aids and protects business through tariffs, monetary loans, grants, and subsidies. It also sets standards in many areas of business operation.

Protective Tariffs

The federal government's earliest effort to aid business was in the form of protective tariffs. A **TARIFF is a charge or duty levied by government against goods imported from other countries.** The very first tariffs levied by the federal government were largely intended to produce revenue for the government. However, early in the nineteenth century tariffs were levied to help some infant industries. Tariffs helped the textile industry during the War of 1812 and the iron industry in the 1840s by protecting them from the competition of foreign goods. Since World War II the federal government has advocated low tariffs and has favored free trade among nations.

Government Loans and Guarantees

For many years the federal government's financial strength has enabled it to provide loans to businesses in one form or another. One of the earliest loans made by the federal government was to the Union Pacific and Central Pacific railroads. These loans helped in the completion of the first transcontinental railroad in 1869. Since 1958 the Interstate Commerce Commission has been authorized to guarantee loans on new equipment purchased by railroads. In the same manner the Maritime Administration has aided ship construction since 1932. In 1961 and 1962 federal funds were employed to aid in the development of urban mass-transportation facilities, including commuter lines. Currently the Chrysler Corporation is operating because the federal government has guaranteed more than a billion dollars of its borrowed funds.

Small Business Administration.

One of the most important government agencies for business is the Small Business Administration. It was created by Congress in 1953 to help small companies meet the rigors of competition. Business and disaster loans are the main type of loans made by the SBA. Chapter 6, "Small-Business Management and Franchising," examines the services furnished to small businesses by the SBA.

Federal Grants and Subsidies

Because transportation has been so vital to the development of this nation, the federal government has made railroads, water carriers, and airlines special objects of support. The westward movement of population encouraged the construction of railroads. Prior to the Civil War the federal government made huge land grants amounting to 180 million acres to several railroads, mostly in the sparsely populated West. Included among the seventy railroads that shared in the grant program were four western roads—Northern Pacific, Santa Fe, Southern Pacific, and Union Pacific. Together they received almost three-fourths of the total. These railroad land-grant programs ended in the 1870s.

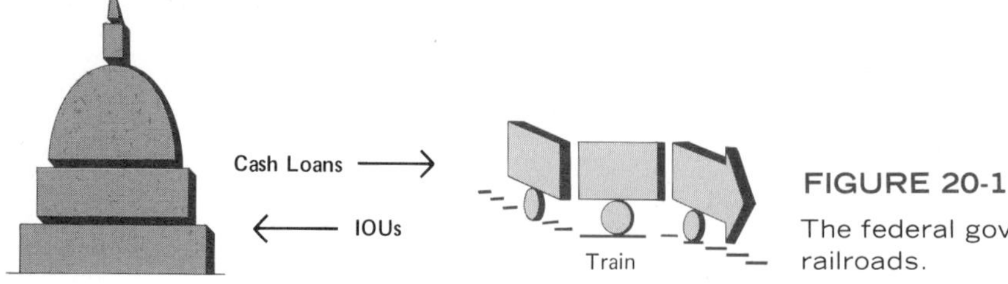

FIGURE 20-1
The federal government subsidized the railroads.

The subsidy. Another form of government aid to business is the subsidy. A **SUBSIDY is a government payment or grant to a private enterprise or institution for the good of the public.** Over the years the federal government has paid subsidies to various groups, such as farmers, railroads, airlines, and shipping companies. For example, President Gerald Ford signed legislation boosting the allowable federal subsidy payments to shipbuilding companies on negotiated building contracts from 35 to 50 percent of the total construction costs. These subsidies helped to maintain American shipbuilding facilities in the face of lower foreign ship construction and repair costs. By subsidizing private enterprise, government acts to improve the economic position of the private group. A subsidy is a means of guaranteeing an entrepreneur a fixed price.

Farm subsidies have been or are being paid to growers of tobacco, corn, wheat, feed grains, sugar cane, and sugar beets. Farmers producing some specific crop are guaranteed a certain minimum price. If the market price falls below the set minimum, the government makes up the difference as a subsidy payment to the farmer.

AN EXAMPLE OF BUSINESS SUBSIDIZING GOVERNMENT

George V. Voinovich was elected mayor of Cleveland in 1979. He immediately invited business to help straighten out the city's financial problems—the city had a $111 million deficit.

At Voinovich's request, E. Mandell de Windt, chairman of Cleveland-based Eaton Corporation, formed a task force of businesspersons to examine the operations of every city department, from the office of the mayor to the dog pound. Sixty-three companies—among them Sohio, Republic Steel, and Reliance Electric—volunteered the full-time services of seventy-five executives. Most were department or division heads in accounting, data processing, purchasing, personnel, and so on. De Windt said that he made a point of recruiting only men and women whose companies would miss them during the twelve weeks that they served the city. These experts were paid by their companies, not the city—a donation by business of about $1 million worth of management time.

Two foundations and 225 companies donated $765,000 in cash to pay the fees of the consulting firm that coordinated the task force, and to provide some $500,000 to help put the task force's recommendations into effect.

PRO AND CONS OF THE SUBSIDY ISSUE

Those in favor of subsidies argue that subsidies are a useful solution for helping the domestic firm compete with foreign companies. Marginal firms are able to remain solvent until they can become large enough to compete effectively. A subsidy may be proposed as a substitute for protection by tariff which does not cause a foreign government to retaliate with a similar tariff.

Subsidy critics contend that subsidy payments are paid to large establishments rather than helping smaller firms that often need more assistance. This is often the case where large corporate-owned farms receive more subsidy than small farms. Subsidy payments encourage marginal firms to continue operating at the expense of taxpayers.

Farmers and business firms are not the only ones subsidized by the federal government. When workers become unemployed because of the competition from imported goods, they are paid unemployment benefits. College students are granted scholarships and low-interest loans, which are subsidies. Hospitals built by nonprofit organizations are given grants, and long-term loans at low interest rates.

Parity. The parity concept has dominated farm price-support legislation since the Agricultural Adjustment Act of 1933. **PARITY is government action designed to maintain the purchasing power of farm income at a certain level.** It is supposed to be an expression of economic justice. Parity means placing farmers' income on a par with the cost of producing their crops. It is intended to entitle the farmer to a living standard by the use of two indexes. One is a price index of things farmers buy. The other is a price index of things farmers sell. The base period selected is arbitrarily determined—farm supporters try to get a base that is favorable to farmers. The first base period was from 1910 to 1914. This period was chosen because members of Congress felt that the trade-off between farm expenses and crop prices then was ideal for farmers. The U.S. Department of Agriculture calculates monthly the price needed to give farmers parity for their crops.

Governments Set Standards

Government standards apply in most industries. The auto manufacturers, for example, are required to meet safety and environmental standards that are set by the federal government. All new automobiles must be equipped with seat belts and shoulder straps. Engines must be equipped with devices that prevent pollution of the air. Businesses and municipalities must meet certain standards

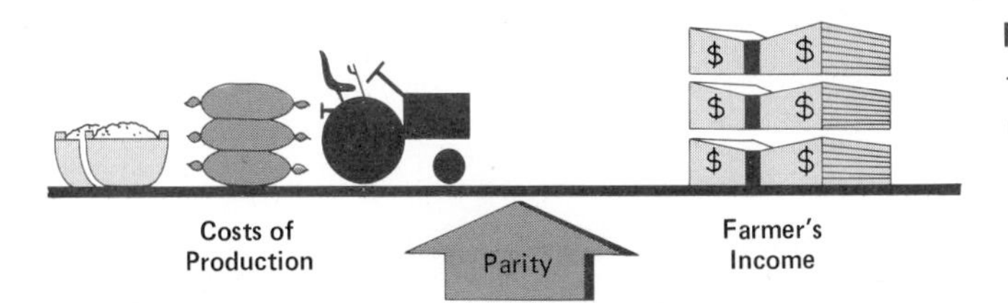

FIGURE 20-2

The federal government guarantees parity prices to farmers.

relative to water purification and waste disposal. The maintenance of these standards is supervised by the Environmental Protection Agency.[1]

You undoubtedly have heard of OSHA. These letters stand for Occupational Safety and Health Administration, an agency established in 1971. It is responsible for regulating safety and health conditions in all workplaces—except those run by government. Stories about OSHA's activities appear regularly in business periodicals.

Whether OSHA is a help or a hindrance is not yet clear. The Bureau of Labor Statistics found that in a recent year, on-the-job fatalities among employers with eleven or more workers rose 20 percent. During the first three years after OSHA began operation, job fatalities declined, but during each of the last three years there have been increases. There is some question as to whether OSHA standards can have much effect.

A recent report by the President's Interagency Task Force on Workplace Safety and Health estimates that only 25 percent of accidents could be prevented through compliance with OSHA rules.

State and local governments inspect hotels, restaurants, barber shops, beauty salons, and so forth, to see that they meet and maintain certain health standards.

GOVERNMENT MAINTAINS A SOUND MONETARY SYSTEM

In the most primitive societies, one good is traded for another. This process is called **BARTER**. In the early history of the American colonies, the fur traders were among the first entrepreneurs. They bartered manufactured articles made in England, France, and Spain for furs and grains produced by the colonies. Barter has great limitations. For example, how do you trade a pair of shoes for half a cow? Almost immediately traders needed some type of a **medium of exchange**. When an acceptable medium is developed into a system, it is called **money**.

A Monetary System

When money is backed by a government, we have an official national monetary system. One of the most important functions of government is to provide a sound money system, which is necessary for conducting business transactions. Here in the United States the basic monetary unit is called the dollar. In Belgium, France, and Switzerland, it is called the franc; in Germany, the mark; and in Britain, the pound.

[1]The various laws relating to the environment are discussed in Chapter 2.

At one time the U.S. dollar was supported by gold. During this period the United States, upon demand, redeemed its paper money with gold. Later paper money issued by the federal government was redeemable in silver. Now our paper money depends only on the credit standing of the government. It is not backed by either gold or silver.

The Value of the Dollar

For a long period in our history the value of the dollar was "fixed" by the government. This means that the number of dollars that would be exchanged for a British pound was set by the federal government. The number of German marks or Swiss francs per dollar was also fixed. But in 1973 the U.S. dollar was freed to *float* against other currencies. The value of the dollar, as measured in other currencies, is now determined by supply and demand. The number of marks, francs, or yens that one can obtain for a U.S. dollar or a British pound is determined in the international money market.

For many years the U.S. dollar has been an "international currency." It has been used as a currency of settlement for business transactions outside the United States. The oil-exporting nations, for example, price their products in dollars. This role has led to a large demand by individuals, institutions, and corporations. They want dollars to be used for trading purposes and as a storehouse of value as well. Occasional "hoarding" or "dishoarding" of privately held dollars abroad is at times an important element influencing the supply and demand of dollars on the foreign-exchange market. This fluctuates from day to day, and foreign-exchange rates are published in the leading daily newspapers.

Monetary Policy

The rules and regulations relating to the money system constitute our official **monetary policy.** Whether the value of a government's money is to be fixed or allowed to "float" depends on government policy. Whether the amount of money in circulation is to be increased or decreased also depends on government policy. Is credit expansion or contraction to be encouraged? Should interest rates rise or decline? Business is very dependent on the government's monetary policies.

In the United States the Federal Reserve Board is responsible for setting a monetary policy in relation to money supply and interest rates. This subject is discussed in detail in Chapter 15, "Credit and the Banking System."

PATENTS, COPYRIGHTS, TRADEMARKS, AND FRANCHISES

The law is an important source of granting monopoly power. Laws covering patents, copyrights, and trademarks have the objective of conferring temporary monopoly control to their holders.

Patents

If you invent a machine or a device, you may apply for a patent. In the United States a **PATENT** is **the exclusive right to own, use, and dispose of an invention** and is granted to the owner for seventeen years. After that period, the patent right expires and is not renewable.

G. WILLIAM MILLER

The Federal Reserve is a unique American institution. It represents a solution to central banking that is typically American where you blend the national responsibilities with local and regional participation. And it is a system that has well stood the test of time.

It operates in an American system that has shown itself to have strength of flexibility . . . . Impacted by many adverse forces it has responded with resilience and the ability to self-correct.

These are the words of G. William Miller on the occasion of his appointment as chairman of the Board of Governors of the Federal Reserve Board in 1978. It shows that he believes in the American system.

At the time of Miller's appointment to the Federal Reserve Board, he was chairman and chief executive officer of Textron, Inc. Textron is a diversified corporation with 180 plants and facilities in the United States, and gross sales of about $3 billion. Miller has been a member of the Business Council and of the Business Roundtable, and chairman of the Conference Board and of the National Alliance of Businessmen. He was appointed secretary of the U.S. Treasury in 1979 by President Jimmy Carter.

Throughout his business career Miller has been active in public service, with emphasis on full employment and nondiscrimination. He once served as chairman of the Industry Advisory Council of the President's Committee on Equal Opportunity.

Miller, a native of Oklahoma, was born in Sapulpa in 1925. He graduated from the U.S. Coast Guard Academy in 1945 and served as an officer in the Pacific. In 1952 he received a J.D. degree from the University of California. He practiced law in New York with the firm of Cravath, Swaine and Moore before joining Textron in 1956 as assistant secretary.

In June 1980 the U.S. Supreme Court ruled allowing patent rights for biogenic discoveries. These may include creation of organisms such as genes in a laboratory. The full impact of this decision may not be apparent for several years.

The General Electric Company has been assigned more than fifty thousand patents. Its fifty thousandth patent covers a process for creating fine grids in semiconductor devices.

The expiration of patents can cause problems, as the manufacturers of prescription drugs recently learned:

> In 1980 eighty-three of this nation's one hundred leading prescription drugs lost their patent protection. The expiration of these patents brought a sudden end to the monopoly that brand-name drug producers have enjoyed for years on popular high-revenue products.
>
> Moving into competition for the market was the manufacture of the so-called generic-equivalent drugs, which cost 15 to 40 percent less. In addition, some forty states now have laws that promote the substitution of generic drugs for brand-name drugs where possible. This is an attempt to cut health-care

costs. The difference between the price of a brand-name drug and the price of its generic equivalent may be considerable. For example, *Librium,* a widely prescribed tranquilizer, carried a wholesale cost of $9.06 per one hundred tablets while its generic substitute cost $1.10 per one hundred tablets.

The U.S. Patent Office examines the owner's application to see whether the invention is new and useful as claimed and whether the application conforms to the law. Copies of patent laws can be obtained from the Superintendent of Documents, Government Printing Office, Washington, D.C. 20402.

A $60 MILLION PATENTED WRENCH

Peter Roberts was a clerk in a Sears, Roebuck store in Gardner, Massachusetts, in 1964. He obtained a patent on a socket wrench that has a quick release, which enables the wrench to be operated with only one hand. In May 1964 Roberts sold the rights to the wrench to Sears for $10,000.

Later Roberts sued Sears to have his contract with the company rescinded. In 1978 a federal jury ruled that Sears had fraudulently obtained Roberts's patent and awarded him $1 million.

Sears appealed this decision to a higher court, and on May 31, 1979, U.S. District Court Judge George Leighton canceled the sales contract and ordered the patent returned to Roberts. Judge Leighton also ruled that Roberts was entitled to all the profits made by Sears on the sale of this wrench.

Since Sears has sold 25 million of these wrenches at a profit of $44 million, this together with the interest will amount to about $60 million.

Copyrights

The word **copyright** literally means the "right to copy." The first American copyright law was passed by Congress in 1790 in keeping with Article I, Section 8, of the U.S. Constitution. A **COPYRIGHT gives an author** (including a designer, a composer, a photographer, a publisher, a sculptor, or an artist) **the exclusive right to publish, print, produce, or copy his or her work.** No one else can do so without his or her permission. Copyrights, like patents, have an obvious importance to business, since they involve the granting of a government-approved monopoly for a limited time. If your copyright is violated, the copyright law gives you the right to seek redress through the courts. This may include an action for damages, an injunction restraining the continued infringement, and the cost of litigation. Copyrights can be obtained from the U.S. Copyright Office of the Library of Congress upon the payment of a fee and the furnishing of two copies of the material to be copyrighted.

It took Congress more than twenty years to pass the Copyright Act of 1976, which became effective January 1, 1978. Under that act the right of copyright covers the lifetime of the individual owner plus an additional fifty years. According to Barbara A. Ringer, register of copyrights at the Library of Congress, the

TABLE 20-1
THE FEDERAL COPYRIGHT LAW

Provisions	Old law	New Law
Term	28 years, renewable for another 28 years	Life of author plus 50 years
Photocopying	Not covered	Permits an individual to copy a limited amount of material for research purposes, but bars "systematic" copying without permission
Cable television	Not covered	Mandates royalty payments on programs and films based on a sliding scale that depends on the TV system's revenues
Phonograph records	Provided flat royalty rate of 2¢ per record	Raises royalty rate to 2.75¢ per record or ½¢ per minute of playing time, whichever is higher. Imposes an $8 annual license fee on every jukebox
Pooled royalty settlements	Not covered	Creates a new, five-person, independent regulatory agency to review license rates periodically and distribute pooled royalties

new copyright law is "a monumental accomplishment compared to the 1909 law that we've been working with." Table 20-1 shows how the copyright law was changed by the 1976 act.

Trademarks

Many firms use the **TRADEMARK—a distinctive symbol, title, or design that readily identifies the company or its product.** By registering the trademark with the Patent Office, the owner is granted the exclusive right to its use for twenty years. The registration can be renewed once for another twenty years. Once the trademark has been registered, the Patent Offiice is empowered to deny the registration of infringing trademarks. The owner must initiate legal action to restrain the use by another if the owner feels that this person unlawfully adopted the trademark.

The major benefit of the trademark is that it is *prima facie* ("on first appearance") evidence of the registrant's exclusive right to use the symbol.

Protecting a trademark symbol. Litigation over trademarks may seem frivolous to most consumers, but to companies owning trademarks protection is no small matter. The legal staffs of corporations scan thousands of articles and advertisements for misuses of brand names and trademark infringements. For example, the Coca-Cola Company retains the services of three lawyers to challenge others who might use the trademark **Coke** in advertising.

In a suit brought before the Court of Customs and Patent Appeals, the Procter & Gamble Company persuaded the judges to reject Certified Chemical & Equipment's claim that involved the use of a stain remover called Mister Stain because it "stimulates the same mental reaction" as P&G's Mr. Clean brand. As we discussed in Chapter 12, the trademark **Formica** is owned by the American

FIGURE 20-3
Many companies use the trademark as a symbol to identify their product or service. When registered with the U.S. Patent Office, trademarks prevent others from using the same name. Some well-known trademarks are shown here. (Courtesy RCA, GE, A&P, and Greyhound.)

Cyanamid Company. In April 1978 the Federal Trade Commission announced that it wanted the Commerce Department's Trademark Trial and Appeal Board to cancel Cyanamid's right to the exclusive use of the name **Formica**. The FTC argued that the name was so widely used to refer to plastic laminated counter tops that it had become a generic term.

A few companies have abandoned efforts to protect their trademark title by allowing it to be used by the public without prior approval. **Nylon** is now dedicated by Du Pont to public use. Some of the most successful trademarks have been lost because of their popularity. They became so firmly entrenched in the language that no single company could legitimately claim ownership. Such casualties have included cellophane, linoleum, mimeograph, and kleenex.

Licenses and Franchises

If you wish to establish a new business enterprise in your community, you must obtain a license from the appropriate governmental agency. Many cities require the licensing of door-to-door salespersons. Professional persons such as teachers, physicians, and lawyers are licensed by state governments. Corporations are "chartered" to do business by state governments.

Franchises for regulated monopolies.

Some business services can be rendered economically only through monopolies. The public utilities (telephone, gas, and electricity) are the best-known examples. Large sums of capital are required to start and maintain a utility system. Local and state governments grant franchises to selected public utilities to provide and distribute these services. A **FRANCHISE** is **an exclusive right to perform a stated business service in a specified geographical area.** It defines the period of time and the territory within such services are to be provided.

Every state has some form of commission or state agency that regulates franchised businesses and supervises the rates they charge.

AMERICAN TELEPHONE AND TELEGRAPH

The American Telephone and Telegraph Company, familiarly known as Ma Bell, operates nationwide. It is the best known of our large regulated corporate monopolies. It has more than 3 million stockholders, and it ranks high among all U.S. corporations in gross revenue and value of assets.

Theodore N. Vail is generally credited with building the AT&T into the company it is today. Vail had been the general manager of Bell Telephone between 1878 and 1887. He became president of AT&T on May 1, 1907, and served as its president until June 1912. John Brooks, in writing about AT&T, said that under Vail, AT&T was no doubt the first large private corporation to adopt a conscious, clearly stated policy of making a profit secondary to providing services to its customers.

GOVERNMENT AGENCIES THAT REGULATE BUSINESSES

At the federal level our government has established many agencies to administer federal laws. These agencies are the regulators of business—especially interstate transactions. They determine which firms may enter the field, what rates they may charge, and what rules must be observed. Table 20-2 lists the most important agencies and commissions.

Space limitations do now allow a detailed explanation of the authority and functions of each of these agencies. Specific ones have already been discussed in previous chapters.

Complaints against government regulation of business continue to increase in volume and intensity. Business's chief complaints relate to the confusion and misunderstanding of purposes and guidelines supplied, the time required to prepare reports, the lack of consideration being given to reports, and the duplication of effort required.

Consumer advocate Ralph Nader observes that

> our unguided regulatory system undermines competition and entrenches monopoly at the public's expense.

TABLE 20-2
WHO ARE THE FEDERAL REGULATORY AGENCIES?

Civil Aeronautics Board	Federal Power Commission
Commission on Civil Rights	Federal Reserve Board
Commodity Futures Trading Commission	Federal Trade Commission
Consumers Product Safety Commission	Food and Drug Administration
Environmental Protection Agency	Interstate Commerce Commission
Equal Employment Opportunity Commission	National Labor Relations Board
Federal Aviation Administration	Nuclear Regulatory Commission
Federal Communications Commission	Occupational Safety and Health Administration
Federal Energy Regulatory Commission	Securities and Exchange Commission
Federal Maritime Commission	

FIGURE 20-4
Government committee holding a hearing.

And New York Congressman Jack Kemp states that

> instead of strangling commerce with costly and counterproductive regulations, we must cut out those that do not serve the public interest . . . we should be reviving the idea of incentives—an idea that we know works, because it is the idea that built this country.

When addressing the annual meeting of shareholders of the Union Oil Company of California, Fred L. Hartley, Chairman of the Board noted:

> Today government priorities are reversed . . . the entangling web of government controls and intervention has now become the most dominant force affecting us. In fact, these events have become of such enormous significance that they threaten our historic and heretofore successful system of private enterprise.

And indeed deregulation is winning some battles. An example follows.

The ICC recently changed its rules to allow railroads to set their rates for hauling fresh fruit and vegetables. The railroads believe that by reducing their rates, they will have a chance to regain business they lost to the truckers.

The Federal Railroad Administration eliminated unnecessary and burdensome maintenance requirements that will save the industry $100 million a year. Further ICC deregulations have helped truckers by allowing them to make deliveries to points that they had been barred from serving.

The FTC is dropping a rule that would have required funeral homes to list the price and display their cheapest-priced coffins. And the EPA decided to allow the use of MMT as a substitute for lead in unleaded gasoline. This is a reversal of an earlier position. This will permit a better grade of unleaded gasoline and a greater supply.

REGULATING MONOPOLIES AND PUBLIC POLICY

The extent to which governments attempt to control business activities is largely determined by what the public seems to want. The doctrine of *laissez faire,* "to let alone," prevailed in this country from about 1780 to 1890. During this period our government did not interfere in the conduct of business. The trend toward government regulation of large businesses, starting about 1890, was presumed to be in the interest of public policy. Thomas Edison said:

> There is far more danger in public than in private monopoly, for when Government goes into business it can always shift its losses to the taxpayers. Government never makes ends meet—and that is the first requisite of business.

Meaning of Public Policy

Congress may formulate public policy, which is the result of public hearings, investigation, and debate. Exactly what the public policy means depends mainly on how it is interpreted by government administrators and judges. Public policy also becomes a matter of what those subject to the law interpret it to mean. Public policy, therefore, is an expression of both public officials and private interests.

A precise definition has not yet been formulated by our courts. As used here, however, **PUBLIC POLICY is a statement or an interpretation of an action that carries the weight of government authority.** It may be used in determining business and political decisions.

Controlling Business Monopolies

Toward the end of the nineteenth century, a group of stockholders in several large companies were persuaded to turn their shares over to a group of trustees. These trustees were then able to control competition and maximize profits at the public expense. These organizations became known as business trusts. A **BUSINESS TRUST is a combination of businesses operated under trust agreements by trustees for the benefit of the members.** Its purpose is to restrain trade.

In 1882 John D. Rockefeller and his associates organized the first large-scale business trust, the Standard Oil Company. Through a series of trust agreements with some forty different corporations, these corporations were placed in the hands of a few Standard Oil Company trustees, although they did not own the shares. Thus it was possible, through the trustees, to take whatever action was necessary to gain a monopoly in oil. A **MONOPOLY exists when a firm has a large enough segment of a particular industry that it can control prices within that industry.**

Similar trusts were formed to control the source and price of sugar, tobacco, whiskey, and cottonseed oil, and machinery for making shoes. By the late 1880s it became obvious that government regulation to prevent monopolies was in the interest of public policy. So in 1890 Congress enacted the Sherman Antitrust Act to control monopolies. This law and its amendments have proved to be milestones in combating trusts and monopolies in the interest of public policy.

Sherman Antitrust Act. Named for U.S. Senator John Sherman (1823–1900), an early sponsor of the act, this legislation became the first to curb monopolies. The act is brief but broad and its two main provisions are as follows:

> Section 1: Every contract, combination in the form of trust or otherwise, or conspiracy, in restraint of trade or commerce among the several states, or with foreign nations, is hereby declared to be illegal . . . .
>
> Section 2: Every person who shall monopolize, or attempt to monopolize, or combine or conspire with any other person or persons, to monopolize any part of the trade or commerce among the several states, or with foreign nations, shall be deemed guilty of a misdemeanor . . . .

Violators could draw a fine of $5,000, a prison term of one year, or both. In 1974 Congress raised the maximum fine to $1 million for corporations and to $100,000 for individuals. Violations became a felony rather than a misdemeanor.

The Sherman Act applies only to firms in interstate commerce (trade between the states), and enforcement is under the Antitrust Division of the Department of Justice, in cooperation with the Federal Trade Commission and the courts. The Antitrust Division investigates about twelve hundred complaints each year.

Between 1890 and 1914 monopolies still flourished, for the Sherman Act was limited in its scope and some corporations found ways to circumvent the law. Finally the Supreme Court evolved the "rule of reason" concept—a merger may be considered legal as long as the intent to monopolize an industry does not exist.

This "rule of reason" applies to corporate mergers as well as to other ways to gain control of another corporation. For instance, two or more companies may agree to merge to achieve a specific purpose: Companies A, B, and C agree to merge; when the merger is completed, A and B go out of business and C remains. In another instance, two corporations desire to combine and form a new corporation. In still another instance, one company decides to purchase enough voting stock to gain control of another corporation. This is called an *acquisition*—an outright purchase of enough voting stock in another corporation to gain control. The corporation, however, may continue to operate under its original charter and use its own name. Today merger activities are carefully reviewed by government agencies before they are approved.

The Clayton Act. This act was passed in 1914, as an amendment to the Sherman Act. It brings within the antitrust laws some abuses that previously were not covered. The Clayton Act preserved competition by stating specifically those things that a business cannot do to achieve business growth. For example, the use of interlocking directorates to bring two companies closer together is illegal, as is price fixing to gain a monopoly. Also, one company cannot acquire stock in a competing company either by amalgamation or acquisition in order to eliminate competition.

The Clayton Act specifically forbids the following:

1. The use of interlocking directorates in companies that compete directly with one another
2. The acquisition by one company of more than a limited amount of stock in another company that competes directly with it
3. Contracts that require the purchaser to buy other items in addition to the product desired

4. The practice of charging different prices among various buyers for goods that are equal in quality or quantity should such action reduce competition or lead to a monopoly

Hundreds of cases have been tried by the Justice Department under the antitrust laws. Probably the most complex case of its kind involves the International Business Machines Corporation. In this case the government is attempting to prove that IBM illegally monopolized the computer industry during the 1960s.

THE GOVERNMENT vs. IBM

The government filed its charge against IBM on January 17, 1969. The trial began on May 19, 1975, and the government rested its case in court in April 1978.

IBM contends that its early dominance in the industry resulted from superior products and business methods.

The record of the case up to April 1978 fills ninety thousand pages of transcript.

IBM made 69 million pages of documents available to the government.

Almost five thousand exhibits were entered as evidence.[2]

Regulating Prices and Practices

The Federal Trade Commission Act. Noting the loopholes that existed in the Clayton Act, Congress in 1914 enacted the Federal Trade Commission Act. This act provides that "unfair methods of competition in commerce are hereby declared unlawful." A five-member commission was established to define and detect unfair trade practices. Included among the unlawful practices are

1. Misbranding goods as to quality, origin, composition, durability, and so on
2. Using false or misleading advertising to deceive the public
3. Bribing a customer's employees to obtain orders or to learn their trade secrets
4. Using containers that give a false impression of an item's size
5. Advertising or selling rebuilt or reconditioned goods as new
6. Using business schemes that are based on chance

The commission has a large staff of accountants, lawyers, and economists who investigate alleged unfair methods of competition and conduct hearings. When necessary, the commission issues cease and desist orders. Table 20-3 shows how legislation has added to the powers of the FTC.

The Robinson-Patman Act. **This act amended the Clayton Act. Passed in 1936, its general purpose is "to make it unlawful for any person engaged in interstate commerce to discriminate in price or terms of sale between purchasers of commodities of like grade and quality."**

[2]Additional details regarding this case can be found in Chapter 19.

TABLE 20-3
GROWING POWER OF THE FEDERAL TRADE COMMISSION

The Legislation	Its Purpose
FTC	Originally an antitrust law, passed in 1914 and broadened in 1938 to let the agency attack "unfair or deceptive acts or practices in commerce"
Clayton	The basic antitrust statute, including antimerger provisions and prohibitions on interlocking directorates
Robinson-Patman	These 1938 amendments to the Clayton Act require that sellers must offer equal deals to all customers
Truth in Lending	Details the information that must be given to a credit customer
Fair Credit Reporting	Establishes a customer's rights in disputes with credit bureaus
Fair Credit Billing	Protects consumers from unfair and inaccurate billing practices
Equal Credit Opportunity	Bars discrimination by sex, race, religion, or age in loans and credit sales
Fair Packaging	Outlaws deceptive packaging or labeling
Fur Products	Requires accurate branding of fur products
Textile Identification	Requires accurate labeling of fiber content of textile products
Webb-Pomerene	Provides antitrust immunity for U.S. companies that band together in joint export efforts
Magnuson-Moss	Extends the agency's reach to local business dealings and confirms its right to regulate by industrywide rules

The FTC conducted investigations showing that large corporate buyers secured discriminatory low prices. These were gained not only on the pretense of quantity discounts but also on getting rebates for brokerage services when no such services were rendered. Large buyers were also using their economic power to extract favorable prices. These were not granted to other less-powerful buyers and not justified by savings to the seller resulting from differences in cost of manufacture, sales cost, or delivery expenses.

The act prohibits indirect discrimination in price through the use of advertising allowances and such services as window displays and demonstrations of merchandise. It is unlawful to pay brokerage fees to agents under the direct control of the buyer. Brokerage fees may not be paid to the buyer, except for services rendered by the buyer.

The Celler-Kefauver Antimerger Act. In 1950 the Celler-Kefauver Act was passed as an amendment to Section 7 of the Clayton Act. Its purpose is to forbid mergers that prohibit competition. Under the Clayton Act of 1914, acquiring the stock of another corporation where the effect might be to reduce competition was prohibited. Subsequent court decisions so weakened this law that it no longer restricted acquisition of assets by merger, acquisition, or amalgamation.

Under the antimerger act, corporations that are major competitors cannot merge in any manner. This amendment extends jurisdiction to all corporations subject to the Federal Trade Commission. In formulating the Celler-Kefauver Act, congressional committees stated that this legislation was not intended to stop the merger of two small companies or the sale of a company that was in a "failing" condition.

Effectiveness of antitrust laws. How effective has the antitrust legislation been in reducing monopolistic business practices? On the positive side, the antitrust laws have contributed enormously toward improving the degree of competition in our system. Those who value the capitalistic way applaud this kind of government intervention.

Each year more cases are being investigated and brought to trial. Some cases are settled without trial if a consent decree is accepted. Defendants deny guilt but agree to abide by the conditions subject to negotiation between them and the Justice Department before the decree is issued. However, American antitrust laws have not been a complete success. But we have only to look at business to realize how much worse off our economy might have been without these laws.

On the negative side, a sizable number of persons, including members of Congress, would like to see these laws broadened. They feel that such organizations as labor unions, professional associations, professional baseball teams, and agricultural cooperatives should be covered by antitrust laws. To some economists and businesspersons, unions are socially irresponsible and uncon-

THE FEDERAL REGISTER

In 1933 Chief Justice Charles Evans Hughes threw a case out of the Supreme Court because it was based on a presidential order that had been revoked months earlier. But the defendants, the plaintiffs, and the lower courts knew nothing about the revocation because it had not been adequately publicized. In the furor that followed, Congress passed the Federal Register Act, requiring the daily publication of all presidential proclamations, executive orders, and federal agency actions.

The importance of the Federal Register Act has grown markedly in recent years as Congress has delegated more and more authority to such rule-making agencies as the Environmental Protection Agency, the Occupational Safety and Health Administration, and the Federal Trade Commission. No action of these agencies is official until it appears in the *Federal Register*. The number of *Federal Register* pages alone dramatizes the incredible increase in regulatory activity. In 1937, the first full year of publication, the *Register* had only 3,450 pages; in 1978, the total was 61,261.

The *Federal Register* provides its readers with critical information on executive pronouncements, and proposed and final rules, as well as upcoming meetings, investigations, application deadlines, and other agency activities. For the businessperson wishing to comply with a newly issued regulation or testify on a proposed rule, or for a state or local government official who is trying to find additional federal aid, there is no better source of up-to-date information.

trollable monopolies. The government has both promoted unions and attempted to curb their powers.

Some thirty-eight thousand organizations and businesses subscribe to the **Federal Register.** In addition, some eleven thousand government offices receive copies regularly.

TAXATION AND BUSINESS

Governments can provide essential services only because they collect taxes. The federal government collects about one-sixth of its total revenue through income taxes on private corporations. In addition, businesses are obliged to pay and collect social security and excise taxes.

Purposes of Taxes

There are several identifiable purposes of taxes, the most important of which are to (1) raise revenue, (2) regulate or influence some aspect of the economy, and (3) transfer or redistribute wealth. Most of our taxes serve at least one of these purposes.

Philosophy of Taxation

There are two basic philosophies in this country as to how the tax burden should be apportioned: (1) the benefit principle and (2) the ability-to-pay principle.

The benefit principle. Advocates of this principle contend that those who benefit from government services should pay for them. No one can argue very loudly that this is not a logical concept. For example, the federal tax on gasoline was passed to provide funds for highways. After all, those who drive benefit most from the highways. However, this principle does have its limitations. For example, assume that public-school taxes were levied on the basis of the number of children that parents have in school. In fact, all people derive some benefit from the public-school system, regardless of whether they have children in school. Thus it would be unsound to tax only those who have children in school.

The ability-to-pay principle. Taxation based on this principle seems to be superior to the benefit principle. But what measures one's ability to pay? Net income received during a given year is probably the most widely accepted criterion. Others prefer to use gross income. But even after a criterion has been agreed upon, there remain the problems of determining the acceptable tax rate.

The income tax is perhaps the best example of applying the ability-to-pay principle. Income taxes are broadly based and are set up on the basis of the government's estimates of the people's ability to pay what is asked of them. A person with a $25,000 income is asked to pay more than one who earns $15,000.

A major problem during periods of high inflation has been the fact that taxes have been rising rapidly. A few years ago when the average family income was $8,000, the prices of food, shelter, and transportation were much lower. Now the average income is more than twice that, but prices of essentials have risen even more than incomes. Yet the tax structure continues to treat current incomes as it did when $8,000 was enough to live on. The ravages of inflation are a major business and government problem. Its impact has led to a major debate on the annual balancing of the federal government budget.

REVENUE SOURCES AND TYPES OF TAXES

Governments obtain their funds from taxes and through borrowing, which is paid back with tax money. Local, state, and federal governments together tax away a large part of the income one earns. The expenditures of the federal government are greater than those of all state and local governments combined.

CURRENT ISSUE

Should the Federal Government Maintain a Balanced Budget?

Senator William Proxmire (Democrat, Wis.), when speaking on the Senate floor in May 1979, said, "If we cannot balance the budget in a year of solid growth, such as we assume in 1980, we will never be able to balance the budget. This is no time for gentle, pitty-pat cure for inflation, but it is time for a tough, sharp, emphatic answer."

By January 1980 thirty states had passed resolutions calling for a constitutional convention to draft legislation requiring a balanced federal budget.

With which of the following statements do you agree and with which do you disagree?

1. We should maintain a balanced budget during periods of sound economic growth.
2. We should work toward a balanced federal budget but reach it gradually.
3. A balanced budget will restrain inflation.
4. High employment and low unemployment support the idea of a balanced budget.
5. A balanced budget would not leave sufficient funds for defense spending, and social and educational programs.
6. A balanced budget would encourage people and build their confidence in government leaders.
7. To require a balanced budget even in normal economic periods does not allow government sufficient fiscal flexibility.

In your opinion, when should the federal government maintain a balanced budget?

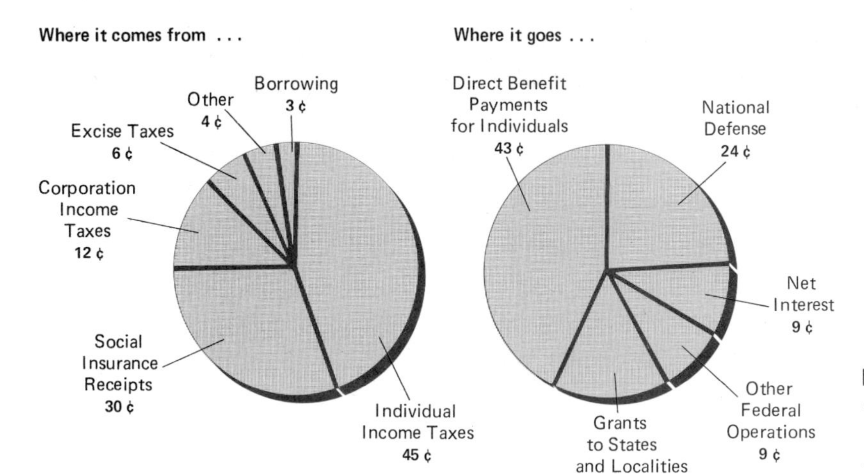

FIGURE 20-5
The budget dollar, fiscal year 1981 estimate. (Source: Data from the President's budget message.)

Figure 20-5 shows where the federal government revenue comes from and where it goes. Notice that business corporations pay a large percentage of the total. Income taxes paid by business proprietorships and partnerships are included in that portion shown as individual income taxes. Businesses also pay approximately one-half of the social security taxes.

Types of Taxes

The principal types of taxes levied by all types of government are summarized in Table 20-4. The table also shows where the effect of the tax finally comes to rest.

TABLE 20-4
PRINCIPAL TYPES OF TAXES

Type of Tax	Description	Probable Incidence (Resting Place)
Personal income	This is a graduated tax levied directly on individual income. Its rates are progressive, and it is based on the ability-to-pay principle.	On the taxpayer.
Corporate income	This tax is levied on the net earnings of corporations. Because stockholders pay taxes on dividends received, this double taxation is a constant source of complaint to members of Congress.	On the corporation.
Property	Cities, counties, and states levy taxes against both real and personal property.	On the property owner. Taxes on rental property can be shifted to tenants. Taxes on business property can be shifted to consumers.
Sales and excise	States and cities levy retail sales taxes on the buyer or consumer. Excise taxes are levied on the producer or seller. Excise taxes are assessed against such items as jewelry, tobacco, beer, and gasoline.	Shifted to consumers.

TABLE 20-4 (Continued)
PRINCIPAL TYPES OF TAXES

Type of Tax	Description	Probable Incidence (Resting Place)
Severance	This tax is levied on the owner of minerals taken from beneath the earth's surface —coal, iron ore, oil, etc.	Passed on to ultimate purchaser.
Estate and inheritance	The federal government levies an estate tax on wealth that is passed on to one's heirs. States use inheritance taxes, since they are assessed against the persons who inherit the wealth.	Both are usually paid out of property left by the deceased.
Corporation franchise	This is a tax levied by the state government that grants the corporation a charter for doing business.	Borne by the company as a cost of operation.

Business Payroll Taxes

Three types of payroll taxes are paid by businesses to provide benefits for their employees: (1) social security, (2) unemployment insurance, and (3) workmen's compensation.

Social security tax. The Social Security Act of 1935 established a national plan to supplement a person's retirement income. In addition to normal retirement pensions, the act now provides for disability payments and health-care payments (medicare). To defray the cost of these benefits, both employers and employees pay a monthly tax. For employees, this tax is deducted from wages. For employers, it is assessed against their payrolls. The rate of the tax and the amount of salary it is assessed against are established periodically by Congress.

Almost everyone who works is covered by the social security program. This includes men and women on active duty in the armed forces. Employees of non-profit organizations may elect to be covered. If the employer and two-thirds or more of his or her employees vote for coverage, the law will apply to them.

Covered employees who become disabled may qualify for benefits regardless of age. Dependents who are eligible for disability or old-age retirement benefits and who have children under eighteen are entitled to monthly payments equal to half the amount of workers' retirement benefits. Benefits stop when the children reach their eighteenth birthday. However, there are two exceptions to this rule. First, when a child becomes totally disabled before age eighteen, that person may continue to collect the benefit as long as the disability lasts. Second, when a child attends school full time, he or she may receive disability payments until age twenty-two.

These payroll taxes have been raised to the point that they constitute a real burden on both businesses and workers. But the additional money is needed to keep the social security system solvent.

Unemployment insurance. Under the Social Security Act of 1935 and the Employment Security Amendments of 1970, all states and the District of Columbia are encouraged to enact unemployment-compensation protection laws. Each state now has its own plan approved by the federal government. In every state except

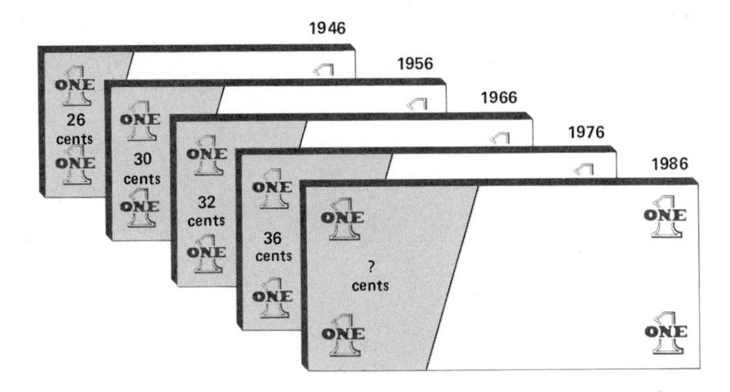

FIGURE 20-6

The cost of government.

All taxes—federal, state, and local—as a percentage of national income. (Source: U.S. Department of Commerce.)

Alaska, Alabama, and New Jersey, the cost of the plan is borne by the employer. In these three states the tax is shared by employer and employee.

A 1970 amendment to the Federal Unemployment Tax Act established a payroll tax rate of 3.2 percent on the first $4,200 of wages paid each employee in the plan. A credit of 2.7 percent of this amount is allowed for payments made to state programs to finance payments to unemployed individuals. The program protects most workers in industry, but few in agriculture. Approximately 80 million jobs in industry, commerce, and government are covered, including those of members of the armed forces. During periods of unusually high unemployment, many state funds become exhausted.

Workers' compensation. Another payroll tax program providing workers' compensation is compulsory in most states. It is a form of accident insurance for employees injured on the job. The employer pays the cost of the program and may elect to buy an insurance policy or join a state-operated program. Workers' compensation insurance is discussed in some detail in Chapter 16, "Risk Management and Insurance."

Some Effects of Taxation

Taxes levied by the federal government are high and of national scope and have a major effect on business. Such business taxes as sales and excise taxes tend to increase the price of goods to the consumers. Corporate-income taxes, which are levied against earnings, reduce profits that might otherwise be distributed to stockholders. Corporate-income taxes also result in the highly controversial problem of double taxation.

Because of the amount of taxes paid, taxation can have an impact on business policy and decisions. For example, corporations with high earnings and a possible increase in income taxes often find it advantageous to buy a company that has been losing money. For tax reasons, corporations may decide to engage in debt financing (bonds) rather than sell stock to raise capital. Interest on bonds is part of the cost of doing business. It is deducted from earnings in computing taxable income. Companies have also been known to move their headquarters from a state with a high property or income tax to one with a low tax.

The cost of government continues to increase as we call upon it for more and more services. Government taxes at all levels—federal, state, and local—now take almost two-fifths of our national income. According to J. B. Hill, any existing waste and extravagance of government will not be eliminated or diminished until people realize that the burden of paying its bills will, through direct or indirect taxation, ultimately fall upon them, their children, or their children's children.

The Value-Added Tax—A Proposed Tax

The **value-added tax** (VAT) is a relatively new concept in this country. It is quite popular in Europe but has received little support in the United States. This is a tax at the manufacturer's level, based on the amount of value that is added to each stage of the product as it goes through the production or manufacturing process. In principle, it taxes the market value a business adds to a product at each stage of production. It resembles a sales tax in that it can easily be passed on to the ultimate consumer. But in terms of what the consumer pays, the effect of a 5 percent value-added tax could be the same as a 5 percent sales tax. For this reason, the VAT is referred to as a national sales tax, although it can be adopted by a state and applied to manufacturing concerns operating in that state.

The main criticism of the VAT is that it is mildly regressive, falling more heavily on the poor than on the rich. Its chief advantages are that it falls alike on the incorporated and unincorporated, on the efficient and inefficient, and that there is no easy tax shelter from it—except to spend less of one's income.

This tax has been adopted by France, West Germany, Belgium, the Netherlands, Luxembourg, Denmark, Sweden, Norway and Italy. It was recommended by the Committee for Economic Development several years ago. More recently it has been recommended by both the chairman of the Senate Finance Committee and the chairman of the House Ways and Means Committee. They use this as a way to reduce other federal taxes, especially the social security tax.

SUMMARY OF KEY CONCEPTS

The power and authority of government legislation come from the Constitution and the interpretation of laws.

Government encourages and protects businesses through tariffs, loans, grants, and subsidies.

The exchange of trade requires an acceptable *medium of exchange.* The federal government provides this through a national monetary system.

A business may gain a temporary monopoly of an invention, a writing, or an idea, through a patent, a copyright, or a trademark.

Issuing licenses and franchises provides a simple and direct way to control businesses.

To protect the public interest, government must regulate business.

Government functions and services depend on successful businesses. In order to sustain competition and protect businesses, monopolies must be prevented or controlled.

Revenue to pay for government comes largely from taxes. A variety of taxes are levied against both individuals and businesses:

Income	Estate
Property	Inheritance
Sales	Severance
Excise	Franchise

Some special taxes are levied against businesses, which adds considerably to their cost of operation:

- Social security taxes
- Unemployment insurance
- Workers' compensation

Taxes have a tremendous impact on business. In fact, intelligent business decisions can only be made within the framework of governmental rules and public policy.

BUSINESS TERMS

You should be able to match these business terms with the statements that follow:

a. Barter
b. Business trust
c. Copyright
d. Estate tax
e. Franchise
f. Money
g. Monopoly
h. Parity
i. Patent
j. Public policy
k. Subsidy
l. Tariff
m. Trademark

1. A charge or duty levied by the government against imported goods
2. A government grant to a private enterprise for the good of the public
3. Placing farmers' income on a par with the cost of producing their crops
4. The exclusive right to own, use, and dispose of an invention
5. The right of an author or a publisher to own, sell, or use written material
6. A distinctive symbol, title, or design that readily identifies a company or product
7. The trading of one good for another
8. A governmental system establishing a legal medium of exchange as payment for goods or services
9. The exclusive right to perform a particular type of business service in a specified geographical area
10. A statement or an interpretation of an action that carries the weight of governmental authority
11. A combination of businesses operated under agreement by trustees on behalf of the members
12. A situation where a firm (or a few firms) has a large enough segment of an industry that it can control prices
13. A tax levied against wealth passed on to heirs by one deceased

REVIEW QUESTIONS

1. From where does the federal government receive its power and authority?
2. In what specific ways does the federal government encourage and assist businesses?
3. In what areas does the government set standards for business?
4. How do patents, copyrights, and trademarks aid businesses?
5. What is the chief purpose of a government franchise?
6. What is the meaning of the term *public policy* as it relates to business?

DISCUSSION QUESTIONS

1. What is the purpose of parity and how does it work?
2. Why is a sound monetary policy important to business?
3. How do you feel about government regulatory agencies? Do we have enough or too many?
4. What in your opinion constitutes a good tax policy?
5. What specific effects do taxes have on business decisions and consumers?

BUSINESS CASE 20-1

Evers Products and the Justice Department

Harris Industries, a close corporation chartered under the laws of New Mexico, operates a lightweight steel products manufacturing plant in Seattle, Washington, which serves a sixteen-state area west of the Mississippi River. Annual sales represent about 49 percent of the market for woven-wire fence, reinforcing rods, small seamless pipe, and galvanized sheets. The Western Steel Company and Evers Products, Inc., also close corporations, are competitors, along with a Japanese company that exports competing products. Western Steel and Evers each furnish about 18 percent of the total demand for this area, and the Japanese company furnishes about 12 percent. Competition from eastern steel companies is very slight.

About three years ago Western Steel had a long labor strike that set the company back. Last year it was rumored that the company might shut down. Two months ago the directors of Harris Industries discussed the matter of acquiring Western. They voted to make the company a tender offer to consolidate, with payment in cash and in Harris common stock, details to be worked out between the two companies. What happened as a result of the proposal was not released to the public, but Evers Products requested that the Justice Department conduct a hearing by the Antitrust Division staff.

1. What factors must exist to support the fears expressed by Evers Products?
2. Do you agree that Evers should have filed a complaint?
3. What advantages does consolidation offer to Harris and to Western Steel?

BUSINESS CASE 20-2

Government to the Rescue

Hart's Textiles, located in New England, is a small independent operation that employs 180 workers. Hart's Textiles is incorporated, but most of the stock is owned by persons who live in the immediate and surrounding area. For the past six years the company has lost money and has paid no dividends. The two largest stockholders are urging that the company be sold, moved, or liquidated. They have found a suitable location in one of the southeastern states. Labor in this state is plentiful and cheaper than in New England. The city government in this potential location has offered to forgive the payment of property taxes for the first five years. It has also offered to build the new plant and lease it to the corporation.

Since hearing this news, the presently employed labor force is urging its local government to buy the plant and forgo the payment of property taxes. A small group has suggested that the workers buy the plant and operate it as a cooperative.

Thus the alternatives considered so far are

a. Continue as now organized
b. Move to a southern location
c. Sell out to the local government
d. Sell to the workers and operate as a cooperative

1. Do you see other alternatives?
2. What is the plant's importance to the local government?
3. Assume that the local government has sufficient money to buy the plant. Would it be better off to do so or should it offer tax concessions for a period of years, thus enabling the company to continue to be privately owned?
4. What would be the determining factors in deciding whether to operate the company as a cooperative?

INTERNATIONAL BUSINESS

21

STUDY OBJECTIVES

WHEN YOU HAVE FINISHED READING THIS CHAPTER YOU SHOULD BE ABLE TO

ONE Recognize how world trade can benefit those countries that engage in it

TWO Name the kinds of products that the United States lacks and must obtain from other countries

THREE Identify the leading trading partners of the United States, considering both imports and exports

FOUR Explain how one nation gains an advantage over others in production through world trade

FIVE Describe the chief barriers to international trade

SIX Define the term tariff and summarize the advantages of free trade between nations

IN THE NEWS IN THE NEWS IN THE NEWS IN THE NEWS IN THE NEWS IN THE NEWS IN THE NEWS IN THE NEWS IN THE NEWS

U.S. Health Care is Becoming a Big Export Item

U.S. health-care expertise has boomed as a U.S. export. Developing nations with many petrodollars want modern health care. But there is a demand from Western Europe as well. Many Europeans who are tired of socialized medicine are demanding alternatives. This was dramatized recently by a British woman who "hijacked" a hospital bed after waiting months for a gallbladder operation.

According to Royce Diener, president of American Medical International, U.S. health care is viewed as the best in the world. Most developing nations lack expertise in hospital design, staff recruiting and training, equipment selection, systems development and management, and preventive health care.

Entrance into foreign markets has speeded the growth and broadened the business base of the U.S. hospital management industry. However, the costs and risks are great. One company estimates that it requires three times as much capital to go "international" as it does to market only in the United States. High travel and living expenses and the time required to build local relationships add a great deal to the costs. Furthermore, political instability, potential nationalization, changing currency rates, and inflation add to the risks.

Most developing nations prefer to administer their own hospital and other health-care facilities. But without an existing health-care structure, they do not know where to start. American Medical International uses five prerequisites for choosing foreign markets: Does the government of the country really want to improve health care? Can the government afford it? Will private enterprise be accepted? Is the political climate moderate? And is the governmental bureaucracy workable?

IN THE NEWS

Free trade is just another word for open competition and protection is just another word for monopoly. Whether we are talking about commerce on a national scale or a world scale, the more competition and the less monopoly we have, the better.

HENRY FORD

Trade with other nations is essential to the existence and welfare of this nation. Jobs and profits at home depend upon our ability to buy goods from abroad that we do not produce in this country. Today it seems that almost every large corporation does business overseas, and many foreign companies are investing in American property and business.

Doing business abroad merits special study because these transactions are conducted in a different environment. Business conducted in a foreign country is subject to laws and customs different from ours and often involves many currency systems. In order to sell goods to a foreign country, there must be some kind of understanding and system acceptable to both parties.

This chapter begins with the idea that trade between nations is a two-way street. We will learn why international trade is necessary and how it is conducted and financed. We will also discuss such topics as tariffs, foreign exchange, marketing channels, balance of payments, and career opportunities in international trade. Throughout this chapter the terms **international trade, world trade,** and **international business** are used interchangeably.

THE DYNAMICS OF WORLD TRADE

Considered in its broadest sense, **world trade** covers not only merchandise but also services, financial investments, and monetary transactions between residents of different countries. However, the bulk of international economic transactions involves exports and imports of merchandise.

HENRY HEIDT

Henry Heidt is the owner-manager of Heidt Metal Products Ltd. in Waterloo, Ontario. Heidt was born in Hungary where he attended both public school and high school. He was deported to East Germany in 1946 because of his German heritage. (The Socialist-Communist governments confiscated all properties and belongings.) Within that same year he moved to West Germany. He soon found employment in a metal shop where he learned the welding trade. Two years later he passed the test for welder-fabricator.

Heidt was married in 1953, and in July 1954 he and his wife arrived in Canada with a lot of enthusiasm and $250 in cash. At the age of twenty-four, Heidt was to start on a new job and a new language. The first job he could find in his trade was with a school-furniture manufacturing company. Here he performed many kinds of work: machine operator, assembler in the shipping and spray rooms, and assembler in the woodworking department. Because of the experience he gained there, his future began to shape itself. He was promoted through the regular channels: lead hand, welding foreman, foreman of the complete metal fabricating and finishing department, and finally plant superintendent.

In November 1963 Heidt started his own business, which consisted of doing custom metal work. He was his own salesman and did the costing, purchasing, and actual physical production as well. For the first two months he employed only part-time help (experienced tradesmen).

Eventually the number of his customers increased, as did the staff. Fifteen years later Heidt Metal Products manufactures not only school furniture but library shelving and engineering drafting tables, and it does a considerable amount of custom work to offset the seasonal school trade. There are forty employees, including three sales personnel.

Heidt believes that an honest day's work deserves honest pay and benefits. He cannot understand why everyone does not appreciate free enterprise and a democratic way of life and work. He is proud to be a citizen of a country that promotes freedom in business under a democratic political structure.

Heidt is married to the former Margaret Schroeder, and they have three children.

Since there is an unequal world distribution of resources—food, wealth, population, and technology—the need for international trade is crucial. Fortunately, there is good reason to believe that as nations continue to develop economically, the volume of world trade will increase. This is true because of the growing demand for goods as countries achieve a higher standard of living. It is also true because of the expansion of productive activity and the tendency for nations to specialize.

What is world trade? **WORLD TRADE** can be described as **business transactions between citizens, companies, and governments, conducted on an international scale.** Some nations have resources not found in abundance elsewhere. For example, if one country has tin and another has coal, it becomes

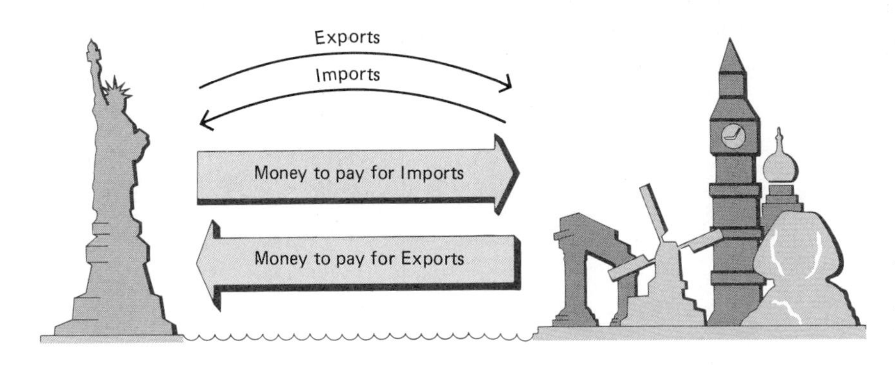

FIGURE 21-1

International trade is a two-way street.

The United States is not self-sufficient. Importing goods from other nations encourages them to import goods from us.

advantageous for them to exchange these materials with each other. An article in FORTUNE, September 15, 1967 states:

> What is taking shape, slowly and tentatively but nevertheless unmistakably, is "one world" of business, a world in which business will truly know no frontiers, in which the paramount rule governing the movement of goods and money will be the rule of the market.

Domestic producers often stand to gain from international trade by way of importing. Importing crude oil from the Middle East has increased the market there for American products. Imported raw materials are often cheaper and more readily available than the same items supplied by domestic sources. Domestic producers also stand to gain from exporting. Exporting gives them a profit on sales and a larger production scale that may result in lower unit costs. About one job in eight in our production industries depends on exports. Everyone in the United States is affected by marketing exchanges with other countries. U.S. President Jimmy Carter in an address in Davenport, Iowa said,

> I think it would be good for us to choose American products whenever they are of high enough quality and reasonably competitive in price. Sometimes you can buy something a little bit cheaper from a foreign country but I think it's good for us to buy American whenever we can.

Thus we see that international trade is indeed a two-way street, as illustrated in Figure 21-1.

Composition of International Trade

Despite the versatility of American business, this nation is completely dependent on other countries for supplies of specific commodities, such as bananas, coffee, tin, natural rubber, and diamonds. Figure 21-2 shows the percentage of selected raw materials that we import. Note that for several of these products we are completely dependent on foreign sources. Other countries depend on us for food, technology, and machinery. We saw in Chapter 10 that the United States depends on other nations for two-fifths of its petroleum energy. In addition, several sectors of American agriculture depend heavily on foreign markets to buy rice, wheat, and cotton grown in America.

Goods and services that are produced in this country and sold abroad are called **EXPORTS.** Raw materials and manufactured products shipped into this country are called **IMPORTS.**

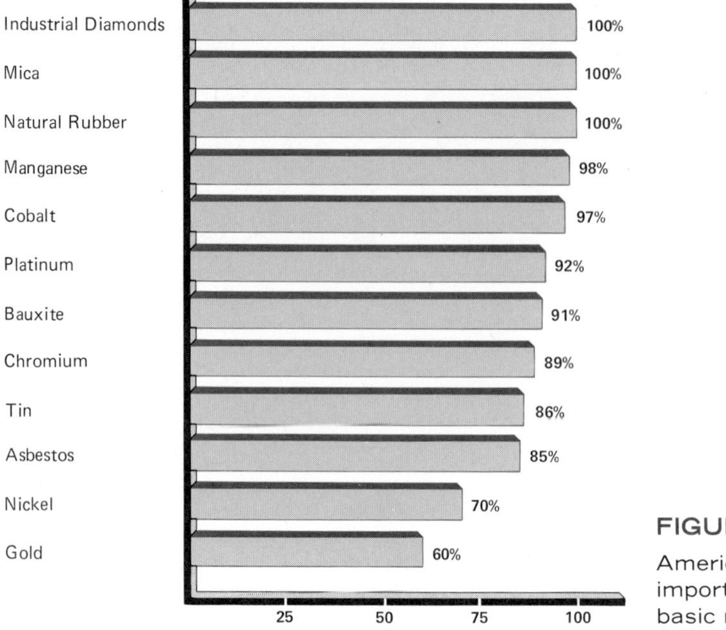

FIGURE 21-2
America depends on imports for many basic raw materials.

Milton Friedman, formerly of the University of Chicago and recipient in 1977 of the Nobel Prize in economics, said this about trade between nations:

> Exports are the cost of trade, imports the return from trade. We should be setting a standard for the world by practicing the freedom of competition, of trade, and of enterprise.

The United States produces and consumes almost 30 percent of the total world supply of goods and services. American industry exports annually about 6 percent of its production, and it imports about 5 percent of the goods consumed in this country. (These percentages fluctuate somewhat from year to year, depending upon economic conditions here and elsewhere.)

International trade is more important for certain sectors of the American economy than for others. We depend upon foreign markets to absorb about 35 percent of our milled rice and its byproducts, 30 percent of our cotton-farm products, and about 32 percent of our mining, construction, and tractor production. The chemical, machinery, and machine-tool industries also sell significant portions of their output abroad.

A comparison of U.S. imports and exports is shown in Figure 21-3.

Who carries on trade with the United States? The largest volume of world trade is among countries with a highly industrialized economy. These countries are able to produce a surplus and to use large quantities of the materials they obtain from other nations. The United States trades mostly with the countries of the Western Hemisphere—Canada, South America, Mexico—and with the European countries and Japan. American firms now export to the USSR as a result of improved political relations, and to Middle East countries as a result of their new wealth. The developing countries of Africa are beginning to engage in world trade, for they have products desired by other nations.

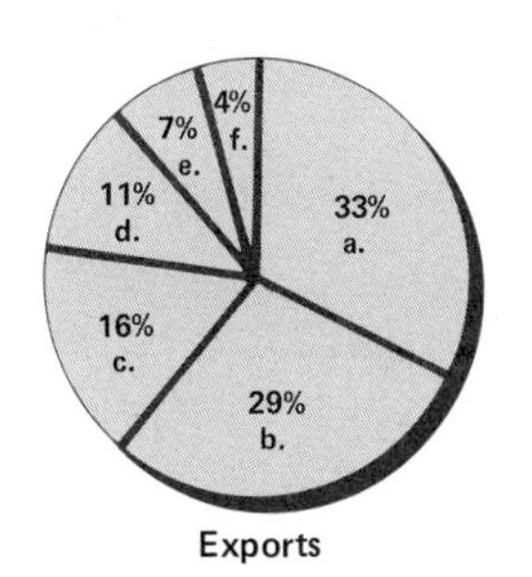

a. Capital Goods, Except Automotive
b. Industrial Supplies and Materials
c. Food, Feeds and Beverages
d. Automotive Goods
e. Consumer Goods
f. All other

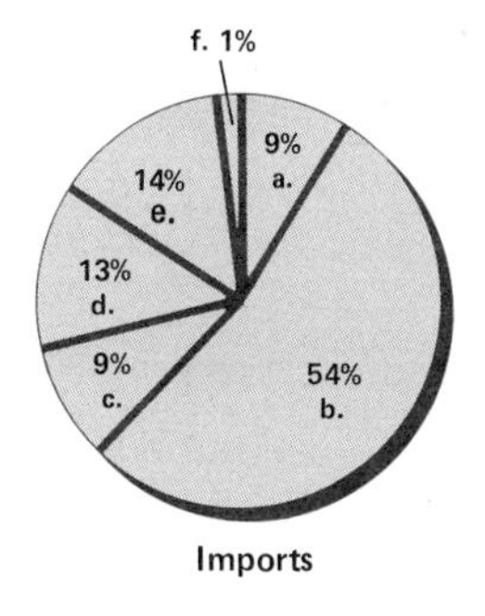

FIGURE 21-3

Composition of United States trade, 1977. (Source: The Conference Board.)

Our leading imports from Canada are paper pulp, agricultural products, and lumber. From Germany we buy automobiles, precision instruments, musical instruments, and textiles. Wines, automobiles, and textiles are some of our major imports from Italy. Japan, our largest customer in Asia, ranks second to Canada in export and import trade with the United States. Japan is a leading manufacturer of radios, televisions, automobiles, and steel products. Because of high labor costs in the United States, most American radio and television parts are made in the Far East under the trade names of American brands and are returned to this country for assembly. Japanese imports of automobiles and the parts to keep them running have been a major item. Several Japanese auto-parts manufacturers, however, are now considering establishing plants in the United States:

> A full-scale invasion of the U.S. auto-parts market is shaping up. The U.S. replacement-part market is about $40 billion a year. Detroit's shift to small cars, almost 7 million Japanese cars on American roads, and several states and cities courting Japanese manufacturers have made the climate here attractive.
>
> Nippon Oil Seal, which controls 80 percent of the market in Japan, has built a plant in LaGrange, Georgia. When the company's sales in the United States reached $13 million, the decision was made to build in America. Totoya Motor Company is Nippon Oil Seal's biggest customer, and many believe that the move foreshadows a move by Toyota to manufacture cars in the United States. Germany's Volkswagen already has a plant in Pennsylvania.

Who Gains from International Trade

When we analyze the dependence of the American economy on both imports and exports, it becomes clear that this nation must continue to promote trade with other countries. Approximately 4.5 million jobs in this country depend directly on import and export trade. Because many of the raw materials we need are not available here, we must seek foreign sources. If we are unable to obtain these scarce materials, it becomes necessary to substitute inferior goods or reduce our production. And in the area of exporting, foreign markets often make the difference between profit and loss for some American companies operating in this country.

Multinational companies are major contributors to this nation's strength. They differ greatly in the goods and services they produce and sell, their sources of raw materials, their capital and labor needs, policies, and practices.

To remain strong, a country must participate in the international marketplace. American companies must either do business abroad or surrender world markets to foreign competition. Economic isolationism obviously would undermine America's position in the Free World. It would seriously impair our domestic economy and destroy the foundation of our influence in world affairs.

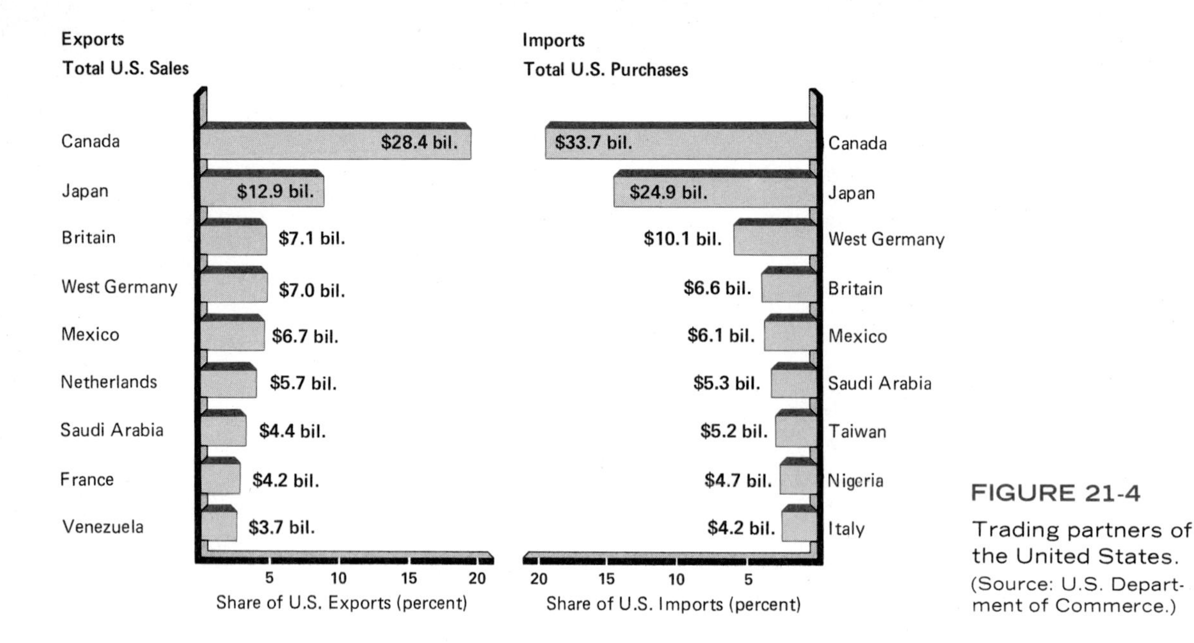

FIGURE 21-4

Trading partners of the United States. (Source: U.S. Department of Commerce.)

No major nation can take an important step in economic policy without affecting business in other countries. The prosperity of each nation depends upon the well-being of others. International trade is an influence for peace by bringing people together in a common economic purpose.

Of the two hundred largest American companies, eighty have more than one-fourth of their sales, earnings, and assets abroad. Of Europe's two hundred largest companies, approximately eighty also conduct more than one-fourth of their business abroad. During the past decade, transatlantic capital investments have increased about 10 percent per year in each direction.

But a company does not have to be big to be an exporter. In fact, three out of five American exporters have fewer than one hundred employees.

A comparison of our exports and imports with those of our major trading partners is shown in Figure 21-4.

THE ECONOMICS OF INTERNATIONAL TRADE

Since many textbooks are devoted exclusively to the economics of international trade, we will deal mainly with the basic economic reasons for having international trade and discuss some of the principles involved.

Principle of Comparative Advantage

What determines the products a country will specialize in? One answer may be found in the principle of **COMPARATIVE ADVANTAGE.** This principle implies what we have been stressing in this chapter: (a) **It is to the economic advantage of a country to specialize in goods that it can produce more cheaply than can other countries;** (b) nations should refrain from producing those items that they can buy more cheaply elsewhere. Comparative advantage may be due to such factors as a well-trained labor force, an abundance of raw materials, modern and efficient plants, and favorable climatic conditions.

The principle of comparative advantage may be explained further by a hypothetical example. Suppose there were only two countries, the United States and Russia. Each country produced only two commodities of mutual interest, wheat and textiles. And suppose the cost ratios between wheat and textiles differed between the two countries as follows:

Unit Cost (Price)	United States (Dollars)	Russia (Rubles)
Of wheat	4.00	16.00
Of textiles	2.00	1.00

Disregarding the exchange rate between the two currencies, the cost ratio of wheat to textiles in the U.S. is 2:1, and for Russia, 16:1. These ratios indicate that the United States would have a comparative cost advantage in the production of wheat and a comparative cost disadvantage in the production of textiles. In Russia, the opposite would exist. *Gainful trade would occur if the United States exported wheat and imported textiles while Russia exported textiles and imported wheat.* The real cost of one unit of wheat in the United States would be half a unit of textiles. In Russia, the opportunity cost of producing one unit of wheat would be five units of textiles. It is obvious that the United States would have a lower opportunity cost of producing wheat and would export it because of the comparative advantage in that commodity.

At this point you might ask, Why shouldn't the United States sell both wheat and textiles to Russia, bringing the dollars home without buying anything from them? The answer is that there would be no dollars in Russia with which to pay for American wheat and textiles, and therefore no dollars to bring home, unless Russians could obtain dollars by selling something to the United States. In other words, we cannot be paid for our goods and services unless we take payment in the form of foreign goods and services. All of this reemphasizes that foreign trade travels on a two-way street.

Principle of Absolute Advantage

Specialization in foreign trade is also encouraged under the principle of **ABSOLUTE ADVANTAGE.** This principle recognizes that the costs of producing commodities differ from country to country. According to this principle, **a nation should specialize in an article when it enjoys the advantages of low costs due to a natural monopoly or some unusual technical development.** As an illustration, Brazil can produce coffee more cheaply than the United States. So as a coffee producer, Brazil has an absolute advantage over this country. On the other hand, we have an absolute advantage over Brazil in making jet aircraft. Both countries will gain from the exchange of American jet aircraft for Brazilian coffee.

Let us compare the principle of absolute advantage with comparative advantage. It often benefits a nation to import goods even when that nation can make them for lower labor costs. Although a nation may have a greater absolute advantage, its *comparative advantage* may dictate that it should specialize in the production of another good. It can then use the income from this production to pay for the good bought from another country. In other words, unless we buy from other countries, they cannot buy from us.

Advantages of International Trade

Aside from these broad aspects of international trade, a high level of commerce with other countries provides individual businesspersons with several specific advantages.

Advantages to importing. American business firms import goods because

1. Foreign prices may be lower than domestic prices on similar goods.
2. Certain goods are not available in this country—or, if they are available, the supply is not sufficient to meet the demand.
3. Ordering goods from foreign firms may encourage them to buy goods from more American firms.
4. Some foreign merchandise is considered to offer more style and prestige than domestic products, and consequently will command higher prices in the United States.

Advantages to exporting. Many American firms engage in exporting because

1. Selling to foreign customers is often less expensive than expanding a new home market.
2. Foreign markets are a way of increasing sales volume and obtaining the economies of large-scale production and lower unit costs.

OVERSEAS INVESTMENT AND JOBS AT HOME

Some people argue that when U.S. companies invest in overseas enterprise, this exports jobs.

The Business International Corporation has undertaken seven special research studies dealing with this question. The most recent study was concluded in 1979 and 124 U.S. firms were surveyed, covering the period 1970–77. This seventh study reached the same conclusion as the first six: There is a direct correlation between investment abroad and job creation at home.

Specifically, Business International found that those businesses with the most foreign investment increased their U.S. employment by 2.3 percent, while those with the least foreign investment decreased their U.S. employment by 4.1 percent.

BARRIERS TO INTERNATIONAL TRADE

Certain barriers to foreign trade make selling in an international market a real challenge.

The Language Barrier

Relatively few Americans are fluent in more than one language, and not all foreign traders speak English. However, English is the second language in many countries, which is helping to lessen the language barrier. Also, an increasing number of American students are learning a second language.

Differences in Social Customs

Each nation has its peculiar social customs and business practices, which often serve as a hindrance to international trade. The Latin American *siesta*—the long lunch hour that makes the workday longer—is not common to other ethnic groups. Many foreigners working in Latin American countries find this custom difficult to observe. For some, driving an automobile on the left-hand side of the road is confusing. Removing your shoes to enter a residence or a religious building is another unique custom. Strange and exotic foods sometimes create a diet problem for the newcomer abroad. On the other hand, the American practice of one-stop shopping in so-called shopping centers is becoming a common practice in many foreign countries.

One common foreign custom that has caused trouble between American business and the federal government is the "entry fee" or bribe that is often expected when dealing with foreign governments.

Mr. Trilli is president of a large Pittsburgh-based engineering and construction firm. He contends that his company was beaten out of a number of big overseas contracts because competitors paid off government officials. One project was a $40 million brick plant in Iraq. Trilli says, "We had it all wrapped up." All terms had been agreed to, and they were told that the contract would be signed in a month. Then out of the blue a German firm got the contract. Trilli says the German firm got the contract because it made a big payment to a high Iraqi official.

Midland-Ross Corporation cited two instances of suspected payoffs involving paper-mill equipment for two west African nations. Midland-Ross was favored by the consulting engineer on the project but lost out at the last minute to an Italian firm.

Congressional committees investigated the activities of the Central Intelligence Agency (CIA) and several American firms operating abroad. It was revealed that cash payments had been made to high government officials in foreign countries. The officials of the American companies testified that such payments were essential in order to secure trade. It was also revealed that such payments were not illegal in many of the countries where such payments were assessed. All of this raises a major issue. If payment to local officials is an accepted practice in a foreign country, is it illegal, immoral, or unethical to make such payments? Or is it just good business for the American firm operating in that country?

In any event, U.S. companies must operate under the provisions of the Foreign Corrupt Practices Act, which makes it an offense to offer a payment to a foreign government official to obtain business. This law provides for prison sentences of up to five years for violators and fines of up to $1 million for companies. Other industrialized nations do not impose such sanctions on their businesses. Indeed a treaty proposed by the United States to eliminate bribery in international transactions has received almost no active support in the United Nations. The U.S. brand of morality has not been accepted in most areas. In many countries "rewarding" the decision maker is common practice.

Differences in Laws

Another barrier to foreign trade is the differences in laws. For example, the cartel is illegal in the United States, but it is not illegal in most other countries. The Organization of Petroleum and Exporting Countries (OPEC) is a cartel familiar to most of us.

A **CARTEL** is an association of individual companies whose purpose is to control prices or the conditions of sale. Cartels are price-fixing monopolies, which are illegal in this country because they violate the Sherman Antitrust Act. Price-fixing by cartels abroad can lead to critical situations in international commerce when an American firm finds it must compete with foreign firms. **Patent laws** of various nations differ more widely than do laws relating to other industrial property. Some countries will not grant patents on certain products—for example, chemical compounds. Others issue patents immediately upon application, but these give protection for different periods of time. And Russia is not a signatory to the International Patent Agreement. In some countries, **copyright laws** are not complied with as they are in the United States. Some nations have laws requiring that a certain number of resident stockholders be maintained by foreign corporations.

Differences in Currencies and Availability of Dollars

Currencies differ throughout the world, which is a barrier to international trade. To illustrate the complications this can create, an American manufacturer who sells goods to a Belgian merchant expects to be paid in dollars. So the Belgian merchant would need to obtain dollars by exchanging Belgian francs on the foreign-exchange market.

There was a period when gold was the common denominator for all currencies. But for several years the gold standard has been almost nonexistent. It is no longer possible to obtain gold when dollars are unavailable. The fluctuation of these currencies in their exchange values does not simplify the situation.

Other problem areas that serve to make international marketing a real challenge are

1. Differences in people's consumption patterns in the various countries
2. Difficulties in obtaining reliable market data
3. Complex and inefficient distribution structures in many countries

MANAGEMENT OF INTERNATIONAL BUSINESS

When an American firm decides to sell abroad, it may do so by choosing one of two widely different methods. One method of marketing is to engage in direct selling by using the company's own export division. This is referred to as direct-export marketing channels. The other method is to sell through independent middlemen located in the United States who specialize in export selling. This is referred to as indirect-export marketing channels.

Using Direct-Export Marketing Channels

Companies that engage in a substantial amount of foreign commerce find that it pays to have their own foreign-distribution facilities. Perhaps they will also have factories abroad.

Foreign branches. Foreign branches are divisions of a domestic company, located in a foreign country. Their operations range from foreign sales, storage, and warehouse operations, to foreign assembly or manufacturing plants.

Foreign subsidiaries. Foreign subsidiaries resemble foreign branches, but they are in fact virtually separate companies owned and controlled by a parent American company. An advantage of this form is that the subsidiary can handle a complete line of products because of its size.

In recent years the multinational corporation has evolved. This **MULTINATIONAL BUSINESS** **is a firm with a number of directly controlled operations in different countries and with a worldwide perspective.** American multinational companies include such firms as International Business Machines; John Deere, a farm-machinery maker with subsidiaries in nine countries; and Procter & Gamble. Ford Motor Company has plants in twenty countries; National Cash Register and Exxon operate worldwide. Of the twenty thousand American companies engaged in international business, about three thousand have subsidiaries and branches in foreign countries. Among non-American multinational corporations, Nestlé, Volkswagen, and Sony are widely known.

The built-in export department. Aside from the two direct-export methods of marketing abroad, a third method is the built-in export department. Where such a system is in effect, export activities are assigned to certain people in the company. These are usually an export manager and one or two clerks. The export manager does the selling or directs it. The traffic department handles documents and transportation, along with other traffic matters for the company. Such other functions as credit and accounting operations for foreign sales are performed by departments that also handle domestic credit and accounting. The built-in export department is generally small. It is well adapted to the manufacturer whose export volume is likewise small in comparison with the total volume of the business.

Using Indirect-Export Marketing Channels

Indirect exporting uses outside organizations located in the home market. Some of these middlemen take title to goods.

The export merchant. The export merchant is an independent middleman who buys and sells abroad on his or her own account. The merchant does both exporting and importing. In exporting, the firm is often known as a trading company because it buys and sells a large variety of products from many companies.

The export agent. The export agent generally represents several noncompeting American firms on a commission basis, without taking title to goods.

Sales are made by the export agent for the manufacturer, who finances and ships the product to the buyer.

Buyers for export. Buyers for export are also independent middlemen. They canvass American markets in search of goods needed by foreign consumers. Buyers for export take orders from foreign clients and are paid a commission by the producer or seller of the goods. The main advantage in selling through export buyers is that there is little marketing expense for the seller.

Joint Ventures

Historically, the wholly-owned foreign subsidiary has been the most common way to do business overseas. Along with complete ownership a company also exercises almost complete control. **Ownership** refers to the supplying of equity capital. **Control** includes operation of the production processes, patent rights, technical knowledge, and marketing procedures. However, in recent years many government leaders in host countries decided that foreign ownership did not serve the best economic interests of their countries. As a result, there has been a constant shift toward more joint ventures by multinational businesses.

A **JOINT VENTURE OVERSEAS** is **an enterprise that is not completely owned and/or controlled by the parent company.** Participation in the host country may be by private enterprise or by the government. In general, the ratio of joint ventures is higher in developed than in underdeveloped nations.

About 83 percent of U.S. direct investments in economically backward countries are wholly-owned subsidiaries, compared with only 76 percent in Europe and 62 percent in Canada. In total, joint ventures represent 31 percent of the investment in industrialized countries and 17 percent in underdeveloped areas.[1]

Although this is the current status, it will not remain that way long. Both the industrial nations and the underdeveloped nations are insisting more and more upon local participation in the enterprise.

Advantages to host country. The joint venture offers several advantages to the host country. First, it provides investment for local capital. It enables local entrepreneurs to acquire needed technological know-how. It also ensures more local influence over production, thereby preventing domination from outside interests. The government policy in India is that "the major interest in ownership and effective control of an industrial undertaking should, as a rule, be in Indian hands." Mexico and Burma both limit foreign ownership to 40 percent in corporations that engage in a wide variety of economic activities. These activities include mining, coal, petroleum, publishing, advertising, and transportation.

TARIFFS AND GOVERNMENT TRADE POLICIES

In this country, goods can be shipped from one state to another with little or no government interference. In international trade, however, the same shipment of goods is subject to various controls established by host governments. These

[1]Endel J. Kolde, *International Business Enterprise,* 2nd ed. (Englewood Cliffs, N.J.: Prentice-Hall, 1973), p. 193.

controls are in the form of tariffs, quotas, embargoes, and price-fixing agreements. These restrict the free play of economic forces.

Definition of Tariff

A TARIFF is **a tax or customs duty levied by a nation on imported goods.** It works both ways. We tax goods entering this country, and other countries tax their imports. In the United States, Congress may levy duties only on imports, according to Article I of the U.S. Constitution. Congress cannot levy duties on exports. Depending upon the political party in power, this nation has had high or low tariffs from the early days of the Republic. Since World War II the emphasis has been on free trade among nations. There are low tariffs for friendly nations that qualify for "favored-nation" treatment.

CURRENT ISSUE

Should American Industry Be Protected through Tariffs?

Large proportions of the American textile and radio and TV manufacture have been moved overseas. The steel industries of England, Japan, and Europe have been accused of dumping goods in the American market below their costs of production (through subsidies by their governments). We should protect protect American industry through tariffs.

With which of the following statements do you agree and with which do you disagree?

1. We should have tariffs in order to keep jobs for our workers "at home."
2. No country is self-sufficient, and therefore free trade is mutually beneficial to all those concerned.
3. Free trade makes it possible for nations to practice the principle of comparative advantage.
4. When we buy goods abroad, we are exporting jobs that should go to American labor.
5. Nations should have tariffs to protect their basic industries but should sell goods to "foreigners" through "duty-free" ports.
6. The U.S. government should maintain tariffs but should encourage U.S. companies to establish subsidiaries overseas.
7. Restrictions against imported goods encourage foreign companies to establish businesses in this country.
8. Instead of having tariffs, the U.S. government should stablish import quotas for goods from other countries.

What major criterion should govern whether we establish tariffs and, if so, how high they should be?

CURRENT ISSUE

Kinds of Tariffs

The two broad categories of tariffs are (1) revenue tariffs and (2) protective tariffs. The two are designed for different purposes. A **REVENUE TARIFF is a tax on imports to produce revenue.** A **PROTECTIVE TARIFF is a tax on imports to protect domestic producers against competition from foreign producers.**

Arguments for and against Tariffs

The first congressional debate on the tariff issue occurred in 1789. Since then Congress has taken the issue up periodically. Some people advocate complete "free trade," which would abolish all tariffs. Others argue for "protection" or for quotas. There are sound arguments to support both points of view.

The infant-industry argument. This is the oldest protariff argument of all. It holds that a new and struggling industry should be protected from foreign competition by a tariff until the industry has become established. Too often, however, even after the infant industry has grown up, new arguments are advanced to retain the high protective tariff.

Arguments for free trade. Free-traders argue that each country should be able to take advantage of its own national specialization and thereby maximize its production. Under free trade, all nations can raise the standard of living of their people. Elimination of trade barriers promotes a free flow of goods between nations.

The wage argument. Labor unions want to maintain high wages. Thus they often see goods coming from low-wage countries as unfair competition. They assert further that tariffs help protect worker's employment. If we keep out imported goods produced by lower-priced labor, it is possible to sell more American-made goods in America, thereby maintaining a higher employment level. On the other hand, to keep out foreign competition restricts our volume of exports. If foreign producers are unable to sell to the American market, they will lack the necessary funds to buy from us. A good example of the controversy regarding tariffs can be found in the U.S. distilled-spirits industry.

A proposed tariff change would lower taxes on huge shipments of Scotch and Canadian whiskey. Such U.S. marketers as Joseph Seagram & Sons and Hiram Walker, Inc., support the change. They are both owned by Canadian-based companies. Other sizable importers of Canadian and Scotch whiskey support the change as well. However, Heublein, American Distilling, National Distillers Products, and several other domestic producers oppose the cut.

The U.S. distillers are concerned that a big tax cut would increase the amount of money available to the foreign producers to advertise their product. The increased advertising would lead to increased sales for the importers. The government has responded: "We recognize that a change in the present system . . . might adversely affect some producers. . . ." However, "These negative factors must be balanced against the value of concessions obtained from other nations."

Foreign-Trade Legislation

The reciprocal trade agreements program. The present American tariff policies are based on the Reciprocal Trade Agreements Act of 1934 (RTA). Then in 1947 the United States and twenty-two other nations agreed upon a system of procedures and rules for studying tariffs, the General Agreement on Tariffs and Trade (GATT). The basic elements of GATT are to

1. Provide rules of nondiscrimination in trade relations
2. Negotiate trade concessions
3. Approve prohibitions against quantitative restrictions on exports and imports

The member countries of GATT meet annually to review recommendations, to settle disputes, and to study ways to reduce tariffs.

In 1962 Congress passed the Trade Expansion Act (TEA). This is a completely new approach to world trade for the United States. This legislation gave the president the power to cut tariffs by 50 percent in negotiating new trade pacts during the five years following its inception. The purposes of the TEA, as expressed in the language of the act, are to

1. Stimulate the economic growth of the United States and maintain and enlarge foreign markets for the products of United States agriculture, industry, mining, and commerce
2. Strengthen economic relations with foreign countries through the development of open and nondiscriminatory trading in the free world
3. Prevent Communist economic penetration

Kennedy Round of Tariff Negotiations. The most sweeping tariff reductions in our history were concluded in 1967. The negotiations involved over fifty member nations of GATT. During the negotiations—called the Kennedy Round of Tariff Negotiations because they were initiated by President Kennedy in 1962—tariff duties were cut on some sixty thousand items. Only a few items, such as zinc, lead, watches, and rugs, were not affected by these agreements.

WHAT "MOST FAVORED NATION" MEANS

The term most favored nation dates back to an agreement signed in Geneva in 1947 by twenty-three of the world's major non-Communist countries. The pact was known as the General Agreement on Tariffs and Trade.

One of its important provisions was the most-favored-nation principle. In essence, the provision states that the signers of the GATT agreement must extend to one another any tariff concession given to any other member country.

U.S. trade law sets tariff rates on thousands of individual products. In general, rates for nations enjoying MFN status are substantially lower than for nations that do not.

The purpose of these tariff cuts was to promote American exports by removing trade barriers. Yet much of the impetus to total world trade can be credited to the spread of international commerce that resulted from these reductions.

U.S. Trade Reform Act (1974). Under this act the president is authorized to enter into trade agreements for modifying tariff rates and liberalizing other barriers to international trade. It also gives the president authority to proclaim import measures, for a period of up to 150 days, for balance-of-payments purposes. The antidumping provisions help promote fair competition.

In 1977 Congress passed the Foreign Corrupt Practices Act. This act was designed to outlaw bribes and "improper" commissions in international trade. Many corporations, particularly among the multinationals, had been pressing for such help. They charged that its absence was forcing them to forgo dealing with countries where such practices are a way of life. The Commerce Department, which is charged with promoting U.S. exports, was equally upset. Congress did not order any guidelines for this act. However, the Justice Department did prepare them.

Tokyo Round of Tariff Negotiations. New discussions on reducing trade barriers began in Tokyo in 1973. Congress committed itself, in the Trade Act in 1974, to vote only yes or no on implementing legislation for the Tokyo Round. These discussions culminated on April 12, 1979, when representatives of the major trading nations initialed the agreement. Ninety-nine nations participated in these multilateral trade negotiations. The agreement was approved by the U.S. Senate on July 23, 1979. (See Figure 21-5.)

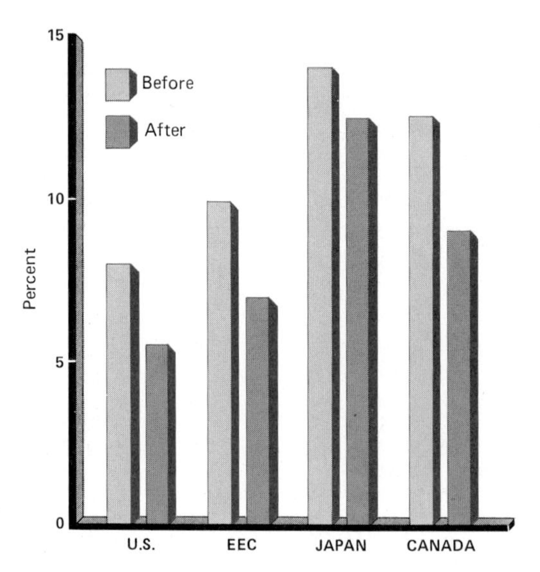

FIGURE 21-5

Changes in tariff rates (Tokyo round)

This represents a 28 percent reduction for Canada; 30 percent for the U.S. and the EEC; and 11 percent for Japan. (Data: Office of the U.S. Special Trade Representative.)

Sir Roy Denman, Common Market commissioner for external affairs, called the agreement "one of the great achievements since World War II." President Jimmy Carter declared:

> The agreements steer us away from destructive protectionism and into a path of greater export opportunities with the prospects of new jobs, improved productivity and increased industrial and agricultural production.
>
> U.S. officials estimate that tariff cuts by the Common Market that will benefit American goods average about 35%; the average U.S. tariff cut on goods coming from Europe is about 34%. Similarly, Japanese tariff cuts on goods exported from the U.S. average 46%, while U.S. tariff cuts on imports from Japan average 32%.

The agreement took effect on January 1, 1980, lowering tariffs on nonfarm imports an average of 33 percent over eight to ten years. The economic benefits to businesses in this country could be as much as $10 billion per year. Administration foreign experts predict that 130,000 additional jobs for American workers will result from these new trade agreements.

THE BALANCE OF INTERNATIONAL PAYMENTS

The most useful tool to explain the interrelations created by foreign trade is a statistical statement called the *balance of international payments.* It is prepared annually by the U.S. Department of Commerce and is also known as the balance of payments. It resembles an income statement rather than a balance sheet, because it shows this nation's sales (exports) and purchases (imports), together with the other forms of receipts and expenditures derived from foreign-trade transactions and foreign relations. An examination of a country's balance of payments would show a country's ability to pay for imported goods. All things considered, a country is either a debtor or a creditor nation.

Transactions between domestic and foreign residents are entered in the balance of payments as either debits or credits. Debit transactions are recorded as payments by domestic residents to foreign residents for imports. Credit transactions are dollars received by domestic residents from the sale of goods to foreign residents.

In addition to the income received by the United States from its exports and the payments made for its imports, the balance-of-payments statement also includes other items. Among these are capital outflow when residents of this country invest abroad, and capital inflow when a foreign resident invests in the United States. Another section shows gold movements, representing gold exports and imports. For years the United States has experienced a deficit in the balance of payments, and gold was used to offset this deficit. Still other transactions include money spent by tourists abroad, military-aid payments, dividends, and grants.

Recent trends in the U.S. balance of trade are shown in Figure 21-6.

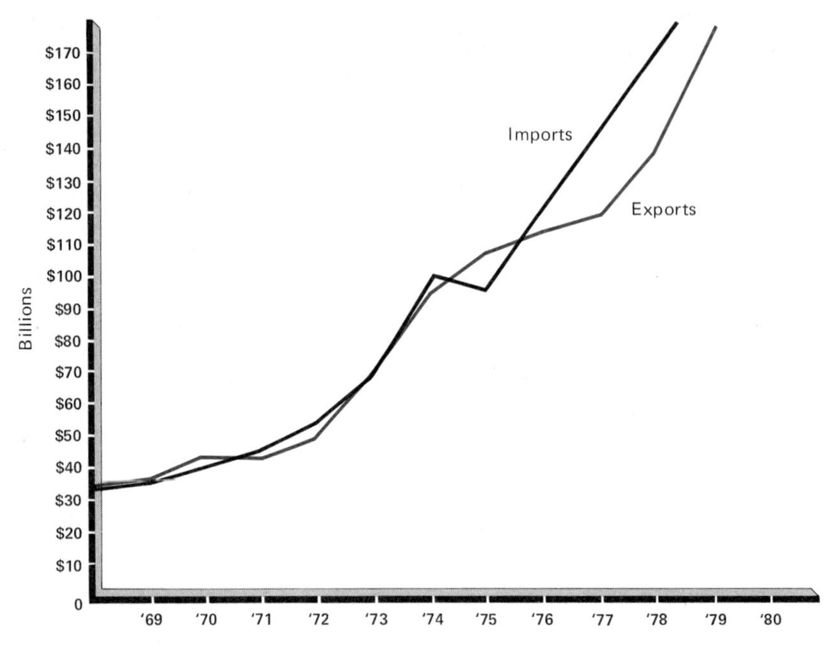

FIGURE 21-6

Trends in the U.S. balance of trade. (Source: U.S. Department of Commerce.)

Favorable Balance of Trade

Balance of trade is a part of international balance of payments. When a nation's exports exceed the value of its merchandise imports, it has a favorable balance of trade. But when a nation's imports exceed the value of exports, it has an unfavorable balance of trade. The idea conveyed by "favorable" or "unfavorable" is misleading. It implies that a nation should always work to export more than it imports.

The U.S. balance of trade between 1965 and 1975 was generally a favorable one, for this nation's exports exceeded its imports. Although the balance of trade was favorable, there was still an unsatisfactory balance of payments. The exporting of surplus goods was not large enough to offset other expenditures, such as grants, loans, gifts, and military expenses abroad. Persistent deficits would drain American gold reserves to the point of danger to our monetary system. The balance-of-payments deficits during the 1970s reached major proportions. As

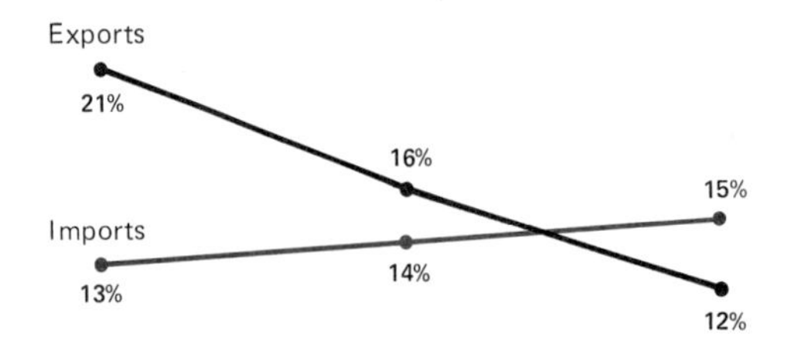

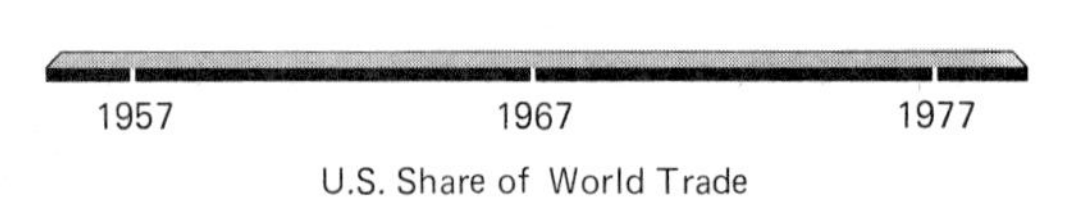

FIGURE 21-7

U.S. share of world trade. (Source: The Conference Board.)

a result, the value of the U.S. dollar abroad dropped substantially as compared with other major currencies. Continued deficits can destroy confidence in the American dollar by jeopardizing the stability of our economy. And they serve to create dollar shortages and inflate the economy.

FINANCING INTERNATIONAL TRADE

As we have already mentioned, one of the complications of international trade is that the seller of goods or services expects to be paid in the kind of money he or she can use in paying debts. But not all nations have the same currency system. English pounds, for instance, must be converted into dollars before an English buyer can pay an American business associate.

Fortunately, buyers and sellers need not meet in order to complete transactions. In this and other countries, there are banks that buy foreign currencies (or claims to them) for use by exporters. Banks also sell foreign currencies to importers who want to make payments in foreign money. These banks charge a commission for buying and selling the currencies or handling the negotiable instruments used in foreign exchange.

Foreign Exchange Market Dealers

Market values for most of the world's currencies fluctuate almost daily. Foreign-exchange dealers, located in large commercial banks in the major financial centers, buy and sell foreign exchange, priced at the prevailing rate for a given day. American importers who expect to buy a foreign article must keep in mind not only the price they must pay for their item abroad but also the price of the foreign currency they must buy to pay for their import. This price is called the **FOREIGN EXCHANGE RATE. This is the rate at which the currency of one country is exchanged for that of another country.** For example, assume that the exchange rate for Mexican pesos is twenty-two pesos to the dollar. An American wishing to obtain a foreign-exchange credit would pay $1,000 in order to receive credit for twenty-two thousand pesos for use in Mexico City. The foreign-exchange rate is the rate at which a foreign currency can be exchanged for American dollars. This rate changes daily.

Figure 21-8 shows which countries are making the largest direct investments in the United States. Figure 21-9 shows where the countries making the major overseas investments are investing their funds. Japanese firms make more color television sets in this country than we import from Japan.

Rates of exchange fluctuate in response to the supply and demand of international money transfers. If our total foreign sales are greater than our total foreign purchases, the foreign demand for dollars to make payments rises. This is because the dollars would sell at a premium in terms of foreign currencies. But if our imports exceed our exports, the dollar will be at a discount in terms of foreign currencies. This illustrates the effect of the balance of trade. Actually, money is rarely shipped to another country to settle a debt. Instead, drafts or bills of exchange are used. These are provided through a bank as a service to its customers.

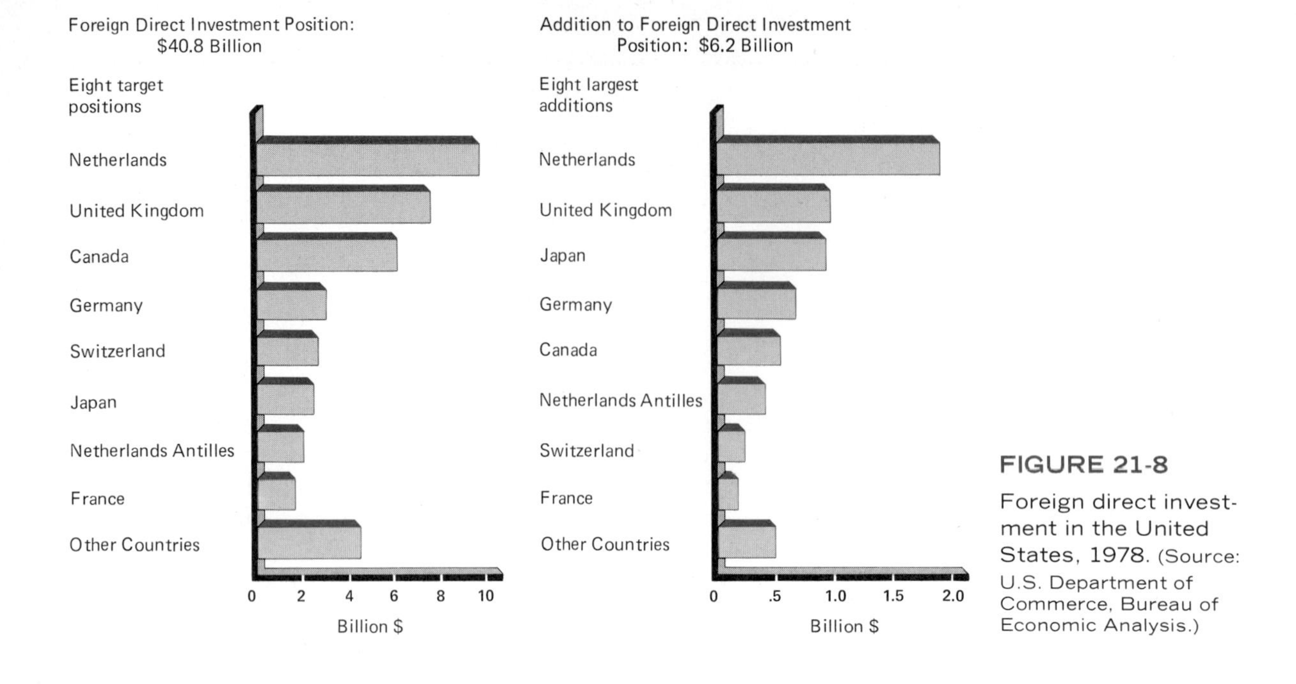

FIGURE 21-8

Foreign direct investment in the United States, 1978. (Source: U.S. Department of Commerce, Bureau of Economic Analysis.)

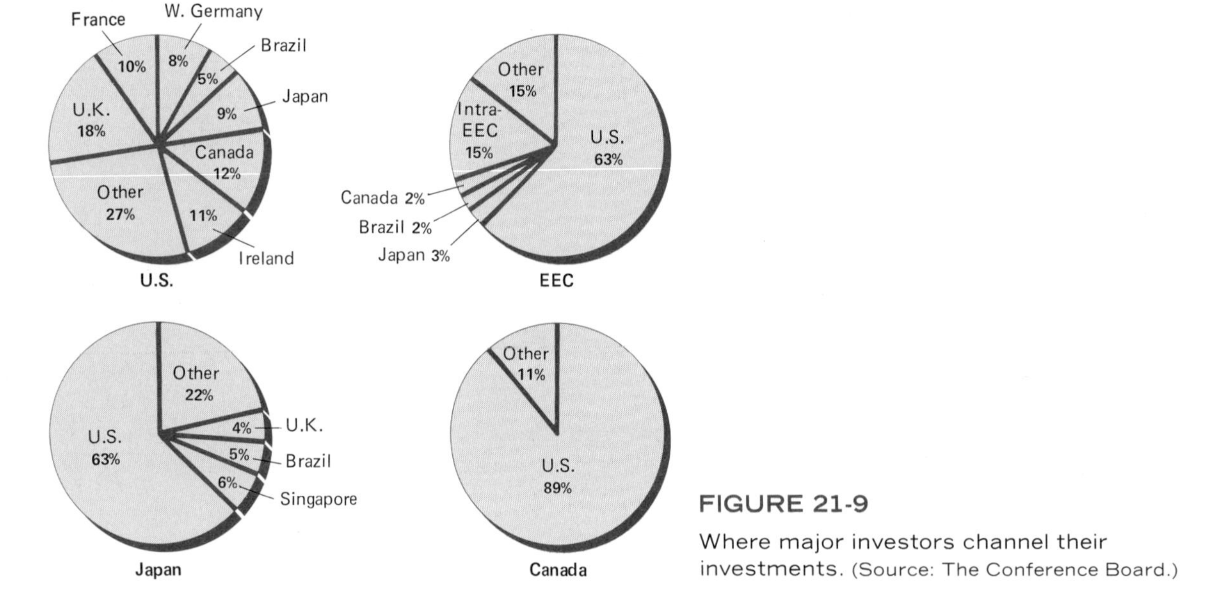

FIGURE 21-9

Where major investors channel their investments. (Source: The Conference Board.)

Financing Exports

Financing is more complicated in international trade than in domestic trade. There is greater risk in extending credit to buyers abroad. The parties may be unknown to each other. Or the seller may want a down payment with the order, with the balance payable on receipt of the shipment.

As a rule, when an exporter sells goods abroad, he or she takes the initiative in obtaining payment by drawing a draft for the amount of the invoice. This instrument is drawn directly on the buyer (importer), who is the debtor. It may be drawn to become due at sight, on arrival of goods, or at a designated future time. It is customary in such a case to use the services of a commercial bank that offers exporting services. In most cases exporters are paid in the currencies of their own countries.

Export documents. The export documents that generally accompany drafts are of the following types:

1. Ocean bill of lading, usually indorsed in blank (lists goods shipped and terms of the contract under which goods are shipped by the transportation agency)
2. Commercial invoice (shows quantities, terms, and prices)
3. Marine insurance certificate
4. Special customs invoice (shows weight, value, destination, and class of goods)
5. Inspection certificate
6. Certificate of origin

On receipt of an order from a foreign customer, the American exporter draws a draft (either in dollars or in the foreign currency) against the importer. The exporter takes the draft and the documents listed above to the bank for further handling.

Customer's draft. The following example illustrates the steps involved in financing a foreign sale by use of a draft. (The use of drafts in domestic trade is discussed in Chapter 15.)

The Tejas Manufacturing & Equipment Company of Houston, Texas sells equipment to Colombiana Importadora, S.A., Bogotá, Colombia.[2] On receipt of an order, the Houston firm (the seller) draws a customer's draft (Figure 21-10) made payable to itself, in the amount of $3,500, on Colombiana Importadora. This instrument instructs Colombiana (drawee and buyer) to pay the amount of the draft to the holder at a specified future date. In this case it is thirty days from the date of the draft.

[2]The abbreviation S.A., used as part of the company title, is derived from the Spanish term *sociedad anónima,* which means "corporation."

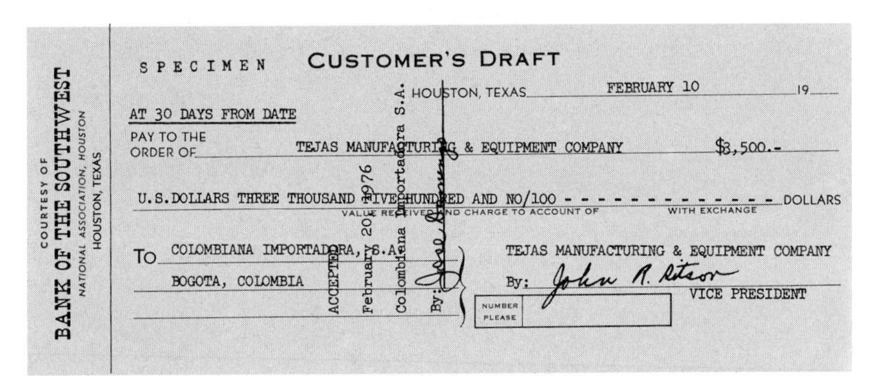
COURTESY OF
BANK OF THE SOUTHWEST
NATIONAL ASSOCIATION, HOUSTON
HOUSTON, TEXAS

SPECIMEN CUSTOMER'S DRAFT

HOUSTON, TEXAS FEBRUARY 10 19

AT 30 DAYS FROM DATE

PAY TO THE ORDER OF TEJAS MANUFACTURING & EQUIPMENT COMPANY $3,500.-

U.S.DOLLARS THREE THOUSAND FIVE HUNDRED AND NO/100 - - - - - - - - - - - - DOLLARS

VALUE RECEIVED AND CHARGE TO ACCOUNT OF WITH EXCHANGE

TO COLOMBIANA IMPORTADORA, S.A.
BOGOTA, COLOMBIA

ACCEPTED February 20 1976 Colombiana Importadora S.A. By:

TEJAS MANUFACTURING & EQUIPMENT COMPANY
By: John R. Ritson
VICE PRESIDENT

NUMBER PLEASE

FIGURE 21-10
A customer's draft used in foreign-trade transactions. (Courtesy The Bank of the Southwest, Houston, Texas.)

The draft is presented to the buyer (drawee) for acceptance. If the drawee chooses to accept it, the drawee writes "Accepted" across the draft, followed by the date and the drawee's signature, and returns it to the drawer. This actually transforms the draft into a trade acceptance. It is customary for American exporters to draw similar drafts, but in dollars. Such a draft is often referred to as a *dollar draft.*

The buyer (drawee) cannot take possession of the goods until certain required documents are released by the bank. Examples of such documents are the bill of lading and the invoice, which are usually attached to the draft. If the Tejas Company decides not to hold the draft the full thirty days for payment, it may discount it to the Houston bank. The discount is charged by the Houston bank for cashing the draft before it is due. This discount is the same as the interest it would charge on $3,500 for the period of time until the draft comes due.

Letters of credit. Another method of payment used in international business is letters of credit. The rather common use of the letter of credit stems from the weakness of the bill of exchange, or draft. Under the draft, the exporter (seller) must bear the entire risk of collecting from the importer (buyer). However, letters of credit have one disadvantage—they are not standardized, and each document must be carefully read. The money to be paid under a letter of credit is obtained by a bill of exchange drawn on a bank.

International Banks

The Export-Import Bank. In 1934 the Export-Import Bank of Washington (D.C.) was established as an agency of the U.S. government to finance American exports. The bank tries to supplement, rather than compete with, commercial banks. It lends only to those ventures in which the ordinary commercial bank is not interested. It tends to confine its loans to financing productive capital equipment, such as special machinery used in agriculture and industry. It guarantees credit and gives financial counseling. How the Export-Import Bank serves business is shown in Figure 21-11.

FIGURE 21-11

How the export-import bank serves world business. (Source: Export-Import Bank.)

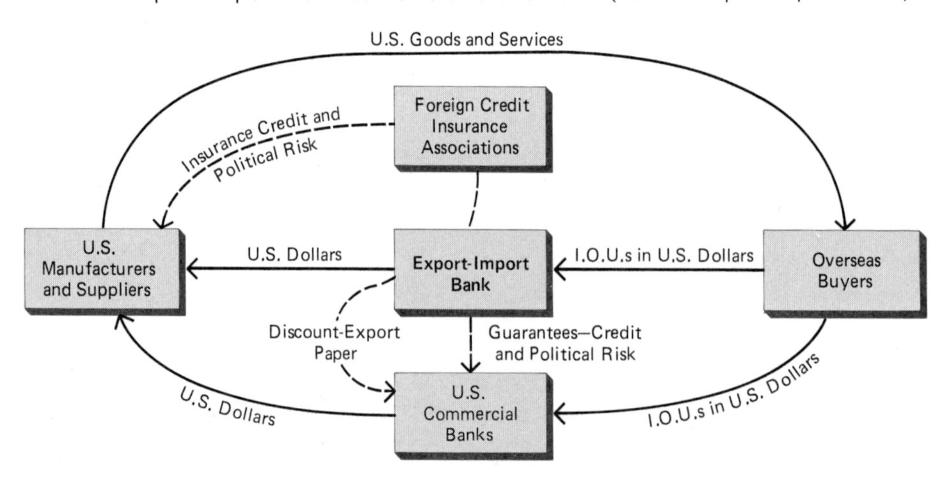

The International Monetary Fund. The International Monetary Fund (IMF) is the world's largest source of quickly available international credit. The purposes of the fund are to

1. Promote international monetary cooperation
2. Help eliminate restrictions on foreign trade
3. Provide funds to meet temporarily unfavorable trade balances between nations
4. Stabilize exchange rates

If country A wants to buy goods from country B but lacks the currency to make the purchases, it can borrow the money from the fund in the currency of country B. Country A pays back its debt to the fund in gold or in currency received through transactions with other nations.

The IMF has currency reserves furnished by 125 member countries. Each country's quota is determined by its relative volume of international trade and its national income.

The World Bank. This bank is more properly named the International Bank for Reconstruction and Development (IBRD). It began operating early in 1946 with slightly more than $9 billion of subscribed capital. Since then the number of countries supporting the bank has grown from 43 to 130.

INTERNATIONAL TRADE COOPERATION

The success of the Marshall Plan in achieving the economic recovery of Europe after World War II further demonstrated the advantages of closer economic cooperation among European nations. One effective way to promote economic cooperation is for European nations to remove their trade barriers by forming a customs union. A **customs union** is a geographical region embracing two or more nations, within which goods can move freely without being subject to customs duties. Customs unions have been formed in both Europe and Latin America.

The European Economic Community

One of the most effective and best-known customs unions is the European Economic Community (EEC), referred to as the Common Market. France, Italy, Belgium, West Germany, Luxembourg, and the Netherlands formed the EEC on January 1, 1958. Those six nations worked toward producing a full integration of their economies by 1970. Beyond that, their goal is to achieve political unity. The EEC is also working toward elimination of restrictions in insurance, banking, and labor laws, and toward the enactment of new laws to regulate the marketing of drugs and pharmaceuticals.

On October 28, 1971, Great Britain's House of Commons voted to join the Common Market effective January 1, 1973. Denmark and Ireland followed Britain in becoming members. In 1975 the people of Britain voted to remain a member of the EEC.

The nine nations that make up the Common Market of Western Europe account for about one-third of the world's trade, including trade among them-

FIGURE 21-12
The European economic community.

selves. Disputes between the United States and the European countries continually arise over tariff rates for specific commodities. An ultimate objective of the EEC is to bring about complete political and economic unity.

CAREER OPPORTUNITIES IN INTERNATIONAL TRADE

Today an increasing number of American corporations are engaged in international business. As a result, career opportunities in this field are on the increase. Or if you want to work for yourself, you may become an independent importer, exporter, broker, commission merchant, or import merchant. There are also opportunities with domestic companies engaged in foreign-freight forwarding.

Generally speaking, there are probably more positions open to the beginner in training programs within domestic companies than for immediate employment abroad.

General Requirements

One of the important skills needed in foreign trade is the ability to speak at least one foreign language. Another is adaptability to a foreign culture, including ways of doing business that are very different from those used in the United States. A college education, preferably with a degree in business administration, is also an important requirement.

Employment in Exporting

The export manager. Experience in business is a necessary prerequisite for this position. The export manager exercises direct supervision over company agents, salespersons, and clerks. He or she must have an understanding of trade documents used in foreign shipments. Such documents include the ocean bill of lading, commercial invoice, marine insurance certificate, and others that we discussed under the subject of financing exports.

The export agent. This is an indirect-exporting position. The export agent is similar to the manufacturer's agent in domestic trade. He or she sells goods in the name of the manufacturer, who finances and ships the goods. The export agent receives a commission. The more successful export agents are those who have lived abroad and know a great deal about foreign-trade operations.

The freight forwarder. There are two types of freight forwarders. One is a domestic-freight forwarder, who consolidates and combines domestic shipments in order to take advantage of the lowest freight rates. The foreign-freight forwarder prepares shipments for foreign countries, usually for companies that ship large amounts abroad and do not require the combining of individual shipments. One of the most important functions of the freight forwarder is to handle documents used in finance and in transportation. Both loading and unloading of shipments can be delayed if the forwarder fails to prepare the documents correctly.

Employment in Importing

The import broker. The broker's function is to bring foreign sellers and American buyers together. This is done in much the same way as the domestic broker, who finds a buyer and then locates a seller with that article. The import broker rarely takes title but is paid a commission and expenses. Much of the Brazilian coffee trade is carried on by import brokers in the United States who deal with export merchants in Brazil.

The import merchant. This person's specialty is buying goods abroad and holding them in either a foreign or an American warehouse until a buyer can be found. The import merchant must take title to the goods until they are sold. On occasion, the merchant sorts, grades, mixes, or blends goods where this must be done for shipment. He or she travels widely in foreign countries to locate goods. Diamonds, rugs, china, liquor, seeds, bulbs, and leather goods are among the many items imported into this country through import merchants.

Opportunities in Foreign-Trade Banking

As we have seen, commercial banks are important in promoting overseas trade. Many large commercial banks located in harbor cities maintain fully staffed trade departments to handle all the details of preparing, processing, and collecting negotiable instruments used in foreign trade. These departments engage in currency exchange, prepare letters of credit, and handle such negotiable instruments as drafts, checks, and promissory notes. Persons interested in this area of banking need a broad background in banking and finance.

SUMMARY OF KEY CONCEPTS

The United States is a leading producer of goods and services. Still, it depends heavily on other countries for many raw materials, goods, and services.

Exporting is a means of selling goods in addition to those sold on the domestic market. It thus expands the market for a company's product.

We import because it is impossible to produce some items in this country or because goods may be purchased abroad at lower prices than at home.

The principle of comparative advantage states that a nation tends to export those goods that it can produce at relatively low costs. And it imports goods for which the costs are relatively high. Countries, therefore, specialize in producing certain products.

International trade is far more complex than doing business at home. There are differences in laws, social customs, and language.

Trade barriers in the form of tariffs and quotas restrict the international movement of goods and services.

Some companies that engage in much foreign commerce find that it pays to have their own marketing outlets. These outlets can be foreign branches, factories, or even foreign subsidiaries located in other countries.

Other companies find that the most efficient export-marketing channels are the export merchants, export agents, and buyers for exports. They are chiefly marketing middlemen who bring the exporter and the exporter's client together.

The two broad categories of tariffs are revenue tariffs and protective tariffs. A *revenue tariff* is a tax on imports to produce revenue. A *protective tariff* is a tax on imports to protect domestic producers against competition from foreign producers.

Reciprocal tariff reductions on a broad scale began in 1947 in Geneva. The result was the General Agreement on Tariffs and Trade.

The Tokyo Round of Tariff Negotiations was concluded in April 1979. In general this far-reaching agreement reduced tariffs by about one-third. Ninety-nine nations participated in the negotiations.

The purpose of such tariff reductions is to stimulate foreign trade by eliminating trade barriers.

The Export-Import Bank makes loans to foreign countries for mining, agriculture, and industrial ventures to promote foreign trade. The International Monetary Fund helps countries stabilize their currencies and promote trade with other nations.

BUSINESS TERMS

You should be able to match these business terms with the statements that follow:

a. Balance of trade
b. Cartel
c. Comparative advantage
d. Exports
e. Foreign exchange
f. Imports
g. Importer
h. Joint venture
i. Multinational business
j. Protective tariff
k. Tariff
l. World trade

1. Business that is conducted between citizens, companies, and governments on an international scale
2. Goods or services produced in this country but sold abroad
3. Where a country, by specializing in specific goods, can produce them more economically than other countries
4. Raw materials or manufactured goods produced abroad but shipped into this country
5. A group of companies working cooperatively to control prices
6. A firm that conducts operations in several countries and has a worldwide perspective

7. An overseas enterprise that is not completely owned and/or controlled by the parent company
8. A tax or customs duty levied by a nation on goods imported from other countries
9. A tax on imports to protect domestic producers
10. Changing the currency of one nation to that of another
11. The difference between a country's imports and exports
12. A person who buys goods abroad and takes possession of them until he or she finds a buyer

REVIEW QUESTIONS

1. Why is world trade important to our nation and to American business?
2. What determines the kinds of products that businesses of any nation export to other countries?
3. What is the difference between *direct-export* and *indirect-export* marketing channels?
4. What is a *joint venture overseas?*
5. Why do governments enact tariffs on imported goods?

DISCUSSION QUESTIONS

1. How does international trade promote a higher standard of living?
2. What specific problems make world trade a challenge?
3. What is the chief argument for free trade among nations?
4. Compare a balance-of-payments statement with a statement of income and expenses.
5. What are the main functions of the International Monetary Fund?
6. What causes foreign-exchange rates to fluctuate?

BUSINESS CASE 21-1

To Build Overseas?

The executive committee of the Newcomb Electronics Company has recommended that the company build an assembly plant in Taiwan. The committee gave as supportive arguments the following:

a. The government in Taiwan will erect the building and lease it back to the company.
b. The company will be given exemption from property taxes on its capital equipment for five years.
c. Labor costs in Taiwan are lower than those in the United States.
d. The company must employ native personnel both in production and in management. But during the first two years, U.S. personnel could be used to train the native workers.

1. **Which of these advantages might be available in this country?**
2. **What arguments can you make for building the new plant in the United States?**
3. **Which of the arguments made in answering questions 2 do you consider to be the most important?**

BUSINESS CASE 21-2

The Harkness Company Proposes to Go International

The Harkness Company of Terre Haute, Indiana, is a manufacturer of household appliances—including vacuum cleaners, electric dishwashers, and electric stoves—under the trade name of Wellbuilt. The company management is considering going abroad to expand sales. Last year its annual sales amounted to $80 million, with earnings at 9 percent of sales. The company is a close corporation owned by the Harkness family.

Ten weeks ago Tom Harkness, the son of the founder, Robert Harkness, attended a conference in Detroit on foreign-trade opportunities in Australia for American firms. At this conference, Tom heard an authority on foreign trade speak about his trip to Australia. In response to Tom's invitation, the authority recently visited with officials of the Harkness Company. He recommended that the company establish an export department to conduct foreign trade with Australian companies. He also recommended that the firm get in contact with the International Monetary Fund, the Export-Import Bank, the International Chamber of Commerce, the International Bank for Reconstruction, and the U.S. State Department about opportunities for trading in Australia.

Assume that you are assigned to make a study of how to set up an export department. Prepare a list of the kind of information you would try to obtain to make the proposed study.

CAREER DEVELOPMENT IN BUSINESS 22

STUDY OBJECTIVES

WHEN YOU HAVE FINISHED READING THIS CHAPTER, YOU SHOULD BE ABLE TO

ONE Define career and explain what a career is not

TWO Identify the steps involved in the career-planning process

THREE Describe the factors that affect people's choice of a career

FOUR Indicate the life stages that careers follow

FIVE Discuss things to be aware of in a job interview situation

SIX Prepare a resume for use when applying for a position

IN THE NEWS

Companies Recognize That the Employee Is Responsible for Career Planning

In a recent interview Douglas M. Reid, Xerox's director of international personnel, pinpointed the change in businesses' approach to career planning:

> I think part of the problem is that in the '50s and '60s most employees expected the company to plan their careers for them. They would work hard, put their heads down and grind away, and if the company said move from Rochester to San Antonio, they packed their bags that weekend and went. Starting in the '70s, however, employees started to speak up. They said, "I don't know if I want to move from this part of the country. I don't know if I agree that this next move makes sense." We spent a lot of time exploring what the issues were, and we have concluded that it's incumbent on us to educate our employees that it's their responsibility to plan their own careers. We can tell them about logical career paths, what the prerequisites for various jobs are, and so on, but each employee is going to have to decide what he or she specifically wants to do and whether to make the investment in training, or whatever it might be, to try to enhance his or her chances of success. With regard to career planning, we have a long way to go before we'll be reasonably satisfied.

Douglas Reid's comments and those of other experts clearly demonstrate a change in approach. The employee must take a more active role in planning his or her own career.

Alice: Will you tell me please which way I ought to go from here?
Cheshire Cat: That depends a great deal on where you want to get to.
Alice: I don't much care.
Cheshire Cat: Then it doesn't matter which way you go.

From LEWIS CARROLL'S Alice in Wonderland

Like Alice in Wonderland, if you don't much *care* where your career is going, almost any road will get you there. But if you do care, then it is important that you take an active role in reaching those goals.

Planning your career is not something that you do just one time and then forget. We live in a world of increasing uncertainty, a world of unstable career choices. The situation is made that way by rapid shifts not only in technology but in economic and social conditions. This means that people must learn how to make and remake career plans despite these changes. Such changes work against "business as usual" and add a certain amount of complexity and frustration to our careers and our lives.

A successful career has *always* been influenced by the economy and by trends in basic business forces. The conditions that influence careers today are not new, but it is important that you recognize them. Planning a career requires integrating your work, career, family, and life education. It is a continuous process of learning throughout life. Deciding what you want your future career to be like can be difficult, but also rewarding. It involves testing the reality of your goals and plans and defining the criteria for career actions and decisions. There are no instant solutions to career-planning choices and problems. However, if we fail to do our homework on careers and on our personal goals, more choices will be made *for us* and they will not all be to our liking.

WHAT IS A CAREER?

Let us consider a few things about a career.

1. The speed with which your career unfolds does *not* necessarily suggest success or failure. What happens during the career, rather than the speed with which it

happens, is more important. The thirty-five-year-old vice-president is not necessarily more successful than the forty-five-year-old vice-president.

2. You are the only one who can determine whether your career has been successful. There are *no absolute criteria* for evaluating a career, yet friends, spouse, and society are all too quick to help you determine whether your career has been successful. It is inappropriate for one person to evaluate another person's career. You are the only one who has the right to make your own life choice.

3. A career is not only what you do but how you feel about what you do. Persons who hate their careers are not successful no matter how much money they make. A person's values, attitudes, and motives change as he or she grows older. Your work is a success or a failure to the degree that it fits your values, attitudes, and motives.

4. A career is a sequence of work experiences, not simply certain jobs. Any work, paid or unpaid, can make up a career. The work you do during your life will constitute your career. It need not be a profession, nor necessarily even paid. It can be volunteer work.

A career includes both your feelings and your activities and the way in which they are related over the span of your life. A career, therefore, is a lifelong series of work-related experiences.

Why Are Careers Important Enough to Study?

Work provides the setting for satisfying many of the needs that all human beings have. The list of human needs identified by Maslow, and discussed earlier in the text, illustrates this well. The whole range of Maslow's hierarchy of needs—physical, safety, social, self-respect, and self-actualization—can be satisfied at work.

What would you do if you suddenly became a multimillionaire? Imagine, for example, that somebody willed you several million dollars and it was no longer necessary for you to work. What would you do with yourself? Most people would probably take a vacation. They might even change jobs and try to find something that they *really wanted to do.* But studies have shown that most people would continue to work rather than sit around for the rest of their lives. Work clearly plays a key role in a person's life. And like other important things in life, you can control it better if you *plan* for it, rather than simply allow it to happen.

Yet many people do not plan well as far as their careers are concerned. George Bennett is a typical example.

George Bennett is one of my students and an advisee. A month before graduation last spring, George decided it was time to look for a job. After two weeks of fruitless hunting, he came to my office for a chat and some advice.

I asked what kind of job he was looking for. George's reply was, "I'm not really sure. I kind of liked my marketing courses so maybe that would be a good field for me. Besides I had sort of hoped that you could give me some ideas about the functional areas, industries, or companies that would offer the best job opportunities."

Most students are like George. They find that as graduation approaches they have no job offers, and panic sets in. Unfortunately, an orderly and effective approach to career planning cannot be done in two weeks.

Job Mobility

At one time people who had changed jobs several times during a career were viewed as unstable. But changing jobs frequently over the course of a career (within reason) is no longer considered a negative factor. It represents a varied experience and often implies a high level of personal drive. Indeed, a person who stays with one organization too long may have difficulty finding and adapting to other work. This is especially true if the technology, economics, or social changes we mentioned earlier force him or her out of the present job.

Studies have shown that the average college graduate changes jobs several times before he or she reaches the age of thirty. Such incresed job mobility suggests that people are willing to change jobs more often today if it gives them a better opportunity to match job characteristics and personal interests.

But other evidence suggests that people are also less willing to make job changes that they find unacceptable. There is a well-documented trend indicating that over the last decade people have been unwilling to take transfers or promotions. This is especially true when it would mean an unfavorable job or location change for them. For example, many people are unwilling to move to undesirable metropolitan locations simply because there is a promotion involved. Other people are unwilling to take jobs that they feel do not fit their personal interests or goals even though it means a promotion.

Matching People and Careers

As you can see in Figure 22-1, the characteristics of the job may be such that the job requires *no* interest in the work to be done. Or it may require a high level of interest. Furthermore, an individual's interest may be low or high in that particular kind of work. The best situation occurs when the job requires a high level of interest and the person is interested in that kind of work. This **match** between person and job is best for the individual and the organization.

Figure 22-2 shows that when the job does not require the values that you hold important, the job is meaningless. But when the job requires certain values that you do hold important, it allows for realization of these values. Figure 22-3 shows that individual talents should be matched with given job characteristics. If a job **requires very little** of a certain talent, and you **have very little** of that talent, the job is not giving you the opportunity to use the talents that you have.

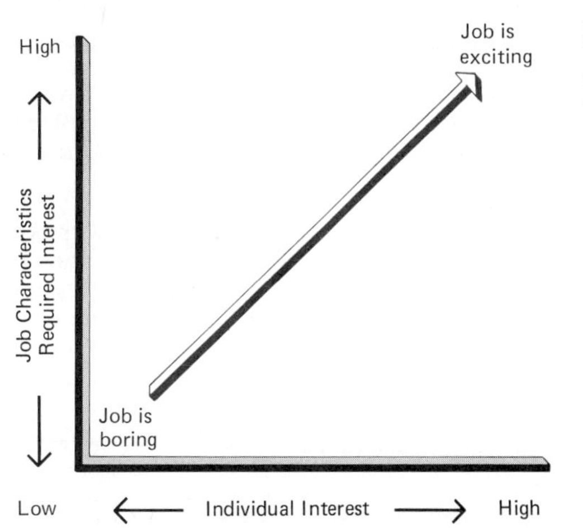

FIGURE 22-1

Matching individual interest with the job.

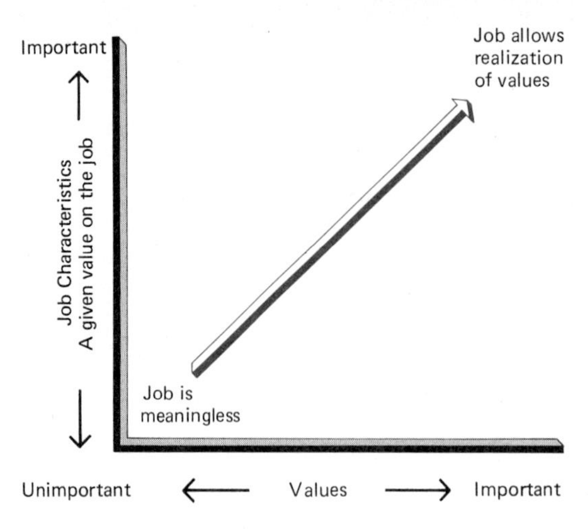

FIGURE 22-2

Matching individual values with the job.

Everyone has a **certain set of talents for doing something.** On the other hand, if the job requires a lot of a certain talent, and you have a lot of that talent to offer, the job is more fulfilling because your talents are being utilized.

THE CAREER-PLANNING PROCESS

Career planning is a process that all individuals must do themselves because each individual is different. The R. G. Barry Corporation of Columbus, Ohio, has prepared a self-guide for its management group to use in doing career planning. This guide is given to all managers, but those managers who wish to take it further than the introductory session must do so on their own.

Robert L. Woodruff, Jr., vice-president of human resources for R. G. Barry, commented as follows about the company's experiences with the self-guided career-planning process prepared for its managers.

> Our experience has been interesting. We had about 15 percent of our management people who took the time—and it would have taken perhaps eight to twelve hours to do it thoroughly—to go through the entire exercise and who then came back to the personnel department for additional information or review or who reviewed their results with their bosses. We didn't restrict them; they could go to anyone they wanted for review. The other 85 percent, as far as I know, never took the time to think through these issues regarding their jobs, their career, their profession, their community responsibilities, their family responsibilities, and the other items that are in the guide.
>
> On the basis of my experience I would say people need a lot more encouragement and help than we gave them in order to get into such a review. It's a heavy kind of thinking process and is probably more work than they do on their regular jobs. The guide required some soul searching: What are your strengths? What are your weaknesses? It's tough to deal with; it really is.

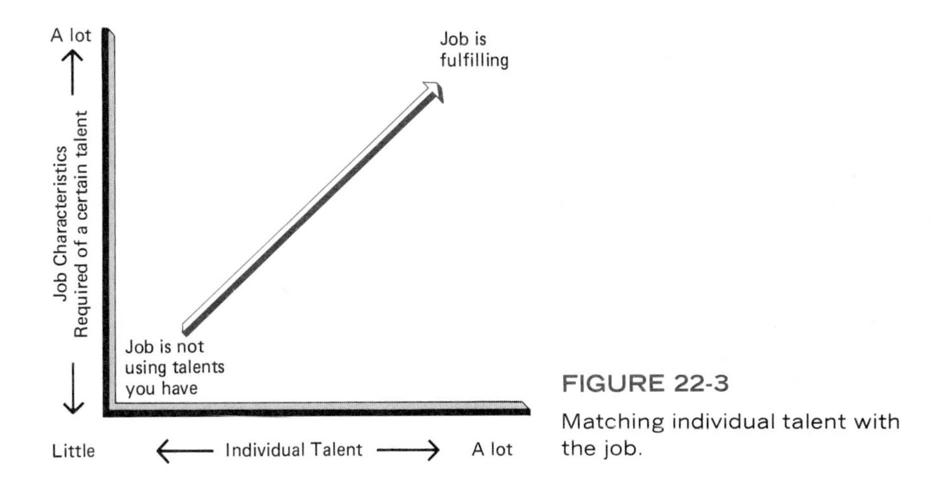

FIGURE 22-3

Matching individual talent with the job.

Career planning consists of four phases: (1) determining personal goals and objectives, (2) evaluating personal strengths and weaknesses, (3) analyzing career opportunities, and (4) reviewing and updating the career plan. We will now consider each of these phases.

Determining Personal Goals and Objectives

In setting personal goals and objectives, you should ask yourself the following questions. What kinds of tasks or activities have I enjoyed the most? What kinds have I enjoyed the least? If I could have **any job I wanted,** what job would it be? The best way to help determine what you really want out of life is to give yourself some honest answers. Some of the factors that must be considered when answering these questions are **income, geographical location, amount of travel, job security, independence, autonomy,** and **company size.** What price are you willing to pay to get ahead? Are you willing to move whenever and wherever your firm dictates? When you honestly answer those questions, you will have a clearer understanding of your goals, values, and priorities. Goal analysis is a frustrating process and takes a lot of time, but without some idea of where you want to go, it is difficult to plan how to get there.

Evaluating Personal Strengths and Weaknesses

When you have established your goals and objectives, an analysis of your personal strengths and weaknesses is in order. The answers to the following questions can help that analysis:

What are my six strongest skills?
What is my greatest accomplishment in life?
Is it salable?
Why should an employer hire me instead of someone else?

Rate yourself on each of the characteristics listed in the accompanying chart. Use the ratings to determine your major strengths and weaknesses. Then go over these strengths and weaknesses with a trusted friend and ask for his or her candid opinion.

Assessing your strengths and weaknesses may be difficult for you, but the chart can help you identify them. A number of appraisal forms are available to

MY STRENGTHS AND WEAKNESSES

Academic achievement (grades)	______
Ingenuity and creativity	______
Administrative knowledge and ability	______
Cooperativeness	______
Ambition and self-motivation	______
Conscientiousness	______
Educational credentials	______
Intelligence	______
Leadership ability	______
Maturity and poise	______
Oral communication skills	______
Written communication skills	______
Prior work experience	______
Sociability	______
Technical competence (marketing, finance, operations, research, personnel, etc.)	______

Rate yourself using the following scale:

5—a major strength
4—a moderate strength
3—neither a strength nor a weakness
2—a moderate weakness
1—a major weakness

help you identify your interests. The Strong and Kuder interest inventories can help immensely.

There are informal ways of learning about yourself too. Ask your instructors or your superior for feedback on your performance. Usually people don't get feedback on themselves unless they go out of their way to ask for it. Ask about areas of strength and weakness and what you might do to improve the weak areas. When you have developed a good list of your basic skills, try to develop a number of ways in which your skills can be used. You will be suprised at how many different types of careers can be built from a given set of skills and interests.

Analyzing Career Opportunities

Now you can begin to consider paths to reach your goals. Include not only promotion opportunities but additional training and learning experiences that might help you get there.

Take a long careful look at the industries and jobs that might be appropriate. Table 22-1 lists certain industry, organization, and job characteristics. You should

TABLE 22-1
INDUSTRY, ORGANIZATION, AND JOB CHARACTERISTICS

I. Characteristics of the industries you are considering:
   A. Structure (Is it dominated by large companies? Is it geographically centralized?)
   B. Profitability
   C. Growth prospects
   D. Relationship to economic and government contracts cycle
II. Characteristics of the organizations you are considering:
   A. Profitability and financial strength
   B. Growth potential
   C. Position in the industry
   D. Management style (democratic, autocratic, bureaucratic, etc.)
   E. Company policies regarding career development
III. Characteristics of the job you are considering:
   A. Reputation and importance of the department in which the job is housed
   B. Financial standing and autonomy of the department
   C. Value of the job as a steppingstone to a higher position
   D. Age and characteristics of the people you will be working with (Are the department heads old and due to retire soon or is the department overstocked with young talent?)
   E. Actual duties, responsibilities you will be assigned

note that jobs change, but company climate and industry health tend to be more permanent. The major criteria for making a choice should be the extent to which the job will help you achieve both your short-term and your long-term career goals.

Reviewing and Updating the Career Plan

At this point you should have a good picture of your objectives, your assets and liabilities, and the career opportunities available to you. Now commit your career plan to *writing*. This written plan could include a listing of your long-term goals and objectives, intermediate goals for achieving the long-term goals, and schedules to make sure each can be reached in a reasonable length of time.

At this point you should also note that career planning is an ongoing process. It is not something you can do once and then have a blueprint to follow the rest of your life. It must continually be updated to account for changes in you and your interests. Many people use the technique of reviewing and updating the career plan once a year. Be sure to save old career plans because they provide a written record of your progression and the changes in your goals and interests.

HOW DO PEOPLE CHOOSE CAREERS?

Recent studies indicate that four general characteristics can affect the career choices that people make.[1]

1. *Interests*—Persons tend to pursue careers that they think match their interests.
2. *Self-identity*—A career is an extension of a person's self-image, as well as a maker of the self-image. People choose careers in keeping with their self-images.
3. *Personality*—This factor includes personal orientation, personal needs, and other personality variables. Again, career choice is usually in keeping with personality.
4. *Social background*—Socioeconomic status and the educational and occupational level of a person's parents can influence a person's choice of a career.

[1]Douglas T. Hall, *Careers in Organizations* (Pacific Palisades, Calif.: Goodyear, 1976), pp. 11–13.

All of these characteristics are important. People clearly try to match their choice of jobs with how they see themselves.

Social background is indeed an important item in determining the type of job that people are likely to consider. UCLA and Korn/Ferry International surveyed seventeen hundred senior executives of U.S. businesses. When the executives were asked to classify their fathers' occupations, 22.2 percent said that their fathers had been professional/technical people; 22.8 percent said that they had held a managerial position; and 16.9 percent said that they had been sole proprietors. Thus 61.9 percent of the sample said that their father's occupations had at least been related to an executive career. Only 20.8 percent said that their fathers had been blue-collar workers.

One obvious factor when choosing a specific company is the available position when you are looking for work. The amount of information you may have about alternative jobs is important too. Beyond these issues, people seem to pick organizations on the basis of the fit between the climate of that organization (as they perceive it) and their own personal characteristics.

CAREER STAGES

The research and literature on careers generally agree that an individual's career follows four stages. These stages correspond to a person's "life stages"—the steps that one goes through in maturing.

The first stage is **establishing an identity.** This is a period of exploration of alternative careers and of getting into the adult world. It may range from age ten to age twenty or later. Establishing an identity includes such things as choice of an education, development of an individual's self-image, and a growing need to test one's ability to work and accomplish real-life tasks.

The second stage is the **growing and becoming established stage.** This is a period when people test several different types of work and finally make a commitment to an occupation. During this stage (generally from age twenty to age forty), the person also establishes a home and family life. This early career stage includes major learning periods about what work is, and what kinds of work an individual might find satisfying. It also includes some "reality shock" about what the world of work is really like.

The third stage is **maintenance and adjustment to self.** This stage may range from thirty-five or forty to age fifty or later. It may include major changes in life plans, such as divorce, changing jobs, or accepting the fact that one's career is at a plateau. This last occurrence may require a reassessment of life objectives and self-concept. If the individual is "succeeding," he or she is probably developing special areas of competence. This may be accompanied by the feeling of having "made it" in the organization.

The fourth stage is **decline.** This includes formal preparation for retirement. It is generally a period of diminishing physical and possibly mental capabilities. This stage is often a result of such socially induced pressures as forced retirement. The individual must learn to accept a reduced role or learn to resist decline.

Within this general career and life-cycle pattern, people make choices that affect their satisfaction with their careers. Now that we have considered how one plans a career and how careers typically progress, let us look at some specific areas that are likely to be good areas for careers in the near future.

ANALYZING THE CAREER ENVIRONMENT

In viewing career opportunities, many different areas should be considered. For example, What is the forecast for long-term economic, social, and political trends that will inevitably influence careers in many fields? Two extensive surveys tried to predict exactly these things recently. One was prepared by the European Common Market Commission, the other by the Organization for Economic Cooperation and Development in Paris.

Both surveys arrived at similar conclusions. They predict a moderate growth of industrial economies through the year 2000, and uneven growth rates in the newly industrialized countries of Asia, the Middle East, and Latin America. The most likely scenario foresees a world that is basically "free-trade" oriented. The rates of productivity growth will decline in the United States but will increase in other industrialized nations. Table 22-2 shows the per capita gross national product for the major economies in 1975 and gives an estimate for the year 2000. One report says that current government attention to environmental problems will be important to help sustain the earth's resources. At the same time it finds that nuclear energy, when it is made safe, will be a key element in shifting world energy use away from oil. Coal and solar energy will also be increasingly important.

Specific Industry Trends

A projection by the U.S. Department of Labor gives the expected growth rate in major industries. Table 22-3 shows that the service industries are expected to have the highest growth rate, while transportation and public utilities will have a low growth rate. Agriculture will actually lose employment through 1985.

TABLE 22-2
PER CAPITA GROSS NATIONAL PRODUCT

	1975	2000*
United States	$5,132	$8,130
Japan	2,371	8,230
European Common Market	2,752	6,110
Latin America	745	2,040
China	256	800

*Estimate.

TABLE 22-3
INDUSTRY TRENDS IN JOBS GROWTH, 1976–85

Services	+40%
Mining	+35
Construction	+32
Finance, insurance, real estate	+30
Government	+22
Trade	+20
Manufacturing	+19
Transportation and utilities	+15
Agriculture	−30

SOURCE: Bureau of Labor Statistics.

Within the industries mentioned, certain jobs will have a higher growth rate than others.

The Bureau of Labor Statistics also projects the outlook for various career opportunities across industries. A summary of these industries is given in Table

TABLE 22-4
JOB OUTLOOK ACROSS INDUSTRIES TO MID-1980s

Occupation	Rate of Increase
Accountant	Average and faster
Computer programmer	Very rapid
Bank officer	Very rapid
Insurance (general)	Very rapid
Hotel manager	Average
City manager	Rapid
Hospital manager	Rapid
Personnel manager	Rapid
Purchasing agent	Rapid
Industrial designer	Average
Advertising	Moderate
Market researcher	Rapid
Sales	Moderate to slow
Real estate sales	Favorable
Retail buyer	Rapid
Transportation manager	Moderate to slow
Lawyers	Rapid

SOURCE: Bureau of Labor Statistics.

22-4. The outlook for many of the professions within the business area is quite good. Others will grow more slowly, as the table indicates.

An interersting study of what people with professional training want from their careers was conducted by four magazines in the "professional group": *MBA, Juris Doctor, Medical Dimensions,* and *New Engineer.* The results were reported in *MBA.*

The study found that there are differences among members of the "professional groups" in the single most important thing they want from their jobs. By area of training they were:

	Business	Law	Engineering	Medicine
Intellectual challenge	1	2	1	3
Money	2	3	3	7
Independence	3	1	4	1
Security	4	4	2	2
Prestige	5	7	6	5
Contribute to society	6	5	5	4
Power	7	8	7	8
Step to another career	8	9	9	9
Social change	9	6	8	6

Notice that business and engineering both ranked intellectual challenge first, while law and medicine ranked independence first.

Working in a Small Business

Many people would prefer to work in a small business rather than a large one. The outlook, however, for small businesses in the United States is somewhat mixed. For certain small businesses, the outlook can be quite good. But for small businesses in general, the overall favorability of the business climate has deteriorated. Small-business owners blame government policies for this situation. Government paper work is a major complaint. It is estimated that this constitutes a $100 billion added cost of doing business each year. More than half of the burden is borne by small businesses.

Unincorporated small businesses may pay a larger percentage of their income in federal taxes than do corporations because of the structure of our tax system. Perhaps the biggest problem for small businesses is their limited ability to raise capital. Financing the small business has always been difficult. But with high interest rates expected to persist throughout the 1980s, and failure of the capital markets to provide capital for smaller more risky firms, obtaining money has become even more difficult. Small businesses, to be successful in the decade of the 1980s, must adopt more professional and better management techniques than they have in the past.

GETTING THE RIGHT JOB

Looking for a job is just plain hard work. But the better prepared you are, the better you will be able to cope with the job-hunting situation. This means preparing yourself through the educational process and doing your "homework" on the kinds of jobs and companies you might consider. It is advisable to specialize in a major area as part of your college education. You should also develop a second and perhaps a third area of specialization. For example: Many students majoring in finance develop a second area of specialization in accounting. Economics majors may find it wise to develop a second area in computer science or one of the business disciplines.

Finding the right position is an active process on your part. There is no substitute for determining the job you want and actively pursuing it. A few students sit back and wait for a job to come to them through the college's placement service or other sources. This may work well in some instances, but it is not the best way to go about getting a good job.

Preparing your Resumé

Some companies will ask you to list your qualifications on a personnel sheet that they have designed. Or the placement office at your college or university may supply a standard data sheet. In either event, it is a good idea to prepare an individual resumé of your experience and education and keep it updated. A good resumé can go a long way toward making a good impression. A really poor one can seriously hurt the chances of an applicant who may be desirable in every other way.

The content and layout of resumés vary widely, and there is no one "best" format. Some general suggestions do apply in every case, however. You will be on firm footing if you keep it short and simple. It must be typed and it must be neat. Spacing can be important, since it can be used to isolate points that you want to emphasize. Crowding too many details too close together results in an untidy appearance as well as a "fine print" appearance, which can turn a reader off.

Most resumés include the following information:

1. A listing of your academic work to date.
2. A listing of your work and life experience that may be related to the work itself.
3. Persons to contact if the company would like a recommendation about your work. These may be people who have known you in a professional sense—professors, employers, and so forth.

Work experience is, of course, the essential ingredient in any resumé. Dates should be given, along with company addresses and a brief description of the work that you did. Your job list should ordinarily begin with the last job you held, and other jobs should be listed in reverse order.

Don't overlook your extracurricular activities. Many jobs are especially fitted for the well-rounded individual. The fact that you have been chosen as a member of an honorary group or elected to professional societies in your field speaks well for your future in that field. If you belong to purely social organizations, list them. A large part of anyone's success in a new job depends on the ability

FIGURE 22-4
A RESUMÉ FORMAT

James E. Doe	Home Address:
10000 University Ave.	3414 Nicollet Ave.
Minneapolis, Minn.	Minneapolis, Minn.
University 1-4296	742-2001
(to June 5, 1981)	

PERSONAL DATA:

Age: 21	Birth Date: February 27, 1958
Height: 6′1″	Weight: 185
Marital Status: Single	
Health: Excellent	

OCCUPATIONAL GOAL:

My goal is a job in the field of sales promotion, with the eventual possibility of a management position.

EDUCATION:

University of Minnesota
Degree: Bachelor of Arts, '81
Major: Psychology
Minor: English Literature
Major subjects: Industrial Psychology, General Psychology, English Literature, Economics, Business Management and Organization, History
Grades: Good to excellent in major subjects; average to good in others

EXTRACURRICULAR ACTIVITIES:

Secretary, Alpha Pi Zeta, honorary social science fraternity
Member of Student Industrial Relations Society
Vice-president and social chairman of the ABC social club
Swimming team

WORK EXPERIENCE:

Summer, 1980—Gunderson Manufacturing Co., 1203 Ryan Ave., St. Paul, Minn. Payroll clerk. While working for Gunderson Co., I received a cash award for a payroll procedure suggestion that resulted in saving time for the company.
Summer, 1979—Wearever Aluminum Co., door-to-door salesman in Minneapolis.
Summer, 1978—Lifeguard, Camp Chippewa, Lake Bemidji, Minn.

to get along with fellow workers. Figures 22-4 and 22-5 show two different resumé formats.

Locating Job Opportunities

A number of sources for job leads are available. Private employment agencies may be used, but they usually charge a fee for their services. State employment agencies can sometimes provide job leads, and they do not charge a fee.

A major source is the classified section of your newspaper. Employers usually list their job openings in the Sunday newspapers. Your college professors can be a source of good leads for jobs in your area of specialization. Friends and relatives who are aware of openings in various organizations can be useful too. Many schools and colleges provide placement services for their students. These can be useful sources of initial contact with several companies and organizations.

FIGURE 22-5
PERSONAL DATA SHEET

NAME: Jane R. Richards

ADDRESS: 1201 Senator Place, Cincinnati, Ohio (to June 5, 1980)

TELEPHONE: 881-5000

HOME ADDRESS: 12 River St., Portsmouth, Ohio

HOME TELEPHONE: 233-4832

AGE: 22 HEIGHT: 5′9″ WEIGHT: 159

MARITAL STATUS: Single

EDUCATION: University of Cincinnati
Degree: Bachelor of Science, '81
Major: Chemical Engineering
Class rank: Upper tenth, Dean's Honor List, 1980–81

Major subjects:

Quantitative Analysis	Physical Chemistry	Physics	Geology
Qualitative Analysis	Organic Chemistry	German	Zoology

I received two scholarships to the School of Chemistry, which paid part of my tuition expenses.

EXTRACURRICULAR ACTIVITIES:

Member of American Student Chemical Society
Independent Student Association

WORK EXPERIENCE:

1979–80 General Chemical Laboratories, 3455 Woodburn Ave., Cincinnati, Ohio. As part of my cooperative education program, I have been working full-time, alternate six-week periods as a laboratory assistant.

Summer Ajax Laboratory Supply Co., Portsmouth, Ohio, Inventory Clerk. Promoted from shipping department after first month.

REFERENCES:

Mr. Henry A. Neff	Mr. Walter J. Schapp	Dr. John O. Ryan
General Chemical Lab.	Ajax Lab. Supply Co.	Professor
3455 Woodburn Ave.	Portsmouth, Ohio	School of Chemistry
Cincinnati, Ohio		U. of Cincinnati
		Cincinnati, Ohio

Preparing for the Interview

An important part of preparing for the interview is to do some research on the company that will be interviewing you. Try to find out when the company was established; where its plants, offices, or stores are located; what its products and services are; what its growth has been; and its future prospects. This will give you something besides yourself to talk about during the interview and will provide a framework for questions you should ask. It will also help to protect your own interests.

Prepare some questions before you go for the interview. There are a number of things that you will want to know about the company. Rather than rely on your memory to supply them, write them down. Most interviewers are favorably impressed by an interviewee who brings in carefully thought out questions. Appropriate business dress and neatness and cleanliness scarcely need to be mentioned. The importance of the initial impression cannot be overemphasized.

To avoid making errors, an individual can choose commonly accepted business dress for an interview.

The Interview

Be ready for at least one surprise question during an interview, perhaps more. A few interviewers always use one of the following:

a. What can I do for you?
b. Tell me about yourself!
c. Why are you interested in this company?
d. What are your weaknesses?
e. What are your strengths?
f. Why do you want to work for us?

If you think those are easy questions to answer without some previous thought, just try it. You don't have time to flounder around. This is where preparation will count.

A few interviewers like to do most of the talking, and they judge you by your reactions. Others hardly talk at all, and for an amateur these are the hardest to deal with. Their attitude is that selling yourself is your job. That is where you will have to rely on your knowledge of yourself and you interest in the work and the company.

Make sure that your good points get across to the interviewer. He or she won't know about them unless you talk about them, but try to appear factual and sincere, not conceited or boastful. Be ready to answer the question, "What do you plan to be doing ten years from now?"—it is a favorite interview question. A popular alternative is, "How much money do you expect to be earning in ten years?" The purpose of the question is to try to determine your ambition and ability to plan ahead and the soundness of your thinking.

Try to avoid giving the impression that you have come in to look over the possibilities and that you are not sure yet of what you want. Avoid "I'll do **anything** if I'm given the chance to learn" or "I don't know what I want to do." Wherever possible, apply for a **specific job** or field or work. If there is no opening in the jobs you want, the way you present what you have to offer may well allow the interviewer to suggest another job or department.

If you get the impression that the interview is not going well and that you have already been rejected, don't let your discouragement show. You have nothing to lose by continuing to appear confident, and you may gain much. The last few minutes often change things. An interviewer who is genuinely interested in your possibilities may seem to discourage you in order to test your reaction.

What happens if an interviewer offers you a job on the spot? If you are absolutely sure it is the one you want, accept it with a definite "Yes." If you have the slightest doubt, or if you do not want to accept it without some further thought or further interviews, ask for more time to consider the offer. You will not embarras the person who has made you the offer. Be courteous and tactful and ask him or her for time to think it over. Set a definite date as to when you can give an answer. This will assure the interviewer that you are giving the offer serious consideration. Above all, don't create the impression that you are playing one company off against the other to drive up the bidding.

Don't be too discouraged if no definite offer is made. The recruiter may wish to communicate with someone else or interview more applicants before making any offer.

Most interviews last between twenty and thirty minutes. A glance at your watch will tell you if your time is almost up. Don't go on talking and talking. Some applicants talk themselves into a job and then right out of it. Be alert for signs from the interviewer that the session is almost at an end.

If you are not successful with your first interview or first several interviews, remember that interviewers, companies, and jobs differ greatly. You will learn much from your first interview, and you will almost certainly do better in succeeding ones. The important thing is to *keep trying.* Figure 22-6 lists the fifty major negative factors that occur during the employment interview. These frequently lead to rejection of the applicant.

FIGURE 22-6
Negative Factors during the Employment Interview Which Frequently Lead to Rejection of the Applicant

1. Poor personal appearance.
2. Overbearing—overaggressive—conceited "superiority complex"—"know-it-all."
3. Inability to express himself clearly—poor voice, diction, grammar.
4. Lack of planning for career—no purpose and goals.
5. Lack of interest and enthusiasm—passive, indifferent.
6. Lack of confidence and poise—nervousness—ill-at-ease.
7. Failure to participate in activities.
8. Overemphasis on money—interest only in best dollar offer.
9. Poor scholastic record—just got by.
10. Unwilling to start at the bottom—expects too much too soon.
11. Makes excuses—evasiveness—hedges on unfavorable factors in record.
12. Lack of tact.
13. Lack of maturity.
14. Lack of courtesy—ill mannered.
15. Condemnation of past employers.
16. Lack of social understanding.
17. Marked dislike for school work.
18. Lack of vitality.
19. Fails to look interviewer in the eye.
20. Limp, fishy hand-shake.
21. Indecision.
22. Loafs during vactions—lakeside pleasures.
23. Unhappy married life.
24. Friction with parents.
25. Sloppy application blank.
26. Merely shopping around.
27. Wants job only for short time.
28. Little sense of humor.
29. Lack of knowledge of field of specialization.
30. Parents make decisions for him.
31. No interest in company or in industry.
32. Emphasis on whom he knows.
33. Unwillingness to go where we send him.
34. Cynical.
35. Low moral standards.
36. Lazy.
37. Intolerant—strong prejudices.
38. Narrow interest.
39. Spends much time in movies.
40. Poor handling of personal finances.
41. No interest in community activities.
42. Inability to take criticism.
43. Lack of appreciation of the value of experience.
44. Radical ideas.
45. Late to interview without good reason.
46. Never heard of company.
47. Failure to express appreciation for interviewer's time.
48. Asks no questions about the job.
49. High pressure type.
50. Indefinite response to questions.

As reported by 153 companies surveyed by Frank S. Endicott, Director of Placement, Northwestern University.

CAREER MANAGEMENT AND WOMEN

Careers in business, especially in the upper levels of business and management in this country, has typically meant men. The overwhelming majority of large business firms in the United States are still managed by men. Most women are primarily concentrated in entry-level, supervisory, or trainee positions.

The **Wall Street Journal** estimates that women hold only 6 percent of all middle-management positions and only 1 percent of all vice-presidential or higher-level positions. However, **changes are occurring.** There are more women in managerial positions, even if at entry level, than there have been in the past. There are more women on corporate boards of directors and more female applicants for professional degrees including the M.B.A. than ever before. The **New York Times** says that women now constitute over one-third of the law-school graduates and an increasing proportion of the top-flight business-school graduates.

As "equal opportunity" for women is becoming a reality, management people in many companies are realizing that some special measures are needed. Some companies provide special training in management to help women move quickly and successfully into the mainstream of managerial action. One recent study suggests that the development of women as managers seems to require an understanding of their special needs as well as the requirements of the business. Research on women managers leads to the following recommendations for speeding their development:

1. Women need help in raising their self-esteem as managers.
2. Women need training to learn new behaviors for managing interpersonal conflict.
3. Women need training to develop leadership and team-building skills.
4. Women need help with career planning.
5. Training for *women only* is often desirable initially.[2]

Such research will undoubtedly result in better managers, **both** male and female, and it is hoped that it will also result in a better use of an important resource: **competent human beings.**

SURVIVING IN AN ORGANIZATION

Douglas T. Hall, in his book "**Careers in Organizations**," suggests the following behaviors for survival in organizations and for making a career successful:

1. Be an outstanding performer.
2. Develop professional mobility. This includes maintaining a wide set of options, trying to keep from being blocked by immobile superiors, and planning for a multicareer.
3. Plan your own and your spouse's careers collaboratively.

[2]J. Steven Heiner, Dorothy McGlauchlin, Constance Legeros, and Jean Freeman, "Developing the Woman Manager," *Personnel Journal*, May 1975, p. 54.

4. Get help in career management.
5. Continually reassess your career.[3]

As you can see from the material that we have covered in this chapter, the point made initially—that career planning is difficult—is indeed true. However, to fail to take an active role in planning your career simply because it is difficult is the weakest of all excuses. With planning and thought, you can have the kind of career that you would like to have.

SUMMARY OF KEY CONCEPTS

If you don't plan your own career, you are at the mercy of luck and circumstance.

The work you do during your life will constitute a career. It need not be for pay, and you are the only one who can determine whether your career has been "successful."

Job mobility is increasing, *but* people are becoming more particular about changing jobs. If the reasons do not fit their own goals and interests, they often will not change.

A job must fit an individual's interests, values, and talents if it is to be a good match.

Career planning consists of a process of determining one's goals, identifying strengths and weaknesses, analyzing career opportunities, and finalizing and updating the career plan.

Career stages follow life stages for most people and include identity, getting established, maintenance, and decline.

Per capita gross national product will remain high in the United States in the foreseeable future, but our rate of productivity will decline.

The service industries will be the fastest-growing industries in the 1980s. Agriculture will actually lose employees.

The outlook for small business is mixed. Many people like to work in small businesses. But getting capital to start or maintain the business is becoming increasingly difficult.

Interviews can be an interesting interchange, but being prepared in advance for likely questions can make the interview pleasant and fruitful. Knowing why interviewers are likely to reject candidates is also helpful.

REVIEW QUESTIONS

1. What is meant by the statement "Only you can define the success of your career"?
2. Describe the steps involved in the career-planning process.
3. How do personality and self-identity affect career choice?
4. Why do career stages follow life stages?
5. Select the five negative factors that you think occur most often during employment.

DISCUSSION QUESTIONS

1. Why, do you think, do people usually leave their careers to chance instead of planning for them?
2. What is your biggest concern about the job search process?

[3]Hall, *Careers in Organizations,* pp. 185–87.

3. Given the predictions made by the European Common Market Commission regarding the world economy through 2000, what do you think the "hot" careers might be?
4. Discuss the pros and cons of "proper business attire" as a necessary condition for getting a job.

BUSINESS CASE 22-1

Dead End

Joe Dogeness received a business degree from a well-known university in 1975 and took a job with a large oil company. His career got off to a good start. By 1981 his salary was $28,000 and he was in charge of a five-person analysis team.

Joe was not happy with his career progress, however. While his salary was satisfactory, his level of responsibility was only slightly greater than it had been during his first year or two with the company. He had been stuck in a staff job at the home office for six years and felt that he would like a change. He requested a transfer to a line-marketing job.

He was told that he was too valuable in his current job to be transferred. He was overpaid for a lower-level line position, and too inexperienced to be promoted to a middle- or upper-level line position.

1. What should Joe do?
2. Why has he gotten into this fix?

BUSINESS CASE 22-2

I Am A Success!!

Roberta Franklin got an M.B.A. in 1974 and went to work for a large New York consulting firm. Within a year she was in charge of major projects throughout the country, which meant that she was away from home much of the time. Roberta assured her husband that this hectic pace would only last a few years and that she could then settle down to a more normal life.

In 1977 she went to work for a client firm as division personnel manager. But the job had been neglected for some years, and Roberta had to work long hours and weekends to straighten things out. By 1981 she had received two more promotions and was earning over $50,000. She was viewed as a real comer by top management.

Roberta paid a price. Her husband seldom saw her, and he finally asked for a divorce. Roberta has begun to question whether this is the kind of life she really wants. Much of the enjoyment she has had from her work is gone, and she feels that her life is being wasted.

1. Roberta is very successful—what is the problem?
2. Where does she go from here?

SELECTED READINGS

PART ONE
BUSINESS AND ITS ENVIRONMENT

Baumol, William J., and Wallace E. Oates, with Sue Anne Batey, **Economics, Environmental Policy, and The Quality of Life,** Englewood Cliffs, N.J.: Prentice-Hall, Inc., 1979.

Bornstein, Morris, **Comparative Economic Systems: Models and Cases,** 4th ed. Homewood, Ill.: Richard D. Irwin, Inc., 1979.

Bradley, Michael, **Economics.** Glenview, Ill.: Scott, Foresman and Company, 1980.

Business Week magazine (September 3, 1979) fiftieth anniversary issue.

Duignan, Peter and Alvin Rabushka, **The United States in the 1980's.** Stanford, Cal.: Hoover Institution Press, 1980.

Fortune magazine, Vol. 101, No. 3 (Feb. 11, 1980) fiftieth anniversary issue.

Galbraith, John Kenneth, **The Age of Uncertainty.** Boston: Houghton Mifflin Company, 1977.

Hailstones, Thomas J., **Basic Economics,** 6th ed. Cincinnati: South-Western Publishing Co., 1980.

Hay, Robert D., and Edmund R. Gray, editors, **Business and Society: Cases and Text.** Cincinnati, O.: South-Western Publishing Co., 1980.

Leftwich, Richard H., **The Price System and Resource Allocation,** 7th ed. New York: The Dryden Press, 1979.

McKenzie, Richard B., and Gordon Tullock, **Modern Political Economy: An Introduction to Economics.** New York: McGraw-Hill Book Company, 1978.

Nader, Ralph, **The Consumer and Corporate Accountability,** New York: Harcourt Brace Jovanovich, Inc., 1973.

Sawyer, George C., **Business and Society: Managing Corporate Social Impact.** Boston: Houghton Mifflin Company, 1979.

Stead, Bette Ann, **Women in Management.** Englewood Cliffs, N.J.: Prentice-Hall, Inc., 1978.

Stokes, Charles J., **Economics for Managers.** New York: McGraw-Hill Book Company, 1979.

PART TWO
OWNERSHIP, ORGANIZATION, AND MANAGEMENT

Aldag, Ramon J., and Arthur P. Brief, **Task Design and Employee Motivation.** Glenview, Ill.: Scott, Foresman and Company, 1979.

Baumback, Clifford M., **How to Organize and Operate a Small Business,** 6th ed. Englewood Cliffs, N.J.: Prentice-Hall, Inc., 1979.

Beer, M., **Organizational Change and Development: A Systems View.** Santa Monica, Cal.: Goodyear Publishing Company, Inc., 1980.

Dale, Ernest, **Management: Theory and Practice.** 4th ed. New York: McGraw-Hill Book Company, 1978.

Ford, R., and C. Heaton, **Principles of Management: A Decision-Making Approach.** Reston, Va.: Reston Publishing Company, Inc., 1980.

Glueck, William F., **Management Essentials.** New York: The Dryden Press, 1979.

Jackson, John H., and Cyril P. Morgan, **Organizational Theory: A Macro Perspective for Management.** Englewood Cliffs, N.J.: Prentice-Hall, Inc., 1978.

Massie, Joseph L., and John Douglas, **Managing: A Contemporary Introduction,** 3rd ed. Englewood Cliffs, N.J.: Prentice-Hall, Inc., 1981.

Mondy, R. Wayne, et al., **Management: Concepts and Practices.** Boston: Allyn and Bacon, 1980.

Sayles, Leonard R., **Leadership: What Effective Managers Really Do . . . And How They Do It.** New York: McGraw-Hill Book Company, 1979.

Stoner, James A. F., **Management.** Englewood Cliffs, N.J.: Prentice-Hall, Inc., 1978.

Truett, Dale B., and Lila F. Truett, **Managerial Economics: Analysis, Problems, Cases.** Cincinnati, O.: South-Western Publishing Co., 1980.

Van Voorhis, Kenneth R., **Entrepreneurship and Small Business Management.** Boston: Allyn and Bacon, 1980.

Webber, Ross A., **Management: Basic Elements of Managing Organizations.** revised ed. Homewood, Ill.: Richard D. Irwin, Inc., 1979.

PART THREE
PEOPLE AND PRODUCTION

Adam, Everett E., Jr., and Ronald J. Ebert, **Production and Operations Management: Concepts, Models and Behavior.** Englewood Cliffs, N.J.: Prentice-Hall, Inc., 1978.

Chruden, Herbert J., and Arthur W. Sherman, Jr., **Personnel Management: The Utilization of Human Resources.** 6th ed. Cincinnati, O.: South-Western Publishing Co., 1980.

Estey, Marten, **The Unions: Structure, Development, and Management.** 2nd ed. New York: Harcourt Brace Jovanovich, Inc., 1976.

Harper, Donald V., **Transportation in America: Users, Carriers, Government.** Englewood Cliffs, N.J.: Prentice-Hall, Inc., 1978.

Jucius, Michael J., **Personnel Management.** 9th ed. Homewood, Ill.: Richard D. Irwin, Inc., 1979.

Lieb, Robert C., **Transportation and the Domestic System.** Englewood Cliffs, N.J.: Prentice-Hall, Inc., 1978.

McClain, John O. and L. Joseph Thomas, **Operations Management: Production of Goods and Services.** Englewood Cliffs, N.J.: Prentice-Hall, Inc., 1980.

Mitchell, Terence R., **People in Organizations: Understanding Their Behavior.** New York: McGraw-Hill Book Company, 1978.

Pigors, Paul, and Charles A. Myers, **Personnel Administration.** 8th ed. New York: McGraw-Hill Book Company, 1977.

Sawhill, John, **Energy Conservation and Public Policy.** Englewood Cliffs, N.J.: Prentice-Hall, Inc., 1979.

Stair, Ralph M., and Barry Render. **Production and Operations Management: A Self-Correcting Approach.** Boston: Allyn and Bacon, 1980.

Strauss, George, and Leonard R. Sayles, **Personnel: The Human Problems of Management,** 4th ed. Englewood Cliffs, N.J.: Prentice-Hall, Inc., 1980.

Taff, Charles A., **Management of Physical Distribution and Transportation.** 6th ed. Homewood, Ill.: Richard D. Irwin, Inc., 1978.

Yoder, Dale, **Personnel Management and Industrial Relations.** 6th ed. Englewood Cliffs, N.J.: Prentice-Hall, Inc., 1970.

PART FOUR
MARKETING

Buskirk, Richard H., and Bruce D. Buskirk, **Retailing.** New York: McGraw-Hill Book Company, 1979.

Diamond, Jay, and Gerald Pintel, **Principles of Marketing.** 2nd ed. Englewood Cliffs, N.J.: Prentice-Hall, Inc., 1980.

Enis, E., **Marketing Principles: The Marketing Process.** Santa Monica, Cal.: Goodyear Publishing Company, Inc., 1980.

Kerin, Roger A., and Robert A. Peterson, **Perspectives on Strategic Marketing Management.** Boston: Allyn and Bacon, 1980.

Kotler, Philip, **Marketing Management: Analysis, Planning, and Control.** 3rd ed. Englewood Cliffs, N.J.: Prentice-Hall, Inc., 1980.

Kotler, Philip, **Principles of Marketing.** Englewood Cliffs, N.J.: Prentice-Hall, Inc., 1980.

Mandell, Maurice, **Advertising.** 3rd ed. Englewood Cliffs, N.J.: Prentice-Hall, Inc., 1980.

McCarthy, Jerome, **Essentials of Marketing.** Homewood, Ill.: Richard D. Irwin, Inc., 1979.

Marquardt, Raymond A., **Retail Management: Satisfaction of Consumer Needs.** 2nd ed. New York: The Dryden Press, 1979.

Nylen, David W., **Advertising: Planning, Implementation, and Control.** Cincinnati, O.: South-Western Publishing Co., 1980.

O'Dell, William F., Andrew C. Ruppel, and Robert H. Trent, **Marketing Decision Making: Analytic Framework and Cases.** 2nd ed. Cincinnati, O.: South-Western Publishing Co., 1979.

Stanton, William J., **Fundamentals of Marketing.** 5th ed. New York: McGraw-Hill Book Company, 1978.

PART FIVE
FINANCING AND INSURING THE ENTERPRISE

Amling, Frederick, **Investment: An Introduction to Analysis and Management.** 4th ed. Englewood Cliffs, N.J.: Prentice-Hall, Inc., 1978.

Blecke, C., and D. Gotthif, **Financial Analysis for Decision Making.** 2nd ed. Englewood Cliffs, N.J.: Prentice-Hall, Inc., 1980.

Brigham, Eugene F., **Financial Management: Theory and Practice.** 4th ed. New York: The Dryden Press, 1979.

Devine, Ronald K., editor, **Successful Investing: A Complete Guide to Your Financial Future.** New York: Simon and Schuster, 1979.

Dorfman, Mark S., **Introduction to Insurance.** Englewood Cliffs, N.J.: Prentice-Hall, Inc., 1978.

Keynes, John Maynard, **The General Theory of Employment, Interest, and Money.** New York: Harcourt Brace Jovanovich, Inc., 1936.

Kamerschen, David R., **Money and Banking.** 7th ed. Cincinnati, O.: South-Western Publishing Co., 1980.

Klein, John J., **Money and the Economy.** 4th ed. New York: Harcourt Brace Jovanovich, Inc., 1978.

Light, Jay O., and William L. White, **The Financial System.** Homewood, Ill.: Richard D. Irwin, Inc., 1979.

Thomas, Lloyd B., Jr., **Money, Banking, and Economic Activity.** Englewood Cliffs, N.J.: Prentice-Hall, Inc., 1979.

Van Horne, James C., **Financial Management and Policy.** 5th ed. Englewood Cliffs, N.J.: Prentice-Hall, Inc., 1980.

PART SIX
INFORMATION AND DECISION MAKING

Bodnar, George H., **Accounting Information Systems.** Boston: Allyn and Bacon, 1980.

Clark John J., et al., **Capital Budgeting: Planning and Control of Capital Expenditures.** Englewood Cliffs, N.J.: Prentice-Hall, Inc., 1979.

Gore, Marvin, and John Stubbe, **Computers and Data Processing.** New York: McGraw-Hill Book Company, 1979.

Gorsline, G. W., **Computer Organization: Hardware/Software.** Englewood Cliffs, N.J.: Prentice-Hall, Inc., 1980.

Grad, Burton et al., **Management Systems: A Guide To The Study and Design of Information Systems.** 2nd ed. New York: The Dryden Press, 1979.

McLaughlin, Frank S., and Robert C. Pickhardt, **Quantitative Techniques for Management Decisions.** Boston: Houghton Mifflin Company, 1979.

Moore, Carl L., and Robert K. Jaedicke, **Managerial Accounting.** 5th ed. Cincinnati, O.: South-Western Publishing Co., 1980.

O'Brien, James A., **Computers in Business Management: An Introduction,** revised ed. Homewood, Ill.: Richard D. Irwin, Inc., 1979.

Smith, Jack L., and Robert M. Keith, **Accounting for Financial Statement Presentation.** New York: McGraw-Hill Book Company, 1979.

Taggart, William M., **Information Systems: An Introduction to Computers in Organizations.** Boston: Allyn and Bacon, 1980.

Tyran, M., **Computerized Accounting Methods and Controls.** 2nd ed. Englewood Cliffs, N.J.: Prentice-Hall, Inc., 1978.

PART SEVEN
GOVERNMENT AND WORLD BUSINESS

Carbaugh, Robert, **International Economics.** Cambridge: Winthrop Publishers, Inc., 1980.

Cateora, Philip R., and John M. Hess, **International Marketing.** 4th ed. Homewood, Ill.: Richard D. Irwin, Inc., 1979.

Corley, Robert N., and William Robert, **Principles of Business Law.** 11th ed. Englewood Cliffs, N.J.: Prentice-Hall, Inc., 1979.

Corley, Robert N., et al., **The Legal Environment of Business.** New York: McGraw-Hill Book Company, 1977.

Fritschler, A., and B. Ross, **Business Regulation and Government Decision Making.** Cambridge: Winthrop Publishers, Inc., 1980.

Grilliot, Harold J., **Introduction to Law and the Legal System.** 2nd ed. Boston: Houghton Mifflin Company, 1979.

Harron, Thomas J., **Law for Business Managers: The Regulatory Environment.** Boston: Allyn and Bacon, 1979.

Keegan, Warren J., **Multinational Marketing Management.** 2nd ed. Englewood Cliffs, N.J.: Prentice-Hall, Inc., 1980.

Kotter, John P., Victor Faux, and Charles McArthur, **Self-Assessment and Career Development.** Englewood Cliffs, N.J.: Prentice-Hall, Inc., 1978.

Kramer, Ronald L., and Ruel C. Kahler, **International Marketing.** 4th ed. Cincinnati, O.: South-Western Publishing Co., 1977.

Reader's Digest Association, Inc., **You and the Law,** revised ed. Pleasantville, N.Y.: The Reader's Digest Association, Inc., 1977.

Rodriguez, Rita M., and E. Eugene Carter, **International Financial Management.** Englewood Cliffs, N.J.: Prentice-Hall, Inc., 1979.

Shepherd, William G., **Public Policies Toward Business.** Homewood, Ill.: Richard D. Irwin, Inc., 1979.

GLOSSARY

ABSENTEEISM Failure of workers to be present at work as scheduled.

ABSOLUTE ADVANTAGE A country's specializing in goods when it enjoys low-cost advantages due to a natural monopoly or some unusual technical development.

ABSTRACT OF TITLE A written summary of all conveyances, mortgages, and liens affecting the title.

ACCOUNTABILITY Holding a subordinate answerable for the responsibility and authority delegated to him or her.

ACCOUNTING Process of recording and reporting financial information about a business.

ADVERTISING Any paid form of nonpersonal presentation and promotion of ideas, goods, or services.

AGENT A person authorized to act for another in transactions with third parties.

ALIEN CORPORATION A corporation doing business in the United States but chartered by a foreign government.

APPRAISAL Evaluation of an employee's performance on the job.

APTITUDE Potential ability to perform satisfactorily a specific type of work.

ARBITRATION Settlement of a labor-management dispute by a third party—both sides agree in advance to abide by the decision rendered.

ARBITRATOR An impartial labor expert who hears and settles grievances.

ASSET Any item of value owned by a business.

AUTOCRATIC LEADER One who makes decisions without consulting subordinates.

AUTHORITY Power to act and make decisions in carrying out assignments.

BALANCE SHEET An accounting statement of the financial condition of a business or institution on a specific date.

BANK DISCOUNT Interest deducted in advance.

BARTER Trading of one good for another good.

BOND A certificate of indebtedness indicating debt that is owed the bondholder by the corporation.

BOOK VALUE The value of stock carried on the company records.

BRAND A word, phrase, or symbol that gives identity to a product or class of products.

BUDGET A financial plan that shows the amounts of anticipated revenues and expenditures during a specified period of time.

BURGLARY Unlawful taking of property from premises with entry made by force.

BUSINESS Organized efforts of enterprises to supply consumers with goods and services.

BUSINESS TRUST Combination of businesses operated under trust agreements by trustees for the benefit of the members.

CAPITAL Money, equipment, and machinery used in business and industry.

CAPITALISM An economic system based upon the right of private ownership and the freedom to make choices.

CAPITAL STOCK Permanently invested capital contributed by the owners (shareholders) either at or subsequent to the time the corporation is organized.

CARTEL An association of companies whose purpose is to control prices or the conditions of sale.

CASHIER'S CHECK A check drawn by a bank against its own funds.

CENTRALIZED MANAGEMENT A system that delegates authority and control to a central area.

CERTIFIED CHECK A check that is guaranteed by the bank both as to signature and as to payment.

CHATTEL MORTGAGE A mortgage pledging tangible personal property.

CIVIL RIGHTS Rights to possess personal liberty with full legal, social, and economic equality under the Constitution.

CLOSE CORPORATION A corporation whose stock is held by a few persons and is not available for purchase by the general public.

COALITION BARGAINING When different unions within a given industry collaborate in bargaining with an employer.

COLLATERAL Property or security deposited with a creditor to warrant payment of a debt.

COLLECTIVE BARGAINING Negotiations between representatives of labor and representatives of management.

COMMON CARRIER A carrier that offers its services to the general public.

COMPARATIVE ADVANTAGE A country's specializing in goods it can produce more cheaply than other countries can.

COMPETITION The practice of striving for something that is also being sought by others.

CONCENTRATION Location of plants in a single geographical area.

CONSIDERATION Something of value pledged in exchange for a promise.

CONSUMER CREDIT Credit granted to consumers to promote personal consumption.

CONSUMERISM A multifaceted movement to inform consumers and protect them from business malpractice.

CONTRACT An agreement between two competent parties in the form required by law that is legally enforceable.

CONTRACT CARRIER A carrier that sells its transport services by individual agreements.

CONTROLLING A procedure for measuring performance against objectives.

CONVENIENCE GOODS Low-priced goods that are easily available.

COOPERATIVE A business organization owned and operated by its user members.

COORDINATION Synchronizing all individual efforts toward a common objective.

COPYRIGHT Exclusive right to publish, print, produce, or copy one's work—usually granted to an artist, author, composer, designer, publisher, or sculptor.

CORPORATION An association of individuals united for some common purpose, permitted by law to use a common name and to change its members without dissolution of the association.

CORRESPONDENT BANK A bank that maintains an account relationship with another bank or engages in exchange of services.

CREDIT The ability to secure goods or services in exchange for a promise to pay later.

CREDIT UNION An organization formed by individuals on a cooperative basis to make loans to its members and encourage them to save.

CRIME A felony or misdemeanor—usually punishable by imprisonment.

CURRENT ASSETS Items of value, owned by a business, that will be converted into cash within a relatively short time.

CURRENT RATIO An accounting ratio found by dividing the total current assets by the total current liabilities.

CUSTOMS UNION Geographical region embracing two or more nations within which goods may move freely (without being subject to customs duties).

DATA PROCESSING That group of operations performed in handling units of data from original to final entry.

DECENTRALIZED MANAGEMENT A systematic effort to delegate to lower levels all authority except that which must be exercised at the highest level.

DEFENDANT The party against whom an action at law is taken.

DELEGATION Giving one person the power and obligation to act for another.

DEMOCRATIC LEADER One who encourages the group's participation in decision making that affects them.

DEVELOPMENT Attempt to use new knowledge in the production of useful products.

DIFFERENTIAL ADVANTAGE Securing one or more favorable features for a product which are not found in competing products.

DIRECTING Achieving organizational objectives by motivating and guiding subordinates.

DISCOUNTER A merchant who sells goods at a price below the regularly established retail price.

DISCOUNT RATE The interest rate charged by Federal Reserve district banks on loans to member banks.

DISPATCHING Preparation and issuance of work orders in manufacturing.

DISPERSION The building of factories and warehouses over a wide geographical area.

DISTRIBUTION CENTER A center for handling and storing goods and preparing them for shipment.

DISTRIBUTION CHANNEL The route that goods follow as they move from the producer to the consumer or from the seller to the buyer.

DIVERSIFICATION Making different products or engaging in a variety of activities.

DOMESTIC CORPORATION A corporation is a **domestic corporation** in the state that granted it a charter.

DORMANT PARTNER A partner who plays no active role in the business and is unknown to the public as a partner.

DRAFT An unconditional written order made by the drawer, addressed to the drawee (second party), ordering the drawee to pay a specific sum to a third party (payee).

ECOLOGY Science of relationships between people and their environments.

ECONOMICS Science that deals with the satisfaction of human wants through the use of scarce productive resources.

EMOTIONAL MOTIVES Incentives to purchase goods whose appeal is subjective and impulsive in nature.

ENTREPRENEUR Chief initiator or organizer of a business enterprise—in a proprietorship the entrepreneur takes the risk.

ENVIRONMENT All external forces surrounding and affecting individuals, businesses, and communities.

EQUITY A branch of unwritten law that grants an adequate or fair remedy. Also the ownership claim to the resources of a business.

EQUITY CAPITAL Funds invested in the business (by the owner) on which there is no legal obligation to repay or pay interest.

ETHICS A code of conduct that guides an individual in dealing with others.

EXCLUSIVE DISTRIBUTION Using only one retailer in any given community to handle a product.

EXECUTIVE A top-level management person responsible for the work performed by others under his or her supervision.

EXPORTS Goods or services produced in some country and sold abroad.

EXPRESS WARRANTY Any statement of material fact, oral or written by the seller, about the characteristics of the goods.

FACTOR OF PRODUCTION Resources essential to produce goods and services.

FIXED CAPITAL Money invested in fixed assets such as land, buildings, and machinery, for use over a long term.

FIXED LIABILITIES Debts that are not due and payable for at least one year.

FORECLOSURE When a person who holds a mortgage against property sues to take title to it.

FOREIGN CORPORATION A corporation is a **foreign** corporation in all states other than the state granting its charter.

FOREIGN EXCHANGE RATE Rate at which the currency of one country is exchanged for that of another country.

FORMAL ORGANIZATION System of jobs, authority relationships, responsibility, and accountability designed by management.

FRANCHISE Exclusive right to perform a stated business service in a specified territory.

FRANCHISEE The dealer in a franchise agreement.

FRANCHISOR The licensing company in a franchise agreement.

FREE-REIN LEADER One who allows most decisions to be made by subordinates with a minimum of direction from the leader.

FRINGE BENEFIT Employee benefits or considerations in addition to wages or salary earned.

GENERAL PARTNERSHIP Two or more owners of a business where each co-owner has unlimited legal liability.

GOVERNMENT Center of political authority having power to govern those it serves.

GRIEVANCE A specific formal dissatisfaction expressed through an identified procedure.

GROSS NATIONAL PRODUCT (GNP) Total value of all finished goods and services produced by an economy in one year.

HARDWARE Computer terminology for machines and equipment that make up a computing center.

HEDGING Taking equal but opposite positions in the cash and futures markets.

HOLDING COSTS Warehousing expenses arising from capital investment in inventories.

HORIZONTAL MERGER The joining together of separate companies engaged in the same business activity.

IMPLIED WARRANTY A warranty that is not specifically stated in certain terms but is implied by law.

IMPORTS Materials and goods shipped into a country.

INCOME The revenues or earnings resulting from business operations.

INDUSTRIAL GOODS Products used by businesses in the manufacture of other goods.

INFORMAL ORGANIZATION A network of personal and social relationships that may have nothing to do with formal authority relationships.

INSIDE DIRECTORS Corporate officers who also serve as directors of the corporation.

INSURABLE INTEREST The opportunity to suffer a financial loss to life, health, or property.

INSURANCE A financial arrangement that redistributes the cost of unexpected losses from risk.

INSURANCE PREMIUM The price paid by the insured for insurance protection.

INTENSIVE DISTRIBUTION Saturating the market by using many wholesalers or retailers.

INTERMITTENT PROCESS Halting factory processes without damaging the finished product.

INVENTORY CONTROL Management of goods and supplies.

INVENTORY TURNOVER The number of times the value of the stock on hand is sold during the year.

INVESTMENT Purchase of securities that offer safety of principal and satisfactory yield equal to the risks.

JOB An organizational unit of work—it is made up of tasks, duties, and responsibilities.

JOB ANALYSIS The use of observation and study to determine pertinent information about the nature of a specific job.

JOB DESCRIPTION A written description of what an employee is to do on a specific job.

JOINT VENTURE An association of two or more persons for a limited purpose, without the usual rights and responsibilities of a partnership.

JUDICIAL SYSTEM The branch of government authorized to hear controversies between parties and to apply the law to these disputes.

LEADERSHIP The ability to influence others to behave in a certain way.

LIABILITY A debt owed by a business; the equity of some creditor in the business.

LIMITED PARTNER One whose personal liability is limited to the amount invested in the partnership.

LIMITED PARTNERSHIP An association in which at least one partner has limited personal liability for the debts of the firm.

LOGISTICS Management's plan for providing an orderly flow of materials and goods to and from the plant.

MANAGEMENT Process of planning, organizing, directing, and controlling activities of an enterprise to achieve certain objectives.

MANUFACTURING Process of using materials, labor, and machinery to create finished goods.

MARKET The exchange of goods or services between buyer and seller at a mutually agreed-upon price.

MARKET ANALYSIS Determining the supply of, and demand for, a given product.

MARKET COMMUNICATION Flow of information back and forth between buyers and sellers.

MARKETING Performance of business activities that direct the flow of goods and services from producer to user.

MARKETING ENVIRONMENT All factors surrounding and affecting selling operations.

MARKETING MIX Blending of strategies involving the four ingredients: product, distribution channels, promotion, and price.

MARKET SEGMENTATION Dividing the total market into submarkets that have similar characteristics.

MARKET VALUATION Cost-benefit analysis of the marketing exchange.

MARKET VALUE The price of bonds or stock shares on the market.

MARKUP The difference between the middleman's cost and his selling price.

MEDIATION The offering of various suggestions by a third party assisting in labor-management negotiations.

MERCHANT WHOLESALER A wholesaler who provides a wide variety of services to retailers.

MICROGRAPHICS Method of filing information on film so that it can be retrieved in seconds.

MIDDLEMAN One who buys and sells goods as an aid in distributing them from the producer to the user.

MINORITY GROUP A small division of the population who share a common historical background and cultural patterns different from those of other segments of society.

MONEY Anything generally accepted in exchange for goods and services.

MONOPOLY Having control of a large enough segment of a particular industry or trade that makes possible the manipulation of prices.

MORALE General attitude and feeling of employees toward their company and their working relationships.

MORTGAGE Property pledged as security for a loan.

MOTION STUDY Breaking down a worker's movements and procedures into all the basic motions used—also, the analysis of this breakdown.

MOTIVATION An internal force that makes people move toward satisfying a need.

MULTINATIONAL BUSINESS Firm with a number of directly controlled operations in different countries with a worldwide perspective.

MUTUAL COMPANY An association, owned by policyholders, organized under state law.

NOMINAL DAMAGE A trifling sum of money awarded to a person in recognition of a technical infraction by the defendant of the plaintiff's rights.

OPEN CORPORATION A profit-making corporation that offers its stock to the public on the open market.

OPEN SHOP A business enterprise in which there is no organized union.

ORGANIZATION A structure of relationships to get work done.

ORGANIZATION CHART Blueprint of the company's internal structure—shows key positions by titles, with lines of authority.

ORGANIZING Coordination of human and material resources within the formal structure.

OUTSIDE DIRECTORS Persons who serve as directors of a corporation but whose business position is outside the corporation.

PARENT COMPANY The company that owns one or more other companies.

PARITY Government action designed to maintain the purchasing power of farm income.

PARTICIPATING POLICY An insurance policy that pays the policyholder a dividend.

PARTNERSHIP An association of two or more persons to carry on as co-owners of a business.

PARTNERSHIP AGREEMENT Written or oral provisions agreed to by business partners.

PAR VALUE The value printed on the stock certificate.

PATENT Exclusive right to own, use, and dispose of an invention.

PLANNING Preparing a plan of action, setting company objectives, determining strategy, and selecting alternative courses of action.

PLANT LAYOUT Arrangement of the work processes to be performed.

PLURALISTIC SOCIETY The combination of diverse groups that influence the business environment to meet societal expectations.

POLICY A written or oral statement that serves as a general guide for decision making.

POLLUTION Deterioration of the natural environment in which we live and work.

PORTFOLIO A collection of investment securities owned by the investor.

POSITION A specific work station occupied by an employee.

PREEMPTIVE RIGHT Stockholders' right to subscribe to additional shares before they are offered to the public.

PREFERRED STOCK Stock that carries certain preferences over common stock.

PRICE The exchange value of a product or service.

PRICE COMPETITION The strategy to sell goods below the going market price.

PRINCIPAL The person for whom the agent acts.

PRIVATE CARRIER A business that transports its own goods.

PRIVATE CORPORATION A business privately operated for profit for the benefit of stockholders.

PRIVATE ENTERPRISE A business system wherein individuals may hold legal title to property and are free to carry on business as they see fit in utilizing their property.

PRIVATE WAREHOUSE A warehouse owned and operated by an individual enterprise.

PROCESSOR The arithmetic or computing unit of a computer installation.

PRODUCT Something that offers a combination of attributes that give it customer appeal, such as style, design, utility, packaging.

PRODUCT DIFFERENTIATION All the ways that buyers and sellers adjust product offers.

PRODUCTION All activities involved in removing natural resources from the earth and processing them into finished goods.

PRODUCTION SHARING Participation of workers in the distribution of profits that result from savings which accrue from reducing production costs.

PRODUCTIVITY Efficiency of production—the amount of output in relation to the input needed to produce it.

PROFIT The net increase in company assets resulting from the operation of an enterprise.

PROFIT SHARING Wage-payment plans to provide remuneration beyond basic pay schedules.

PROGRAM Term used to refer to the instructions to a computer—also called **software**.

PROMOTION A position change that increases one's responsibility and pay. Also, advertising efforts to increase the sale of goods.

PROPRIETORSHIP A business owned and operated by an individual entrepreneur—also known as **sole proprietorship**.

PROTECTIVE TARIFF Tax on imports to protect domestic producers against competition from foreign producers.

PROXY A power of attorney that transfers to a third party the stockholder's right to vote.

PUBLICITY Information about a firm, a product, or an event, made available to the public without charge.

PUBLIC LAW Laws dealing with topics that the public is concerned about.

PUBLIC POLICY A statement or an interpretation of an action that carries the weight of government authority.

PUBLIC WAREHOUSE A warehouse whose services are available to any business wishing to use them.

PURE RISK A risk that involves only a chance of loss.

RATIO A mathematical means of expressing a relationship between two items.

RATIONAL MOTIVES Incentives to buy that appeal to logic or reason.

REAL INCOME Value of wages measured in terms of the goods and services they will buy.

REAL PROPERTY Land and anything permanently affixed to it that in a general way is immovable.

RECESSION A period in which the pace of business activity is very slow.

RECRUITING Process of forming a pool of qualified applicants.

RESEARCH Original investigation aimed at discovering new scientific knowledge.

RESPONSIBILITY The individual's obligation to carry out duties assigned to him or her.

RETAILER A business that sells goods or services to consumers.

RETAINED EARNINGS Profits of the firm that have not been paid as dividends to stockholders.

REVENUE TARIFF A tax on imports to produce revenue.

RIGHT-TO-WORK LAW A state law that forbids some form of compulsory unionism.

RISK Uncertainty associated with an exposure to loss.

RISK MANAGEMENT Planning to deal with potential losses before they occur.

ROUTING Assigning a sequence to the various steps in a manufacturing process.

SCHEDULING Assigning times to production tasks in order to ensure a smooth and constant flow of work along production lines.

SCRAMBLED MERCHANDISING The broadening of one's product lines to include types of goods in addition to the main category handled.

SECRET PARTNER A co-owner of a business whose identity as a partner is not revealed to the public.

SELLING The art of personal persuasion employed to convince others to buy.

SIGHT DRAFT A draft payable on demand.

SILENT PARTNER A co-owner of a business who is not active in the management of the firm.

SHOPPING GOODS Items that are bought only after comparing price, quality, and style.

SHORTAGE COSTS Expenses resulting from failure to have sufficient goods on hand to fill orders.

SMALL BUSINESS An independently owned business that is not dominant in its field.

SOFTWARE Term used to refer to the instructions to the computer—normally called a **program**.

SOLE PROPRIETORSHIP A business owned and operated by one person—also called a **proprietorship**.

SPAN OF CONTROL A limit on the number of positions one person should supervise directly.

SPECIALTY GOODS Specific items that one wants and is willing to search for.

SPECULATION Assumption of above-average risks for which there is anticipation of higher financial returns.

SPECULATIVE RISK A situation in which there is the possibility of either a loss or a gain.

STANDARD OF LIVING People's living level or quality of life—the degree to which their economic needs can be satisfied by family income.

STATE BANKS Commercial banks chartered by the state.

STOCK COMPANY A profit-making corporation organized to sell certain types of insurance.

STOCK DIVIDEND Distribution of profits paid in stock.

STOCK OPTION A privilege given to executives to purchase company stock under certain conditions of price and time.

STOCK SPLIT A division of common stock outstanding into additional units.

STOCK WARRANTS Options to buy a specific number of shares, generally common stock, at a predetermined price.

SUBSIDIARY A company that is owned and controlled by another company which is known as the holding company.

SUBSIDY A government payment or grant to a business enterprise or institution for the public good.

SYSTEM An entity made up of two or more independent parts that interact to form a functioning organism.

TARIFF A tax or customs duty levied by a nation on goods imported from other countries.

TECHNOLOGY Application of scientific knowledge to enhance human effort and increase production.

TENDER-PRICE OFFER Stock price proposed by the offering corporation to the shareholders of another company.

TIME DRAFT A draft payable at a fixed future date.

TIME STUDY Determining the time required for a worker's motions on the job.

TORT A civil (private) wrong. It includes libel, slander, and fraud.

TRADE ACCEPTANCE A draft drawn by a seller of merchandise ordering the buyer to pay the amount of the purchase at a fixed date.

TRADE DISCOUNT Adjusting catalog prices to reflect the cost of a service rendered.

TRADEMARK A distinctive symbol, title, or design that readily identifies a company or its product.

TRANSFER A job shift at the same level of employment, without changing the person's degree of responsibility of rate of pay.

TRUST INDENTURE Contract between the corporation issuing a bond and the bond trustee.

TURNOVER The degree to which employees leave the company.

UNION SHOP A shop in which union membership is required of all employees.

VENDEE The person who buys the goods.

VENDOR The person who sells the goods.

VERTICAL MERGER A consolidation of several firms engaged in different steps of producing the same product.

VOLUNTARY CHAIN A group of individually owned retail stores that pool certain buying and distribution functions.

WAREHOUSE RECEIPT A document used as evidence of the deposit of goods in a warehouse and for a contract for storage.

WAREHOUSING Care, handling, and storage of goods until they are needed.

WARRANTY An express or implied promise made by the seller about the goods to induce the buyer to purchase them.

WARRANTY DEED A written instrument that warrants title to real property without defects.

WHOLESALER A middleman who buys goods for resale, primarily to other businesses.

WORK GROUP A collection of employees who share a common job and view themselves as a group.

WORKING CAPITAL Excess of current assets over current debts (It is a measure of a firm's ability to pay its expenses and buy new merchandise.)

WORLD TRADE Business transactions between citizens, companies, and governments conducted on an international scale.

INDEX

A

D

E

F

G

H

I

J

K

N

O

P

T

U

V

W

X

Y

Z